# *Children's*
# *Writers'*
# *& Artists'*
# YEARBOOK
# 2024

# Children's Writers' & Artists' YEARBOOK 2024

TWENTIETH EDITION

The essential guide for children's writers and artists
on how to get published and who to contact

**BLOOMSBURY YEARBOOKS**

LONDON · OXFORD · NEW YORK · NEW DELHI · SYDNEY

BLOOMSBURY YEARBOOKS
Bloomsbury Publishing Plc
50 Bedford Square, London, WC1B 3DP, UK
29 Earlsfort Terrace, Dublin 2, Ireland

BLOOMSBURY YEARBOOKS, WRITERS' & ARTISTS' and the Diana logo are
trademarks of Bloomsbury Publishing Plc

This edition published 2023

A catalogue record for this book is available from the British Library

ISBN: PB: 978-1-3994-0892-9; eBook: 978-1-3994-0895-0

2 4 6 8 10 9 7 5 3 1

Typeset by DLxml, a division of RefineCatch Limited, Bungay, Suffolk
Printed and bound in Great Britain by CPI Group (UK) Ltd, Croydon, CRO 4YY

MIX
Paper | Supporting
responsible forestry
FSC
www.fsc.org
FSC® C171272

To find out more about our authors and books visit www.bloomsbury.com and sign up for our
newsletters.

**Writers' & Artists' team**
*Editor* Alysoun Owen
*Assistant editor* Eden Phillips Harrington
*Articles copy-editor* Virginia Klein
*Listings editors* Lisa Carden, Rebecca Collins, Lauren MacGowan
*Editorial assistance* Brooke James; Sophia Blackwell (poetry)
*Production controller* Rachel Murphy

This edition of the *Yearbook* is dedicated to the memory of writer and editor Rachel Bladon.

1969–2022

Rachel's article *The learning curve: writing for the children's educational market* starts on page 113.

# About the *Yearbook*

The Editor welcomes readers to this edition of the *Children's Writers' & Artists' Yearbook.*

In one of the new articles in this edition of the *Yearbook*, novelist Beth Reekles (see *How BookTok can help you engage with your readers* on page 361) highlights the importance of community: 'Writing can be a lonely profession, so it's important to find community where you can.' It's a refrain that echoes across the pages of this guide: get to know your readers, find your tribe, get involved with writing groups or creative events locally and nationally. Such involvement will make your writing richer and is likely to improve your wellbeing too. This *Yearbook* is here to promote cooperation and offer support and encouragement to all writers and illustrators – those just dipping their toes into the creative pond as well as more established authors and artists. *Writers' & Artists'* exists to provide information and inspiration across all publishing media and formats (see *More than a book* on page ix) through its online community (www.writersandartists.co.uk) and through the collective voices of the established writers, illustrators, agents and publishers who have contributed articles.

In this year's *Foreword* (see page xv), the Waterstones Children's Laureate, Joseph Coelho, shares his views on what the *Childrens' Writers' & Artists' Yearbook* has to offer, namely 'articles from authors I respected, lists and lists of organisations offering opportunities, and a compendium of agents'. For new writers, it's a guided introduction to the strange and often intimidating world of publishing – an opening up of what Coelho refers to as the 'top secret files'.

I hope this edition will open up the publishing world to you, so that getting your writing noticed will seem a real possibility. Take a look at our other new pieces this year: Elle McNicoll, in *Writing real characters into fiction* (see page 148), makes an impassioned plea to write what you want to – to write your 'truth' when storytelling; there are tips on how to approach an agent with your fantasy or sci-fi children's novel from literary agent Molly Jamieson, in *Submitting your sci-fi/fantasy novel to an agent* (page 205); Bella Pearson gives an insight into the support authors can (and should) expect from their publisher in *Winning opportunities: the role of a small independent publisher*, on page 9; and to ensure you are protecting your work, and are aware of what you can and can't use in your writing from existing texts, consult Sarah Burton's *Copyright 101: top tips* on page 397.

Welcome to our community. We look forward to hearing all about your own writing and publishing experiences through our website: www.writersandartists.co.uk/community.

**Alysoun Owen, Editor**

# More than a book

The Writers & Artists **website** (www.writersandartists.co.uk) offers more free content and resources than ever before.

Here you will find hundreds of **articles** on the writing and publishing process, regular **writing competitions**, and a **community** space to share your work or ask questions about the entire creative process. Brand new features, such as being able to annotate and bookmark pages, can be accessed by creating your **free user account.** As a registered member of the Writers & Artists community, you will receive – straight to your dashboard – exclusive discounts on books, events and editing services and regular content to match your particular interests.

You can find details of our range of **editing services** as well as our **writing courses** and **masterclass evenings**. A selection of bursaries are available as well as payment installment plans.

Our **Listings subscription** provides access to the entire database of contacts in the latest editions of the *Writers' & Artists' Yearbook* and the *Children's Writers' & Artists' Yearbook*, as well as hundreds of additional online-only entries.

Whatever your needs, we hope that *Writers' & Artists'* resources, whether delivered in an ebook, print, online or at our events, will provide you with the information, advice and inspiration you are looking for.

## Short story competition

The annual *Writers' & Artists' Yearbook* Short Story Competition offers published and aspiring writers the chance to win a place on an Arvon Residential Writing Week (worth £850). In addition, the winner's story will be published on the Writers & Artists website.

**To enter** the competition, submit a short story (for adults) of no more than 2,000 words, on the theme of 'risk' by 12 February 2024 to waybcompetitions@bloomsbury.com. For full details, terms and conditions, and to find out more about how to submit your entry, visit www.writersandartists.co.uk/competitions.

You can find details of competitions for children's writing under *Children's book and illustration prizes and awards* on page 333.

**ARVON** hosts residential creative writing courses in three rural writing houses in the UK. With the opportunity to live and work with professional writers, participants transform their writing through workshops, one-to-one tutorials, time and space to write. Five-day courses and shorter courses are available in a wide range of genres and have provided inspiration to thousands of people at all stages of their writing lives. An online programme of writing courses, masterclasses and live readings also runs year-round. Find out more and book a course online at www.arvon.org.

# Contents

# Praise for the *Yearbook*

'Take the great advice that's in this *Yearbook*.'
**David Almond**

'[An] impressive raft of advice and notes on every aspect of the business.'
**Quentin Blake**

'Riffle these pages and turn your dream into an ambition.'
**Frank Cottrell Boyce**

'To find your way as a children's author, *CWAYB* should be your first port of call.'
**Sarah Crossan**

'Between the covers of this book is everything you need to know to get published.'
**Julia Donaldson**

'Contains a wealth of essays, articles and advice.'
**Frances Hardinge**

'A wonderful resource – *the* resource for writers'
**Sally Green**

'Every writer has to take a first step, make the
*Children's Writers' & Artists' Yearbook* yours.'
**Meg Cabot**

# Praise for the *Yearbook*

'Stuffed full of useful facts to help you get writing (and drawing).'
**Liz Pichon**

'Whenever people ask me about how to get their work for children published ... the first words to come out of my mouth are always: *Children's Writers' & Artists' Yearbook.'*
**Michael Rosen**

'A goldmine of invaluable information.'
**Francesca Simon**

'Filled with practical and creative advice.'
**William Sutcliffe**

'I wish you all the luck in the world. Don't be a ninny like me, practically giving up at the first rejection. Consult the excellent *Children's Writers' & Artists' Yearbook.'*
**Jacqueline Wilson**

'It's rare to find a book that's as useful as it is inspiring ... essential reading.'
**M.G. Leonard**

'A one-stop welcome to the world of publishing ... worth its weight in gold.'
**Smriti Halls**

'How to get published? 1. Write a good book. 2. read a good book – this one.'
**Charlie Higson**

# Foreword

Joseph Coelho

You should put this book back where you got it! Honestly – put it back, back up on the shelf and step away. That way everything can stay exactly the same and you'll be safe ... You're still here! Ok – so you're prepared for the consequences of flicking through these pages, of delving into this book's knowledgeable depths? You have been warned ... your life is about to be changed.

When I first started putting pen to paper in the early noughties, it was as a performance poet. I took to the stage at Battersea Arts Centre or the Poetry Society or some other gig in a cafe or bar, rushing from my day job selling advertising in my ill-fitting suit and shakily putting my name down on the open mic list. And the reward for my careering around central London? A chance to read my poems to a live audience and sometimes, *sometimes* I might get paid for my efforts. Getting paid was rare, but it didn't matter – I had the writing bug and a little thing like rarely 'getting paid' wasn't going to stop me. I gigged for years, mainly around central London, and spent my days running from one horrible job to the next – working as a transport planner, gym instructor and (during a low period) tequila boy. Slowly but surely, I started to get known on the circuit and would be invited to perform at paid gigs. Through the brilliant performance poetry organisation Apples and Snakes, I found a whole host of paid opportunities, from doing R&D (research and development) as a writer for theatre shows to leading creative writing sessions in schools to engage young people with poetry. Life was good but, in order to make ends meet, I found I was saying yes to every opportunity going. Most of these gigs were educational – wonderful, rewarding educational gigs – but not necessarily taking my career in the direction I needed it to go.

It was at this juncture I started to actively look for ways of being published as a writer and playwright. I started googling, started to attend workshops and to take advantage of mentoring schemes run by organisations like Spread the Word and Arvon. I got speaking to other writers who had somehow managed to get a play put on or to get a book deal, and I found that they all kept mentioning one book – this book, the book you now hold in your hands.

Flicking through the pages of the *Children's Writers' & Artists' Yearbook* felt conspiratorial, like I was glimpsing top secret files. There were articles from authors I respected, lists and lists of organisations offering opportunities, and a compendium of agents. I started to research the playwrights and authors whose work was similar to the sort of things I was writing. I made lists of top agents to approach, and I started to send out my pitches. Whereas before I had been sending approaches to agents out in the dark, now I was focused – I knew who represented who and, when I started to get replies and meetings, I knew how to impress. I was wise to the industry I wanted to be a part of, and that was in no small part because of the information gifted to me by the *CWAYB*.

Since those early days thumbing through the *Children's Writers' & Artists' Yearbook* over 15 years ago, much has changed: I'm now a fully-fledged author and playwright with over 30 books under my belt, and many plays besides; and I'm the current Waterstones

Children's Laureate – an honour that the nervous young writer who first picked up a volume of this book could never have imagined. It's been a long and a bumpy road carving out space for myself as a writer, but I have loved and continue to love every minute of it. It's not easy and it's not for everyone – but not everyone makes the effort to get to know the industry. You, dear reader, are not like everyone; you have this book in your hands, which already tells me a lot about you. You are actively researching, you are finding out about an industry which wants and needs your voice, your stories, your illustrations, your poems, plays, TV series and films. So ... write, illustrate, put ink to paper, finger to keyboard and use the knowledge contained in these pages to set you on your course. It will be difficult, there will be rejection, and at times you'll wonder: 'Why am I doing this?'. But deep down you know why – it's because you can't *not* do it, because something is calling you on this adventure. And there is no treasure without trial, so rise to the challenge, dearest of readers, and know that you have already taken that first essential step.

**Joseph Coelho** is the Waterstones Children's Laureate 2022-24, an award-winning performance poet, playwright and children's author. His first poetry collection *Werewolf Club Rules* was published by Frances Lincoln in 2014 and won CLPE CLiPPA Poetry Award 2015. His other books include the critically acclaimed *Luna Loves...* series (Andersen Press 2017–), *If All the World Were* (Lincoln Children's Books 2018), the CLiPPA-shortlisted collection of poems, *Overheard in a Tower Block* (Otter-Barry Books 2017), *The Girl Who Became a Tree* (Otter-Barry Books, 2019), which was shortlisted for the 2021 CILIP Carnegie Medal, the middle-grade series *Fairytales Gone Bad* (Walker 2020) and YA novel *The Boy Lost in the Maze* (Otter-Barry Books 2022). Joseph has also published non-fiction titles including *How to Write Poems* (Bloomsbury 2017). For more information see www.thepoetryofjosephcoelho.com. Follow him on Twitter @JosephACoelho.

# Books

## The publishing process

# Authentic inclusion in children's books

Beth Cox, inclusion and equality consultant, shares advice on how to make books authentically inclusive, based on her 20 years' experience in publishing, most of them doing just that, and explores why inclusion is vital for the wellbeing of all children.

There is no doubt that inclusion and diversity are at the forefront of everyone's mind in publishing. But what do we mean by inclusion and diversity and are the terms interchangeable? There are two core approaches in this area when it comes to the content of books: books that focus on or teach about 'diversity' or a particular facet of it, and books that just happen to include a diverse range of characters. The former certainly have a place – they help us understand things that we don't have lived experience of, they open up conversations, and they show the challenges that many marginalised people face. However – and it's a big however – if books 'about' diversity are all that children are exposed to, they are still 'othering'; they still say, 'This is different', 'This is unusual', 'People with this experience only have challenges and face suffering, never joy'. I refer to these types of books as 'diverse books'.

What we need most, what I'm passionate about, and what my work focuses on are 'inclusive books'. These are great stories (or high-quality content if non-fiction) that include a diverse range of characters incidentally. In such books, the reason that characters are traditionally marginalised is incidental or only a minor part of the plot, the characters are fully rounded and more than the aspect(s) that make them 'different'. Because all humans are different. All humans are diverse. Talking about 'diverse books' suggests there is a 'norm' – a white, heterosexual, male, cisgender, nuclear family norm. But there is no such thing. Normal is subjective.

At this point I want to emphasise that, when I talk about inclusion and diversity, I'm referring to all facets of diversity and the many ways in which all humans are 'different'. A lot of the time the focus is solely on ethnic diversity, but no one facet exists in isolation, and they often intersect, which impacts experiences of marginalisation.

## Why is inclusion so important?

The most common answer to this question is the 'windows and mirrors' explanation, first introduced by Emily Style in 1988 and expanded on by Rudine Sims Bishop in 1990 to include the further analogy of sliding doors. The phrase explains that books should be windows onto that which is outside a reader's experience and mirrors for them to see themselves. The sliding door is a metaphor for how books allow a reader to step into and experience a world created by an author. Now, there is absolutely nothing wrong with this analogy, but it's only part of the reason inclusive books are important. They do so much more than this.

The limitation with the windows and mirrors analogy is that, even if such a book exists, a reader might not come across a book that reflects their personal experience. Books that present a stereotypical 'norm' again and again and again suggest there is just one way of being. However, if books represent a multitude of ways of being, if books show that there are a multitude of ways to be happy, readers will see, regardless of whether their own precise experience is reflected, that it's okay and safe for everyone to be exactly who they are. That whoever they are – that's okay. They are of value. They are enough. They belong. Inclusion in books isn't just important as a way of challenging marginalisation and discrimination, it is important for the mental wellbeing of every child (and adult).

I've been working in publishing for 20 years and since 2005, when I joined the steering group for Scope's 'In The Picture' project, I've been committed more than ever to making books inclusive. Thankfully, the way inclusion is thought about and approached in the industry has changed a lot in that time. When Alexandra Strick and I founded Inclusive Minds in 2013, our focus was very much on convincing publishers of the need for incidentally inclusive books and exploring the barriers they faced in creating these, as well as seeking solutions. More recently, Inclusive Minds has been able to focus on supporting authors and publishers to ensure authenticity, mainly through its network of Inclusion Ambassadors – young people with lived experience of marginalisation who are willing to be connected with publishers, authors and illustrators to help them build authentic characters and plots.

It's important to be clear that Inclusion Ambassadors are NOT sensitivity readers. Sensitivity readers are too often brought in at a very late stage in the publishing process to 'check' that there is nothing in a book that could 'cause offence', but this isn't an effective approach. Not only is it too late in the publishing process to make large changes, should core problems be identified, but it can lead to authors feeling as though they are being censored because they had already pretty much finalised their text. Working with people with lived experience should happen much earlier, as part of the research and development process. When authors are building characters and working out plots, they should be having conversations with people who have real experience similar to that of their characters to enable them to sense-check the authenticity of their ideas and build in nuance that only someone with lived experience would know about. This will result in a much more authentic representation than doing a sensitivity check at the end of the book.

## So, where do you start?

The first piece of advice I always give is to **focus on similarities first**, not differences. Often when a traditionally marginalised character appears in a book there is an emphasis on what makes them different. But this approach 'others' them further. The way readers initially engage with characters is by identifying things they have in common. This is what builds empathy – a reader's sense that 'Oh, *I* do/feel/think that' (or that someone they know does). Once a connection with a character has been made, it's easier to explore or understand what might make that character different, if that's even necessary, without danger of them being othered. After all, this is how we make friends. We initially connect with people because of something we have in common, and then, as a friendship develops, we find out how we are different; we have conversations that might challenge our thinking; we understand how their 'normal' is different from ours.

Very closely linked to this is **ensuring that your characters are fully rounded** – that they are more than the aspect for which they are marginalised. Humans are multifaceted and should be treated as such. Everyone has a multitude of hopes, interests, passions, concerns, fears. Know who your character is, inside and out. Even if that isn't all explored in the text, it will ensure that they come across as a real person rather than a caricature.

**Be aware of your world-view and any privilege you may hold**. Regardless of how much research you do and how many people you speak to, you will still write or approach a project from your own personal world-view and experience. It's important therefore to try to look at your work, dispassionately if you can, and consider how your writing might come across to someone with a different lived experience from yours. This isn't an easy thing to do, but the more you understand about inclusion and the various facets of diversity, and the more you try, the easier it becomes. Overthinking is a positive skill here. You need to think about all the possible ways that something could be perceived, and whether one of these interpretations will perpetuate a stereotype. Of course, there will be a point where you have to accept that one book can't do everything, and times when you might decide that, although a character could perpetuate one stereotype, they challenge many others. And that's fine. The important thing is for that to be a conscious decision.

**Consider what you have done to ensure authenticity**. Basing a character on what you've been exposed to in other media isn't enough, as the media is often based on stereotypes. What research has gone into the plot and character to ensure that these will ring true?

## Further resources

- **The Danger of a Single Story**
Chimamanda Ngozi Adichie's TED Talk
    www.ted.com/talks/chimamanda_ngozi_adichie_the_danger_of_a_single_story

- **Inclusive Minds**
Organisation with a large network of Inclusion Ambassadors, who can be connected to book creators to help them.
    www.inclusiveminds.com

- **Inclusion and equality training and consultancy**
Including the Inclusion Incubator (for publishers) and Foundations for Inclusion (for freelancers, authors and illustrators) which combines training, implementation tasks and consultancy.
    www.bethcox.co.uk

- **What is intersectionality?**
A simple explanation from Kimberlé Crenshaw who coined the word.
    www.youtube.com/watch?v=ViDtnfQ9FHc

- **Inclusive and accessible to all? An evaluation of children's picture books and their representation of physical disability**
Dissertation by Caroline Linnea Oestergaard
    https://whatcarolineread.co.uk/inclusive-and-accessible-to-all

- **#BAMEOver – Statement for the UK**
Inc Arts guide to terminology, based on a survey of and discussion by and of people with lived experience of racism.
    https://incarts.uk/%23bameover-the-statement

- **Reflecting Realities**
The 2019 report has a useful section on exemplifications of good practice and reiterates in detail the various 'degrees of erasure' by which ethnically marginalized characters are kept in the background. The section on ensuring children's literature reflect realities provides useful questions to ask when producing or working on inclusive books.
    https://clpe.org.uk/research/reflecting-realities

Finally, remember that **this is a constant learning journey**. After so many years I'm still learning all the time. I also look back at some of the things I've done in the past with the awareness that I would do them differently now. You might still get something wrong; in that case the most important thing is to apologise and ask, or see, how you can learn from it.

## Where can you get support?

The good news is that you don't have to go on this journey alone. I realised, after working on numerous books over the years, that if authors, illustrators, editors, designers and publishers understood the basic principles of inclusion, the children's book landscape could be transformed much more quickly. So I designed a programme based on everything I've learned, not just about inclusion, diversity and equality, but also about creating books and, most importantly, about combining the two.

**Foundations for Inclusion** offers a unique combination of training, implementation tasks, mindset work and live group sessions with me to help anyone who is self-employed in the children's book world, including authors and illustrators, understand and explore those basic principles. I also deliver a version of this programme, the Inclusion Incubator, to publishers, along with tailored training and consultancy.

And if you want to explore the best inclusive books, I'd highly recommend becoming a member of and purchasing books from **Letterbox Library**, who curate the most authentic inclusive books and sell them individually or in collections. But please do support by buying from them, as their sales fund their valuable curation work.

**Beth Cox** is an inclusion and equality consultant (and editor) who has been working in the publishing industry since 2003. She worked at Child's Play International Ltd for almost eight years before becoming self-employed. From 2005–08 she was on the steering group for the lottery-funded Scope 'In the Picture' project. She is the co-founder of Inclusive Minds alongside Alexandra Strick and speaks on inclusion at conferences across the UK and overseas. Beth is the author of four books in the *Level Headers* series published by B small publishing. For more information visit www.bethcox.co.uk and follow her on LinkedIn and Instagram @BethCInclusion.

## See also...

• *A message for under-represented writers: We Want You*, page 212

# What are children's publishers looking for?

Editorial director Rebecca Hill highlights the key ingredients that combine to produce a children's book that will inspire the passion of an editor, publishing team and readers. She urges writers to focus on their craft, knowing that a great book relies on a great story, one with its own fully developed world that captures the reader from start to finish.

Stories! Each year publishers send thousands of books out into the world, into the hands of eager children, so how can you make sure your story gets to the top of a publisher's pile? Every editor is a fan of reading, but the truth is we get sent more material than we can hope to acquire. What we are all looking for when we open up a new manuscript is a story that allows us to do what we love best … *read*.

It really is that simple. What I'm looking for when I start a story is to be that writer's biggest fan. The books we publish at Usborne have all given me that feeling of wanting to shout about them from the rooftops: 'Listen to this sentence, everybody! Turn the page and gasp, dear reader … Hide under the covers and tremble, if you dare dive into this one.' Stepping into a world that is thoroughly developed, and has characters that live and breathe, is a feeling unlike any other. So, if a book can hook me in and make me laugh, make me cry, affect me more than anything else I've read that week, I know that's the one to be passionate about. And passion is what every editor needs – first at an editorial meeting, then at an acquisition meeting and at every available opportunity after that, until that book ends up on a bookseller's table.

As an editorial director, when I'm building Usborne's list I'm always aware of providing a book for every reader. After all, there are lots of tastes that need catering for. But it is essential to see a company's passion for each and every book – from the very first editorial meeting when a submission is discussed. That is exactly what is needed to make a book a success because, beyond the editor's door, a whole team of people will need to love and champion a book: the cover designer, the sales teams, the publicist, the rights team and the marketing department. Without company-wide passion a book could disappear, but with it a book will fly, because we come together to become its superfans.

But before editors even start reading a story and becoming superfans, we make judgements based on your **title**. The title is the crucial 'first sell' of your book to the reader; I can't emphasise enough that a title needs to work hard, and you need to work hard on making it right. As publishers, we are not looking for a set of clumsily arranged buzz words – *The Secrets of the Forbidden Girl in the Magical Dragon Kingdom with Unicorns* – but we are looking for a title that tells us what kind of book you are writing. Strong titles should shine a light on something about your novel, be that the character, the tone or the central interest. Great titles should make us want to know what your book is about. Great titles should make us want to read on.

After the title, the **start** of your story is essential. I so often find myself getting distracted from the story in front of me by a plot that doesn't quite know where it is heading, or a character that doesn't leap out from the pages to ensure I don't return to the demands of office life. Make sure your opening is as strong and grabby as you can make it, without throwing the whole of the kitchen sink in there. Openings are the reason we carry on but, more importantly, they are the reason *children* carry on reading, and that is who we, as editors, are always thinking of when we read. Child readers are harsher than any editor, so make sure you work on making your opening as perfect as you can get it. That prologue – do you actually need it? Where should the first chapter start? Often the story gets going just before your inciting incident, so make *that* the kicking off point!

And carry that **guiding light**; ask yourself, what was it that made you want to write this book? What idea? What theme? What was it you wanted to say? What is it you want children to feel? Make sure you keep those things with you when writing and editing, and keep coming back to them, because what editors want to see, when looking for books to acquire, is authors who are in control of their material; authors who understand how their world is built and understand who their characters are; authors who will tell me at some stage of the editing process: *No, no! My character would never do that, but they would do this instead.*

Always, always think about your **audience**. The children's book market is split into age groups, and you need to be aware of what works for those categories – what content is appropriate, what subjects appeal and what word counts are expected.

Then there's the **ending**: this is another area that I often work hard on with authors. Plan where you want your story to go, and what message and emotion you want to leave the reader with. Make sure that when we finish your book we want to thrust it straight into someone else's hands to read!

## But how do publishers *really* decide what to publish?

There are many important things for a publisher to consider when acquiring a book. Will children love it? Will international publishing partners want to buy the rights? Does the author have many more stories to tell? If it is a series, how quickly can the author write the next book? Does this book fit the type of publishing house that we are? Is this something that is missing on our list, or is it something that the competition is doing well with? I always hope the answer to all of these questions is 'Yes', but the truth is, my mind is set when I'm about a third of the way through a book – because by then I have fallen in love with the story.

After that comes the editing, the positioning, the building up of the campaign, the writing of sales material, the development of a cover... These things all combine to help make a great story into a great book. Great stories will always find readers, because stories make us who we are, and help us to become what we want to be.

So, how *do* you make sure your book gets to the top of the editor's pile? Focus on your craft! When the market is ever-changing, do publishers really know what trend is coming next? Can we look into a crystal ball and see what will become a bestseller? I'll let you into a secret here: the answer is no and ...erm... no. But I do know a good story, as soon as it arrives on my desk. I open it up, settle down, and then I read, and read and read – doing what every editor loves best. All I want is a story that won't let me stop reading.

**Rebecca Hill** is fiction editorial director at Usborne Books. She was named Editor of the Year at the British Book Awards 2019, the first children's editor ever to win this coveted prize. Rebecca has acquired and published bestselling authors Holly Bourne, Peter Bunzl, Sophie Anderson and P.G. Bell alongside award-winning titles such as *After the Fire* by Will Hill, winner of the 2018 YA Book Prize, and *Kick* by Mitch Johnson, winner of the Branford Boase Award 2018.

# Winning opportunities: the role of a small independent publisher

Bella Pearson tells of the goals and values that drive her work as a children's publisher, and the excitement and reward of bringing the work of talented creators to fruition, as well as the hard work and resilience required by authors, illustrators and publishers alike. She advises aspiring writers and artists to focus on developing creative confidence and an authentic voice, to be open to all possibilities and ready for ups and downs on the journey to publication and success.

I have worked in children's publishing for nearly 25 years (can that really be true?!) and the landscape now is so very different to when I started. After working in an independent children's bookshop and completing an MA in Children's Literature, my first job was as editorial assistant to publishing director Philippa Dickinson at Transworld Children's Books in 1999. This was followed by an almost 17-year stint working with David Fickling at David Fickling Books in Oxford, firstly when it was an imprint of Random House Children's Books and then as an independent company. And then, lo, in 2018 I was presented with the opportunity to set up my very own publishing company. Setting up Guppy Books single-handedly was the hardest thing I've ever done, but also the most exciting and rewarding (not counting giving birth to my children, by the way!). From the age of 12, I had wanted to be a publisher (as a child I thought that meant I could read all the time – and oh how I wish that was the case…) and the concept of curating my *very own* list of children's books was a dream. So I took the plunge, deciding that – based on my track record – if I could continue acquiring the same kind of books I had previously, I would be able to create a sustainable, communicative, transparent and innovative publishing company that would provide a good home for authors and illustrators from around the world.

Guppy Books is small and independent, producing between eight and ten books of fiction each year for children aged 5-18 – entertaining, thought-provoking, eclectic, original and inclusive books for young readers of all ages, ability, background. We produce a selection of books that will comfort, stimulate, illuminate, or provide escape for young readers (as well as their carers), individual books that stand out from the crowd and create readers of the future. If (… another dream here) in ten years' time, any child was to wander into a Guppy Bookshop, they would find something that they loved to read. That's the aim. Reading brings SO much value to lives, in so many ways, and children's books are simply the best. Our books range from highly illustrated texts for five-to-eight year-olds (such as the *Ghost Scouts* series (2021-) by Taylor Dolan) to comical intertextual series for emerging readers (e.g. *Knight Sir Louis* by the Brothers McLeod, 2020-); high-octane adventures for the more confident reader (e.g. *Ghostlight* (2022) by Kenneth Oppel) to the stunning *Maggie Blue* fantasy trilogy (2021-) by Anna Goodall for children aged 10+, to thought-provoking novels for young teens, such as *Song Beneath the Tides* (2020) by Beverley Birch. We also look at different ways of telling stories: *Tsunami Girl* (2021), written by Julian Sedgwick and illustrated by Chie Kutsuwada, is a part-prose part-manga novel for readers aged 12+; the *Bronte Mettlestone* series (2017-) by Jaclyn Moriarty is an intricately-woven magical series for readers wanting to be transported into an accessible fantasy world; and Louisa Reid's verse YA novels are quick and immersive reads for young adults, highly impactful and beautifully crafted.

At the time of writing, Guppy has published 32 titles in just under four years. We have been shortlisted for almost all the key children's book awards (the Costa Children's Book Award, the Yoto Carnegie Medal, the Branford Boase Award), as well as recently winning the Waterstones Overall Book Prize in 2023 (… more about that exciting moment below). (See *Children's book and illustration prizes and awards* section starting on page 333.) We've had five *Sunday Times* Book of the Week slots, as well as our other titles receiving reviews in all the broadsheets; our authors are out there doing school events and attending book festivals (Edinburgh, Hay, Cheltenham, Young Adult Literature Convention (YALC) to name a few); we've sold translation rights and optioned film rights; and this year Guppy was shortlisted for the Newcomer of the Year in the Independent Publishers Guild Awards.

Okay, that's enough boasting! Because it's not all prizes and glory. Publishing is a very strange business. And it can be a very difficult one for all involved, especially for you, the creators – the authors and illustrators. It can be lonely, it can feel as if the industry is closed, opaque and, on top of that, everyone else seems to be doing it better. It's easy to watch other creatives having success and to feel left behind – though I can guarantee that they, too, will have had their insecure moments. An aspiring writer or artist's journey goes up and down; there is no simple upward trajectory, unfortunately, even for the most successful. And then, getting a deal is far from the end of the road. Even when you are published – at that stage, perhaps, by foreign publishers or film companies – it can feel like a long process of rejection: book sales aren't as strong as you hoped; there's an award shortlisting you aren't included on. As a small independent publisher, we try to help our authors through this process as much as we can. We aim to be as communicative and transparent as possible. We're small – we keep in regular touch with our authors and illustrators; we try to provide as much clarity as possible, especially to debut authors when they first set out. It is so important to us that all our authors have a positive experience of being published by Guppy. Although we can't control everything that happens when the book goes out in the world, we can be there every step of the way on the journey – to do our very best for each title individually and to be supportive when things don't work out quite as planned.

We also want to be small enough to remain concentrated on our backlist – we don't intend simply to move on each month. Indeed, it's a backlist that provides the bedrock of a small publishing company – and to ignore this would be foolish. Although I would never say to any author/artist that we want to publish everything they write or illustrate, we are there for the long term rather than for a single book. When Guppy takes on a book, we take on the author and hope to sustain a relationship with them (though, equally, we would completely understand the need to move on when the time is right).

The other thing I was intent on, when setting up Guppy, was to be as open as possible to the multitude of writers out there who neither have an agent or have been previously published. But as a small publisher (or to be honest, even as a larger publisher), it is impossible to be open to submissions all year round. The number received would be so high that, in order to respond to everyone, we simply wouldn't have time to do the actual work of producing any books. But there is another way … In the spring of 2020, when suddenly the world had shut down and the summer was stretching out ahead of us in a very different way, it felt like the perfect time to hold the first Guppy Open Submission competition. Over the course of a week, we invited unpublished and unagented writers to submit the first 2,000 words or so of their young adult novels (one year we ask for YA, and the following year for middle grade). In that first pandemic year we had nearly 400 submissions. We whittled this down to a longlist of around 35, and subsequently a shortlist of ten which was read by a selection of expert judges. I also offered an editorial session for all shortlisted authors. We then went on to choose a winner who was offered a contract with Guppy Books. It was an overwhelming but incredibly exciting experience – to receive so many submissions in one week, and of such high quality too.

In 2020, 23-year-old law student, Nadia Mikail, won the prize with her extraordinary YA post-apocalyptic novel, *The Cats We Meet Along the Way*, which Guppy published in February 2022. And just over a year later, in 2023, this very novel went on to win the hugely prestigious Waterstones Children's Book Prize (see page 342). Florentyna Martin, head of children's buying at Waterstones, said: 'Booksellers were overwhelmed by the tenderness woven through each chapter; the moments of silence between the characters are as truthful and evocative as their conversations. Mikail has ultimately crafted a novel of hope, set against an eventful road trip, that encourages us to share stories and dreams.' We have sold rights all over the world, and the book comes out in America this autumn. What an extraordinary achievement for Nadia! And for Guppy too – all as a result of remaining open to the huge wealth of talent which does not come via the traditional, agented route. The following year the competition was open to middle-grade writers, and James Dixon's evocative and tender book, *The Billow Maiden* (2022), was crowned the winner, while runner-up Carrie Sellon's *Pizza Pete and the Perilous Potions* (illustrated by Sarah Horne) will be published later in 2023. And in 2024 we'll be publishing Olivia Collard's fabulously funny LGBTQ YA novel, *Apocalypse Cow*. I have no doubt that all these talented writers will be names of the future, and all through this open and inclusive process. I can't wait for the next one!

So what advice do I have for writers and artists trying to get a break? Well, most of all, have confidence in your own voice/style. I can't remember how many times I've been asked what 'voice' is, and what makes one voice work when another doesn't; frankly, I wish I had an easy answer. It's different for everyone. But confidence and authenticity have a big part to play – don't try to be someone or something you're not. Write from the heart, and tell the story YOU want to tell. And it is important to remember that your voice/style might not be right for one editor, but it could be right for another. I also suggest you watch what is out there for reference, context, and enjoyment! But don't restrict yourself as a result. We didn't choose to publish *The Cats We Meet Along the Way* because it was *like* something else or was '*the next* … [insert your favourite title]'. No, it was an outstanding book in its own right and showed an originality of storytelling, a strong and compulsive spine and authenticity of voice.

It's important to recognise that everyone's journey is different. Author A might have a six-figure deal one year and five years later find themselves looking for a new publisher; Author B might submit over years and finally land a small deal, before winning a huge award; Author C might never publish traditionally and decide to self-publish with great success. There's a whole myriad of possibilities, and everyone's journey is different. But they have one thing in common: they keep going, keep writing, keep illustrating – and hopefully will go on doing so for a very long time.

**Bella Pearson** has worked in children's publishing for over 20 years. After working in an independent children's bookshop, she completed an MA in children's literature and then moved into publishing at Transworld Children's Books. In 2001 she began work as an editor with David Fickling, helping set up his eponymous list under the umbrella of Random House, leaving as publishing director in 2018 to set up her own publishing company Guppy Books. Bella won the Branford Boase Award for Siobhan Dowd's *A Swift Pure Cry* (Penguin Random House 2006) in 2007 and has been shortlisted a further six times. For three years she was as a mentor at The Golden Egg Academy, and has also edited for many children's publishers including Puffin, Chicken House and Oxford University Press. See https://guppybooks.co.uk for more information and follow on Twitter @guppybooks.

## See also...
- *Children's book and illustration prizes and awards*, page 333
- *Finding your voice and point of view*, page 85
- *What are children's publishers looking for?*, page 7

# Getting published: the author's story

In this, the first of three articles tracking the course of her debut novel, *29 Locks* (HopeRoad 2021), from concept through to publication and beyond, author Nicola Garrard describes what motivated her to write it, the steps, decisions and people involved in each stage of the process, and the highs and lows encountered along the way.

My journey to publication was unplanned. I'd been a secondary English teacher since 1998, but I never thought to write a novel until 2017, when one of my loveliest students was stabbed to death in London. I started writing with a clear intention: to show how poverty, knife crime and child criminal exploitation rot childhoods but also how young people resist and succeed. Having taught boys groomed by gangs for many years, I was able to illustrate the pressures to which they are exposed and celebrate their many special qualities which are often unappreciated by wider society.

These early attempts at writing developed into the story of an inner-city teenager, Donny, who was raised in poverty and exploited by gangs, but who gets the opportunity to leave London, learn about boats and make friends with rural teenagers. He then returns, via the eponymous 29 canal lock gates, to take his revenge on the drugs importers who have hurt his family, friends and community. I wrote the first draft rapidly when my young children were asleep and hit 'send' to literary agents as soon as it seemed 'finished'. I wouldn't advise you to do this but, perhaps because of its emotive subject and the passion with which I wrote, a number of agents quickly replied with variations of 'This is important but needs work … Try this …' and I was thrilled to be telephoned by a top agent. Encouraged by 'revise and resubmit' requests, I returned to the manuscript and worked with Islington teenagers and former students who had been groomed by gangs to make sure my representations of their lived experience and London dialect were respectful and accurate.

A few months later, I submitted a draft to the Lucy Cavendish Fiction Prize and the Mslexia Children's Novel Award; both competitions shortlisted *29 Locks*. At this point I was made four offers of representation. I met the agents and chose The Good Literary Agency, which was founded by Nikesh Shukla and Julia Kingsford to promote under-represented voices, such as BAME, working class, disabled and LGBTQ+ writers. I was star-struck when Nikesh Shukla appeared with the TGLA team for coffee and signed my copies of his YA novels. I had never met a novelist before! The other agencies were equally impressive, but I wanted my writing to generate income that would one day be reinvested into under-represented writers. As a teacher committed to social justice, I needed my writing career to align with those values.

After signing with TGLA I completed a new draft, taking on board the editorial suggestions of the agency team which works collegiately on their titles. Next, my agent Abi Fellows pitched in person to publishers. There was immediate interest. Abi took me to meetings with a publishing director, head of PR and commissioning editor at 'Big 5' publishing house in central London. Sadly, *29 Locks* did not clear the acquisitions stage. This is an aspect of publishing that is seldom acknowledged: that a writer can find literary representation yet still not find a publisher. Having sailed through all the milestones – prize shortlistings, signing with an agent, submission to publishers – my Young Adult novel stumbled at the last post.

But my agent didn't give up. I was delighted when, many months after I had accepted the idea that *29 Locks* might never be published, Abi phoned with an offer from Rosemarie Hudson at HopeRoad. It was a perfect fit. When I looked up HopeRoad, I discovered that their remit is to further Asian, Caribbean and African diaspora stories, and to fight negative cultural representations. As a Black publisher, with decades of experience, Rosemarie was uniquely placed to champion *29 Locks* and its multicultural cast of characters. She was also keen to build opportunities in publishing, such as commissioning a young illustrator whose degree portfolio was inspired by the Bristol Black Lives Matter movement. HopeRoad's editor, Joan Deitch, brought decades of publishing experience to bear on the final stages of structural revision, copy-editing and preparation of the manuscript for publication. My overwhelming sense was that the entire team of this small, award-winning independent publisher wanted to make my novel the best it could be and to bring Donny's story to readers.

Since publication, throughout the publicity and promotion phase, Rosemarie and her friendly team give ongoing support. Rosemarie sends encouraging texts before I do an event or interview, and recently called to give me a much-needed pep talk about writing my next novel. I'm told that this level of attention would be unlikely with a large publisher, and I am very grateful for her kind and supportive introduction to the industry. As a result, my experience of publishing has been enormously fulfilling and *29 Locks* was soon recognised in literary prizes, such as the Branford Boase Award (see page 335), and reviews, making the *Financial Times* 'Best Books of 2021' list.

Abi, an enthusiastic but pragmatic agent who manages my expectations, is always available to answer questions about publishing, contracts and marketing, and to guide my next steps following a successful debut. We were both very excited to be consulted in the choice of actor for the upcoming audiobook of *29 Locks* and, as a rule, I follow her advice whenever opportunities arise. I would advise aspiring authors to be open to independent publishers, and to manage their expectations because – even with an outstanding manuscript – there remains a huge element of luck. Say yes to all promotional opportunities sent your way, be energetic in generating your own, and remember that the right agent and publisher for you are the ones who care deeply about your story's intentions and the readers for whom it was written.

As a small indie, HopeRoad doesn't have the budget of large publishers to place their titles in trade publication listings, supermarkets and on bookseller's shop tables, but their high-quality production values, personal touch and passionate belief in *29 Locks* has already inspired support from award-winning authors, reading organisations, librarians, teachers, reviewers, grass-roots youth organisations and the readers who matter: teenagers seeking to make sense of the world, develop empathy with others, and most importantly, find hope. I am deeply grateful to Abi and Rosemarie who have brought my story to their hands.

**Nicola Garrard** is a teacher and author. Her debut novel, *29 Locks* (HopeRoad 2021), was shortlisted for the Lucy Cavendish Fiction Prize and the Mslexia Children's Novel Competition, longlisted for the 2022 Branford Boase Award, and included in the *Financial Times* Best Books 2021. Nicola has taught in secondary schools for 23 years, including 15 in an Islington comprehensive. She studied English Literature, with a focus on representations of race in Early Modern theatre. Nicola grew up in Devon, France and Sussex, and now lives in Sussex with her partner, three children and a Jack Russell terrier. For more information see https://nicola-garrard.co.uk. Follow her on Twitter @nmgarrard.

## See also...

- *Choosing the right agent*, page 198
- *Getting published: the agent's story*, page 15
- *Getting published: the publisher's story*, page 18

# Getting published: the agent's story

Abi Fellows, in this second of three articles tracking the course of Nicola Garrard's debut novel *29 Locks* from concept to publication, recounts how she came to sign Nicola as one of her first authors at The Good Literary Agency (TGLA) and to support her along that journey. She describes the qualities she looks for in books to add to her list, and in their authors, and what her multifaceted role as literary agent entails.

Often, when I do workshops and panels, writers ask that golden question: what are agents looking for? For me personally, as an agent, what is most important is the potential for impact. Because I work across fiction and non-fiction, for adults and for children, this potential can manifest in a number of ways. My list is very diverse, but what unites my authors is their commitment to, and passion for, creating narratives that spark conversation, raise awareness, advocate for positive change and engender hope – narratives for readers who haven't seen themselves, their histories and their stories in books before, or enough.

The importance of representation is at the forefront of my mind when I'm considering children's publishing specifically. When I first read the manuscript of *29 Locks*, I had been volunteering as a school governor in southeast London schools for several years and was acutely aware of the issues that Nicola's writing shone a spotlight on: grooming, gang violence and knife crime. I also knew that teachers were always looking for ways to open up conversations with their students about the realities of young people's lives, realities which are – sadly – often challenging and bleak, in a way that British-originated YA fiction doesn't always acknowledge. The thing that struck me most on my first reading of *29 Locks* was the impact it could have in terms of raising awareness about issues which have been neglected by politicians but which impact a huge number of teenagers, and younger children too. To jump forward for a moment, this was hammered home to me when Nicola told me about the number of safeguarding referrals made at one of the schools she visited, after 29 Locks was published, for a session with the students. It is devastating that the novel's themes and plot resonate with so many young people, but also heartening to know that, because of seeing themselves in the novel, some youngsters felt better equipped to ask for help.

Authors often wonder whether agents are more moved by polish than by potential. Potential is the thing that excites me, personally, coupled with talking to the writer and believing they have the tenacity and persistence writers need to progress from manuscript to published book. Most agents these days will do some editorial work (some more than others), and, to be sure that your vision is aligned with theirs, I would always advise writers to ask any prospective agents about this. I'm lucky enough to be able to invest both my own time and energy and the support of colleagues when giving editorial feedback, and I was able to use this collegiate approach when working with Nicola ahead of submission.

Working on an edit – or more often several edits – before submitting a book to publishers is one of my favourite parts of the job. While my client is hard at work redrafting, based on the feedback that I have given them, I am busy perfecting my pitch and drumming up some buzz with editors. Cultivating relationships with editors is a vital part of an agent's job, as we need to keep up to date with what editors are looking for and how their lists are evolving. Alas, this is not all 'Call my Agent'-style long lunches and parties (although we're grateful to see some of these events returning); it also involves phone calls, Zooms, office meetings, reading published books to keep an eye on the market, and a little bit of stalking editors on Twitter. But even with the most enthusiastic pitch and a superb manuscript, submissions don't always go quite as we agents hope. In Nicola's case, wider conversations about the market at that time were a tricky road bump that we had to navigate. The least fun part of an agent's job is having to make the call to say that an anticipated offer has not come through after all – but it's where we go together, as agent and author, from that point that is important.

Rejection is a part of an agent's life, just as it is an author's, and we don't talk about this enough as an industry. In fact, I think we are overly keen to give the impression that all debuts sell overnight in massive pre-empts. Would it were so! There are many routes to publication, not all of them quick or direct, and resilience is a huge necessity of life for most authors. It's important to be aware that the journey to publication can have unexpected hiccups along the way. But we agents are a tenacious species, and the key thing is to find an ally and champion of your work who will hold tight during these challenging times. As agents we are here to give moral support to our authors whilst they are waiting for news of an offer. This can be a time in a writer's career when working on something else is a great distraction. In Nicola's case, she was buzzing with new ideas so it made sense to start exploring those, talking together about her wider goals and what the strategy for her career should look like moving forward.

Choosing an agent is generally a decision that is made in a moment of excitement, and it marks a great stage of achievement in a writer's life. It's important to consider what kind of advisor that person is going to be in the tougher moments and how you will communicate when things are tricky. It's worth remembering that it is not always an author's first book to go on submission that lands a deal. This can be down to shifting trends and tastes more than the quality of the work itself. I'm a great believer in never giving up on a project and will always keep my ear to the ground for unexplored opportunities, new imprints and editors. And that is how I ended up having a very fortuitous conversation with Rosemarie at HopeRoad about *29 Locks*. Key for both Nicola and I was to hold on to our belief in what made *29 Locks* special and the impact it could have, a belief which – happily – Rosemarie and her team at HopeRoad shared. We knew we needed a publisher who would put this book out into the world sensitively and in a way that would enable both the book and Nicola to have the impact that had motivated her to write it.

Agents are often thought of as the 15-percenters who do the deal, keep their commission, and move on. But our work encompasses so much, both before and after the deal is done. Once the contract is signed, the agent's role shifts into one of overseeing, occasional troubleshooting, and a lot of cheerleading. In the case of *29 Locks*, (HopeRoad 2021) the publishers made my job very easy. One of the things that I love about working with independent publishers is the personal touch and the shared vision that runs through the team, along with the vast amount of energy that goes into every single launch. Particularly important was that the team fully supported Nicola's wish to use the book to create opportunities for up-and-coming creatives, such as the artist who designed the cover and the young actor who voiced the audio edition.

I am thrilled that, in HopeRoad, we found powerful advocates and collaborators who shared our vision of the impact *29 Locks* could have. Its publication is a wonderful example of how author, agent and editor can work together as a team.

**Abi Fellows** is a literary agent who has worked at the Good Literary Agency since 2019. She has previously worked as a literary agent at Georgina Capel Associates, a literary scout at Rosalind Ramsay Ltd, and also as a bookseller at Blackwell's and on the sales team at Faber & Faber. Abi has a BA in English Literature from Bristol University and an MA in English Literature from UCL. See www.thegoodliteraryagency.org/about/abi for more information, and follow her on Twitter @AbiRFellows.

## See also...
- *A message for under-represented writers: We Want You*, page 212
- *Choosing the right agent*, page 198
- *Getting published: the author's story*, page 13
- *Getting published: the publisher's story*, page 18
- *What do agents do for their commission?*, page 191

**Books**

# Getting published: the publisher's story

Following on from the author's story and that of the agent, Rosemarie Hudson, publisher at HopeRoad, describes her role and experience as commissioning editor of *29 Locks* by Nicola Garrard, and gives advice for other new authors on how to tackle the publishing process.

On my first reading of the manuscript for *29 Locks*, I was immediately struck by the relevance of the content and also deeply moved by the loving relationship between the main protagonist, Donny, and his addicted mother. The story was written with so much passion – passion, and sometimes anger, at the suffering of the young hero and his contemporaries in their real-life settings of inner-city deprivation. By publishing *29 Locks* (HopeRoad 2021), I hoped the story would inspire young readers *not* to take up the knife or a life of drugs. I vowed to do my very best for this book, because it was story that was worth telling and sharing. There was no need to give the manuscript out to any of our readers, nor to spend much time deliberating about my decision – you see, I fell in love with Nicola's story immediately and by the end of Chapter One I knew it was perfect for HopeRoad's Young Adult list. The story reminded me so much of award-winning and now well-established author Alex Wheatle's debut novel *Brixton Rock* (which I published in 1999 and has been republished by others since) in its rawness and in its depiction of Brenton Brown's struggles in that book. Alex, in fact, later read the proofs of *29 Locks* and gave us a lovely quote for the front cover of the book, saying that the text 'crackles off the page'.

From the very start, I could see that *29 Locks* had a distinct selling point: I knew I could promote it well to the public and get it into schools, libraries and bookshops. Teachers and librarians, as well as booksellers, are real experts when it comes to knowing what readers want and what sells well, so asking them for their views and tapping into their knowledge is an important part of being a publisher. Publishers have an eye on book prizes, as being longlisted, shortlisted or winning one can propel a title up the sales charts. I sensed that *29 Locks* would shine in the YA fiction category of some of our most prestigious prizes. Suzi Feay, writing for the *Financial Times*, loved it and it became one of her Best Books for YA readers for 2021. At the time of writing, *29 Locks* is on the longlists for the Branford-Boase Award 2022 (see page 335) and the Berkshire Book Award. At HopeRoad we feel that *29 Locks* is a classic book that will continue to sell.

It is worth noting that we did not use many professional reviewers pre-publication; these can be especially valuable for quotations and endorsements to use in marketing. Instead, we sent the proofs out to real 'beta' teenage readers, and to reading groups in young offenders' institutions, from whom we received original and enthusiastic feedback. The book resonated with these readers in a way that is truly authentic; many could see their own lives, and choices they had made, reflected in the text. As publishers, we are really grateful for their input as it helped confirm my own views about Nicola's manuscript and to hint at a receptive market for her story.

To sign Nicola up as one of our authors, I swiftly contacted her literary agent Abi Fellows at the Good Literary Agency. We negotiated and arrived at an agreement that worked well for all of us. The cover design for the book was hugely important – it is what readers see first, so needs to have impact and compel them to pick it up. We needed a cover that properly reflected the content and was fresh as well as enticing. Our brilliant designer, James Nunn, working alongside his gifted mentee Olivia Anthony, came up with our fabulous design, which sums up exactly the mood of the novel.

Nicola is a dream author to work with; this was her first book, so she was a little anxious at first but adapted speedily to the publishing process. An extremely hard worker, Nicola's own ideas come thick and fast, and she's a great communicator. It's important for publisher and author to work well together, and especially key in finding the right copy-editor to work with an author – someone who is on their wavelength. When Nicola learned that Joan Deitch had worked on *Brixton Rock* back in the day, she was reassured; they loved working together. One of the high points of the whole process for me was the launch event, which took place on 'Word on the Water', the London Bookbarge on the Regent's Canal towpath. I also enjoyed reading the reviews that confirmed our own high regard for the book. It was a joy to watch Nicola talking about her book during interviews. With her talent at communication, she takes great pleasure in visiting schools and discussing the book and its themes.

Were there any downsides to the whole process? Yes! Thanks to Covid, the book had to be put back from a summer publication to an autumn one. Getting everything done on time, when staff illness (which had an impact throughout the industry) was delaying deadlines and causing breaks in the chain of production, caused quite a bit of panic. Schedules were turned upside down. And, of course, during Covid we couldn't take advantage of public events, as they were cancelled (and Zoom will never replace face-to-face!).

Here is my top advice for all new authors:
• **Know the market**. Know who you are writing for – who is your book aimed at? Who is your reader? Make sure you have a good story to tell, one that is believable, and write it well. Persevere. Rejection and dejection are part of the learning curve; they are not the end of the world. And success does not always come with the first book.
• **Research and read**. Know where to look for information about publishers who produce books like your own. This book, *Children's Writers' & Artists' Yearbook*, is a key resource. Also, do plenty of research in the bookshops and online. Find out who is publishing what. Read lots.
• **Get your work edited**. You need to have it edited by a professional before you send it out to an agent or publisher. A good copy-editor will help with presentation and polish. Always check the Acknowledgement pages at the end of books in the same genre as your own, as they can give valuable clues about the copy-editors and agents that the author worked with.
• **Work hard**. Be prepared to work hard both at the editing stage and at publication. Once your book has been acquired, the work does not stop there. Social media helps to sell books, so be on top of your game. Post publication, be prepared to do interviews, to be in the public eye and travel to events to promote your book. Don't be shy. Your publisher and their team will support you at all times. And finally ...
• **Keep writing.**

**Rosemarie Hudson** is a publisher and commissioning editor, and the founder and managing director of HopeRoad (www.hoperoadpublishing.com).

## See also...
● *Getting published: the agent's story*, page 15
● *Getting published: the author's story*, page 13

# The hybrid author: you can do it all – your way!

Shelli R. Johannes explains what it is to be a hybrid author, explores the pros and cons of traditional publishing and self-publishing, and describes how an author can enjoy the best of both worlds.

## My journey

When I was a little girl, I never believed there was only one way of doing things. So I grew up trying to accomplish things in a different way. As you can imagine, my parents weren't always thrilled about me 'thinking outside the box'. Years later, nothing has changed. I feel the same way about publishing. As a writer, people told me there was a right way and a wrong way to tear down the walls in the secret society of publishing. Like many writers, I stood outside the closed doors to publishing, banging my head against invisible barriers. If I couldn't find my way in, I decided to carve my passage.

In 2011, when I first decided to self-publish, it was considered 'taboo' in the publishing industry. To many, taking that route meant I was cheating the system – that maybe I wasn't good enough to barge through the front door of traditional publishing. In my heart, I knew that wasn't true. I had an agent who loved my writing. My books had made it to acquisitions at several publishing houses. But as many of you know, writing is like any art – it's subjective and it's competitive. Hundreds of other manuscripts are vying for that opening at a publishing house at any given time. I started to think that self-publishing was the only way inside a tough industry

To date, I have sold over 250,000 ebooks of my *Nature of Grace* series. I have self-published five novels to date and plan to continue. Not only did I sell well, but I also loved the whole process – the control in creating my own covers, the excitement of watching my sales numbers, and choosing where and when I wanted to publish. I got to nurture my own books. However, although I loved the process, I still wanted to publish traditionally because I wanted the experience of working with a big publisher. Again, people in the industry told me I had to choose – it was one way or the other. In addition to self-publishing, I have sold 18 children's pictures and chapter books to Greenwillow, HarperCollins, PRH, Philomel, Viking, and Capstone.

At the time, there wasn't a word or a title for authors who straddled both sides of the great divide. Now, we call it *hybrid publishing*.

### Self-publishing: pros and cons

**PROS**
- control over the process
- retain rights
- higher royalties
- digital printing options
- fast to market
- timely topics

**CONS**
- minimal distribution
- stigma
- tough marketing
- publishing expense
- author handles business end-to-end
- hard to find direct readers

## What is a hybrid author?

A hybrid author is someone who publishes through many different media. For example, hybrid authors can self-publish some books while selling others to a traditional publisher.

I realized publishing doesn't have to be one way or the other. I wavered between playing them all at once or deciding which one to play first for a long time. With so many pros and cons to each channel, everything was exciting and new.

So, what are the pros and cons of being a hybrid author? A hybrid author generally benefits from the traditional advance, professional editing, distribution and marketing. But they also get the self-publishing benefit of creative control, flexible pricing, and the opportunity to write and publish timely titles for immediate earnings (see boxes: *Self-publishing/Traditional publishing: pros and cons*).

## How to be a successful hybrid author

As authors, we have no reason to stay in one lane. We can do it all. But an author must understand what they are getting into and how to do it right. Before diving into hybrid publishing, research is critical – do your homework and seek advice. Here are a few points to keep in mind when preparing your action plan:

### 1. Write a fantastic book

Always have a book in your queue. I like to write for my agent first because the traditional path tends to be much slower than the self-publishing channel. Once my book is on submission or in my agent's hands, I develop my novels for self-publishing. This way, I'm always working on something that can move my career forward. It's also critical to 'go for high-quality' in all your writing. Every piece of work should be your absolute best. Being a hybrid author isn't a shortcut to writing; it's a different path to market. So, write the best book possible and *then* figure out how to publish it. Bad writing doesn't sell in *any* market or channel – no matter how you publish.

### Traditional publishing: pros and cons

**PROS**
- advance
- team makes the book
- mass print distribution
- validated
- access to TV, film, etc
- access to reviewers

**CONS**
- sells rights
- little marketing
- lower royalty
- slower to market
- risk averse regarding the type of book published
- decreasing revenue

### 2. Be prepared to run a business

To be a successful hybrid author, you must manage your writing as a business. You will have to juggle many different processes at the same time. Traditional publishing will include the basics in editing and marketing; you do those things in self-publishing too. However, self-publishing also demands business acumen and an entrepreneurial spirit to keep everything moving forward. You must learn about, and manage, the book's production (covers, editing, jacket copy, etc), plus the business side of publishing, such as inventory, sales, distribution, finances, marketing, and more. Some people don't mind this part – but it can be overwhelming. It also takes away from your writing time, so you must be efficient and organised. Find out what works for you. Being a hybrid author requires a different business mindset from traditional publishing because you have to juggle simultaneous processes across multiple channels. Don't be scared – it can be done, but it is a challenging process. You will have to try new things, so do not fear failing or taking risks. It's part of the process.

**3. Do yourself a favour and get an agent!** Even if you think you will be a hybrid author, I still believe you need an agent. Many authors may disagree. But I feel agents can help you navigate both sides and help you decide which books are best for each publishing path. They know the market. They can also help you navigate other tasks, like contract negotiation and managing other rights – foreign, subsidiary, etc. Of course, you need an agent who believes in the hybrid model. You must find the right agent/agency that truly believes there are viable sales on both pub-

> **How an agent can help you succeed:**
>
> • **Channel management** – Helps decide which path is best for your books.
>
> • **Contract negotiation** – Reviews any issues that might surface.
>
> • **Editorial advice** – Provides manuscript revisions and edits.
>
> • **Market knowledge** – Gives insight into the various markets/channels.
>
> • **Networking** – Has access to a variety of resources.
>
> • **Rights management** – Can facilitate the sale of other rights.
>
> • **Trusted partner** – Offers advice on whole career and portfolio.

lishing paths. Make sure they are experienced in digital publishing and open to supporting any opportunities that arise. I have had two excellent agents in the past and recently signed with my third agent, Laurel Symonds at KT Literary because agents are crucial in this business. Today, many agents understand and value the possibilities of the self-publishing model. You need someone in your corner with your best interest and career in mind. Trust me, agents are worth their 15%! (See box *How an agent can help you succeed.*)

**4. Make a book plan**

Decide which books you want to publish traditionally and which ones you want to publish yourself. My agent helps me choose the best path for each book idea. Because, let's be real, self-publishing does *not* work for all books, and traditional publishing doesn't work for everything, either. For example, my picture books (such as *Cece Loves Science*) and science chapter books are much better suited for traditional publishing. In contrast, some of my YA material that is based on a timelier topic (such as *ReWired* cyber-thriller series) or that target a niche audience (such as the *Nature of Grace* wilderness thriller series), may be better suited for self-publishing. So, decide what you want to write, then figure out the best channel; consider time, topic, and level of control.

**5. Always keep writing**

The indie world is very fast paced, while the traditional model is much slower. Doing both can bog you down in tasks, project management and marketing. But it's essential always to keep writing. It is the best way to build a back-list that will continue to sell. When one book is in edits, work on a new idea. When one manuscript is in your agent's or critique partner's hands, move onto your next book. Never sit and wait for something to happen. Make something happen. It's all worth it in the end!

Going forward, I want to continue my hybrid career because I love the traditional and self-publishing options for different reasons. I value the flexibility and control that self-publishing offers. But I also enjoy the collaborative process of working with an editor and team at a publishing house. As I develop as a writer, I want to remain open to ANY writing opportunity or path available. I want to pave my own way in this exciting, frustrating, challenging and wonderful industry. Because at the end of the day, I just want to write great books and reach people of all ages with my words. I'm proud to be a hybrid author – one who publishes my work, my way.

Remember, there is no right way to make this journey; there's only *your* way!

**Shelli R. Johannes** co-authors the popular science picture book series *Loves Science* (Greenwillow/HarperCollins) and *Penny, The Engineering Tale of the Fourth Pig* (Capstone). She also authors her picture book series, *Theo Thesaurus* (Philomel/Viking) and *Shine Line a Unicorn* (HarperCollins). Her newest book is *Florence Nightingale* in Chelsea Clinton's *She Persisted* series. Shelli also writes middle-grade and YA fiction, and has self-published five novels, selling over 250,000 ebooks. After earning an MBA specializing in marketing and working in corporate America as a senior vice president, Shelli traded in her heels and suits for flip-flops and jeans to follow her passion for writing. For more information, visit www.srjohannes.com and hang out with her on Twitter or Instagram @srjohannes.

Books

# Listings

# Children's book publishers UK and Ireland

There are changes to listings in this section every year. We aim to provide a comprehensive list of publishing imprints, the name or brand under which a specific set of titles are sold by a publisher. Any one publisher might have several imprints, which are included either under a publisher's main entry or in some cases as entries themselves. Information is provided in a way that is of most use to a reader. The listings that follow are updated by the Writers' & Artists' editors based on information supplied by those listed.

*Member of the Publishers Association or Publishing Scotland
†Member of Publishing Ireland, the Irish Book Publishers' Association
‡Member of the Independent Publishers Guild
sae = self-addressed envelope
MS = manuscript (MSS = manuscripts)

## Acair Books*

An Tosgan, 54 Seaforth Road, Stornoway,
Isle of Lewis HS1 2SD
*email* info@acairbooks.com
*website* https://acairbooks.com/
*Facebook* www.facebook.com/acairbooks
*Twitter* @acairbooks

Publishes Scottish Gaelic children's books and a wide range of titles in Scottish Gaelic and English. Founded 1977.

## Alanna Max

38 Oakfield Road, London N4 4NL
*email* info@alannamax.com
*website* www.alannamax.com
*Co-publisher* Fay Erek, *Editor-At-Large* Anna McQuinn

Children's picture books. See website for submissions guidelines. Founded 2012.

## Amgueddfa Cymru – National Museum Wales‡

Cathays Park, Cardiff CF10 3NP
*tel* 029-2057 3235
*email* post@museumwales.ac.uk
*website* www.museumwales.ac.uk
*Twitter* @AmgueddfaBooks
*Head of Publishing* Mari Gordon

Books based on the collections and research of Amgueddfa Cymru for adults, schools and children, in both Welsh and English. Founded 1907.

## Andersen Press Ltd*

20 Vauxhall Bridge Road, London SW1V 2SA
*tel* 020-7840 8703 (editorial) / 020-7840 8701 (general)

*email* anderseneditorial@penguinrandomhouse.co.uk
*website* www.andersenpress.co.uk
*Managing Director* Mark Hendle, *Publisher* Klaus Flugge

Children's publisher of picture books, fiction for 5–8 and 9–12 years and YA fiction. Publisher of the *Elmer* series by David McKee, the *Little Princess* series by Tony Ross, *The Proudest Blue* by Ibtihaj Muhammad, S.K. Ali and Hatem Aly, *The Bolds* series by Julian Clary and David Roberts, as well as award-winning fiction by Phil Earle and Kwame Alexander. Founded 1976.

## Arachne Press

*email* cherry@arachnepress.com
*website* https://arachnepress.com/
*Director* Cherry Potts

Small, independent publisher of award-winning short fiction, poetry and select non-fiction, for adults and children. Founded 2012.

## Arcturus Publishing Ltd

26–27 Bickels Yard, 151–153 Bermondsey Street, London SE1 3HA
*tel* 020-7407 9400
*email* info@arcturuspublishing.com
*website* www.arcturuspublishing.com
*Editorial Manager* Joe Harris (children's)

Children's non-fiction, including activity books, reference, education, practical art, geography, history and science. No unsolicited MSS. Founded 1993.

## Aurora Metro‡

80 Hill Rise, Richmond TW10 6UB
*tel* 020-8948 1427
*email* submissions@aurorametro.com
*website* www.aurorametro.com
*Facebook* www.facebook.com/AuroraMetroBooks

Books

*Twitter* @aurorametro
*Managing Director* Cheryl Robson

Adult fiction, YA fiction, biography, drama (including plays for young people), non-fiction, theatre, cookery and translation. Submissions: send synopsis and three chapters. Runs a biennial competition for women novelists (odd years): Virginia Prize for Fiction. Entry fee for submission of either adult or YA novel. Imprints include Aurora Metro Books and Supernova Books. Founded 1996.

## Award Publications Ltd

The Old Riding School, The Welbeck Estate, Worksop, Notts. S80 3LR
*tel* (01909) 478170
*email* info@awardpublications.co.uk
*Facebook* www.facebook.com/awardpublications
*Twitter* @award_books
*Instagram* @award.books

Picture story books, fiction, early learning, information and activity books for 0–12 years. No unsolicited material. Refer to social media sites for details of submission windows. Founded 1972.

## b small publishing limited*‡

*website* www.bsmall.co.uk
*Managing Director* Catherine Bruzzone, *Publisher* Sam Hutchinson

Activity books and foreign language learning books for 2–12 years. Written in-house. No unsolicited MSS. Founded 1990.

## Badger Learning*

Oldmedow Road, King's Lynn, Norfolk PE30 4JJ
*tel* (01553) 816083
*email* info@badgerlearning.co.uk
*website* www.badgerlearning.co.uk
*Publisher* Sarah Rudd

Specialists in publishing high interest/low reading age fiction and non-fiction for ages 7–16. The range also includes educational and teacher resources. Series include *Making the Team, Wow Facts, Teen Reads, YA Reads, Papercuts, Between the Lines, The League of Enchanted Heroes, Full Flight* and *Graphic Novels.* Email for submission guidelines. Founded 2001.

## Barrington Stoke*‡

18 Walker Street, Edinburgh EH3 7LP
*tel* 0131 225 4113
*email* info@barringtonstoke.co.uk
*website* www.barringtonstoke.co.uk

Fiction for reluctant, dyslexic or under-confident readers: fiction for children 8–12 years with a reading age of 8+, fiction for teenagers with a reading age of 8+, fiction for 8–12 years with a reading age of below 8, fiction for teenagers with a reading age of below 8, non-fiction for children 8–14 years with a reading age of 8+, graphic novels. Resources for readers and their teachers. Acquired by HarperCollins (page 34) in 2023. No unsolicited MSS. All work is commissioned from well-known authors and adapted for reluctant readers. Founded 1998.

## Big Picture Press

Victoria House, Bloomsbury Square, London WC1B 4DA
*tel* 020-3770 8888
*email* hello@bonnierbooks.co.uk
*website* www.bonnierbooks.co.uk
*Twitter* @BigPicturePress
*Publisher* Jo McInerney

Publishes a boutique range of illustrated gift books. An imprint of Bonnier Books UK (page 29). Founded 2013.

## Bloomsbury Publishing Plc*‡

50 Bedford Square, London WC1B 3DP
*tel* 020-7631 5600
*website* www.bloomsbury.com
*Founder & Chief Executive* Nigel Newton

A leading independent publishing house with authors who have won the Nobel, Pulitzer and Booker prizes. Bloomsbury has offices in London, New York (page 56), New Delhi, Oxford and Sydney (page 46). MSS must normally be channelled through literary agents, with the exception of academic and professional titles. Founded 1986.

### BLOOMSBURY CONSUMER DIVISION
*Managing Director* Ian Hudson

Imprints include: Absolute Press, Bloomsbury Children's Books, Bloomsbury Circus, Bloomsbury Press, Raven Books, Bloomsbury Tonic (wellbeing), Head of Zeus-Zephyr (page 35).

### Bloomsbury Children's Books
*Publishing Director & International Editor-in-Chief* Rebecca McNally

Authors include J.K. Rowling, Louis Sachar, Neil Gaiman, Sarah J. Maas, Sarah Crossan, Brian Conaghan. No unsolicited MSS.

### Bloomsbury Education
*Head of Education* Helen Diamond, *Editorial Director* Hannah Rolls (educational fiction & poetry), *Senior Commissioning Editor* Joanna Ramsay (early years & CPD), *Commissioning Editor* Emily Badger (primary & CPD)

Publishes around 75 print titles per year: educational fiction, children's poetry, teacher resource books and CPD titles. Imprints include ABC-CLIO, Andrew Brodie, Featherstone Education. No submissions by email. Look at recently published titles and catalogues to gauge current publishing interests. Much of the list is educationally focused and publishes in series. Allow 8–10 weeks for a response.

## Bog Eyed Books Ltd

39 Coptefield Drive, Belvedere DA17 5RL
*email* info@bog-eyed-books.com
*website* https://bog-eyed-books.com
*Facebook* www.facebook.com/bogeyedbooks
*Twitter* @bogeyedbooks
*Instagram* @bogeyedbooks
*Directors* Gary Northfield, Nicky Evans

Publishes children's comic books of all genres, mystery, historical, bizarre. Hosts events in comic bookshops. Founded 2016.

## Bonnier Books UK*

Victoria House, Bloomsbury Square,
London WC1B 4DA
*tel* 020-3770 8888
*email* hello@bonnierbooks.co.uk
*website* www.bonnierbooks.co.uk
*Ceo* Perminder Mann

Publishes across a wide variety of genres for different ages. From crime to reading group fiction; memoir to self-help; activity to reference. Publishes a number of imprints. Adult trade: Blink Publishing, Echo Publishing, Embla Books, Eriu, Heligo Books, Ithaka, Lagom, Manilla Press, Nine Eight Books, Twelve Point Audio, Zaffre. Children's trade: Big Picture Press (page 28), Hot Key Books (page 35), Piccadilly Press (page 40), Studio Press (page 43), Templar (page 44). Founded 2015.

## The Book Guild Ltd

Unit E2 Airfield Busines Park, Harrison Road,
Market Harborough, Leics. LE16 7UL
*tel* 0800 999 2982
*email* info@bookguild.co.uk
*website* www.bookguild.co.uk
*Facebook* www.facebook.com/thebookguild
*Twitter* @BookGuild
*Managing Director* Jeremy Thompson

Offers traditional and partnership publishing arrangements, with all titles published being funded or co-funded by The Book Guild Ltd (does not offer self-publishing). MSS accepted in fiction, children's and non-fiction genres, see the website for details. The Book Guild is part of parent company Troubador Publishing Ltd. Founded 1996.

## Boom House Books‡

8 Chapel Street, Derby DE56 1AR
*email* hello@boomhousebooks.co.uk
*website* https://boomhousebooks.co.uk/
*Facebook* www.facebook.com/boomhousebooks
*Founders* Jo Leigh, Sascha Landskron, Zoe McCullagh-George

Children's fiction and non-fiction publisher with a focus on the local area, health, diversity and sustainability. Also publishes books for adults on parenting. Founded 2021.

## Boxer Books Ltd

*email* info@boxerbooks.com
*website* www.boxerbooks.com
*Publisher* David Bennett

Publishes innovative baby board books, picture books, young fiction and stunning story collections. No unsolicited MSS in any form unless via a recognised agency. Acquired by Sterling Publishing in 2022. Founded 2000.

## Bright Red Publishing*

Mitchelston Drive Business Centre,
Mitchelston Drive, Kirkcaldy KY1 3NB
*tel* 0131 220 5804
*email* info@brightredpublishing.co.uk
*website* www.brightredpublishing.co.uk
*Facebook* www.facebook.com/BrightRedBooks
*Twitter* @_BrightRed
*Instagram* @bright_red_publishing
*Directors* John MacPherson, Alan Grierson

Educational publishing for Scotland's students and teachers. Founded 2008.

## Brilliant Publications Ltd*‡

Unit 10, Sparrow Hall Farm, Edlesborough,
Dunstable LU6 2ES
*tel* (01525) 222292
*email* info@brilliantpublications.co.uk
*website* www.brilliantpublications.co.uk
*Facebook* www.facebook.com/Brilliant.Publications
*Twitter* @Brilliantpub, @BrillCreative
*Managing Director* Priscilla Hannaford

Publishes easy-to-use educational resources, featuring engaging approaches to learning, across a wide range of curriculum areas, including English, foreign languages, maths, art and design, thinking skills and PSHE. No children's picture books, non-fiction books or one-off fiction books. See guidelines on website before sending proposal. Founded 1993.

## The British Museum Press

Great Russell Street, London WC1B 3DG
*tel* 020-7323 8000
*email* publicity@britishmuseum.org
*website* www.britishmuseum.org/publishing
*Head of Publishing* Claudia Bloch

Publishes books for children, young readers and families, in collaboration with award-winning publisher Nosy Crow (page 39). Titles range across picture books, activity books and illustrated non-fiction. Founded 1973.

## Buster Books

16 Lion Yard, Tremadoc Road, London SW4 7NQ
*tel* 020-7720 8643
*email* enquiries@mombooks.com
*website* www.mombooks.com/buster
*Facebook* www.facebook.com/BusterBooks
*Twitter* @BusterBooks
*Instagram* @buster_books

Reference, activity, fiction and picture books for 0+ years. Publishes approx. 60 titles a year. Buster's publications include puzzle books, including the bestselling *Clever Kids* series, and a wide selection of children's illustrated non-fiction, colouring, drawing, sticker, activity, fiction and picture books. Titles range from enlightening books such as *The Wild Life of Animals, A Day in the Life of a Caveman, A Queen and Everything In Between* and *Dr Maggie's Grand Tour of the Solar System* to quirky books such as *Does a Bear Poo in the Woods?, The Dinosaur Department Store, Feeling Good About Me* and *Sherlock Bones and the Case of the Crown Jewels*. Bestselling colouring books include the *I Heart Colouring* series and the *Kerby Rosanes* series. No unsolicited MSS. Founded 1985.

## Cambridge University Press & Assessment*‡

University Printing House, Shaftesbury Road, Cambridge CB2 8BS
*tel* (01223) 358331
*email* directcs@cambridge.org
*website* www.cambridge.org
*Facebook* www.facebook.com/CambridgeUniversityPress
*Twitter* @CambridgeUP
*Chief Executive* Peter Phillips; *Managing Directors* Mandy Hill (academic), Jill Duffy (UK education), Rod Smith (international education)

For children: curriculum-based education books and software for schools and colleges (primary, secondary and international). For adult and younger learners: ELT. Founded 1534.

## Campbell – see Pan Macmillan

## Candy Jar Books

Mackintosh House, 136 Newport Road, Cardiff CF24 1DJ
*tel* 029-2115 7202
*email* submissions@candyjarbooks.co.uk
*website* www.candy-jar.co.uk/books
*Facebook* www.facebook.com/CandyJarLimited
*Twitter* @Candy_Jar
*Head of Publishing* Shaun Russell

Non-fiction and fiction for children aged 7+. Will consider unsolicited MSS. Check website for submission details. Founded 2010.

## Cassava Republic Press‡

9 Eri Studio C11, Mainyard Studios, 94 Wallis Road, London E9 5LN
*email* info@cassavarepublic.biz
*website* https://cassavarepublic.biz/
*Facebook* www.facebook.com/CassavaRepublic
*Twitter* @cassavarepublic
*Instagram* @cassavarepublicpress
*Publishing Director* Bibi Bakare-Yusuf

Publishes contemporary Black and African writing. Aims to bring high-quality fiction and non-fiction for adults and children to a global audience. Has offices in Abuja and London. Founded 2006.

## Caterpillar Books – see Little Tiger Group

## Catnip Publishing Ltd

320 City Road, London EC1V 2NZ
*tel* 020-7138 3650
*email* editorial@catnippublishing.co.uk
*website* www.bouncemarketing.co.uk/publisher/catnip-publishing
*Twitter* @catnipbooks
*Managing Director* Robert Snuggs

New and previously published titles from picture books to teen fiction. Acquires new titles from overseas publishers, reissues out-of-print titles by top authors and commissions original fiction for 7–9 years, 9–12 years and YA readers. Publishes 15–20 books a year. Recently published books by Pippa Goodhart, Jason Beresford, Berlie Doherty, Sarah Baker, Sophie Plowden, Joan Lingard, Keris Stainton and Anne Booth. Will only consider agented submissions. Founded 2005.

## CGP

Coordination Group Publications, Broughton House, Broughton-in-Furness, Cumbria LA20 6HH
*tel* (01229) 715766
*email* ewt@cgpbooks.co.uk
*website* www.cgpbooks.co.uk

Educational books centred around the National Curriculum, including revision guides and study books for Reception, KS1, KS2, KS3, GCSE, iGCSE and A level. Subjects include maths, English, science, history, geography, computing, ICT, computer science, psychology, business studies, economics, religious studies, design and technology, PE, music, French, German, Spanish, sociology, 11+, 13+ and functional skills. On the lookout for top teachers at all levels, in all subjects. Potential authors and proofreaders should fill in the application form found on the website, ready for when a project comes up in their subject area. Founded 1996.

## Chicken House

2 Palmer Street, Frome, Somerset BA11 1DS
*tel* (01373) 454488
*email* hello@chickenhousebooks.com
*website* www.chickenhousebooks.com
*Twitter* @chickenhsebooks
*Instagram* @chickenhousebooks
*Managing Director & Publisher* Barry Cunningham, *Deputy Managing Director* Rachel Hickman

Fiction for 7+ years and YA. No unsolicited MSS. Successes include James Dashner (the *Maze Runner* series), Cornelia Funke (*Inkheart* and *Dragon Rider* series) and Kiran Millwood Hargrave (*The Girl of Ink & Stars*). See website for details of The Times/ Chicken House Children's Fiction Competition for unpublished writers. Part of Scholastic Ltd (page 42). Founded 2000.

## Child's Play (International) Ltd

Ashworth Road, Bridgemead, Swindon, Wilts. SN5 7YD
*tel* (01793) 616286
*email* office@childs-play.com
*website* www.childs-play.com
*Facebook* www.facebook.com/ChildsPlayBooks
*Twitter* @ChildsPlayBooks
*Chair* Adriana Twinn, *Publisher* Neil Burden

Children's educational books: board, picture, activity and play books; fiction and non-fiction. Founded 1972.

## Christian Education

5/6 Imperial Court, 12 Sovereign Road, Birmingham B30 3FH
*tel* 0121 472 4242
*email* sales@christianeducation.org.uk
*website* https://shop.christianeducation.org.uk/, www.retoday.org.uk
*Facebook* www.facebook.com/RETodayServices
*Twitter* @IBRAbibleread

Incorporating RE Today Services and International Bible Reading Association. Publications and services for teachers and other professionals in religious education including *REtoday* magazine, curriculum booklets and classroom resources. Also publishes bible reading materials. Founded 2001.

## Cicada Books*

Unit 9, 6 Cliff Road, Cliff Road Studios, London NW1 9AN
*email* info@cicadabooks.co.uk
*website* www.cicadabooks.co.uk
*Twitter* @cicadabooks
*Instagram* @cicadabooks

Independent publisher specialising in highly illustrated books for children. Publishes between ten and 12 titles a year. Founded 2009.

## Colourpoint Creative Ltd†

Colourpoint House, Jubilee Business Park, 21 Jubilee Road, Newtownards, Co. Down BT23 4YH
*tel* 028-9182 6339 (within UK) / +353 (0)48 91846339 (Republic of Ireland)
*email* sales@colourpoint.co.uk
*website* www.colourpointeducational.com
*Twitter* @colourpointedu
*Commissioning Editor* Wesley Johnston

Textbooks for Northern Ireland CCEA board. Educational textbooks for KS3 (11–14 years), KS3 Special Educational Needs (10–14 years), GCSE (14–16 years) and A Level/undergraduates (age 17+). Not primary. Subjects include, but not limited to,

biology, business studies, chemistry, design and technology, English, French, geography, history, HE, ICT, Irish, life and health sciences, LLW, MVRUS, PE, physics, politics, RE and science. Full submission by email only including details of proposal, sample chapter/section to show ability to connect with target age group, qualification/experience in the subject, full contact details. Textbooks, workbooks and electronic resources all considered. Founded 1993.

## Cranthorpe Millner Publishers

9 Hills Road, Cambridge CB2 1GE
*tel* 020-3441 9212
*email* kirsty.jackson@cranthorpemillner.com
*website* www.cranthorpemillner.com
*Facebook* www.facebook.com/CranthorpeMillner
*Twitter* @CranthorpeBooks
*Instagram* @CranthorpeMillner
*Managing Director* Kirsty Jackson

Titles include fiction and non-fiction: memoir, celeb autobiographies, history, sci-fi, YA, historical fiction, crime/thriller, literary fiction. Founded 2018.

## Critical Publishing Ltd‡

3 Connaught Road, St Albans AL3 5RX
*tel* 07791 607373
*email* admin@criticalpublishing.com
*website* www.criticalpublishing.com
*Facebook* www.facebook.com/CriticalPublishing
*Twitter* @criticalpub
*Directors* Di Page (sales & marketing), Julia Morris (editorial)

Award-winning publisher of books for teachers – from trainee through CPD and on to leadership. Titles are practical but research-based and are suited for those teaching across all age ranges. Founded 2012.

## Crown House Publishing Ltd*‡

Crown Buildings, Bancyfelin, Carmarthen SA33 5ND
*tel* (01267) 211345
*email* books@crownhouse.co.uk
*website* www.crownhouse.co.uk
*Facebook* www.facebook.com/CrownHousePub
*Twitter* @CrownHousePub
*Instagram* @crownhousepub
*Directors* David Bowman, Karen Bowman

Award-winning independent publisher specialising in the areas of education, coaching, business training and development, leadership, NLP, hypnotherapy, psychotherapy, self-help, personal growth and children's books. Founded 1998.

### Independent Thinking Press
*email* books@independentthinkingpress.com
*website* www.independentthinkingpress.com
Publishes CPD books and resources for teachers and school leaders, including business, training and development, coaching, health and wellbeing, NLP, hypnosis, counselling and psychotherapy. Publishes a range of children's books.

### Dinosaur Books Ltd
*tel* 020-7737 6737
*email* info@dinosaurbooks.co.uk
*website* www.dinosaurbooks.co.uk
*Twitter* @dinosaurbooksco
*Director* Sonya McGilchrist

Chapter books for children 5–14 years. Submissions by email only: submissions@dinosaurbooks.co.uk. Founded 2014.

### DK*
One Embassy Gardens, 8 Viaduct Gardens, London SW11 7BW
*tel* 020-7139 2000
*website* www.dk.com
*Ceo* Carston Coefeld

A member of the Penguin Random House UK (page 40) division of Bertelsmann, publishing illustrated books for adults and children: travel, licensing, reference, education, gardening, food and drink. Founded 1974.

### Dogberry Ltd
13 The Rafters, Nottingham NG7 7FG
*email* contact@memoirist.org
*website* www.dogberrybooks.com
*Publisher* Auriel Roe

English-language publisher of humorous literary fiction, YA fiction and memoir. Founded 2020.

### Dorling Kindersley – see DK

### Dref Wen
28 Church Road, Whitchurch, Cardiff CF14 2EA
*tel* 029-2061 7860
*website* www.drefwen.com
*Directors* Roger Boore, Anne Boore, Gwilym Boore, Alun Boore, Rhys Boore

Welsh-language publisher. Original, adaptations and translations of foreign and English-language full-colour picture story books for children. Also activity books, novelty books, Welsh-language fiction for children 7–14 years, teenage fiction, reference, religion, audiobooks and poetry. Educational material for primary and secondary school children in Wales and England, including dictionaries, revision guides and Welsh as a Second Language. Publishes approx. 50 titles a year and has 450 in print. No unsolicited MSS. Founded 1970.

### The Educational Company of Ireland
Ballymount Road, Walkinstown, Dublin D12 R25C, Republic of Ireland
*tel* +353 (0)14 500611
*email* info@edco.ie
*website* www.edco.ie

Educational (primary and post-primary) books in the Irish language. Publishes approx. 60–70 titles each year and has 600–700 in print. Ancillary materials include digital resources, concrete resources and CDs. A member of the Smurfit Kappa Group Plc. Submissions to: amolumby@edco.ie. Please include: a brief description of the project's scope and content; table of contents; sample chapter and biographical details. Allow three months for response. Founded 1910.

### EK Books
Unit 11, 201 Main Street, Gosford NSW 2250
*website* www.ekbooks.org
*Facebook* www.facebook.com/ekbooksforkids
*Twitter* @ekbooksforkids
*Instagram* @EK_Books
*Ceo* Gareth St John Thomas

An imprint of Exisle Publishing. Independent children's publisher on a mission to publish books with heart on issues that matter. Publishes fiction and non-fiction for ages 0 to YA, on themes including mental health, environmentalism and creative learning. Founded in 2013.

### Electric Monkey – see HarperCollins Publishers

### Elsewhen Press
Alnpete Limited, PO Box 757, Dartford, Kent DA2 7TQ
*tel* 07956 237041
*email* info@elsewhen.co.uk
*website* https://elsewhen.press
*Facebook* www.facebook.com/ElsewhenPress
*Twitter* @elsewhenpress
*Instagram* @elsewhenpress
*Managing Director* Alison Buck, *Editorial Director* Peter Buck

Small independent publisher, delivering new talents in speculative fiction (including sci-fi, fantasy, paranormal, horror, alternative history), for ages YA upwards. Digital-first publisher. For submission guidelines see website. Founded 2011.

### Everything with Words Ltd
16 Limekiln Place, London SE19 2RE
*tel* 020-8771 2974
*email* info@everythingwithwords.com
*website* www.everythingwithwords.com
*Managing Director & Publisher* Mikka Bott

Children's fiction for 5 years to YA. Accepts unsolicited MSS. Founded 2016.

### Faber & Faber Ltd*‡
Bloomsbury House, 74–77 Great Russell Street, London WC1B 3DA
*tel* 020-7927 3800
*website* www.faber.co.uk
*Twitter* @FaberChildrens
*Publisher* Leah Thaxton (children's)

Award-winning, independent publisher of high-quality picture books, fiction, middle grade, YA, non-fiction and poetry. Publishes books to support teachers, libraries and book clubs with relevant, inclusive and necessary stories. Authors include Emma Carroll, Jason Reynolds, Kieran Larwood, Swapna Haddow, Marissa Meyer, Kacen Callender, Kate Saunders, Bonnie-Sue Hitchcock and Natasha Farrant. Founded in 1929.

## CJ Fallon
Ground Floor, Block B, Liffey Valley Office Campus, Dublin D22 X0Y3, Republic of Ireland
*tel* +353 (0)16 166400
*email* editorial@cjfallon.ie
*website* www.cjfallon.ie
*Executive Director* Brian Gilsenan

Educational textbooks. Founded 1927.

## Farshore Books – see HarperCollins Publishers

## David Fickling Books‡
31 Beaumont Street, Oxford OX1 2NP
*tel* (01865) 339000
*website* www.davidficklingbooks.com
*Publisher* David Fickling, *Publishing Director* Liz Cross

Independent publisher of picture books, novels and non-fiction for all ages, as well as graphic novels. Currently not accepting unsolicited MSS. Founded 1999.

## Fincham Press*
University of Roehampton, School of Humanities, Fincham Building, Roehampton Lane, London SW15 5PH
*email* finchampress@roehampton.ac.uk
*website* https://fincham.press/
*Facebook* www.facebook.com/finchampress
*Twitter* @finchampress

Based at the University of Roehampton. Titles are commissioned, edited and published by a team based in English and creative writing, part of the School of Humanities and Social Sciences. Publishes creative writing anthologies, a journalism anthology, a book on representations of the professor in children's literature and a book on YA writing by a pre-eminent practitioner of the form. Founded 2014.

## Firefly Press Ltd*‡
Britannia House, Caerphilly Business Park, Van Road, Caerphilly CF83 3GG
*email* hello@fireflypress.co.uk
*website* www.fireflypress.co.uk
*Facebook* www.facebook.com/FireflyPress
*Twitter* @fireflypress
*Publisher* Penny Thomas, *Editor* Janet Thomas

Award-winning publisher of fiction for ages 5–19. Founded 2013.

## Fisherton Press
*email* general@fishertonpress.co.uk
*website* www.fishertonpress.co.uk
*Facebook* www.facebook.com/FishertonPress
*Twitter* @fishertonpress
*Director* Ellie Levenson

A small, independent publisher producing picture books for children under 7 years. Not currently accepting proposals but illustrators are welcome to send links to a portfolio. Founded 2013.

## Five Quills*
93 Oakwood Court, London W14 8JZ
*website* www.fivequills.co.uk
*Facebook* www.facebook.com/www.fivequills.co.uk
*Twitter* @5Quills_kids
*Publisher* Daniela Schneider, *Editorial Director* Natascha Biebow

An independent children's book publisher. Publishers picture books and chapter books for young readers 3–9 years. Currently not accepting submissions. Founded 2017.

## Floris Books*
Canal Court, 40 Craiglockhart Avenue, Edinburgh EH14 1LT
*email* floris@florisbooks.co.uk
*website* www.florisbooks.co.uk
*Facebook* www.facebook.com/FlorisBooks
*Twitter* @DiscoverKelpies
*Commissioning Editors* Sally Polson, Eleanor Collins

Children's board books, picture books, story anthologies. Approx. 50 titles each year. Founded 1976.

### Kelpies
*website* www.discoverkelpies.co.uk
Contemporary Scottish children's books – picture books (3–6 years), young readers series (6–8 years) and novels (8–15 years). Successes include *The Nowhere Emporium* by Ross MacKenzie and *There Was a Wee Lassie Who Swallowed a Midgie* by Rebecca Colby. Annual Kelpies Prize, see website.

## Flying Eye Books Ltd*
27 Westgate Street, London E8 3RL
*tel* 020-7033 4430
*email* info@nobrow.net
*website* www.flyingeyebooks.com
*Twitter* @flyingeyebooks

Publishes picture books, illustrated fiction and non-fiction and graphic novels. Founded 2013.

### Nobrow
*email* info@nobrow.net
*website* www.nobrow.net
*Twitter* @NobrowPress
Comics and graphic novel imprint. Fiction and non-fiction. Founded 2008.

## Galore Park Publishing Ltd*

Carmelite House, 50 Victoria Embankment,
London EC4Y 0DZ
*tel* 020-7873 6412
*website* www.galorepark.co.uk

Educational textbooks and revision guides for
students studying at independent schools. *So You
Really Want To Learn* range of textbooks for children
11+ years and *Junior* range for children 8–10 years.
Courses include Latin, French, English, Spanish,
maths and science. Founded 1999.

## Graffeg

24 Stradey Park Business Centre, Mwrwg Road,
Llangennech, Llanelli SA14 8YP
*tel* (01554) 824000
*email* croeso@graffeg.com
*website* https://graffeg.com/
*Facebook* www.facebook.com/graffegbooks
*Twitter* @graffeg_books
*Founder* Peter Gill

Publishes non-fiction illustrated books about food,
art, music, culture and heritage, architecture, gardens,
photography, sport and lifestyle, and illustrated
fiction for children. Imprint: Cadno (middle grade
fiction, books in English with Welsh content).
Founded 2003.

## W.F. Graham

2 Pondwood Close, Moulton Park,
Northampton NN3 6RT
*tel* (01604) 645537
*email* books@wfgraham.co.uk
*website* www.wfgraham.co.uk

Activity books including colouring, dot-to-dot, magic
painting, puzzle, word search and sticker books.
Founded 1956.

## Guppy Publishing Ltd*‡

Bracken Hill, Cotswold Road, Oxford OX2 9JG
*tel* 07884 068983
*email* bella@guppybooks.co.uk
*website* www.guppybooks.co.uk
*Facebook* www.facebook.com/guppybooks
*Twitter* @guppybooks
*Instagram* @guppypublishing
*Director* Bella Pearson

Publishing children's and YA fiction for 5–18 years.
Illustrated books for newly emerging readers, fiction
for middle-grade readers and novels for YA. Poetry,
prose, graphic novels. No unsolicited submissions
outside the Guppy Open Submission Competition
(run annually in May). Founded 2019.

## Hachette Children's Group*

Carmelite House, 50 Victoria Embankment,
London EC4Y 0DZ
*email* editorial@hachettechildrens.co.uk
*website* www.hachettechildrens.co.uk
*Facebook* www.facebook.com/hachettechildrens
*Twitter* @HachetteKids
*Instagram* @Hachettechildrens
*Ceo* Hilary Murray Hill, *Senior Trade Publisher* Ruth
Alltimes, *Trade Publisher* Emma Blackburn,
*Education Publisher* Paul Rockett, *Publishing Director*
Leah James (colour non-fiction)

Hachette Children's Group is one of the largest
children's publishers in the UK, publishing baby and
preschool books, picture books, illustrated gift,
fiction, non-fiction, series fiction, books for the
school and library market and licensed publishing.
Comprising of imprints Hodder Children's Books;
Laurence King Children's Books; Little, Brown Books
for Young Readers; Orchard Books; Orion Children's
Books; Quercus Children's Books; Pat-a-Cake; Wren
& Rook; Franklin Watts; Wayland Books; and
Welbeck Children's Books. Owner of Enid Blyton
Entertainment. Generally only accepts submissions
sent via an agent. Occasionally holds periods of open
submissions for a limited time or a specific genre. See
social media channels for details. Founded 1986.

## Hachette UK*

Carmelite House, 50 Victoria Embankment,
London EC4Y 0DZ
*tel* 020-3122 6000
*website* www.hachette.co.uk
*Ceo* David Shelley

Part of Hachette Livre SA since 2004. Hachette UK
group companies: Hachette Children's Group (see
above); Hachette Ireland; Hachette Australia
(page 47); Hachette New Zealand; Headline Book
Publishing; Hodder Education Group; Hodder &
Stoughton; Hodder Faith; Illuminate Publishing
(page 36); Little, Brown Book Group; John Murray;
Orion Group; Octopus Group. Founded 1986.

## Happy Yak

1 Triptych Place, London SE1 9SH
*tel* 020-7000 8084
*website* www.quartoknows.com/happy-yak

A children's imprint of the Quarto Group, Inc.
(page 41). Publishes preschool, picture books and
illustrated non-fiction for children from birth
upwards, with a focus on fun, accessible content and
contemporary illustration. Founded 2021.

## HarperCollins Publishers*

The News Building, 1 London Bridge Street,
London SE1 9GF
*tel* 020-8741 7070
*Alternative address* Westerhill Road, Bishopbriggs,
Glasgow G64 2QT
*tel* 0141 772 3200
*website* www.harpercollins.co.uk
*Ceo* Charlie Redmayne, *Managing Director* Kate
Elton, *Executive Publishers* Sarah Emsley, Kimberly
Young

For adults: fiction (commercial and literary) and
non-fiction. Subjects include history; celebrity

memoirs; biographies; popular science; mind, body & spirit; dictionaries; maps and reference. All fiction and trade non-fiction must be submitted through an agent. Owned by News Corporation. Founded 1817.

## Collins
*website* www.collins.co.uk
*Managing Director* Alex Beecroft

Reference publishing, including dictionaries and atlases, as well as the National Trust and *The Times* lists. Collins is also an education publisher for UK and international school curriculums, and publishes extensive revision and home learning support for parents and children.

## Farshore Books
*website* www.farshore.com
*Executive Publisher* Cally Poplak, *Publishing Directors* Lindsey Heaven, Melissa Fairley, John Packard

Children's fiction, YA (Electric Monkey), picture books, non-fiction (Red Shed), film/TV, toy and gaming. Previously known as Egmont UK.

## HarperCollins Audio
*Group Technology & Digital Director* Joanna Surman, *Audio Publishing Director* Fionnuala Barrett

Publishes various audio formats. Leading publisher of trade fiction and non-fiction audiobooks for children and adults, as well as standalone audio projects. Publishes in excess of 75,000 audiobooks each year.

## HarperCollins Children's Books
*Executive Publisher* Cally Poplak; *Publishers* Nick Lake, Juliet Matthews

Activity books, novelty books, preschool brands, picture books, pop-up books and book and CD sets. Fiction for 5–8 and 9–12 years, YA fiction and series fiction; film/TV tie-ins. Publishes approx. 265 titles each year. Picture book authors include Oliver Jeffers, Judith Kerr and Emma Chichester Clark, and fiction by David Walliams, Michael Morpurgo, David Baddiel and Lauren Child. Books published under licence include *Dr Seuss*, *Bing*, *Twirlywoos* and *Paddington Bear*. No unsolicited MSS: only accepts submissions via agents.

## Hawthorn Press*‡
1 Lansdown Lane, Stroud, Glos. GL5 1BJ
*tel* (01453) 757040
*email* info@hawthornpress.com
*website* www.hawthornpress.com
*Director* Martin Large

Publishes books and ebooks. Series include *Early Years*, *Steiner/Waldorf Education*, *Crafts*, *Storytelling* and *Parenting*. Founded 1981.

## Head of Zeus - Zephyr*‡
Clerkenwell House, 5–8 Hardwick Street, London EC1R 4RG
*tel* 020-7253 5557
*email* hello@headofzeus.com
*website* www.headofzeus.com
*Facebook* www.facebook.com/headofzeus
*Twitter* @_ZephyrBooks
*Ceo* Anthony Cheetham

Children's imprint of Bloomsbury Publishing Plc (page 28). Founded 2002.

## Hogs Back Books Ltd‡
34 Long Street, Devizes, Wilts. SN10 1NT
*tel* (01483) 506030
*email* enquiries@hogsbackbooks.com
*website* www.hogsbackbooks.com

Children's picture books and teenage fiction. Welcomes texts and submissions from illustrators but cannot return material without prior arrangement. Founded 2009.

## Hopscotch
St Jude's Church, Dulwich Road, London SE24 0PB
*tel* 020-7501 6736
*email* orders@hopscotchbooks.com
*website* www.hopscotchbooks.com
*Associate Publisher* Angela Morano Shaw

A division of MA Education. Teaching resources for primary school teachers. Founded 1997.

## Practical Pre-School Books
*website* www.practicalpreschoolbooks.com

Early years teaching resources.

## Hot Key Books*
Victoria House, Bloomsbury Square, London WC1B 4DA
*tel* 020-3770 8888
*email* hello@bonnierbooks.co.uk
*website* www.hotkeybooks.com, www.bonnierbooks.co.uk
*Twitter* @HotKeyBooksYA
*Executive Publisher* Emma Matthewson

Publishes original and thought-provoking teen and YA fiction, some books also suitable for an adult audience. An imprint of Bonnier Books UK (page 29). Founded 2012.

## I Am a Bookworm*
35 Manor Close, Templecomb, Somerset BA8 0LA
*email* hello@iamabookworm.co.uk
*website* www.iamabookworm.co.uk
*Facebook* www.facebook.com/iamabookwormuk

An independent packager and publisher of children's novelty books, board books, activity books and light books for children aged 0–5 years. Founded 2011.

## Igloo Books Ltd
Cottage Farm, Mears Ashby Road, Sywell, Northants. NN6 0BJ
*tel* (01604) 741116

Books

*email* customerservices@igloobooks.com
*website* www.igloobooks.com
*Twitter* @igloo_books

Children's: fiction (adult), licensed books, novelty, board, picture, activity books and education. Not currently accepting submissions. Founded 2005.

## Illuminate Publishing

Carmelite House, 50 Victoria Embankment, London EC4Y 0DZ
*tel* (01235) 827720
*email* sales@illuminatepublishing.com
*website* www.illuminatepublishing.com

An award-winning publisher of teaching and learning resources. Publishes across a wide range of secondary subjects: academic and vocational. Part of Hachette UK (page 34). Founded 2010.

## Imagine That Publishing Ltd

Marine House, Tide Mill Way, Woodbridge, Suffolk IP12 1AP
*tel* (01394) 386651
*email* customerservice@imaginethat.com
*website* www.imaginethat.com
*Facebook* www.facebook.com/ImagineThatPublishing
*Twitter* @imaginethatbook
*Instagram* @imaginethatbook
*Chairman* Barrie Henderson, *Managing Director* David Henderson

Children's activity, novelty, picture, reference, character, gift and early learning books. Founded 1999.

**Top That**
Books plus kits.

## IWM (Imperial War Museums) Publishing

Lambeth Road, London SE1 6HZ
*tel* 020-7416 5000
*email* publishing@iwm.org.uk
*website* www.iwm.org.uk
*Facebook* www.facebook.com/iwm.london
*Twitter* @I_W_M

IWM tells the stories of people who have lived, fought and died in conflicts involving Britain and the Commonwealth since 1914. Produces a range of books, drawing on the expertise and archives of the museum. Books are produced both in house and in partnership with other publishers. Founded 1917.

## Jolly Learning Ltd*‡

77 Hornbeam Road, Buckhurst Hill, Essex IG9 6JX
*tel* 020-8501 0405
*email* info@jollylearning.co.uk
*website* www.jollylearning.co.uk
*Director* Christopher Jolly

Educational: primary and English as a Bilingual Language. Publishes approx. 25 titles each year and has 300 in print. Successes include *Jolly Phonics Extra*, *My Jolly Phonics* and *Jolly Dictionary*. Imprint: Jolly Phonics. Unsolicited MSS are only considered for add-ons to existing products. Founded 1987.

## Miles Kelly Publishing

Harding's Barn, Bardfield End Green, Thaxted, Essex CM6 3PX
*tel* (01371) 832440
*email* hello@mileskelly.net
*website* www.mileskelly.net
*Director* Gerard Kelly

High-quality illustrated non-fiction and fiction titles for children and family: activity books, board books, story books, picture books, poetry, reference, posters and wallcharts. Age groups: preschool, 5–10, 10–15, 15+. Founded 1996.

## Kelpies – see Floris Books

## Knights Of*

97 Granville Avenue, Brixton Village, London SW9 8PS
*website* https://knightsof.media
*Twitter* @_KnightsOf
*Managing Director* Aimée Felone, *Editorial Director* Eishar Brar

Children's commercial fiction publisher, championing authors and illustrators from diverse backgrounds. Founded 2016.

## Kube Publishing Ltd

Markfield Conference Centre, Ratby Lane, Markfield, Leics. LE67 9SY
*tel* (01530) 249230
*email* info@kubepublishing.com
*website* www.kubepublishing.com
*Managing Director* Haris Ahmad

Publishes books of a Muslim interest. Founded 2006.

## Ladybird Books

One Embassy Gardens, 8 Viaduct Gardens, London SW11 7BW
*tel* 020-7139 3000
*email* ladybird@penguinrandomhouse.co.uk
*website* www.ladybird.co.uk

Ladybird publishes books across a wide range of formats for children ages 0–7. They include tactile books for babies, nursery rhymes, classic fairy tales and reading schemes, alongside licensed character publishing. Part of Penguin Random House UK (page 40). Founded 1867.

## Lantana Publishing

Clavier House, 21 Fifth Road, Newbury RG14 6DN
*email* info@lantanapublishing.com
*website* https://lantanapublishing.com/
*Facebook* www.facebook.com/lantanapublishing
*Twitter* @lantanapub

*Instagram* @lantana_publishing
*Ceo* Alice Curry, *Commissioning Editors* Holly Tonks, Katrina Gutierrez

An award-winning children's book publisher and social enterprise, publishing inclusive books by authors from under-represented groups. Looking for inclusive picture books for babies and toddlers, and fiction for 5–8 years and 9–12 years. Authors should send full MS, illustrators their portfolio and link to their website and author-illustrators a complete book dummy. See submissions page on website for how to submit. Founded 2014.

## Leckie*

103 Westerhill Road, Bishopbriggs G64 2QT
*email* leckiescotland@harpercollins.co.uk
*website* www.leckiescotland.co.uk

Publishes education textbooks and revision guides specifically for the Scottish Curriculum for Excellence. Founded 1989.

## Lexus Ltd

47 Broad Street, Glasgow G40 2QW
*tel* 0141 556 0440
*email* peterterrell@lexusforlanguages.co.uk
*website* www.lexusforlanguages.co.uk
*Director* P.M. Terrell

Publisher of language books. Publishes *Lexus Travelmate* series and *Chinese Classroom* series; *Insider China*; and *UK4U*. Also dual-language books: *Cross Over into Gaelic* series; *Scottish Folk Tales in English and French*; *Scottish Folk Tales in English and Spanish*; and *ScotlandSpeak*. For children: dual-language books for young children. Founded 1980.

## Frances Lincoln

The Old Brewery, 6 Blundell Street, London N7 9BH
*tel* 020-7700 6700
*email* peter.marley@quarto.com
*website* www.quarto.com/Frances-Lincoln-Children's-Books
*Pubsliher* Peter Marley

Imprint of The Quarto Group (page 41). Children's books. Founded 1977.

## Frances Lincoln Children's Books

1 Triptych Place, Second Floor, London SE1 9SH
*tel* 020-7700 9000
*email* peter.marley@quarto.com
*website* www.quartoknows.com/Frances-Lincoln-Children's-Books
*Facebook* www.facebook.com/Quartokids
*Twitter* @QuartoKids
*Publisher* Peter Marley

Imprint of The Quarto Group (page 41). Illustrated children's books: arts and the great outdoors, visual storytelling and cultural diversity. Founded 1983.

## Lion Hudson Ltd‡

Prama House, 267 Banbury Road, Summertown, Oxford OX2 7HT
*tel* (01865) 302750
*email* info@lionhudson.com
*website* www.lionhudson.com
*Managing Director* Suzanne Wilson-Higgins

Bible story retellings, prayer books, picture storybooks, illustrated non-fiction and information books on the Christian faith and world religions. Also specialises in gift books, occasion books, seasonal books for Christmas and Easter and bible activity books. Children's submissions: hard copy with sae if return required. Part of the SPCK Group. Founded 1971.

## Little Door Books

*email* submissions@littledoorbooks.co.uk
*website* www.littledoorbooks.co.uk
*Twitter* @littledoorbooks

Award-winning independent publisher specialising in children's books. Publishes four or five books a year. Not currently accepting unsolicited MSS. Founded 2016.

## Little Tiger Group*

1 Coda Studios, 189 Munster Road, London SW6 6AW
*tel* 020-7385 6333
*email* contact@littletiger.co.uk
*website* www.littletiger.co.uk
*Group Publishing Director* Thomas Truong, *Publisher* Jude Evans

Owned by Penguin Random House (page 40). Founded 1987.

### Caterpillar Books

*website* www.littletiger.co.uk/imprint/caterpillar-books
*Editorial Director* Pat Hegarty

Books for children, including novelty board and picture books.

### Little Tiger Press

*website* www.littletiger.co.uk
*Editorial Director* Eleanor Farmer

Children's picture books, board books and novelty books for preschool up to 7 years. See website for submissions guidelines.

### Stripes

*website* www.littletiger.co.uk/imprint/stripes-publishing
*Editorial Director* Lauren Ace

Fiction for children 6–12 years and YA. Quality standalone titles and series publishing in all age groups. Will consider new material from authors and illustrators; see website for guidelines.

**360 Degrees**
*website* www.littletiger.co.uk/special/360degrees
*Editorial Director* Pat Hegarty
Non-fiction novelty for children aged 5–12 years.

## LOM ART
16 Lion Yard, Tremadoc Road, London SW4 7NQ
*tel* 020-7720 8643
*email* enquiries@mombooks.com
*website* www.mombooks.com/lom
*Facebook* www.facebook.com/MichaelOMaraBooks
*Twitter* @OMaraBooks
*Managing Director* Lesley O'Mara

Illustrated non-fiction for children. Publishes approx.
ten titles a year. Titles include *Fantomorphia, Maybe
the Moon, The Van Gogh Activity Book* and *Life
Lessons I learned From My Cat*, plus a range of artist-
led drawing, colouring and picture book titles.
Unable to guarantee a reply to every submission
received, include a sae if submission to be returned.
Imprint of Michael O'Mara Books Ltd.
Founded 2015.

## Longman – see Pearson UK

## Mabecron Books Ltd
3 Briston Orchard, St Mellion, Saltash,
Cornwall PL12 6RQ
*tel* (01579) 350885
*email* ronjohns@mabecronbooks.co.uk
*website* www.mabecronbooks.co.uk
*Twitter* @mabecronbooks

Award-winning publisher. Produces children's
picture books and books with a Cornish or West
Country subject. Linked to bookshops in Falmouth,
St Ives and Padstow. Founded 1998.

## McGraw-Hill School Education*
8th Floor, 338 Euston Road, London NW1 3BH
*tel* (01628) 502730
*email* helpme@mheducation.com
*website* www.mheducation.co.uk
*Facebook* www.facebook.com/UKSchoolsMHE
*Twitter* @UKSchoolsMHE

Educational publisher for primary and secondary
education in English, maths, science, humanities and
other subject areas, including intervention and
learning support. Founded 1888.

## Magic Cat Publishing*‡
Unit 2, Empress Works, 24 Grove Passage,
London E2 9FQ
*email* marketing@magiccatpublishing.co.uk
*website* www.magiccatpublishing.co.uk
*Instagram* @magiccatpublishing
*Directors* Jenny Broom, Rachel Williams

A small, independent children's publisher. Publishes
family-focused non-fiction and gift books.
Founded 2019.

## Mama Makes Books Ltd‡
49 Newlands Road, Tunbridge Wells, Kent TN4 9AS
*tel* 07790 468405
*email* info@mamamakesbooks.com
*website* www.mamamakesbooks.com
*Facebook* www.facebook.com/mamamakesbooks.com
*Twitter* @mamamakesbooks
*Instagram* @mamamakesbooks
*Director* Penny Worms

A small, independent children's publisher of
illustrated books for children 0–8 years: baby books,
novelty, early learning and non-fiction.
Founded 2020.

## Mantra Lingua Ltd
Global House, 303 Ballards Lane, London N12 8NP
*tel* 020-8445 5123
*email* info@mantralingua.com
*website* https://uk.mantralingua.com/
*Facebook* www.facebook.com/Mantralingua
*Twitter* @mantralingua
*Managing Director* R. Dutta

Publishes bilingual picture books and educational
resources for UK, US, Swedish and German
audiences. Looking for illustrators with ability to
draw racially diverse faces and authors and
storytellers with ability to interpret or imagine
modern city lives. Commission and royalty-based
relationships with print runs covering between 10
and 15 language editions. Translators and audio
narrators, tel: 0845 600 1361. Founded 2002.

## Maverick Books
Studio 11, City Business Centre, 6 Brighton Road,
Horsham, West Sussex RH13 5BB
*tel* (01403) 256941
*email* submissions@maverickbooks.co.uk
*website* www.maverickbooks.co.uk
*Facebook* www.facebook.com/Maverick-Childrens-
Books
*Twitter* @maverickbooks
*Managing Director* Steve Bicknell, *Managing Editor*
Kimara Nye

Publishes titles across the formats of picture books,
early readers, graphic reluctant readers, junior fiction
and middle grade. For submissions, please see
submission guidelines page on website. Submissions
by email only. Founded 2009.

## Kevin Mayhew Ltd
Fengate Farm, Rattlesden, Suffolk IP30 0SZ
*tel* (01284) 374495
*email* info@kevinmayhew.com
*website* www.kevinmayhew.com
*Director* Barbara Mayhew

Christianity: prayer and spirituality, pastoral care,
preaching, liturgy worship, children's, youth work,
drama, instant art, educational. Music: hymns, organ
and choral, contemporary worship, piano and

instrumental, tutors. Read submissions section on website before sending MSS/synopses. Founded 1976.

## The Mercier Press[†]

*email* info@mercierpress.ie
*website* www.mercierpress.ie
*General Manager* Mary Feehan

Books for adults and children. Subjects include Irish literature; folklore; history; politics; humour; current affairs; health; mind, body & spirit; general non-fiction. Founded 1944.

## Moonlight Publishing*

Garden House at Vine House, Chapel Square, East Hendred, Oxon OX12 8JN
*email* info@moonlightpublishing.co.uk
*website* https://moonlightpublishing.co.uk/

An independent, family-run company specialising in illustrated information books for children 4–10 years. Founded 1980.

## Neem Tree Press*[‡]

95A Ridgmount Gardens, London WC1E 7AZ
*tel* 020-7993 5581
*website* www.neemtreepress.com
*Facebook* www.facebook.com/neemtreepress
*Twitter* @neemtreepress
*Ceo & Publisher* Archna Sharma, *Head of Marketing & PR* Divia Kainth, *Project Manager & Creative Lead* Lisa Cohen, *Marketing Executive* Jade McGrath

Award-winning fiction, non-fiction and children's/ YA books including translation and short stories. Diverse and inclusive with the aim to inspire, inform and provoke. See website for submission guidelines. Founded 2013.

## Nosy Crow*[‡]

Wheat Wharf, 27A Shad Thames, London SE1 2XZ
*tel* 020-7089 7575
*email* hello@nosycrow.com
*website* www.nosycrow.com
*Group Ceo* Kate Wilson, *Publishing Directors* Kirsty Stanfield (fiction), Louise Bolongaro (picture books), Rachel Kellehar (non-fiction, preschool & activity)

Independent children's publisher. Publishes child-focused, parent-friendly children's books. Also children's publisher for The National Trust and The British Museum. Founded 2010.

## The O'Brien Press Ltd[†]

12 Terenure Road East, Rathgar, Dublin D06 HD27, Republic of Ireland
*tel* +353 (0)1 4923333
*email* books@obrien.ie
*website* obrien.ie
*Directors* Ivan O'Brien, Kunak McGann

Children: picture books; fiction for all ages; illustrated fiction for ages 3+, 5+, 6+, 8+ years, novels (10+ and YA): contemporary, historical, fantasy. Non-fiction.

No poetry or academic. Unsolicited MSS (sample chapters only), synopses and ideas for books welcome – submissions will not be returned. Further information available on website. Founded 1974.

## Old Barn Books*[‡]

Warren Barn, Bedham Lane, Fittleworth, West Sussex RH20 1JW
*tel* (01798) 865010
*email* ruth@oldbarnbooks.com
*website* www.oldbarnbooks.com
*Facebook* www.facebook.com/oldbarnbooks
*Twitter* @oldbarnbooks
*Instagram* @oldbarnbooks

Independent publisher of picture books and fiction for children up to 14 years and the occasional gift book for adults. Interested in the natural world and promoting empathy. Not currently accepting unsolicited submissions. Founded 2015.

## Otter-Barry Books Ltd[‡]

Little Orchard, Burley Gate, Herts. HR1 3QS
*tel* (01432) 820915
*email* info@otterbarrybooks.com
*website* www.otterbarrybooks.com
*Twitter* @otterbarrybooks
*Publisher* Janetta Otter-Barry

Publishes illustrated books for children 0–11+ years. Authors and illustrators include Jackie Morris, Joseph Coelho, Chitra Soundar, Petr Horáček and Ken Wilson-Max. Founded 2015.

## Owlet Press[‡]

*tel* 07920 446328
*email* sam@owletpress.com
*website* www.owletpress.com
*Facebook* www.facebook.com/owletpress
*Twitter* @owletpress

Independent publisher of children's books. Works with established and new, under-represented authors and illustrators. Founded 2017.

## Oxford University Press*

Great Clarendon Street, Oxford OX2 6DP
*tel* (01865) 556767
*email* enquiry@oup.com
*website* www.oup.com
*Ceo* Nigel Portwood

Archaeology, architecture, art, belles lettres, bibles, bibliography, children's books (fiction, non-fiction, picture), commerce, current affairs, dictionaries, drama, economics, educational (foundation, primary, secondary, technical, university), encyclopedias, ELT, electronic publishing, essays, foreign language learning, general history, hymn and service books, journals, law, medical, music, oriental, philosophy, political economy, prayer books, reference, science, sociology, theology and religion; educational software; *Grove Dictionaries of Music & Art*. Trade paperbacks published under the imprint of Oxford Paperbacks. Founded 1478.

**Children's and Educational Division**

Picture books, fiction, poetry and dictionaries. Authors include Tim Bowler, Gillian Cross, Julie Hearne and Geraldine McCaughrean.

## Palazzo Editions

15 Church Road, London SW13 9HE
*email* info@palazzoeditions.com
*website* www.palazzoeditions.com
*Facebook* www.facebook.com/palazzoeditions
*Twitter* @palazzoeditions
*Publishers* Rob Nichols, Jon Rippon

Publisher of high-end illustrated non-fiction. Founded 1998.

## Pan Macmillan*

6 Briset Street, Farringdon, London EC1M 5NR
*tel* 020-7038 5000
*email* publicity@macmillan.com
*website* www.panmacmillan.com
*Ceo* Joanna Prior

For children: fiction and non-fiction including popular reference. Founded 1843.

**Campbell**

Early learning, pop-up, novelty, board books for the preschool market.

**Kingfisher**

Illustrated non-fiction books for children.

**Macmillan Children's Books**

Imprint for Macmillan Children's Books.

**Tor**

Sci-fi and fantasy published in hardback and paperback.

**Two Hoots**

Illustrated children's books.

## Pearson UK*

Edinburgh Gate, Harlow, Essex CM20 2JE
*tel* 0845 313 6666
*email* schools@longman.co.uk
*website* www.pearsoned.co.uk
*Ceo* Andy Bird

Consists of five divisions: Virtual Learning, Higher Education, English Language Learning, Workforce Skills and Assessment and Qualifications. Imprints include: Addison-Wesley Professional, Adobe Press, Allyn & Bacon, BBC Active, Benjamin Cummings, Causeway Press, Cisco Press, Edexcel, Exam Cram, FT Press (formerly FT Prentice Hall), Ginn & Company, Edwin Ginn, Harvester Wheatsheaf, IBM Press, InformIT, LifeBound, Macromedia Press, Maths Champs, MySQL Press, New Riders, Novell

Press, Oliver & Boyd, Payne Galway, Peachpit, Pearson Custom Publishing, Pearson Longman (formerly Longman), Penguin Books, Pi Press, Pitman, Prentice Hall, Prospero, Puffin, Que Publishing, Rigby, SAMS Publishing, VangoBooks, Wharton School Publishing and York Notes. Founded 1998.

## Penguin Random House Children's UK*

One Embassy Gardens, 8 Viaduct Gardens,
London SW11 7AY
*tel* 020-7139 3000
*website* www.penguin.co.uk/company/publishers/
penguin-random-house-children-s
*Managing Director* Francesca Dow

Part of Penguin Random House UK (see below). Children's paperback and hardback books: wide range of picture books, board books, gift books and novelties; fiction; non-fiction, popular culture, digital and audio. Preschool illustrated developmental books for 0–6 years; licensed brands; children's classic publishing and merchandising properties. No unsolicited MSS or original artwork or text. Imprints: Ladybird (page 36), Puffin, Penguin. Founded 2013.

## Penguin Random House UK*

One Embassy Gardens, 8 Viaduct Gardens,
London SW11 7BW
*tel* 020-7139 3000
*website* www.penguin.co.uk
*Ceo* Tom Weldon

Penguin Random House UK group companies which publish books for children: Penguin Random House Children's UK (see above). Founded 2013.

## Phaidon Press Ltd

2 Cooperage Yard, London E15 2GR
*tel* 020-7843 1000
*email* enquiries@phaidon.com
*website* www.phaidon.com
*Editorial Director* Tracey Smith, *Vice-President & Publisher* Deborah Aaronson, *Associate Publisher, Children's Books* Maya Gartner.

Visual arts, lifestyle, culture and food. Founded 1923.

## Piccadilly Press*

Victoria House, Bloomsbury Square,
London WC1B 4DA
*tel* 020-3770 8888
*email* hello@bonnierbooks.co.uk
*website* www.bonnierbooks.co.uk
*Twitter* @PiccadillyPress
*Managing Director* Helen Wicks

Publishes books primarily for readers 5 to 12 years old. Titles can be standalone stories or part of a series. Imprint of Bonnier Books UK (page 29). Founded 1983.

## Pikku Publishing‡

7 High Street, Barkway, Royston, Herts. SG8 8EA
*tel* (01763) 849656
*email* info@pikkupublishing.com
*website* https://pikkupublishing.com/
*Twitter* @pikkupublishing

Publishes original, illustrated books for 3–13 years. Founded 2020.

## Poolbeg Press Ltd

123 Grange Hill, Baldoyle, Dublin D13 N529, Republic of Ireland
*tel* +353 (0)18 063825
*email* info@poolbeg.com
*website* www.poolbeg.com
*Directors* Kieran Devlin, Barbara Devlin

Children's and teenage fiction. Imprints: Poolbeg, In a Nut Shell. Founded 1976.

## Priddy Books

The Stables, 4 Crinan Street, London N1 9XW
*tel* 020-7418 5515
*website* www.priddybooks.com
*Publisher* Roger Priddy

Specialises in baby/toddler and preschool books: activity books, board books, novelty books, picture books. Founded 2000.

## Prim-Ed Publishing

Unit 2A, Block E, Waterford Road Business Park, New Ross, Co. Wexford Y34 NC82, Republic of Ireland
*tel* +353 (0)5 1440075
*email* marketing@prim-ed.com
*website* www.prim-ed.com
*Managing Director* Seamus McGuinness

Educational publisher specialising in copymasters (photocopiable teaching resources) for primary school and special educational needs. Books written by practising classroom teachers. Founded 1993.

## Puffin – see Penguin Random House Children's UK

## Pure Indigo Ltd

Publishing Department, 17 The Herons, Cottenham, Cambridge CB24 8XX
*tel* 07981 395258
*email* ashley.martin@pureindigo.co.uk
*website* www.pureindigo.co.uk/publishing
*Commissioning Editor* Ashley Martin

Currently closed to submissions. Children's books: develops innovative junior series fiction. Also develops software products that complement the product range. The junior series fiction titles are developed in house and on occasion authors and illustrators are commissioned to complete project-based work. Founded 2005.

## Pushkin Press*

New Wing, Somerset House, Strand, London WC2R 1LA
*email* books@pushkinpress.com
*website* www.pushkinpress.com
*Facebook* www.facebook.com/PushkinPress
*Twitter* @pushkinpress
*Publisher* Adam Freudenheim, *Deputy Publisher* Laura Macaulay, *Commissioning Editor* Daniel Seton

Publishes European classics of the 20th century and novels, essays, memoirs, children's books (Pushkin's Children's Books). Imprints: Pushkin Press, Pushkin Children's Books, Pushkin Vertigo, ONE. Founded 1997.

## The Quarto Group, Inc.

The Quarto Group, Inc., 1 Triptych Place, Second Floor, London SE1 9SH
*tel* 020-7700 9000 / 020-7700 8066
*email* dan.rosenberg@quarto.com
*website* www.quarto.com
*Chairman* Peter Read, *Group Ceo* Alison Goff

Composed of three publishing divisions: Quarto International Co-editions Group, Quarto Publishing Group US and Quarto Publishing Group UK. Quarto has nine children's imprints: Quarto International Co-editions Group (Quarto Children's Books', QED Publishing, Ivy Kids, small world creations, Happy Yak (page 34), Marshall Children's Books, Quarto Publishing Group UK (Wide Eyed Editions) (page 45), Frances Lincoln Children's Books (page 37) and Quarto Publishing Group US (Walter Foster Jr.). Founded 1976.

## Ransom Publishing Ltd*‡

Unit 7, Brocklands Farm, West Meon GU32 1JN
*tel* (01730) 829091
*email* ransom@ransom.co.uk
*website* www.ransom.co.uk
*Managing Director* Jenny Ertle, *Creative Director* Steve Rickard

Children's fiction and non-fiction, phonics and school reading programmes, and books for children and adults who are reluctant or struggling readers. Range covers high interest age/low reading age titles, quick reads and reading schemes. Currently not accepting any unsolicited submissions. Founded 1995.

### Raven Books

Publishes fiction and non-fiction for children 8–14 years.

## Really Decent Books

156 Newbridge Road, Bath BA1 3LE
*tel* (01225) 334747
*email* info@reallydecentbooks.co.uk
*website* www.reallydecentbooks.co.uk
*Facebook* www.facebook.com/reallydecentbooks

Books

*Twitter* @ReallyDecent
*Publisher* Phil Dauncey

Independent publisher of books for babies, toddlers and children. Founded 2012.

## Red Bird Publishing

Kiln Farm, East End Green, Brightlingsea, Colchester, Essex CO7 0SX
*tel* (01206) 303525
*email* info@red-bird.co.uk
*website* www.red-bird.co.uk

Innovative children's activity packs and books produced with a mix of techniques and materials. Activity books, novelty books, picture books, painting and colouring books, teaching books, posters, hobbies, nature and the environment, science. Age groups: preschool, 5–10, 10–15. Authors are specialists in their fields. No unsolicited MSS. Founded 1998.

## Rockpool Children's Books Ltd

6 Kitchener Terrace, Ferryhill,
Co. Durham DL17 8AX
*tel* 07711 351691
*email* stuarttrotter3@gmail.com
*website* www.rockpoolchildrensbooks.co.uk
*Facebook* www.facebook.com/
RockpoolChildrensBooks
*Twitter* @rockpooltweets
*Instagram* @rockpool_childrens_books
*Publisher & Creative Director* Stuart Trotter

Independent publisher of quality children's picture books. Founded 2006.

## Ruby Tuesday Books Ltd‡

6 Newlands Road, Tunbridge Wells, Kent TN4 9AT
*tel* (01892) 557767
*email* shan@rubytuesdaybooks.com
*website* www.rubytuesdaybooks.com
*Twitter* @RubyTuesdaybk
*Publisher & Author* Ruth Owen

Publishes children's books. Founded 2008.

## SAGE Publishing*‡

1 Oliver's Yard, 55 City Road, London EC1Y 1SP
*tel* 020-7324 8500
*email* info@sagepub.co.uk
*website* www.sagepublishing.com
*Facebook* www.facebook.com/SAGEPublishing
*Twitter* @SAGE_Publishing
*Instagram* @sage_publishing

Journals, books and library products for the educational, scholarly and professional markets. Founded 1965.

## Scallywag Press Ltd*

10 Sutherland Row, London SW1V 4JT
*tel* 07910 278462

*email* publisher@scallywagpress.com
*website* www.scallywagpress.com
*Twitter* @scallywagpress
*Instagram* @scallywagpress
*Contact* Sarah Pakenham

Publishes works by newcomers as well as established authors and illustrators. Currently not accepting unsolicited MSS. Founded 2018.

## Schofield & Sims Ltd*

7 Mariner Cour, Wakefield, West Yorks. WF4 3FL
*tel* (01484) 607080
*email* editorial@schofieldandsims.co.uk
*website* www.schofieldandsims.co.uk

Educational: nursery, infants, primary; posters. Founded 1901.

## Scholastic Ltd*

Euston House, 24 Eversholt Street,
London NW1 1DB
*tel* 020-7756 7756
*website* www.scholastic.co.uk
*President & Ceo* Peter Warwick

Children's fiction, non-fiction and picture books, education resources for primary schools. Owned by Scholastic Inc. Founded 1964.

### Chicken House

See page 30.

### Scholastic Children's Books

*tel* 020-7756 7761
*email* submissions@scholastic.co.uk
*website* www.scholastic.co.uk
*Twitter* @scholasticuk
*Fiction Publisher* Lauren Fortune, *Non-Fiction Publisher & Licensing* Elizabeth Scoggins, *Editorial Director, Illustrated Books* Felicity Osborne

Activity books, novelty books, picture books, fiction for 5–12 years, teenage fiction, series fiction and film/TV tie-ins. Successes include *Tom Gates* series by Liz Pichon, *Horrible Histories* by Terry Deary and Martin Brown, *His Dark Materials* by Philip Pullman, *The Hunger Games* by Suzanne Collins, and picture books by Julia Donaldson and Axel Scheffler including *Stick Man*, *Zog*, *Tiddler* and *The Highway Rat* , and *Wonky Donkey* by Craig Smith and Katz Cowley. Imprints: Scholastic, Alison Green Books. No unsolicited MSS. Unsolicited illustrations are accepted, but do not send any original artwork as it will not be returned.

### Scholastic Educational Resources

Book End, Range Road, Witney, Oxon OX29 0YD
*tel* (01993) 893456
*Publishing Director* Robin Hunt

Professional books, classroom materials, home learning books and online resources for primary teachers, and GCSE support material.

## Scripture Union

Trinity House, Opal Court, Fox Milne,
Milton Keynes MK15 0DF
*tel* (01908) 856000
*email* hello@scriptureunion.org.uk
*website* www.scriptureunion.org.uk
*Director of Ministry Development (Publishing)* Terry
Clutterham

Christian books and bible reading materials for
people of all ages; educational and worship resources
for churches; adult fiction and non-fiction; children's
fiction and non-fiction (age groups: under 5, 5–8
years, 8–10 years and youth). Publishes approx. 40
titles each year for children/young people and has
200–250 in print. Successes include the *Bible
Storybook* series and *Essential 100* by Whitney
Kuniholm. Will not consider unsolicited MSS.
Founded 1867.

## SEN Press Ltd

1 Necton Road, Wheathampstead AL4 8AT
*tel* (01582) 833205
*email* info@senpress.org
*website* www.senpress.org
*Publisher* Janie Nicholas

Literacy and life skills resources for 14–19 years with
special educational needs. Founded 2003.

## Shepheard-Walwyn (Publishers) Ltd‡

107 Parkway House, Sheen Lane, London SW14 8LS
*tel* 020-8241 5927
*email* books@shepheardwalwyn.com
*website* www.shepheardwalwyn.com,
www.ethicaleconomics.org.uk
*Facebook* www.facebook.com/
ShepheardWalwynPublishers
*Twitter* @SWPublishing
*Instagram* @swpublishers
*Director* M. Lombardo, *Marketing Manager* T.
Kerrigan, *Production Manager* K. Toth

Publishes books for children with a focus on the
environment. Publishing partner of The School of
Philosophy and Economic Science, London. IPG
member. Hosts a podcast: https://
shepheardwalwyn.podbean.com. Founded 1971.

## Simon & Schuster UK Ltd*

222 Gray's Inn Road, London WC1X 8HB
*tel* 020-7316 1900
*email* enquiries@simonandschuster.co.uk
*website* www.simonandschuster.co.uk
*Facebook* www.facebook.com/simonschusterUK
*Twitter* @simonschusteruk
*Directors* Ian Chapman (Ceo), Rachel Denwood
(managing director, children's), Ali Dougal
(publishing director, children's)

Children's and YA fiction, picture books, novelty,
pop-up and licensed character. Founded 1986.

### Simon & Schuster Audio

*website* www.simonandschuster.co.uk/audio
*Publisher* Dominic Brendon

Fiction, children's, YA and non-fiction audiobooks.
Authors include Graham Swift, Philippa Gregory,
Bruce Springsteen and Anita Anand.

## Smart Learning

Unit 2, Aston Way, Middlewich, Cheshire CW10 0HS
*tel* (01423) 206200
*email* admin@smart-learning.co.uk
*website* www.smart-learning.co.uk

High-quality teaching and learning resources for both
teachers and children – from Foundation Stage
through to KS3. Publishes software and books to
enhance the teaching and learning of ICT, phonics,
literacy, PSHE and citizenship and English.
Founded 2012.

## SRL Publishing Ltd*

*email* admin@srlpublishing.co.uk
*website* www.srlpublishing.co.uk
*Facebook* www.facebook.com/srlpublishing
*Twitter* @srlpublishing
*Instagram* @srlpublishing

A climate-positive publisher. Titles range from YA,
new adult, contemporary fiction and crime/thriller to
non-fiction. Founded 2014.

## Stacey Publishing Ltd

14 Great College Street, London SW1P 3RX
*tel* 020-7221 7166
*email* info@stacey-international.co.uk
*website* www.stacey-international.co.uk
*Founder* Tom Stacey

Illustrated books for children 3–12 years. Publishers
of the *Musgrove* series. Founded 1974.

## Strident Publishing Ltd

22 Strathwhillan Drive, Hairmyres, Glasgow G75 8GT
*tel* (01355) 220588
*email* info@stridentpublishing.co.uk
*website* www.stridentpublishing.co.uk

Fiction for children 7–18 years. Publishes approx. 15
books a year. Works closely with authors who present
in schools and at festivals. Email proposed blurb
together with the first three chapters and covering
letter stating why book is likely to appeal to readers.
Founded 2005.

## Stripes – see Little Tiger Group

## Studio Press*

Victoria House, Bloomsbury Square,
London WC1B 4DA
*tel* 020-3770 8888
*email* hello@bonnierbooks.co.uk
*website* www.bonnierbooks.co.uk
*Twitter* @StudioPress
*Executive Director* Helen Wicks

Publishes a diverse range of books for all ages. Subjects include: pop culture trends and health, well-being and environmental issues. Publishing partner to major brands including Disney, Marvel and Harry Potter. An imprint of Bonnier Books UK (page 29). Founded 2015.

## Sweet Cherry Publishing*‡

Unit 4u18, The Book Brothers Business Park, Tolwell Road, Leicester LE4 1BR
*tel* 0116 253 6796
*email* info@sweetcherrypublishing.com
*website* www.sweetcherrypublishing.com
*Facebook* www.facebook.com/sweetcherrypublishing
*Twitter* @sweetcherrypub
*Director* A. Thadha

Award-winning specialist in children's fiction series. Children's picture books, novelty books, gift books, board books, educational books and fiction series for all ages. Also welcomes YA novels and series. See website for submission guidelines. Imprints include Clock Tower and Cherry Stone. Clock Tower aims to champion marginalised voices and values diversity, inclusivity and representation. Founded 2011.

### Clock Tower

Champions marginalised and diverse voices, aiming to bring readers a range of trade fiction for all ages, including standalone and series titles.

## Tarquin Publications

Suite 74, 17 Holywell Hill, St Albans AL1 1DT
*tel* (01727) 833866
*email* info@tarquinbooks.com
*website* www.tarquinbooks.com

Mathematical models, puzzles, codes and logic and paper engineering books for children. Publishes 7–8 titles each year and has over 100 in print. Successes include *Magic Moving Images* and *Mini Mathematical Murder Mysteries*. Do not send unsolicited MSS. Send a one-page proposal of idea. Founded 1970.

## Taylor & Francis Group*

4 Park Square, Milton Park, Abingdon, Oxon OX14 4RN
*tel* 020-7017 6000
*email* enquiries@taylorandfrancis.com
*website* https://taylorandfrancis.com/
*Ceo* Annie Callanan, *Managing Director* Jeremy North (Taylor & Francis, Academic Learning)

Academic and reference books, including education. Imprints include CRC Press, Routledge, and Taylor & Francis. Founded 1798.

## Templar Books*

Victoria House, Bloomsbury Square, London WC1B 4DA
*tel* 020-3770 8888
*email* hello@bonnierbooks.co.uk
*website* www.bonnierbooks.co.uk
*Twitter* @templarbooks
*Publisher* Sophie Hallam

Children's imprint. Series include the *Ology* series, *Jonny Duddle's Gigantosaurus* titles and the *Amazing Baby* range of board and novelty books. Imprint of Bonnier Books UK (page 29). Founded 1978.

## Tiny Owl Publishing Ltd

6 Hatfield road, London W4 1AF
*email* info@tinyowl.co.uk
*website* www.tinyowl.co.uk
*Facebook* www.facebook.com/tinyowlpublishing
*Twitter* @TinyOwl_Books
*Publisher* Delaram Ghanimifard

An independent publisher of global children's literature. Publishes high-quality picture books for children 3–11 years. Aims to promote diversity and human rights values. Founded 2015.

## Troika*

Troika Books Ltd, Well House, Green Lane, Ardleigh, Colchester, Essex CO7 7PD
*email* info@troikabooks.com
*website* www.troikabooks.com
*Publisher* Martin West, *Publicity, Marketing & Editorial* Roy Johnson

Publishes picture books, poetry and fiction for all ages, with an emphasis on quality, accessibility and diversity. Founded 2012.

## UCLan Publishing

Victoria Street, Preston PR1 2HE
*email* uclanpublishing@uclan.ac.uk
*website* https://uclanpublishing.com/
*Facebook* www.facebook.com/uclanpublishing
*Twitter* @publishinguclan
*Publisher* Hazel Holmes

Supporting students at the University of Central Lancashire, not-for-profit publishers of early years, middle grade, teen and YA fiction. Currently closed to submissions. Founded 2010.

## Usborne Publishing Ltd‡

Usborne House, 83–85 Saffron Hill, London EC1N 8RT
*tel* 020-7430 2800
*email* mail@usborne.co.uk
*website* www.usborne.com
*Ceo* Peter Usborne, *Directors* Nicola Usborne, Jenny Tyler (editorial), Andrea Parsons

An independent, family publisher of books for children of all ages, including baby, preschool, novelty, activity, non-fiction and fiction. Looking for high-quality imaginative children's fiction. No unsolicited MSS. Founded 1973.

## Wacky Bee Books*

Riverbank House, 1 Putney Bridge Approach, London SW6 3JD
*tel* 020-7801 6300

email hello@wackybeebooks.com
website www.wackybeebooks.com
Facebook www.facebook.com/wackybeebooks
Twitter @wackybeebooks
Director Louise Jordan

Publishing books with a buzz for children 3–12 years. Picture books for 3+ years, early readers for 5–7 years, general fiction for 8–12 years. Submission enquiries by email to submissions@wackybeebooks.com. Founded 2014.

## Walker Books Ltd*‡

87 Vauxhall Walk, London SE11 5HJ
tel 020-7793 0909
website www.walker.co.uk
Facebook www.facebook.com/walkerbooks
Twitter @walkerbooksuk
Instagram @walkerbooksuk
Editors Karen Lotz, Jane Winterbotham, Denise Johnstone-Burt, Annalie Grainger

An independent company with a global reach, publishing activity books, novelty books, picture books, fiction for 5–8 years and 9–12 years, YA fiction, series fiction, film/TV tie-ins, plays, poetry, digital and audio. Publishes approx. 300 titles each year and has 2,000 in print. Continuing successes include the *Alex Rider* series by Anthony Horowitz, *Chaos Walking* by Patrick Ness, *Maisy* by Lucy Cousins, *Where's Wally?* by Martin Handford, the *Mortal Instruments* series by Cassandra Clare and a wide range of award-winning novels and picture books by other authors and illustrators. Imprints: Walker Books, Walker Studio, MIT Kids Press, MITeen Press and Walker Entertainment. Write to the editor, enclosing sae, and allow six months for response. Founded 1980.

## Welbeck Publishing Group*

20 Mortimer Street, London W1T 3JW
tel 020-7612 0400
email enquiries@welbeckpublishing.com
website www.welbeckpublishing.com

No unsolicited MSS; synopses and ideas welcome, but no fiction or poetry. Acquired by Hachette UK (page 34) 2022. Founded 2019.

### Mortimer

Children's entertainment, licensing and gaming.

### Welbeck Flame

*Associate Publisher* Felicity Alexander
Children's fiction.

## What On Earth Books*‡

The Black Barn, Wickhurst Farm, Leigh, Tonbridge, Kent TN11 8PS
tel (01732) 464621

email info@whatonearthbooks.com
website www.whatonearthbooks.com
Twitter @whatonearthbook
Founder & Ceo Christopher Lloyd Publisher & Editor-in-Chief Nancy Feresten

Publishes children's non-fiction books that engage their natural curiosity and passion for learning. Founded 2010.

## Wide Eyed Editions

The Old Brewery, 6 Blundell Street, London N7 9BH
tel 020-7700 6700
website www.quartoknows.com/Wide-Eyed-Editions
Publisher Georgia Amison-Bradshaw

Imprint of the Quarto Group, Inc. (page 41). Creates original non-fiction for children. Founded 2014.

## Y Lolfa Cyf

Talybont, Ceredigion SY24 5HE
tel (01970) 832304
email ylolfa@ylolfa.com
website www.ylolfa.com
Director Garmon Gruffudd, Editor Lefi Gruffudd

Welsh language books and English books of Welsh and Celtic interest, popular biographies and sports books. Founded 1967.

## ZigZag Education

Unit 3, Greenway Business Centre, Doncaster Road, Bristol BS10 5PY
tel 0117 950 3199
email submissions@publishmenow.co.uk
website www.zigzageducation.co.uk, www.publishmenow.co.uk
Development Director John-Lloyd Hagger, Strategy Director Mike Stephens

Secondary school teaching resources: English, maths, ICT, geography, history, science, business, politics, P.E., media studies. Founded 1998.

## ZunTold

email elainebous@gmail.com
website https://zuntold.com/
Facebook www.facebook.com/zuntoldbooks
Twitter @zuntold
Instagram @zuntold_books
Director Elaine Bousfield

Publishes new fiction for children and young people. Also supports young people in their own writing. Interested in middle-grade fiction (9–12), teens, YA and crossover fiction. Agent submissions send a copy of synopsis and the first three chapters. Submissions opened for authors without an agent in June (for YA, new adult, crossover fiction) and in December (for middle grade). Does not work with picture books. Founded 2016.

# Children's book publishers overseas

Listings are given for children's book publishers in Australia (below), Canada (page 48), France (page 50), Germany (page 51), Italy (page 52), the Netherlands (page 52), New Zealand (page 52), South Africa (page 53), Spain (page 55) and the USA (page 55).

sae = self-addressed envelope
MS = manuscript (MSS = manuscripts)

## AUSTRALIA

*Member of the Australian Publishers Association*

### ACER Press*

19 Prospect Hill Road, Private Bag 55, Camberwell, VIC 3124
*tel* +61 (0)3 9277 5555
*email* proposals@acer.org
*website* www.acer.org/au

Publisher of the Australian Council for Educational Research. Produces a range of books and assessments including professional resources for teachers, psychologists and special educational needs professionals. Founded 1930.

### Affirm Press*

28 Thistlethwaite Street, South Melbourne, VIC 3205
*tel* +61 (0)3 8695 9623
*email* info@affirmpress.com.au
*website* https://affirmpress.com.au/
*Facebook* www.facebook.com/affirmpress
*Twitter* @affirmpress
*Ceo & Publishing Director* Martin Hughes

Non-fiction, fiction and young fiction. Founded 2010.

### Allen & Unwin Pty Ltd*

83 Alexander Street, Crows Nest, NSW 2065
*Postal address* PO Box 8500, St Leonards, NSW 1590
*tel* +61 (0)2 8425 0100
*website* www.allenandunwin.com
*Chairman* Patrick Gallagher, *Ceo* Robert Gorman,
*Publishing Directors* Jane Morrow (Murdock Books),
Eva Mills (children & YA), Cate Paterson (Atlantic Books)

Fiction for children 5–9 and 10–13 years, teenage fiction, series fiction and narrative non-fiction. Also adult/general trade books, including fiction and broad-ranging non-fiction. Imprints include: Allen & Unwin, Albert Street Books, Atlantic Books, Inspired Living, Crows Nest, House of Books, Murdoch Books, Pier 9. Submission guidelines: will consider unsolicited MSS (but not picture book texts). Will only accept MSS through the electronic Friday Pitch system. Founded 1990.

### Bloomsbury Publishing Pty Ltd*

Level 6, 387 George Street, Sydney, NSW 2000
*tel* +61 (0)2 8820 4900
*email* au@bloomsbury.com
*website* www.bloomsbury.com/au
*Facebook* www.facebook.com/
bloomsburypublishingaustralia
*Twitter* @BloomsburySyd
*Managing Director* Cristina Cappelluto

Supports the worldwide publishing activities of Bloomsbury Publishing: caters for the Australia and New Zealand territories. Bloomsbury Publishing Plc founded 1986.

### Brolly Books*

Suite 330, 45 Glenferrie Road, Malvern, VIC 3181
*tel* + 61 3 95338863
*email* andrew@brollybooks.com
*website* https://brollybooks.com

An independent Australian publishing house specialising in Australian children's books, boxed picture jigsaws and general non-fiction. Founded 1997.

### Cambridge University Press & Assessment Education Australia*

477 Williamstown Road, Private Bag 31, Port Melbourne, VIC 3207
*tel* +61 (0)3 8671 1400
*email* enquiries@cambridge.edu.au
*website* www.cambridge.edu.au/education
*Executive Director* Mark O'Neill

Academic, educational, reference, ESL. Founded 1534.

### Cengage Learning Australia*

Level 7, 80 Dorcas Street, South Melbourne, VIC 3205
*tel* +61 (0)3 9685 4111
*website* www.cengage.com.au

Educational books. Founded 2007.

### ELK Publishing

PO Box 2828, Toowoomba, QLD 4350
*tel* +61 (0)4 0030 1675 / +61 (0)4 7592 3670
*email* contactus@elk-publishing.com
*website* www.elk-publishing.com
*Facebook* www.facebook.com/elkpublishing

*Twitter* @elkpublish
*Instagram* @elkpublishing
*Founder & Ceo* Selina Kucks

An Australian-grown, independent publishing house of children's and educational literature. Established in Korea, the company is presently based in Queensland, Australia. ELK Publishing creates children's and educational books, provides opportunities for unknown artists and illustrators to collaborate with in-house authors and offers internships to university students who are presently engaged in literary scholarship. Founded in Seoul, Korea, 2009.

## Hachette Australia Pty Ltd*

Level 17, 207 Kent Street, Sydney, NSW 2000
*tel* +61 (0)2 8248 0800
*email* auspub@hachette.com.au
*website* www.hachette.com.au
*Ceo* Louise Stark

General, children's: picture books, fiction for children 5–8 and 9–12 years, teenage fiction and series fiction. Accepts MSS via website. Founded 1971.

## Hardie Grant Children's Publishing*

Ground Floor, Building 1, 658 Church Street, Richmond, VIC 3121
*tel* +61 (0)3 8520 6444
*email* info@hardiegrantchildrenspublishing.com.au
*website* www.hardiegrantchildrens.com

The young readers' division of one of Australia's largest independent publishers. Publishes a diverse list of fiction, non-fiction, graphic novels and picture books, including two imprints of illustrated titles: Little Hare and Bright Light. Check website for details of when submissions are accepted. Founded 2010.

## HarperCollins Publishers (Australia) Pty Ltd Group*

*Postal address* PO Box A565, Sydney South, NSW 1235
*tel* +61 (0)2 9952 5000
*website* www.harpercollins.com.au

Literary fiction and non-fiction, popular fiction, children's, reference, biography, autobiography, current affairs, sport, lifestyle, health/self-help, humour, true crime, travel, Australiana, history, business, gift, religion. Founded 1989.

## McGraw-Hill Australia Pty Ltd*

Level 2, 82 Waterloo Road, North Ryde, NSW 2113
*Postal address* Private Bag 2233, Business Centre, North Ryde, NSW 1670
*tel* +61 (0)2 9900 1800
*website* www.mcgraw-hill.com.au
*Facebook* www.facebook.com/MHEducationANZ
*Twitter* @MHeducationAU

Educational publisher: higher education, primary education and professional (including medical,

general and reference). Division of the McGraw-Hill Companies. Founded 1964.

## New Frontier Publishing*

Suite 83/20-40 Meagher Street, Chippendale, NSW 2008
*tel* +61 (0)2 9660 4614
*email* info@newfrontier.com.au
*website* www.newfrontier.com.au

Aims to uplift, educate and inspire through its range of children's books. Activity books, board books, picture books, middle-grade fiction, dictionaries, textbooks. Caters for children 2–12 years. Unsolicited MSS accepted. Understanding of existing list crucial. Downloadable submissions pack available via website. Founded 2002.

## Pan Macmillan Australia Pty Ltd*

Level 25, 1 Market Street, Sydney, NSW 2000
*tel* +61 (0)2 9285 9100
*email* pan.reception@macmillan.com.au
*website* www.panmacmillan.com.au
*Publishing Director* Ingrid Ohlsson

Commercial and literary fiction; children's and YA fiction; non-fiction and character products; general non-fiction; sport; cooking and lifestyle. Founded 1843.

## Penguin Random House Australia Pty Ltd*

*Sydney office* Level 3, 100 Pacific Highway, North Sydney, NSW 2060
*tel* +61 (0)2 9954 9966
*email* information@penguinrandomhouse.com.au
*Melbourne office* 707 Collins Street, Melbourne, VIC 3008
*website* www.penguinrandomhouse.com.au
*Ceo* Julie Burland, *Publishing Directors* Holly Toohey, Laura Harris (Penguin Young Readers), Karen Reid (Launch Title)

General fiction and non-fiction; children's, illustrated. MS submissions for non-fiction accepted, unbound in hard copy addressed to Submissions Editor. Fiction submissions are only accepted from previously published authors, or authors represented by an agent or accompanied by a report from an accredited assessment service. Imprints: Arrow, Bantam, Ebury, Hamish Hamilton, Knopf, Michael Joseph, Penguin, Viking, Vintage and William Heinemann. Subsidiary of Bertelsmann AG. Founded 2013.

## University of Queensland Press*

PO Box 6042, St Lucia, QLD 4067
*tel* +61 (0)7 3365 7244
*email* reception@uqp.com.au
*website* www.uqp.com.au

Publishes children's and YA as well as fiction, non-fiction and poetry for all ages. Founded 1948.

Books

## R.I.C. Publications Pty Ltd

5 Bendsten Place, Balcatta, WA 6021
*tel* +61 (0)8 9240 9888
*website* www.ricpublications.com.au

Educational publisher specialising in blackline master or copymasters and student workbooks for schools and homeschoolers. Founded 1986.

## Rhiza Edge

PO Box 302, Chinchilla, QLD 4413
*tel* +61 (0)7 3245 1938
*email* editor@rhizaedge.com.au
*website* www.rhizaedge.com.au
*Facebook* www.facebook.com/rhizaedge
*Commissioning Editor* Emily Lighezzolo

Publishes issue-based stories for YA readers. Imprint of Wombat Books (below). Founded 2018.

## Scholastic Australia Pty Ltd*

76–80 Railway Crescent, Lisarow, Gosford, NSW 2250
*tel* +61 (0)2 4328 3555
*website* www.scholastic.com.au
*Chairman* David Peagram

Children's fiction and non-fiction. Founded 1968.

## Wombat Books*

PO Box 302, Chinchilla, QLD 4413
*tel* +61 (0)7 3245 1938
*email* website@wombatrhiza.com.au
*website* www.wombatrhiza.com.au
*Facebook* www.facebook.com/wombatbooks
*Publisher* Rochelle Manners

An independent publisher of children's picture books and books for early readers. YA and adult imprint: Rhiza Edge (above). Founded 2009.

# CANADA

*\*Member of the Canadian Publishers' Council*
*†Member of the Association of Canadian Publishers*

## Annick Press Ltd†

388 Carlaw Avenue, Suite 200 Toronto, ON M4M 2T4
*tel* +1 416-221-4802
*email* annickpress@annickpress.com
*website* www.annickpress.com
*Owner & Director* Rick Wilks

Preschool to YA fiction and non-fiction. Approximately 25% of books are by first-time authors. Founded 1975.

## Breakwater Books†

PO Box 2188, St John's, NL A1C 6E6
*tel* +1 709-722-6680
*email* orders@breakwaterbooks.com
*website* https://breakwaterbooks.com/
*Facebook* www.facebook.com/breakwaterbooksltd

*Twitter* @breakwaterbooks
*President & Publisher* Rebecca Rose

Publishes award-winning writing in all literary genres: fiction, non-fiction, poetry, drama, art, YA and children's books, as well as cookery, guidebooks and educational resources. Founded 1973.

## Dundurn Press†

1382 Queen Street E, Toronto, ON M4L 1C9
*tel* +1 416-214-5544
*email* submissions@dundurn.com
*website* www.dundurn.com
*Facebook* www.facebook.com/dundumpress
*Twitter* @dundumpress

YA fiction. Founded 1972.

## Fitzhenry & Whiteside Ltd

209 Wicksteed Avenue, Unit 51, East York, ON M4G 0B1
*tel* +1 905-477-9700
*email* hdoll@fitzhenry.ca
*website* www.fitzhenry.ca
*Facebook* www.facebook.com/FitzWhits
*Twitter* @FitzWhits
*Ceo* Sharon Fitzhenry

Fiction and non-fiction (biography, environment, social studies, visual arts). Publishes first-time authors. Emphasis is on Canadian authors and illustrators, subject or perspective. Will review MS/illustration packages from artists. Submit outline and copy of sample illustration. For illustrations only, send samples and promotional sheet. Founded 1966.

## HarperCollins Publishers Ltd*

22 Adelaide Street West, 41st Floor, Toronto, ON M5H 4E3
*tel* +1 416-975-9334
*email* hcOrder@harpercollins.com
*website* www.harpercollins.ca

Literary fiction and non-fiction, history, politics, biography, spiritual and children's books. Founded 1989.

## House of Anansi Press and Groundwood Books†

128 Sterling Road, Lower Level, Toronto, ON M6R 2B7
*tel* +1 416-363-4343
*email* publicity@houseofanansi.com
*website* https://houseofanansi.com/
*Facebook* www.facebook.com/groundwoodbooks
*Twitter* @GroundwoodBooks
*Publisher* Karen Li

Groundwood Books publishes books for all ages, including fiction, picture books, graphic novels and non-fiction. Founded 1978.

## Kids Can Press Ltd†

25 Dockside Drive, Toronto, ON M5A 0B5
*tel* +1 416-479-7000

*email* customerservice@kidscan.com
*website* www.kidscanpress.com
*Facebook* www.facebook.com/kidscanbooks
*Twitter* @kidscanpress
*Editorial Director* Yvette Ghione

Middle-grade/YA fiction and non-fiction. Publishes picture books, young readers, middle readers and YA titles. Approximately 10–15% of books are by first-time authors. Submit outline/synopsis and between two and three sample chapters. See website for submission guidelines. Founded 1973.

## McGraw-Hill Canada*

145 Kings Street West, Suite 1501,
Toronto ON M5H 1J8
*tel* +1 800-565-5758
*website* www.mheducation.ca
*Facebook* www.facebook.com/mcgrawhillcanada
*Twitter* @mcgraw_canada

Educational and trade books. Founded 1972.

## Nelson Education*

2005 Sheppard Ave E, Suite 700, Toronto,
ON M2J 5B4
*tel* +1 416-752-9448
*website* www.nelson.com
*President & Ceo* Steve Brown

Educational publishing. Canada's leading K–12 educational publisher, founded on equitable, inclusive and engaging learning. Creator of Edwin, a revolutionary digital platform. Founded 1914.

## Nimbus Publishing†

PO Box 9166, Halifax, NS B3K 5M8
*tel* +1 800-646-2879
*website* https://nimbus.ca/
*Facebook* www.facebook.com/nimbuspub
*Twitter* @nimbuspub

Publishes children's picture books and fiction, literary non-fiction, social and cultural history, nature photography, current events, biography, sports and cultural issues. Founded 1978.

## Oberon Press

203–105 Spruce Street, Ottawa, ON K1R 6P1
*tel* +1 613-238-3275
*email* oberon@sympatico.ca
*website* www.oberonpress.ca

General fiction, short stories, poetry, some biographies, art and children's. Only publishes Canadian writers. Currently not accepting unsolicited MSS. Founded 1985.

## Orca Book Publishers†

1016 Balmoral Road, Victoria, BC V8T 1A8
*tel* +1 800-210-5277
*email* orca@orcabook.com
*website* www.orcabook.com
*Facebook* www.facebook.com/orcabook

*Twitter* @orcabook

Books for children and YA. Will consider MSS from Canadian writers only. No submissions by fax or email. See website for submission guidelines. No poetry. Founded 1984.

## Pajama Press†

11 Davies Avenue, Suite 103, Toronto, ON M4M 2A9
*website* https://pajamapress.ca/
*Facebook* www.facebook.com/pajamapress
*Twitter* @pajamapress
*Publisher* Gail Winskill

Children's: picture books, new sturdy books for the very young, early chapter books for new readers, middle-grade novels, YA novels for pre-high school audiences, and literary non-fiction. Publishes 18 to 20 titles a year. Not currently open to unsolicited submissions. Founded 2011.

## Pearson Canada*

26 Prince Andrew Place, North York, ON M3C 2T8
*tel* +1 800-361-6128
*website* www.pearson.com/ca/en.html

Academic, technical, educational, children's and adult, trade. Founded 1998.

## Penguin Random House Canada Ltd*

320 Front Street West, Suite 1400, Toronto,
ON M5V 3B6
*tel* +1 416-364-4449
*website* www.penguinrandomhouse.ca
*Ceo* Kristin Cochrane

Literary fiction, commercial fiction, memoir, non-fiction (history, business, current events, sports), adult, teen and young readers. No unsolicited MSS; submissions via an agent only. Imprints: Allen Lane Canada, Anchor Canada, Appetite by Random House, Bond Street Books, Doubleday Canada, Emblem, Hamish Hamilton Canada, Knopf Canada, McClelland & Stewart, Penguin Canada, Penguin Teen, Portfolio Canada, Puffin Canada, Random House Canada, Seal Books, Signal, Strange Light, Tundra Books, Viking Canada, Vintage Canada. Subsidiary of Penguin Random House. Founded 2013.

## Rebel Mountain Press†

*email* rebelmountainpress@gmail.com
*website* www.rebelmountainpress.com
*Facebook* www.facebook.com/rebelmountainpress
*Twitter* @rebelmountain1
*Publisher* Lori Szwydky

Publishes children's and YA literature, anthologies and poetry that feature characters and authors who are BIPOC, LGBTQIA2S+ and/or have disabilities. Founded 2015.

## Red Deer Press

209 Wicksteed Avenue, Unit 51 Toronto,
ON M4G 0B1
*tel* +1 800-387-9776

*email* rdp@reddeerpress.com
*website* www.reddeerpress.com
*Facebook* www.facebook.com/reddeerpress
*Twitter* @reddeerpress
*Publisher* Sharon Fitzhenry, *Children's Editor* Beverly Brenna

Literary fiction, sci-fi, non-fiction, children's illustrated books, YA fiction, teen fiction. Publishes books that are written or illustrated by Canadians and that are about or of interest to Canadians. Imprint: RJS (Robert J. Sawyer) Books (sci-fi). Publishes 14–18 new books a year. Children's picture books MSS from established authors with a demonstrable record of publishing success are preferred. Currently accepting new MSS. Founded 1975.

## Ronsdale Press[†]

125A–1030 Denman Street, Vancouver, BC V6G 2M6
*tel* +1 604-738-4688
*email* ronsdale@shaw.ca
*website* www.ronsdalepress.com
*Facebook* www.facebook.com/ronsdalepress
*Twitter* @ronsdalepress
*Director* Veronica Hatch

A Canadian publisher based in Vancouver with some 300 books in print. Not currently accepting picture books. Founded 1988.

## Scholastic Canada Ltd*

175 Hillmount Road, Markham, ON L6C 1Z7
*tel* +1 800-268-3860
*email* custserv@scholastic.ca
*website* www.scholastic.ca
*Facebook* www.facebook.com/ScholasticCanada
*Twitter* @scholasticCDA
*Instagram* @scholasticcda
*Art Director* Andrea Casault

Serves children, parents and teachers through a variety of businesses including Scholastic Reading Club and Book Fairs, Scholastic Education, Classroom Magazines, Trade and Éditions Scholastic. Publishes recreational reading for children and young people from preschoolers to teens and educational materials for kindergarten to Grade 8 in both official languages. Its publishing focus is on books by Canadians. Wholly owned subsidiary of Scholastic Inc. Scholastic Canada is currently interested in reviewing unpublished material by writers from under-represented communities, including Black writers, Indigenous writers, writers of colour, writers with disabilities, LGBTQIA2S+ writers and writers who identify with other marginalised groups. Canadian artists may submit electronic samples of their work along with their website/contact information to the art director. Never send originals. Please see website for submission guidelines. Founded 1920.

## Second Story Press[†]

20 Maud Street, Suite 401, Toronto, ON M5V 2M5
*tel* +1 416-537-7850
*email* info@secondstorypress.ca
*website* https://secondstorypress.ca/
*Facebook* www.facebook.com/secondstorypress
*Twitter* @secondstory

Publishes feminist-inspired fiction and non-fiction for adults, children and YA. Founded 2015.

## University of Toronto Press

800 Bay Street, Mezzanine, Toronto, ON M5S 3A9
*tel* +1 416-978-2239
*email* publishing@utpress.utoronto.ca
*website* www.utorontopress.com
*Facebook* www.facebook.com/utpress
*Twitter* @utpress

Imprints include: Aevo UTP; New Jewish Press; Rotman-UTP Publishing. Publishers of non-fiction, monographs, textbooks and academic books, ESL/EFL, teacher reference, adult basic education and school texts. Founded 1901.

## Tundra Books[†]

320 Front Street West, Suite 1400, Toronto, ON M5V 3B6
*tel* +1 416-364-4449
*email* submissions@tundrabooks.com
*email* art@tundrabooks.com
*website* www.penguinrandomhouse.ca/imprints/TU/tundra-books
*Facebook* www.facebook.com/tundrabooks
*Twitter* @TundraBooks

Publisher of high-quality children's picture books and novels, renowned for its innovations. Publishes books for children to teens. A division of Penguin Random House Canada Ltd (page 49). Founded 1967.

# FRANCE

## l'école des loisirs

11 rue de Sevres, 75006 Paris
*tel* +33 (0)1 4222 9410
*email* edl@ecoledesloisirs.com
*website* www.ecoledesloisirs.fr
*Facebook* www.facebook.com/ecoledesloisirs
*Twitter* @ecoledesloisirs
*Managing Director* Louis Delas

Specialises in children's literature from picture books to YA fiction. Founded 1965.

## Flammarion

82, rue Saint-Lazare CS 10124, 75009 Paris
*tel* +33 (0)1 4051 3100
*website* https://editions.flammarion.com
*Facebook* www.facebook.com/Editions_Flammarion
*Twitter* @Ed_Flammarion
*Ceo* Gilles Haéri

Leading French publisher. Children's imprints include: Albums du Père Castor, Castor Poche, Tribal, Etonnants Classiques, GF – Flammarion, Chan – OK. Founded 1875.

### Père Castor

Children's picture books, junior fiction, activity books, board books, how-to books, comics, gift books, fairy tales, dictionaries and records and tapes. Covers 0–16 years.

## Gallimard Jeunesse

5 rue Gaston Gallimard, 75328 Paris
*tel* +33 (0)1 4954 4200
*website* www.gallimard-jeunesse.fr
*Children's Publisher* Hedwige Pasquet

Publisher of high-quality children's fiction and non-fiction including board books, novelty books, picture books, pop-up books. Founded 1911.

## Hachette Livre/Gautier-Languereau

Building Louis Hachette, 58 rue Jean, Bleuzen, CS 70007 – 92178 Vanves
*tel* +33 (0)1 4392 3030
*website* www.gautier-languereau.fr

Picture books for children. Imaginative stories for children 2–10 years. Publishes approximately 55 titles each year. Will consider unsolicited MSS. Allow four months for response. Contacts on website. Founded 1885.

## Kaléidoscope

11 rue de Sèvres, 75006 Paris
*tel* +33 (0)1 4544 0708
*website* www.editions-kaleidoscope.com
*Facebook* www.facebook.com/editionskaleidoscope
*Twitter* @kaleidoscope
*Children's Publisher* Isabel Finkenstaedt

Specialises in up-market picture books for children 0–6 years. Founded 1989.

## Editions Sarbacane

35 rue d'Hauteville, 75010 Paris
*tel* +33 (0)1 4246 6207
*email* e.beulque@sarbacane.net
*website* www.editions-sarbacane.com

High-quality activity books, board books, picture books and YA fiction, fiction for children from preschool age to adult. Founded 2001.

## Le Sorbier

25 boulevard Romain Rolland, 75014 Paris
*tel* +33 (0)1 4148 8000
*website* www.editionsdelamartiniere.fr
*Twitter* @ed_LaMartiniere

High-quality picture books for children up to 10 years and illustrated reference books for 9–12 years. Imprint: De La Martinière Jeunesse.

# GERMANY

## Carlsen Verlag

Postfach 50 03 80, 22703 Hamburg
*tel* +49 (0)40 398040
*email* info@carlsen.de
*website* www.carlsen.de
*Facebook* www.facebook.com/kanaeleWE
*Twitter* @carlsen_verlag
*Directors* Renate Herre, Joachim Kaufmann

Children's picture books, board books and novelty books. Illustrated fiction and non-fiction. Teenage fiction and non-fiction. Publishes both German and international authors including Stephenie Meyer, J.K. Rowling and Philip Pullman. Publisher of the *Harry Potter* series. Imprint: Chicken House Deutschland. Age groups: preschool, 5–10, 10–15, 15+. Unsolicited MSS welcome but must include a sae for return. Do not follow up by phone or post. For illustrations, submit no more than three colour photocopies and unlimited b&w copies. Founded 1953.

## dtv Verlagsgesellschaft mbH & Co. KG

Tumblingerstraße 21, 80337 Munich
*tel* +49 (0)89 38167282
*email* verlag@dtv.de
*email* junior@dtv.de
*website* www.dtvjunior.de
*Facebook* www.facebook.com/dtvVerlag
*Twitter* @dtv_verlag
*Editor-in-Chief (Early Teen, Young Adult & Young General Fiction)* Susanne Stark

Fiction and non-fiction for children, teenagers, YA and young general fiction. Authors include Yuval Noah Harari, Kate DiCamillo, Kevin Brooks, Colleen Hoover, Sarah J. Maas, Tracy Wolff, Eva Ibbotson. Founded 1971.

## Carl Hanser Verlag

Vilshofener Straße 10, 81679 Munich
*tel* +49 (0)89 998300
*email* info@hanser.de
*website* www.hanser-literaturverlage.de
*Facebook* www.facebook.com/HanserLiteraturverlage
*Twitter* @hanserliteratur
*Instagram* @hanserliteratur, @hanser.hey
*Children's Publisher* Saskia Heintz

High-quality hardback books for all ages from preschool to YA. Board books, picture books, fiction and non-fiction. Age groups: 3–10, 10–15, 15+. Founded 1993.

## Ravensburger Buchverlag

Robert-Bosch-Straße 1, 88214 Ravensburg
*tel* +49 (0)751 860
*email* buchverlag@ravensburger.de
*website* www.ravensburger.de

Activity books, novelty books, picture books, fiction for children 5–8 and 9–12 years, teenage fiction, series fiction and educational games and puzzles. Publishes approx. 450 titles each year and has 1,500 in print. Will consider unsolicited MSS for fiction only. Allow two months for response. Founded 1883.

## ITALY

### De Agostini Editore

Via Giovanni da Verrazano 15, 28100 Novara
*tel* +39 02-380861
*website* www.deagostini.it

Illustrated and children's books. Founded 1901.

### Edizioni Arka srl

Via Milano 73/75, 20010 Cornaredo Milan
*tel* +39 02-4818230
*email* daisy.zonato@edizioniel.it
*website* www.arkaedizioni.it
*Publisher* Ginevra Viscardi

Picture books and some general fiction for preschool children and children up to 10 years.

### Edizioni El/Einaudi Ragazzi/Emme Edizioni

Via J. Ressel 5, 34018 San Dorligo della Valle TS
*tel* +39 040-3880311
*email* edizioniel@edizioniel.it
*website* www.edizioniel.com
*Children's Publisher* Orietta Fatucci

Activity books, board books, picture books, pop-up books, non-fiction, novels, poetry, fairy tales, fiction. Age groups: preschool, 5–10, 10–15, 15+.

### Giunti Editore S.p.A.

Via Bolognese 165, 50139 Florence
*tel* +39 055-50621
*email* info@giunti.it
*website* www.giunti.it
*Facebook* www.facebook.com/GiuntiEditore
*Twitter* @GiuntiEditore
*President* Sergio Giunti

Activity books, board books, novelty books, picture books, colouring books, pop-up books and some educational textbooks. Founded 1841.

### Arnoldo Mondadori Editore S.p.A. (Mondadori)

Via Mondadori 1, 20090 Segrate, Milan
*tel* +39 02-75421
*email* stampalibri@mondadori.it
*website* www.mondadori.it

Activity books, board books, novelty books, picture books, painting and colouring books, pop-up books, how-to books, hobbies, leisure, pets, sport, comics, poetry, fairy tales, education, fiction and non-fiction.

Age groups: preschool, 5–10, 10–15, 15+.
Founded 1907.

### Adriano Salani Editore S.p.A.

Via Gherardini 10, 20145 Milan
*tel* +39 02-34597624
*email* info@salani.it
*website* www.salani.it
*Children's Publisher* Simona Scandellari

Picture books, how-to books, comics, gift books, fiction, novels, poetry, fairy tales. Age groups: preschool, 5–10, 10–15, 15+. Founded 1862.

## THE NETHERLANDS

### Lemniscaat BV

Vijverlaan 48, 3062 HL Rotterdam
*tel* +31 10-2062929
*email* info@lemniscaat.nl
*website* www.lemniscaat.nl
*Publisher* Jesse Goossens

Well-known independent children's book publisher. Publishes picture books, juvenile novels and YA literature. Founded 1963.

### Rubinstein Publishing

Prinseneiland 43, 1013 LL Amsterdam
*tel* +31 20-4200772
*email* info@rubinstein.nl
*website* www.rubinstein.nl
*Publisher* Irene Kunst

Independent publisher specialising in audiobooks for children. Also produces novelty books. Founded 1985.

### Van Goor/Van Holkema & Warendorf

PO Box 23202, 1100 DS Amsterdam
*tel* +31 20-2364200
*website* www.de-leukste-kinderboeken.nl, www.bestofyabooks.nl

High-quality picture books, learn-to-read books, middle-grade and (literary) fiction and non-fiction, YA. Founded 2009.

## NEW ZEALAND

*Member of the New Zealand Book Publishers' Association*

### Black Chook Books*

PO Box 137, Waimauku, Auckland 0842
*email* info@blackchookbooks.co.nz
*website* www.blackchookbooks.co.nz
*Facebook* www.facebook.com/blackchookbooks
*Publisher* Martin Bailey

Publishes children's fiction, specialises in board books. Founded 2020.

## Cengage Learning New Zealand*

Unit 4B, Rosedale Office Park, 331 Rosedale Road,
Albany, North Shore 0632
*Postal address* PO Box 33376, Takapuna,
North Shore 0740
*tel* +64 (0)9 415 6850

Educational books. Founded 2007.

## The Cuba Press

Level 6, 138 Wakefield Street, Te Aro,
Wellington 6011
*email* hello@thecubapress.nz
*website* www.thecubapress.nz
*Co-directors* Mary McCallum, Sarah Bolland,
*Publisher* Paul Stewart

Fiction, creative non-fiction, poetry, memoir,
biography, social history, children's fiction and
poetry. Founded 2018.

## Edify Ltd*

PO Box 36502, Northcote, Auckland 0748
*tel* +64 (0)9 972 9428
*email* mark@edify.co.nz
*website* www.edify.co.nz
*Ceo* Adrian Keane

A publishing, sales and marketing business providing
its partners with opportunities for their products and
solutions in the New Zealand educational market.
Exclusive representatives of Pearson and the
educational publisher Sunshine Books.
Founded 2013.

## Gecko Press*

PO Box 9335, Marion Square, Wellington 6141
*tel* +64 (0)4 801 9333
*email* office@geckopress.com
*website* www.geckopress.com
*Publisher* Julia Marshall

Children's books: picture books, junior fiction and
non-fiction. Translates and publishes award-winning
children's books from around the world and a small
number of own titles. Selects books strong in story,
character, illustration and design. See website for
submission guidelines. Founded 2005.

## HarperCollins Publishers (New Zealand) Ltd*

Unit D, 63 Apollo Drive, Rosedale, Auckland 0632
*tel* +64 (0)9 443 9400
*email* publicity@harpercollins.co.nz
*Postal address* PO Box 1, Shortland Street, Auckland
1140
*website* www.harpercollins.co.nz

Publishes a range of high-quality non-fiction titles
each year by New Zealand authors. Submissions can
be sent digitally to
nz.submissions@harpercollins.co.nz. Founded 1989.

## McGraw-Hill Book Company New Zealand Ltd

Level 8, 56–60 Cawley Street, Ellerslie, Auckland 1005
*Postal address* Private Bag 11904, Ellerslie,
Auckland 1005
*tel* +64 (0)9 526 6200
*website* www.mcgraw-hill.com.au
*Facebook* www.facebook.com/MHEducationANZ
*Twitter* @MHEducationAU

Educational publisher: higher education, primary and
secondary education (grades K–12) and professional
(including medical, general and reference). Division
of the McGraw-Hill Companies. Always looking for
potential authors. Has a rapidly expanding publishing
programme. See website for author's guide.
Founded 1974.

## New Zealand Council for Educational Research

Box 3237, Education House, 178–182 Willis Street,
Wellington 6140
*tel* +64 (0)4 384 7939
*email* info@nzcer.org.nz
*website* https://www.nzcer.org.nz

Education, including educational policy and practice,
early childhood education, educational achievement
tests, Māori education, schooling for the future,
curriculum and assessment. Founded 1934.

## Penguin Random House New Zealand Ltd*

Private Bag 102 902, North Shore, Auckland 0745
*tel* +64 (0)9 442 7400
*email* publishing@penguinrandomhouse.co.nz
*website* www.penguin.co.nz
*Facebook* www.facebook.com/
PenguinBooksNewZealand
*Twitter* @PenguinBooks_NZ
*Instagram* @penguinbooksnz
*Head of Publishing* Claire Murdoch

Adult and children's fiction and non-fiction.
Imprints: Penguin, Vintage, Black Swan, Godwit,
Viking, Puffin Books. Part of Penguin Random
House. Founded 2013.

# SOUTH AFRICA

*Member of the Publishers' Association of South Africa*

## Cambridge University Press & Assessment, Africa*

Unit OW3A Old Warehouse Building,
Black River Park, 2 Fir Street, Observatory,
Cape Town, 7925
*tel* +27 (0)21 412 7800
*email* cambridge-sa@cambridge.org
*website* www.cambridge.org
*Publishing Director* Johan Traut

Textbooks and literature for sub-Saharan African countries, as well as primary reading materials in 28 African languages. Founded 1534.

## Educat Publishers Pty Ltd

4 Clifford Street, Ottery, Cape Town
*tel* +27 (0)21 697 3669
*email* takeeducat@gmail.com
*website* www.educat.co.za

Educational products including science and maths, product designs for schools and retail, as well as mass markets. Age groups: preschool, 5–10, 10–15, 15+.

## Human & Rousseau

12th Floor, Naspers, 40 Heerengracht, Roggebaai 8012
*tel* +27 (0)21 406 3033
*email* nb@nb.co.za
*website* www.humanrousseau.com

General Afrikaans and English titles. Quality Afrikaans literature, popular literature, general children's and youth literature, cookery, self-help. Founded 1959.

## Macmillan Education South Africa

4th Floor, Building G, Hertford Office Park, 90 Bekker Road, Vorna Valley, Midrand 1685
*tel* +27 (0)11 731 3300
*Postal address* Private Bag X19, Northlands 2116
*website* www.macmillan.co.za
*Managing Director* Preggy Naidoo

Educational titles for the RSA market. Founded 1843.

## NB Publishers (Pty) Ltd*

12th Floor, Media24 Centre, 40 Heerengracht, Cape Town 8001
*tel* +27 (0)21 406 3033
*email* nb@nb.co.za
*website* www.nb.co.za

General: Afrikaans fiction, politics, children's and youth literature in all the country's languages, non-fiction. Imprints: Tafelberg, Human & Rousseau, Queillerie, Pharos, Kwela, Best Books and Lux Verbi. Founded 1950.

## New Africa Books (Pty) Ltd*

Unit 13A, Athlone Industrial Park, 10 Mymoena Crescent, Cape Town 7764
*tel* +27 (0)21 467 5860
*email* info@newafricabooks.co.za
*Postal address* PostNet, Suite 144, Private Bag X9190, Cape Town 8000
*Contacts* Dušanka Stojaković, Nerina van Wyngaarden Lindhout, Cheraldine Smit

Winner of Best Children's Publisher in Africa Award 2022 (Bologna Children's Book Fair), member of IBBY and member of the UN SDG Publisher's Compact. An independent publisher of picture books publishing approx. 60 titles per year. Publishes fiction, non-fiction and comics with South African content in all South African languages. Award-winning writers and illustrators include Sindiwe Magona, Gcina Mhlophe, Richard Rive, Elinor Sisulu, Lebohang Masango, Paddy Bouma, Loyiso Mkhize, Subi Bosa, Nokuthula Mazibuko Msimang, Nicolaas Maritz, Lorato Trok and Xolisa Guzula. Founded 1971.

## Oxford University Press Southern Africa*

Vasco Boulevard, N1 City, Goodwood, Cape Town 7460
*tel* +27 (0)21 596 2300
*email* oxford.za@oup.com
*Postal address* PO Box 12119, N1 City, Cape Town 7463
*website* www.oxford.co.za
*Managing Director* Hanri Pieterse

One of the leading educational publishers in South Africa, producing a wide range of quality educational material in print and digital format. The range includes books from Grade R to Grade 12, as well as TVET textbooks, textbooks, school literature, dictionaries and atlases. Founded 1586.

## Pearson South Africa*

4th Floor, Auto Atlantic Building, Corner Hertzog Boulevard and Heerengracht Boulevard, Cape Town 8001
*Postal address* PO Box 396, Cape Town 8000
*tel* +27 (0)21 532 6008
*email* pearsonza.enquiries@pearson.com
*website* https://za.pearson.com/

Pearson South Africa provides learning materials, technologies and services for use in schools, TVET colleges, higher education institutions and in home and professional environments. Founded 2010.

## Shuter and Shooter Publishers (Pty) Ltd*

110 CB Downes Road, Pietermaritzburg, KwaZulu-Natal 3201
*tel* +27 (0)33 846 8700
*email* sales@shuters.com
*Postal address* PO Box 61, Mkondeni, KwaZulu-Natal 3212
*website* www.shuters.co.za
*Ceo* Primi Chetty

Core curriculum-based textbooks for use at foundation, intermediate, senior and FET phases. Supplementary readers in various languages; dictionaries; reading development kits, charts. Literature titles in English, isiXhosa, Sesotho, Sepedi, Setswana, Tshivenda, Xitsonga, Ndebele, isiZulu and Siswati. Founded 1925.

## Via Afrika Publishers

11th Floor, 40 Heerengracht, Cape Town 8001
*Postal address* PO Box 5197, Cape Town 8001
*tel* +27 (0)21 406 3528

*email* customerservices@viaafrika.com
*website* www.viaafrika.com
*Ceo* Christina Watson

Educational materials for South African schools and FET colleges, for all learning areas and subjects at all grades/levels: in all official languages of South Africa. Imprints: Acacia, Action, Afritech, Afro, Atlas, Bateleur Books, Collegium, Idem, Juta/Gariep, KZN Books, Nasou, Stimela, Van Schaik (literature), Via Afrika. Founded 1949.

## SPAIN

### Grupo Anaya

C/Juan Ignacio Luca de Tena 15, 28027 Madrid
*tel* +34 913 938 800
*website* www.anaya.es

Non-fiction: education textbooks for preschool up to 15+ years. Part of Hachette Livre. Founded 1984.

### Editorial Cruilla

C/Roger de Llúria 44, 4th, 08009 Barcelona
*tel* +34 902 123 336
*email* editorial@cruilla.cat
*website* www.cruilla.cat
*Facebook* www.facebook.com/SMEspana
*Twitter* @SM_Espana

Activity books, novelty books, fiction for children 5–8 and 9–12 years, teenage fiction and poetry. Publishes approx. 120–130 titles each year. Successes include *El Vaixell de Vapor* (series), *Vull Llegir!* and *Molly Moon Stops the World/Molly Moon's Incredible Book of Hypnotism*. Subsidiary of Ediciones SM. Founded 1984.

### Destino Infantil & Juvenil

Carrer de Llull 51, 60–4A, 08005 Barcelona
*email* info@librosdelzorrorojo.com
*website* www.librosdelzorrorojo.com
*Children's & Young Adult Director* Marta Bueno Miró

Fiction for children 6–16 years. Picture books, pop-up books, fiction and some unusual illustrated books.

### Libros del Zorro Rojo

Carrer de Llull 51, 6–4, 08005 Barcelona
*email* rights@librosdelzorrorojo.com
*website* www.librosdelzorrorojo.com
*General Director* Fernando Diego García, *Editorial Director* Diana Hernández Aldana

Independent publisher specialized in illustrated titles for readers of all ages. Founded 2004.

### Editorial Libsa

C/ Puerto de Navacerrada, 88, Pol. Ind. Las Nieves, Madrid
*tel* +34 916 572 580
*email* libsa@libsa.es
*website* www.libsa.es

Publisher and packager of highly illustrated mass market books: activity books, board books, picture books, colouring books, how-to books, fairy tales. Founded 1980.

### Penguin Random House Grupo Editorial

Luchana 23, 1A, 28010 Madrid
*tel* +34 915 358 190
*website* www.penguinrandomhousegrupoeditorial.com
*Facebook* www.facebook.com/penguinlibros
*Twitter* @penguinlibros

Preschool activity, novelty and picture books through to YA fiction. Also a packager and printer. Part of Penguin Random House. Founded 2013.

### Vicens Vives SA

Avenida Sarriá 130–132, 08017 Barcelona
*tel* +34 932 523 700
*email* rrhh@vicensvives.es
*website* www.vicensvives.com

Activity and novelty books, fiction, art, encyclopedias, dictionaries, education, geography, history, music, science, textbooks, posters. Age groups: preschool, 5–10, 10–15, 15+. Founded 1960.

## USA

*\*Member of the Association of American Publishers Inc.*

### Abingdon Press

810 12th Ave South, Nashville, TN 37203
*tel* +1 800-251-3320
*website* www.abingdonpress.com
*Facebook* www.facebook.com/AbingdonPress
*Twitter* @AbingdonPress
*President & Publisher* Neil Alexander

General interest, professional, academic and reference, non-fiction and fiction, youth and children's non-fiction and Vatican Bible School; primarily directed to the religious market. Imprint of United Methodist Publishing House with tradition of crossing denominational boundaries. United Methodist Publishing House founded 1789.

### Harry N. Abrams, Inc.

195 Broadway, 9th Floor, New York, NY 10007
*tel* +1 212-206-7715
*email* abrams@abramsbooks.com
*website* www.abramsbooks.com

Art and architecture, photography, natural sciences, performing arts, children's books. Imprints include: Abrams, Abrams Appleseed, Abrams Books for Young Readers, Abrams ComicArts, Abrams Image, Abrams Noterie, Abrams Press, Amulet Books, Amulet Paperbacks, Cernunnos, Magic Cat, The Overlook Press. Founded 1949.

### Abrams Books for Young Readers
*tel* +1 212-519-1200
*website* www.abramsyoungreaders.com

Fiction and non-fiction: picture books, young readers, middle readers, YA. For picture books submit covering letter and complete MS, for longer works and non-fiction send query and sample chapter with sase.

### Aladdin Paperbacks – see Simon & Schuster Children's Publishing Division

### All About Kids Publishing
7680 Monterey St. #307, Gilroy, CA 95020
*tel* +1 408-337-1152
*email* lguevara@allaboutkidspub.com
*website* www.allaboutkidspub.com
*Publisher* Mike G. Guevara, *Editor* Linda L. Guevara

Fiction and non-fiction picture books and chapter books. Successes include *Don't Let the Dead Bugs Bite!* by Stephen Zmina (picture book) and *Cold Waves, Cold Blood* by Patrick Doherty (teen novel). See website for submission guidelines. Founded 2000.

### Astra Publishing House
19 West 21st Street, #1201, New York, NY 10010
*email* info@bmkbooks.com
*website* www.boydsmillsandkane.com
*Facebook* www.facebook.com/BMKbooks
*Twitter* @kanepress
*President* Leying Jiang

Activity books, picture books, fiction, non-fiction and poetry for 18 years and under. Publishes 80 titles each year. Check website for submission guidelines. Imprints: Astra House, Astra Young Readers, Calkins Creek, Hippo Park, Kane Press, minedition US, Toon Books, Word Song. Founded 1991.

### Atheneum Books for Young Readers – see Simon & Schuster Children's Publishing Division

### Avon – see HarperCollins Publishers

### Barefoot Books
23 Bradford Street, Concord, MA 01742
*tel* +1 617-576-0660
*email* publicity@barefootbooks.com
*website* www.barefootbooks.com
*Facebook* www.facebook.com/barefootbooks
*Twitter* @BarefootBooks
*Editorial Director* Emma Parkin

Currently not accepting MS submissions or queries. Accepts illustrator samples via mail only. Please mail samples (no original artwork) for the attention of the editor. Successes include *Mindful Kids* by Whitney Stewart, illustrated by Mina Braun; and *The Barefoot Book of Children* by Kate DePalma and Tessa Strickland, illustrated by David Dean (3–7 years,

picture book). Length: 500–1,000 words (picture books), 2,000–3,000 words (young readers). US branch founded 1998.

### Bloomsbury Publishing USA*
1385 Broadway, New York, NY 10018
*tel* +1 212-419-5300
*email* Contact-USA@bloomsbury.com
*website* www.bloomsbury.com/us
*President* Adrienne Vaughan, *Publishing Director* Mary Kate Castellani

Supports the worldwide publishing activities of Bloomsbury Publishing Plc: caters for the US market. For submission guidelines see website. Established in 1998 as an American subsidiary of Bloomsbury Publishing Plc. Founded 1986.

### Calkins Creek Books – see Astra Publishing House

### Candlewick Press*
99 Dover Street, Somerville, MA 02144
*tel* +1 617-661-3330
*email* bigbear@candlewick.com
*website* www.candlewick.com
*President & Publisher* Karen Lotz, *Creative Director & Associate Publisher* Chris Paul, *Executive Editorial Director & Associate Publisher* Liz Bicknell, *Editorial Director & Director of Editorial Operations* Mary Lee Donovan

Books for babies through teens: board books, picture books, early readers, first chapter books, novels, non-fiction, novelty books, poetry, graphic novels. Publishes 70 picture books, 40 middle readers and 30 YA titles each year. Founded 1991.

#### Candlewick Entertainment
*Group Editorial Director* Joan Powers

Media-related children's books, including film/TV tie-ins.

### Charlesbridge Publishing
9 Galen Street, Watertown, MA 02472
*tel* +1 617-926-0329
*email* development@charlesbridge.com
*website* www.charlesbridge.com

Fiction and non-fiction board books, picture books and middle-grade books for preschool up to 14 years. YA novels for readers 14+ years. Dedicated to diversity and new voices across genres. Non-fiction list specialises in nature, concept, history and science. Publishes roughly 60% non-fiction, 40% fiction. Send full MSS for board books and picture books; send first three chapters and plot summary for MSS longer than 30 pages; no queries; electronic submissions only (childrens.submissions@charlesbridge.com). Responds to MSS of interest. For illustrations, send art postcards or electronic query with samples, pdf or jpg portfolio, and website

(design.submissions@charlesbridge.com).
Founded 1980.

## Chicago Review Press

814 North Franklin Street, Chicago, IL 60610
*tel* +1 312-337-0747
*email* frontdesk@jpg.com
*website* www.chicagoreviewpress.com
*Publisher* Cynthia Sherry

General publisher. Non-fiction activity books for
children. Imprint Zephyr publishes professional
development titles for teachers. Interested in hands-
on educational books. See website for submission
guidelines. Founded 1973.

## Chronicle Books*

680 Second Street, San Francisco, CA 94107
*tel* +1 415-537-4200
*email* hello@chroniclebooks.com
*website* www.chroniclebooks.com,
www.chroniclebooks.com/titles/kids-teens
*Facebook* www.facebook.com/chroniclekidsbooks
*Twitter* @ChronicleKids
*Instagram* @chroniclekidsbooks
*Chairman & Ceo* Nion McEvoy

Traditional and innovative children's books. Looking
for projects that have a unique edge – in subject
matter, writing style or illustrative technique – that
will add a distinctive flair. Interested in fiction and
non-fiction for children of all ages as well as board
books, decks, activity kits and other unusual or
'novelty' formats. Publishes 60–100 books each year.
Also for adults: cooking, how-to books, nature, art,
biographies, fiction, gift. For picture books submit
MS. For older readers, submit outline/synopsis and
three sample chapters. No submitted materials will be
returned. Response approx. three months.
Founded 1967.

## Clear Light Books

823 Don Diego, Santa Fe, NM 87505
*tel* +1 505-989-9590
*website* www.clearlightbooks.com

For adults: art and photography, cookbooks, ecology/
environment, health, gift books, history, Native
America, Tibet, Western Americana. Non-fiction for
children and YA: multicultural, American Indian,
Hispanic. Looking for authentic American Indian art
and folklore. Send complete MS with sase.
Founded 1997.

## David C Cook

4050 Lee Vance View, Colorado Springs, CO 80918
*tel* +1 719-536-0100
*website* www.davidccook.com
*President & Acting Ceo* Rick Rekedal

Christian education resources for preschool to
teenagers. Founded 1875.

## Dawn Publications

P.O. Box 4410, Naperville, IL 60567-4410
*tel* +1 800-432-7444
*website* www.sourcebooks.com/dawn-
publications.html

Dedicated to inspiring in children a deeper
understanding and appreciation for all life on Earth.
The aim is to help parents and teachers encourage
children to bond with the Earth in a relationship of
love, respect and intelligent cooperation, through the
books published and the educational materials
offered online. Dawn Books is an imprint of
Sourcebooks eXplore, the children's non-fiction
division of Sourcebooks. Founded 1979.

## Dial Books – see Penguin Young Readers

## Doubleday – see Penguin Random House

## Dover Publications, Inc.

31 East 2nd Street, Mineola, NY 11501
*tel* +1 516-294-7000
*website* https://store.doverpublications.com/
*Facebook* www.facebook.com/doverpublications
*Twitter* @doverpublications

Activity books, novelty books, picture books, fiction
for children 5–8 and 9–12 years, teenage fiction,
series fiction, reference, plays, religion, poetry, audio
and CD-Roms. Also adult non-fiction. Will consider
unsolicited MSS but write for guidelines.
Founded 1941.

## EDCON Publishing Group

9316 East Raintree Drive, Suite 120, Scottsdale,
AZ 85260
*tel* +1 800-826-4740
*email* info@edconpublishing.com
*website* www.edconpublishing.com

Supplemental instructional materials for use by
education professionals to improve reading and
maths skills. Includes early reading, *Classics* series,
*Easy Shakespeare*, fiction and non-fiction, reading
diagnosis and vocabulary books. Founded 1970.

## Eerdmans Publishing Company

4035 Park East Court SE, Grand Rapids, MI 49546
*tel* +1 616-459-4591
*website* www.eerdmans.com
*President & Publisher* Anita Eerdmans

Independent publisher of a wide range of religious
books, from academic works in theology, biblical
studies, religious history and reference to popular
titles in spirituality, social and cultural criticism and
literature. Founded 1911.

### Eerdmans Books for Young Readers

*website* www.eerdmans.com/youngreader
Picture books, biographies, and middle reader fiction
and non-fiction. Publishes 18–22 books a year.

Stories that celebrate diversity, stories of historical significance and stories that relate to current issues are of special interest. Accepts unsolicited submissions. Send to Acquisitions Editor; responds in four months only to submissions of interest. For illustrations, send photocopies or printed media and include a list of previous illustrated publications. Send to Art Director. Samples will be kept on file; they will not be returned.

## Enchanted Lion Press

248, Creamer Street, Studio 4, Brooklyn, New York, NY 11231
*website* https://enchantedlion.com/
*Facebook* www.facebook.com/enchantedlion
*Twitter* @EnchantedLion
*Publisher* Claudia Zoe Bedrick

An independent children's book publisher based in Brooklyn, New York, publishing illustrated books from around the world. Founded 2003.

## Encyclopaedia Britannica Inc.

325 North La Salle Street, Suite 200, Chicago, IL 60654-2682
*tel* +1 312-347-7159
*email* contact@eb.com
*website* www.britannica.com

Encyclopedias, reference books, almanacs, videos and CD-Roms for adults and children 5–15+ years. Founded 1999.

## Enslow Publishers, Inc.

29 East 21st Street, New York, NY 10010
*tel* +1 800-398-2504
*email* customerservice@enslow.com
*website* www.enslow.com
*Owner* Roger Rosen

Provides fiction and non-fiction content across the K-12 space. Aims to inspire readers to become lifelong learners. Founded 1976.

## Evan-Moor Educational Publishers

18 Lower Ragsdale Drive, Monterey, CA 93940
*tel* +1 800-714-0971
*email* marketing@evan-moor.com
*website* www.evan-moor.com
*Founder & Ceo* William E. Evans

Educational materials for parents and teachers of children (3–12 years): activity books, textbooks, how-to books, CD-Roms. Subjects include maths, geography, history, science, reading, writing, social studies, art and craft. Publishes approx. 50 titles each year and has over 500 in print. Less than 10% of books are by first-time authors. Query or submit outline, table of contents and sample pages. Responds to queries in two months; MSS in four months. See website for submission guidelines. For illustrations, send résumé, samples and tearsheets to the Art Director. Primarily uses b&w material. Founded 1979.

## Farrar, Straus Giroux Books for Young Readers

175 Fifth Avenue, New York, NY 10010
*website* https://us.macmillan.com/fsg

An imprint of Macmillan Children's Publishing Group. Books for toddlers through to YA: picture books, fiction and non-fiction for all ages, and poetry (occasionally). Publishes 70 hardcover originals plus 10 paperback reprints each year and has approx. 500 titles in print. Approx. 10% of books are by first-time authors. No unsolicited MSS. Founded 1946.

## The Feminist Press

365 Fifth Avenue, Suite 5406, New York, NY 10016
*website* www.feministpress.org
*Facebook* www.facebook.com/feministpress
*Twitter* @feministpress
*Publisher* Margot Atwell

Publishes books that ignite movements and social transformation. Publishes 12 to 15 books a year and specialises in an array of genres including cutting-edge fiction, activist non-fiction, literature in translation, hybrid memoirs and children's books. Founded 1970.

## Flux

2297 Waters Drive, Mendota Heights, MN 55120 *tel* +1 888-417-0195
*email* publicity@northstareditions.com
*email* submissions@northstareditions.com
*website* www.fluxnow.com
*Facebook* www.facebook.com/FluxBooks
*Twitter* @FluxBooks
*Senior Editor* Meg Gaertner

YA. See website above for submission guidelines. Accepts electronic submissions only. Flux is an imprint of North Star Editions, Inc. Founded 2006.

### Flux Books (imprint)

*email* submissions@northstareditions.com
*website* www.fluxnow.com

YA fiction for ages 12+ in all genres. Particularly interested in out-of-the-box narratives with a fresh premise and a unique voice. Flux is an imprint of North Star Editions, Inc.

## Free Spirit Publishing

6325 Sandburg Road, Suite 100, Golden Valley, MN 55427
*tel* +1 612-338-2068
*email* acquisitions@freespirit.com
*website* www.freespirit.com
*Facebook* www.facebook.com/freespiritpublishing
*Twitter* @freespiritbooks

Award-winning publisher of non-fiction materials for children and teens, parents, educators and counsellors. Specialises in self-help materials for kids and teens which empower young people and promote positive self-esteem through improved social and emotional health. Topics include self-esteem and self-awareness, stress management, school success, creativity, friends and family, peacemaking, social action and special educational needs (i.e. gifted and talented, children with learning differences). Publishes approx. 18–22 new products each year, adding to a backlist of over 200 books and posters. Free Spirit authors are expert educators and mental health professionals who have been honoured nationally for their contributions on behalf of children. Founded 1983.

## Fulcrum Publishing

3970 Youngfiled Street, Wheat Ridge, CO 80033
*tel* +1 303-277-1623
*email* orders@fulcrumbooks.com
*website* https://fulcrum.bookstore.ipgbook.com/

Publishes a wide variety of educational non-fiction texts and children's books, also books and support materials for teachers, librarians, parents and elementary through middle school children. Subjects include: science and nature, literature and storytelling, history, multicultural studies, and Native American and Hispanic cultures. Founded 1965.

## Gale, part of Cengage Group*

27555 Executive Drive, Suite 270, Farmington Hills, MI 48331
*tel* +1 248-699-4253
*website* www.gale.com

Education publishing for libraries, schools and businesses. Serves the K–12 market with the following imprints: Blackbirch Press, Greenhaven Press, KidHaven Press, Lucent Books, Sleeping Bear Press, UXL. Founded 1954.

### Greenhaven Press

29 East 21st Street, New York, NY 10010
*website* https://greenhavenpublishing.com/
High-quality non-fiction resources for the education community. Publishes 220 YA academic reference titles each year. Successes include the *Opposing Viewpoints* series. Approx. 35% of books are by first-time authors. No unsolicited MSS. All writing is done on a work-to-hire basis. Send query, résumé and list of published works. Founded 1970.

### KidHaven Press

Non-fiction references for younger researchers.

### Lucent Books

Non-fiction resources for upper-elementary to high school students. Successes include *Women in the American Revolution* and *Civil Liberties and the War on Terrorism*. No unsolicited MSS. Query with résumé.

### Sleeping Bear Press

*email* sleepingbearpress@cengage.com
*website* www.sleepingbearpress.com
High-quality picture books.

## Gibbs Smith

570 N Sportsplex Drive, Kaysville, UT 84037
*tel* +1 800-835-4993
*email* info@gibbs-smith.com
*website* www.gibbs-smith.com

An employee-owned, independent, Utah-based publisher. Its book and gift division publishes home reference, cookery, non-fiction, and children's titles. The Gibbs Smith Education division is the nation's leading publisher of state history programs. All unsolicited queries, submissions and correspondence should be via email. Responds only to projects of interest. Founded 1969.

## Greenhaven Press – see Gale, part of Cengage Group

## Gryphon House, Inc.

PO Box 10, 6848 Leon's Way, Lewisville, NC 27023
*tel* +1 800-636-0928
*email* info@gryhonhouse.com
*website* www.gryphonhouse.com
*President* Jennifer Lewis, *Executive Editor* Stephanie Roselli

Early childhood (0–8 years) resource books for teachers and parents. Looking for books that are developmentally appropriate for the intended age group, are well researched and based on current trends in the field, and include creative, participatory learning experiences with a common conceptual theme to tie them together. Send query and/or a proposal. Founded 1971.

## Hachai Publishing

527 Empire Boulevard, Brooklyn, New York, NY 11225
*tel* +1 718-633-0100
*email* info@hachai.com
*website* www.hachai.com

Jewish books for children 0–8+ years. Welcomes unsolicited MSS. Specialises in books for children 2–4 years and 3–6 years. Looking for stories that convey the traditional Jewish experience in modern times or long ago, traditional Jewish observance and positive character traits. Founded 1988.

## Hachette Book Group*

1290 Avenue of the Americas, New York, NY 10104
*tel* +1 212-364-1100
*website* www.hachettebookgroup.com

Publishing groups: Grand Central Publishing; Hachette Nashville; Little, Brown and Company; Little, Brown Books for Young Readers; Orbit; Perseus Books; Workman Imprints: Grand Central: Balance; Forever; Forever Yours; Legacy Lit; Twelve; Vision. Hachette Nashville: Center Street; Ellie Claire; FaithWords; Worthy Books; WorthyKids. Little, Brown and Company: Little, Brown Audio; Back Bay Books; Little, Brown Spark; Mulholland Books;

Voracious. Little, Brown Books for Young Readers: Christy Ottaviano Books; JIMMY Patterson; LB Kids; LBYR+; Poppy. Orbit: Redhook. Perseus Books: Avalon Travel, Basic Books; Black Dog & Leventhal; Bold Type Books; Hachette Books; Hachette Go; Moon Travel; Rick Steves; RP Studio; Running Press; Running Press Kids; PublicAffairs; Seal Press. Founded 1996.

## Handprint Books

413 Sixth Avenue, Brooklyn, New York, NY 11215–3310
*tel* +1 718-768-3696
*email* cmf@handprintbooks.com
*website* www.handprintbooks.com
*Publisher* Christopher Franceschelli

A range of children's books: picture and story books through to YA fiction. Imprints: Handprint Books, Ragged Bears, Blue Apple. Welcomes submissions of MSS of quality for works ranging from board books to YA novels. For novels, first query interest on the subject and submit a 7,500-word max. sample. Accepts MSS on an e-submission basis only. Artwork should be sent as small jpg files; artists' website addresses may also be submitted. No series fiction, licensed character (or characters whose primary avatar is meant to be as licences), 'I-Can-Read'-type books or titles intended primarily for mass merchandise outlets. Founded 2000.

## HarperCollins Publishers*

195 Broadway, New York, NY 10007
*tel* +1 212-207-700
*website* https://corporate.harpercollins.com/us/
*President & Ceo* Brian Murray

For children, publishes fiction (literary, juvenile poetry) and non-fiction (education, history). No unsolicited material; all submissions must come through a literary agent. Founded 1817.

## History Compass LLC

25 Leslie Road, Auburndale, MA 02466
*tel* +1 617-332-2202
*email* info@historycompass.com
*website* www.historycompass.com

Publishes the history of the USA presented through the study of primary source documents. Also historical fiction for younger readers. Successes include *Get a Clue!* (grades 2–8) and *Adventures in History* series (grades 4–8). Other series include *Perspectives on History* (grades 5–12+) and *Researching American History* (8–15 year-olds and ESL students). Founded 1990.

## Holiday House, Inc.*

120 Broadway, New York, NY 10271
*tel* +1 212-646 5025
*email* info@holidayhouse.com
*website* www.holidayhouse.com

General fiction for children. Publishes 35 picture books, ten young reader, 15 middle reader and eight YA titles each year. Successes include *Lafayette and the American Revolution* by Russell Freedman. Approx. 20% of books are by first-time authors. Send entire MS. Only responds to projects of interest. Will review MS/illustration packages from artists: send MS with dummy and colour photocopies. Founded 1935.

## Houghton Mifflin Harcourt

3 Park Avenue, Floor 19, New York, NY 10016
*tel* +1 212-598-5730
*website* www.hmhco.com

Reference, fiction and non-fiction for adults and young readers. Also educational content and solutions for K–12 teachers and students. Founded 1832.

### Clarion Books

Picture books, fiction, poetry and non-fiction for children, preschool through to high school. Successes include *Mr. Wuffles!* by David Wiesner. For fiction and picture books, send complete MS. For non-fiction, send query with up to 3 sample chapters. Founded 1965.

### Houghton Mifflin Harcourt Books for Young Readers

*website* www.hmhbooks.com

Picture books, fiction, poetry and non-fiction for children, preschool through to high school. Successes include *The Testing* by Joelle Charbonneau and *Sleep Like a Tiger* by Mary Logue and illustrated by Pamela Zagarenski. Imprint: Clarion Books. For fiction, submit complete MS. For non-fiction, submit outline/synopsis and sample chapters. Responds only if interested. For illustrations, query with samples (colour photocopies and tearsheets). Responds in four months.

## Hyperion Books for Children*

237 Park Avenue, New York, NY 10017
*tel* +1 212-633-4400
*website* www.hyperionbooks.com

Board and novelty books, picture books, young readers, middle grade, YA non-fiction (all subjects at all levels). Successes include *Don't Let the Pigeon Drive the Bus*, written and illustrated by Mo Willems, *Dumpy the Dump Truck* series by Julie Andrews Edwards and Emma Walton Hamilton (3–7 years) and *Artemis Fowl* by Eoin Colfer (YA novel). Imprints include Michael di Capua Books, Jump at the Sun, Volo. Approx. 10% of books are by first-time authors. Only interested in submissions via literary agents. For illustrations, send résumé, business card, promotional literature or tearsheets to Art Director to be kept on file. Founded 1990.

## Impact Publishers Inc.

5674 Shattuck Avenue, Oakland, CA 94609
*tel* +1 805-466-5917
*email* customerservice@newharbinger.com

*website* www.newharbinger.com/about-us/impact-publishers

Psychology and self-improvement books and audio tapes for adults, children, families, organisations and communities. Imprint of New Harbinger Publications. Only publishes non-fiction books which serve human development and are written by highly respected psychologists and other human service professionals. Rarely publishes authors outside of the USA. See website for guidelines. Founded 1970.

## Incentive Publications by World Book

180 N. LaSalle, Suite 900, Chicago, IL 60601
*tel* +1 888-482-9764
*website* https://incentivepublications.com

Produces supplemental resources for student use and instruction and classroom management improvement materials for teachers. Specialises in supplemental resources for middle-grade students and teaching strategies for grades K–12. More than 300 titles are available. Send a letter of introduction, table of contents, sample chapter and sase for return of material. Acquired by World Book in 2013. Founded 1969.

## Jolly Fish Press

2297 Waters Drive, Mendota Heights, MN 55120
*tel* +1 888-417-0195
*email* publicity@jollyfishpress.com
*email* submit@jollyfishpress.com
*website* www.jollyfishpress.com
*Facebook* www.facebook.com/JollyFishPress
*Twitter* @JollyFishPress

Dedicated to promoting exceptional, unique new voices in middle-grade fiction and jump-starting writing careers. See website above for submission guidelines. Accepts electronic submissions only. Imprint of North Star Editions, Inc. Founded 2011.

## Just Us Books, Inc.

395 Pleasant Valley Way, Suite B, West Orange, NJ 07052
*tel* +1 973-672-7701
*email* info@justusbooks.com
*website* https://justusbooks.com/
*Publishers* Cheryl Hudson, Wade Hudson

Publishers of Black-interest books for young people, including preschool materials, picture books, biographies, chapter books and YA fiction. Focuses on Black history, Black culture and Black experiences. Imprint: Sankofa Books. Currently accepting queries for YA titles, targeted to 13–16 year-old readers. Work should contain realistic, contemporary characters, compelling plot lines that introduce conflict and resolution, and cultural authenticity. Also considers MSS for picture books and middle reader chapter books. Send a query letter, one-to-two page synopsis and a brief author biography that includes any previously published work, plus an sase. Founded 1988.

## Kaeden Books

PO Box 16190, Rocky River, OH 44116
*tel* +1 800-890-7323
*email* info@kaeden.com
*website* www.kaeden.com

Educational publisher specialising in early literacy books and beginning chapter books. Accepts samples of all styles of illustration but is primarily looking for samples that match the often humorous style appropriate for juvenile literature. Vocabulary and sentence structure must be appropriate for young readers. No sentence fragments. See website for complete guidelines. Founded 1986.

## Kane Press – see Astra Publishing House

## KidHaven Press – see Gale, part of Cengage Group

## Alfred A. Knopf – see Penguin Random House

## Lee & Low Books, Inc.

95 Madison Avenue, Suite 1205, New York, NY 10016
*tel* +1 212-779-4400
*email* general@leeandlow.com
*website* www.leeandlow.com
*President* Tom Low

Children's book publisher specialising in multi-cultural literature that is relevant to young readers. The company's goal is to meet the need for stories that children of colour can identify with and that all children can enjoy and which promote a greater understanding of one another. Focuses on fiction, non-fiction and poetry for children 5–12 years, for middle graders and YA 13–18 years. Of special interest are realistic fiction, historical fiction and non-fiction with a non-white protagonist, a distinct voice or unique approach. Does not consider folktales or animal stories. Offers two writing contests per year for debut picture book writers and novelists. Writers of colour and/or of Native nations are especially encouraged to submit. Imprints: Lee & Low, Lee & Low Games, Bebop Books, Cinco Puntos Books, Tu Books, Children's Book Press, Dive Into Reading, Shen's Books. Please visit website to see current guidelines and needs. Potential authors will be contacted by email or phone within six months if interested. Founded 1911.

## Lerner Publishing Group

241 First Avenue NorthMinneapolis, MN 55401
*tel* +1 800-328-4929
*email* info@lernerbooks.com
*website* www.lernerbooks.com
*Publisher* Adam Lerner

Independent publisher of high-quality children's books for K–12 schools and libraries: picture books, fiction for children 5–8 and 9–12 years, teenage fiction, series fiction and non-fiction. Subjects include biography, social studies, science, sports and curriculum. Publishes approx. 300 titles each year and has about 1,500 in print. Publishing Group includes: Carolrhoda Books, Carolrhoda LAB, Darby Creek, ediciones Lerner, First Avenue Editions, Graphic Universe, Kar-Ben Publishing, Lerner, Lerner Classroom, Lerner Digital, Millbrook Press, Twenty-First Century Books, Zest Books. Publishing Group Partners include: Anderson Press, Big & Small, Cheriton Children's Books, Creston Books, Full Tilt Press, Gecko Press, Hungry Tomato, Intergalactic Afikoman, JR Comics, Knowledge Books, Lantana Publishing, Live Oak Media, Lorimer Children's & Teens, Maverick Arts Publishing, New Frontier Publishing, Page Education Foundation, Planting People Growing Justice Press, Quarto Library, Red Chair Press, Ruby Tuesday Books, Souring Kite Books, We Do Listen. No unsolicited submissions for any imprint. Founded 1959.

## Lightbox Learning Books

276 5th Avenue, Suite 704 #917, New York, NY 10001
*tel* +1 866-649-3445
*website* https://openlightbox.com

Educational publisher: children's non-fiction titles. Successes include *The AV2 Collection* (av2books.com). Founded 1979.

## Little, Brown and Company

1290 Avenue of the Americas, New York, NY 10104
*tel* +1 212-364-1100
*email* lbpublicity.Generic@hbgusa.com
*website* www.littlebrown.com
*Facebook* www.facebook.com/littlebrownandcompany
*Twitter* @littlebrown
*Senior Vice-President & Publisher* Bruce Nichols

General literature, fiction, non-fiction, biography, history, trade paperbacks, children's. Founded 1837.

### Little, Brown Spark

Publishes books for young people and adults that spark ideas, feelings and change. Looking for authors who are experts and thought leaders in the fields of health, lifestyle, psychology and science.

## Lucent Books – see Gale, part of Cengage Group

## Margaret K. McElderry Books – see Simon & Schuster Children's Publishing Division

## McGraw-Hill Professional*

1325 Avenue of the Americas, 7th Floor, New York, NY 10019
*website* www.mhprofessional.com
*Facebook* www.facebook.com/mcgrawhilleducation
*Twitter* @MHEducation
*Associate Publisher* Donya Dickerson

Divisions and imprints include: Business, Education and Test Prep, International Marine and Ragged Mountain Press, Medical, Open University Press. To find individual editorial contacts check website. Founded 1966.

## Macmillan Publishers, Inc.

120 Broadway, New York, NY 10271
*tel* +1 646-307-5151
*email* press.inquiries@macmillanusa.com
*website* https://us.macmillan.com/

Imprints for children: Macmillan Children's Publishing Group, FSG Books for Young Readers, Feiwel & Friends, First Second, Holt Books for Young Readers, Kingfisher, Neon Squid, Odd Dot, Priddy Books, Roaring Brook, Starscape/Tor Teen, Square Fish, Swoon Reads, Young Listeners. Founded 1843.

## Marshall Cavendish Education

800 Westchester Avenue, Suite N-641, Rye Brook, NY 10573
*email* mc@marshallcavendish.com
*website* https://www.marshallcavendish.com

Non-fiction books for young, middle-grade and YA readers. Subjects include: American studies, the arts, biographies, health, mathematics, science, social studies, history, world cultures. Non-fiction subjects should be curriculum-related and are published in series form. Length: 1,500–25,000 words. Send synopsis with one or more sample chapters and sample table of contents. Founded 1968.

## Mitchell Lane Publishers, Inc.

2001 S.W. 31st Avenue, Hallandale, FL 33009
*tel* +1 800-223-3251
*email* customerservice@mitchelllane.com
*website* www.mitchelllane.com
*President* Phil Comer

Non-fiction titles for young readers, middle readers and YA. Founded 1962.

## Mondo Publishing*

501 Grant Street, Union Trust Building, Suite, 1075 Pittsburgh, PA 15219
*tel* +1 877-401-2527
*email* info@mondopub.com
*website* www.mondopub.com

Classroom materials and professional development for K–5 educators. Part of Carnegie Learning. Founded 1986.

## Thomas Nelson Publisher*

PO Box 141000, Nashville, TN 37214
*tel* +1 800-251-4000
*email* publicity@thomasnelson.com
*website* www.thomasnelson.com

Bibles, religious, non-fiction and fiction general trade books for adults and children. Acquired by HarperCollins in 2012. Founded 1798.

## North Star Editions, Inc

2297 Waters Drive, Mendota Heights, MN 55120
*website* www.northstareditions.com

Publishes Flux (page 58), a YA fiction imprint, and Jolly Fish Press (page 61), a middle-grade fiction imprint. Also distributes juvenile non-fiction titles in various imprints, including Focus Readers, Little Blue Readers, Press Box Books, Apex, and NSE Classroom. Founded 1939.

## NorthSouth Books

600 Third Avenue, 2nd Floor, New York, NY 10016
*tel* +1 917-699-2079
*website* www.northsouth.com
*Publisher* Herwig Bitsche, *Associate Publisher* Andrew Rushton, *Editor* Beth Terrill, *Managing Director* Riky Stock

Publishes 35 titles a year. Publishes fresh, original, picture books with universal themes that could appeal to children 3–8 years. Accepting agented picture book submissions from US authors and illustrators. Guidelines on submissions: accepts picture book MSS (1,000 words or less); typically, does not acquire rhyming texts (although have been exceptions for simple/original text); authors do not need to include illustrations. Illustrators can send work for consideration via postcards/pdfs emailed to: submissions@northsouth.com. Successes include: *The Rainbow Fish* by Marcus Pfister; *Little Polar* by Hans de Beer; *Einstein – The Fantastic Journey of a Mouse Through Space and Time* by Torben Kuhlmann; *Peace* by Baptiste Paul, Miranda Paul, and Estelí Meza; *The Field* by Baptiste Paul and Jacqueline Alcántara; *Frida Kahlo and Her Animalitos* by Monica Brown and John Parra; and *Surf's Up* by Kwame Alexander and Daniel Miyares. Founded 1961.

## Richard C. Owen Publishers, Inc.

PO Box 585, Katonah, NY 10536
*tel* +1 914-232-3903
*website* www.rcowen.com
*Publisher* Richard C. Owen

Books for grades K–6. All work must be submitted as hard copy. Books for young learners: seeks high-interest stories with charm and appeal that children 5–7 years can read by themselves. Interested in original, realistic, contemporary stories, as well as folktales, legends and myths of all cultures. Non-fiction content must be supported with accurate facts. Length: 45–1,000 words. Also beginning chapter books up to 3,000 words.

## Pearson Education*

One Lake Street, Upper Saddle River, NJ 07458
*tel* +1 201-236-7000
*email* communications@pearsoned.com
*website* www.pearsoned.com

Educational secondary publisher of scientifically researched and standards-based instruction materials for today's grade 6–12 classrooms. Subjects include: arts, mathematics, modern and classical languages, science, social studies, careers and technology. Part of the Curriculum Division of Pearson Education, Inc. Founded 1966.

## Pelican Publishing

990 N. Corporate Drive, Suite 100, New Orleans, LA 70123
*tel* +1 504-684-8976
*email* editorial@pelicanpub.com
*website* www.arcadiapublishing.com
*Publisher & President* Scott Campbell

Gulf South children's books. Also biographies, holiday books, local cookery, history. Email a query letter, outline if chapter book, and résumé. No unsolicited MSS for chapter books. Most young children's books are 32 illustrated pages when published; their MSS will be 1,100 words maximum. Proposed books for middle readers (8+ years) should be at least 90 pages. Brief books for readers under 9 years may be submitted in their entirety. Founded 1926.

## Penguin Random House*

1745 Broadway, New York, NY 10019
*tel* +1 212-782-9000
*website* www.penguinrandomhouse.com
*Interim Ceo* Nihar Malaviya

Consists of 300 independent imprints and brands, more than 15,000 new print titles and close to 800 million print, audio and ebooks. Committed to publishing adult and children's fiction and non-fiction print editions, and is a pioneer in digital publishing. Its book brands include storied imprints such as Doubleday, Viking and Alfred A. Knopf (USA); Ebury, Hamish Hamilton and Jonathan Cape (UK); Plaza & Janés and Alfaguara (Spain); and Sudamericana (Argentina); as well as the international imprint DK. Founded 2013.

## Penguin Young Readers*

1745 Broadway, New York, NY 10019
*tel* +1 212-366-2000
*website* www.penguin.com/children
*Facebook* www.facebook.com/penguinkidsbooks
*Twitter* @penguinkids
*President* Jen Loja

A leading children's book publisher in the USA. The company owns a wide range of imprints and trademarks including Dial Books; Dutton; Grosset & Dunlap; Kathy Dawson Books; Kokila; Nancy Paulsen Books; Penguin Workshop; Philomel; Puffin; G.P. Putnam's Sons; Razorbill; Speak; Viking; and Frederick Warne. Penguin Young Readers is a division of Penguin Group LLC, a Penguin Random House company. Founded 1935.

## Puffin – see Penguin Young Readers

## Quarto Publishing Group – Walter Foster Publishing

100 Cummings Center, Suite 265D, Beverly, MA 01915
*tel* +1 978-282-9590
*email* walterfoster@quarto.com
*website* www.walterfoster.com
*Group Publisher* Anne Landa, *Senior Managing Editor* Karen Julian

Imprint of The Quarto Group. Instructional art books for children and adults. Also art and activity kits for children. A division of Quarto Publishing Group US. Founded 1976.

## Random House Children's Books*

1745 Broadway, New York, NY 10019
*tel* +1 212-782-9000
*website* www.rhcbooks.com,
www.randomhouse.com/teachers
*President & Publisher* Barbara Marcus

An English-language children's trade book publisher. Creates books for preschool children through YA readers, in all formats from board books to activity books to picture books, graphic novels, novels and non-fiction. Imprints: Dragonfly, Ember, Laurel-Leaf, Little Golden Books, Make Me A World, Princeton Review, Random House Books for Young Readers, Random House Graphic, Rodale Kids, Schwartz & Wade Books, Sylvan Learning, Wendy Lamb Books, Yearling Books. Part of Penguin Random House (page 63). Founded 1925.

## Razorbill – see Penguin Young Readers

## Roaring Brook Press

120 Broadway, New York, NY 10271
*tel* +1 646-600-7861
*website* https://us.macmillan.com/publishers/roaring-brook-press/
*Publisher* Jennifer Besser

Picture books, chapter books, novels and graphic novels in fiction and non-fiction for young readers, 0–18 years. Publishes about 70 titles a year. Division of Holtzbrink Publishers. Part of Macmillan Children's Publishing Group. Does not accept unsolicited MSS or submissions in print or digital. Founded 2002.

## Rowman & Littlefield

4501 Forbes Boulevard, Suite 200, Lanham, MD 20706
*tel* +1 301-459-3366
*email* customercare@rowman.com
*website* www.rowman.com
*Facebook* www.facebook.com/rowmanuk
*Twitter* @rowmanuk
*President & Ceo* James E. Lyons

An independent publisher specialising in both academic publishing in the humanities and social sciences and trade non-fiction publishing. Founded 1925.

## Running Press Book Publishers

2300 Chestnut Street, Suite 200, Philadelphia, PA 19103
*tel* +1 215-567-5080
*email* perseus.promos@perseusbooks.com
*website* www.runningpress.com
*Facebook* www.facebook.com/runningpressbooks
*Twitter* @running_press

General non-fiction, science, history, children's fiction and non-fiction, cookbooks, pop culture, lifestyle, illustrated gift books, Miniature Editions. Imprints: Running Press Adults, Running Press Kids, Running Press Minis, Running Press Studio. Member of the Perseus Books Group which is an imprint of Hachette Book Group (page 59). Successes include *You Are a Badass* by Jen Sincero, *Ripe* by Cheryl Sternman Rule, *Cats in Hats* by Sara Thomas and *Slow Beauty* by Shel Pink. Founded 1972.

### Running Press Kids

Picture books, activity books, YA fiction. Successes include the *Doodles* series.

## Sasquatch Books

1904 Third Avenue, Suite 710 Seattle, WA 98101
*tel* +1 206-467-4300
*email* custserv@sasquatchbooks.com
*website* www.sasquatchbooks.com
*Facebook* www.facebook.com/SasquatchBooksSeattle
*Twitter* @sasquatchbooks

Publishes a variety of non-fiction books, as well as children's books under the Little Bigfoot imprint. Will consider queries and proposals from authors and agents for new projects that fit into the company's West Coast regional publishing programme. Imprints: Sasquatch Adult, Little Big Foot, Spruce Books. Founded 1986.

## Scholastic, Inc.*

557 Broadway, New York, NY 10012
*tel* +1 212-343-6100
*email* news@scholastic.com
*website* www.scholastic.com
*Facebook* www.facebook.com/scholastic
*Twitter* @scholastic

The world's largest publisher and distributor of children's books and a leader in education technology and children's media. Divisions: Scholastic Book Clubs, Scholastic Book Fairs, Scholastic Education, Scholastic International, Media, Licensing and Advertising, Scholastic Trade Publishing. Imprints include: Arthur A. Levine Books, The Blue Sky Press, Cartwheel Books, Chicken House, David Fickling Books, Graphix, Orchard Books, Point, PUSH, Scholastic en español, Scholastic Focus, Scholastic Licensed Publishing, Scholastic Nonfiction, Scholastic Paperbacks, Scholastic Press and Scholastic Reference. In addition, Scholastic Trade Books includes Klutz, a highly innovative publisher and creator of 'books plus' for children. Founded 1920.

### Scholastic Trade Books, Children's Book Publishing

Award-winning publisher of original children's books. Publishes over 600 new titles a year including bestselling brands such as *Harry Potter*, *Captain Underpants*, *The Hunger Games*, *Clifford The Big Red Dog*, *I Spy* and *The Magic School Bus*.

## Scholastic Education*

557 Broadway, New York, NY 10012
*tel* +1 212-343-6100
*website* www.scholastic.com

Educational publisher of research-based core and supplementary instructional materials. A leading provider in reading improvement and professional development products, as well as learning services that address the needs of the developing reader – from grades pre-K to high school. Publishes 32 curriculum-based classroom magazines used by teachers in grades pre-K–12 as supplementary educational materials to raise awareness about current events in an age-appropriate manner and to help children develop reading skills. Scholastic Education has also developed technology-based reading assessment and management products to help administrators and educators quickly and accurately assess student reading levels, match students to the appropriate books, predict how well they will do on district and state standardised tests and inform instruction to improve reading skills. Founded 1923.

## Simon & Schuster Children's Publishing Division*

1230 Avenue of the Americas, New York, NY 10020
*tel* +1 212-698-7200
*website* www.simonandschuster.com/kids
*President & Publisher* Jon Anderson

Preschool to YA, fiction and non-fiction, trade, library and mass market. Imprints: Aladdin Paperbacks, Atheneum Books for Young Readers, Beach Lane Books, Little Simon, Margaret K. McElderry Books, Salaam Reads, Simon & Schuster Books for Young Readers, Simon Pulse, Simon Spotlight, Paula Wiseman Books. Division of Simon & Schuster, Inc. Founded 1924.

### Aladdin Books

*Vice-President & Publisher* Valerie Garfield

Publishes commercial middle grade fiction with an emphasis on adventure, fantasy and humor. Accepts query letters with proposals for middle-grade series and single-title fiction, middle-grade and commercial non-fiction. Send MS for the attention of the Submissions Editor.

### Atheneum Books for Young Readers

*Vice-President & Publisher* Justin Chanda

Picture books, chapter books, mysteries, biography, sci-fi, fantasy, graphic novels, middle-grade and YA fiction and non-fiction. Covers preschool–YA. Approximately 10% of books are by first-time authors. No unsolicited MSS. Send query letter only. Responds in one month.

### Margaret K. McElderry Books

*Vice-President & Publisher* Justin Chanda

Picture books, easy-to-read books, fiction (8–12 years, YA), poetry, fantasy. Covers preschool to YA. Approximately 10% of books are by first-time authors. No unsolicited MSS. Responds in three months. Samples returned with sase.

### Simon & Schuster Books for Young Readers

*Vice President & Publisher* Justin Chandu

Publishes a wide range of contemporary, commercial, award-winning fiction and non-fiction that spans every age of children's publishing. Seeking challenging and psychologically-complex YA novels; also imaginative and humorous middle-grade fiction. No unsolicited MSS. Send query letter only. Responds in two months.

### Paula Wiseman

*email* paulawiseman@simonandschuster.com
*Vice-President & Publisher* Paula Wiseman

Publishes award-winning and bestselling books, including picture books, novelty books and novels. The imprint focuses on stories and art that are childlike, timeless, innovative and centered in emotion. Approximately 10% of books are by first-time authors. Submit complete MS. Length: picture books – 500 words; others standard length. Considers all categories of fiction. Will review MS/illustration packages from artists. Send MS with dummy.

## Sleeping Bear Press – see Gale, part of Cengage Group

## Sourcebooks, Inc.

PO Box, 4410, Naperville, IL 60567-4410
*website* www.sourcebooks.com
*Editorial Director* Todd Stocke

A leading independent publisher in a wide variety of genres including fiction, romance, children's, YA, gift/calendars and college-bound. E-commerce businesses include *Put Me In the Story*, the number one personalised books platform. Imprints include: Cumberland House, Dawn Publications, Little Pickle Press, Poison Pen Press, Simple Truths, Sourcebooks, Sourcebooks Casablanca, Sourcebooks Fire, Sourcebooks Kids, Sourcebooks Landmarks. Founded 1987.

### Sourcebooks Kids

Publishes notable fiction and non-fiction projects including board books, picture books, chapter books and middle-grade works with the hope of engaging children in the pure fun of books and the wonder of learning new things.

## Tachyon Publications

1459 18th Street, #139, San Francisco, CA 94107
*tel* +1 415-285-5615
*email* Tachyon@tachyonpublications.com
*website* https://tachyonpublications.com/
*Facebook* www.facebook.com/Tachyon-Publications
*Twitter* @TachyonPub
*Publisher* Jacob Weisman

A publisher of smart sci-fi, fantasy and horror, as well as occasional mysteries, memoirs, YA and literary fiction. Founded 1995.

## Teacher Created Resources

12621 Western Avenue, Garden Grove, CA 92841
*tel* +1 800-662-4321
*email* custserv@teachercreated.com
*website* www.teachercreated.com

Educational materials. See website for guidelines. Founded 1977.

## Union Square & Co.

33 East 17th Street, New York, NY 10003
*tel* +1 800-367-9692
*email* editorial@sterlingpublishing.com
*website* www.unionsquareandco.com

Adult non-fiction and children's board books, picture books and non-fiction. Imprints include: Union Square & Co., Union Square Kids, Sterling Ethos, Puzzlewright Press, Flashkids, Hearst Books. Founded 1949.

## Viking – see Penguin Young Readers

## Walker Books US

99 Dover Street, Somerville, MA 02144
*tel* +1 617-661-3330
*website* www.walkerbooksus.com,
www.candlewick.com
*Facebook* www.facebook.com/CandlewickPressBooks
*Directors* Susan Van Metre (editorial), Maria Middleton (art)

Great storytelling and instant reader appeal in fiction, graphic novels and illustrated non-fiction. Titles range from YA to picture books, with emphasis on middle-grade and YA works. Walker Books US is a division of Candlewick Press (page 56). Founded 2017.

## Albert Whitman & Company

250 South Northwest Highway, Suite 320, Park Ridge, Illinois, IL 60068
*tel* +1 847-232-2800
*email* marketing@albertwhitman.com
*website* www.albertwhitman.com

Books that respond to cultural diversity and the special educational needs and concerns of children and their families (e.g. divorce, bullying). Also novels for middle-grade readers, picture books and non-fiction for children 2–12 years. For submissions guidelines see website. Founded 1919.

## Paula Wiseman – see Simon & Schuster Children's Publishing Division

## Word Song – see Astra Publishing House

## Workman Publishing Company*

225 Varick Street, New York, NY 10014
*tel* +1 212-254-5900
*email* info@workman.com
*website* www.workman.com
*Facebook* www.facebook.com/workmanpublishing
*Twitter* @workmanpub
*Publisher & Editorial Director* Susan Bolotin

General non-fiction for adults and children. Calendars. Owned by Hachette Book Group (page 59). Founded 1968.

## World Book, Inc.

180 North LaSalle Street, Suite 900, Chicago, Illinois 60601
*tel* +1 800-729-5800
*email* international@worldbook.com
*website* www.worldbook.com
*Facebook* www.facebook.com/WorldBook
*Twitter* @worldbookinc

A leading publisher of authoritative, age-appropriate and reliable print and digital educational and reference materials for children and adults. Trade companies include children's book publisher Bright Connections Media and Incentive Publications which specialises in supplemental resources for children and teachers. Founded 1917.

## WorthyKids

830 Crescent Centre Drive, Ste 450, Franklin, TN 37067
*email* IdealsInfo@hbgusa.com
*website* www.worthykids.com
*Facebook* www.faccebook.com/worthykidsbooks

An imprint of Hachette Book Group. Picture books, board books, and middle-grade novels for children (1–12 years). Email to request submission guidelines. Digital submissions not accepted. Due to the large volume of submissions, the company only responds to those that are of interest to the publishing program. Potential authors should become familiar with current books before submitting. Agents welcome. Founded 1944.

## Yen Press

150 W 30th Street, 19th floor, New York 10001
*email* yenpress@hbgusa.com
*website* www.yenpress.com
*Facebook* www.facebook.com/yenpress
*Twitter* @yenpress

Graphic novels and manga in all formats for all ages. Founded 2006.

# Children's audio publishers

Many of the audio publishers listed below are also publishers of print and electronic books.

## Audible

*email* partners-uk@audible.co.uk
*website* www.audible.co.uk
*Twitter* @audibleuk

Producer and seller of digital audio entertainment, including fiction and non-fiction audiobooks for adults and children. Publishers interested in exploring business opportunities with Audible may email the address above, or find out more about turning print books into audiobooks at www.acx.com. Founded 1995; acquired by Amazon 2008.

## Audiobooks.com

*email* acquisitions@audiobooks.com
*website* www.audiobooks.com
*Facebook* www.facebook.com/audiobookscom
*Twitter* @audiobooks_com

Subscription audiobook service, offering a wide range of fiction and non-fiction genres, as well as some children's titles. Publishers interested in having their titles included in the company's library may get in touch via the email address above.

## Barrington Stoke – see page 28

## BookBeat

*email* info@bookbeat.com
*website* www.bookbeat.com/uk
*Twitter* @BookBeatUK
*Instagram* @bookbeat

Digital streaming service for adult and children's audiobooks across a variety of fiction and non-fiction genres. Monthly subscription model (from £5.99). Owned by Bonnier. Founded 2017.

## Dref Wen

28 Church Road, Whitchurch, Cardiff CF14 2EA
*tel* 029-2061 7860
*website* www.drefwren.com
*Directors* Roger Boore, Anne Boore, Gwilym Boore, Alun Boore, Rhys Boore

Welsh-language and dual-language children's books. Founded 1970.

## The Educational Company of Ireland

Ballymount Road, Walkinstown, Dublin D12 R25C, Republic of Ireland
*tel* +353 (0)1 4500611
*email* info@edco.ie
*website* www.edco.ie
*Chief Executive* Martina Harford

Irish language CDs. Trading unit of Smurfit Kappa Group – Ireland. Founded 1910.

## W. F. Howes Ltd

Unit 5, St George's House, Rearsby Business Park, Gaddesby Lane, Rearsby, Leicester LE7 4YH
*tel* (01664) 423000
*email* info@wfhowes.co.uk
*website* www.wfhowes.co.uk

Audiobook and large-print publisher, distributing its content through consumer and library vendors. Catalogue includes over 6,500 titles, including authors such as Danielle Steel, Val McDermid, Dan Jones, V. E. Schwab, Mark Dawson, Julia Quinn and Nicci French. UK subsidiary of RBmedia. Founded 1999.

## Kobo

*website* www.kobo.com/gb/en
*Twitter* @kobo

Audiobook streaming service, for a monthly fee. Offers fiction, non-fiction, adult, children's and YA titles.

## Naxos AudioBooks

5 Wyllyotts Place, Potters Bar, Herts. EN6 2JD
*tel* (01707) 653326
*email* info@naxosaudiobooks.com
*website* www.naxosaudiobooks.com
*Twitter* @NaxosAudioBooks
*Managing Director* Anthony Anderson

Recordings of classic literature, modern fiction, non-fiction, drama and poetry. Founded 1994.

## Penguin Random House UK Audio (Children's)

Penguin Studios, One Embassy Gardens, Nine Elms Lane, London SW8 5BL
*website* www.penguinrandomhouse.co.uk
*Producer and Composer* Kate MacDonald

Contemporary and classic literature for younger listeners. Authors include Malorie Blackman, Charlie Higson, Roald Dahl and Eoin Colfer.

# Children's book packagers

Many illustrated books are created by book packagers, whose particular skills are in the areas of book design and graphic content. In-house editors match up the expertise of specialist writers, artists and photographers who usually work on a freelance basis.

## Aladdin Books Ltd

PO Box 53987, London SW15 2SF
*tel* 020-3174 3090
*email* sales@aladdinbooks.co.uk
*website* https://simonandschusterpublishing.com/aladdin/
*Editorial Director* Kirstin Gilson

Full design and book packaging facility specialising in children's non-fiction and reference. Part of Simon & Schuster (page 43). Founded 1980.

## Nicola Baxter

16 Cathedral Street, Norwich NR1 1LX
*tel* (01603) 766585 / 07778 285555
*email* nb@nicolabaxter.co.uk
*website* www.nicolabaxter.co.uk
*Director* Nicola Baxter

Full packaging service for children's books in both traditional and digital formats. Happy to take projects from concept to finished work or supply bespoke authorial, editorial, design, project management or commissioning services. Produces both fiction and non-fiction titles in a wide range of formats, for babies to YA, and experienced in novelty books and licensed publishing. Founded 1990.

## Brown Bear Books Ltd

Unit 1/D, Leroy House, 436 Essex Road,
London N1 3QP
*tel* 020-3176 8603
*website* www.windmillbooks.co.uk
*Children's Publisher* Anne O'Daly

Specialises in high-quality illustrated reference books and multi-volume sets for trade and educational markets. Opportunities for freelancers. Imprint of Windmill Books. Founded 1967.

## Global Blended Learning Ltd

Singleton Court, Wonastow Road,
Monmouth NP25 5JA
*tel* (01993) 706273
*email* hello@globalblendedlearning.com
*website* www.globalblendedlearning.com

Primary, secondary academic education (geography, science, modern languages) and co-editions (travel guides, gardening, cookery). Multimedia (CD-Rom programming and animations). Opportunities for freelancers. Founded 1985.

## Graham-Cameron Publishing & Illustration

59 Hertford Road, Brighton BN1 7GG
*tel* (01273) 385890
*email* enquiry@gciforillustration.com
*Alternative address* The Art House, Uplands Park, Sheringham, Norfolk NR26 8NE
*tel* (01263) 821333
*website* www.gciforillustration.com
*Partners* Helen Graham-Cameron, Duncan Graham-Cameron

Offers illustration and editorial services for picture books, information books, educational materials, activity books, non-fiction and reference books. Do not send unsolicited MSS. Founded 1985.

## Hawcock Books

242 Bloomfield Road, Bath BA2 2AX
*tel* 07976 708720
*website* www.hawcockbooks.co.uk
*Twitter* @DavidHawcock

Designs and produces highly creative and original pop-up art and 3D paper-engineered concepts. Most experience is in developing, providing editorial assistance, printing and manufacturing pop-up books and novelty items for the publishing industry. Also undertakes demanding commissions from the advertising world for model-making, point-of-sale and all printed 3D aspects of major campaigns.

## I Am a Bookworm*

35 Manor Close, Templecomb, Somerset BA8 0LA
*email* hello@iamabookworm.co.uk
*website* www.iamabookworm.co.uk
*Facebook* www.facebook.com/iamabookwormuk

An independent packager and publisher of children's novelty books, board books, activity books and light books for children aged 0–5 years. Founded 2011.

## Little People Books

The Home of BookBod, Knighton,
Radnorshire LD7 1UP
*tel* (01547) 520925
*email* littlepeoplebooks@thehobb.tv
*website* www.littlepeoplebooks.co.uk
*Directors* Grant Jessé (production & managing)

Packager of audio, children's educational and textbooks, digital publications. Parent company: Grant Jessé UK.

## Orpheus Books Ltd

2 Hewlett Place, Cheltenham, Glos. GL52 6DQ
*tel* (01993) 774949
*email* info@orpheusbooks.com
*websites* www.orpheusbooks.com, www.Q-files.com
*Executive Directors* Nicholas Harris, Sarah Hartley

Produces children's books and ebooks for the international co-editions market: non-fiction and reference. Orpheus Books are the creators of Q-files.com, the online educational resource for schools and libraries. Founded 1993.

## The Puzzle House

Ivy Cottage, Battlesea Green, Stradbroke,
Suffolk IP21 5NE
*tel* (01379) 384656
*email* puzzlehouse@btinternet.com
*website* www.thepuzzlehouse.co.uk
*Partners* Roy Preston, Sue Preston

Editorial service creating crossword, quiz, puzzle and activity material for all ages. Founded 1988.

## Storymix

The Wenta Business Centre Colne Way, Watford,
Hertfordshire WD24 7ND
*email* jasmine@storymix.co.uk
*website* www.storymix.co.uk
*Facebook* www.facebook.com/storymixstudio
*Twitter* @storymixstudio
*Director* Jasmine Richards

Inclusive children's fiction studio. Works with minority ethnic communities in children's books and offers paid writing opportunities to writers and illustrators of colour. Actively looking to add emerging and established talent to our database of creatives. Apply here: www.storymix.co.uk/write-for-us. Founded 2019

## Toucan Books Ltd

128 Aldersgate Street, Suite 106, London EC1A 4AE
*tel* 020-7250 3388
*website* www.toucanbooks.co.uk

International co-editions; editorial, design and production services. Founded 1985.

## David West Children's Books

11 Glebe Road, London SW13 0DR
*tel* 020-8876 1405
*email* lynn@davidwestbooks.com
*website* www.davidwestchildrensbooks.com
*Proprietor* David West, *Partner* Lynn Lockett

Packagers of highly illustrated children's non-fiction books. Specialises in science, art, geography, history, sport and flight. Produces 20 titles each year. Opportunities for freelancers. Founded 1986.

## Working Partners Ltd

9 Kingsway, 4th Floor, London WC2B 6XF
*tel* 020-7841 3939
*email* enquiries@workingpartnersltd.co.uk
*website* www.coolabi.com/books
*Managing Director* Chris Snowdon

Creators of children's and YA fiction: animal fiction, fantasy, horror, historical fiction, detective, magical, adventure. Unable to accept any submissions. Pays advance and royalty; retains copyright on all works. Selects writers from samples based on specific brief provided. Founded 1995.

**Books**

# Children's bookshops

The bookshops in the first part of this list specialise in selling new children's books and are good places for writers and illustrators to check out the marketplace. Most of them are members of the Booksellers Association and are well known to publishers. A list of secondhand and antiquarian children's bookshops follows. Independent Booksellers Week usually takes place each year in June or July, but check online for further information (https://booksellers.org.uk/Campaigns/independentbookshopweek).

## The Alligator's Mouth
2A Church Court, Richmond, Surrey TW9 1JL
*tel* 020-8948 6775
*email* info@thealligatorsmouth.co.uk
*website* www.thealligatorsmouth.co.uk
*Facebook* www.facebook.com/alligatorsmouth
*Twitter* @alligatorsmouth

Independent children's bookshop stocking works for all ages from babies to teenagers. Runs regular story-time sessions, book clubs and author events.

## Bags-of-Books
1 South Street, Lewes BN7 2BT
*tel* (01273) 479320
*email* bagsofbooks@bags-of-books.co.uk
*website* https://bags-of-books.co.uk
*Twitter* @BagsofBooks
*Instagram* @bagsofbookslewes
*Proprietor* Rachel Givertz

Independent children's bookshop situated within a 16th-century building. Extensive selection of fiction and non-fiction from babies up to age eighteen. Hosts author visits and runs a books-for-schools programme.

## Bert's Books
54 Goodwin Court, Swindon SN1 4BB
*email* bert@bertsbooks.co.uk
*website* https://bertsbooks.co.uk/
*Facebook* www.facebook.com/BertsBooks
*Twitter* @BertsBooks
*Founder* Alex Call

Online bookshop with a focus on diversity. Offers books in monthly bundles, including young adult titles. A bricks-and-mortar shop opened in May 2022. Founded 2019.

## Blackwell's Bookshop, Children's Dept
Blackwell's Bookshop, 50 Broad Street, Oxford OX1 3BQ
*tel* (01865) 333694
*email* oxford@blackwell.co.uk
*website* https://bookshop.blackwell.co.uk/bookshop/home
*Facebook* www.facebook.com/blackwellbooks

Based on the first floor of Blackwell's flagship bookshop, the children's department stocks over 10,000 titles for younger readers and holds a regular events programme, including author visits to schools.

## The Blue House Bookshop
10 Bootham, York YO30 7BL
*tel* (01904) 927838
*email* karen@thebluehousebookshop.co.uk
*Facebook* www.facebook.com/bluehousebookshop
*Twitter* @bookishkids
*Instagram* @thebluehousebookshop
*Proprietor* Karen Walker

Independent children's bookshop in the historic heart of York. Offers a range of fiction and non-fiction to young readers. Supplies books for schools and can advise on book choices. Supporter of the Yorkshire Dales Millennium Trust. Founded 2019.

## The Book Burrow @ Aardvark Books & Café
The Bookery, Manor Farm, Brampton Bryan, Bucknell SY7 0DH
*email* aardvaark@btconnect.com
*website* www.aardvark-books.com
*Facebook* www.facebook.com/AardvarkBooks
*Twitter* @AardvarkEthel
*Instagram* @aardvarkbookscafe
*Proprietors* Sheridan and Sarah Swinson

Bookshop and play space with a castle, enchanted forest, pirate cabin and princess seat. Extensive range of books, mostly new but some secondhand and rare. Children's events throughout the year. BA member.

## Book Corner
24 Milton Street, Saltburn-by-the-Sea TS12 1DG
*tel* (01287) 348010
*email* jenna@bookcornershop.co.uk
*website* www.bookcornershop.co.uk
*Facebook* www.facebook.com/people/Book-Corner-Saltburn/100069049526679/
*Twitter* @BookCornerShop
*Proprietor* Jenna Warren

Independent bookshop with dedicated children's section, stocking books for all ages from babies to young adults. Also stocks fiction and non-fiction for adults, and hosts author visits.

## The Book House

93 High Street, Thame, Oxon OX9 3HJ
*tel* (01844) 213032
*email* anybook@thebookhousethame.co.uk
*website* www.thebookhousethame.co.uk
*Instagram* @the_book_house
*Proprietor* Brian Pattinson

Specialises in children's books alongside a wide range of titles for all ages.

## The Book Nook

First Avenue, Hove BN3 2FJ
*tel* (01273) 911988
*email* info@booknookuk.com
*website* www.booknookuk.com
*Twitter* @booknookhove
*Proprietors* Vanessa Lewis, Julie Ward

Specialist children's bookshop set in a child-friendly environment with author events, regular story-time, book clubs, café and pirate ship. Previous winner of Children's Bookseller of the Year category at *The Bookseller* Industry Awards.

## Booka Bookshop and Café

26–28 Church Street, Oswestry, Shrops. SY11 2SP
*tel* (01691) 662244
*email* hello@bookabookshop.co.uk
*website* www.bookabookshop.co.uk
*Facebook* www.facebook.com/bookabookshop
*Twitter* @bookabookshop
*Proprietors* Carrie and Tim Morris

Independent bookshop and café offering a wide range of books, cards and gifts. Hosts a regular programme of author talks and signings, organises themed events, runs bookclubs and works with schools and the local library. Previous winner of Independent Bookshop of the Year category at *The Bookseller* Industry Awards.

## Bookbugs and Dragon Tales

41 Timberhill, Norwich NR1 3LA
*tel* (01603) 964022
*email* leanne@bookbugsanddragontales.com
*website* https://bookbugsanddragontales.com
*Facebook* www.facebook.com/people/Bookbugs-and-Dragon-Tales/100039029726821/
*Twitter* @Bookbugsdragon1
*Instagram* @bookbugsdragontales
*Proprietors* Dan and Leanne Fridd

Independent bookshop offering a wide range of books and events for children and their families. An events space that hosts bookclubs, classes and other interactive opportunities is also available. Founded 2019.

## The Broadway Bookshop

6 Broadway Market, London E8 4QJ
*tel* 020-7241 1626
*email* books@broadwaybookshophackney.com
*website* www.broadwaybookshophackney.com
*Proprietor* Jane Howe

General independent bookshop specialising in literary fiction with a strong selection of children's books for all ages.

## Browns Books For Students

5 Redcliff Road, Melton, East Yorkshire HU14 3RS
*tel* (01482) 384660
*email* enquiries@brownsbfs.co.uk
*website* www.brownsbfs.co.uk
*Facebook* www.facebook.com/BrownsBFS
*Twitter* @BrownsBFS
*Instagram* @BrownsBFS

Supplier of books and educational resources across the UK and internationally. Offers next-day delivery, an extensive ebook catalogue, in-house stock selection team and shelf-ready book servicing.

## Chicken & Frog

30 Crown Street, Brentwood, Essex, CM14 4BA
*tel* (01277) 230068
*email* info@chickenandfrog.co.uk
*website* https://chickenandfrog.com
*Twitter* @chickenandfrog
*Instagram* @thechickenandfrog
*Proprietors* Jim and Natasha Radford

Independent bookshop and tuition centre. Weekly rhythm and rhyme, creative writing and handwriting sessions. Regular events for children and families, book clubs (in person and online), school supply and consultation.

## Children's Bookshop (Huddersfield)

*tel* (01484) 658013
*email* hello@childrensbookshuddersfield.co.uk
*website* www.childrensbookshuddersfield.co.uk
*Twitter* @Lindley_Books
*Contact* Nicola Lee

Independent bookshop stocking a wide selection of titles for children, from picture books to YA. Also offers services to schools. New premises planned during 2023; see website for details.

## Children's Bookshop (Muswell Hill)

29 Fortis Green Road, London N10 3HP
*tel* 020-8444 5500
*email* admin@childrensbookshoplondon.co.uk
*website* www.childrensbookshoplondon.com
*Facebook* www.facebook.com/ChildrensBookshopLondon
*Twitter* @childrensbkshop
*Instagram* @childrensbookshoplondon

Oldest-running children's bookshop in the UK. Stocks approximately 12,000 titles and 25,000 books for children from newborn to young adult. Offers services for schools, charities, and individual companies, as well as an events programme. Founded 1974.

### DRAKE The Bookshop

26–27 Silver Street, Stockton-on-Tees TS18 1SX
*tel* (01642) 909970
*email* books@drakethebookshop.co.uk
*website* www.drakethebookshop.co.uk
*Twitter* @drakebookshop
*Proprietors* Richard Drake, Melanie Greenwood

Independent bookshop with strong children's offering, as well as events and initiatives aimed at young readers and schools. The shop runs three children's book groups (Teen Readers, High-Rise Readers and Young Bookworms) and offers a selection of dyslexia-friendly titles. Founded 2015.

### ebb & flo bookshop

12 Gillibrand Street, Chorley, Lancs. PR7 2EJ
*tel* (01257) 262773
*email* diane@ebbandflobookshop.co.uk
*website* www.ebbandflobookshop.co.uk
*Facebook* www.facebook.com/ebbandflobookshop
*Twitter* @ebbandflobooks
*Proprietor* Diane Gunning

Small independent bookshop stocking books for children and adults, plus toys, cards and gifts. Supplies books to local schools, including library restocks and topic boxes. Organises author visits. Hosts a regular story-time for preschool children (call ahead to book) as well as author events and holiday workshops.

### The Edinburgh Bookshop

219 Bruntsfield Place, Edinburgh EH10 4DH
*tel* 0131 447 1917
*email* mail@edinburghbookshop.com
*website* www.edinburghbookshop.com
*Facebook* www.facebook.com/EdinBookshop
*Twitter* @EdinBookshop
*Proprietor* Marie Moser

Four-time Scottish Independent of the Year winner. Events programme includes author visits, book signings, book clubs and a twice-weekly story-time for the under 5s. Founded 2007.

### Far from the Madding Crowd

20 High Street, Linlithgow EH49 7AE
*tel* (01506) 845509
*email* info@maddingcrowdlinlithgow.com
*website* www.maddingcrowdlinlithgow.com
*Facebook* www.facebook.com/
FarFromTheMaddingCrowdLinlithgow
*Twitter* @Furtherfrom

Independent bookshop with eclectic range of titles, including children's and preschool in the dedicated Little Owls section. Strong influence from Scottish publishers. Free storytelling on Fridays at 3pm: tickets must be booked in advance.

### Foggie Toddle Books

18 North Main Street, Wigtown DG8 9HL
*tel* (01988) 402896
*email* hello@foggietoddlebooks.co.uk
*website* https://foggietoddlebooks.co.uk
*Facebook* www.facebook.com/FoggieToddleBooks
*Twitter* @FoggieToddler
*Instagram* @foggietoddlebooks
*Proprietor* Jayne Baldwin

Independent children's bookshop and publisher named after the Scots word for bumblebee. Stocks new, second-hand and vintage books for age groups from babies to young adults. Local art and crafts also available; a different artist or crafter is featured every month. Member of the Booksellers Association.

### Ginger and Pickles Children's Bookshop

51 St Stephen Street, Edinburgh EH3 5AH
*tel* 0131 285 8069
*email* hello@gingerandpicklesbookshop.com
*website* www.gingerandpicklesbookshop.com
*Facebook* www.facebook.com/
gingerandpickleschildrensbookshop
*Instagram* @gingerandpicklesbookshop

Independent children's bookshop catering for young readers from birth to teenage years. Also offers professional advice to schools on stocking and ordering key titles. Currently preparing events programme and a schools department. Founded 2020.

### Glowworm Books & Gifts Ltd

Unit 2, 5 Youngs Road, East Mains Industrial Estate, Broxburn, West Lothian EH52 5LY
*tel* (01506) 857570
*website* www.glowwormbooks.co.uk

Specialises in supplying books for children, especially those who find reading difficult due to physical or special educational challenges.

### Golden Hare Books

68 St Stephen Street, Edinburgh EH3 5AQ
*tel* 0131 225 7755
*email* mail@goldenharebooks.com
*website* www.goldenharebooks.com
*Twitter* @GoldenHareBooks
*Instagram* @goldenharebooks
*Owner* Mark Jones

Stocks books for readers of all ages. Holds regular book groups and author events. Runs a book subscription and offers bookshop membership. Previous winner of Independent Bookshop of the Year at the British Book Awards.

### Harbour Bookshop

2 Mill Street, Kingsbridge, Devon TQ7 1ED
*tel* (01548) 857233
*email* hello@harbourbookshop.co.uk
*website* www.harbourbookshop.co.uk
*Twitter* @HarbourBookshop
*Proprietor* Jane Fincham, *Manager* Louise Sanders

Well-established independent bookshop with an extensive range of children's books for all ages. Next-day delivery available. Also works with primary and secondary schools and holds children's book events and celebrations.

## Heath Educational Books

Willow House, Willow Walk, Whittaker Road, Sutton, Surrey SM3 9QQ
*tel* 020-8644 7788
*email* orders@heathbooks.co.uk
*website* www.heathbooks.co.uk
*Proprietor* Richard Heath

Supplies books to schools and teachers throughout Europe. Large showroom.

## Jacqson Diego Story Emporium

444 London Road, Westcliff on Sea, Essex SS0 9LN
*tel* (01702) 344262
*email* stories@jacqsondiego.com
*website* www.jacqsondiego.com
*Facebook* www.facebook.com/jacqsondiego
*Twitter* @jacqsondiego
*Instagram* @jacqsondiego

Independent bookshop specialising in fiction and non-fiction for children and young people. Regular events include bookclubs and writing groups. Also runs bespoke book-related services for schools and nurseries, including author visits, library audits, consultancy and workshops. BA member. Founded 2011.

## Madeleine Lindley Ltd

Book Centre, Broadgate, Broadway Business Park, Chadderton, Oldham OL9 9XA
*tel* 0161 683 4400
*email* books@madeleinelindley.com
*website* www.madeleinelindley.com
*Twitter* @teacher_books

Supplies books to schools and nurseries, provides information services and runs open days and training courses for teachers. Hosts author/publisher events for teachers and children.

## The Little Bookshop

47 Harrogate Road, Chapel Allerton, Leeds LS7 3PD
*tel* 0113 212 3465
*email* hello@thelittlebookshopleeds.co.uk
*website* www.thelittlebookshopleeds.co.uk
*Facebook* www.facebook.com/
thelittlebookshopleedskids
*Instagram* @thelittlebookshopleeds
*Proprietor* Cheryl Duffield

Independent bookshop specialising in books for children; also stocks adult titles. Carries a wide range of diverse and inclusive books and also provides subscription service for readers of all ages. Holds regular author events for children and adult. Also has storytimes Monday, Wednesday and Friday at 11am outside of school holidays, and daily craft sessions weekdays during school holidays. Offers services for

schools, including creating and ordering book lists, as well as arranging author events and book fairs. Founded 2017.

## The Mainstreet Trading Company

Main Street, St Boswells, Scottish Borders TD6 0AT
*tel* (01835) 824087
*email* info@mainstreetbooks.co.uk
*website* www.mainstreetbooks.co.uk
*Facebook* www.facebook.com/
Mainstreet.Trading.Company
*Twitter* @mainstreethare
*Instagram* @mainstreethare
*Proprietors* Rosamund and Bill de la Hey

General bookshop with a particular focus on children's books. Previous winner of Independent Bookseller of the Year category at the *The Bookseller* Industry Awards.

## Moon Lane Ink CIC

300 Stanstead Road, London SE23 1DE
*tel* 020-3489 7030
*email* info@moonlaneink.co.uk
*website* www.moonlaneink.co.uk
*Facebook* www.facebook.com/moonlaneink
*Twitter* @moonlaneink
*Instagram* @moonlaneink

Community-interest company dedicated to raising equality in children's books; equality of access, representation and roles in the publishing industry. In addition to a bookshop, runs enterprise workshops for children as well as a range of events. Founded 2018.

## Nickel Books

9 Merlin Close, Sittingbourne ME10 4TY
*tel* 07731 152089
*email* enquiries@nickelbooks.co.uk
*website* www.nickelbooks.co.uk
*Twitter* @NickelBooks
*Instagram* @nickelbooks
*Proprietor* Andrea Don

Mail-order, school books supply, visits, fairs, fetes and events. Specialises in children's books, from birth to teenage; also books for parents.

## Norfolk Children's Book Centre

Church Lane, Alby, Norwich NR11 7HB
*tel* (01263) 761402
*email* marilyn@ncbc.co.uk
*website* https://ncbc.co.uk
*website* https://uk.bookshop.org/shop/NorfolkCBC
*Facebook* www.facebook.com/NorfolkCBC
*Twitter* @NorfolkCBC
*Instagram* @NorfolkCBC

Independent bookshop established for over 35 years, specialising in books for children and teachers. Offers storytelling and school booksales within East Anglia, and nationwide conference book displays and mail order. Other services include school library assessment and rejuvenation, and topic-based approval collections.

## Octavia's Bookshop

24 Black Jack Street, Cirencester, Glos. GL7 2AA
*tel* (01285) 650677
*email* info@octaviasbookshop.co.uk
*website* www.octaviasbookshop.co.uk
*Twitter* @octaviabookshop
*Proprietor* Octavia Emanuel

Independent bookshop in which more than half the stock is dedicated to children's titles, from buggy books to teen fiction and classics. Previous winner of the Children's Independent Bookseller of the Year category at the *The Bookseller* Industry Awards.

## The Oundle Bookshop

13 Market Place, Oundle, Peterborough PE8 4BA
*tel* (01832) 273523
*email* oundlebookshop@colemangroup.co.uk
*website* www.colemans-online.co.uk/oundle-bookshop.html

General bookshop with extensive children's selection.

## Owl and Pyramid

10 Fore Street, Seaton EX12 2LA
*tel* (01297) 598030
*email* owl.pyramid@yahoo.com
*website* www.owlandpyramid.co.uk
*Facebook* www.facebook.com/owlpyramid
*Twitter* @OwlPyramid
*Instagram* @owlandpyramidbookshop

Independent children's bookshop stocking fiction and non-fiction for young readers from babies to teenagers. Also runs four book clubs for different age groups. Small but growing section of adult fiction and non-fiction. Founded 2014.

## Peters Ltd

120 Bromsgrove Street, Birmingham B5 6RJ
*tel* 0121 666 6646
*website* www.peters.co.uk
*Facebook* www.facebook.com/Petersbooksbirmingham
*Twitter* @petersbooks
*Instagram* @petersbooks

Specialist supplier of children's books and library furniture to schools, nurseries, academies and public libraries, with a book and furniture showroom, online ordering facilities and ten specialist children's librarians. Also provides a library design and installation service and hosts regular professional development events for teachers and librarians, featuring speakers, authors and illustrators.

## Pickled Pepper Books

10 Middle Lane, Crouch End, London N8 8PL
*tel* 020-3632 0823

*email* info@pickledpepperbooks.co.uk
*website* www.pickledpepperbooks.co.uk
*Twitter* @pickledbooks
*Instagram* @pickledpepperbooks
*Proprietors* Urmi Merchant, Steven Pryse

Family-run specialist children's bookshop with a weekly programme of events for preschoolers including baby sensory sessions, music and drama sessions, Italian and French classes, and storytimes. After-school events include both middle grade and teen book clubs, and illustration classes. Also hosts regular interactive author events, as well as theatre and puppet shows in the upstairs performance space. Works closely with nurseries, primary schools and secondary schools to deliver bespoke author talks and books to support reading.

## The Rabbit Hole

21 Market Place, Brigg DN20 8LD
*tel* (01652) 408534
*email* therabbithole.brigg@outlook.com
*website* www.therabbitholebrigg.com
*Facebook* www.facebook.com/therabbitsbrigg
*Twitter* @Therabbits21
*Instagram* @therabbithole.brigg
*Proprietors* Mel and Nick Webb

Community-focused bookshop with a strong emphasis on children's books. Also runs events and workshops and offers a range of services to schools. Named Midlands Bookshop of the Year at the 2023 British Book Awards. Founded 2017.

## The Rocketship Bookshop

5 Bridge Street, Salisbury SP1 2ND
*tel* (01722) 237172
*email* info@rocketshipbookshop.co.uk
*website* https://rocketshipbookshop.co.uk
*Facebook* www.facebook.com/rocketshipbookshop
*Twitter* @rshipbshop
*Instagram* @rocketshipbooks

Independent bookshop catering predominantly for children and young people, although a specially curated selection of adult titles is also available. Hosts author events and supports Salisbury International Arts Festival.

## Round Table Books

97 Granville Avenue, Brixton Village, London SW9 8PS
*email* bookshop@roundtablebooks.co.uk
*website* www.roundtablebooks.co.uk
*Facebook* www.facebook.com/RoundtableBookshop
*Twitter* @BooksRound
*Instagram* @roundtablebooks
*Co-Directors* Aimée Felone, Meera Ghanshamdas

Inclusive children's bookshop, launched by the Knights Of, an independent children's publisher that champions authors and illustrators from diverse backgrounds. Founded 2019.

## Seven Stories – see page 309

### Seven Stories Bookshop

30 Lime Street, Ouseburn Valley,
Newcastle upon Tyne NE1 2PQ
*tel* 0300 330 1095
*email* bookshop@sevenstories.org.uk
*website* www.sevenstories.org.uk/shop
*Twitter* @7StoriesBooks

Independent children's bookshop and part of the
National Centre for Children's Books. School
accounts are available, as is advice on library stock.

### Simply Books

228 Moss Lane, Bramhall, Cheshire SK7 1BD
*tel* 0161 439 1436
*email* enquiries@simplybooks.info
*website* www.simplybooks.info
*Twitter* @simplybooksNo1

Independent bookshop with strong children's
selection, as well as regular events and reading groups
for adults and children readers.

### Storytellers, Inc.

7 The Crescent, St Anne's on Sea, Lytham St Anne's,
Lancs. FY8 1SN
*tel* (01253) 781690
*email* info@storytellersinc.co.uk
*website* www.storytellersinc.co.uk
*Twitter* @storytellersinc
*Proprietors* Carolyn Clapham, Katie Clapham

Independent bookshop with dedicated children's
section. Supplies books to local schools. Regional
winner (North) in the Independent Bookshop of the
Year category at *The Bookseller* Industry Awards 2015.

### Tales On Moon Lane

25 Half Moon Lane, London SE24 9JU
*tel* 020-7274 5759
*email* info@talesonmoonlane.co.uk
*website* www.talesonmoonlane.co.uk
*Twitter* @talesonmoonlane
*Instagram* @talesonmoonlane
*Proprietor* Tamara Macfarlane

Specialist children's bookshop which runs yearly
children's literature festivals in February and
October, as well as weekly storytelling sessions for
preschool children.

### Through the Wardrobe Books

2 Nettleton Road, Mirfield, West Yorks. WF14 9AA
*email* hello@throughthewardrobebooks.co.uk
*website* www.throughthewardrobebooks.co.uk
*Facebook* www.facebook.com/
throughthewardrobebooks
*Twitter* @WardrobeBooks
*Founders* Leanne Yeomans, Samantha Ward

Specialist children's and young adults bookshop.
Open Monday to Saturday. Founded 2019.

### West End Lane Books

277 West End Lane, London NW6 1QS
*tel* 020-7431 3770
*email* info@welbooks.co.uk
*website* www.welbooks.co.uk
*Twitter* @WELBooks
*Instagram* @westendlanebooks

Independent family-owned bookshop, carrying
fiction and non-fiction books and stationery. Offers
twice-weekly story-time sessions for preschool
children. Hosts regular author talks, reading groups
and school events.

### Winstone's Hunting Raven Books

10 Cheap Street, Frome, Somerset BA11 1BN
*tel* (01373) 473111
*email* winstonebooks3@gmail.com
*Facebook* www.facebook.com/HuntingRavenBooks
*Twitter* @HuntingRavenBks
*Instagram* @huntingravenbooks
*Proprietor* Wayne Winstone, *Manager* Tina Gaisford-
Waller

Award-winning independent bookshop with
extensive range of books and gifts for all ages and a
strong children's section. Holds events and signings
throughout the year. South-West Independent
bookshop of the year 2020. Other Winstone's
bookshops can be found in Sidmouth and Sherborne.

### Wonderland Bookshop

64 Carolgate, Retford DN22 6EF
*tel* (01777) 948580
*email* hello@wonderlandbookshop.co.uk
*website* https://wonderlandbookshop.co.uk
*Facebook* www.facebook.com/WonderlandBookshop
*Twitter* @Wonder_Bookshop
*Instagram* @wonderlandbookshop
*Proprietor* Helen Tamblyn-Saville

Specialist children's bookshop stocking titles for
readers from birth to teens (also orders in titles for
adults on request). Includes dyslexia-friendly and
LGBTQI+ shelves. Also offers services for schools,
including library advice, author visits (in person or
online) and school wishlists. Named independent
Bookshop of the Year (Midlands region) 2022 and
Highly Commended Children's Bookshop of the Year
2022 at the British Book Awards. Founded 2019.

## BOOKSELLERS FOR COLLECTORS

### Blackwell's Rare Books

48–51 Broad Street, Oxford OX1 3BQ
*tel* (01865) 333555
*email* rarebooks@blackwell.co.uk
*website* https://blackwells.co.uk/rarebooks/
*Twitter* @blackwellrare

Deals in early and modern first editions of children's
books, among other subjects.

## Bookmark Children's and Illustrated Books

Orchard Close, Wye Lane, Marlborough,
Wiltshire SN8 1PJ
*tel* (01672) 512415
*email* leonora.f.smith@gmail.com
*Contacts* Leonora Smith, Anne Excell

Mail-order bookseller, specialising in books for collectors, ranging from antiquarian to modern. A wide range of first editions, novelty and illustrated books, chap-books, ABCs, annuals, etc. Also a selection of vintage toys, games, greetings cards and illustrated postcards, dolls and nursery china. Member of PBFA, selection of stock on PBFA website, occasionally exhibiting at PBFA book fairs in London, Bristol, York, Devizes, Brighton and Oxford. Established 1973

## The Children's Bookshop – Hay-on-Wye

Toll Cottage, Pontvaen, Hay-on-Wye,
Herefordshire HR3 5EW
*tel* (01497) 821083
*email* sales@childrensbookshop.com
*website* https://childrensbookshop.com/
*Twitter* @childrnsbkshop
*Proprietors* Judith and Colin Gardner

Second-hand and antiquarian children's books.

## Henry Sotheran Ltd

2–5 Sackville Street, Piccadilly, London W1S 3DP
*tel* 020-7439 6151
*email* rh@sotherans.co.uk
*website* www.sotherans.co.uk
*Facebook* www.facebook.com/sotherans
*Twitter* @Sotherans
*Instagram* @sotherans_piccadilly

Large showroom with hundreds of important children's books spanning two centuries, specialising in first editions and illustrated works by pivotal artists. Opening hours: Mon–Fri 9:30am–6:00 pm. Two specialist catalogues issued annually, available free on request.

## Stella & Rose's Books

Monmouth Road, Tintern,
Monmouthshire NP16 6SE
*tel* (01291) 689755
*email* enquiry@stellabooks.com
*website* www.stellabooks.com
*Twitter* @stellarosebooks

Specialists in rare, out-of-print children's and illustrated books, also carrying a large and varied general stock (over 25,000 books in stock). Stock available for sale via website. Specialist lists issued regularly. Open seven days a week; see website for opening hours. Single items or collections purchased. Founded 1991.

# Books, sites and blogs about children's books

These listings include some of the best print and online resources about children's books for readers, writers and illustrators.

## BOOKS

### The Oxford Companion to Children's Literature

Edited by Daniel Hahn
Published by Oxford University Press (2015, 2nd edn)
ISBN 978-0-1987-1554-2

An indispensable reference book for anyone interested in children's books. Over 900 biographical entries deal with authors, illustrators, printers, publishers, educationalists and others who have influenced the development of children's literature. Genres covered include myths and legends, fairy tales, adventure stories, school stories, fantasy, science fiction, crime and romance. This book is of particular interest to librarians, teachers, students, parents and collectors.

### The Reading Bug – and how you can help your child to catch it

by Paul Jennings
Published by Penguin Books (2004)
ISBN 978-0-1413-18400

Paul Jennings is a well-known children's author. This book explains, in his unique humorous style, how readers can open up the world through a love of books. He cuts through the jargon and the controversies to reveal the simple truths, which should enable adults to infect children with the reading bug.

### Sticks and Stones: The Troublesome Success of Children's Literature from Slovenly Peter to Harry Potter

by Jack Zipes
Published by Routledge (2002)
ISBN 978-0-4159-38808

Jack Zipes – translator of the Grimm tales, teacher, storyteller and scholar – questions whether children ever really had a literature of their own. He sees children's literature in many ways as being the 'grown-ups' version' – a story about childhood that adults tell kids. He discusses children's literature from the 19th century moralism of Slovenly Peter (whose fingers get cut off) to the wildly successful *Harry Potter* books. Children's literature is a booming market but its success, this author says, is disguising its limitations. *Sticks and Stones* is a forthright and engaging book by someone who clearly cares deeply about what and how children read.

### 1001 Children's Books You Must Read Before You Grow Up

Edited by Julia Eccleshare
Published by Cassell Illustrated (2009)
ISBN 978-1-8440-36714

This aims to provide an introduction to the best of children's literature, ranging from international classics to contemporary writers. Reviews of each book are accompanied by line drawings and artwork from the books themselves. A number of authors including Michael Morpurgo and Jacqueline Wilson also write about their favourite books. The reviews are ordered according to the book's publication date, from past to present, and age range of the reader.

### The Ultimate Book Guide

Edited by Leonie Flynn, Daniel Hahn and Susan Reuben
Published by A&C Black (2009)
ISBN 978-1-4081-04385

Over 600 entries covering the best books for children aged 8–12, from classics to more recently published titles. Funny, friendly and frank recommendations written for children by their favourite and best-known authors including Anthony Horowitz, Jacqueline Wilson, Celia Rees, Darren Shan, David Almond and Dick King-Smith. Plus features on the most popular genres.

### The Ultimate First Book Guide

Edited by Leonie Flynn, Daniel Hahn and Susan Reuben
Published by A&C Black (2008)
ISBN 978-0-7136-73319

Comprehensive reference to help children aged 0–7 with their first steps into the world of books. Covers board books and novelty books, through to classic and contemporary picture books, chapter books and more challenging reads. It includes recommendations and features from top authors and experts in the field of children's books, including former Children's Laureate Michael Rosen, Tony Bradman, Malachy Doyle and Wendy Cooling. There are also special features on a variety of topics and themed lists, and a selection of cross-references to other titles children may enjoy. See page 342.

## The Ultimate Teen Book Guide

Edited by Daniel Hahn and Leonie Flynn
Published by A&C Black (2010, 2nd edn)
ISBN 978–1–4081–04378

Listings of over 700 books that might interest teenage readers, recommended and reviewed by authors such as Melvin Burgess, Anthony Horowitz, Meg Cabot, Eoin Colfer and Philip Pullman. Reviews cover the classics to cult fiction, and graphic novels to bestsellers, and each is cross-referenced to other titles as suggestions of what to read next. The book also contains essays on areas of teenage writing including *Race in Young Adult Fiction* by Bali Rai and *Off the Rails* by Kevin Brooks. There are also the results of a national teen readers' poll, plus reviews from teen readers.

## ONLINE

## Armadillo

www.armadillomagazine.co.uk

An online magazine about children's books, including reviews, interviews, features and profiles. New issues are posted at the end of March, June, September and December. It was founded in 1999 by author Mary Hoffman as a review publication for children's books.

## BBC Bitesize

www.bbc.co.uk/bitesize

Information about UK schools' curriculum. Useful for those wishing to write for educational publishers but also for keeping abreast of curricular topics.

## The Bookbag

www.thebookbag.co.uk

A UK-based website focused on great reviews about children's books, there are also booklists and information about book awards, as well as articles and author interviews.

## Books for Keeps

http://booksforkeeps.co.uk

Featuring a quarterly online magazine for children's books including book reviews and features.

## The Bookseller

www.thebookseller.com

A magazine for the publishing industry, sharing news on author deals, book launches and industry features to subscribers. Some content is available for free, including the fortnightly *Chapter and Verse: The Art of Selling Children's Books* podcast.

## BookTrust

www.booktrust.org.uk

Dedicated children's reading charity, this is a useful site for professionals working with young readers. Information on events, prizes, books, authors, etc.

## BookTrust Great Books Guide

www.booktrust.org.uk/books-and-reading/our-recommendations/great-books-guide

BookTrust's independent annual 'pick of the best' in children's paperback fiction published in the previous calendar year. It is designed to help parents and those interested in children's reading to select books for children, from babies to teenagers.

## Branford Boase Award

www.branfordboaseaward.org.uk

The website for the annual children's book award dedicated to debut children's writers and their editor. Includes a writing competition for young people.

## CBBC

www.bbc.co.uk/cbbc

Website of the CBBC channel with games, activities and news for children.

## The Children's Book Council

www.cbcbooks.org

The Children's Book Council in the USA is dedicated to encouraging literacy and the enjoyment of children's books. The website includes reviews of children's books published in the USA, forthcoming publications and author profiles. A good site for checking out the US marketplace.

## Children's Laureate

www.booktrust.org.uk/what-we-do/childrens-laureate

Official website of the Children's Laureate with resources and activities for children.

## Children's Literature

http://childrenslit.com

US website of the Children's Literature Comprehensive Database (CLCD), a subscription database with over 120,000 reviews of children's books. Plus links to US author and illustrator websites.

## Yoto Carnegie & Kate Greenaway Medals

http://yotocarnegie.co.uk

This website follows the only UK children's book award where the winners are selected by specialist children's librarians. The website includes a shadowing' area for schools to leave their comments about the books, plus interviews with shortlisted authors.

## The Federation of Children's Book Groups

http://fcbg.org.uk/

The FCBG runs an annual children's book award, judged by children, and a network of local groups for those interested in finding out more about children's books and authors. See page 311.

## Good Reads for Children

www.goodreads.com/genres/childrens

The Amazon-owned website supports consumer reviews about books for children that can be researched by categories including middle grade and picture books, etc.

## The Horn Book

www.hbook.com

US website hosting *The Horn Book Guide Online*, a comprehensive, fully searchable database of over 70,000 book titles and reviews for children and young adults. Also includes a regular newsletter sharing an interview with an author or illustrator, *Authors & Illustrators talk with Roger*, and and a monthly e-newsletter for parents, *Notes from the Horn Book*.

## Quentin Blake Centre for Illustration

https://qbcentre.org.uk

The brainchild of author and illustrator Quentin Blake, it celebrates all forms of illustration, runs regular talks and events and supports schools-based activities. See page 318.

## National Literacy Trust

www.literacytrust.org.uk

The organisation is focused on developing literacy among adults and children and its website documents its activities. See page 313.

## Picture Book Den

http://picturebookden.blogspot.com

An independent website created by professional children's authors based in the UK and Ireland where they share their passion for picture books, with blogs on getting published and creating picture books.

## ReadingZone

https://readingzone.com

A magazine-style website, created with Arts Council support, dedicated to children's books including monthly book reviews by teachers and librarians as well as children, chapters to download, author interviews, news, activities and a regular newsletter. There are distinct areas for teachers, librarians, families, children and teenagers.

## Scottish Book Trust

www.scottishbooktrust.com

Information on books for children of all ages in Scotland plus a national programme of events with children's writers: author tours, festivals, writing competitions and exciting activities.

## Seven Stories

www.sevenstories.org.uk

The Seven Stories National Centre for Children's Books, based in Newcastle, provides regular events and exhibitions dedicated to children's literature which are highlighted on its website. See page 309.

## The Story Museum

www.storymuseum.org.uk

Stories from around the world to watch, hear, read and tell.

## Toppsta

https://toppsta.com

A children's book review website that invites children and adults to review books for children and teenagers.

## Words & Pictures

www.wordsandpics.org

The online magazine of SCBWI British Isles, an organisation of writers and illustrators of children's books, with advice on writing, illustrating, news, blogs and activities. See page 305.

## World Book Day

www.worldbookday.com

Providing a range of resources for children and teenagers, from writing and illustration masterclasses to quizzes, activities and reading ideas.

# Inspiring writers

# Making a writer

Sarah Crossan describes what led her to take her writing seriously, put her secret dream of being a writer into practice and – with time and resolve – achieve her goal.

I never thought a person like me could be a writer. I was an incredibly ordinary child, have become an even more ordinary adult and believed many untruths about writing and writers. Firstly, I didn't come from a family connected to the literati, which I perceived as a major problem, though at the time I probably hadn't even come across the word 'literati'. Secondly, I wasn't privately educated and didn't have anything close to a BBC newsreader's accent – grand drawback. Finally, and perhaps most importantly, I didn't own a serious-looking scarf. You know the ones. All proper artists own them.

When I went to university, to study Philosophy and Literature, my fears about what went into making a writer were compounded as I carefully stalked the creative writing students: they all seemed aloof, important and occasionally sad, hanging out in the humanities building, wearing oversized jumpers and, yes, their scholarly scarves.

After my undergraduate degree, convinced writing wasn't for me (and secretly hating all those creative writing students who'd spent three years smugly impersonating Margaret Atwood), I went off to study teaching. It was a way to make books a part of my daily life. And I was actually really good at it. The students fell in love with words and sentences, with poems and novels. I even convinced a class of hardened Shakespeare haters (one of whom offered to steal my car for £50 so I could pick up the insurance money!) to perform scenes from *Romeo and Juliet*, as well as partake in some Renaissance dancing. I loved teaching – my job was about books and kids, words and relationships.

Then came an afternoon that changed everything – a lesson that had an outcome missing from my planning notes. I was teaching poetry, encouraging students to write about their dreams, their hopes, how they saw their lives developing. I believed in those kids. I knew they could be anything they wanted to be if they just puffed out their chests and did some hard work. They wrote wonderful poems. They wrote moving poems. And then, at the end of the lesson, one child put up his hand and asked a question: 'Have you always wanted to be an English teacher, Miss?'. Now, a more sensitive person might have read some subtext into this, namely '*Why are you a teacher, Miss? You're terrible at your job.*' But I don't think that's what he meant. He genuinely wanted to know whether or not I'd lived my dreams, so shyly I explained that, as well as being a teacher, I wanted to be a writer, a poet and a novelist, but that I didn't think I quite had what it took. The boy frowned, as did a few other students, and angrily replied, 'Well you have a bit of cheek then, don't you, telling us to live our dreams when you haven't even done it yourself. Have you even tried?'

Despite being young, I was a strict teacher; I never tolerated rudeness, but in that moment I was dumbstruck – because he was right. Who was I to lecture them on bravery and risk when I had never taken myself nor my own desires seriously? Instead of asking him to leave the room, where I could speak to him about his tone of voice, I quietly said, 'You're right. I've been too afraid to try.'

On the basis of that very bald conversation, I applied to go back to university and study creative writing – which I did the very next year, annoying the head teacher who had to find a replacement for the next academic year at short notice.

And so I began to write. And I began to take my writing seriously. Rather than going to the cinema when friends asked, I started to say, 'Sorry, I can't. I'm writing.' When they seemed irritated by my resolve, I didn't care. If I wanted to achieve my dream of writing for a living, I had to believe in myself, otherwise no one else would. I found a way out of my shame and into a pattern of work that I loved.

That doesn't mean a contract came quickly; it didn't. It was another ten years of graft and fine-tuning my skills before I found an agent, listed in the *Writers' & Artists' Yearbook* in the children's section, who seemed to fit the bill. I sent her my book and astonishingly she took me on within days. We are still together, for better or for worse, and when I start to flounder and find myself wondering if I should pack it all in, she reminds me that I don't need anything to succeed except a dash of self-belief and a bit of hard work. Oh, and my serious writerly scarf, of course. Everyone needs one of those!

**Sarah Crossan** is the award-winning author of the young adult novel *One* (Bloomsbury 2015) which won the CILIP Carnegie Medal, the YA Book Prize, the CBI Book of the Year Award and the CLiPPA Poetry Award in 2016. Also published by Bloomsbury, her books *The Weight of Water* (2011) and *Apple and Rain* (2014) were both shortlisted for the CILIP Carnegie Medal. Sarah's other children's novels are *Breathe* (2012), its sequel *Resist* (2013), *We Come Apart* (co-authored with Brian Conaghan 2017) and the free verse novel *Moonrise* (2017), which was shortlisted for the Costa Children's Book Award, the YA Book Prize and the CBI Book of the Year Award. Her latest books are *Toffee* (Bloomsbury 2019), a free verse novel for adults *Here is the Beehive* (Bloomsbury Circus 2020) and a collection of contemporary and classic poetry *Tomorrow is Beautiful* (Bloomsbury 2021). Sarah was Laureate na nÓg, the Irish Children's Laureate, from 2018-20.

# Finding your voice and point of view

Anna Wilson looks at the importance of finding your own distinctive voice as a writer and at the impact and technical considerations involved in choosing a particular point of view to tell your story. She shows how much this choice of viewpoint influences your reader's perceptions, enabling you to 'be the director of your own movie'.

When, as a teenager, I asked someone what it would take to become a writer, they said rather grandly, 'You need to find your voice'. This felt like an important pronouncement, so I nodded sagely, having absolutely no idea what they meant or how I was going to be able to do this for myself. I thought that finding my voice must go hand in hand with having a Muse, or Inspiration, or Life Experience. These were all things I had read that writers should have – and all things which seemed far out of reach to a grammar school kid living in suburbia, where the most exciting thing ever to happen was when Deirdre-next-door got ideas above her station and had a conservatory built.

What I didn't realise was that, to be a writer, I didn't need to do anything other than to write, and I had been doing that ever since I could pick up a pencil. I still have some of my early scribbles – drawings of people, mostly, to whom I would chatter endlessly, creating conversations and adventures for them; these soon morphed into cartoons influenced by my love of the *Beano*, and from there I started writing my own 'proper stories'. By the time I had reached my early teens I had already filled innumerable notebooks with angsty thoughts and records of what I had been up to at school and elsewhere. And I was becoming conscious, through my obsessive reading, that 'becoming a writer' was something that I could aspire to. Yet how to achieve this? How on earth was I to 'find my voice'?

We all have a voice. And if we all started out doing as the great scriptwriter Russell T. Davies does – 'writing how you speak', each of us would soon see our own voice appearing on the page straight away. One of the first mistakes emerging writers tend to make (I include my younger self in this) is that they try too hard to nail down a voice, and end up writing something that rings false. Looking back at my journals, I can see I had a distinctive voice emerging then: the cadence and rhythm of my writing is 100% me, and it has found its way into so much of my children's fiction via characters who bear a striking resemblance to that bored suburban kid who lived in her head and dreamed of better things.

In writerly terms, 'voice' is the combination of **what** is said and **how** it's said. Anyone reading this will be able to think immediately of books with a voice so real it leaps off the page and keeps on talking inside your head long after you've stopped reading. I am thinking of Lauren Child's *Clarice Bean* series (1999–) or Louise Rennison's inimitable Georgia Nicolson in her teen books such as *Angus, Thongs and Full-Frontal Snogging* (Piccadilly Press 1999) or McKay Tambo in Alex Wheatle's *Crongton Knights* trilogy (Little, Brown 2017–). In picture books, voice will come through as strongly in the illustrations as it does in the text. Think of the way the mouse looks out from the pages of *The Gruffalo* (Macmillan 1999); Axel Scheffler's illustrations make sure that the mouse is saying as much with his eyes as Julia Donaldson's words have him say with his mouth.

Much of what constitutes voice will come down to 'point of view', which can often be another minefield. In fact, this seems to get emerging writers into more of a tangle than almost any other technical issue, and it's certainly something that I struggle with every single time I sit down to write a new book. Should I write in the first person and thereby show the whole story through one immutable lens? Should I step back and have an omniscient narrator who can move silently and god-like through my story and have a finger in every pie, a foot in every room, an eye in every meeting-place? Or should I choose one character to take my reader through the story, but keep a pace behind them by writing in third person whilst also staying close to their experiences? In other words, where am I allowing the narrator to stand? From which point of view am I allowing my reader to see things?

All books are written by people, about people – even when they're apparently about animals: any child reading *The Gruffalo* will recognise the power of the mouse's cunning over the other animals' fear and stupidity, and thus the mouse is really a human in disguise. And any being, human or otherwise, can perceive certain things through their senses – and not perceive others. As visual animals we talk about 'view', but good writing in fact uses all the senses, not only sight. Therefore, 'point of view' will necessarily include all the senses. We can't physically see behind our own heads, but we can smell the bakery behind us. We can't see someone six floors up, but we might hear, from the open window, the music they are playing. In writing, as in the rest of life, this idea of what a particular being can and can't perceive widens to include how they understand it, how it makes them feel, what else they know about the world, what they think of it all, what they say, and – crucially – what they don't say about it. All of this is point of view.

When I was writing my *Vlad the World's Worst Vampire* series (Stripes Publishing 2017–), I wanted to keep close to Vlad's experiences. He was going out into the human world for the first time and discovering that it was very different from the terrifying pictures his parents had painted of it. I wanted the reader to see things through his eyes and to taste human food as he tasted it, to see human school and human relationships as he saw them. I therefore chose to write the stories in 'close third', rather than from the perspective of an all-seeing, all-knowing, distant third-person narrator. I could have chosen first person, of course, but I rejected this as I didn't want to use such a limited viewpoint that my reader had only Vlad's voice in their heads. Also, as this is a series for confident young readers who are just becoming adept at reading alone, I didn't want to stray too far from the storytelling voice that they would be used to from most picture books and early readers. So I had many considerations in mind when choosing this 'close third' point of view.

However, I knew there were some things to be aware of in choosing this slightly limited viewpoint: the reader could only ever know what Vlad knew, could only ever see what Vlad saw; and I risked letting him stay in his thoughts too long if I left him on his own for any length of time. This led to me to invent a character who was nearly always with him – his pet bat, Flit. Flit acted like Vlad's own conscience, helping him work through problems or challenging him when he was about to do something stupid (pets can be useful like that in children's fiction, even if they don't actually speak!).

A final note on point of view: whichever voice you choose, and from whichever standpoint you prefer to allow your characters to speak, try to 'vary the camera angles' in your writing. By this I mean, don't always be showing your reader an intense close-up where we are so inside the character's head that we have lost sight of what is going on outside it – this can be a very claustrophobic experience for the reader. Equally, don't swamp the reader with continual long 'wide-angle' shots that give pages and pages of scene-setting;

these can take the reader away from the action and from what the characters are thinking, saying and doing in the moment. Think of yourself as the director of your own movie, particularly when it comes to editing. Ask yourself: has my character spent too long walking down that path wondering what they are going to have for dinner? Or: has the narrator spent too long sitting in a car looking out of the window on the way to their auntie's, taking in the scenery and describing the whole, boring journey beat by beat? Remember that the reader needs to see only the things that matter. Think of how a director uses 'jump-cuts' to move us from one scene to the next. As the American writer Colum McCann says in his wonderful book *Letters to a Young Writer* (Random House 2017):

It is a good trick to assume that you have a number of changeable lenses. Be fish-eye. Be wide-angle. Be telephoto. Zoom in. Zoom out. Distort. Sharpen. Divide. Imagine yourself into the actual camera. Find the words that are glass and shutter both.

It's all about the degree to which we are inside a character's head. And the choice of which 'person' we choose to write in, or which point of view we choose, will have an impact on how close in we are, right from the off. In first person we are clearly right in the thick of things – we are, as McCann says, 'glass and shutter both'. In third person, there is an immediate element of detachment, but there are degrees of closeness too; you only have to think of how Hilary Mantel writes from the point of view of Thomas Cromwell in *Wolf Hall* (Fourth Estate 2009) to see that 'he' can easily transubstantiate into 'I'.

If all this sounds like too much, and you still have no idea how to find your voice or which point of view is right for your work in progress, step away from the manuscript and give yourself a little exercise to loosen things up. Think yourself into your main character's shoes. If you've been writing in the first person, swap to third – close or omniscient, it's up to you. If you've been using third person, swap to first. Now have a think about a scene that you're struggling to inject some energy into; maybe your character is too much in their head, or they seem to be taking an age to get from A to B and frankly, even you, their creator, is feeling pretty bored with them now. Flip the point of view and see what happens. Has it brought you closer to a character you were struggling to bring alive on the page? Has it given you a perspective that has shown your character in a startling new light? Do you prefer this new piece written from this point of view, or has your writing become stodgier? Why do you feel the way you do about these shifts of perspective?

Above all, have fun! It is in constantly trying things for size that we improve and grow as writers. And it is in playing around like children chattering to their first made-up scribbled pictures, that we learn to find our voice.

**Anna Wilson** is the author of over 50 books for children, including novels, non-fiction, poems, short stories, picture books and early readers. Her most recent picture books for children are *Shine Like the Stars* (Andersen Press 2023) and *Grandpa and the Kingfisher* (Nosy Crow 2023). Anna's latest non-fiction title is *A Story of the Seasons* (Nosy Crow and the National Trust 2024). Her latest fiction series is *Vlad the World's Worst Vampire* (Stripes Publishing 2019). Anna runs creative workshops for the Arvon Foundation and is a coach for the London Writers' Salon. Read her blog on acwilsonwriter.wordpress.com

# Parent your inner child: what kind of writer are you?

Lucy van Smit explores how to thrive as a writer in uncertain times and overcome anxiety, self-doubt and self-criticism. She explains how to apply four key principles of parenting to help you understand, boost and nurture your inner writer.

## Your shadow is what you don't know about yourself

Heads up, I'm a dyslexic author who didn't know I had ADHD until after publication. And what should have been the best of times became months of Dark Nights, until my shiny, writerly soul forced me to stop and listen to my life. Luckily, I did, before a virus flipped our world inside out with a pandemic. The solution is always to know who you are and what happened to you. What created the repeat pattens in your life?

## What has this to do with your writing career?

As an author, I wish I'd seen overwhelm coming. I was unprepared for the anxiety that infected me and my writing friends. Do you struggle to soothe yourself when fear, rejection, procrastination and writer's block strike? Writers need to be able to regulate their emotions. Here's the kicker: maybe you don't see yourself as anxious? I didn't. I am cheerful, friendly, witty, clever, spiritual; I love life. And I'm tough. Really tough. After all, I'd been a successful TV producer who made documentaries on famous authors. I survived ten miscarriages, the stillbirth of our darling Luke; I'm an expert at getting a severely dyslexic boy through pushy London day schools; a wife of 30 years, an artist, a writer, a close friend, a great mother (something I didn't learn growing up – sorry Mum, but you were rubbish). Parental self-care can take a long time to learn.

## Pre-publication oblivion

Neurodiversity shines at outwitting problems. In TV, I applauded myself for working 20-hour days, in the Philippines living on chocolate and orange juice for six weeks – classic shadow, ADHD behaviour. Gabor Maté says what we admire is often what kills us. Niceness disguises suppressed feelings, and our overworking is labelled success.

Speed forward a decade or three, in the run-up to publication; already an insomniac, I had several nights a week with no sleep. I still didn't get it. Eventually, at the awesome age of 60, it occurred to me that my lifelong insomnia, since childhood, was anxiety. My niece sniggered when I told her my revelation. The thing is, unlike you lovelies, we didn't have the word 'anxiety' when I was growing up. We self-medicated with alcohol and distraction; from love affairs to careers.

Older, wiser, I read more. Energy Medicine (yes, my teenage son scoffed too, until the virus), Yoga, Flow Psychology, Nutrition, Spirituality, Podcasts, Writing Workshops. Bought loads more books. The arrogance of a conceptual brain – you try everything … except talking and listening to your intuitive self.

## When *Writers'* & *Artists'* asked for a YA workshop

I wanted to share skills from the Family Links Parenting Programme I ran at my son's school. Its focus is emotional intelligence for otherwise cerebral, articulate, ambitious parents, whose kids behaved in mystifying ways. Who knew rebellion is a child's response to feeling powerless? Maybe procrastination is our rebellion against powerlessness in the publishing industry? Four parenting tools are great for writers:

## 1. Know yourself

I am so busted. Did you know that Socrates ridiculed you if you studied any subject before you took the time to have a good hard look at yourself? In his *Four Quartets*, T.S. Eliot got it: 'We shall not cease from exploration./And the end of all our exploring./ Will be to arrive where we started./And know the place for the first time.' To be a good author, you need to know what makes you tick.

### What don't you know about yourself?

As writers, not knowing our shadow often shows up as our Perfectionist Archetype. This Archetype is a coping mechanism that manages cultural shame, those feelings of never being good enough and can sabotage your dreams by never finishing that book.

Archetypes are patterns of behaviour. Beliefs. Which ones are pulling your strings? Caroline Myss says we all share four Survival Archetypes; Child, Victim, Saboteur, and Prostitute – how you negotiate your life. Everyone has a Child Archetype – but which one? Invisible Child? Nature Child? Rejected Child? We are often unconscious how we abandon ourselves later in life. Writers abandon their own voice when they write what others want. Do you rate others' approval above your own? This is central in writing for young adults; teenagers often abandon themselves to fit in with their peers. It was the core theme for my debut YA novel, *The Hurting* (Chicken House 2018). Abandoned as a baby by her mother, Nell abducts baby Ulv Pup to win a boy's approval. Redemption comes when her greatest flaw becomes her greatest strength. Nell must choose between eco-warrior Lukas, the love of her life, or saving the abandoned baby from wolves on his wild Norwegian mountain. She needs to learn that No Boy is Worth Your Soul.

### You know the power of words

Do you notice how you speak to yourself? Mean or kindly? Words like 'blame', 'I don't deserve this' or 'I'm entitled' are the language of your Victim Archetype. We are more powerful when we edit them out of our vocabulary. Goethe knew that once you 'decide' to do anything the universe steps in behind you. Intention is everything.

### Are you a conceptual or an intuitive writer?

Know your inner writer. Are you an intuitive or a conceptual one? We veer towards one or the other. Knowing your obstacles helps you get your work to a publishable standard. Have you ever been told your writing is beautiful, and wondered why you're not signed? Do your characters sing off the page with originality? Do agents love, love, love your voice, but they don't snap you up?

Maybe, often, it's because the promise of your voice sputters out. Your story rambles; agents give up, confused. Somehow your right brain can't seem to fix your story problem; you add more events to add a bit of structure, only to make the narrative flat, linear. You struggle with the dynamics of drama, conflict. But everyone loves your characters, you wail. You brought them to life. They're so real. Of course. You poured your soul into them. But still … your story doesn't sell.

### A conceptual writer is the exact opposite

You've read every writing craft book going. You can hit the Inciting Incident on page one – hey, you can hit it in the opening paragraph. You can write a mesmerising Hook. You nail your story in a 25-word logline (one-sentence summary) and have all those important beats, conflict, climax, rising tension, a great ending. You know exactly what happens to your protagonist at Midpoint. You know her 'flaw' and her basic 'need'. But you don't get snapped up. Why? Maybe, often, agents don't care enough about your characters. Readers don't feel for them, because *you* didn't feel anything when you wrote them. You can't access emotion from your left brain.

We tend to play to our strengths and hide weaknesses, which makes them worse. Learn to use both sides of your brain, but not at the same time. This is why you don't stop to edit when you write your first draft. Editing is a left-brain activity. Switching between two brain hemispheres is a skillset every writer can learn.

Screenwriting guru, Corey Mandell, calls the process 'creative integration'. He advocates an arduous training; conceptual writers are not allowed to structure or plot, for months! Intuitive writers must stop creating dialogue (ouch) until you can crack structure. I don't buy Mandell's theory that your *corpus callosum*, the bit facilitating communication between brain hemispheres, can't work them both at the same time, nor that it takes ages to re-train writers. Practice builds neural pathways, so write. Stop avoiding what you don't like to do – outlining, for instance. Think of it as eating your greens as a kid. A little goes a long way, and there are new tools to help. My favourite tool is 'energy medicine' – brilliant for connecting both sides of your brain, fast. It works by crossing and strengthening the energy pathways in your body. I practise Donna Eden's Daily Energy Routine (https://edenenergymedicine.com/donnas-daily-energy-routine) before I start to write. It calms even a bonkers brain like mine.

Music is another activity that uses both parts of the brain simultaneously. Conceptual writers, try meditating before you start: dance, create a sacred space, breathe, focus on your body, set an intention that tunes you into your creative right brain. You know, by the language you use, which part of the brain you are firing.

As a general principle, intuitive writers do best if they outline first. Keep it simple. Sketch, map it out, just so you know where you're going. Think … what is best for your story? Best for your characters? And best for you to write? When that all aligns, it feels like flow … fun! But conceptual writers, hold off planning. Play first, and discover your characters, before you work on your brilliant plot. Make us *care* first.

## 2. Empathy

To be a good parent, you need the ability to empathise with your child and put yourself in their shoes. Pixar have a formula to enable conceptual writers to write emotion for their protagonist:

$$EC = EM (R+P^2) +H +A +ES +(MS)$$

Don't panic … it's easier than it looks!

To create Empathy (EM) with your reader you need to find the Emotional Core (EC) of your character. What drives them? Fear? Love of a sister? Pixar creates empathy through Recognition (R) and heaping obstacles, so we pity the Protagonist ($P^2$), makes them seem Human (H) and gives them a skill for us to Admire (A), like bravery. Also create high Emotional Stakes (ES) … what happens if your protagonist fails? The final element (MS) stands for Meaning: the 'why' of your story. Make readers care what happens to your characters and empathise with what they desperately want or need.

## 3. Appropriate expectations

The third principle of good parenting. Do you have Appropriate Expectations of your inner writer? (What? … I hear you say.) How long have you been writing? Ten years? Two? Do you assume your inner writer should behave with the maturity of your chronological age – even if you've only been writing for a year or two?

Inappropriate Expectations cause a lot of unnecessary stress. Would you say to a toddler, 'Get up, you Dummy!' when they fall down? But you say that to yourself all the time. There's a reason why Enid Blyton locked her kids away – so she could write. And why Barbara Hepworth dumped her triplets on friends – so she could sculpt. Do you work? Do you have a young family? Or elderly parents? Do you have Appropriate Expectations of what you can get done … or of where you think your writing career should be? My simple rule is: if you are stressed, your expectations are inappropriate. As a writer, have compassion for yourself. Rest.

## 4. Positive discipline

Positive Discipline means praise. We praise children in order to focus on what they are doing right. Good teachers praise. Constant self-criticism doesn't help you perform better or love writing more. We forget how to praise ourselves. Practise. Praise your inner writer for showing up. Praise switches off that constant inner critic that says you're not good enough at this writing malarkey.

You can't praise and criticise yourself at the same time. So praise yourself – when you think like a writer, when you read as a writer, when you sit down to write. We don't compare our children, so don't compare yourself to published authors. Praise yourself for just being you, not for doing more or achieving more. Success will happen naturally, joyfully. Play more. Fun breeds success.

While it's useful to think of parenting your inner writer child, don't take it as an excuse to baby yourself, to have unlimited duvets days, or to 'snowflake', as my teenager calls it. Writing needs a lot of self-discipline to sit down and write. When it gets tough, finish what you have started. Breathe. Exercise. Play. Journal. Know what kind of writer you are before you even think about getting published. I promise that knowing yourself better helps you write better. And when you do send your work out, don't wait to hear back; write something new, don't wait for approval. End of story.

Former TV producer and artist, **Lucy van Smit's** latest book is *A Writer's Journal Workbook* (Bloomsbury 2022). Lucy won the Bath Children's Novel Award with her debut novel, *The Hurting* (Chicken House 2018), pitched as 'Nordic Noir Wuthering Heights'; she is currently working on *The Hurting* film script. She has a BA Hons in Fine Art and received a Distinction in her MA in Creative Writing. She offers one-to-one creative recovery coaching and workshops. Follow Lucy on Twitter and Instagram @Lucyvansmit or see her website www.lucyvansmit.com.

# Words are my happy place

Award-winning children's novelist Smriti Halls demonstrates how her love for words has grown into a lifelong desire to write.

Words are my happy place. Playing with them, nudging them, giving them a little squeeze. From as far back as I can remember they've been my companions, filling me to the brim with joy. It wasn't much of a surprise, then, that they became the tools of my trade – as teacher, copywriter, staff writer and editor. Any excuse to keep tinkering. The surprising bit was that those same words started prodding at *ME* – playing with me, nudging me, giving *me* a little squeeze … Soon they were filling me to the brim with stories of my own that I felt compelled to write – books that reflected my own passions, preoccupations and perspectives; stories I wanted the world to hear, written in my own voice.

Pursuing this path seemed neither sensible nor sane and, at first, I tried to ignore it, knowing full well that I didn't have the luxury of an office or even a desk at home – much less the idyllic writer's shed, den or hut to retreat to. But those mischievous words wouldn't let me go. I quickly realised that writing in my spare time, around a full-time job, daily commute and three gorgeous children, was not sustainable. And so, gathering all my courage, I plunged into the life of a full-time, freelance writer.

How I longed for a room of my own (frankly I'd have made do with a small cupboard) – just somewhere to shut the door and concentrate for five minutes together – but that simply wasn't an option. Instead, I focused on grabbing the moments I could, in the space that was available. I negotiated with my husband for some clear working days and accepted every offer of help. I paid for a childminder (and tried not to be put off by the sound of pound coins clinking into an invisible jar, for every word not written). And little by little, one by one, with comedic haphazardness, my books began to be written – at the library, in my sister's spare bedroom, on the train, in waiting rooms and coffee shops. I wrote at the kitchen table, kneeling up to the sofa, with babies asleep in the back of the car, whilst on holiday, and once (only once) I got out of bed and wrote the first draft of a picture book at three in the morning. On one memorable camping trip, I charged across several fields in the rain, was pursued by a bull and lost a shoe in a ditch – all in pursuit of a pub where I could use the WiFi to send off a manuscript. Naturally, the minute I got there, out of puff, dishevelled and smelling fragrantly of manure, the laptop ran out of charge.

It's now exactly ten years since my first picture book was published and, in that time, that has grown from one to 50 titles – brought to life by a host of incredible illustrators. Some have seen success, others none at all, but I'm proud of every single one. Each is fingerprinted with love and is a snapshot of my life at a single moment. Together, they are a photo album of the joys, the tears – and the tantrums, too! The books I write are created right in the centre of my topsy-turvy, everyday life. That obviously brings significant challenges (*No, you may not build a den out of my proofs!*), but whenever I bemoan the lack of space to escape to, I remember that I wrote a Number One bestseller standing up in my living room with a child on one hip and another toddling on the floor – which helps lend a bit of perspective.

I'm humbled to know that some of the words I've written have walked alongside people in their deepest, most profound moments. They've been used in beauty and brokenness, used as marriage vows and as last rites; I sometimes wonder whether their creation, amidst the idiosyncrasies and imperfections of my own life, imbues them with something that speaks into the real-life moments of other people's lives. I don't know. What I *do* know is that not a word would have been written if I'd waited for what I foolishly believed were the ideal circumstances.

So, my advice? a) Don't waste time trying to get everything in order – embrace the chaos and roll with it. b) Enjoy your work and the pleasure it brings you. c) Even if the path might not look as you expected, it might be leading somewhere spectacular ... You won't find out unless you get started, so get going and enjoy the journey!

And if you need just one trusty friend for the road, you won't find better than the *Children's Writers' & Artists' Yearbook*. It was placed into my hands when I first started out and I recommend it to everyone who asks me for advice. It's a one-stop welcome to the world of publishing – an invaluable guide to who's who and what's what. For anyone new to the business, it's worth its weight in gold.

As for me, I'll still daydream about my writing room (and you have an open invitation to come and visit me there one day), but for now I'll be content living in and out of words. *They're* my happy place.

**Smriti Halls** is an award-winning, bestselling children's author. She published her first picture book in 2012. Her books include the bestselling *I Love You Night and Day* (Bloomsbury 2014), *I'm Sticking with You* (Simon & Schuster 2020), *Elephant in My Kitchen!* (Egmont UK 2020), *The Little Island* (Andersen Press 2020) and *Rain Before Rainbows* (Walker Books 2021). Smriti formerly worked in children's publishing and television for 12 years, as a writer and commissioning editor. She now works widely with children and adults in schools, libraries, festivals, bookshops and prisons to bring a love of reading and stories to the widest possible audience. Her books have been published in more than 30 languages. Smriti has been a judge for several awards and prizes, including the Stratford Salariya Prize, Faber's FAB Award and the BookTrust Lifetime Achievement Award, and was BookTrust Writer in Residence 2020–21. She lives in London and is also published as Smriti Prasadam-Halls. See www.smriti.co.uk for more information.

# If at first you don't succeed...

Frances Hardinge describes the steps she took, as a hopeful young writer, to brave rejection, persevere and grow in confidence, and the friends and resources that helped her find where her writing belonged and gain that first momentous book contract.

I was in my teens when I bought my first copy of the *Writers' & Artists' Yearbook*. Back then, the *Children's Writers' & Artists' Yearbook* didn't exist. But in those days I wasn't an adult writing children's fiction, I was a teenager trying my hand at adult fiction.

Buying the book felt significant – a little intimidating, in fact. I sensed that I was making a promise to myself. I wouldn't keep my stories safely hidden away. I would send them off to be judged, and expose my fragile, iridescent bubble-dreams to the jagged edges of the real world. In effect, I had *bought* some of my cowardly excuses into non-existence: '*I can't send my work off, I don't know where to start!*'; '*I don't know what to send, or where!*'. Well, now I did.

And whenever I let schoolwork or other commitments eat up all my time, I'd spot the *Yearbook* on my shelf, fire-engine red. A silent, insistent reminder of my promise to myself. A gentle but much-needed boot in the rear.

I meticulously typed out my stories on the roaring, ill-tempered electric typewriter I'd bought from my sister for five pounds. Every time I made an error and had to perform Tipp-Ex surgery, I agonised over it and considered typing the whole page again.

And all the while I was gripped by a crippling fear that my first submission might be my only chance, and that if I messed it up badly all would be lost. The submissions editor would look coldly at my clunkiest metaphor, or scowl at my Tipp-Ex, and then stride away to the dark chamber where the editor collective kept the Terrible Tome of Authors We Must Never Publish. They would add my name to the list, and from that moment all my other submissions would be doomed. Prospective editors would consult the book, see my name in blood-red letters, shake their heads and throw my manuscript in the bin.

Only after a few trembling submissions did I start to suspect that the Terrible Tome didn't actually exist. Rejection slips arrived in the post, but didn't bring the apocalypse with them. Occasionally there was an actual rejection letter. (My favourite of these effectively said: 'We rather liked your story, and we wish we knew what it was about.') Eventually I realised that I had nothing to lose but the cost of two stamps and a spoonful of pride. If I was turned down it didn't matter. All that mattered was that I kept trying.

By my twenties, I was subscribing to *Writers' News* and *Writing Magazine* to supplement the *Yearbook*. I now typed my stories on a little Franken-puter that my boyfriend had cobbled together from parts of discarded, elderly computers. My friends and I set up a small writers' group, which gave me a regular deadline to keep me writing. With their feedback I became more confident, and less precious about editing my work.

And one day, after sending a short story to a little independent magazine, I received an answer that wasn't a 'no'. This was the first in a series of 'not-no' responses. However, when I received my first book contract a few years later, it was thanks to my good friend Rhiannon Lassiter. She realised something I hadn't – that my peculiar dark fairy tales were actually children's fiction. Rhiannon persuaded me to try writing a children's novel, then wrested my first five chapters from my unwilling hands and marched off with them to her editor.

The *Children's Writers' & Artists' Yearbook* would have been invaluable to me as a young, aspiring children's writer, if I'd had the sense to realise that that was what I was. The latest editions of the *Yearbook* are even richer and more useful than those I bought in my teens and twenties, with more information on agents, prizes, courses, conferences, digital publishing and self-publishing, and a wealth of essays, articles and advice.

Even now, when I look at the *Writers' & Artists' Yearbook*, I still recall everything it symbolised for me. It looks too heavy for the shelf, packed to the binding with hunger, trepidation, determination and hope. It's still a little intimidating. Opportunities often are.

**Frances Hardinge** is the award-winning author of *Fly by Night* (Macmillan Children's Books 2005), winner of the 2006 Branford Boase Award, *Twilight Robbery* (Macmillan Children's Books 2011), shortlisted for the Guardian Children's Fiction Prize, and *Cuckoo Song* (Pan Macmillan 2014), which won the Robert Holdstock Award for Best Novel at the British Fantasy Awards 2015. *The Lie Tree* (Macmillan Children's Books 2015) won the Costa Book of the Year 2015 award, the 2016 UKLA Book Award (12–16 category), the 2016 *Boston Globe* Horn Book Fiction Award and the 2016 *Los Angeles Times* Young Adult Literature Prize and was also shortlisted for the Independent Booksellers Week Award 2015, the *Guardian* Children's Fiction Prize 2015 and the 2016 Carnegie Medal. The sequel, *A Skinful of Shadows* (Pan Macmillan 2017), won the Dracula Society's Children of the Night Award. Her other books include *Gullstruck Island* (Macmillan Children's Books 2009) and *A Face Like Glass* (Pan Macmillan Children's 2012). Her latest book is *Unraveller* (Macmillan 2022). She was nominated for the 2021 Astrid Lindgren Memorial Award. Find out more at http://www.franceshardinge.com/.

# How stories shape you as a writer

Patrice Lawrence reflects on how she found her voice through the stories she read.

I'm writing this in rather unexpected circumstances. I had originally planned a few paragraphs about my love of reading and how privileged I feel now that my own books are on the shelves of libraries and shops and in the hands of readers. I do still feel incredibly privileged, but as we're coming to understand the long-term global impact of the Covid-19 virus, it's impossible not to reflect further.

Like many full-time writers, I smiled knowingly in the early days of the pandemic lockdown. Stay inside? That's what we do anyway, isn't it? Hanging around in our pyjamas, staring mystically into space and occasionally tapping a laptop. But, actually, for me that's just a small part of the story. Many of my books are set in London – a city crammed full of history. If I look up, I see Hercules taming horses on the Royal Mews, a pterodactyl on the Natural History Museum and angels on the Apollo Theatre. When I look down, I see clay pipe stems on the Thames foreshore and fragments of pottery that were held by hands hundreds of years ago. So many stories, waiting to be collected and assembled. London also – usually – vibrates with the clamour of many different voices. There are moments of drama happening everywhere. And when I'm not eavesdropping and scribbling notes, I'm visiting schools, learning from the children and young people I write for and about.

It has been an uncertain, frightening time, but what has become clear is the absolute importance of stories. Writers and illustrators have been sharing their stories online; children and young people encouraged to tell their own tales. Struggling to write or even read fiction, I've lost myself in audiobooks, finding comfort in books being read to me.

Stories, though, have shaped me for as long as I can remember. I'm part of the first generation of Caribbean-heritage people to be born in the UK. I have lived in households that were often different from those around me – multi-ethnic, or lone parent, or in a private foster arrangement. I've never lived in a family where we're all the same colour. I was a passionate reader from very young, but there were never stories featuring families like mine.

I started writing. I wrote and illustrated stories about a giant purple rabbit for my toddler brother. I delivered my Year 7 history homework about the Saxons in rhyming couplets (thank you, Mr Mann, for the A). When I was 13, I hit pay dirt when my poem published in the *Brighton Evening Argus* earned me a £1 postal order. At sixth-form college, my 1980s version of *The Wizard of Oz* was performed on stage, complete with Michael Jackson-esque Thriller zombies with releasable arms!

During my 20s, I fell in love with short stories. I managed to get a couple of stories published in teenage romance magazines, greatly helped by the *Writers' & Artists' Yearbook*; I'd read every listing for UK magazines, every detail of every agent, and wondered how on earth I could ever be part of that world. As a young person growing up in Sussex suburbia, it seemed impossible.

Three things happened that inadvertently propelled me into the world of children's publishing. Firstly, I moved to London in my late 20s to be a mature student at Goldsmiths' College. London seemed unfathomable and terrifying for a long time, but gradually I realised I was inside an endless whorl of stories and started noting down vignettes and ideas. Prompted by one of those scraps, I submitted a short story to a competition for unpublished writers and it was included in a high-profile anthology. Although it was adult writing, my characters were teenagers and it led me to my wonderful agent, Caroline Sheldon.

Secondly, I joined a writing group. It was brutal and empowering and, through critiquing and being critiqued, I am an infinitely better writer. We supported and commiserated with each other, we even ran continual professional development sessions to up our game. Last of all, and most important for me, I found my voice. At that time there were no working-class, multi-ethnic British families in children's books – and only a few in adult books. I internalised the message that I was not allowed to write from my own perspective.

Then, one winter afternoon in 1999, I turned on the TV and discovered Malorie Blackman. It was the BBC adaptation of her novel *Pig Heart Boy* (Doubleday 1997). A story about a black family who weren't the Cosbys or in *The Fresh Prince of Bel-Air*? A story set in England? A door opened for me and I stepped through … and eventually wrote *Orangeboy* (Hodder Children's Books 2016). It was shortlisted for the Costa Children's Award and won other prizes. But, do you want to know a secret? It was the fifth book I'd actually written. It took a while!

So, keep at it. Write. Find your voice. Keep improving and, like me, you'll get there.

**Patrice Lawrence** MBE is an award-winning writer of picture books, middle grade and young adult books. She has won many prizes including the YA Prize, the Waterstones Prize for Older Children's Fiction, the Crimefest YA Prize twice and the inaugural Jhalak Prize for Children and Young People. She has been nominated for the Carnegie Award seven times.

# My way into a different world

Sally Green describes how, in middle life, she found herself hooked on the creative process of writing and, by applying hard work and good advice, made her way into the world of the professional writer.

I remember the beginning of my writing career quite clearly. It was a sunny afternoon in June 2010, I was 48 years old and doing housework and I had an idea for a story. I'd never written anything before (no diary, no dabbling in short stories, no childhood dreams of being an author), but what did I have to lose other than a few hours of my time? Anything had to be more interesting than hoovering, and no one would ever read the story but me, so I sat down and wrote.

At school I'd learnt the basics of grammar and punctuation, but I always felt inhibited about my writing and that I lacked imagination. Now I realize that everyone has imagination, but being brave and comfortable enough to risk expressing it is the hard thing. By June 2010 schoolgirl inhibitions were a distant memory, although learning wasn't, as the previous year I'd begun to study Social Sciences with the Open University. Because of the OU course I had developed the habit of writing – I had to produce regular assignments and I enjoyed closing the door on the outside world and immersing myself in a new topic. I loved the process of putting ideas and words together and creating something, even if it was only a rather poor essay on politics.

So that June afternoon, with no more essays to write, I repeated the procedure but instead of an essay I began a short story about a girl who didn't know that she was a witch. I didn't have much of a plan – I just wrote, and I continued the next day and the next. After two weeks of this I had to admit to myself that the story wasn't that short; in fact I was probably writing a novel, and it was now taking up all my time. I was hooked. Possibly I was in love too – with my characters. I was obsessed with them, thinking about what they'd do and how, and why. I carried on writing and by September 2010 my story was complete and definitely not short (136,000 words). It wasn't atrocious but there were things wrong with it, though I wasn't even sure what those things were (the narrative point of view was jumping all over the place). I was desperate to improve and so I switched my OU course to Creative Writing, studying hard and all the while working on my manuscript.

I never really believed I'd be a published writer – it seemed less likely than winning the lottery – but I believed in my story. I wanted to try to get it published, but I had a problem: I didn't know a thing about the publishing world. However, I had heard about the *Writers' & Artists' Yearbook* and I found a rather battered copy at my local library. As soon as I started leafing through it I knew I'd found a book I could trust. I devoured its advice. It became my Bible, a source of knowledge and comfort. It was my way into a different world – the world of the professional writer.

I decided to try the traditional route of getting an agent who would then help me find a publisher, and so I listed the agents who accepted manuscripts for YA books, googled them and chose a few I thought might be interested in my story. I submitted to eight agents and within a few months received five brief replies saying 'No' (though the non-replies were fairly clear No's too). However, one reply was different: it was still a 'No', but the agent said she liked my writing style though the story 'didn't have the necessary edge for today's market'. I was delighted. OK – it was a rejection, but an agent from a prestigious London literary agency liked my writing style! I was over the moon. Better yet, I was fired up – I knew I could do edgy better than most people, and I knew that I could improve on the manuscript that I'd sent out. My mindset, once I decided I'd try to get published, was that I would write at least three novels before I'd give up, so starting again didn't daunt me. I gave myself a year to rewrite the story and immediately set to work. Best of all, I'd been released from the cage that I hadn't realised I was still in; I'd been told to be edgy, and to do that I had to let go of my writing inhibitions and make the story mine.

A year later I was back in the library with the *Writers' & Artists' Yearbook*, following its advice about covering letters and synopses (much better advice than the, often American, tips I'd seen online) for what turned out to be my first published novel.

I would have been lost without *Writers' & Artists' Yearbook* to guide me, and I'm delighted there is now this *Children's Writers' & Artists' Yearbook*. It's a wonderful resource – it's *the* resource for writers.

**Sally Green** is the author of two internationally acclaimed, award-winning trilogies of young adult fantasy novels, *Half Bad* (*Half Bad*, *Half Wild* and *Half Lost*) and *The Smoke Thieves* (*The Smoke Thieves*, *The Demon World* and *The Burning Kingdoms*) published by Penguin Random House in the UK. *Half Bad* (2014), Sally's debut novel, was named Waterstones Best Book for Teenagers 2015 and was shortlisted for the YA Book Prize 2015 and for the 2015 Branford Boase Award, and was adapted for a Netflix series released in 2023. Sally is on Instagram at @SallyGreenWriter, Twitter @Sa11eGreen, and her website is at www.SallyGreenWriter.com

## See also...
● *Writing for teens*, page 261

**Books**

# How do you do it?

After more than two decades as a published author William Sutcliffe has only one answer to the often-asked question 'How do you do it?'. He shares the most important piece of advice he has to offer and reminds writers to enjoy every step of the long journey they are embarking upon.

In the 24 years that I have been writing and publishing books I have been to scores of literary events, both as a speaker and an audience member. If I had to agglomerate all the questions I've heard put to authors into one overarching meta-question, it would be this: 'How do you do it?'. Sadly, my agglomerated meta-answer to that question would have to be 'I don't know.' Every published writer frequently gets asked for advice, and most of them have only one truly essential tip to offer: buy the *Writers' & Artists' Yearbook*. The key turning point in every professional writer's life is when writing shifts from being a hobby or a dream into a source of income. For making that transition, this book is the Bible.

To get published, you don't have to know someone; you don't have to know someone who knows someone; you don't have to live in Hampstead; and you don't need a degree in English literature. You do, however, need to understand that publishing is a business and that, like every other business, it operates in a way that seems obvious and transparent to insiders, but is opaque and confusing to outsiders. This is what makes the *Writers' & Artists' Yearbook* an essential reference book for everyone who hopes to make a living as a writer. Trying to get published without it is like setting off on a hike without a map.

When put to a writer, the question 'How do you do it?' can mean two things. If it means 'How do you get published?', you are holding the answer in your hands right now. Not everyone who hopes to find a publisher will achieve that, not by a long shot, but if you want to give your work in progress the best possible chance of finding an agent and ultimately a publisher, all the answers you need are right here. Of course, the other thing that question often means is 'How do you write a good book?'; and for that one, there are no clear-cut answers. Moreover, when it comes to key questions such as getting started, editing, plotting, characterisation and getting unstuck when you are stuck, for every writer there is a different solution. There is a right and a wrong way to make a submission to an agent; there isn't a right and a wrong way to write a novel. Everyone finds their own method.

The fascinating essays in this volume contain a wealth of experience from many of Britain's finest children's authors. You will find Jacqueline Wilson on 20 years of perseverance before her big breakthrough; J.K. Rowling on rejection letters; Michael Rosen analysing who children's writers write for; and many more fascinating pieces. None of these essays will tell you how to write like those authors, but they will open your thoughts onto how you should write – how to get your personality onto the page; how to tell a unique story in an original way; how to navigate your own path through the craft of writing. These essays are the second-best resource there is for hearing the secrets of good children's writing. The best resource, of course, is the novels themselves.

Read them. Read them once as a reader, then again as a writer – which is to say with the eyes of a hyena. Pull the books to pieces. Think about the word choices, the structure, the characterisation, the pacing, the world-building. Read the books you love ruthlessly and critically. Read the books you don't love in the same way, and hone your sense of where your literary taste sits. There is no objective scale of good and bad. You need to make your own. This gimlet-eyed reading is essential, because only when you have done it to others will you be able to do it to your own prose. To write for children you have to tap into a playfulness in your imagination, but when it comes to editing and rewriting you have to be brutal. Any word or sentence that isn't doing a useful job has to go.

This book is filled with practical and creative advice for writers at every stage of a writing career, but I would like to leave you with the simplest and most important advice there is: enjoy it. When you write, pour yourself into the work. Think of the blank page not as a scary place but as a path to freedom. Writing can take you anywhere. If you really apply yourself to the task, whether you get published or not, that journey will be worthwhile.

**William Sutcliffe** writes for adults, young adults and children and is the author of 12 novels, including three titles in his *Circus of Thieves* series, published by Simon & Schuster Children's: *Circus of Thieves and the Raffle of Doom* (2014), *Circus of Thieves on the Rampage* (2015) and *Circus of Thieves and the Comeback Caper* (2016). His YA books are *The Wall* (2014) which was shortlisted for the CILIP Carnegie Medal, *Concentr8* (2016), shortlisted for the YA Book Prize, *We See Everything* (2017), *The Gifted, The Talented and Me* (2019) and *The Summer We Turned Green* (2021), all published by Bloomsbury. William's novels for adults include the international bestseller *Are You Experienced?* (Hamish Hamilton 1997), *New Boy* (Penguin 1996), *Bad Influence* (Hamish Hamilton 2004) and *Whatever Makes You Happy* (Bloomsbury 2008), which was adapted into a Netflix film with the new title *Otherhood*, in 2019. He is also a screenwriter. His work has been translated into 28 languages. Follow him on Twitter @Will_Sutcliffe8.

Books

# Writing and translating children's fiction

Clémentine Beauvais explains the special satisfaction, pleasure and value to be found in translation, with its concentrated focus on language. She urges all writers to use translation to develop and re-energise their reading and writing skills.

This article is about writing children's fiction and translating children's fiction, and the peculiar kinds of pleasure and knowledge that arise when you do both. Let's start by stating the obvious: there shouldn't be any stark distinction between 'writing' and 'translating' children's fiction. Translating is an act of writing. Some translators actually prefer to call themselves 'writers of translations'. As Kate Briggs puts it beautifully, translated texts 'come to us twice-written'. Aren't we lucky, as readers of translations, that not just *one*, but *two* writers, gave their time and applied their talent to that text?

I was a children's writer long before I became a literary translator, and these days I spend roughly half of my time doing 'my' writing and half of my time translating – namely, redoing someone else's writing. Many people are surprised that I would choose to halve what they see as my 'real writing' time, a thought which you could well translate as: 'Surely translation is something you only do when you can't *really* write?'

My view, of course, is that you should translate only if you can *really* write. And only if you can *really* read. And the more you do it, the more it transforms your writing and reading. I want to convince you that if you wish to be a writer, you should *absolutely* write translations. Even if you don't speak another language fluently. Even though it will never bring you fame or money. Even if no one ever reads your translations. Translate. Do it for yourself, for your writing. Do it as a secret pleasure. Do it as a way of learning to write and read better. Here's why.

## Translating is writing, rewriting and rewiring your writing

Translating forces you to focus on language, and only on language. I shiver to write this, because of course there's no such thing as 'only' language: it is literally the *only* stuff literature is made of. But when you write a whole novel, you need to keep a million things in mind at the same time: narrative structure, characterisation, audience considerations, chapter length, ideological aspects, the logistics of seriality. And that's even before the editorial dance starts.

When you're translating, you have one task: language. The story's in place, the characters are there; you have a global view of them, in their finished form. Your task is to focus on the words, and to make sure that, in the target language, each of them does the job of propping up this whole fictional world. By 'each of them' I do mean each word, and this is why translating is close to the purest kind of writing: rarely in one's writerly life does one get the luxury of 'angsting' so much over every single word. You think about every word at least twice – in the source language, and in the target one – when the equivalence is obvious. But it seldom is. So you think of each word many times. It is precision work, a series of micro-decisions, adjusting and tweaking language. That's your only job and it's a colossal one.

Doing so will show you two things that are crucial to developing your writing. Firstly: you are never an expert in your native language. All my qualms about writing in English collapsed when I realised I was working from an erroneous assumption – that I knew French. French fails me just as often as English does. We can never write perfectly in any language, nor even approach perfection. Those little failures of language, of any language, are literature.

Secondly: translating changes your writing by forcing you out of your writerly reflexes. My writerly self is lazy. There are certain character types, certain places, certain genres or certain voices it doesn't write because it can't be bothered to venture out of its comfort zone. And my writerly self is ignorant – it doesn't write about things it doesn't know. My translating self cannot afford such whimsicality. It needs to write a text full of those things my writerly self usually avoids or simply doesn't know about. When I translated Sarah Crossan's *Moonrise* (Bloomsbury Children's 2017), I had to write a whole novel about the American prison system; I ended up having, effectively, written it. I never knew anything about it before; I have now learnt not just facts but a way of writing them. Translating is one of the most enlightening acts of writing you can do, because it forces you into the writerly reflexes and comfort zones of someone else.

And it changes your writing, of course, because there's no way you can survive the experience and not acquire new practices, a new way of looking at structure, at character, at style. It inspires you and re-energises your writing. It gives you a glimpse of what your writing-from-scratch could be like if you tried out something entirely different.

## Translating is reading, rereading and learning to read

At the same time, translating is also an act of reading – arguably one of the most reverent, attentive and generous acts of reading. I was, so to speak, a professional reader before I became a translator – as an academic specialising in children's fiction – and those skills are evidently useful when reading-for-translation; it's helpful to be able to notice and name the literary devices, and know roughly what the equivalent ones would be in the other language. For instance, I know that an iambic pentameter in English is like the French twelve-footed alexandrin; both are the classic, solemn rhythms at which the hearts of those cultures beat.

Those reading skills, however, are activated not just for analysis and description, but in close relation with writerly decisions. If I'm looking for equivalence of *effect*, the TaDAM TaDAM TaDAM TaDAM TaDAM of my English iambic pentameter could become the tadadadadaDAM tadadadadaDAM of the French alexandrin. It is equivalently lulling, pleasant and familiar. But wait – perhaps I want my French reader to feel that English beat, to be slightly puzzled by that poetic rhythm from beyond the sea? And there I'll wrench my French into an awkward five-footed line.

I decide. I'm in charge. When you're reading-for-translation, you're exercising your critical reading skills and making that interpretation matter for writing. Thus translating teaches you a special kind of reading practice. You read with the eyes of a critic and a creator. Of course, all writers should read as widely as possible in their chosen genres and beyond, but when we say this we generally mean that they should do this for their own edification and/or for pleasure. Reading for translation adjusts a different kind of lens to your readerly eye; this is active reading, in the sense of reading activated by the writing that must come next.

So when I translated Meg Rosoff's minuscule novel *Moose Baby* (Barrington Stoke 2013), I needed to understand how she packed so much humour in so little space, and it was a free lesson in the mechanics of humour in literature. I learned to spot exactly where funny dwells, at the level of sentence, paragraph, page. But it was no academic exercise; none of this would have mattered unless I also thought about where to reinject that humour in the French rewriting. This is more than close reading – it's intimate reading: you reread the same sentence many times, holding in your head analytical considerations of literary devices, writerly considerations of effect and your own sensitivity as a reader. In so doing, you learn to read better, and more precisely, as you start to develop a sense for the composition and aesthetics of even the tiniest units of text.

## So go away and translate

So please: go away and translate. If you're lucky enough to have another language, use it for your writing. Write translations. Pick a book you love in the other language and translate it into your own. Not for money, not for networking, not for any kind of profitability as measured by normal standards. No one will thank you for it; you probably won't be paid for it. But it will teach you so much about reading and writing. It will teach you the amazing focus on language that only translating can afford – the aesthetic epiphanies brought about by the most minute of tweaks; the fact that so much in a good piece of literature depends on the right word; character, plot and the way words pull them in this direction or that. The intense attention to words is a lesson you'll never learn better than when translating.

If you are unlucky enough to be monolingual, learn another language. I'm serious – do it. How can you claim to see what your own language can do if you can't watch it from the vantage point of another? All writers, if they really care about words and language – which is the stuff their work is made of, and therefore a professional requirement – should yearn to feel that estrangement, that distancing which brings understanding, knowledge and the destabilising sense that you can't say everything in your own language.

Careful – I'm not saying 'go away and become bilingual'. Fun fact: not all translators are fluent in the languages they translate *from*. Many can't actually hold a conversation. Translating is an act of writing and reading, not dazzling everyone with your perfect accent. Anyway, even bilinguals don't speak two languages perfectly. Even monolinguals don't speak their one language perfectly. Learn another language precisely, *because you'll never speak it perfectly*.

Start small. Pick up a picture book in whatever language you did at school, ages ago. Translate a few lines, painstakingly, using dictionaries and the internet. From that ugly literal translation, make a beautiful literary one. There you go. It's at the same time much more and much less difficult than it sounds.

People are awed by translators because they think 'they're really good at languages', whereas they should really be awed by thinking 'they're really good at writing'. You're good at writing, and that's all that matters: go and write translations. The more you do it, the more you'll develop that superpower and the better you'll write and the better you'll read. And one day you, too, will join that underground league of people who secretly think: 'Hey, writers. We know our stuff ... *and* yours. Here we are, in your writing, taking your words, making them our words. No one's read you like we have. No one's rewritten you like we have. You are mine now.'

**Clémentine Beauvais** is a Senior Lecturer in English in Education at the University of York. She is also a writer for children and young adults in French, and a literary translator from English to French. Her books written in English include the *Sesame Seade Mysteries* series (Holiday House), *The Royal Babysitters* series (Bloomsbury Children's), *Piglettes* (Pushkin Press 2017, self-translated from the French) and *In Paris With You* (Wednesday Books 2019, translated by Sam Taylor). Her translation of J.K. Rowling's children's book, *The Ickabog*, was published in French as *L'Ickabog* (Gallimard 2020). She is also the French translator of Sarah Crossan, Elizabeth Acevedo and some works by Meg Rosoff. For more information visit www.clementinebeauvais.com/eng.

# Writing for different genres and markets

# Finding new readers and markets

Tom Palmer shows how, by seeking out unexpected working partnerships, a children's author can open up mutually rewarding and productive markets and draw in new young readers.

I have managed to make a living as a full-time children's author for 14 years. As everyone who has tried it knows, it is not easy to earn enough money to live on from being a writer. You're forever in fear. Forever asking yourself questions ... How long will people want to buy your books? Will school events dry up as finances tighten and the political landscape changes? There is little respite, even if you are living the dream. Which I am.

That's why I spend a lot of time trying to think of ways I can attract interest to my books, so that people will continue to buy and borrow them. And so schools will keep paying me to visit. One of the most successful ways I have found to do this is to *give*.

## Looking for partnerships

There are a lot of organisations, charities and companies who would benefit from working with a children's author. But who are they? What can you give them? And, what can they give you? I have developed relationships with several organisations – large and small – giving and taking. In partnership. As a result of those partnerships, I have boosted my longevity as a children's author.

Each partnership is different and each evolves in its own unpredictable way. But it usually starts with a series of questions that I ask myself, and which I suggest you ask *yourself*. Here is a plan of action:

• Think about what you've written. List subjects, settings, themes, ideas. And dig deep. Text your friends and family. Your readers. Ask them what *they* think you write about.

• Now look at your list. Are there natural partners for your work? (For instance, Beatrix Potter might have chosen the RSPCA, a pet shop chain or *Animals & You* magazine. Or she might not.)

> ### How to approach potential partners
>
> 1 The more you know about the possible partner the better. That includes researching the right person to contact.
> 2 Offer to do as much of the set-up and admin work as you can. They are likely to be under massive time-pressure with their job already.
> 3 When you meet for the first time, try to make it open and creative. Set it up as a thinking/sharing session, not just a blast of ideas from you.
> 4 You probably have to be willing to give first, to do stuff for free to demonstrate that your partnership could help them. Then, as your relationship evolves, the balance will tip back in your favour.

• Suss out one or more partners whose work is linked to what you write about. Again, stretch it. Brainstorm; be creative. Have ideas that are stupid. Cross them out. Have more. There might be one that fits.

• Think carefully about those potential partners. Go to their website. Watch them. What do they do? What do they want to achieve? Can you help them?

• Now think about what you could ask for from *them*. How can they help you to promote your books? Or, how can your link with them help you to promote your books?

## Case studies

Over the last decade I have worked successfully with the RAF Museums, England Rugby, the Premier League, Divine Chocolate, Leeds Schools Library Service, Leeds United, the

Anne Frank Trust and many others. Below are three different examples. They could help you see how to identify suitable partners that fit the writing and themes of your own books.

## Fair trade chocolate

I was writing a book about football and fair trade for Puffin. It's called *Off Side* and includes storylines relating to the trafficking of young African footballers and to fair-trade cocoa bean farming. I needed help to write it. A lot of help. From people who knew about football and chocolate in Africa.

So I did a bit of research. In fact, my wife did. She came up with Divine Chocolate who work with fair-trade farmers so that the likes of us can give them a fair wage for what they farm. I identified the Right to Dream football academy in Ghana. They look after gifted young child footballers and help protect them from being exploited by corrupt football agents. I contacted both, suggesting that I could help raise awareness of what they do. Could they explain it to me? Could they help me research and write a meaningful book? They said they could.

I went to Ghana at my own expense. I saw everything I needed to see. It was amazing. When I got home I promoted Divine and Right to Dream and the great work they do through writing my story. And my book continues to sell well because it was properly researched and I knew what I was talking about. Job done.

But relationships evolve. When *Off Side* was published, Divine wanted me to tell the story of how fair trade makes a difference. They gave me a PowerPoint. I used it as part of my talk in schools. I did this for free, of course. But it enhanced my school events, made them more meaningful. As a result, more schools wanted to book me to go in and talk to their pupils, meaning my book became better known in schools with fair-trade status and beyond. More book sales. More paid school events. And the raising of awareness of very important issues.

Ask yourself:
– *Does my book deal with an issue or a cause?*
– *Which charity or campaign group might be interested in working with me?*
– *How can I help that cause through my book and events?*

## The Royal Air Force

I was writing a series about children going back in time to fly famous RAF aeroplanes. I approached three organisations to ask if they'd like to work with me. Two did not reply. The RAF Museums did.

The RAF Museums have some amazing artefacts in their collections at Hendon and Cosford: tiny kite-like planes from the First World War; terrifying giants like the Vulcan bomber. But the RAF Museums are always looking for ways to bring those planes to life. For ways to tell the story behind them, and about the men and women who flew them. That was what they needed. A way of telling more stories. That's what I could give.

I volunteered to do a school event for them for free, to see if we could work together. It was a success, and they offered to pay me for the next one. Six months later, they had a new exhibition called 'First World War in the Air'. They asked me how we could work together to tell a story about the pilots. One of their exhibits is of the possessions of a 19-year-old pilot, Kevin Furniss, who was killed on his second sortie. His gloves. His shaving equipment. His Bible. His pipe. Letters home. These items were poignant enough on their own, but I suggested writing a story about Furniss using those objects before his fateful flight. The museum then used the story in schools to attract visitors. And I was paid for the story.

Now I am the museum's Children's Writer in Residence. I do four school and public events a year for them, based around the three important planes from their collections that I have since – with their help – written books about: the Sopwith Camel; the Spitfire; and the Eurofighter Typhoon. My book is on sale in their shops. They promote my events and books to the many RAF and aeroplane interest groups that they work with. We bring schools into their museum and run writing workshops based around their aircraft and artefacts.

Ask yourself:
– *Is there subject matter in my books that relates to a museum, gallery, festival, interest group?*
– *Which ones should I research and what might they be interested in from me?*
– *How could I or my book help them?*
– *Can we work together?*

## England Rugby

I had a trilogy of rugby stories published in 2015 by Barrington Stoke (*Rugby Academy: Combat Zone*; *Rugby Academy: Dead Locked*; and *Rugby Academy: Surface to Air*). We timed their publication to tie in with the Rugby World Cup, hosted in the UK that year.

I contacted the education people at England Rugby, the RFU, in the hope that I could apply for money to create literacy interventions. With the RFU as a partners, I'd have a good chance. I suggested that the RFU and I apply for money to tour an event at the library near each of the 13 Rugby World Cup venues. I also suggested a set of literacy resources linking rugby to reading for pleasure and writing. And I said that I could write a live story to be read in schools as the Rugby World Cup was on. Would they be interested?

They were. My ideas met their needs because the RFU are keen to get into schools. They want to use the interest in the game to encourage children to read and write. They want to spread the culture of their five core values. And they want to start more rugby teams in schools to help create players for the future. So they offered to pay for it all direct, with no need to apply for funding.

I now work regularly with the RFU, performing events, creating resources and writing stories that they publish on their website. This has led to my *Rugby Academy* series becoming very well-known in rugby circles. Which goes a long way to explaining how all three sold out their advance within a year of publication.

Ask yourself:
– *Is there an activity or interest at the centre or on the margins of my book?*
– *Does a national or regional body administer that interest?*
– *Who can I work with? Who would be interested in my book?*

Working with partners has been a massive boon for my career. If I had not sought out those partners, I think that my full-time writing career may well have ground to a halt. In addition, I have been able to promote the joys of reading for pleasure to children and families I might not have reached without the help of those partners. And that is deeply satisfying and very much on my agenda. One downside could be that – in always working with partners – I am a slave to *their* agenda. I try to overcome that by making sure the books I write with partners always meet whatever my obsession of the moment is. Also, the good money I make from working with partners buys me time to write other work that is 100% what I want to do.

**Tom Palmer** is the author of 59 books for children. He has been published by Puffin, Barrington Stoke and others. *Foul Play* was shortlisted for the 2008 Blue Peter Book Award. His recent books *Armistice Runner* (2018), *After the War* (2020), *Arctic Star* (2021) and *Resist* (2022) were each nominated for the Carnegie Medal. *Armistice Runner* (2018) and *D-Day Dog* (2019) both won the UK Children's Book Award in 2019 and 2020. Tom is Children's Writer in Residence at the RAF Museum and Leeds United FC. Tom was awarded the Ruth Rendell Award for his contribution to literacy in 2019. Find out more at http://tompalmer.co.uk, and follow him on Twitter @tompalmerauthor.

# Troubador
## Publishing Limited

*The home of* **Matador**

## ABOUT US...

We help authors get published with bespoke, market-leading self-publishing services – taking authors and their books from manuscript to market.

## WITH AUTHORS AT THE HEART OF ALL WE DO

We work in partnership with authors to design, create, publish, market, distribute and sell quality books across print and digital formats, putting customers at the heart of what we do. We use our 30 years' experience and expertise to give the best self-publishing experience – working with our authors to publish and sell beautiful books, making publishing dreams come true.

## PRODUCTION, MARKETING, SALES AND DISTRIBUTION

We have unparalleled experience in book production. But far more, we have a retail trade and PR marketing department that can actively promote your work; and we have real bookshop distribution.

Our aim is to publish a book that you are proud of and then to get it sold.

## OUR SERVICES...

**BOOK PRODUCTION**

From manuscript through editing, typesetting, design and print, we produce high-quality books using our market-leading services.

**MARKETING**

Our marketing experts use their experience to make retail buyers aware of your book and to get the media talking about it.

**SALES AND RETAIL DISTRIBUTION**

Our own warehousing, bookshop distribution and sales teams ensure seamless fulfilment of bookshop orders.

**EBOOKS AND AUDIOBOOKS**

Publishing your ebooks and audiobooks to the highest standard and distributing them worldwide.

## NEXT STEPS?

Get started with a no-obligation conversation with one of our publishing team about what you want to achieve and how we can help you. What you'll get:

- The opportunity to ask a publishing professional anything about self-publishing
- Helpful advice from the best in the business on the options available to you
- Honest advice based on 30 years in the self-publishing business
- No obligation, commitment or hard sell.

 Phone
**0116 279 2299**

 Email
**books@troubador.co.uk**

 Website
**www.troubador.co.uk**

# Specialising in creating Children's Books

We offer the complete package! From initial ideas, layout design, unique illustrations, character design and logo design. Here at Happydesigner, we do it all!

# www.happydesigner.co.uk

# STORYMIX
## THE INCLUSIVE FICTION STUDIO

## WITH YOUR HELP AND TALENT STORYMIX CREATES INCLUSIVE CHILDREN'S FICTION FOR PUBLISHERS.

### WE'RE LOOKING FOR CREATIVES WHO:

- Are keen to write or illustrate for children;
- Can work collaboratively and to a brief;
- Are from a Black or Minority Ethnic background.

Less than 2% of published authors and illustrators in the UK are British people of colour.

Storymix imagines differently.

We work with agented and unagented, published, self-published and unpublished creatives to make heroes for all kids.

## STORYMIX.CO.UK

## CBC
### CURTIS BROWN CREATIVE

THE WRITING SCHOOL FROM THE
MAJOR LITERARY & TALENT AGENCY

# Craft brilliant stories for children & young adults

**200+**
former students with
publishing deals

*I went in an enthusiast, but left with a much more professional outlook... I'm a better writer for it*

**MICHAEL MANN**
*Ghostcloud*
Hachette Children's Group

*The course took me from being a solitary writer to one with a trusted group of critique partners*

**CYNTHIA MURPHY**
*Last One to Die*
Scholastic

## Unlock your imagination
## with an online course
www.curtisbrowncreative.co.uk

# The learning curve: writing for the children's educational market

Rachel Bladon shares her experience of writing children's educational books and describes the appeal and value of this sector, with its broad range of content and skills, and the satisfying creative challenges and rewards it offers a writer.

Any kind of children's writing involves putting yourself in a young person's shoes and viewing the world through their eyes – that is one of the key attractions and challenges of working for this age group. But for writers like me, who are pitching our stories at the educational rather than trade market, there are quite a lot of extra considerations to take on board. It's not just a question of how old your readers are likely to be, but also what level they are working at, what kind of setting they are learning in, and above all, if you write for international markets, where in the world they are.

Children's educational publishing takes many forms. There are textbooks for every subject in UK schools, of course, plus a multitude of extra resources in print, digital and audio format; and, as any parent who's had to support their child with reading will know, there's also an abundance of literacy schemes out there. Then there's the home-learning market, and the sector I have ended up in: ELT (English Language Teaching) publishing, with its vast array of materials for the world's 1.5 billion English language learners.

## The appeal of the role

Having your name on a textbook probably doesn't give quite the same hit a writer gets from seeing their lovingly crafted children's story make its way onto the shelves of a bookshop. But for me, this highly market-driven kind of publishing has always had a draw. I'd started out as a writer of information books with a well-known children's publisher, and it was a fun and vibrant place to work. I would sit at my desk writing a children's guide to beginner's German, of which I spoke not a word, while colleagues around me emerged occasionally from heaps of wool, crepe paper, straws and plasticine to write the next spread of a bestselling craft guide or a children's book on science experiments. I loved making a living from crafting words, surrounded by a buzz of creativity, but there was something missing for me in this desk-based existence, and in the broadness and freedom of the brief – which amounted to whatever notes you scribbled down during a short, white-knuckled meeting at the start of every project with the formidably capricious director, in his office on the top floor.

When I became aware of the thriving publishing industry that exists around ELT, something I'd got a qualification in and spent a year earning money from in France when fresh out of university, I realized I'd found something that really appealed to me. What better than travelling the world (and I really did), observing classes, talking to teachers and trying to get under the skin of a different country's education system, then coming home and writing books that would one day be used in those classrooms to help children learn English and thus access a wider world? I became an editor in children's ELT publishing at first, so not officially writing – but the authors of the books I was editing were often teachers with a reputation in their respective countries who had little writing experience, so there was always a lot of rewriting involved. Once I had a family and decided to go freelance, it was easy to make the hop across from editing into actually writing myself. I've always relished, and still do, the many different elements of my role: needing to understand the particular market I'm writing for; applying a particular methodology to the structure of the material; and researching and creating a wide range of content – from topical texts about issues of the moment, 'realia' (concocted newspaper articles, etc used to expose learners to 'real English') and self-contained stories to activities, exercises and tests, as well as scripts for audio and video (and now, of course, digital) components. And then there's the visual side: with the complexity of a textbook and its many constituent parts, the design is absolutely key, so collaborating closely with designers, artists, picture researchers and photographers is an essential part of the job.

## Cultural sensitivities

As an ELT author and xenophile, one of the things I love most about writing for international markets is what you learn about the different cultures you are tailoring your materials for. There was a furore in the British press a few years ago when it was unearthed that we in the ELT world abide by a code of taboos called PARSNIPs, which denotes the various things we avoid at all times in our writing: Politics, Alcohol, Religion, Sex, Narcotics, 'Isms' (such as Communism), and Pork. In actual fact, there's a host of other things that we steer clear of, and in the course of my career I've been asked to avoid everything from ghosts and magic to aardvarks and crows. I never got to the bottom of what it is about aardvarks that makes them off-limits, but fortunately that particular taboo has never constrained me too greatly!

Critics have said that, by keeping these things out of our books, we're sanitising them and stifling opportunities for debate, discussion and the broadening of minds. But, while I would draw the line at anything that ventured into the realm of censorship, it has always seemed obvious to me that in books that are going to be used in the classroom, cultural sensitivity is essential. Partly this is a commercial necessity: in many countries, textbooks won't sell unless they are included in approved ministry lists, and anything that's seen as breaching cultural norms is not going to make the grade. But it also seems to be common sense, if you're creating a book for students in another part of the world, to show respect for their culture. In the same way that we'd be unlikely to show a child spitting in the street or smoking in a UK textbook, so teachers in China don't want to see pets in the kitchen (which they consider unhygienic), and a class of children in the Middle East will balk at a picture of someone showing the soles of their feet.

## Graded readers

These days, I generally find myself writing for a global market that might typically include Brazil, Poland, Spain, Italy, Japan and Egypt. I've wiggled my way down into a particularly narrow niche in the world of ELT, writing 'graded readers' for students who are learning English. These are simplified storybooks, with the language and vocabulary carefully controlled so that an English language learner can read them fluently, at any level from beginner to advanced, consolidating and expanding their language skills as they do. One of the best things for me about writing graded readers is the freedom to write across different literary genres, and for a wide range of age groups. I've written everything from original fiction for pre-schoolers and adaptations of modern and classic titles for children aged 6–12, to non-fiction for teens and young adults – and in the past few years my smorgasbord of writing work has included new stories based around the TV characters *Dora the Explorer* and *Paw Patrol*, a book about the life and diaries of Anne Frank, an adaptation of the story of Don Quixote, and a young person's guide to the global issues of the 21st century.

For the 'grading' itself, I have a syllabus and vocabulary list on my desk at all times, bespoke for every different series; these tell me exactly what language I can and can't use at any particular level. Some writers might find it limiting and frustrating to work within such constraints, but I love the extra challenge, and I often feel there's something of the cryptic crossword about it – you think of the word that you need to convey a particular thought or idea, but if it doesn't fit your other criteria (in this case the syllabus) you then have to find some other way of saying what you want ... it gives the brain a good stretch. The grading comes very much on top of all the requisites for any piece of storytelling; our number one priority is to engage and captivate the reader, so – as for all good stories – the prose needs to be sharp, the dialogues need to flow naturally, the characters have to jump out of the page, and there needs to be a clearly defined story arc. For adaptations, which are a big component of the graded reader library, there are the added challenges of deciding what from the original can be cut or condensed, and of trying to retain the author's original voice in simplified form.

## The value and rewards

Writing for children in any format is intrinsically rewarding, of course, but a definite advantage of educational publishing is that the benefits are quantifiable. Research into the effectiveness of graded readers has shown what a huge impact they can have on language learning, and I've been really humbled on the occasions when I've actually seen my books in use in the classroom – this is quite a powerful reminder of the need to get things right and to put together the very best story you possibly can, in the hope of engaging a disaffected student or passing on the tiny nugget that might ignite something in a young mind.

Educational writing is also a lot easier to find a way into than the trade market, I think, especially if you're coming from a teaching background. Most practising teachers are too busy or exhausted to write new materials and, unless you have teaching experience or are a very engaged parent, you're unlikely to have a clear picture of what kind of resources are needed – or might work well – in a classroom setting. So if you do have the background, and the ideas, and are able to get them down on paper well, publishers might be very interested in what you can offer, particularly if you have some standing in your segment of the educational sector. There's also the advantage that sales can be quite substantial, because schools will usually buy class sets; this means every adoption might mean an order of tens or even hundreds of copies, still more if it's made by a big educational chain. Royalties are quite hard to come by these days, at least in the ELT world, but if you can secure them they're likely to hold up reasonably well. The world's bestselling ELT course-book, *Headway* (Oxford University Press), has sold more than 70 million copies, and is still going strong in its fifth edition!

Some might see educational writing for schools as the poor cousin of children's fiction, but I've found it a field with plenty of scope for creativity, in which you can foster a broad range of writing skills and dip your toe into other sides of the publishing process, like marketing and design. If, like Nelson Mandela, you believe that education is 'the most powerful weapon which you can use to change the world', you might just feel that as an educational writer, you're doing something that has value too.

**Rachel Bladon** was an EFL editor and writer, the author of more than 80 graded readers for adults and children, including *White Fang* (Macmillan Readers 2008), *Mulan* (Oxford Classic Tales 2017) and *The Life and Diaries of Anne Frank* (Oxford Bookworms 2018), winners of the ERF (Extensive Reading Foundation) Language Learner Literature Award. She was series editor of the *Oxford Bookworms Library*.

# Writing adventures in the real world: children's non-fiction

Isabel Thomas explores the exciting world of children's non-fiction, and shares her tips for writing the perfect pitch.

## Why write non-fiction?

Children's non-fiction is so much more than 'books with facts'. It's a different way for writers to reach young readers, to take them on a journey that makes them laugh, or cry, or bubble over with enthusiasm. It inspires children to explore their world – and to change it.

The last decade has seen an exciting renaissance in the genre. Dozens of new children's non-fiction imprints have launched, and publishers are investing in lavish illustrations and large formats. Bookshops and libraries have reconfigured their shelves to make space for titles big enough to dive into. Children's non-fiction titles appear in bestseller charts, award shortlists and festival programmes. Readers – and their families – are demonstrating a huge appetite for bold and beautiful adventures in the real world.

It's an exciting time to write and illustrate children's non-fiction, and the scope for creativity is huge. I've written picture books, comic strips and biographies where text and illustrations play together on the page. I've created coffee table tomes, activity books packed with paper engineering, and hands-on crafts and experiments.

All these books have something in common: a good children's non-fiction book is nothing like a textbook. It's an opportunity to tell a complete story that helps children connect bite-sized facts with the bigger picture.

## Where do I begin?

Find something that excites YOU, and then work out the best way to pass that excitement on to young readers. For me, it's science and nature.

Next, get specific. My first book was about blue and purple foods, an extension of an existing series. As debuts go it was low key. But it gave me the confidence to offer my services as a science writer to other publishers. Finding your niche is useful for winning that first commission, but it's not enough to know your subject area in depth. To make a topic irresistible to children, you need to know your readers too.

Spend time with children and immerse yourself in their world. Not just literature, but TV, films, apps and playground trends. Children's non-fiction competes with all of these things. I volunteer as a school governor and STEM Ambassador, roles that keep me in touch with curriculum change, and the influences that shape children's lives. I also read at libraries and run school events. 200 books into my career, I've become an expert in thinking like an eight-year-old.

## Finding your angle

The value of a non-fiction book lies not just in the information delivered – which must of course be accurate and up-to-date – but in the way it's presented. How will you hook your reader, so that your book educates *and* entertains? Play with ideas, make connections and take your readers on a journey. It might be through humour, adventure or quirky details. Or it might be by making a complex topic simple enough to give a child that 'wow' moment.

An original angle is essential if your book is to stand out on a crowded shelf. Instead of listing facts about space, weave them into an alien's guide to the solar system, or a book of rocket science for beginners. If you're writing about life cycles, how about a zookeeper's handbook, or a hypothetical battle of lion versus tiger?

## Developing your idea

At this point, a fiction author would write the first draft, ready to polish to perfection. The advice for non-fiction is rather different: don't write the book!

Children's non-fiction is usually a team effort, combining the author's ideas with those of talented editors, illustrators and designers to create something extraordinary. Unless you are pitching a picture book, there is usually no need to write the entire manuscript up front. Instead, develop a proposal and a few sample spreads, and make these as polished as possible. Once your idea has been commissioned, the editor will work with you to refine the approach, perfect the pacing of content and finalise the text features.

Don't forget to visit bookshops and libraries as you develop your idea. Holding the latest children's non-fiction books in your hands is much more revealing than looking at covers online. Get a feel for the typical extent and word count for each age group. How will you build knowledge and understanding over 48, 64 or 96 pages? Will you write a picture book with 20 words per page, or a reference book with 200? Read as many examples as you can to absorb the language level. Make a note of the page features that non-fiction writers use to break up the text into manageable chunks.

## Writing a proposal – dos and don'ts

Children's non-fiction authors work with publishers in several different ways. The first will be familiar if you already write fiction. Pitch an original idea and negotiate an advance and royalty. Some non-fiction authors work with literary agents; others pitch directly to publishers. When I worked as a non-fiction commissioning editor, I was equally happy to hear from both. I worked without an agent for the first decade of my writing career, and used the excellent Society of Authors (see page 297) for advice on contracts.

Even if your initial idea is not the right one at that time, pitching is a good way to introduce yourself. Editors often come to non-fiction writers with a subject in mind and ask for a text treatment – a fresh new approach that will work for their market. In this case, the remuneration may be a one-off fee, higher than the advance for a similar title. Either way, your first task for each new title is to write a concise and engaging proposal to make the case for your idea.

Begin with an **overview** that showcases your style and tone. It should be good enough to become the back-cover blurb (and it often does). Follow this attention-grabbing intro-duction with a longer **description**. Explain why the book is timely, perfect for the target age group and why you are the best person to write it. There's no need to send the whole manuscript (unless you are writing a short picture book). Instead provide a **breakdown of the structure**, showing how you build engagement and understanding. Finally, include two or three pages of **sample text** to bring the idea to life.

## DO:

• **Explain why you are pitching to this publisher**. Visit bookshops and scour catalogues, including the rights catalogues that publishers produce for book fairs. Find out what makes their books special. Then show why your idea and their list are a perfect match.

• **Come up with an attention-grabbing title** that hints at both subject matter and approach. Humorous and irreverent or lyrical and atmospheric? Hands-on activities or narrative adventure?

• **Point out anything that might drive sales**, such as anniversaries, curriculum links or exhibitions. Remember to work at least 18–24 months ahead – illustrated non-fiction takes around a year to journey from manuscript to shelf.

• **Showcase your voice**. Ten years ago, children's non-fiction often had a formal tone, edited to match house style. Today, a unique voice will help you stand out.

## DON'T:

• **Claim that there is no competition**. More often than not, this points to a lack of research. Competition can prove that a topic is in demand. Publishers will always offer books on dinosaurs, space and animals, and are hungry for creative new approaches to these popular themes. Compare your idea to existing titles – ideally successful ones! Explain why your approach will be different (and better).

• **Include illustrations**. Unless you're an author-illustrator, it's the publisher's role to find an illustrator that the audience will love (often, but not always, with your approval). Instead, note down ideas about the type of illustrations you think would work well, as part of your overall vision for the book.

• **Mention how much your family and friends like the idea**. Publishers get many proposals saying 'tested on my kids'. It's better to showcase the skills and experience that make you an expert in your subject area or target audience – or both!

## Writing the book – three golden rules

### 1. Research is key

One of the best things about writing for a living is the chance to dive into a subject. You might be writing for ten-year-olds, but you'll need to understand your topic in much greater depth. To avoid introducing errors, track down original sources. If you read an interesting article, find the original research too. Better still, interview the author. Insist on – and carefully record – at least two sources for every fact (and never make one of those sources Wikipedia). And be warned – when you're interviewing stuntwomen, scientists or astronauts, job envy is an occupational hazard!

### 2. Be playful

Hooking the audience doesn't end with a creative angle. Every page, paragraph and sentence must work hard to weave in the information you'd like to cover, while keeping readers engaged.

Make good use of text features, such as infographics, charts, text boxes and quotes. They can help you to bring interesting facts to the fore, enticing a reader to explore the rest of the page. They also help to pace the flow of information, making complex topics or arguments easier to follow.

Resist the temptation to include everything. First drafts are often double the length of the final text, and the real work comes in deciding what to leave out.

### 3. Think visually

Illustrations are a key ingredient in children's non-fiction. Sourcing these illustrations (whether buying photographs or commissioning illustrators) is the job of the publisher. But briefing them is the job of the author.

Think like an art director – how will information be broken up into chunks and displayed on the page? What diagrams will help you to explain a difficult concept? Will you include cartoons and visual jokes? An information book might need simple photo briefs, while a graphic text demands detailed descriptions of every panel. Create a wish list, to be realized by a talented illustrator and designer.

## Building a writing career

Children's non-fiction authors develop valuable skills: the ability to carry out in-depth research, to build bridges between prior knowledge and new information, and to craft a story that educates and entertains. These skills are in demand outside book publishing – by companies, charities and organisations that want to create outreach resources, by children's magazines, museums and science centres, and by producers of educational websites, blogs and vlogs. Writing other types of non-fiction content helps you keep your voice and ideas fresh. It can also be another way to reach your audience if you have an idea that's close to your heart, but find that there is no commercial demand for it in book form.

Promoting your books is another area where creative ideas and an appetite for pitching will help you to shine. As a non-fiction author, you are well placed to **design and run** events linked to your writing. For example, write and introduce yourself to to organisations and museums linked to the subject(s) you write about; suggest topics for radio or podcast discussions; pitch magazine and newspaper articles; offer to run hands-on sessions in bookshops and public libraries; help children unleash their own non-fiction writing power in an educational workshop. Events are a direct way to keep in touch with your readers, and you'll come away with dozens of ideas for new books.

Nothing beats the feeling of discovering something wonderful for the first time. Whether I'm writing a biography, an activity book or a picture book, I aim to give readers the same feeling. If I can encourage children to pick up a book, think 'wow', and keep reading, I know I've done a good job. But if they read something that encourages them to close the book, head outside and explore the world ... well, then I know I've done a *great* job.

Where will your next non-fiction adventure take you?

**Isabel Thomas** has written more than 200 non-fiction titles for young audiences, published by Bloomsbury, What on Earth? Books, Oxford University Press, Puffin, Laurence King, Ladybird, Collins, Pearson, Phaidon, DK, Rising Stars, Raintree, Schofield & Sims, QED, Welbeck, Weldon Owen, Wide Eyed and Wren & Rook in the UK, and translated into more than 30 languages around the world. Her narrative non-fiction picture books *Moth: An Evolution Story* and *Fox: A Circle of Life Story* (both published by Bloomsbury) were winners of the AAAS Subaru Prize for Excellence in Science Books. Isabel's most recent publications include *The Bedtime Book of Impossible Questions* (Bloomsbury), a *Guardian* Book of 2022, *Full of Life: Exploring Earth's Biodiversity* (Phaidon) and *Thirty Trillion Cells* (Welbeck). Isabel's short online course in developing and pitching non-fiction for young audiences is available via Domestika. Find out more at www.isabelthomas.co.uk and follow her on Twitter @isabelwriting and Instagram @isabelthomasbooks. ks.

## See also...

- *Finding new readers and markets*, page 109

# Connecting with your readers

Clare Povey explores how a writer can reach out and grow valuable connections with a wider readership. She shares her tips on how best to establish and maintain a strong author–reader relationship, through web content, social media, teachers, schools, libraries and bookshops.

Every writer wants to be read. I believe that every writer writes the book that they want to read themselves. Why else would we spend hours of our lives typing or scribbling away, with no guarantee that anyone other than ourselves (and a few lucky family members or friends) will get to see it? Connecting with your readers has to start with yourself. It's essential that you, the writer, find the story that you are most passionate and excited about because, without this, you will struggle to engage with your readers. Believe me, children can sniff out insincerity.

The first proper story I wrote was one I absolutely wanted to read. For full disclosure, it was my own take on *Holes* (Bloomsbury Children's 2015) by Louis Sachar. In my version, a girl character named Clara (we'll ignore how this is one letter off my own name) is sent to Camp Green Lake and shakes things up. It was my very own fan fiction; I reread it until the pages started to wear thin and tear. Since then, I have carried that same energy into all the stories I've written. So, although my first piece of advice seems simple, I can assure you that being genuine is a starting point for any meaningful author–reader relationship.

How do you successfully reach beyond your one-person audience and find wider readers for your work? Every writer – whether agented or un-agented, whether they have published with a larger publisher or an independent, or have self-published – can feel this an overwhelming task, but the advice in this article should be relevant.

My debut middle-grade book *The Unexpected Tale of Bastien Bonlivre* (Usborne) was published in September 2021. While bookshops were open then (thankfully), there were still certain restrictions in place. I wasn't able to get into schools immediately, and I also work full-time, so it was a challenge to organise school events to promote the book. This meant that, for the first six months of my book being out in the world, I had to find and use different ways of connecting with potential readers.

## Promotional disclaimer

I must acknowledge, at this point, that I was lucky enough to receive the September 2021 slot for Waterstones Children's Book of the Month. This promotional opportunity definitely helped my book reach a really wide audience in its early days – the size of audience that any author, especially a debut author, would dream of. It meant that my book sat in the window of every Waterstones bookshop across the UK (all 283 of them), as well as being clearly placed on tables and displayed next to the till for a whole month. It was an opportunity that I will be forever grateful for, but I appreciate that it is also something that a writer has no control over; your publisher pitches your book to Waterstones and the head team of retail experts decides which story gets the coveted slot.

But, as a writer, establishing connections and maintaining them is something you need to grow for a lifetime, not just a single month. So much of the publishing world is out of your control, so it is important to focus on the things that you can do and take accountability for yourself. How, then, can you connect with your readers? Beyond summoning the bookish child inside you and demanding an answer, here are my five top tips on how you can connect and communicate best with your readers. All of these tips are interconnected, but I've broken them down into five separate points for clarity.

## 1. Create and organise your own content

A writer does not necessarily need a website (it's something you will have to pay for, as well as maintain and update), but you do need to build up a bank of content. By content, I mean blogs, articles, Q&A features, short videos or audio clips … anything that can be used for promotional purposes. Having a variety of content available to offer to teachers, librarians and parents is a great way to expand the scope of your book. I have a Resources area on my website that allows me to put worksheets, links to articles and blogs, reading lists, historical facts and much more all in one place. Teachers can directly download resources for their classrooms, as well as access the first chapter of my book. I'm planning to record a series of videos about different aspects of the writing process that I can share with interested teachers.

You don't need to be an expert video editor or design whizz to create content. I use the free versions of Canva (www.canva.com) and Clipchamp (https://clipchamp.com) and am learning as I go. But I do keep my publishers in the loop about what I'm up to. I created a 'villain' worksheet for my school events (see section on School visits below) and the Usborne marketing and design team redesigned it into something much more professional looking. Communication is key – because, even though I love learning new skills, I'm not an expert designer or video editor. If you need help, ask for it.

## 2. Find your corner of Twitter

Social media isn't for everyone. If you're reading this and thinking 'Nope, not going anywhere near that cesspool,' that's your choice. But, be aware that the online children's fiction writing and book community contains some of the most supportive people you could ever hope to meet. I have met so many writers, book bloggers, booksellers, librarians and teachers through Twitter. I'll go into more detail about each one of these communities below, but I cannot overstate how useful and rewarding it has been to connect with others digitally. I have found my own tiny corner of Twitter that is generous, kind and supportive.

While you might not be reaching your main readership through Twitter, especially if you are writing for children up to the age of 12, you will still connect with the people who buy books for your younger readers. Other children's fiction writers are not your competition, but your co-workers. They will support your book and recommend you to their own readers, and in turn you can shout about their writing and make friends for life.

## 3. Reaching out to teachers and librarians

There are so many brilliant primary school teachers and librarians who are incredibly engaged with the children's publishing world. They truly care about making sure that every single child feels seen. I've met a number of teachers, mainly through Twitter, who are passionate about literacy and want authors to get involved. Here are some ways that have allowed me to connect:

• Ask if any schools would like to enter an author pen-pal correspondence with you. You could contact a local school or even get in touch with your old primary school.

• Go to your local library to discover what reading resources are especially useful for children. Accelerated Reader (www.renaissance.com/products/accelerated-reader), for example, is a great programme that is used in many schools to encourage reading for pleasure.

• Get involved in online chat and keep an eye out for hashtags such as: #teachertwitter, #edutwitter, #primaryschoolbookclub.

## 4. The brilliance of bookshops and booksellers

It's well worth calling up or going into your local bookshop(s) and introducing yourself. It's hypocritical of me to tell you not to be shy because, even after visiting dozens upon dozens of bookshops, I still quietly mutter, 'My name's Clare and I wrote that book over there...' (*points ambiguously to a shelf in the distance*). Bookshops can't stock every single book that has been published (unless they're a Tardis in disguise). I guarantee they will want to hear from you and, if they don't have copies of your book in store, be assured that they will be ordering after your visit.

Once you connect with a bookseller, you can ask whether they might be interested in running an event with you or organising a signing. For all of the big glossy promotions and huge marketing and publicity campaigns, bookseller recommendations are still one of the most useful selling tools. How many times have you walked into a bookshop, only planning to buy just one book on your list, and then left with a dozen new recommendations from a friendly bookseller? Booksellers help your books to live a long and happy life, and to be read by new readers time and time again.

## 5. School visits

A school visit is one of the most direct ways to connect with your readers. In the *Writers' & Artists' Guide to Writing for Children and YA* (Bloomsbury 2019), author Linda Strachan has written a comprehensive guide for writers on how to navigate school visits. I do implore you to get that book and read it, so you can make the most out of any school visits you organise.

I am writing this article a few days after my first ever World Book Day Week in March 2022 as an author. I visited five different schools over the course of four days; I led assemblies on writing and the author life, as well as classroom workshops on creating authentic villains in a responsible way. Villains are a big part of my book and I always give a reading of my main villain – the bestselling author Olivier Odieux – and then immediately follow it up with a 'Guess the Villains' quiz, where I include villains from other books, films and TV shows. Think about what strands of your story would work best for a school event and how this will relate to your readers.

Not every writer is able to visit schools in-person, but there are still other ways of connecting with schoolchildren. Virtual workshops and Q&As are more popular than ever, and this is a great way to reach your readers from your home office desk or kitchen table. Alternatively, if you don't have time in your working day to offer virtual school visits, creating pre-recorded videos – whether it's a five-minute creative writing exercise challenge or a much longer workshop session – is another great way to maintain a connection with schools. You can also reuse any recordings as content for other schools or organisations, or upload it to your website.

## A note to remember:

You can do as much or as little of this as you want. You might agree to write a blog for free; you might offer a visit to a school in a low-income area that would love to have an author visit but just doesn't have the financial means. As an author, you are in control of what you say 'Yes' and 'No' to. You never have to do anything you feel uncomfortable with. I always remind myself that connecting and growing readers is a marathon, not a sprint. Focus on what you can control and enjoy it – because, when you're having fun, your readers will too.

**Clare Povey** is an author and the editorial and communities manager of the Writers & Artists website. She fell in love with France as a child, inspired by the stories in her local Barking & Dagenham Library, and by discovering the vocabulary in Usborne's *First Thousand Words in French* (1995). The magic of speaking another language eventually led to her living and working in France, and writing her debut, *The Unexpected Tale of Bastien Bonlivre* (Usborne 2021), which was a Waterstones Children's Book of the Month. The sequel, *The Bad Brothers*, published in July 2022. Her next book will be published in 2024. For more information see www.clarepovey.com. Follow her on Twitter @ClareFPovey or Instagram @ClareFPovey.

## See also...
- *Finding new readers and markets*, page 109
- *Why teachers make great children's writers*, page 208

# Keeping going: the ups and downs of being a published writer

Theresa Tomlinson shares the emotional and creative highs and lows, opportunities and hurdles an author may encounter during a long writing career. She tracks the course of her career – through finding and losing a trusted editor, writing fiction for children, adults and YA, and moving from traditional publishing to self-publishing.

As a child I had no ambitions to write, but I loved reading and delighted in magical escapes to Narnia. I failed the eleven-plus, and rather struggled at my convent boarding school, but discovered I had some facility for drawing and painting. I spent two years at Hull Art College but left without completing my graphic design course. Unsure of what to do next, I trained to be an infant teacher and it was in that role that I discovered the sheer joy of storytelling (in those days both children and teachers could look forward to a blissful story session at the end of each day).

Later, as the mother of three young children, I started to put together simple picture books, initially focusing on the artwork rather than the words. As time passed the stories grew longer; my interest in the artwork faded and I began to write somewhat obsessively. Visits to the local library provided huge inspiration as I discovered new and exciting children's writers; it was almost like finding a new version of Narnia. Discovering Jane Gardam was a revelation – not only did I love her humour, sensitivity and clear writing style, but I recognised many of the settings based on the part of the north-east coast where I grew up. I knew every street, garden and house in the background of *A Long Way from Verona* (Abacus 1997), heard familiar cadences in the dialogue and experienced once again the familiar tang of steelworks built close to the sea. I began to feel that I, too, had stories to tell.

Having discovered a local writers' workshop, tutored by Berlie Doherty, I settled to work more seriously as a writer; five years of hard work followed, including three inspiring Arvon courses. There were many rejections, but things started to look up when I was awarded a Yorkshire Arts Bursary to help me finish a book in progress – *The Flither Pickers* (1987) – stories of fishing families set on the north-east coast, along with an offer of publication from John Killick of the Littlewood Press, based at Hebden Bridge. Although it was a limited print run, it meant that I had a well-produced example of my work to send to publishers. Fairly soon after that I got my first (modest) offer from a London publisher – for a magical children's story set in the industrial seaside village that I had lived in as a child. The offer came from Julia MacRae, a highly respected publisher with her own imprint within Walker Books and – best of all – she was Jane Gardam's publisher! I was thrilled.

Over the next 20 years, with the support of Julia and my fabulous editor, Delia Huddy, I flourished. One book followed another. Historical themes appealed to me and were appreciated by schools. Julia MacRae moved to Random House and took me with her, though happily Walker Books continued to publish my younger-age 'time-slip' books, which allowed modern children to slip magically back through time to experience an earlier period. I was hugely encouraged when *Riding the Waves* (1990) a more modern novel, set on the north-east coast, was recommended for the Carnegie Medal and my young adult novels were translated into several languages and sold in the USA. I was regularly shortlisted for the Sheffield Children's Book Award (Michael Palin memorably turned his back on me and folded his arms when I was called up onto the stage twice in an award ceremony!); it was such good fun.

Publishing contracts were now becoming rather complicated for me to deal with, so I looked for an agent; persuading Caroline Walsh of David Higham to take me on turned out to be one of the best things I ever did. Educational publishers were asking for more historical time-slip stories and when again one of these, *Meet Me By The Steelmen* (1997), was shortlisted for the Carnegie Medal, I thought my future was secure … But then gradually things started to change: schools became short of funds and invitations to visit grew scarce, ebooks appeared on the scene and time-slip stories seemed to fall out of favour. However, I still had the backing of my editor and a sympathetic agent.

For some time I had longed to use Anglo-Saxon Whitby as a setting for a story so, having moved to Whitby, I set out to write a trilogy of YA mystery/adventures with Hild's famous monastery as the setting. The research process was sheer pleasure and it was inspiring to be living in sight of the location. *Wolf Girl* (Corgi Children's 2006) was the first book completed and we had almost finished the editing process when my editor Delia suddenly died. The book was published but it didn't sell widely and Random House concluded that readers were not interested in Anglo-Saxon settings, but by then I had become passionately interested in the period; my bookshelves were filled with studies of food, clothing, language and crafts of the time – I'd persuaded my husband that our travels must include Sutton Hoo, West Stow Anglo-Saxon village, Durham, Bede's World (now Jarrow Hall), Yeavering, Bamburgh Castle and Lindisfarne.

By then, fortunately, trying to earn a living by writing had become less of a priority, but it was a depressing time; I almost considered giving up altogether. A few months of ignoring the computer, though, made me realise that it would be even more depressing not to write; for my own wellbeing, I needed to do it. Hearing that Whitby had a writers' group, I went to join them. It was like starting at the beginning again, and there was something rather exciting about that.

I couldn't let my Anglo-Saxon obsession go and began work on an adult murder mystery with the same setting as my YA book and with a theme somewhat similar to Ellis Peters' Cadfael series, but with a 7th-century half-pagan herb-wife, rather than a monk. Creating a much older protagonist was something I'd wanted to try for a while and the character of Fridgyth was already present in *Wolf Girl*, waiting to step forward into the limelight. Whitby Writers Group provided practical criticism and friendly encouragement and my pleasure in writing returned. A difficult decision had to be made when the manuscript was completed: whether to try to get it published traditionally or go down the self-publishing route. I talked it through with my agent and it became clear that, although I'd had some success as a children's writer, that wouldn't mean much when tackling the competitive, adult, historical crime fiction market. Even acceptance by a traditional publisher might mean waiting years for publication.

I was then in my 60s and felt time might be running out, so I decided to experiment with self-publishing. My agent negotiated a contract with Acorn Independent Press. They provided discerning editing, and I enjoyed having lots of input into the cover design. The book was well produced as a print-on-demand (POD) and ebook edition and Acorn helped with marketing and distribution. *A Swarming of Bees* (2012) was put forward for an Amazon promotion and within a few weeks it reached number three in the historical bestsellers chart – I was briefly placed between Hilary Mantel and C.J. Sansom and couldn't have been happier. I recovered my costs fairly quickly and local bookshops still sell copies at a steady pace, which I supply them with.

I set about writing a sequel and I also had a straightforward historical novel published, *The Tribute Bride* (2014), this time with a 6th-century setting. Self-publishing seemed to be working for me, so I began to look at my backlist of out-of-print titles. Two of my short novels, *The Flither Pickers* and *The Herring Girls*, focusing on the harsh lives of the fishing families of the north-east coast, were published in a paperback edition in 2017, illustrated with atmospheric Victorian/Edwardian photographs by Frank Meadow Sutcliffe. York Publishing Services (www.yps-publishing.co.uk) produced the book and it was a real benefit to be able to discuss the project face to face before agreeing to go ahead and at any point during the production process. YPS produced a Kindle version that displays the photographs beautifully and the books are selling steadily in local shops. YPS suggested an initial print run of 250 copies and I'm now into my second run.

However, self-publishing hasn't been all plain sailing. When the manuscript for my 'herb-wife' sequel was finished, Acorn were happy to put the book together but had decided to withdraw from providing marketing services. Once again, my agent came to the rescue: Caroline negotiated a rather different contract with Acorn, and David Higham Agency agreed to take on the setting up and management of a Kindle version and POD facility themselves. *Queen of a Distant Hive* (2017) was produced and has gathered positive reviews – not least from fellow historical writers. I sense that there is more interest in the Anglo-Saxon period now and I have discovered a good community of support out there, especially from those writing in a similar genre. Bloggers invite me to appear as their guest and provide reviews – Annie Whitehead (http://anniewhiteheadauthor.co.uk), Helen Hollick (https://discoveringdiamonds.blogspot.com) and Carla Nayland (http://carlanayland.blogspot.com) are three active examples.

I haven't entirely given up on traditional children's publishing and am working on a YA novel set in Victorian Whitby. At the age of 72 my ambitions are modest. I have a small pension, a supportive husband and a loyal agent – it's a privileged position to be in. I'm grateful simply to be able to sit down at my computer and still spend a few magical hours in Narnia – or any other time or place that I fancy.

**Theresa Tomlinson** is known for her YA and children's historical novels, particularly those set on the north-east coast of England. Her books include *The Flither Pickers* (1987), *Summer Witches* (1991), and five *Time Slip* adventures including the republication of *Meet Me By the Steelmen* (Award Publications Ltd 2019), which was followed by a sequel, *Forged in Steel* (Award Publications Ltd 2020), shortlisted for the 2021 Sheffield Children's Book Award. Under her own imprint, The Old Print Workshop, she published her latest novel, *Dark Fortune* (2021), and in 2022 republished the *Forestwife* trilogy – *The Forestwife, Child of the May* and *Path of the She-Wolf*. Theresa's other books include the *Troy and the Warrior Women* series – *The Moon Riders* (2002) and *The Voyage of the Snake Lady* (2004). Theresa has been shortlisted twice for the Carnegie Medal and for the Sheffield Children's Book Award. For more information and Theresa's blog, see www.theresatomlinson.com.

# How to write a picture book

Tessa Strickland highlights the enduring value of picture books, both educational and emotional, for young children in today's world, and offers advice for writers wishing to engage in the child's world on the process, practices, qualities and skills they will need to succeed.

A picture book is a child's first theatre. It's likely to be the first time a child experiences the drama of storytelling as the spoken word, accompanied by glorious illustration and skilful design. As on a theatre stage, several disciplines come together. The result is an art form whose impact on the imagination can extend well beyond childhood. I remain inspired by my favourite childhood picture books, among them Golden MacDonald's evocative Hebridean story *The Little Island* (Doubleday 1946), Kay Thompson's badass heroine *Eloise* (Simon & Schuster 1955) and Barbara Cooney's Caldecott-winning 1959 version of *Chanticleer and the Fox* (Crowell 1958). Decades later, the picture books that were my own children's favourites still take pride of place on the shelves of my family library.

Picture books are not just about entertainment: they play a crucial role in establishing basic literacy skills, emotional intelligence, acquisition of language, appetite for learning and enjoyment of art. Of course, the child is not reading the text, it is being read to her. But as she listens, she knows that the adult reader is decoding those curious black marks that run along the page. She knows too that these marks, these words, are the key to what is happening in the illustrations. So, the heart of the picture book is this marriage between the text and the illustration – each depends on the other.

## Where to start

The starting point is the story. Picture books are short (publishers typically require a text of less than 1,000 words), so it's dangerously easy to think that they are easy to write. In fact, the opposite is the case. Writing a picture book presents the same challenges as writing a poem. Your aim is to achieve a sense of balance and harmony between the story as music and as meaning. Small children will experience the storytelling as sound first, sense later. As long as the sound of the language is congruent with its meaning, they will happily let themselves be carried along by the emotional momentum of the narrative.

If you want to have a go at picture book writing, it is a very good idea to spend dedicated time with children under five. You may have children of your own; you may teach in an early-years setting; you may simply like the idea of storytelling for this enthusiastic and receptive age group. Consider volunteering to read aloud at your local preschool, primary school or library. This will help you to get a sense of what stories the children enjoy listening to AND what kind of stories you most enjoy telling. Notice what the children are doing and saying when they play (children come into the world knowing instinctively that play is work. This is how they learn, and their interactions reveal their major interests and preoccupations).

As well as engaging with the child's world, try to remember what you felt like as a child. Get these feelings into your storytelling. This will make your writing authentic. Children see straight through sentimentality, yet an alarming number of adults shy away from the intensities and terrors of childhood and try to sugar-coat it. This won't work.

## Practice and peer groups

Write as often as you can. If it's not possible for you to write every day (for many of us, it isn't), then choose at least a couple of hours a week and make this your personal, uninterruptable writing time. Writing is a craft and, like any craft, the more you practise, the better you get. Look for a supportive writing group – the excellent Society of Children's Book Writers & Illustrators (see page 305) has many local chapters and there are also all kinds of courses online and masterclasses at literature festivals (see *Children's writing courses and conferences*, page 392). Peer support groups can be transformative and you will learn a lot, not only about your potential as a writer but also about how to give and receive feedback. Very few of us can write to please everyone. So, like any professional writer, one of your challenges will be how to decide what to retain because you instinctively believe that it works, and what to revise or discard based on other people's feedback.

## Finding your thread

Aristotle was right when he said that a story needs a beginning, a middle and an end. When you have an idea for a story, you may be surprised by how difficult it is to start, to get a beginning that really *is* a beginning.

Once you *have* started, it can be tricky to tell the story you thought you were going to tell. Don't worry! This is a good sign. Writing is a creative act. Your characters may well take on lives of their own and decide they are going to get up to all kinds of antics you had not predicted. Be prepared to fool around for a good many drafts, to get to know the characters you are writing about, to give them a back story. The back story won't necessarily appear on the page, but by creating it you will ground your narrative and make it more convincing than it would otherwise be.

Some writers start with their characters and go from there. What ages are they? What are their strengths and weaknesses, likes and dislikes? What do they need or crave? Try writing about two strongly contrasting characters: exaggerate their traits and explore the different ways in which they communicate. You may surprise yourself, and if you do this in a group, you will be fascinated by the different ways in which this one-to-one exchange can be unpacked.

Other writers prefer to start with a situation and then decide who they are going to conjure up to resolve it. This is also a sound strategy and every good story needs a problem. If your characters live in a trouble-free dream world or a happy-ever-after hedgerow, your readers are going to be bored and unconvinced, because life is not like this. So, to engage your young audience, you need a situation which quickly becomes problematic. Then you need a way of resolving the problem that is transformative for your main character. The problem may be internal (for example, your character may be afraid of something) or it may be external (for example, a storm is coming). And you may well find that solving one problem leads to another ... learning how to find your thread AND hold onto it will require you to redraft and redraft.

## Staying true to life

The infant's journey from birth to the age of five is the most formative in its entire life. As babies grow into toddlers and then into children, they live among giants, with adults and perhaps older siblings, looming above them and exerting tremendous power. This is why stories about larger-than-life characters resonate so powerfully in young children's minds.

There is something of a trend in contemporary children's publishing to avoid scaring children. In my view, this is a mistake. Fear and rage, pain and sorrow are as familiar to children as cornflakes at breakfast. They are often scared or infuriated and by hearing stories in which scary things happen and are successfully dealt with, they learn that there are ways of navigating and mastering their feelings. Often, successful children's writers tackle these feelings through symbol and metaphor; territory in which most children are naturally at ease.

## Using humour

One of the most valuable resources in the picture book writer's toolkit is humour. It is like medicine, and it can take many forms: it may be dry; it may be quiet; it may be outrageous. Understatement can go a long way with children. By contrast, irony and sarcasm tend to be too sophisticated for little ones. So, if you are using humour, keep it straightforward. It can be tempting, as the writer, to introduce layers of tongue-in-cheek humour that are evident to the adult, who is also, after all, the one who is likely to have paid for the book in the first place, and this can be wonderful. Just be careful that it is not at the expense of the child for whom you are writing.

## Writing in verse

Aspiring writers can find themselves utterly bewildered by conflicting advice about whether or not to write in verse. My experience both as a publisher and as a writer is that verse is hugely popular. However, it's a common misperception among beginners that verse means no more than having a rhyme scheme. To write in verse, you need to have an ear for metre and for the relationship between metre, tone and meaning. The rhyme is secondary. It is certainly valuable in all kinds of ways – children and adults alike take enormous pleasure in guessing and remembering the word that completes a rhyming couplet, and unexpected rhymes are particularly delightful. But without a convincing metre, verse becomes flat-footed. If you want to write in verse, read and decode the masters, and be prepared to do a lot of re-writing to get it right. One false note will kill your endeavour.

## Going to market

You have been diligently writing for a year or two and you now have three or four manuscripts you are happy with. It is time to gird your loins and pitch your work to an agent or a publisher. It is certainly not essential to have an agent, but if you do go this route, a good agent will know what different publishers are looking for and be able to negotiate terms on your behalf. Also, the UK children's publishing industry is a small world. Agents who do well on behalf of their clients do so because they keep up to date on changing trends and know who is looking for what.

You don't need to find an illustrator; the publisher will do this. You just need to have a selection of short manuscripts that are skilfully crafted, that surprise and delight the editor who will read them first and that show you have a distinctive voice. Before you make your submissions, check what is on the market and make sure someone else hasn't already had your idea (you will be surprised by how often this happens). Check the agent's or publisher's website, so that you have a sense of what kind of taste they have and what their successes are.

Be professional. Follow the agent's or publisher's submission guidelines and keep your cover letter brief. You will not help your cause by saying that your children or grandchildren love your writing. Of course they do, but they are not the ones taking the commercial risk.

Persist. Many of the most successful picture book writers have endured years of rejection. They have succeeded not only because they are talented but also because they have been prepared to work very hard and to persevere.

## The international picture book market

Picture books are expensive to develop. This is one of the reasons why only a few new picture books appear on UK publishers' lists each year. The expense of sourcing and commissioning artwork, then paying for full-colour origination and printing, quickly runs well into five figures. To recover this investment, UK publishers typically seek out publishing partners overseas, from the USA to China. Economies of scale mean that the more copies a publisher prints, the lower the unit cost. Because the UK market is a small one, publishers here usually seek to sell co-edition licences to as many partners as possible before they go to press.

This process takes time. So, do not give up your day job! The period between having your manuscript accepted and seeing it in the world as a printed book can be anything between one and three years.

## Picture books in a changing world

The coronavirus lockdown era is now, thankfully, behind us. But we live in a world that has changed immeasurably. It's still too early fully to assess the impact of the pandemic on children, but many primary school teachers in this country report that their young charges have less vocabulary and more fear of the wider world than pre-pandemic children. This can't come as a surprise. Lockdown took away the chance for preschool and older children to gain the social skills which would otherwise have come to them naturally. Play is at the heart of learning for little ones and, for many, the experience of playing with peers dwindled to near-oblivion. As well as the effects of the pandemic, we are all grappling with the implications of climate crisis, war in Europe and economic instability. So where do picture books fit into this era of unprecedented challenges?

Well, not everything is doom and gloom. In 2021, sales of picture books exceeded sales of children's fiction for the first time. This says a lot about the sound instincts of parents, teachers and other caregivers. It's as if adults with children in their care just know in their bones that, by sharing picture books with children, they can create a multi-sensory learning environment where the child feels safe, cared for and, we hope, entranced by the book they are helping to hold and the words and pictures that are unfolding before them. There is now a surge in demand from picture book editors for new manuscripts. And there are some interesting emergent trends: for books which could almost be called self-help; for texts that sit in the opaque area between fiction and non-fiction; and for stories that challenge cultural stereotypes. The perennial childhood themes – funny stories, bedtime stories, fairy tales, aliens, journeys east of the sun and west of the moon – remain in demand. But alongside them on the shelves of bookshops and libraries sit new picture books on nature and wildlife, on homelessness, and on moving ... not just to a new house but to a new continent. Picture books, like other genres, reflect our times – now, perhaps, more than ever.

**Tessa Strickland** is the co-founder and advisory editor of independent children's publisher Barefoot Books. As Stella Blackstone, she has written many internationally acclaimed picture books. Her writing has been translated into over 30 languages. Tessa's latest picture book, *The Mystery of the Golden Feather*, was published in May 2023 by Dorling Kindersley. For details of her courses for picture book writers, contact her at tessa@challiscombe.com.

# Writing short stories for children

Julia Green describes the power and the pleasure of a well-written children's short story, and its essential attributes. She encourages aspiring short story writers to read, study, practice, experiment and aim high.

Primary School. I'm maybe eight or nine. We're reading a short story in class, from an ancient hardback collection of stories and poems illustrated with line drawings, with a faded blue and green cover. I can't remember the title of the anthology, but I do remember one story, about a lonely man making sand sculptures on the beach – Weymouth, in my memory. And the atmosphere – slightly melancholy, a sense of loss, the way that I often felt as a child when it was time to leave the beach – the tide coming in, late afternoon, the beach emptying out. The man walks away, the sea washes in and erases the sculptures… Later on, aged 13 or 14, in an English lesson we read Ted Hughes' short story *The Rain Horse*, which is all atmosphere – a field, the rain, the threatening horse, a young man's sense of terror.

Why have these particular short stories stayed in my mind over so many years, out of all the others we read as children? Perhaps it's the strong sense of place, the use of vivid detail to create a landscape and a moment in time through the appeal to all the senses. And a strong *feeling*: sadness, sense of loss, fear. It's partly in what is *not said*; an effective short story doesn't waste words. It leaves a space for the reader to imagine, to fill in the gaps. We enter into the story world, stay a short time, and leave again – but as a reader, we're left with the sense that something has changed forever. We've glimpsed something, felt something, of lasting significance. The short story as 'an arrow in flight', as the Irish writer Mary Lavin described it.

We are talking here about **the short story as a form in itself**; not a short book for children, like a picture book, or an illustrated story for young children which is short in length but is in essence a short novel – though much of what I am saying here would apply to these forms of story, too. And we are thinking of the **audience** as children aged from about four, when a child might be listening to the story being read aloud rather than reading for themselves, to about 12. Publishers and booksellers classify readers older than that as 'teen' or 'young adult' rather than children. It is helpful for a new writer to be aware of this. Writing for a four- or five-year-old is obviously very different from writing for someone of 9-12 years. Think about how appropriate the theme or experiences and emotions in your story would be for the age group you want to write for. Alternatively, first write the story you want to write, and *then* think about that question of audience. The problem for many new or unpublished writers is a mismatch between the style/language/content of the story and the age and interest of the 'audience': the child reader. Of course there are many notable exceptions to this, but as a *beginner writer* it's helpful to think about making the age of your main character just a little older than the age of your readers. You will need to be aware of the language and style, too, to make it appropriate for the intended audience.

If you want to write short stories for children, the important thing, of course, is to *read* many! Immerse yourself in the form. You might reread stories you enjoyed as a child, to re-experience them with your adult 'writer' mind, namely reading as-a-writer, alert to the way the story has been written. Examine closely: 1) the language, the way words and sentences work, how much or little description there is, how dialogue is used, how much or how little 'action' or 'plot'; 2) the pace (how quickly do things move along?); 3) what the story is actually 'about'; 4) the form of the short story, studying this is the best way of learning how to do it yourself (not so that you write in exactly the same way – we can only ever write authentically as ourselves – but to help you think about the different options open to you, and the tools of your trade). Make notes for yourself in a notebook.

Read contemporary short stories for children, too, to see what is being published now. Fashions change. Haunt bookshops and libraries. Look at anthologies of short stories published for children, such as *Moonlight Magic* (Stripes 2016) or *My Kind of School* (A&C Black 2008), edited by Tony Bradman; collections for different age groups, such as *The Puffin Book of Stories for Five-Year-Olds* (Penguin 1996) edited by Wendy Cooling, or *Funny Stories for 5-Year-Olds* (Pan Macmillan 2016), edited by Helen Paiba. These contain stories by different writers, new and old.

Read collections of short stories by individual authors, too. These are usually by established authors (it is very rare for a brand-new writer to have a collection of stories accepted for publication):

• Nicola Davies' *Up on the Hill* (Walker 2008) consists of three separate short stories about children who live in the country.
• Michael Morpurgo wrote a memorable collection, published as *The White Horse of Zennor and other stories* (Mammoth 1982).
• Leila Berg's wonderful *Little Pete Stories* (Methuen) for very young children written in the 1950s were groundbreaking in their time for the way she showed 'real' children, feeling strong emotions including anger.
• Emma Carroll's *When We Were Warriors* (Faber 2019) contains three short stories linked to her popular historical novels for children.
• David Almond's collection *Counting Stars* (Hodder Children's 2000) illustrates the richness of the short story form in the hands of a master storyteller. These layered, rich, strange and beautiful stories are based on his childhood in Felling in the North-East of England and transcend the usual publishing boundaries of 'age groups'. Almond wrote them before he wrote the prize-winning *Skellig* (Hodder Children's 1998), but they weren't published until after he was established as a successful novelist for young people.

Read these stories and then, as a 'writing exercise' in your writing notebook (of course you have one of these!), take real incidents or experiences from your own childhood as the material for a short story, so as to get in touch with the real, raw emotions of childhood and to help you find an authentic voice in your writing. (Note: this might end up as a short story '*about* childhood' as distinct from a story '*for* children', two subtly different things.)

One of the great satisfactions of writing a short story is that sense of having the complete story in your hand, so you can 'see' it all at once, with its beautiful, honed shape. You can polish and perfect it, and learn much that will help you with all your writing, particularly about precision and brevity, voice and tone, and about the significance of endings. Aim high. Only the very best writing is good enough for children.

As children's writers, we have other things to consider as well as mastery of the short form. A contemporary short story for children is likely to be commissioned by an editor, via an agent, on a particular theme, to be published alongside other stories by other writers on that same theme. For example, I have been asked to write stories about children and animals suitable for several 'winter' anthologies, about the experience of primary school and on the theme of friendship for children of primary school age (up to age 11). The challenge is to write a story that will be original and different enough from the others in the collection, that will appeal to the age group, be accessible, reflect the diversity of the world we live in and be enjoyable and engaging. The story needs to feel complete, to give the reader that satisfaction of a happy (or happy/hopeful *enough*) ending. It needs to take the reader into its world and introduce the main character (in my case always a child) swiftly and immersively, and to do this within a word limit (in these examples, 1500 words).

So, like a novel but in very condensed form, the story has to establish a character, a setting and a situation. It must take the reader on some kind of 'journey' with ups and downs, as the character does things (takes certain actions) to try to resolve the 'situation' (problem/issue). And then it must swiftly reach an ending – in such a way that the situation you established at the beginning is either resolved or changed in some way. You might ask yourself these questions: What does my character want? What do they DO, to try to get it? How does it all work out? (Do they get what they wanted ... or something else, unexpected?)

In a story for children, it is usually a good idea to put the child at the centre of the action, to make them ACTIVE (rather than passive, having things done TO them). **Write from the child's perspective**. Find a voice that feels fresh and authentic and contemporary. Experiment with first person or close-up third person as a way of bringing your child reader close to the action. Children want to immerse themselves in the story.

I write realistic stories, but a short story might be in any genre: fantasy, science fiction, supernatural, funny, historical. It can be a good way to **try out something new**, in terms of style or genre, before committing to a longer project. And some ideas just come as 'short'; you know that's the form they need to take. After I'd written a commissioned short story about a girl and a seal pup, I went on to write a novel, *Seal Island* (OUP 2014). The short story had led me into a longer story in a similar setting with a similar central character, but with more incidents, more characters, more developed themes and the longer time-frame that a novel allows.

When we are learning, nothing we write is ever wasted, whether it gets published or not. We write first and foremost for ourselves. **Practising the short story form will improve all your writing.** There are short story competitions which can give you the benefit of a deadline, and sometimes a subject or theme, too. Having the constraints of a word count can be strangely liberating. Set yourself a deadline, a word count, and a subject, and see what magic happens. The mind plays games. A character will arrive, and a place – all stories have to happen somewhere – and before you know it, the story will start to emerge. Keep asking questions: *What if…? Supposing she….* Write it, one word, one sentence at a time. Write the first draft, fast. Then – cut, cut, cut! Polish. Make it beautiful. Make it the best story it can be. Write the story only *you* can write.

**Julia Green** is the author of more than 20 novels and short stories for young people. She is Emeritus Professor in Writing for Young People at Bath Spa University and founded the MA Writing for Young People, which has launched the careers of more than 65 writers for children and young adults. Her most recent novels for children are *The House of Light* (2019) and *The Children of Swallow Fell* (2020), both published by OUP Children's, and a picture book *The Boy Who Sailed the World* (David Fickling Books 2022). She is currently writing a collection of short stories and a new novel for young people. For more information see www.julia-green.co.uk.

# Writing magic into fiction

Kiran Millwood Hargrave recommends the techniques she uses to feed and inspire her magical stories, and guides us through each stage of the process that allows a writer's fantastical ideas to come to fruition.

All fiction is a kind of magic: a conjuring. From your imagination, you are building whole people, whole worlds, making them so vivid and tangible your reader will be able to touch them, see them, wish they lived in your stories – but how do you layer magic upon magic and introduce a fantastical strand to your story? Perhaps you call it fabulism, perhaps magical realism, perhaps fantasy. They are all branches of the same enchanted tree, and here are my experiences of reading – and rooting my own stories in – magic.

## Roots

My earliest love was the *His Dark Materials* trilogy by Philip Pullman. Read first when I was ten, much of it admittedly flew over my head, but I didn't mind because *how* it flew! Like witches on yew twigs, like swan daemons swirling, like angels stirring the clouds. I believe we all have 'books of power', as I term them, often discovered when we are young, that are keystones for the sort of stories we wish to write.

When I look at my own 'books of power', they largely fall into what I used to call magical realism. This was incorrect, as I've recently learned magical realism refers to those writing in the South American tradition, which addresses issues of colonialism. The better term is fabulism. Alongside Pullman's epic trilogy are: *Skellig* by David Almond, the *Chrestomanci* books by Diana Wynne Jones, *The Wolves of Willoughby Chase* by Joan Aiken, *Journey to the River Sea* by Eva Ibbotson and the ubiquitous *Harry Potter* series by J.K. Rowling. All hold very different, varying systems and approaches to 'magic', and often my first task when writing a novel is to decide where I want my book to sit within that spectrum. My debut, *The Girl of Ink & Stars* (Chicken House 2016), plunges into fully-fledged fantasy; my second novel, *The Island at the End of Everything* (2017) finds magic in nature, and my third, *The Way Past Winter* (2018), is folkloric in its telling and so sits on the border of fabulism.

My first challenge to you is to ask: what are your 'books of power'? Do they tell you about the sort of books you love, and give you an insight, as I believe, into the sort of books you should probably be writing? Some of you will be fantasy fans, while others may prefer that world to be recognisable but knocked slightly ajar to let some magic in. I like to keep my 'books of power' on my desk throughout my current writing project (the books change from project to project). It's an excellent procrastination exercise, but also an inspiring one.

## Shoots

Your books of power are on your desk; perhaps you're listening to a film soundtrack (Enya is my writing jam); maybe you have a scented candle wafting snatches of 'Mystical Forest' towards you – and now you're ready to write. It's all possibility … like new shoots of green life emerging in spring. Some of you will plunge straight in, others will plan your narrative to within an inch of its life, but as a self-confessed 'pantser' (as in by-the-seat-of-your-pants vs 'planner') I wholly condone the former. There is nothing more exciting to me than plunging into the adventure alongside your characters and, as they take on more life, letting them make the decisions.

That said, I started my writing life as a poet; a bit of structure has always helped me and I give this to myself in the form of a map. This piece of advice is probably most useful to those of you writing a quest narrative – something where the characters travel through landscape – but I've also worked on maps of houses, or schools or streets. As soon as the perimeters of the places your characters will inhabit are solid, your imagination can run wild. Often these places also help to define the sort of magic you'll encounter in your world: if it's rife with mountains and dragons, you're probably reaching for an alternate universe, the rules of which you get to decide; if it's a secret door in an otherwise ordinary garden, you've got a beautiful set-up for fabulism. But my main advice at this stage is not to worry about labelling *what* sort of magic you're choosing. Let your story tell you what will work.

When I say 'draw a map', it does not need to be a work of art. My map for *The Girl of Ink & Stars* was a clumsily drawn circle with childish landmarks, with the routes of my characters plotted through the landscape in different colours for each. The plan for *The Way Past Winter* was even more basic: a house, some trees, some mountains, the sea and an arrow pointing 'North'. Think of it as storyboarding, as they do for films. You have your whole story on one piece of paper – and you can always rip it up and start again.

## Rings

I can only speak to describe my own experience of writing – and everyone is different – but I like to charge through my first draft, full pelt towards the conclusion. This results in very short, fast-paced first drafts, but it means that the fear of the blank page is conquered. Something is easier to improve than nothing, so I would encourage you to write your first draft quickly, too. Then, the real work begins.

A tree grows rings as it ages, and so too will your story. These next drafts are for firming up its core, and finding the confidence to set down more firmly what you perhaps only gestured at in first drafts. I would argue this is not the time for brutal editing. Rather, luxuriate in bringing your story more fully into being. If you've written a fantasy, full of mermaids and talking animals, give them their back stories. If you've written in magical objects that transport your character into parallel worlds, think about how they feel, smell, look, where they came from. Put in all those details you would want as a reader: colour your world in. Check that your characters' names suit them and the world they inhabit. Research any asides that observant readers will appreciate and think how clever you are. Enjoy playing around, giving credence to ideas that may not quite be working, but that you think *could* – with just one more draft (or three).

This stage takes the longest for me, but it is also the most fun. It's when I experiment and learn the most about myself as a writer, and about what I want this story to do, and what I want a reader to take from it.

## Branches

This next stage may appear to be misleadingly titled, as it implies growth when actually it's very likely that your manuscript will shrink – but editing really *is* like growing branches; it's also a little bit about hacking off the weaker ones.

As a reformed poet, editing holds a special place in my heart. I love it, because finally I know what my story is, and editing will help me get it there. But I know not everyone shares my enthusiasm for hacking at sentences or scenes that took weeks/months/years to write. So my advice to you is this: look at it as *giving* your story something, not taking something away. Only by editing can you find the sub-plots worth growing, and those that need pruning. Only by editing can you find the heart of your story, and make it sing.

## Buds

Now you're ready to submit (I hugely dislike this word: when I was on 'submission' to agents I made a spreadsheet to keep track of where/when/who and my husband changed all the headings to things like 'date soul delivered' to denote when I sent out the manuscript, and 'poop or not poop?' to indicate whether I got a full request or a meeting/rejection ... humour helps!). Speaking from experience, the waiting is possibly the worst bit of all. Even when you're waiting to hear from, and often being rejected by, publishers, at least you and your agent are in it together. So hang in there, and give yourself the best possible chance of success by taking special care when choosing which agents you send to.

I made a list from the *Children's Writers' & Artists' Yearbook* and thoroughly researched this shortlist, breaking it into a top-tier I wanted to send to first, and then a second to help me get straight back on the horse if those initial queries bore no fruit. Look at those who represent the writers of your 'books of power', and pop them on the list too. Aim high. I did, and I ended up with my first choice of agent. But there was something I did not do right, and that I would urge you to do – that is to classify what exactly I had written.

I've mentioned that one of my 'books of power' was *His Dark Materials* by Philip Pullman, but another was *One Hundred Years of Solitude* by Gabriel Garcia Marquez and a third was *The Border Trilogy* by Cormac McCarthy. If that sounds like a confused list, it was, and it made for a confused manuscript. Fraught with long descriptions of landscape, and far too much pathetic fallacy, I wasn't sure what I had written. This showed in my query letter, which announced *The Girl of Ink & Stars* (then *The Cartographer's Daughter*) as a 'magical-realist YA/crossover adventure story'... Yes, I really did write all that down, and press 'send'. Luckily, my wonderful agent saw past it, but you can help yourself enormously by really pinning down what sort of book you've written. This is the only point at which this really matters, I would argue. Until you send your book to agents, just follow your instincts and write in whatever way your story needs you to write it. Once you have an agent, they can help you nail down what exactly you've written. We sent *The Girl of Ink & Stars* out as an adventure story and let the fantasy element come as a surprise.

That's why I've called this section 'buds' – it's about making your story look as appealing as possible, making it impossible for them *not* to want to represent you, and showing that you really know what you're talking about and are taking this seriously. So, finesse what you call your book. Perhaps it's a 'YA coming-of-age story with magic', like Harry Potter, or a 'fast-paced action adventure story' like Percy Jackson. Comparisons to other successful books on the market are always a good idea, but you should highlight how your book differentiates itself too.

Know that you are not alone in your fear and trepidation ... or your big dreams. I look forward to reading your no-doubt magical stories.

**Kiran Millwood Hargrave** is an award-winning writer and poet. Her children's books include *The Girl of Ink & Stars* (2016), winner of the British Book Awards Children's Book of the Year and the Waterstones Children's Book Prize 2017; Costa and Blue Peter Book shortlisted *The Island at the End of Everything* (2017); *The Way Past Winter* (2018), winner of Blackwell's Children's Book of the Year 2018; and *A Secret of Birds & Bone* (2020), which was a Waterstones, *Guardian,* and Big Issue Book of the Year (all published by Chicken House). *Julia and the Shark* (Hachette Children's Group 2021), illustrated by Tom de Freston, won the Waterstones Children's Gift of the Year 2021. YA Book Prize shortlisted and Carnegie longlisted *The Deathless Girls* (Hachette Children's 2019) was her debut for YA readers. For adults, she has written the *Sunday Times* bestselling *The Mercies* (Picador 2020) and *The Dance Tree* (Picador 2022). For more information see www.kiranmillwoodhargrave.com. Follow her on Twitter @Kiran_MH.

**Books**

# Reinventing old stories for new readers

Deirdre Sullivan shares her fascination for retellings of fairy tales and the possibilities that arise from looking with fresh eyes at these stories, reworking their age-old power to inspire, influence and connect with young adult readers.

I think we all remember the first stories that spoke to us – however we encountered them, from the mouths of teachers or caregivers or by ourselves. Different voices speak to different readers, and Hans Christian Andersen's *The Little Mermaid* and Oscar Wilde's *The Nightingale and the Rose* spoke to me. I had learned to expect a 'happily ever after', in the way we all do, so these melancholy stories defied my expectations and lodged themselves in my heart, like a shard of the Devil's mirror.

In college I was introduced to the work of Jack Zipes and his anthology, *Don't Bet On The Prince* (Gower 1987) by a friend (to whom the book is dedicated), and I became acquainted with a greater breadth of fairy-tale retellings, in female voices. I had encountered feminist fairy tales before (a small Irish publisher, Attic Press, had published a children's series of these that I used to hunt for in libraries and secondhand bookshops), but revisiting them at the tail end of my adolescence was as potent as a poisoned comb to the skull. Fairy tales have always had what Marina Warner calls a 'suspect whiff of femininity', but I had been raised on stories told by men. Soon I was discovering Madame Leprince de Beaumont and Dortchen Wild. Female tellers had been there all along, it seemed, if you only took the care to look more closely. From then on, fairy-tale motifs wound themselves through my writing, both subtly and explicitly. I became hungry for more fairy-tale retellings, and devoured stories by the likes of Emma Donoghue, Robin McKinley, Neil Gaiman, Aimee Bender, Francesca Lia Block, Isabel Allende and Margaret Atwood.

In the summer of 2015 my publisher, Little Island, approached me about publishing a collection of my fairy-tale retellings. I was instantly excited about it. It felt right. I dusted off some old stories and began work on some new ones. As the collection progressed, though, I ended up writing 12 brand-new retellings, to ensure the themes and voice felt uniform. It wasn't a hardship. When I write, I feel like I am in conversation with myself and with the stories I have been told about the world around me. I run my hands over their edges, and I try to notice new details I am drawn to. I write what I know, but also what I fear and what I love.

*Tangleweed and Brine* (Little Island 2017) is a book that centres the female experience of the world within the fairy-tale realm. I wanted to write about bodies, and how terrifying and messy they can be. I wanted to talk about being a woman in a society built by and for men. I wanted to talk about fear, but also anger. I wanted to write about the lessons that the world teaches girls, drip by drip or all at once. I was 12 when the last Magdalene laundry closed, and until 2018, I had lived my whole life in the shadow of the eighth amendment. My country was structured in a way that let me know, that let us all know – over and over again – how little women's lives mattered. That casts a shadow, and when I began to piece together the stories for the collection it was largely women in the shadows I was drawn to

– women with bodies that didn't fit societal expectations, women used as pawns for political gain, women who try to find the right thing in a wrong world. It is a sad book, and an angry book, but there are moments of freedom there as well.

… Because there is a witchcraft to being female. From the whisper networks to tampons slipped underneath a cubicle by some kind hand, we find support in each other. There's a shared struggle that binds us. And no one knows that more than a teenage girl. Adolescence can be a very dangerous and lonely place, but there is a power in it, too, an alchemy: changing bodies, fluctuating emotions, the dawning realisations; it's a heady time, and an intense one. It's that mixture of dependence and independence, of forging your own path and being guided along the one envisioned for you. It is a time in my life I remember sharply, and a time that will continue to inspire me. I facilitate creative writing workshops for teenagers, and they are incisive and passionate readers who can enjoy books while recognising their faults. Recently someone asked me when I would write a book 'for adults'; this happens every now and then and is generally framed as a compliment. I brush it off quietly, saying things like 'Oh, you never know', but I'm fairly sure I do know. I write for young adults because I want to, and for the same reason that I tell the stories I do – because they inspire me.

I'm aware that *Tangleweed and Brine* came out at an opportune moment. There was something of a fairy-tale zeitgeist in the air, as well as increased discussion of feminism with the #MeToo movement started by Tarana Burke gaining traction in 2017, when the book had just been published. People, and young people in particular, were becoming increasingly comfortable confronting and unpacking previously unspoken things, looking at the way the world worked and articulating why that wasn't good enough. Whispers were becoming shouts. And my book was not alone – around that time Melissa Albert, Sarah Henning, Louise O'Neill and Daniel Lavery also had books out that reworked or built on old stories and turned them into something of their own. There was something in the air that made writers look at the tales they had been told and hold them up to the light with fresh eyes. And each of us saw something different and built something that was our own from that. There may be a lot of talk about trends in YA but we are all living in the same world; we experience a lot of similar things, consume a lot of the same media, hear the same news headlines. The same inspiration can take two people on very different journeys … I love that.

My advice for someone who wants to rewrite fairy tales would be to be aware of what is out there – to read and reread to give you a sense of what can be done and has been done. Then to listen to yourself. In tarot readings, there are the prescribed meanings of the cards, but sometimes a reader will find themselves drawn to a detail or a symbol; they may not know why, but something about it calls to them. That sense of moving away from what a story is supposed to be towards what it could become for you in this moment – that little, precious space is inspiration. And it's worth worrying at those details like a dog, until you've chewed it into something that's yours alone. With old stories, the more familiar people are with them, the more of a shorthand you can use; a shoe, a wolf, an apple becomes symbolic. Whatever world you put it into, the old story will be humming underneath like a familiar tune. The reader will sense it pulling at them, making them remember when it first spoke to them and all the ways it has spoken to them since. When you retell a fairy tale, you are invoking something very old and very powerful; there's a responsibility to get it right, but a satisfaction when something clicks.

I had two big 'clicks' of this kind when writing *Tangleweed and Brine*. One of them came from years of trying and the other came to me in a dream. The second way was far easier, but I think the first was more satisfying. I had put a lot of 'Little Mermaids' into the collection at first, as it's a story I'm drawn to time and time again. As someone who feels like they spend a lot of time on the outside wondering how people work, I found the mermaid character spoke to me. I grew up beside the ocean, and the tang of salt air was never far away when I was small. The story of *The Little Mermaid* brought me my first sad ending and my first Disney princess, and both of those left small dents on my heart. I had to cull a fair few mermaids as I drafted *Tangleweed and Brine*, but I remember sitting in a café thinking that I could just have my mermaid kill the prince and return to the ocean, and feeling so happy for her. I'm not normally in favour of murder, but I wanted that little tongueless girl – who'd walked on glass for love – to choose herself. And so, in my story, I asked her to do that – and she did. The child I was when I first encountered that story wouldn't have been fond of it ending in a stabbing, but it made sense for me to follow the path not taken in the Andersen story ... and to send my mermaid home. The second magic click came with *Bluebeard*. I didn't know what to do; I'd written what was turning into a tender little love story, but the fairy tale demanded a roomful of murdered wives and I just didn't think the *Bluebeard* I had written would do that (#notallbluebeards). I worried and wondered about it for ages, tweaking other stories while I did (one of my favourite things to do when I get blocked on a project is to start something else, even a ridiculous thing; it provides the distance you need to stand back and see what must be done to set things right). It took a dream to point me in the right direction. I woke up with an image seared into my brain: a room full of dead men. And that gave me the key I needed to unlock my version of the story, where the secret is not the things that Bluebeard has done, but who he is and what he has survived.

I care a lot about these old stories. I have tried to inhabit them respectfully, but my experience is only one experience, and that's not enough for such an intricate world. The stories we tell matter. They can and should change. Your voices matter. I look forward to the next retelling and the next one – the same old story, through a different lens, a different heart.

**Deirdre Sullivan** is an award-winning writer and teacher from Galway. She has written eight acclaimed books for young adults, including *Savage Her Reply* (Little Island 2020), *Perfectly Preventable Deaths* (Hot Key Books 2019), and *Tangleweed and Brine* (Little Island 2017), as well as a collection of short fiction for adult readers, *I Want to Know That I Will Be Okay* (Banshee 2021). Her latest book, *Weave* (Skein Press 2022), is a collaborative work with Oein Debhairduin and Yingge Xu, which again draws on folklore and legend, this time to explore the Wheel of the Year.

# Journey to publication: the summit is worth the climb

M.G. Leonard shares the obstacles she faced on her journey to publication, how she overcame them and what she learnt about the requirements for middle-grade novels along the way.

To me, the feat of becoming a published author was as daunting as climbing Mount Everest … people say they want to do it but the odds of getting to the top are slim and the probability of getting hurt is high. Few people try and even fewer succeed.

Stage One of my ascent was to have the idea for my book – and it crawled into my brain on six legs with an exoskeleton and two pairs of wings. My story was going to be about beetles, an ecological entomological adventure, and so I enthusiastically began researching the bugs – which I thought would take a couple of weeks but actually took six years, because there are over 400,000 known species of beetle and I hadn't known that.

Stage Two was to write the book. During this time, I bought the *Writers' & Artists' Yearbook* and put it on a shelf beside my desk. I would flick through the pages inhaling the smell of an industry I longed to be a part of. Foolishly, I didn't read it. Including false starts and real-life obstacles to creativity, like getting divorced and being a single working mum, it took me four years to complete a draft of my manuscript.

Finally, I was moving to Stage Three of the climb – getting an agent! I'd fantasised about finding my literary best friend, the Clyde to my Bonnie, who would belay for me on the toughest part of the ascent – submitting to publishers. But then I got the fear. What if I sent my book to every single agent in the *Writers' & Artists' Yearbook* and they all hated it? I would crash to earth, a failure (cue sad music). I chose procrastination as my avoidance technique: I took the *Yearbook* and went through every agent, putting the ones I thought looked good (all of them) into a spreadsheet; I typed out all their details into columns (there was absolutely no need to do this), including their submission preferences. Then one day I'd completed my long list of possible agents … there was nothing else I could do other than submit.

At this point, I must confess that I presumed my book about a 13-year-old boy and a sentient giant rhinoceros beetle was for adult readers. I have no defence for this other than I thought: I am an adult, the story came out of my brain, so it must be for adults. As you might guess from this assumption, I hadn't got a clue about how the publishing industry worked. Despite spending a large percentage of my life in libraries and bookshops, I hadn't considered the categories books are sorted into or where my story might fit amongst them. I hadn't thought about what happened after you got an agent. I figured my agent would tell me that. This was an error.

I submitted to four agents on my list. Three rejected me with no feedback. I added a column to my spreadsheet in which to put insults about agents who rejected me. The fourth agent asked for the full manuscript and I sent all 120,000 words of it to them, only to receive a swift reply telling me my book was middle grade (I didn't know what this meant) and that they only represented adult fiction and YA (I didn't know what this meant either). They informed me a middle-grade debut shouldn't exceed 60,000 words and politely suggested I do some market research and edit my book accordingly.

I fell to the ground with a sickening thud. But I'm not a quitter, and a year later, on maternity leave, I began submitting again. This time I'd bought a copy of the *Children's Writers' & Artists' Yearbook* and focused my attention on understanding the rock face I was climbing. I read the whole book, cover to cover, learning about the business and drawing courage from author essays about their journey to publication. It's rare to find a book that's as useful as it is inspiring, but this book is essential reading for aspiring children's authors. Equipped with new knowledge, I began my second ascent, able to see the hand- and footholds that others had used before me.

Once again, I submitted to four agents; once again, three of them rejected me. One said a book on beetles wouldn't sell. Another was rude about my protagonist. I was rude about both of them in my spreadsheet. However, I took on board the agent's concerns about my protagonist and revised my opening chapters. The fourth agent requested my full manuscript. I submitted my 60,000-word book, with a more likeable protagonist, and held my breath … Eventually, I was rewarded with a real-life phone call! Unfortunately, I had a six-month-old baby, so it went to voicemail.

I can still remember repeatedly listening to that voicemail. It was surreal, like getting a message from the other side. The agent said they liked my beetle book and that I could write, but that the manuscript needed work; it had a flabby fourth act and a problematic ending. They told me to call the Golden Egg Academy. This was not the news I'd been hoping for, but it was a crevice into which I could insert my fingers and heave myself a little further up the mountainside. At the Golden Egg Academy, I discovered I'd written a middle-grade book with a YA ending and got a lesson in story structure. I edited my book again. Finally, I had a manuscript fit for submission, and the Golden Egg Academy helped me find both my agent and my first publishing deal.

My journey to publication would have been easier and quicker if I'd read the *Children's Writers' & Artists' Yearbook* before I began my epic climb, but I got here in the end. So, dear climber, put this book in your backpack and don't just smell it, read it from cover to cover. Heed the advice you're given, only be rude in spreadsheets, and don't give up. See you at the top.

**M.G. Leonard** is the bestselling, award-winning writer of children's books *Beetle Boy* (2016), *Beetle Queen* (2017) and *Battle of the Beetles* (2018), published by Chicken House, the *Adventures on Trains* series with Sam Sedgman (Macmillan Children's 2019-22) and *The Twitchers* series (Walker Books 2021–4). Her books have been translated into over 40 languages and *Beetle Boy* is being developed as a live-action series for TV. *Beetle Boy* won the Branford Boase Award (2017), and was shortlisted for the Waterstones Children's Book Award and longlisted for the Carnegie Medal. *The Highland Falcon Thief* (Macmillan Children's 2020), the first in the *Adventures on Trains* series, won the Books Are My Bag Readers Award 2020 for Children's Fiction and the Children's Fiction Book of the Year 2021 in the British Book Awards. The series has won international awards and been nominated for two Edgar Awards. *Twitch* (Walker Books 2021), the first in *The Twitchers series*, won the Sainsbury's Fiction Children's Book Award in 2021 and was nominated for the Carnegie Medal. She wrote the much acclaimed *The Ice Children* for Audible's 2022 Christmas title. Find out more at www.mgleonard.com and follow M.G. on Twitter @MGLnrd.

# Plotting and pace in your middle-grade adventure

Christopher Edge understands the highs and lows, twists and turns that are needed to hold the attention of middle-grade fiction readers with a thirst for adventure. Here he shares valuable advice on how to structure a plot and drive forward an emotionally engaging storyline that has all the essential elements.

'Adventure is just bad planning.' So said the great Norwegian explorer, Roald Amundsen, who was the first man to reach both the North and South poles but who, as far as I know, never wrote a single word of children's fiction – so I really wouldn't go listening to him when it comes to planning your middle-grade adventure.

But what is a 'middle-grade adventure'? Well, the first part is easy to define, as middle grade is the term the publishing industry uses to describe novels for children aged 9–12. Now, I'm a subscriber to C.S. Lewis's dictum that the best children's books which can be enjoyed at the age of ten are equally worth reading at the age of 50 and beyond, so when we talk about middle-grade we're definitely not talking about fiction that is any way middle-of-the-road or second-rate. These are the stories that can shape young readers' lives, opening doors into new realities, allowing them to escape into other lives, and inspiring them to step boldly forward to mark their own place in the world. And as for adventure, I'd argue it's not so much a genre but more an attitude that's woven into the fabric of children's fiction. Whether it's fantasy, mystery, historical, contemporary, science fiction or even comedy, from Lewis Carroll's *Alice's Adventures in Wonderland* (Macmillan 1865) to *Rowley Jefferson's Awesome Friendly Adventure* by Jeff Kinney (Penguin Random House 2020), the drumbeat of adventure can always be heard as we turn the pages of the novels we find on the bookshelves labelled 'Fiction 9–12'.

This is certainly true of my own fiction. I find it difficult to pin the stories I write down to a single genre, but adventure is an 'ever-present'; from *The Many Worlds of Albie Bright* (Nosy Crow 2016) where Albie climbs inside a cardboard box to travel to parallel universes in search of his mum, to *The Infinite Lives of Maisie Day* (Nosy Crow 2018) where Maisie's adventures are contained within the four walls of her home after the universe outside her front door disappears. In children's fiction there are no hard-and-fast rules about where adventure can be found and, in stories such as *The Longest Night of Charlie Noon* (Nosy Crow 2019) which begins, 'Once upon a time, three kids got lost in the woods', I've enjoyed twisting familiar tropes into unexpected new shapes. But why do readers of middle-grade fiction have such a thirst for adventure? In surveys about children's reading habits, such as Scholastic's biennial *Kids & Family Reading Report*, children aged 9–12 respond that they want books that have characters that look like them; this reaffirms the need for all readers to find themselves represented in the fiction they read, but also that they want characters they wish they could be like because they're smart or strong or brave. So this thirst for adventure could be viewed as a form of wish fulfilment, as young readers seek out stories in which they can see idealised reflections of themselves, placed in exciting and dangerous situations. For these readers, reading can be role-play, their identification with the heroes and heroines of middle-grade fiction offering them a vicarious agency they might not be able to find in their everyday lives.

I think another reason why such a rich thread of adventure runs through middle-grade fiction can be found in the world-view of its readers. Still shaping their understanding of the world around them, these are curious readers who read with fearless eyes. Their tastes aren't fixed in the same way that an adult readers often are. This isn't a jaded audience, but it is an audience with high expectations who will only keep turning the pages of a story if it delivers on its promise of adventure. So how can you craft a middle-grade adventure that will keep these readers turning the pages? The first thing to consider is plot. Now plot is just another name for story – it's the sequence of events that take place in a narrative. And the plotting stage is where you decide exactly what these events will be and the best way to structure them. This is a stage of writing that I love. For me, stories rarely land in my brain fully formed. The initial spark of inspiration might arrive in the form of a character, a situation, or a setting. For *The Infinite Lives of Maisie Day*, I had an image of a girl opening her front door to find an infinite darkness outside. Like any spark of inspiration, this image initially existed in what Russell T. Davies dubs 'the quantum state of Maybe' – with seemingly infinite possibilities it could spawn in terms of the story sparking in and out of existence inside my mind. Through a process of asking questions, researching ideas, and making connections, I started to shape these possibilities into a definitive storyline.

But how could I be sure that the plot I was building was taking the right shape? Lots of theories about story structure come from the world of film. From the three-act structure of set-up, confrontation and resolution, with key scenes that tip the story from one act to the next, to mythic structures such as the 'Hero's Journey' where a protagonist heeds a call to adventure, faces tests, trials and challenges before seizing their reward, screenwriting formulas seemingly offer a short cut to crafting the perfect plot. However, I must admit I don't consciously hold any theories like these in the front of my mind when plotting my adventures. For me, the plot always grows from character or, more accurately, plot and character grow together.

Stories are about change and change is driven by character. Examining your protagonist's motives can help you to build your plot, as you consider the actions they might pursue as they try to attain their goal. In *The Many Worlds of Albie Bright*, the motive that spurs Albie to set out on his adventure is his desire to see his mum again, with this goal fuelling his creation of the Quantum Banana Theory – the invention that enables him to travel into parallel worlds. Handily, this universe-hopping device also gave me a skeleton structure for the story, as Albie journeys through these alternate universes in search of the one where his mum is still alive. Now if your protagonist achieves their primary goal straight away, there's not much of a story – so you need to think about what's going to stand in their way. This could be an antagonist whose own motives and goals place them in conflict with your protagonist. In every adventure there needs to be obstacles, complications and confrontations which your protagonist has to navigate to get closer to their goal. Some scenes might shine brightest in your mind at this point, but thinking about the cause-and-effect of these key moments can trigger ideas for other scenes and help you start to sequence these into a coherent plot. I sometimes draw a flow chart to plot the action of the story – this helps me to visualise the links between different events and keep track of how characters develop.

Every scene should have a purpose that drives the plot forward; deciding what this is can help you to focus on the details that matter when you start writing. Begin each scene as far into the action as possible and as soon as the purpose is achieved that should be your signal to end the scene. Each scene should contain the seeds of the next and, as the story moves forward, you want to keep raising the stakes – but you also need to vary the rhythm of the story so that it doesn't become predictable for the reader. Think about the rhythm you want to create, perhaps balancing action-packed scenes with quieter moments of description and dialogue that slow the narrative pace and give the reader a chance to catch their breath.

Now every adventure must come to an end. Some authors only discover the ending of a story through the act of writing it, but I usually find mine before I even write the very first line. At the outset I have a clear picture in my mind of the opening scene and also the climax of the story, with these two moments tracing the emotional arc of my protagonist's adventure. In *The Many Worlds of Albie Bright*, Albie's journeys through different parallel worlds show him the alternative lives he could have lived, and these experiences change Albie and help him to come to an understanding of what he's really searching for as the story reaches its climax. An adventure isn't just an action-packed sequence of events but an emotional journey too, as characters make discoveries, find out things about themselves, and are changed by their experiences.

Writing itself can be an adventure, so don't be afraid to follow your own path. There will be trials and challenges along the way, and you may even feel lost at times as you hack through the thickets of a first draft – but always try to take pleasure in the journey. And when you make it to the end, the reward you find can be greater than any treasure hoard: it's the sight of a young reader turning the pages of your story, their eyes shining with excitement as they escape into a world of adventure.

**Christopher Edge** is an award-winning author whose novels for children include *Twelve Minutes to Midnight* (2012), *The Many Worlds of Albie Bright* (2016), *The Jamie Drake Equation* (2017), *The Infinite Lives of Maisie Day* (2018), *The Longest Night of Charlie Noon* (2019), all published by Nosy Crow, and *Space Oddity* (Chicken House 2021). His latest novel is the bestselling *Escape Room* (Nosy Crow 2022). He is also the author of guides to creative writing for children and teenagers, *How to Write Your Best Story Ever!* (OUP 2015) and *How To Be A Young #Writer* (OUP 2017), and works as a freelance publishing and education consultant. For more information see his website www.christopheredge.co.uk. Follow him on Twitter @edgechristopher.

## See also...
• *Writing mystery and adventure stories*, page 154

# Writing real characters into fiction

Elle McNicoll explores what is meant by describing fictional characters as 'real', a quality that is achieved through 'the exposure of the human condition within an imagined story' in a truthful and relatable way. She relates her experience as a neurodivergent author and how her authentic, lived experience is portrayed in her fiction, and asks other writers to examine their own truth as authors.

As an author, I'm not entirely settled upon what 'real' means anymore. In children's publishing, writing 'real characters' may refer to an author choosing to write contemporary fiction, with characters whose fictional world – or rather the one that the author feels they inhabit – greatly resembles our own and there are no fantastical elements involved. That's not on my résumé.

So why have I been asked to write about creating 'real characters'? Sometimes this refers to an author who chooses to use historic events and people as a stimulus for their story. Perhaps their children's novel is set aboard the Titanic, or maybe it uses WWII as a background. Patience Agbabi brilliantly incorporated Samuel Johnson into her fabulous trilogy for children, *The Leap Cycle* (Canongate Books 2020–23). That is not on my résumé, either. I have not written gritty, realistic novels, nor have I used historical figures as members of my ensemble cast. Both are noble pursuits, but they have not been mine. So again, why have I been asked to write about 'real characters'? It's because I'm neurodivergent and my fiction is unapologetically so. Every author is different, and every author has their own point of view. It's why we read. Books are windows into other people's minds, a way to view how fellow travellers see the world. No literary window looks out onto the exact same landscape as another, so every author brings individuality.

With that disclaimer out of the way, let me say that some viewpoints are promoted more than others. Some writers are considered the default, while the rest of us are treated as charming novelties. A writer with a neurodevelopmental disability, for example, will be asked to talk about their personal life, and even their trauma, far more than their work. Your book may win every literary prize, won on literary merit and awarded by your peers and readers, but the press will only ever want to hear about which parts are 'true' and which are 'made up'. I'm a bestselling, award-winning children's author, with a CBBC adaptation of my debut novel (*A Kind of Spark*; Knights Of 2020) which was described as 'ground-breaking', but I'm mostly asked about my darkest moments. I'm asked about my diagnosis, something that every neurodivergent person should be allowed to hold close to them. I'm asked about how my brain works in comparison to my neurotypical peers, who make up the majority (but not all) of the publishing industry. My neurotypical colleagues on panels answer questions about character development and plot structure. I'm asked to explain why children who are like me deserve to be in stories. I'm asked about what is 'real'.

If you are reading this, we are peers or perhaps even colleagues. I won't presume to tell you how to write, how to publish, how to illustrate. But I am here to tell you that there is no such thing as 'real' in what I do. I use my authentic, lived experience to portray neurodiversity in my books, that is true. Perhaps that is as real as anything *can* be in a children's story. I hope so. I'm heartened and moved by the many letters I receive from readers saying, 'Addie is just like me!' or 'Cora is like me at school'. Good writing, like great acting, needs the truth. A great story is an imagined circumstance, narrated authentically. I don't necessarily believe in the maxim 'Write what you know' – unless we're discussing marginalised people.

So many neurotypical writers have had a go at writing about my brain. I woke up one day and decided it was time *I* actually tried it. And it felt very exposing. Telling all my secrets about dancing hands, heightened senses, masking and processing difficulties. Bad handwriting, social exclusion and the sky falling over things others don't even see. It was vulnerable. It was frightening. But it was truthful. It was, I suppose, real.

It was one candid nettle in a garden of fictional flowers.

But why does the industry insist on treating majority writers like authors and marginalised writers like biographers? We are imaginers, too – perhaps more than anyone; I'll return to that later. It is the truthful and relatable aspects of any fictional character that makes them 'real', not the life of the author. Othello is real to us because his jealousy is something that has spiralled out of control, but it comes from a place that many of us own in our hidden hearts. We love Anne Shirley of L.M. Montgomery's *Anne of Green Gables* (L.C. Page & Co. 1908) because we have all, at some point, wished our hair were a different colour or our face another face. Jo March is not real. In the literal sense. But, to millions, she is real in the soul. Her ambition, her bluster, her clumsy manners. Her yearning for something more.

It is the exposure of the human condition within an imagined story that makes characters 'real' – the vulnerable and brave choice of the author to say, 'I see the world like this. Perhaps people like this exist? Perhaps a world like this is real to you, as it is to me. Or maybe we could make it.'

Every story, no matter the trimmings, asks: 'What am I? Who am I when the light goes out?'. A checklist or a cheat sheet cannot accomplish this kind of portrayal, and it will not connect with the reader. An expert on birds will never truly know what it feels like to fly. So, what is your truth as an author? Not your past, not your biography, but your *truth*? The truth is not synonymous with fact when it comes to storytelling.

So I'll ask again: What is your truth? What do you know to be true? Or believe to be true? What is your point of view? I could have written a novel containing the facts of my life. I could have written a memoir disguised as a children's story. Instead, I plucked a hidden, painful handful of truth dust from my ribs and scattered it onto the page, alongside plenty of imagination. Readers are archaeologists. They can always find and connect with the truth and the 'real' parts … if they're really looking. I wrote about a young witch who could see through the supernatural veil of an ancient city, but what made her real to people was her struggle in school. Her stubbornness. Her pride. Her learning difficulty and her refusal to let people shame her for it. The truth, as I know it.

You can write about the most magical, the most impossible. In children's fiction, there is no impossible. But if you want people to connect with your fiction, add a little of your truth. And again – remember that the truth, in stories, is not objective. I write books where children who have been historically oppressed and miscounted are the heroines: I know that can be true.

I write about characters who learn about their own prejudice and prove in their actions that people can change and grow and make the world a more encouraging place: I know that will be true.

I write about worlds that can be changed by these incredible children and the courage they inspire in others. I write about things that may not have happened but that, in telling them, I can reach through the pages and show young readers they are not alone, they can chart the course. They can decide the path. I can give them permission to be brave: I know that is true.

None of it is real. As a storyteller, I'm not interested in real. I'm tired of remembering things that were real. I'm interested in the truth. And you should be, too. Only in telling the truth in our stories can we create something real for the reader. Our humanity, our fingerprint, our unique view on the human condition and our fellow passengers to the end of the story – that is the only thing that can make your writing 'real'.

**Elle McNicoll** is a bestselling and award-winning Scottish children's author, currently living in North London. Her debut novel, *A Kind of Spark* (Knights Of 2020) won the Blue Peter Book Award and the Waterstones Children's Book Prize. Her second novel, *Show Us Who You Are* (Knights Of 2021) was one of *The Bookseller*'s Best Books of 2021. Her third book, *Like a Charm*, was published in 2022 and its sequel, *Like a Curse*, in February 2023. Elle is also co-writer for the *A Kind of Spark* CBBC series. Neurodivergent herself, Elle is an advocate for better representation of neurodiversity and disability in publishing and the media; she founded the Adrien Prize, to recognise children's fiction that explores the disability experience. For more information see https://ellemcnicoll.com.

# Creating your cast of characters

Aisling Fowler considers the power of fictional characters to engage young readers, and gives advice on how to know and develop your characters fully, in a way that draws readers with them on an emotional journey.

The breadth of children's literature is enormous, but no matter what type of book a child loves to read, one thing remains constant: it's the characters that take our young readers by the hand to lead them through the story. Authors hope that their fictional characters will engage a reader emotionally, compelling them to devour chapter after chapter. But how, as writers, can we create characters who feel *real* enough to do this? I think there are two parts to this: 1) not to think of your characters purely as made-up creations, but as people just as real as anyone you might know – with all the depth, complexity and con-tradictions that go along with that; 2) getting to know those characters inside out, so their authenticity sings off the page when you write them.

In my case, it was the main character of the *Fireborn* series (HarperCollins 2021-), Twelve, who was the first spark of the story for me. She sprang into my imagination with her axes in hand and full of a fiery anger that took me by surprise. She immediately felt strong – but getting to know her thoroughly took a while. I started by asking her questions such as: Why are you so angry? Where is your family? What are those axes for? Through this, Twelve's personality, back story, and many features of the fantastical world of Ember pulled into focus.

When I started writing my first draft, I thought I knew Twelve well. But by the end she was vastly different – not purely because of the journey she'd been on, but also because I'd got to know her better through the act of writing her story. She was no longer abstract; I'd seen her in a variety of situations and discovered her responses to different characters. She felt more complete, more authentic, more three-dimensional. I was delighted – until I realised this meant rewriting how she was portrayed earlier in the book.

For some of us, perhaps those who lean more towards being 'pantsers' (seat-of-the-pants types) than plotters, this is how we ultimately get to know our main characters: we write them and discover them on the page. For those more organised individuals who want to have a clearer idea before they begin, though, there are a multitude of possible methods. You could interview your character, or write test scenes – which is particularly useful, in my opinion, for working out group dynamics. How about reading your char-acter's horoscope, writing diary entries for them, or even giving them the Myers–Briggs personality test? Your imagination is the limit here … anything goes. This will all help you discover your character's strengths and weaknesses, their personality and backstory. But to identify what truly drives them, their goals and motivations for behaving the way they do, you will have to go even deeper, and ask trickier questions: What do they want most? Or even, what do they *think* they want but what do they *actually* want? What do they need (whether acknowledged by them or otherwise)?

Once you've achieved this deep knowledge of your main character, it's time to start thinking about their story arc through your book. How will their experiences change them? How will they grow? This might be immediately obvious or take some careful thought, but your character's emotional journey is every bit as important as their physical one. It's worth thinking about it in conjunction with your plot to make sure these two crucial aspects of the story are working together to draw your reader ever onwards. In *Fireborn*, Twelve is haunted by her past, tormented by the guilt of what happened to her family and obsessed with thoughts of revenge. I knew almost immediately that her arc needed to be a journey towards acceptance and self-forgiveness, one that would allow her to open up enough to allow friendship to blossom. In a way, her entire quest to rescue a kidnapped girl is a vehicle which lets that emotional shift take place in her. Many of the decisions I made about the plot were informed by how Twelve would react and whether that reaction moved her closer to or further from the goals of greater inner peace and friendship.

I can't think of many children's books (or any?) where there is a single, solitary character. At some point, you'll need to consider the wider cast, those sidekicks who'll be beside your main character on their journey. It's definitely worth getting to know these secondary characters just as well as you know your protagonist. Ideally, each of them needs to feel entirely distinct, with their own desires and story arcs through the book – these might end up being important sub-plots. As you did for your main character, identify their personalities and back story as well as their goals and motivations. Ask yourself how they differ from the main character and from each other. What sets each character apart?

In any group, real or imagined, there are usually complex dynamics at play. The chances are that this is true in your story too. Does everyone get on equally well, or are some closer than others? Does anyone feel left out? Do your characters bring out the best in each other, or the worst? Does one of them compensate for a lack of a particular trait in another? These are things worth thinking about carefully and I'll illustrate this with a couple of examples from *Fireborn*. Twelve has almost-impenetrable defensive walls around herself and is very prickly towards the other characters. I wanted the story to end with her having made friends, but it was very clear to me that Twelve herself would not be building any bridges. That meant I needed at least one of the other characters to be both kind and persistent enough to do that for her. These ended up being key traits in a secondary human character called Six. Another example involves Twelve's pet squirrel, Widge. I was worried that, because of those walls I mentioned, a reader would find Twelve unlikeable. I wanted to show there was more to her than raw anger. The solution came through Widge, who at the start of the story is her only friend. Early on, it's only through him that we see a different, softer side to Twelve. As he was a non-human character, I didn't feel I was compromising the coherency of Twelve's determination to remain alone – he's a squirrel: different rules apply than to the human characters.

In both examples, the sidekicks are compensating for flaws in my main character, working under cover to make her more relatable, while also (hopefully) staking their own claim on the reader's affections. It's important to remember that, with each new character, there's another chance to engage your young reader – another opportunity for them to find something they relate to, something that speaks to them and makes them care about your characters on a deeper, emotional level. It's this that can make a story utterly compelling. We can probably all think of a book that kept us up way past our bedtime, one that we couldn't stop reading because we had to know what happened to the characters we cared about so much. But, as writers, how do we invite this degree of connection? My take on it is this: we can like a character for their strengths and admire them for their triumphs, but to *love* them, to root for them with every fibre of your being, to cry for them, you need to see their vulnerabilities, their fears, their moments of weakness and the way they face adversity. Almost inevitably, this means putting them in difficult situations. Although this article is about creating characters, don't forget that it's your plot which showcases them. The two things can (and perhaps should) develop in tangent. Don't be afraid to think something like: 'My character is brave – how can I use the story to show this?'

Let's take a step back. You now have your cast of characters and you know each of them well. It's time to consider how they can be portrayed clearly on the page. Remember that, particularly in the early chapters, their every word and action should be reinforcing who they are, drawing a clear, defined picture in your reader's mind. Consider what you know about each character: how will those things affect the way they speak, the language they choose to use? What about the way they dress, or their attitude towards others? Perhaps even the names you choose for them can help show who they are. This doesn't mean your characters can't have hidden depths, or behave surprisingly, but you need coherence in terms of who you know they are and the journey they're on, both individually and together. From the very first page, you want every character – but especially your main character – to feel as three-dimensional as possible.

In early drafts of *Fireborn*, I found differentiating subsidiary characters difficult. This was because I didn't know them well enough and needed to spend more time with them one-on-one. Later, to make each one feel more unique, I gave them habits or quirks unique to them. For example, one of my characters has a stutter, another constantly uses 'obviously' in his sentences, Twelve bites her lip when she's nervous, and Widge nibbles her hair. These are small things, but if you choose the traits carefully in a way that is authentic to the character, they can act as a shorthand which builds a clearer picture for your reader.

Creating believable characters is at the very heart of what we do as writers for children. Through your characters, young readers will experience ways of thinking and living that are different to their own – and perhaps, through that lens, they'll make more sense of their own lives and beliefs. Maybe your characters will even encourage young readers to question the world around them, show them that they can make a difference, empower them to be the people they want to be. The characters *you* create can do this. So, create them with love, don't be afraid of making them deep or complex and, above all, enjoy the process.

**Aisling Fowler** is the author of *Fireborn: Twelve and the Frozen Forest* (HarperCollins 2021), her debut novel. *Fireborn: Phoenix and the Frost Palace*, the second book in her middle-grade fantasy trilogy, was published in spring 2023. Aisling worked as a support worker and then as a nurse, before rediscovering her childhood love of writing. Follow her on Twitter @fowler_aisling and Instagram @aislingfowler.

# Writing mystery and adventure stories

H.L. Dennis shares her own imaginative method of creating and refining a story, and bringing adventures and emotions fully to the page, using the structure and inspiration of a film-maker's craft.

I'm going to tell you a secret. I'm not a writer at all ... actually, I'm the Chief Executive of my very own Imagination Headquarters. It's a game I play, and it makes writing such an adventure that I'm going to let you in on the mystery of how it works. Not everyone will like this method, but you just might ... so I hope you'll enjoy it too.

I've never been to film school – but being the Ceo of Imagination HQ is like being an entire studio working on a film. After all, a good book plays like a film inside our heads. We watch as characters experience triumph and despair, happiness and pain. And, if the story is a good one, we feel those emotions too. That's my aim: to generate emotion in the reader, to make them laugh, gasp or cry. I want readers to feel, to believe, to remember. I hope they'll adventure with me, racing through the pages of my story as the mystery unfolds.

So now let me show you how it works – in Imagination HQ – as I try to achieve this.

## Time for popcorn ...

It begins with the 'popcorn stage'. This is a time that fuels my spirit – when I'm reminded of the power of good stories. I watch film and TV avidly, re-watching sections, trying to understand the storyteller's craft. I analyse moments when I'm on the edge of my seat, and I break down scenes where I'm sobbing or screaming at the screen. I try to establish exactly how the lighting, music and camera angles make me feel. Then I use exactly the same close analysis on my favourite books; I reread extracts over and over, in precisely the same analytical way. I immerse myself in adventures and mysteries well told. Only then am I ready to start work myself.

## Stage One: Development

**1. Find the theme** – First of all, your story needs to get the 'green light'. You must know why this story needs telling and why it's you who needs to tell it. The theme is the light that guides all the decisions later. It's why the story is emotionally significant. Your job isn't to preach, but to explore a theme that matters to you

My series *Secret Breakers* (Hodder Children's 2012-) was about children's hidden potential. Working as a teacher at the time, I was concerned about how education rated some skills more highly than others. You, too, need to find an area that fascinates, angers, worries or intrigues you. Find something that makes you *feel*; this will become the 'why' that lights your way.

**2. Choose your story world** – In *Secret Breakers* I wanted to celebrate the abilities of children to do more than adults thought possible. The world of code-cracking was a perfect fit. You might choose to explore the theme of fairness, for example, through the world of sport or science, theatre or space travel. So find a world where you can explore your theme. Ground your adventure in this particular, chosen world.

**3. Prepare the trailer** – Film trailers pare back films to their basic elements. Trailers give us a sense of the story's 'palette'. They prepare us for high octane, thrilling action or quiet, sinister mystery. We know what to expect because trailers sell us emotions the film promises to deliver. Your adventure could be created in a range of different tones, so establish the emotional impact you want by analysing film trailers. Then attempt to write a basic summary of a story, noting what you want the reader to feel as they read.

## Stage Two: Pre-production

**1. Select your locations** – If you can set your story anywhere – real or imagined – be purposeful and selective about every single location you use. In my *River of Ink* series (Hodder Children's 2017-) I explored the theme of what makes a life worth living. I chose the world of alchemy to do this and, as the elixir of life was central to this theme, I focused on river locations for my adventure. You need to make every location work to support the story. Choose contrasting locations, intriguing locations, locations that will provoke emotion! Work as a 'location scout', visiting places you can't visit in reality – via guidebooks or the internet.

**2. Cast the characters** – We care about stories because we care about characters. Make sure you rigorously audition every member of your cast, to be certain they're worthy of screen time. The hero of an adventure becomes such after she is tested and because of the difficult choices she makes. We must feel for the characters – even the villains. Make us cheer on an underdog, empathise with the lost soul, root for the character who is scared just like us.

You need characters who give elements of contrast to your theme. In *River of Ink*, a girl with a life ruled by schedules would learn the value of spontaneity. Characters must change as a result of their adventures, so think about how you'd like your character to be in the final stage of your story, then work backwards to create your character at the beginning. Audition a cast of contrasting characters and show us what they're truly like, through their actions and interactions, decision-making and discoveries.

*I like to set up Pinterest boards at this stage – with pictures of locations, sketches of characters and quotes that support my theme. This helps create a sense of tone and sets me up for the more technical stages ahead.

## Stage Three: Production

**1. Prepare the shooting schedule** – You can now begin to sketch out the major arc of an adventure. Think about: an inciting incident; times of crisis when all hope seems lost; then the ultimate life-changing climax. Why is the mystery your characters are trying to solve so important? What obstacles are in the way? What is there to gain or lose? Just as you didn't settle for mediocre locations or cast, make sure the stakes are as big as possible, as meaningful as they can be and the most likely to provoke emotion. We need our characters to be scared about losing everything in order for the adventure to mean everything to us.

**2. Compose the storyboard** – By this I don't mean a drawn storyboard (although this might be just your thing); take the schedule and break it into scenes. It's important, particularly in mysteries, to work out what needs to be revealed when and in what order. You might also have an idea about some key set pieces, and indeed the finale which you're working towards. I envisioned one particular scene, at the end of *Secret Breakers* Book Six, before I ever wrote the words 'Book One: Chapter One'. I was always striving towards this culmination of the adventure – a point when the characters were at their most desperate, and the risk of making the wrong decision the most intense. I could see the weather in the scene, and even hear the musical soundtrack in my head. Here my characters' emotions were at their most raw (and hopefully the reader's would be too!).

The big reveal of the mystery must be worth the pay-off, so give the finale a massive amount of your time, energy and thought. Your ending must deliver all the emotional punch you planned from the trailer stage. Be sure to build anticipation as your storyboard develops; keep the adventure moving, the characters changing, and the stakes increasing.

**3. Rehearse the scenes** – Now I've worked out the gist of what will happen in each scene and, finally, I get to rehearse. A film director might shoot the same scene many times – you can too.

Don't offer your reader your first thoughts about how to show that scene. Try lots of different ways of 'staging' it. For this, I find the 'record card' system really satisfying: on record cards, jot down how variations of each scene could look. Experiment by changing camera angles and focusing on one character more than others or elevating one emotion over another. Try different ways of revealing character through dialogue and actions. The aim of these rehearsals is to choose a version of the scene that will best generate the suspense, worry, fear or elation in the reader you hoped for. Don't settle. Be the director who demands the ultimate take.

**4. Make a rough cut** – By this stage I've worked through all the angst of how best to show something; I've built up tension by heightening anticipation; I've put characters through the very worst situations they (or I) could imagine. So now I cut together the ultimate version of each scene and begin to type them out in a document labelled 'My Book'. This is my Director's Cut – and now it's ready for editing.

## Stage Four: Post-production

**1. Add effects** – Every single scene must be worthy of the reader's time. So I cut, I tighten, I search for the most powerful phrase, the truest character reaction, the most poignant beat to build emotion. You can speed up shots or change the lighting to get closer to the characters and show their emotions more clearly. It's fun to scrutinise every page, every paragraph and every sentence, to make sure it's the best it can be.

**2. Check continuity** – Now I ask whether the whole thing hangs together as one seamless piece. Does the internal logic of the whole adventure make sense? Does the mystery unfold without stuttering or confusing? It's time to ask if you've done everything you promised the reader you would. The record cards are packed away and it's time to focus on the whole story you've created, splicing together the joins so no-one can see the technicalities of your craft!

## Stage Five: Distribution

**Release** – This is it. You've created a story. You've written an adventure full of emotion, twists, turns and cliffhangers, which all build to the solution of your mystery and the emotional punch you guaranteed! Now, at last, it's time to grab your copy of the *Children's Writers' & Artists Yearbook* and – if you have any of those record cards left – use them to jot down a list of agents to approach. It's time to send your story out into the world to find its audience.

## Time for popcorn again

And now you wait ...

Remember though – some people might dislike my suggestions about how to create a story; some fear that such a technical approach might clutter the magic of creation. There's also a chance your story might not resonate with all who read it, but that is part of the adventure – the mystery of the power of words. I personally believe magic *can* come from design, emotion from knowing direction and a powerful story through purposeful attention to detail.

So, if at every stage of the operation of Imagination HQ you've worked hard and refused to settle for mediocre, then you need to relax now and trust in your process. You *will* find an audience. The right reader is waiting. Just enjoy another bowl of popcorn, while your story makes its way out into the world to find them.

**Helen Dennis** is the award-winning author of the *Secret Breakers* six-book series and the *River of Ink* quartet, both published by Hodder Children's Books. *Secret Breakers: The Knights of Neustria* (2013) was nominated for the Carnegie Medal and the series has been optioned for a live action TV series. *River of Ink: Genesis* was selected as a BookBuzz book by BookTrust 2016 and included in their Deaf Awareness Week Recommendation List 2019. Helen worked for 20 years as a junior school teacher before becoming a full-time writer. She has an MA in Creative Writing Education and the Arts from Sussex University. For more information see www.helendennisbooks.com and www.hldennis.com. Follow her on Twitter @HLDennisauthor.

# World-building in your fantasy fiction

L.D. Lapinski explores the creative art of world-building, with its imaginative potential and hidden depths, and has advice on how writers can bring their fantasy worlds, and the characters that navigate through them, to life in a way that engages and absorbs young readers.

World-building is such a strange and magical thing: using just your mind, you are bringing entire populations, places and universes almost to life. Creating a new reality that can feel as precious and vulnerable and enticing as the one we live and breathe in is a fantastic exercise, and one that – given how little we have been able to travel recently due to the global pandemic – seems increasingly tempting. The world you build is not an empty set; it can have as much character as your hero, or as much menace as your villain. The world you create takes your reader on a journey which can be as close to home or as far flung as you desire.

I have always created imaginary places and worlds. Reading and writing have been my creative escape for as long as I can remember (and possibly even further back than that), and I have very fond memories of spending a rainy holiday in a caravan hunched over, drawing a detailed map and plotting a vast history for 'The World of Bunny Rabbits'. The real world wasn't appealing right then, so I made my own. And I'm still doing it. My first novel for children 9+, *The Strangeworlds Travel Agency* (Orion Children's 2020), arrived in bookshops at the start of the pandemic and, though it was a very unexpected baptism, I hope it offered an escape to young readers looking for ways to get away from our world and into others.

However, simply hurling a new world at a reader does not a story make. Novels are, at their very heart, entertainment. The story needs to seize us by the wrist and drag us along a journey, not simply abandon us, mapless, in a new place with no sense of direction. Any world you create is there to work with and for your characters – it is a backdrop that you can change to fit and make the most impact in your story and, although your characters may navigate it with ease, the world they explore and tell the reader about still needs to be strong and 'real' enough to support their narrative journey. And this support is quite a literal concept when it comes to fantasy worlds!

Picture a penguin. Add the David Attenborough narration, if you like, as the camera pans back to reveal that the tiny penguin has hitched a ride on the top of an iceberg, and the iceberg drops deep into the depths below, far more of it below the waterline than above it. This iceberg, and the penguin, is your world-building. As you might expect, there is always so much more going on below the surface when writing fantasy books, but in this analogy what's really important for you to focus on isn't the iceberg at all. It's the penguin. As the writer, that tiny wee penguin is the amount of world-building you're actually going to have the space and words to include in your children's book. The iceberg above the surface is the amount and detail that you, your editor, and your agent will know. And, sadly, that huge mass below the surface is everything that not one other person will ever, ever, see. You might not even write it down.

Then surely we can get rid of it? Well, you could do. Take the iceberg away and the penguin would be able to swim for a bit. But it wouldn't be able to keep it up forever, and eventually it would get eaten by a sea leopard. The iceberg, even the unseen and unwritten part, protects and supports the penguin on its journey. In the same way, your characters and their journey could not carry on for very long without the supporting detail and facts of your world-building.

## Tell me again how a world should feel

In *The Strangeworlds Travel Agency* series so far, Flick and Jonathan have travelled to 14 different worlds in the space of two books. Hardly a great feat for them, given that there are 743 magical suitcase-portals in the travel agency, but certainly a challenge for me to keep a handle on when writing. Such a plethora of worlds could rapidly have felt overwhelming and difficult to keep track of, but – rather than begin an encyclopaedic collection of notes – I consciously crafted the worlds so that each one would appear distinct, without having to deep-dive into the history of each one, particularly since some of the characters' visits are rather fleeting.

I designed each individual world to evoke a specific emotional reaction from both the characters and the reader, and in such a way that each reaction would not be deliberately repeated. I created one world written to be deliberately frightening, another to be innocently joyful, one to be calm and soothing, and so on. In doing so, I was able both to show off the vast potential of *The Strangeworlds Travel Agency*'s magical suitcases, and to ensure that each of the worlds visited by the reader would be memorable. Even if the name of the place was forgotten, a younger reader might remember that one world was 'the scary one' and another 'the funny one', because they will relate to the world in the same way that Flick and Jonathan do. The characters' emotional reaction would be tied to the setting and what happened there, and will be mirrored by the reader, who wants to find out more and find out what will happen next.

## Fantasy rules! Okay...?

Who runs the world? Well, you do! The great thing about fantasy world rules is you get to make them up. And they can be as 'normal' or as outlandish as you like. They don't even have to serve a purpose beyond being entertaining! If everyone has to stand on their chair and shout 'WAHOOEY!' after eating, you can make that a rule. Perhaps this is never explained – and that's completely fine too. But how many of those rules you want to include is dependent on several factors: firstly and most importantly, your readers (and probably your characters) are children. Whether they are visiting this world for a brief visit like in *Strangeworlds*, or they live there full time, they are only going to focus on the aspects of their world that are the most pressing and interesting to them – the parts of their world that are driving their story, and their journey, forward. And if this element is shouting WAHOOEY, your characters might not bother mentioning the complex political systems of their world. Thinking again of the penguin atop the iceberg of world-building and how aware it may be about what's going on below it, remember that, however much you might know your fantasy world inside and out, your reader wants your characters to navigate the world you have built, not to read a travel guide about it.

Secondly, the amount of description you have space to include will always be restricted by the word count. There's nothing wrong with having enough world-building potential to fill a 500,000-word book, but editors and agents generally prefer shorter books (and it helps to keep printing costs down!). Tell readers what they need to know straight away, and use the rest of your imagined rules as iceberg-style unseen support for the story. It's still important, it's just out of sight.

**Books**

## Think fast!

Anyone familiar with video games will know that at the start of a game there is often a video, less than three minutes long, in which the world of gameplay is introduced – a few minutes of speedy world-building for games that can take dozens of hours to complete. I checked a few of these out, and on average an introductory video accounts for about 0.1% of total gameplay time. That's like doing all your introductory world-building in the space of a paragraph that takes up about one third of a page. That sounds pretty extreme, doesn't it?

Actually, no. A decent chunky paragraph at the start of a book can work extremely hard, just as the intro to a video game might. That initial chunk of world-building description introduces what sort of world this is, whether there's anything readers can recognise and relate to, whether there's magic or not, and it sets the scene for other, smaller bits of world-building which can be 'confettied' through the rest of the story. A first world-building paragraph has to be enticing; it may be the deciding factor as to whether someone carries on reading your book or not, having picked it up in a shop to browse through. The first impressions the reader of your fantasy world receives need to be rich, engaging … and brief. Readers should want, nay *need*, to know how your characters are going to navigate this wonderful or terrifying new place. They may even have an initial idea about the sort of problems they may encounter or the fun they might have. That early paragraph of world-building is advertising the journey your characters are about to go on; show off the best bits, and leave the details for later. And if, as in *The Strangeworlds Travel Agency*, the concept of your world is what you want to showcase rather than a description of a place, remember to hint at the richness of its potential but leave the reader hungry for more. Your character's journey is to get from A to B (whether this is physically or emotionally), but your reader's journey is to find out the details and to get thoroughly lost in your new world of fantasy and magic.

To be able to build a world for young readers to explore is a wonderful thing. Whether or not we can ever throw open the doors to our fantasy worlds completely, by writing them down at all we are inviting readers to wander within, to make up their own minds about the potential dangers or excitements – and inspiring them to create escapes of their own.

**L.D. Lapinski** is the author of *Jamie* (2023), and *The Strangeworlds Travel Agency* trilogy (2020–22), with an additional story, *Adventure in the Floating Mountain*, being selected as a 2023 World Book Day Book. They have an MA in Creative Writing from Nottingham Trent University, and are an ambassador for the National Literary Trust's Connecting Stories campaign. For more information see www.ldlapinski.com. Follow them on social media @ldlapinski.

## See also...

• *Writing magic into fiction*, page 136

# Dealing with tough issues in YA fiction

Holly Bourne shares advice for YA authors on how to deal with sensitive and difficult issues through fiction in a responsible, truthful and supportive way that provides 'a safe space for teenagers to explore the dark'.

The YA author has an undeniable influence on their readers, which is why it is vital that they write sensitively and responsibly. I believe that the right book given to a teenager at the right time can change – maybe even save – their life.

Puberty is a pretty ruthless stage in life; it is when weird things happen to your body, a time of first love and first heartache, of first-time sex, and maybe when bullying, loneliness, exam stress or mental illness cast a shadow over your life (75% of people who develop mental illness in their lifetime do so before the age of 18). In short, it is a period when you are grappling with your sense of identity, trying to figure out *who you are*. Being a teenager can be exhausting, exhilarating and terrifying, and I believe fiction can offer both refuge and respite during this time. The best stories don't only provide a gripping plot but also help young readers to make sense of their lives or to feel less alone.

As a YA writer, you must convey essential truths about the teen experience for your stories to have any hope of connecting with your readership. Teenagers are not naive about the hardships of their existence. I travel to schools all over the country to talk about books and mental health and I'm always blown away by how sensitive teenagers are to emerging social issues. There's not much darkness they're not already hugely aware of or personally wrestling with. They're hugely grateful to have books that shed light on the concerns that preoccupy them. Remember that teenagers are legally children and therefore, as a YA writer, you have a responsibility to tell the truth *safely*; you must ensure your story is truthful but not harmful. This delicate balancing act is something it can be tricky to get right.

Before I became a full-time author, I spent five years working as an advisor for young people at a charity called The Mix. This experience gave me a concrete understanding of teen issues and how to engage with young people about their problems within a rigorous safeguarding framework. This has provided me with an invaluable background to my fiction career, in which I feel able to tackle the darkest subject matter in a way I know is as safe for readers as possible. In my novels I've tackled suicide, self-harm, abusive relationships, rape and sexual assault, obsessive compulsive disorder, alcoholic and neglectful parents and many other 'tough issues'. If you research your topics intensively and remember any safeguarding training you have had and expert advice at all times, there are no limits to how dark you can go in your fiction. In fact, teenagers may be grateful that you have.

This safeguarding underpinning must be there at all times. Never let your writerly ego, or the thrill of writing the more dramatic bits on the page, seduce you away from your responsibility to provide a safe space for teenagers to explore the dark. Whatever issues you decide to tackle, you'll need to research them more vigorously than simply reading this article, but I hope the following guidelines will be a useful starting point. Now, where's the torch?

## Writing suicide safely

I'm starting at the very darkest of where the dark can go. That's because it's a hugely common theme running through YA books and one that can have literally fatal consequences if tackled insensitively. Unfortunately, many YA books that have handled this topic dangerously have gone on to achieve huge publishing success. Rather than making it a free-for-all, we need to learn lessons from this – educating ourselves and trying to do better. Any author who wants to explore this issue should research its copycat nature and how getting it wrong can cost someone's life. For instance, Google searches for 'how to commit suicide' rose by 26% after Netflix released the first season of *13 Reasons Why*.

Strong starting-points for research include the Samaritans guidance for covering suicide, as well as the World Health Organization's media guidelines for preventing suicide. Here are some of the most important guidelines:

### • Try not to include any detailed suicide methodology

Leave out any technical details about how a character may take their own life, such as how many pills to take, and never discuss the 'success rate' of any method. Never imply there's any quick or painless way of completing suicide.

### • Never show suicide as a solution to a problem

I once heard suicide described as 'a very permanent solution to a temporary problem.' Even if that is what's going on in a character's head, avoid glamorising the fatal notion that suicide is an 'answer' to life's hardships. Instead perhaps strive to show a character who overcomes this suicide idealisation, gets help and goes on to enjoy happiness. This is something I did in my novel *Are We All Lemmings and Snowflakes?* (Usborne Publishing 2018) which opened with my protagonist Olive in a suicidal state, but ended with her in a much better place. I was also careful to focus mostly on Olive's suicidal 'feelings' rather than showing her detailed thoughts.

### • Avoid giving characters who have completed suicide 'notoriety'

The element of notoriety that may result when someone takes their own life is something that can glamorise it and cause copycat behaviours, which young people are particularly susceptible to.

### • Suicide is never triggered by just one thing

It's is a hugely complicated behaviour, with no a + b = c formula behind it, so it's important not to give a reason 'why' a character was triggered to take their own life.

The right book can save someone's life. Suicide is certainly not a subject to avoid; just ensure you take the time and consideration to write about it safely – there can be catastrophic consequences if you don't.

## What is 'triggering'? And how to avoid it

Triggering is a word with a huge amount of misunderstanding and stigma attached to it. Currently we're seeing a backlash against so-called 'sensitive snowflakes' who demand 'trigger warnings' in art. To some extent it is true that you cannot produce any art that doesn't trigger someone, somewhere, somehow, but the term 'triggering' does actually relate to known psychological responses to trauma which it is important to write about safely. No, you can't keep every reader safe from being triggered, but the following guidelines will certainly minimise any unintentional harm in your writing:

## • Self-harm

This is a behaviour that, like suicide, can have a copycat element to it, and reading descriptions of it can 'trigger' people to self-harm. Try to keep any description of self-harm off the page, focusing instead on the *feelings* rather than the behaviour itself. Certainly never describe the method a character uses to harm themselves, and avoid graphic descriptions of bleeding.

## • Disorder eating

When writing about someone who overeats or under-eats, never actually state that character's specific weight or dress size. This can cause the reader to compare themselves with that character, triggering shame and further disordered eating. The same goes for calories consumed and calories burned by a character's exercise regime – giving these specifics can be very unhelpful, especially as they're so easily avoided.

## • PTSD

The phenomenon most commonly associated with the word 'trigger' is when something triggers a devastating flashback in somebody suffering with Post Traumatic Stress Disorder. A memory of trauma is not stored in the brain in the same way as other memories and therefore, for a PTSD sufferer, reading something similar to what they've been through can cause a flashback. A flashback is when the victim essentially feels like they're reliving their trauma in the present moment, which is obviously hugely upsetting. Although people may be triggered by many different things, I feel it's wise at least to try and minimise graphic descriptions of violence, and especially sexual violence, in your writing. Sadly, many young people are living with trauma and sexual trauma – one in 13 young people have PTSD by the age of 18 – so keep that in mind when writing about these subjects. You don't need to explicitly 'go there' in order for your story to be powerful. If you get published, do flag the parts of the book you're worried about with your editor. They can then hire a sensitivity reader to check the manuscript, as well as putting a trigger warning on the cover. This is something we've decided to do in my book *The Places I've Cried in Public* (Usborne 2019) which has an off-page rape in it. My publisher hired a psychologist specialising in sexual violence triggers to go through the manuscript and the tweaks she suggested didn't impact the narrative in any way.

## Remember mental illness does not exist in a vacuum

Recently there's been a welcome shift away from a simplistic biological explanation for mental illness. The World Health Organization has stated that it is inexplicably linked to human rights issues, and leading experts are campaigning for us to ask people 'What happened to you?' rather than 'What's wrong with you?'. The causes of mental illness might be environmental, socioeconomic or biological, so make sure your character's illness makes sense in the context of the wider world they live in. This is what I tried to explore in *Am I Normal Yet?* (Usborne 2015) about a girl called Evie who has OCD. The book explored both mental illness and gender inequality, making links between the two. I was careful to make sure Evie was never just characterised by her mental illness but was depicted as a fully rounded character who happened to have a mental illness.

## An issue isn't a story

Just as a character is not merely representative of a single attribute or one defining feature, a single 'issue' is never a good substitute for an engaging, well-structured plot. It's completely natural that, when writing for and about teenagers, you should want to include tough issues, simply a realistic interpretation of a teenager's life, but the fundamentals of successful storytelling must not be lost.

## Always offer hope

I feel a responsibility as a children's writer to ensure my novels have a hopeful tinge, especially when dealing with the tougher stuff. Though I'm careful never to perpetuate unhelpful fantasies such as *Love can cure mental illness*, I do want teen readers who see aspects of themselves in my characters to believe that light can emerge from the darkness. Whether that's through caring parents, the power of good friendships or showing positive experiences of teenagers using mental health services, I believe a YA writer should always offer hope, and that your book should be a light that guides them towards it.

**Holly Bourne** is a bestselling author whose YA books, all published by Usborne Publishing, include the award-winning *Spinster Club* series: *Am I Normal Yet?* (2015), *How Hard Can Love Be?* (2016), *What's a Girl Gotta Do?* (2016) and *And a Happy New Year?* (2016). Her other books include *Soulmates* (2013), *It Only Happens in the Movies* (2017), *Are We All Lemmings & Snowflakes?* (2018) and *The Places I've Cried in Public* (2019). Her latest books are *The Yearbook* (Usborne 2021) for young adults and *Girl Friends* (Hodder & Stoughton 2022) for adults. Holly has worked as a news journalist, an editor, relationship advisor and 'agony aunt' for The Mix, a youth charity which helps young people with their relationships and mental health. She is an ambassador for Women's Aid. Follow her on Twitter @holly_bourneYA.

## See also...
● *Writing about love and loss for children*, page 168

# Writing hopeful climate fiction

Bestselling author and self-confessed literary activist Lauren James has advice for writers on how to promote climate awareness and avoid potential pitfalls when dealing with climate change and the planet in children's fiction.

From the beginning of my writing career, I've wanted to write about climate change. But my writing is focused on character and story. It's funny and romantic. For a long time, writing a book about a topic that is discomforting at best and soul-crushing at worst felt impossible.

The turning point came when I realized that I could focus on characters who are actively working to slow climate change. I'm not interested in dark dystopias about a climate-ravaged planet. We know the dangers already – and I feel strongly that in children's and YA literature we should not be telling a generation that their future is broken. I want to read – and write – inspiring, optimistic stories. After all, the books that reach the widest audiences, that have the best chance of spreading awareness, are enjoyable ones.

After seven years of writing, my sixth novel, *Green Rising* (Walker Books 2021), was the result. It centres on teenagers who can grow plants from their skin. These 'Greenfingers', as they are called, use their powers to rewild the planet, and stand up to profit-hungry corporations. The novel shows how positive environmental changes – involving kelp forests, peatlands, reforestation – can help store carbon in huge quantities. I expected the writing process to be depressing. But, in fact, immersing myself in the climate debate helped me to stop feeling helpless. Instead of trying desperately to ignore the monster looming in the corner of my vision, I was facing it head-on. I was doing something.

Writing the novel, and another climate novella, *The Deep-Sea Duke* (Barrington Stoke 2021), led me to setting up the Climate Fiction Writers League. I was inspired in part by the Women Writers Suffrage League, a UK-based awareness-raising organization, founded in 1908 and disbanded in 1918 after the UK granted (some) women the right to vote. The League's prospectus asserted that 'A body of writers working for a common cause cannot fail to influence public opinion'. This has become our own League's guiding principle. Fiction is one of the best ways to inspire passion, empathy and action. We also partner with many other climate activism groups at events and panels, and by publishing essays and interviews.

## Researching the climate crisis

I'm not great at reading scientific publications – it feels too much like homework. But I am good at wasting time on social media. So I tricked myself into researching climate change through online resources although, often, the science has been obscured by politics or disinformation campaigns. Take geoengineering – slowing the global temperature increase by, for instance, using a solar mirror in space, or spraying chemicals into the atmosphere to reflect light away from the planet. These ideas are supported by the fossil fuel industry, which wants to be able to continue selling its products while ostensibly supporting climate action. However, we have no firm idea what knock-on effects geoengineering might have on the planet.

I wanted to explore *Juliana v. US* – an ongoing legal case in which young plaintiffs have argued that the US government has violated their constitutional rights by failing to act on climate change. I'm interested in the way youth activist groups like Extinction Rebellion are treated by the press – as extremist terrorists and moral heroes standing up for the planet, often simultaneously. I also wanted to investigate how billionaires are investing money in accessible space tourism, rather than fixing Earth, and how the new, trendy NFT (non-fungible token) art and bitcoin use huge amounts of power to create cryptocurrency. I wanted to highlight the issues related to carbon emissions, like metal poisoning from coal ash, microplastics and the garbage patches in the ocean. And I wanted to do it all in a positive way, in a book for teenagers. It was a lot to tackle.

## Representing all views

I tried to look at both sides of the debate, because the way that climate deniers talk about the topic can often be really helpful for creating narratives. (Why not let them do the hard work of being creative with arguments?) The Ceo of an oil company, a billionaire trying to launch a space mission or a politician with investments in fossil fuels don't see themselves as the 'bad guys'. To them, they're community-builders, providing jobs and energy to keep the world running. I tried to put myself in their shoes so I could write characters who felt the way they might. For example, space-race billionaire Elon Musk recently tweeted that he didn't want to pay tax on his companies' profits because: 'My plan is to use the money to get humanity to Mars and preserve the light of consciousness'. In my novel *Green Rising*, space-race billionaire Edgar Warren uses a similar justification in an argument with the novel's teenage protagonist Theo.

I also subscribed to a very niche geoengineering forum. Eavesdropping on scientists' highly technical bickering gave me a lot of insight into the people working at the forefront of this issue, on both sides of the equation.

## Making science engaging

In the writing, I tried not to get bogged down in the science. Story always has to come first. I looked for ways to tie science into other fields, like archaeology or linguistics. In *Green Rising*, for instance, my characters plan to use their 'Greenfingers' powers of growing plants to launch an illegal protest against fossil fuel companies, power plants and vehicle manufacturers. I wrote extracts from their online discussions in an activists' forum, dramatising their doubts concerning the science of such topics as solar seeding.

I keep an eye out for interesting, well-known science stories that might provide a way to talk about something more complicated, and for debunked or disproven theories from the past that tell us a lot about people's knowledge level – and motivations – at the time. I also try to think about big concepts in terms of historical events. How can we look at archaeology to get a new perspective on climate change? How might the present day look from a far-future or far-past point of view? Has something like this ever happened before on Earth? What might a climate disaster look like in a far-future world set on another planet? In my novella *The Deep-Sea Duke*, butterfly-like aliens are forced to flee their planet after burning fossil fuels has raised the temperature too high for their caterpillar offspring to survive. Problems arise when the planet they migrate to has the wrong type of environment (fully oceanic) and the butterflies introduce an invasive species to their new home (a rambunctious ferret pet). The book is aimed at ages 8+, and uses this humorous lens to comment on real-world issues.

## Should fiction be political?

Ultimately, climate change is a political topic. It's unavoidable. The end of the world is profitable. From trading stock market futures on water scarcities, to increased crop yields in extreme weather, business will thrive as the planet collapses. My characters are angry they're being told to reduce their climate footprint, that they're being made to feel guilty about their personal pollution when industry is responsible for the vast majority of emissions.

From a legal perspective, there were things I couldn't do – I wasn't allowed to mention real life companies or people by name, and had to create fictional versions of certain things. But in *Green Rising*, I tried to capture the feeling of being part of the ongoing green revolution, to show what it feels like to grow up in a time of unprecedented existential fear. I wanted to write about young people who are turning that fear into hope and action, pushing against the enormous weight of the existing establishment.

## Writing advice

My top tips for writers who want to include climate change in their work:
• Read climate fiction in a variety of genres, not just science fiction and fantasy.
• Consider the activism going on outside the very vocal UK/US groups. Activists from the countries most affected by climate change are often ignored in the media.
• Inspire activism – but be aware that readers don't want to be made to feel guilty.
• Convey the seriousness of the situation without making action seem futile.
• Show how climate change is no longer a long-term issue but something happening right now.
• Use your frustration in your writing – but be aware that most people don't want to read an angry book.
• Remember that hope and optimism will inspire more action than anything else. Fiction can inspire a huge amount of empathy, which is a force that can be used collectively to inspire change on a global level.

### Hopeful climate fiction reading list

*A Cloud Called Bhura: Climate Champions to the Rescue* by Bijal Vachharajani (Speaking Tiger 2019)

*Amara and the Bats* by Emma Reynolds (Simon & Schuster 2021)

*Beauty and the Bin* by Joanne O'Connell (Pan Macmillan 2021)

*How to Save the World with a Chicken and an Egg* by Emma Shevah (Chicken House 2021)

*The Summer We Turned Green* by William Sutcliffe (Bloomsbury 2021)

*The Tale of a Toothbrush* by M.G. Leonard (Walker Books 2020)

**Lauren James** is the bestselling author of many YA novels, including *Green Rising* (2021), *The Reckless Afterlife of Harriet Stoker* (2020), *The Quiet at the End of the World* (2019) and *The Loneliest Girl in the Universe* (2017), all published by Walker Books. Lauren is a Royal Literary Fund Royal Fellow, freelance editor and screenwriter, and founder of the Climate Fiction Writers League. For more information see https://laurenejames.co.uk.

A version of this piece first appeared in *The Author*, the journal of the Society of Authors (Spring 2022 Vol. 133.1).

# Writing about love and loss for children

Natasha Farrant considers the responsibility shouldered by authors who write about love and loss for children and teenagers and how such novels can be a valuable opportunity for young readers to explore challenging emotions and life experiences.

Years ago, when I started out working in children's publishing and before I was published myself, I went to a lecture given by Anne Fine. A member of the audience asked her what the difference was between writing for children and writing for adults. She replied that you could write about all the same subjects, whatever the age of your readers, but that you would tell the story differently. It was all a question, she said, of the angle at which you shone the light. I want to explore that question here in relation to writing about loss and love, because these are subjects I have returned to again and again in my own books.

Even as I write this, I read in *The Bookseller* that authors John Boyne, Malorie Blackman and Sam Copeland, presenting their titles at the Penguin Random House Children's Showcase, 'spoke of transgender issues, experiences of psychosis and how to cope with anxiety as a small child'. And this focus on difficult themes is by no means new to children's literature. From *The Railway Children* to *The Secret Garden*, *Matilda* to *Journey to the River Sea* and *Harry Potter*, authors have dealt with parental imprisonment, poverty, bereavement, loneliness, persecution, child neglect – all huge issues; all, one way or another, connected with loss.

'Struggle and hardship are the essential ingredients of narrative', writes Trisha Lee, theatre director and founder of MakeBelieve Arts, in *Princesses, Dragons and Helicopter Stories* (Routledge 2015). She goes on to quote Kieran Egan in *Teaching as Storytelling* (University of Chicago Press 1989) who believes that it is our desire to explore global concerns with binary opposites – good and evil, fair and unfair, cruel and kind – that engages us with fiction. This is true whatever age the reader. It's up to us, the reader, to make that exploration as engaging, accessible and, dare I say it, as age-appropriate as possible.

My first book for young people, *The Things We Did For Love* (Faber 2012), is a Second World War love story based on the massacre which took place at Oradour-sur-Glane, near Limoges in South West France, in 1944. Years later, a friend still hasn't got over my writing this: 'A children's book! About a massacre!' Well, it wasn't a children's book, as was made clear by the cover. I have no desire to give it to a child – frankly, there are gentler ways for them to learn about man's brutality to man. But teenagers are a different matter. The novel deals with subjects most teens I know are familiar with: sex and desire, jealousy, shame, the awareness that although they long to do the right thing they often feel coerced by social pressure to do the opposite. Most teenagers, by dint of the online world we live in, do know about war. My book offers them a chance to reflect further on what it means.

What, though, makes it a book for teens, and not for adults? It's a tricky question. A book for young people doesn't mean adults can't enjoy it too. It doesn't mean it can't have adult characters. It doesn't mean, for example, that the characters can't have sex. Sex! How often have I heard book pitches along the lines of 'It's a love story, but don't worry, it's for teens so it doesn't have sex in it' – as if teenagers didn't have sex! In *The Things We Did For Love* my teenage protagonists Arianne and Luc have sex. In fact, Arianne uses sex, rather naively thinking that if she sleeps with Luc, he won't join the Resistance and leave her. I don't show them having sex. I show rose petals leading up to a door (corny, but I couldn't resist), and I show that door closing. But we know perfectly well what is happening, and it's the sort of device that's used in plenty of grown-up fiction.

So again, if I can show torture and I can (sort of) show sex, what makes this a book for teens rather than adults? How have I shone the light? Well, there's the characters, I guess – three of the main protagonists are teenagers; one is a child (and one is a fully-grown man, but we'll put that to one side). They have teen and childhood preoccupations, like falling in love and doing homework. Arianne is trying to fill the gap left by her dead mother and her imprisoned father. She believes she may have found her answer in Luc. She believes she can use her love for him to keep him from harm. And the unnamed teenage narrator, after the massacre, writes that the lovers will be together forever. As adults, we suspect that this is unlikely. As teenagers, it's important (I think) to believe that it is true. Maybe that is the key – that belief in the redemptive power of love.

One of my golden rules, when writing for young people, is this: do not leave the reader without hope. Do not destroy that belief that the world can do better. It's difficult, if you're writing about certain subjects. Climate change is a classic example. But I would suggest that if you see no future for humanity yourself, then perhaps writing for young people is not for you. There are various forms of redemption to be found in *The Things We Did For Love*. They were hard to find, in the bleakness of that event, but the focus of the book (and indeed its inspiration) is the small acts of heroism I discovered in the course of my research and which give the book its title. Because writing for children comes with a certain responsibility.

Scientific research has shown that 'when we connect with a story, parts of our brain related to a particular emotion or action light up, and our neurons start firing as if we were engaged in the activity ourselves' (Kieran Egan; *Princesses, Dragons and Helicopter Stories*). And what is true for us as adults is even more true for a child, during the plastic years of brain formation. Philip Pullman writes about his experiences of playing at Davy Crockett in the suburbs of Adelaide when he was growing up: 'When we children play at being characters we admire, doing things we value, we discover areas and depths of feeling it would be hard to reach otherwise. Exhilaration, heroism, despair, resolution, triumph, noble renunciation, sacrifice: in acting these out we experience them in miniature or, as it were, in safety' (*Daemon Voices: Essays on Storytelling*, David Fickling Books 2017). He goes on to write that, through play, he was 'building patterns of behaviour and expectation into my moral understanding'.

As children play, so they read. They *live* the books they love, and these books offer tremendous opportunity to learn about love and loss and everything in between. They will shape their young readers and make them who they are. And yet, remember this. When you are writing for children, know that you are writing for some of the toughest, most critical readers there are, who will not suffer unnecessary babble. Know that that babble includes you pontificating on love and loss, on how sad your heroine is, or how hard she is crying, or how slowly time is passing. Never forget that other golden rule: 'Show don't tell.' *Show* the loss. *Show* the emotion. *Show* the redemptive love. Use every writing trick at your disposal – metaphor, imagery, leitmotiv – to make them come to life. They're never going to live your book if they're bored.

My middle-grade book *The Children of Castle Rock* (Faber 2018) traces the grief of the main protagonist, Alice, as she mourns the death of her mother. The book opens as she prepares to leave her family home forever. Rather than linger on Alice's emotions, I choose to focus on her refusal to leave without taking her mother's commemorative rosebush, which is dug up and squished into the car. The rosebush then reappears periodically – on a balcony, as a watercolour and eventually in a new garden – in a way which shows the reader without spelling it out that Alice, without forgetting, is nevertheless learning to move on.

As I wrote the story, I asked myself these questions: What has Alice lost? What does she want? What does she need? These are the questions which drive the plot. Alice has lost her mum, her dad is completely unreliable and her home is sold. She needs to rebuild a sense of family, she wants her dad to do this for her but she needs to understand that he never will. These are the questions which give the novel emotional depth and a sense of purpose. They are not what make it an exciting read, though. The excitement comes from the fact that, in her pursuit of these needs, Alice runs away from boarding school, camps on a Scottish beach, almost drowns, breaks into a house and gets chased onto a stack of rocks by a bunch of Italian gangsters, where she gets cut off by the tide … and in the end conquers both her fear of losing her dad and her fear of heights by abseiling down a cliff.

Even as I write this, I'm aware how complex this question of responsibility is. It is absolutely not about watering down difficult subjects, but it's about rendering them in such a way that a child can explore them – as Pullman writes in the quote I cited earlier – in safety. Children, like all readers, will take what they can and what they need from a story. A child who has experienced severe loss will be alive to Alice's grief. A child with less experience of loss may simply enjoy the adventure. The story may lead to greater understanding; it may simply entertain. All forms of reading are valid.

In *The Children of Castle Rock*, as in all my other books, I have tried to acknowledge that bad things do happen, that the people you love are not always reliable, but that there are others who love you if you can open your eyes and heart to them. I have also tried to fulfil my other responsibility as a writer, which is to make my story as cohesive, exciting and as good as I possibly can. But there my task as a writer is finished. Alice's story is in the world, to be completed in as many ways as there are readers. Which is just as it should be.

**Natasha Farrant** is a writer and literary scout. Her books include the Costa winning *Voyage of the Sparrowhawk* (Faber 2020), *The Children of Castle Rock* (Faber 2018), *Eight Princesses and a Magic Mirror* (Zephyr 2019), *The Girl who Talked to Trees* (Zephyr 2021) as well as *The Things We Did for Love* (2012) and four titles in her popular children's series *The Diaries of Bluebell Gadsby*: *After Iris* (2013), *Flora in Love* (2014), *All About Pumpkin* (2015) and *Time for Jas* (2016), all published by Faber & Faber. Her latest book is *The Rescue of Ravenwood* (Faber 2023). For more information visit www.natashafarrant.com, and follow her on Twitter @NatashaFarrant1.

# Series fiction: writing as part of a team

Writer Lucy Courtenay spills the beans on the profitable world of series fiction: its fictional authors, the publishers and packagers, and the skilled teams of editors and writers that create and produce it.

Once upon a time, a group of editors sat around a table, brainstorming ideas for a new children's series for girls aged 6–9. It needed to be collectable with a strong series identity. One editor put up her hand. 'I had an idea for a series when I was seven years old,' she said. 'It was about seven fairies. One for each colour of the rainbow.'

The series, *Rainbow Magic* by Daisy Meadows, has since spawned over 200 titles. There are mini-series of four or seven interconnected titles within the overarching series which share common themes: the rainbow, the weather, the ocean, popstars and parties and animals, to give a few examples. Sales of the series currently stand at over ten million copies worldwide.

You might assume, on those statistics, that *Rainbow Magic* has made its author rich. It has, but not in the way you might imagine. If you remember, it was an editor's idea. Daisy Meadows herself doesn't exist. She is an amalgamation of dozens of different writers and editors, all of whom have taken a share of her profits. She is successful because she is the product of professional, dedicated teams who know how to produce books that children love. The same is true of Lucy Daniels – whose *Animal Ark* series could be said to have started the whole series fiction phenomenon in the 1990s – and Adam Blade, more recently of the *Beast Quest* series. There are plenty of other examples, but these are perhaps the best known. When people first learn this, they are often surprised and baffled. What is the point? Why do publishers produce books in this way? Shouldn't they be supporting original talent, promoting original authors?

A fictional author has no rights over a series, which makes that series more flexible and profitable for a publisher or a packager. A fictional author can also write six or more books at the same time, which does wonders for a publisher's production line and (you've guessed it) profits. A fictional author can be designed to fit a niche in the market. They can be given an alphabetically appropriate name to meet a browser's eye level or queue-barge on to the shelf ahead of the direct competition. They can be designed to fit as many commercial platforms as possible, should opportunity present: clothing, online games, stationery. They can also enjoy lives far more exotic than those of real authors. Adam Blade's biography charmingly gives him a pet capuchin monkey called Omar, while Lucy Daniels apparently lives in Yorkshire with Russian Blue cats.

If this seems hard-nosed and commercial, it is. Publishing is a business, and it has to think like a business in the current climate where books fight to be heard above the clamour of YouTube. And, as if the competition weren't tough enough, publishing is an industry with very low margins. A book is cheap compared to a games console; it's cheap compared to a pair of decent socks. In order to turn a profit these days, publishers need to sell a lot of books. A title ideally needs to shift around 10,000 copies a year. More if it's an expensive full-colour book.

Adam Blade, Daisy Meadows and friends sell in these quantities. Their success bankrolls the quieter titles, the books that publishers love but which won't set a financial spreadsheet alight: the standalones, the ones with sad endings and quirky illustrations and unusual production values, the literary prizewinners and the poetry, and all the things which keep a publishing list energised and wide-ranging.

There are dozens of well-known authors now established in their own right who have written packaged series fiction at some point in their careers. Advances aren't high, but the steady stream of royalties and the great and glorious mysteries of PLR income (see *Public Lending Right*, page 369) often mean that the projects are worthwhile. It is a dependable source of income in an unreliable industry. Or 'gas-bill money', as literary agent Lesley Hadcroft once put it.

Publishers are wise to the series-fiction juggernaut and regularly design their own series, commissioning authors and illustrators. But series fiction also originates with packagers. Packagers are an intermediary business. They produce ideas and source writers. But they still have to pitch those ideas to publishers for publication and distribution. In that respect, they are in the same boat as the author rapping on doors to get a commissioning editor's attention. However, publishers take packagers with good track records more seriously than they might a first-time author. Working Partners, for example, has produced some of the biggest series in recent years, including *Rainbow Magic* and *Beast Quest*.

Packagers employ teams of highly experienced editors who have regular meetings to exchange ideas for series, like the meeting described in my opening paragraph. When an idea has been agreed, they will either find a publisher to take it on the strength of the idea (a rare Holy Grail) or, more often, they will ask writers to produce some sample material to fit the concept before presenting it to publishers. The writer is given character names, scenes and complete chapter breakdowns by the packager, with express instructions to fill out the characters and develop the scenes as energetically as possible. There is no fee for sample material, but writers are usually happy to oblige in the knowledge that a little free work can sometimes net a paid project. In terms of cold hard cash, there is usually a small advance if the project is accepted, with around one-third of the royalty charged by the packagers going to the writers.

And here's the good news. Commercial fiction packagers don't need established names to write for them. They simply need writers who can write, and who are able and happy to follow a detailed brief. What's more, they actively recruit them. Go to the website for Working Partners (www.workingpartnersltd.co.uk) and it's hard to miss the great big button shouting APPLY NOW! There are forms to fill in regarding experience and interests, and you are asked to submit some sample writing. Not everyone will make the cut, but if you can turn a phrase and hold a story together, you have as good a chance as anyone else.

It's important to note that packagers are not interested in your magnificent idea about a talking wombat. They are only interested in the mechanics of your writing. In the world of team fiction, it is up to them to produce the ideas. Your job is to fill in the gaps as fluently and excitingly as you can. As such, writing as part of a series team can be a humbling exercise. You might produce your best joke or most moving sentiment in years, but if it doesn't fit the flavour of the series you are writing for, it will be binned as swiftly and unthinkingly as old yoghurt. A successful team writer is the person who can produce writing that fits seamlessly into the whole, not the person with the individual edge.

If your ego can take it, writing series fiction is an incomparable crash course in how to write. I learned a vast amount at the coalface as Lucy Daniels/Adam Blade (yes, I'm both) about pacing, plotting, cliffhangers, world-building, character development and all those other building blocks of successful storytelling. You work closely – often line by line – with expert industry editors, whose practical advice and guidance can feel like a creative writing course without the fee. Instead, miraculously, you are the one who gets paid. There's even a published book to show for your efforts at the end of it all. Writing in this way can be a valuable apprenticeship for the big bad world of author-led fiction that all writers hope lies in their future. Bring an open mind and a flexible pen to the process, and you will find that the craft of writing will lose several of its many mysterious layers.

You will note that producing series fiction in this way is about the writer, not the illustrator. Illustration and design for this type of series fiction lies strictly with the publisher who buys the concept. If you are an illustrator or author-illustrator, the series-fiction route probably isn't for you. If you are a writer: Hello, opportunity!

**Lucy Courtenay** has been writing children's fiction for over 20 years, working as a team writer on series such as *Animal Ark* and *Beast Quest*. She has several series under her own name, most recently *Mermaid School* (2020–22) for Andersen Press with illustrator Sheena Dempsey, and has also written contemporary teen romances for Hodder Children's. She is the Senior Commissioning Editor for Fiction at Farshore, a freelance editor of children's fiction for Cornerstones Literary Consultancy and Curtis Brown Creative, and the author of *Get Started in Writing an Illustrated Children's Book* for the *Teach Yourself* series (John Murray 2016). She tweets @LucyCourtenay1.

# The long and winding road to publication

Paul Stewart tells how he achieved his childhood dream of becoming a writer, championing illustrated books for children, and shares his experience of the submission process, rejection and success, and finding the ideal collaboration.

When I was at school, other boys in my class wanted to be footballers or train drivers. One wanted to be an astronomer. Me, I didn't have a clue. Possibly a singer in a band. Then, when I was eight, I was given a prize by a music teacher. Her husband worked for Collins and the prize was a book: *The Phantom Tollbooth* by Norton Juster, with illustrations by Jules Feiffer (Collins 1962). She apologised that it was an uncorrected proof, but thought I would love it. She was right. The novel took me to somewhere wonderful and, from that moment on, I knew I wanted to be a writer.

I started work on my own children's novel – as well as drawing the pictures to accompany it. I soon discovered two things: writing was more difficult than I'd thought, while illustrating was beyond me. I abandoned the project, but I never lost that new-found enthusiasm for my future career.

At university I studied English, choosing Lancaster because they offered a unit in Creative Writing. Then I applied for a (then almost unknown) writing MA at UEA, run by Malcolm Bradbury and Angela Carter. By the end of the course I had a folder of 20 short stories and an idea for a novel. One of those stories – a reimagining of Andersen's *The Snow Queen*, called *Ice* – was published in a literary magazine, *Bananas*. I still remember the thrill of reading their letter of acceptance: '… we'd like to use it in the next issue due out at the end of this month.' It was my first short story in print. I'd arrived.

I hadn't, of course. The other 19 stories – separately and as a collection – were not published, and the novel remained an idea. I decided that if it was indeed true that you should write about what you know, then I needed to know more. It was time to go travelling.

This was back before computers. Up until then I had been writing on an olive-green Olympia SM3 – allegedly a portable typewriter, but Charles Atlas would probably have had problems lugging it about. So I bought a lightweight Olivetti Lettera 32 and, following Malcolm's parting comment – 'I don't have the address but it is, like all the other addresses, in the *Writers' & Artists' Yearbook*' – got hold of a copy. Then I set off.

I lived in Greece, Germany and Sri Lanka; I travelled through Europe, India, parts of the Far East, Australia, the US, Kenya. I had numerous jobs – factory packer, security guard, fork-lift truck driver, bank operative, translator, EFL teacher, you name it – and I wrote something every day. The typewriter went everywhere I went, and each time I completed a piece of writing, I would search through the *Yearbook* for an appropriate publication. A growing number of magazines and publishers in the UK received examples of my work.

Most, to their credit, were kind in their rejections. Many offered advice. I always tried to match the manuscript to the publication, though not always successfully. A leading women's magazine responded to one story with the comment: 'The idea was ingenious but ... we do try to keep death out of our stories.'

I also discovered that I was receiving letters from people I'd actually heard of: Robert McCrum, Bill Buford, Paul Samwell-Smith (ah, yes ... still nurturing dreams of singing in a band, I'd also submitted a cassette of songs for appraisal). The thrill of communicating with famous people was tempered by the fact that they were sending me rejection letters – one after the other they arrived, enough to paper my walls, and I was feeling increasingly disheartened, though unable to stop writing.

It was this optimistic response from Tom Maschler of Jonathan Cape that set me back on track: 'The above said [i.e. the inevitable rejection], I don't like to lose sight of you because frankly I am convinced that you will make it as a serious writer, and think it likely that we would want to publish you in the future if we had the opportunity.'

I was in Sri Lanka in the '80s when civil war broke out. The school I'd been teaching in was closed, and I returned to England to find that the adult novel I'd almost completed over there suddenly seemed flippant and superficial. So I went back to the children's book I'd been musing over for more than two decades and, three months later, *The Thought Domain* was finished. Published by Viking in 1988, it was my first children's novel in print. For a second time, I'd arrived.

Largely on the strength of that published book, I was taken on by a literary agent. This took a lot of the hard work – and inevitable heartache – out of the process of trying to find a home for my scribblings. I now had someone to do it for me. Three years later, a deal was secured for a book I'd been researching. Based on a true story I'd stumbled upon in Kenya, it was accepted by – yes – Jonathan Cape. In 1991, my first adult book, *Trek*, was duly published. I'd *arrived* ...

Apart from that one book (and even *Trek* itself reads like a *Boy's Own* tale of gung-ho misadventure), it was children's literature that I pursued. I liked the discipline of writing for a younger audience, as well as the rigour, clarity and sincerity it demands. My early books were our-world-but-with-a-twist fantasies, often starting with a simple What if...? premise. What if there was a dimension where our thoughts were stored? What if a child was born able to communicate with animals? What if a video machine could record our nightmares?

After the publication of *The Thought Domain*, I submitted fresh proposals in the form of the first three chapters of the new work, a rough outline of the entire novel and a working title, in order to gauge whether my primary editor thought it had legs. If he didn't, my agent would send it to other publishers. I had, by this time, given up teaching EFL to devote myself to writing full time. I did not intend to return to the classroom. Not only did I generate my own stories, but I also started taking on commissions – writing to order, following briefs. I wrote football stories, puzzle adventures books, graded readers, horror and fantasy novels; I had short stories published in themed anthologies.

All these pieces of work, even the ones for older children, were illustrated. I considered this a good thing; I still do. There is, I believe, something perverse about using pictures to lure children into the world of books and then, when they've cracked reading, to remove them. It feels almost like a punishment. If I'd been able to I would have illustrated my own texts but, since I wasn't good enough, the next best thing was to find an illustrator I could work closely with.

This proved far from easy. Publishers often keep authors and illustrators apart. An American editor once explained that this was company policy, as authors 'tend to bully illustrators'. A likely story! Had there been closer cooperation between me and my various illustrators, however, maybe a scene I'd written about a boy on a bike being attacked by a slavering dog wouldn't have been depicted by an old bicycle leaning up against a wall. I mentioned my disappointment to my editor and was given a new illustrator – based in Tasmania ...

It was at a publisher's party in London that I first got talking to Chris Riddell. Beforehand, we had seen each other at the nursery our two sons went to, but we'd never spoken. On our train journey home that evening we talked about working together and, after a couple of false starts, produced a picture book about a rabbit and a hedgehog: *A Little Bit of Winter* (Andersen Press). It was my first picture book and my first collaboration.

The year was 1998, and that wasn't the only work we had published ... Working together on *Rabbit and Hedgehog*, we'd both realized how much we enjoyed the collaborative process. Chris drew me a fantasy map entitled The Edge: 'Here's the world,' he said. 'What happens in it?'. It was at this stage that we tested our ability to work together to the max. This wasn't a 12-page spread picture book; it would be a long novel for 11-year-olds, illustrated throughout. There were times when we both wondered whether it would ever be completed, but finally, 15 months later, *Beyond the Deepwoods* (Doubleday 1998) – the first of what would become a 13-part fantasy series, *The Edge Chronicles* – was on the shelves. I'd arrived. Again!

Oddly, the series nearly didn't happen. I'd spoken to my editor at the time about the idea. She thought pictures would make the fantasy look too young. 'Not Chris's pictures', I assured her and, though unconvinced, she suggested I send in the proposal. In the usual way, I printed up the three chapters we'd completed, plus a rough synopsis of the book and outline of the world, and included a wad of Chris's pictures. The envelope came back return of post. Being a writer with a string of rejections under his belt, I naturally assumed they'd dismissed it out of hand as a rubbish idea. It was two days later when a tentative phone enquiry revealed that a youngster on a Youth Opportunities scheme had decided to tidy up the office and sent back all the manuscripts that were lying around – ours included. I've often fantasized about other novels that might have been rejected in the same batch ...

Chris and I have written and illustrated more than 40 books together to date. One of us will come up with a very general idea, then we talk, talk, talk. If that initial idea starts to fly, we set about building a self-contained world – with maps, characters, names, back histories – for the two of us to immerse ourselves in; a place where we discover the stories that will turn into books. A flying box containing an ominous warning became the first *Far-Flung Adventure* – *Fergus Crane* (Doubleday 2004); a Victorian delivery lad with an insight into the supernatural became the *Barnaby Grimes* novels; a trio of aliens on a spurious mission to Earth became *The Blobheads*; humans versus killer robots – *Scavenger*; cowboys and dragons – *Wyrmeweald*.

Since Chris and I come to a piece of work from different perspectives, the text itself goes through many revisions. Although it is immensely enjoyable working with someone else – the writing, the events, the festivals, plus the fact that 'writer's block' is impossible if two of you are working together on a piece – collaboration is never easy. If we had tried working together when we'd first left college, it might not have worked. By the time we did start, I think we were both old enough to realize that the finished item was of far more importance than our individual egos. And certainly, none of the books we produced together could have been done by either of us alone.

Looking back on my writing career, it seems to have been so arbitrary. I kept thinking I'd arrived, only to discover that it was not my final destination – that there was always somewhere else to go to. All I know is that, ever since first realizing that 'I wanted to be a writer', everything has been geared towards making that a possibility. Publishing is currently changing. I wonder where I will arrive at next …

**Paul Stewart** is a bestselling author of children's and adult books. He is co-creator (with Chris Riddell) of the *Edge Chronicles* series, the *Far-Flung Adventures* series including *Fergus Crane* (Gold Smarties Prize winner), *Corby Flood* and *Hugo Pepper* (both Silver Nestlé Prize winners), as well as the *Barnaby Grimes* series (published by Penguin Random House), and the *Free Lance*, *Wyrmeweald* and *Scavenger* trilogies. His other books include two *Muddle Earth* adventures and the *Blobheads* series (for younger readers), published by Macmillan Children's, and the *Rabbit and Hedgehog* picture books (Andersen Press). *Brian the Brave* (Otter-Barry Books 2019), the second picture book he has worked on with illustrator Jane Porter, won the 2020 Derby Children's Book Award, while *A Little Bit of Hush* was published in 2022. Barrington Stoke has re-issued both the *Free Lance* trilogy and his *Football Mad* series. Paul has written six titles for OUP's *Hero Academy* series and a biography of footballer Alex Oxlade-Chamberlain (Scholastic 2021). For more information see www.edgechronicles.co.uk.

# Murderous inventions

Robin Stevens reveals how her murder mystery books, written for her 12-year-old self, have tapped into children's fascination for the nasty parts of life. When so much of a writer's career depends on chance, she stresses the value of following your instinct and of finding exactly the right agent and editor to share one's vision and passion.

It's probably not surprising that I'm an author. I grew up in a family that believed in books, and there's never been a moment of my life that I haven't told stories. I have always known with absolute determination that I wanted to have those stories published – but as a child I also wanted to own a zoo, be a wizard and live inside an Eva Ibbotson novel, and all of those ambitions seemed about as likely as each other. So no, it's not surprising that I'm an author – but all the same, I still wake up delighted every single morning by my bewildering good fortune, because *Murder Most Unladylike* (Corgi 2014) was not supposed to be the book that got me published.

I wrote the first draft of it in 2010, during NaNoWriMo (National Novel Writing Month). I really want to stress that I did not have even the smallest insight into the children's book market at the time. The simple fact was that there was no story that made more sense to me. I had discovered Agatha Christie's murder mysteries aged 12 and was then sent to Cheltenham Ladies' College aged 13. Detective stories and boarding schools are in my blood, and so deciding to write a murder mystery set at a boarding school was as obvious as falling in love – a feeling of: ... *Oh, of course it's you.*

*Murder Most Unladylike* let me work through all my confused memories of a boarding-school life that was neither as good nor as bad as Enid Blyton had promised it would be. The structure of its detective story felt like a reassuring arm around my shoulders in an adult world which was turning out to be far less organised that I had been expecting. I knew no one else would want this story, but I realised that I really needed it.

That sounds like a fairy tale, but of course the truth of writing an actual book is not a fairy tale at all. I wrote the first 50,000 words in a wild rush unlike anything I'd done before. I had a full-time job at the time, and so I had to hammer out my word count during lunch breaks, early in the morning and late at night. Daisy and Hazel were the only characters who had names, and they spent long scenes just chatting emptily to each other because I didn't know what was supposed to happen next. I wrote that first draft in 30 days, but I spent two years heavily working and reworking my text before I felt confident enough to actually send the book out to agents.

Once I'd decided to do that, though, I truly realised that I had no idea how to go about it. How did people find agents for their books? And, for that matter, what *was* my book? It was about children who solved a murder – so did that make it for children, or for adults? The only thing I did know was that when I thought about my favourite authors, they wrote for children. So off I marched to a bookshop, bought a copy of the *Writers & Artists' Yearbook 2012* (I still own it) and began to randomly pick children's agents from its pages.

I know now that this was a terrible idea. I should not have just been looking for an agent who works on children's books. I should have looked for children's agents who had specific experience in the type of book I had written. I *should* have been seeking out agents with a specialty in adventurous crime stories that centre on female characters. Hindsight is obviously a wonderful thing, but I wish I could take my younger self by the hand and gently explain to her that genres are important, that picture books are not the same as children's fiction which is not the same as YA fiction, that there are differences between commercial books and prize winners.

Of course, I got a lot of rejections – partly because what I was pitching was a murder mystery for kids, but mostly because I was approaching the wrong people. I have learned since that this is really the cause of almost every 'No' you'll ever get: the people rejecting you are not stupid, or cruel, or wicked – they are simply not obsessed with what you have written. An agent doesn't just need to *like* your book, they need to *love* it with every fibre of their being. They need to be able to spend five, or ten, or twenty years of their lives so wild about it that they will collar random strangers at parties to tell them how brilliant it is. As an author, you shouldn't want an agent that isn't perfect for you – and I was lucky enough (it really was the most incredible luck) to find the perfect agent in Gemma Cooper.

One day I stumbled on a blog post Gemma had written about how much she loved shows like *Murder She Wrote* and *Poirot*, and how she'd love to find a book like that for children – and I suddenly realised where I'd been going wrong. I sent my manuscript to her, not as a random children's agent but as a lover of murder mysteries who understood the children's book market. And it worked. Gemma met me and bowled me over with her enthusiasm for my book and her keen business sense. I signed with her a week later and she helped me trim my flabby and chaotic 80,000-word manuscript (this word count makes me wince to remember it) into a 60,000-word crime novel squarely aimed at children. We sent the book out to UK publishers in the spring of 2013.

Again, we got a lot of rejections. I want to stress that if any author tells you no one ever rejected them, they are either lying or the luckiest human on the planet. Everyone gets rejected. I was personally rejected repeatedly, and the publishers who rejected me were not wrong. They were just not the right publishers for my book. If one of them had bought *Murder Most Unladylike*, they would not have cared about it with enough passion to propel it higher into the bestseller charts with every title. I would not be writing this piece now, ten years later.

Only Random House offered for *Murder Most Unladylike*, because only my editor Natalie Doherty was right for my book. She was besotted with it ten years ago, and she's still wild about it today, which is how I know this is true. She believed so passionately that a children's book about murder would sell that she convinced her publicity team and sales team, and they convinced booksellers, and then … the book sold.

I need to be very honest here and say that I was not expecting *Murder Most Unladylike* to do this well. By the time it came out, in June 2014, I was working in children's publishing myself. I knew the size of the market, and I was realistic about a debut author's chances. Most books – and aspiring authors should prepare themselves for this – sell about 1,000 copies. If you are selling more than 100 books a week you are doing very well indeed. If you sell more than 300 copies a week your publishers will have a small party at their desks in your honour. There are a lot of books on the market, and most of them get lost in the noise. And that was what I was prepared for. I'm still pinching myself that this is not what happened.

I was helped by a lot of things that I had nothing to do with: I had a great cover; I got a few nice reviews; my second book was chosen as the Waterstones Children's Book of the

Month in February 2015; and then I won the Waterstones Prize for Younger Fiction in March. I could not have influenced those events, but I'm not sure I would have been able to write a nine-book series if even one of them had not occurred. A lot of what happens to an author happens outside their orbit – all you can do is react as calmly as possible to the news in your inbox every morning. This lack of control is slightly horrific, and it's a lot to take on board. In fact, what I have realised is that there is only one aspect of my writing career that is within my control – as it is in the control of every writer in the world: the books I write. And I think the content of those books certainly helped me, because the truth is that children *love* thinking about murder.

As adults (or at least, as the good sort of adults), we work very hard to keep children safe. The world is a horrible, stressful place that we struggle to deal with ourselves, and so we put a lot of effort into making sure children do not realise how awful it is until they are grown up and it is too late. Children, on the other hand, spend pretty much every waking hour trying to work out everything they can about the nastiest parts of life. Children are *desperate* to know what adults do to each other, why they behave the way they do, why bad things happen and what those bad things look like.

When you write for children, you have to stop being an adult and remember what it's like to be a child. Children want to understand and explore the darkest places in the universe, and as authors we can let them do that. (We always make sure that we leave behind invisible safety trails, of course, but they're more for us than for our audience). And children also want to be shown that sometimes small is powerful; that kids can be strong and brave and save the day, even when they feel weak and scared; that sometimes adults are good, and sometimes adults are bad; and that it's possible to work out the difference.

I didn't consciously know I was doing all of this when I wrote *Murder Most Unladylike*, of course I didn't. I'm not that clever. But watching how children respond to my series, I've realised this is the key to its success, and to the success of every good children's book ever written. I thought I didn't know who I was writing for, but of course I was lying to myself. I wrote for that 12-year-old Robin who was very grown up but also not grown up at all, who wanted life to be okay and worried that it wasn't, who cared very deeply about crime and justice. This is the only key to success as a children's author that I can pass on to you. *So* much is down to chance and circumstance. You can't hope to give the market what it wants. All you can do is write the book that would have set your younger self's world on fire, and trust that we're all very similar underneath.

**Robin Stevens** is the author of the *Murder Most Unladylike* mystery series (these include *Murder Most Unladylike* (2014), *First Class Murder* (2016) and *Death Sets Sail* (2020), all published by Puffin), and five *Wells and Wong Mysteries*, reissued by Simon & Schuster. She is also the author of *The Guggenheim Mystery* (Puffin 2017), from an idea and characters by Siobhan Dowd. Her latest book is the first in a new series, *The Ministry of Unladylike Activity* (Puffin 2022). Born in California, Robin came to live in England at the age of three. She worked as an editor in children's publishing before becoming a full-time writer. For more information see https://robin-stevens.co.uk, and follow her on social media @redbreastedbird.

# Poetry
## Writing poetry for children

Rachel Rooney reflects on how she re-engaged with a childhood passion and sought out valuable educational and competitive opportunities and challenges to sharpen her poetic skills. With advice for new poets, she sees how both serendipity and tenacity played their part on her path to publication and award-winning success.

I fell in love with poetry twice – once as a bookish child and again, much later, as a middle-aged woman. Maybe it was the 27-year hiatus that fuelled my desire to become a poet for young people, an urge to pick up from where I'd left off. With my third son starting school, and while taking a short break in my teaching career, I signed up to a weekly Writing for Children course run by Roger Stevens, the founder of the online children's website The Poetry Zone (https://poetryzone.co.uk). It ran over three terms, with the main focus on fiction writing, but it quickly became clear that my strengths lay in poetry. I rediscovered a pleasure in its rhythms, rhymes and patterning, and found a natural tendency to condense ideas rather than expand on them.

Soon I became hooked and began to experiment with different forms and styles. I read widely for inspiration, from childhood favourites such as Christina Rossetti and Charles Causley through to contemporary poets. Then I sought out the winning collections from the CLPE Poetry Award (now named the CLiPPA Award; see page 336) as well as those from its predecessor, The Signal Poetry Award. While admiring playful, sharp wordplay and well-crafted light verse, I was also drawn to the 'adult poets' such as Matthew Sweeney, Philip Gross and Carol Ann Duffy, those who turned their skills to the writing of subtle, weighted poems for a younger audience. The scope of children's poetry was opening up to me – from early infant lullabies through to teen/adult crossover free verse, and I was keen to embrace it all.

It was at this time I first had a poem published in an anthology, which had been submitted as part of a challenge organised by the tutor. The early 2000s was a barren era for single-poet collections, but there was a proliferation of anthologies for children and, as an emerging poet trying to get a toehold in the publishing industry, it was perfect timing. My details were soon passed to other anthologists who keep informal lists of poets to contact when calling for submissions. The submission briefs sent out tend to be specific in nature, targeting a particular age range and dictating the subject matter to be covered. While this can feel a little restrictive at times, it serves well as a homework-type exercise and a handy writing prompt. Assuming that the most obvious angles and poetic forms would be covered, I learned to submit poems from slant, unusual perspectives, increasing the likelihood they'd be chosen. The fee offered is low – for as long as I can recall it has mysteriously remained at an average of £50 per poem. As the saying goes, there's no poetry in money and no money in poetry. But I gained a fairly decent strike rate and soon became an established contributor.

By now I had a notion to publish a collection for children, but this was overshadowed by a desire to learn more about the art itself. I felt driven to explore 'adult' poetry, with all its nuance, variations and complexities. So, while juggling a return to special needs teaching, motherhood and a crumbling marriage, I attended a year-long evening class, followed by a part-time two-year Creative Writing certificate at University of Sussex, both under the excellent tutorage of the poet and novelist Ros Barber. Her rigorous teaching helped sharpen up my technical skills and deepened my appreciation of the art. Workshopping poems taught me to accept critical feedback and to constructively critique the writing of others. And in the process I developed supportive relationships with those at a similar stage in their writing careers, some of which continue to this day. After completing the certificate, I refocused on children's poetry. I entered the Belmont Prize, which at the time was the only national poetry competition for a single children's poem. Getting shortlisted in this was an early highlight and gave me reassurance that I was on the right path. The Belmont is now sadly defunct, but two other national single-poem competitions have taken its place: the Caterpillar Poetry Prize (see page 335), run by the children's magazine *The Caterpillar*, and the YorkMix Poems for Children Competition (https://yorkmix.com/yorkmix-poems-for-children-competition). There may also be other local and regional competitions to be found.

I'd accumulated a healthy number of poems over four years but had come to a frustrating impasse. While I was confident I had the basis of a decent collection, I was at a loss to know how to proceed. Most publishers weren't willing to accept unsolicited manuscripts and securing an agent as an unknown poet was unlikely, especially as there was little demand for single-poet collections back then. But I was determined to be published – why, I'd even written 'Win CLPE Poetry Award' on my list of Things I Must Do, hadn't I? To keep myself buoyant, I splashed out on an Arvon residential course (see page 187), Writing Poetry for Children, run by Carol Ann Duffy. These courses don't come cheap, but spending five full days (and evenings) immersed in all things poetic, free from real-life distractions and with the perfect tutor, was a magical and productive experience.

Despite Carol Ann's encouraging response to my writing, I fell back into a despondent personal place. So I decided to channel this feeling into a rhyming picture book text titled *A Patch of Black* – a night-time lullaby about fear of the dark. I made multiple submissions to publishers I thought might suit; although none were taken up I did receive a few positive-sounding rejections and this spurred me on to source a mentor, the late Gerard Benson, whose poetry I admired. Having contacted him through his publisher Smith|Doorstop, I sent him a selection of my poems to see if we'd be a 'good fit' and he agreed to critique my work for a reasonable fee. Gerard was a perceptive reader and an assured editor. We developed an email correspondence over several months and met up at a few poetry events. At one event – a children's poetry showcase at The Society of Authors – he introduced me to a few industry employees including Suzanne Carnell, then the Editorial Director at Macmillan Children's Books. Gently prompted by Gerald, I mentioned that I'd submitted *A Patch of Black* but hadn't heard anything back. Suzanne gave me her business card and suggested I contact her directly, which I duly did. Though I wasn't aware at the time, I had just engaged in what some might term 'networking', thanks to Gerard's generous manoeuvres.

Eventually, *A Patch of Black*, illustrated by Deborah Allwright, was taken up by Macmillan and was to be published in 2010. Now, the hunt for an agent was on. I had no idea where to begin, so I rifled though the *Writers' & Artists' Yearbook* and selected several potential agents to contact. I was delighted to eventually be taken up by Caroline Walsh at David Higham and we've worked together happily ever since. I struck lucky here; after all, poets aren't the most lucrative clients to take on. And, again, the timing was good – Janetta-Otter Barry at Frances Lincoln (now Quarto) was setting up a rare single-poet poetry list and was looking to launch new poetry voices. My agent pitched my work, and *The Language of Cat* was published by Frances Lincoln in 2011, along with a wonderful endorsement from Carol Ann Duffy herself. It was longlisted for the Carnegie Medal and also went on to win the CLPE Prize. Two more poetry collections have followed, both shortlisted for the CLiPPA, with one winning the North Somerset Teachers' Award. *Hey, Girl!*, a collection for young teens, was published by Otter-Barry Books in August 2021 and a picture book, *The Fears You Fear*, is currently in production – the last in a set of three rhyming stories based around emotions, illustrated by the wonderful Zehra Hicks.

My publishing journey reads like a dream come true, and in retrospect I think it has been. However, that isn't the whole story – or poem, if you will. There have been real challenges along the way. Many times it has felt like an uphill struggle, a salutary lesson in remaining tenacious. As in the careers of most published writers, there has been an element of serendipity at play, of chance meetings and fortuitous timings. Unfortunately, you can never factor these in when you set out. In recent years, the publishing landscape has altered somewhat. Children's poetry is inhabiting a more central position, and social media platforms such as Twitter and Instagram provide visibility and exposure for newcomers and established writers alike. Online courses and readings are now commonplace and accessible to most. And the children's poetry world is a relatively small and welcoming one, especially when raw talent is spotted.

So, what advice might I give a poet starting out? I remember once meeting an editor who told me she had real difficulty sourcing new poets for her list. When I asked her why, she told me it was because writing children's poetry is deceptively difficult and most people think it an easy thing to do. With this in mind, my foremost advice is to focus on the craft itself; if your poetry is strong enough, it's sure to get noticed eventually. Good luck!

**Rachel Rooney** is a trained teacher in Primary and Special Education. Her first poetry collection *The Language of Cat* (republished by Otter-Barry Books 2021) won the CLPE Poetry Award and was longlisted for the Carnegie Medal in 2011. Her other collections, *My Life as a Goldfish* (Quarto 2014) and *A Kid in My Class* (Otter-Barry Books 2018) have both been shortlisted for the CLiPPA Award. Her last collection, *Hey, Girl!* (Otter-Barry 2021) was nominated for the Carnegie Medal. She has performed at festivals and for The Children's Bookshow. In 2017 she was the Chair of Judges for the CLiPPA and has judged the Betjeman Poetry Prize. See her website www.rachelrooneypoet.com for more information and follow her on Twitter @RooneyRachel.

## See also...

**Poetry**

# Poetry organisations

Below are some organisations which provide budding poets with opportunities to develop their skills, and to perform and engage with audiences and other poets. Many poetry events are once more happening in person, but there may be an online component to some: please check websites for details.

## WHERE TO GET INVOLVED

A range of organisations – from local groups to larger professional bodies – exists at which emerging and established poets can access support or learn more about others' work. A concise selection appears below.

### Literature Wales

Glyn Jones Centre, Wales Millennium Centre,
Bute Place, Cardiff CF10 5AL
*tel* 029-2047 2266
*email* post@literaturewales.org
*website* www.literaturewales.org

National company for the development of literature in Wales. Working to inspire communities, develop writers and celebrate Wales' literary culture. Activities include the Wales Book of the Year Award, the Children's Laureate Wales and Bardd Plant Cymru schemes, creative writing courses at Tŷ Newydd Writing Centre, writer's bursaries and mentoring, and the National Poet of Wales initiative. The organisation is a member of the Arts Council of Wales' Arts Portfolio Wales.

### The Poetry Book Society

Milburn House, Dean Street,
Newcastle Upon Tyne NE1 1LF
*tel* 0191 230 8100
*email* enquiries@poetrybooksociety.co.uk
*website* www.poetrybooks.co.uk
*Facebook* www.facebook.com/poetrybooksoc
*Twitter* @poetrybooksoc

Book club for readers of poetry founded in 1953 by T.S. Eliot. Every quarter, expert poet selectors choose one outstanding publication (the PBS Choice), and recommend four other titles; these are sent to members, who are also offered discounts on other poetry books. The PBS also produces the quarterly membership magazine, the *Bulletin* (available to all members), which contains the poet selectors' reviews of the Choice and Recommendations, interviews with international poets, reviews and listings. Also offers a range of educational memberships for secondary school libraries with expert teaching tips and posters to inspire students with a love of poetry.

### The Poetry Business

Campo House, 54 Campo Lane, Sheffield S1 2EG
*tel* 0114 438 4074

*email* office@poetrybusiness.co.uk
*website* www.poetrybusiness.co.uk

Publishes pamphlets by young poets between the ages of 17 and 24 under The New Poets List imprint; runs the literary magazine, *The North*. Also organises a national pamphlet competition for young poets, writing days and residential courses.

### Poetry Ireland

11 Parnell Square East, Dublin D01 ND60,
Republic of Ireland
*tel* +353 (0)1 6789815
*email* info@poetryireland.ie
*website* www.poetryireland.ie

Organisation committed to achieving excellence in the reading, writing and performance of poetry throughout the island of Ireland. Poetry Ireland receives support from The Arts Council (An Chomhairle Ealaíon) and The Arts Council of Northern Ireland and enjoys partnerships with arts centres, festivals, schools, colleges and bookshops at home and abroad. Its commitment to creating performance and publication opportunities for poets at all stages of their careers helps ensure that the best work is made available to the widest possible audience. Poetry Ireland publishes the well-regarded journal, *Poetry Ireland Review*.

### The Poetry Society

22 Betterton Street, London WC2H 9BX
*tel* 020-7420 9880
*email* info@poetrysociety.org.uk
*website* www.poetrysociety.org.uk

A leading voice for poets and poetry in Britain. Founded in 1909 to promote a more general recognition and appreciation of poetry, the Society has nearly 4,000 members. With innovative education, commissioning and publishing programmes, and a packed calendar of performances, readings and competitions, the Society champions poetry in its many forms.

The Society also publishes education resources for teachers and educators; organises high-profile events including an Annual Lecture and National Poetry Day celebrations; runs Poetry Prescription, a critical appraisal service; and provides an education advisory service, INSET packages for schools and networks of schools, a poets in schools service, school membership, youth membership and a website.

Competitions run by the Society include the annual National Poetry Competition, with a first prize of £5,000, and the Foyle Young Poets of the Year Award.

## Tower Poetry

Christ Church, Oxford OX1 1DP
*tel* 07849 625906
*email* tower.poetry@chch.ox.ac.uk
*website* www.chch.ox.ac.uk/towerpoetry
*Facebook* www.facebook.com/towerpoetry
*Twitter* @towerpoetry

Exists to encourage and challenge everyone who reads or writes poetry. Funded by a generous bequest to Christ Church, Oxford, by the late Christopher Tower, the aims of Tower Poetry are to stimulate an enjoyment and critical appreciation of poetry, particularly among young people in education, and to challenge people to write their own poetry.

## WHERE TO GET INFORMATION

Your local library is a good first port of call and should have information about the poetry scene in the area. Many libraries are actively involved in spreading the word about poetry as well as having modern poetry available for loan.

## Alliance of Literary Societies (ALS)

*email* allianceoflitsocs@gmail.com
*website* www.allianceofliterarysocieties.org.uk
*Facebook* www.facebook.com/allianceofliterarysocieties
*Twitter* @alliancelitsocs
*Instagram* @alliancelitsocs
*Chair* Marty Ross

Umbrella organisation for literary societies and groups in the UK. It provides support and advice on a variety of literary subjects, as well as promoting cooperation between member societies. Its publications include a twice-yearly members' newsletter, *Not Only But…*, and an annual journal, *ALSo*. ALS holds an AGM weekend which is hosted by a different member society each year, moving around the UK, or online. Founded 1973.

## Arts Council England

*tel* 0161 934 4317
*email* enquiries@artscouncil.org.uk
*website* www.artscouncil.org.uk

National development agency for the arts in England, providing funding for a range of arts and cultural activities. It supports creative writing including poetry, fiction, storytelling, spoken word, digital work, writing for children and literary translation. It funds a range of publishers and magazines as well as providing grants to individual writers. Contact the enquiries team for more information on funding support and advice.

## Arts Council of Wales

Bute Place, Cardiff CF10 5AL
*tel* 0845 873 4900
*email* information@arts.wales
*website* https://arts.wales
*Facebook* www.facebook.com/celfyddydau
*Twitter* @Arts_Wales_

Independent charity, established by Royal Charter in 1994. It has three regional offices and its principal sponsor is the Welsh Government. It is the country's funding and development agency for the arts, supporting and developing high-quality arts activities. Its funding schemes offer opportunities for arts organisations and individuals in Wales to apply, through a competitive process, for funding towards a clearly defined arts-related project.

## Manchester Poetry Library

Manchester Metropolitan University, Grosvenor Building, Cavendish Street, Manchester M15 6BG
*email* poetrylibrary@mmu.ac.uk
*website* www.mmu.ac.uk/poetry-library
*Twitter* @mcrpoetrylib
*Instagram* @mcrpoetrylibrary
*Director* Becky Swain

Public poetry library: free and open to all. Aims to expand access to poetry and to encourage the writing of it at all levels, from primary school to professional publication. Core collection includes 19th- to 21st-century poetry in English from around the world, as well as poetry in translation. Audio and print versions available. Runs events that celebrate the role of local communities and languages.

## National Association of Writers' Groups

Old Vicarage, Scammonden, Huddersfield HD3 3FT
*email* info@nawg.co.uk
*website* www.nawg.co.uk

Aims to bring cohesion and fellowship to isolated writers' groups and individuals, promoting the study and art of writing in all its aspects. There are many affiliated groups and associate (individual) members across the UK.

## National Poetry Library (Children's Collection)

Level 5, Royal Festival Hall, Southbank Centre, London SE1 8XX
*tel* 020-7921 0943
*email* info@poetrylibrary.org.uk
*website* www.nationalpoetrylibrary.org.uk
*Facebook* www.facebook.com/NationalPoetryLibrary
*Twitter* @natpoetrylib
*Instagram* @nationalpoetrylibrary

Comprises thousands of items for young poets of all ages, including poetry on audio and film. The library

Poetry

has an education service for teachers and writing groups, with a separate collection of books and materials for teachers and poets who work with children in schools. Group visits can be organised, allowing children to interact with the collection in various ways, from taking a Poetry Word Trail across Southbank Centre, to exploring how the worlds of science and poetry interact, engaging with war poetry via the Letters Home booklet, or becoming a Poetry Library Poetry Explorer. Children of all ages can join for free and borrow books and other materials. A special membership scheme is available for teachers to borrow books for the classroom. Contact the library for membership and opening time details.

## Northern Poetry Library

The Chantry, Bridge Street, Morpeth, Northumberland NE61 1PD
*tel* (01670) 620391
*email* mylibrary@northumberland.gov.uk
*website* http://northernpoetrylibrary.org.uk
*Twitter* @nplpoetry

Largest collection of contemporary poetry outside London, housing over 15,000 titles and magazines covering poetry published since 1945. Founded 1968.

## Scottish Poetry Library

5 Crichton's Close, Canongate, Edinburgh EH8 8DT
*tel* 0131 557 2876
*email* reception@spl.org.uk
*website* www.scottishpoetrylibrary.org.uk

Houses over 45,000 poetry-related items: books, magazines, pamphlets, recordings and the Edwin Morgan Archive (featuring rare works by Morgan and others). The core of the collection is contemporary and classic poetry written in Scotland – Scots, Gaelic and English – but classic Scottish poetry as well as contemporary works from almost every part of the world are also available. All resources, advice and information are readily accessible, free of charge. The SPL has its own shop and holds regular exhibitions and poetry events, including reading and writing groups and outreach projects throughout the nation, details of which are available on the library website. Closed Saturday and Sunday. Founded 1984.

## ONLINE RESOURCES

There is a wealth of information available for poets at the click of a mouse; the suggestions below are a good starting point.

## The Children's Poetry Archive

*website* https://childrenspoetryarchive.org

World's premier online collection of recordings of children's poets reading their work. Visitors to the website may listen, free of charge, to the voices of contemporary English-language poets and of poets from the past. Featured poets include Allan Ahlberg,

Michael Rosen and Valerie Bloom, but the Archive is added to regularly. The website has a range of search options, so that users can search by theme, poet name, lyric, and so on.

## LoveReading4Kids.co.uk

*website* www.lovereading4kids.co.uk

Independent literature recommendation site designed to inspire and inform parents about the Sets out to inspire and inform parents about the best new reads in children's publishing from toddlers to YA, including poetry. Now features an online bookstore with social purpose where 25% of money spent can be donated to a school of the buyer's choice, to spend on books. Features include: filter by age range and interest; downloadable opening extracts; exclusive reviews from children's book experts; and authentic reader reviews from children.

Recently merged into LoveReading4Kids, the LoveReading4Schools portal supports schools across the UK wanting to embed a reading for pleasure culture. On their school dashboard, they can create their own recommended reading lists and share these with their pupils' parents, so that they can make better informed purchasing decisions for their children both at home and at school. Eligible schools can also apply for between £1,000–£5,000 credit to spend on books through the LoveReading4Kids Funding For Schools Scheme. Founded 2005.

## The Poetry Kit

*email* info@poetrykit.org
*website* www.poetrykit.org
*Twitter* @thepoetrykit

Collates a wide variety of poetry-related information, including events, competitions, courses and more for an international readership.

## Poetry Space

*email* susan@poetryspace.co.uk
*website* www.poetryspace.co.uk

Specialist publisher of poetry and short stories, as well as news and features, edited by Susan Jane Sims. Operates as a social enterprise with all profits being used to publish online and in print, and to hold events to widen participation in poetry. Submissions of poems, stories, novel extracts, photographs and artwork accepted all year for Young Writers' and Artists' Space (18s and under; work by under-16s particularly welcomed).

## Seven Stories – National Centre for Children's Books

*email* info@sevenstories.org.uk
*website* www.sevenstories.org.uk
*Twitter* @7Stories
*Chief Executive* Wendy Elliott

Seven Stories is the only place in the United Kingdom dedicated to the art of children's books. Its website features a blog and online catalogue that may be of use to researchers and authors.

## Teachit: English Teaching Resources

Spaces, Northgate House, Bath BA1 1RG
*tel* (01225) 788850
*website* www.teachitenglish.co.uk
*Twitter* @TeachitEnglish

Resource website for teachers, with over 20,000 pages of classroom worksheets, PowerPoint presentations and activities that have been written and edited by experienced English teachers. The website offers free pdfs as well as teaching packs, classroom posters and books designed for Key Stages 3, 4 and 5.

## WHERE TO CELEBRATE POETRY

Festival information should be available from Arts Council England offices (see page 315). See also *Children's literature festivals and trade fairs* on page 349.

## The British Council

British Council Customer Service UK, Bridgewater House, 58 Whitworth Street, Manchester M1 6BB
*tel* 0161 957 7755
*email* uk-literature@britishcouncil.org
*website* https://literature.britishcouncil.org
*Twitter* @litbritish

Information on events, authors and projects.

## Imagine: Writers and Writing for Children

Southbank Centre, London SE1 8XX
*tel* 020-7960 4200
*website* www.southbankcentre.co.uk/whats-on/festivals-series/imagine-childrens-festival
*Twitter* @southbankcentre
*Takes place* February

Annual festival celebrating writing for children featuring a selection of poets, storytellers and illustrators.

## Ledbury Poetry Festival

The Master's House, St Katherine's, Bye Street, Ledbury HR8 1EA
*tel* (01531) 636232
*email* director@poetry-festival.co.uk
*website* www.poetry-festival.co.uk
*Artistic Director* Chloe Garner
*Takes place* July and throughout the year

The UK's biggest celebration of poetry and spoken word, attended by poets from all over the world. Established and upcoming talents take part in a wide variety of events, from masterclasses, walks, talks and films through to breakfasts, music, exhibitions and bike rides. International Poetry Competition launches every February.

## WHERE TO WRITE POETRY

## Arvon

Lumb Bank – The Ted Hughes Arvon Centre, Heptonstall, Hebden Bridge, West Yorkshire HX7 6DF
*tel* (01422) 843714
*email* lumbbank@arvon.org
Totleigh Barton, Sheepwash, Beaworthy, Devon EX21 5NS
*tel* (01409) 231338
*email* totleighbarton@arvon.org
The Hurst – The John Osborne Arvon Centre, Clunton, Craven Arms, Shrops. SY7 0JA
*tel* (01588) 640658
*email* thehurst@arvon.org
*website* www.arvon.org

Hosts residential creative writing courses and retreats in three rural writing houses. With the opportunity to live and work with professional writers, participants transform their writing through workshops, one-to-one tutorials, time and space to write. Five-day courses and shorter courses are available in a wide range of genres, including writing for children and young adults, fiction, poetry, theatre and creative non-fiction. An online programme of writing courses, masterclasses and live readings also runs year-round. Grants and concessions are available to help with course fees. Founded 1968.

## City Lit

1–10 Keeley Street, London WC2B 4BA
*tel* 020-7831 7831
*email* writing@citylit.ac.uk
*website* www.citylit.ac.uk/courses/history-culture-and-writing/writing
*Twitter* @citylit

Offers classes and courses (online and in-person) on poetry appreciation and writing for children, as well as a wide range of other topics.

## The Poetry School

Somerset House, Strand, London WC2R 1LA
*tel* 020-7582 1679
*website* www.poetryschool.com

Teaches the art and craft of writing poetry, with courses in London and around the UK, ranging from evening classes, small seminars and individual tutorials, to one-day workshops, year-long courses and an accredited MA. Activities for beginners to advanced writers, with classes happening face-to-face and online. Three termly programmes a year, plus professional skills development projects and CAMPUS, a social network for poets.

## Tŷ Newydd Writing Centre

Llanystumdwy, Criccieth, Gwynedd LL52 0LW
*tel* (01766) 522811
*email* tynewydd@literaturewales.org
*website* www.tynewydd.wales

Tŷ Newydd, the former home of Prime Minister
David Lloyd George, has hosted residential creative
writing courses for writers of all abilities for over 30
years. Open to everyone over the age of 16. Courses
cover everything from poetry and popular fiction to
writing for the theatre, developing a novel for young
adults. No qualifications are necessary. Staff can
advise on the suitability of courses, and further details
about each individual course can be obtained by
visiting the website, or contacting the team by phone
or email. Tŷ Newydd also offers courses for schools,
corporate courses and away days for companies. Tŷ
Newydd is also home to Nant, the writers' retreat
cottage located on site. Tŷ Newydd Writing Centre is
run by Literature Wales, the national company for
the development of literature in Wales.

## HELP FOR YOUNG POETS AND TEACHERS

## National Association of Writers in Education (NAWE)

Tower House, Mill Lane, off Askham Fields Lane,
Askham Bryan, York YO23 3FS
*tel* 0330 333 5909
*email* admin@nawe.co.uk
*website* www.nawe.co.uk

National membership organisation which aims to
advocate for creative writing: enhancing knowledge
and understanding of the subject, supporting writers
and good practice in teaching and facilitation in all
settings. NAWE promotes creative writing as both a
distinct discipline and an essential element in
education generally. Its membership is national and
international and includes those working in Higher
Education, freelance writers working in schools and
community contexts, and the teachers and other
professionals who work with them. It runs a national
directory of professional members offering
workshops, talks and other services, produces a
weekly opportunities bulletin, publishes two journals –
*Writing in Education* and *Writing in Practice* – and
holds a national conference (this was online in 2023).
Professional Membership includes public liability
insurance cover.

Professional Graduate Membership is available for
university creative writing students who have recently
graduated and aims to support the move from
student to working as a professional writer in
education and the community, offering the benefits
of Professional Membership at a discounted rate.

## Poetry Society Education

The Poetry Society, 22 Betterton Street,
London WC2H 9BX
*tel* 020-7420 9880
*email* educationadmin@poetrysociety.org.uk
*website* www.poetrysociety.org.uk

An arm of The Poetry Society aiming to facilitate
exciting and innovative education work. For over 30
years it has been introducing poets into classrooms,
providing comprehensive teachers' resources and
producing accessible publications for pupils. It
develops projects and schemes to keep poetry
flourishing in schools, libraries and workplaces,
giving work to hundreds of poets and allowing
thousands of children and adults to experience poetry
for themselves.

Through projects such as the Foyle Young Poets of
the Year Award and Young Poets Network, The
Poetry Society gives valuable encouragement and
exposure to young writers and performers.

Schools membership offers a range of benefits,
including quarterly Poetry Society publications,
books and posters, and free access to the Poets in
Schools placement service. Youth membership is also
available (for ages 11–18; from £25 p.a.) and offers
discounts, publications, poetry books and posters.

## Young Poets Network

*email* educationadmin@poetrysociety.org.uk
*website* https://ypn.poetrysociety.org.uk
*Facebook* www.facebook.com/YoungPoetsNetwork
*Twitter* @youngpoetsnet

Online resource from The Poetry Society comprising
features about reading, writing and performing
poetry, plus new work by young poets and regular
writing challenges. Open to anyone under the age of
25.

## YOUNG POETRY COMPETITIONS

Children's competitions are included in the
competition list provided by the Poetry Library: this
is free online at www.nationalpoetrylibrary.org.uk/
write-publish/competitions. Further information on
literary prizes can be found on the BookTrust website
(www.booktrust.org.uk/what-we-do/awards-and-
prizes).

## Foyle Young Poets of the Year Award

The Poetry Society, 22 Betterton Street,
London WC2H 9BX
*tel* 020-7420 9880
*email* fyp@poetrysociety.org.uk
*website* https://foyleyoungpoets.org/
*Facebook* www.facebook.com/thepoetrysociety
*Twitter* @PoetrySociety

Annual competition for writers aged 11–17. Prizes include publication, mentoring and a residential writing course. Deadline 31 July. Free to enter. Founded 2001.

## Christopher Tower Poetry Competition

Christ Church, Oxford OX1 1DP
*tel* 07849 625906
*email* tower.poetry@chch.ox.ac.uk
*website* www.chch.ox.ac.uk/towerpoetry
*Twitter* @TowerPoetry

Annual poetry competition (open from October to February) from Christ Church, Oxford, aimed at students aged between 16 and 18 in UK schools and colleges. The poems should be no longer than 48 lines, on a different chosen theme each year. Free to enter. Prizes: £5,000 (1st), £3,000 (2nd), £1,500 (3rd). There will also be ten commended awards of £500 each.

## Further reading

Addonizio, Kim, *Ordinary Genius: A Guide for the Poet Within* (W.W. Norton 2012)

Bell, Jo and Jane Commane, *How to Be a Poet: A 21st-Century Guide to Writing Well* (Nine Arches Press 2017)

Bell, Jo and guests: *52: Write a Poem a Week – Start Now, Keep Going* (Nine Arches Press 2015)

Blackwell, Sophia, *Writers' & Artists' Poetry Writers' Handbook* (Bloomsbury, 2022)

Chisholm, Alison, *A Practical Guide to Poetry Forms* (Compass Books 2014)

Fairfax, John and John Moat, *The Way to Write* (Penguin Books, 2nd edn revised 1998)

Greene, Roland et al., *Princeton Encyclopedia of Poetry and Poetics* (Princeton University Press, 4th edn 2012)

Hamilton, Ian and Jeremy Noel-Tod, *The Oxford Companion to Modern Poetry in English* (Oxford University Press, 2nd edn 2014)

Kowit, Steve, *In the Palm of Your Hand: A Poet's Portable Workshop* (Tilbury House, 2nd edn 2017)

Maxwell, Glyn, *On Poetry* (Oberon Books 2017)

Oliver, Mary, *Rules for the Dance: Handbook for Writing and Reading Metrical Verse* (Houghton Mifflin 1998)

Padel, Ruth, *52 Ways of Looking at a Poem: A Poem for Every Week of the Year* (Vintage 2004)

Padel, Ruth, *The Poem and the Journey: 60 Poems for the Journey of Life* (Vintage 2008)

Roberts, Philip Davies, *How Poetry Works* (Penguin Books, 2nd edn 2000)

Sampson, Fiona, *Poetry Writing: The Expert Guide* (Robert Hale 2009)

Sansom, Peter, *Writing Poems* (Bloodaxe 1993, repr. 1997)

Whitworth, John, *Writing Poetry* (A&C Black, 2nd edn 2006)

**Poetry**

# Literary agents
## What do agents *do* for their commission?

Generally, literary agents take 15% of their clients' earnings as their commission. Julia Churchill explains what she does in her role of literary agent in return for that percentage.

My role as a literary agent is to help my authors have successful careers. I endeavour to make money in as many rights streams as possible (with an eye on the long term), and enable an easier professional life for my clients so that they can focus on writing. My job involves spotting talent, helping to develop it and selling it.

Some of my clients came to me as established authors wanting to take their careers up a gear, but most have come via my slush pile, as debut writers. I get well over 100 submissions a week, and I may take on a new writer every few months (if I'm lucky). Spotting talent is often where my job starts. I think I have good taste, and I know that my taste isn't unique. If I love a book, it is likely that there are others who will love it too.

I tend not to follow trends, but I am aware of them. There are two markets to consider, and a good agent will have a clear understanding of both. The first is what I focus on when I sell books to publishers. The editor is the buyer and I need to think about their enthusiasms and needs for their list. Then there's the real market, which is reflected in what people are buying from booksellers right now. Both these markets change constantly and part of my job is to keep up to date with trends, and the preferences of individual editors. This knowledge feeds into my decision-making when considering new authors and guidance for my existing clients, although there are also many opportunities outside of obvious trends. To some extent I'm looking for what's fashionable, but more than anything I'm looking for what may be evergreen.

## What I am looking for

When I read a manuscript, I'm looking to connect with a voice, a concept, a character and a story, a book with something to say. I'm looking for clarity and intent in the storytelling, and to be taken somewhere new.

Most debut manuscripts that arrive in my office are not yet ready to sell to a publisher, and I may work with the author to focus on what's best about the character(s) and story. Every edit is different. We may sit down together with a cup of tea and talk through the book, exploring such questions as: What does the writer do best? Where does the story lose focus? How can we keep raising the stakes? Why does this section not work? Is it needed? Is the story pulling in too many directions? What is the book about, in the small ways and the big ways?

Before I offer to represent an author, I'll talk them through the work that I think their manuscript needs. I want to be sure, for the author's sake as well as my own, that we're pointed in the same direction and in sync with our ambitions. It's my job to help the author bring out what is best in the manuscript. Sometimes these conversations are about the architecture of the book, and at other times just the interior design. I do what's necessary to maximise the chance of achieving a book deal and the value of that deal.

When I'm satisfied that the book is ready, I submit it to editors. On occasion, I may approach just one editor, and one publishing house, if there is a very specific reason why this would be the best possible outcome for the author. This is matchmaking. More often, I send out the manuscript widely in order to find the publisher with the most passion for the book and the best plan for it.

## Selling the book

My favourite aspect of being a literary agent is seeing talent before the rest of the world does. The publishing business relies on having champions for books and an agent is the first professional champion. The agent shares their passion about a book with editors, who in turn pass it on to sales and marketing experts, publicists, reviewers, bloggers, librarians, booksellers and then finally readers.

Sometimes it takes just a few days to sell a book and for other books it can take months – on occasion it has taken years. An auction is lively, but more than anything it's a logistical challenge and requires being organised and systematic. Auctions provide an opportunity for the agent and author to see each publisher's vision, and they give maximum leverage for the best possible deal. Although the idea of an auction may sound exciting, I probably get as much professional satisfaction from humbly selling a book that's been very tough to place as I do from an eight-publisher auction that takes days to tie up.

## Looking at contracts

Being a literary agent is not all about passionate pitches, editorial chats over cups of tea and champagne celebrations. There is some glamour to our business, but in many ways an agent's job is quite mundane and is taken up with working on contracts between publishers and authors. A contract has a long life and it requires rigour and experience to convert a publisher-friendly contract into one that is author-friendly. Negotiating contracts is not confined to increasing the advance and pushing for the best royalty and high discount rates, although that is where an agent is likely to show the most immediate value. It's also about ensuring that the author gets their rights back if the book stops selling above a certain level, that the pay-out is staggered in a way that favours the author, that certain sub-rights revert if they are unexploited, that the delivery and acceptance terms are favourable, that in a multi-book deal the books are accounted separately, that the split of sub-rights are as good as they possibly can be, that there is total clarity on what electronic rights the publisher has and that they don't cut across the author's reserved rights. The list of considerations is long: there is a lot to cover in a contract.

An agency will often sell translation rights, and television and film rights. Some of my clients make more money in Brazil or Norway than they do in the USA or UK. And while some markets shrink, others thrive, so for books with reach, it's important to have a strong international team and relationships with film scouts and production companies.

As in any career, a writer is faced with opportunities and decisions to make. Some are small and possibly of little consequence, and some are big and important to get right. Every now and then, there are huge forks in the road which require bravery, clear-minded counsel and an ally. The role of an agent is to be informed and to guide each of their authors to make the best decisions. On behalf of the author, an agent is responsible for talking through grievances, ensuring that publishers deliver what has been promised, feeding into conversations about strategy regarding their work, saying 'no' when it's appropriate, finding work and pushing back.

While everyone concerned in the publishing process wants a book to succeed, my interests as an agent are the same as those of my client. Publishers' interests obviously dovetail with those of the author, but they aren't identical. This is why we generally find ourselves harmonious and in accord with the process, but occasionally in conflict with it. It's my job to have the necessary conversations to look after my authors, to do everything I can to ensure they have the career they want. We are in it together.

**Julia Churchill** is the children's agent at A.M. Heath Ltd. She is always on the lookout for new writing talent, from picture book texts through to young adult fiction, and considers the slush pile to be the greatest place on earth. Follow her on Twitter @JuliaChurchill.

## See also...
- *Choosing the right agent,* page 198
- *Children's literary agents UK and Ireland,* page 218
- *Children's literary agents overseas,* page 231
- *Society of Authors,* page 297

Literary agents

# Submission to a literary agent (the when, what and how...)

Hannah Sheppard offers practical advice on the process of submitting your finished work to a literary agent and provides top tips and inside knowledge on how to find the representation that might be right for you.

Congratulations! You've finished your novel. This is a huge achievement – not everyone manages to see the task through to completion (I know this from experience ... twice). But, what should you do next?

At the risk of being a complete bore – unless you've already done this, now you need to *get back to work and start editing*.

## Honing your final manuscript

The first rule of submitting to literary agents is: ***don't* submit your first draft**. It's time to read your work objectively. Where does the pace drop? Where do the characters do things that don't fit with their motivations? Remember that section you really love but know, if you're honest, isn't moving the plot forward? Cut it.

Find a critique partner (Twitter and local writers' groups can be a good place to start); read and give feedback on their novel in return for feedback on your own. You'll learn as much from exercising your inner editor on someone else's work as you will from the feedback they give you.

Go back and re-write. Do it again. Do it until, hand on heart, you cannot see another thing that might need changing. Then print your freshly edited story in a font you haven't seen it in before (alternatively stick the manuscript on your e-reader or phone, or read it aloud to yourself); this will help you see the words with fresh eyes and make it easier to spot any lingering typos, word repetitions or slightly awkward sentences, so you can fix those. Only now are you ready to start thinking about submitting to a literary agent, and first, you'll need to decide who to submit to.

## Making your agent list

The second rule of submitting to literary agents is: ***don't* send your work to everyone**. Agents have different tastes and specialisms and there's enough information out there to help you narrow down a list of those who might be suitable for your manuscript. The amount of time authors spend waiting for a response to submissions would be a lot shorter if everyone stuck to this rule!

Luckily, you currently have in your hand the fount of all knowledge when it comes to literary agents – well done. Make your way through the *Children's Writers' & Artists' Yearbook* (but not yet, finish reading this first) looking for agents who represent your genre, and make yourself a longlist. Then look these agents up online – nearly all will have a website, many will also have Twitter accounts, and if you keep hunting you might find articles they've written and also their manuscript wish lists. All of this will give you some clues as to whether each agent might be right for you and your work.

It's also worth thinking about what's important to you when it comes to this relationship. Do you want someone who is a cut-throat dealmaker who is all about the business side of publishing, or someone a little more approachable? (If I'm honest, they're all pretty lovely – I haven't met many of the first kind.) Do you want someone who will be hands-on editorially or do you feel like you've got that covered? My top piece of advice is to find someone you can ask basic questions to without feeling stupid ... because there are going to be a lot of those. Quite honestly, there's no reason you *should* know all about how this industry works. Publishing can be flummoxing at times – even for someone who's been working in it for over 20 years.

After researching everyone on your longlist, put them into some sort of order – from those who feel like the closest fit in terms of their list and who you think you might gel with personally, down to those who could be a bit of wild card but are not completely beyond the realms of possibility. But if an agent says they don't represent your genre, it's unlikely they're going to start doing so just because of *your* book; this is about their publishing contacts as much as anything – and you want an agent who knows the right editors to sell your work.

## Putting together a submission package

After selecting the agents to approach, you'll need to prepare your submission package, and the third rule of submitting to literary agents is: ***always* follow their guidelines**. As well as your *manuscript* (usually the first three chapters or 10,000 words, and always from the beginning of your manuscript), the submission package should generally include a *synopsis* and a *cover letter*. But it's important to check exactly what each agent wants and how they want it sent. These may be different for every agent on your list. Yes, that may be tiresome, but the guidelines are there to enable your chosen agent to get through their inbox as fast as possible (they've worked out a system that works for them) and get an answer to you. And if an author appears to think they're above following the guidelines, I ask myself – why would I want to work with someone who doesn't respect me? Could I feel confident promoting them to editors I have good working relationships with? The harsh truth is, I don't even need to read the material in these cases.

There's a lot of great advice online about writing a synopsis (see for example, www.writersandartists.co.uk/advice/synopsis) but, in short, this should be one page of A4, size 12 font (typically Times New Roman or something similarly readable), single-spaced. Don't play with the margins or shrink the font; think about the person who has to read it – if it's tiny, densely packed text, you've probably lost them. White space on the page is always good.

A synopsis should be a very functional overview of your protagonist's emotional journey. This isn't about trying to wow an agent with your style (but be sure to proofread – try using the different font trick mentioned above). You don't need to include every plot point or introduce every character, but agents do need to know the cause-and-effect structure of your plot – all of it. We *want* the spoilers here please. An agent needs to know that the mechanics of your story work; from this they can see where there might be structural issues to address.

For your cover letter, it's good to strike a professional yet personable tone. This isn't a casual approach, but an agent does want to see some of your personality, to judge whether you're someone they might work well with. Overleaf is the kind of letter I like to see – the focus is very much on the character and story, rather than themes or why the author wrote it.

(1) Dear Hannah/Ms Sheppard

(2) I'm writing to submit *Romeo and Juliet*, a tragic love story for YA readers, complete at 75,000 words.

(3) When Romeo Montague and Juliet Capulet fall in love, it enrages their feuding families. Can they find a way to be together before Juliet is married off to someone else?

(4) Juliet can't even remember what started the argument between her family and the Montagues, it's been going on so long, and as a result she hasn't seen her childhood friend Romeo for years. But when fate brings them together at a school dance which Romeo and his friends have gate-crashed, the connection is immediate. They are meant to be together. Surely their families will see that? But they don't. And in an effort to keep Romeo and Juliet apart, Juliet's family arrange a marriage between Juliet and a friend of her father. Horrified, Romeo and Juliet hatch a plan to escape together, but a series of mixed messages and missed connections lead to disaster.

(5) *Romeo and Juliet* will appeal to readers of *Othello* and *Antony and Cleopatra* and fans of Christopher Marlowe.

(6) I am a debut writer who has …

(7) I am submitting to you because …

(8) Yours sincerely/Regards …

(1) I'm happy with either style. Some agents prefer more formality … but, above all, spell it correctly.

(2) Clearly state your title, target market and word count.

(3) This is your short elevator pitch – it's great to have something like this prepared for chance encounters with an agent, but also for post-publication when you're at promotional events in front of an audience and you're asked to introduce your book. A useful structure is: When A (inciting incident) happens, B (protagonist) must do C (action) otherwise/before D (stakes) happen.

(4) This gives you a chance to expand a little on the story. You want to focus on the main story line and the emotional journey of your protagonist, making sure that the stakes are clear – knowing what the character stands to lose is important for emotionally engaging your reader. Think of this paragraph a little like the blurb on the back of a book; you want to make me care about the character and intrigue me. The synopsis is where you give the full story.

(5) This is your chance to position your work within the market and demonstrate that you understand the area you're writing into. Try not to include only the mega-sellers, as that suggests you don't read widely in the market – and it's important that you do.

(6) We don't need a huge amount of information about you at this point, but try to include anything pertinent, e.g. have you joined SCBWI; are you part of a writers' group; have you completed a writing course or won a writing competition? None of this is essential, but anything you have done will show how seriously you're taking your writing. My top tip here is **keep it positive**. So, for example, if you haven't won any writing competitions, just don't mention them.

(7) Show that you've done your research and understand a little about the particular agency and agent you're submitting to. Have you read an article in which I talked about my love for the type of story you've written? Does it fit with something my agency has mentioned on its manuscript wish list? Are you a huge fan of one of our existing clients and feel your mutual fandom of that body of work suggests we might like yours too?

(8) Polite sign off … Use your actual name, not just initials or a pseudonym, even if that's what you want to write under. The agent is going to have a working relationship with you.

A few final top tips:

• Use your own, professional email address – almost all submissions are via email now. My agency does not accept hard copy submissions, and many agencies have the same policy. Don't use an email address you share with your partner or one that was funny when you were a student. Email accounts are easy and free to set up, so have a separate one for your work.

• Make attachment file names as useful as possible... 'synopsis for Hannah' is not very helpful (I receive hundreds with a similar description). Instead include your name and the title of your book.

• Try testing the water by contacting four or five agents initially, to see what response you get. That will give you the chance to tweak your submission. Maybe start midway down the list you drew up of those to contact. If you start getting positive reactions, you can always quickly send the submission to the agents at the top of the list too.

• Brace yourself for a long wait. Agents don't do this to torture you; we're very busy and we use our office time working for our existing clients. This means reading submissions happens in the evenings and at weekends. I typically receive ten submissions a day.

• Start writing your next book, so that you're not focused solely on the fate of the first one you send out. This should ideally be something new rather than a sequel, just in case your first submission doesn't work out.

• Usually a gentle nudge is fine if you haven't heard back within the time stated on the agent's website, but always stay polite. Definitely update an agent if you've had a full manuscript request elsewhere or have been offered representation, and withdraw the submission if you accept that representation.

• If you get feedback, take it seriously. I'm so busy that I rarely give personalised feedback and only when I think there's something easy to fix which would make a significant difference to an author's chances.

• Remember that rejections are part of the process. They don't always mean your book or your writing is bad; they can simply mean that yours wasn't the right book for that agent at that time. There's a lot of luck and serendipity involved here too.

• If all you are getting are standard rejections, take some time out to think about whether you need to do more work. Perhaps you should get a professional assessment on your manuscript? Or maybe it's time to begin a different project (luckily you followed my earlier tip and have already started one, right?).

• Keep an open mind, the right agent for you might not be the person you initially put at the top of your wish list. How you get on at a personal level when you chat with an agent will be important.

So that's it ... you're ready to start submitting. Good luck, hold your nerve and keep trying.

Literary agent **Hannah Sheppard** worked as an in-house editor with Macmillan Children's Books and Headline Publishing Group before joining the DHH Literary Agency in 2013. In 2023, she launched the eponymous Hannah Sheppard Literary Agency. She represents authors across children's fiction and commercial adult fiction. For more information, visit www.hs-la.com and follow Hannah on Twitter and Instagram @hannah_litagent.

# Choosing the right agent

Literary agent Gill McLay describes some of the differences between big and small agencies, and identifies some of the ways you can discover which might be the right one for you to approach and to sign up with if you are offered representation.

After completing my marketing and publishing degree I moved to London and went straight into my first publishing job. Over 25 years later I am still in publishing. I have worked for small, independent publishers and large global publishers, always on the publicity, marketing and sales side of the business. Then, about 15 years ago, I decided I wanted to work for myself. One of the many things I did was to set up the Bath Festival of Children's Literature, the largest festival in Europe devoted exclusively to books, authors, illustrators and readers of children's books – from picture books right up to young adult. I knew it had to start big if it was to compete in the already vibrant and well-developed literary festivals calendar. After our success with the festival, we have evolved again to establish, Events of Wonder (www.eventsofwonder.com) which stages events for children in Bath, Bristol and beyond. Creating these magical moments for children and families remains very close to my heart and having a wider range of partners has meant we can now reach so many more people. It has also allowed us to stage art exhibitions, other festivals and develop clubs that ensure we work at a truly grassroots level.

It was while I was working more closely with authors, through the festival, that I started to be asked for publishing advice. I would frequently recommend agents that fledging writers could approach and was repeatedly asked why I didn't offer an agent service myself. Being an agent is an all-encompassing job and I knew it would need me to be full-time, so I decided that when my son started school I would do it!

At the time, I was running media training courses for authors and was always surprised by the questions they asked (or hadn't dared or thought to ask). I decided that if I was to be an agent, I would manage careers rather than projects and I would allow authors to become a fully engaged part of my agency. For me, part of surviving in this tough and competitive business is to help my clients be prepared, and to share my knowledge of why decisions are made and how. As well as showing respect for my authors' writing and other creative work, I set out to establish working relationships based on mutual respect, understanding and gratitude for the respective skills of both author and agent; from such close links, greater successes emerge. *Teams* of people create books, and I wanted to put this team spirit right at the heart of my agency.

The Bath Literary Agency is a relatively small company that offers a very hands-on style of management for writers and illustrators of children's books. We are one of many small literary agencies based outside London, the main publishing metropolis, and we like to think that we offer authors something different to what a larger agency provides. The agency is now over ten years old and continues to go from strength to strength, due to my clients who work incredibly hard to deliver saleable books. Together we are always working on our next project.

## How can *you* find the right agent?

I believe that having an agent is essential. Once you are lucky enough to find your publishing home, it makes a big difference if you can focus on the creative side and let your agent focus on the business aspects of your writing.

This doesn't mean you don't get involved. You *must* be involved. It does, however, mean that you can talk through things with your agent and ask all the questions you like without fear of asking the wrong thing – which might not be the case if you were talking directly to a publisher. It also gives you a greater understanding of which things to challenge and which to accept, both contractually and creatively. There is a huge difference between writing for yourself and writing to be published; an agent can help you navigate this fine line.

## What are the differences between small and large agencies?

Bigger agencies, London-based agencies, multimedia agencies and small boutique agencies (with only one or two agents, say) all offer different things. They each have their strengths and weaknesses; the most important thing for you, as a new author, is to get the right agent for *your* books and *your* needs.

The size of the agency is actually irrelevant in many ways, because everything comes down to the relationship you have with one person: your own agent.

That relationship should be symbiotic, with writer and agent coming together to make the strongest possible offering to a publisher, and thus ultimately to your readership or market. Your respective strengths and weaknesses should complement each other.

This is why you need to know your agent's experience. Agents come from all

> ### In a nutshell
>
> **Know what you want:**
> - Do you want to be a big fish in a small pond?
> - Do you write across several genres; if so, does the agent represent them all?
> - Do you want an agent with editorial skills to help shape your writing?
> - Do you want personal support or purely business/commercial help?

sorts of different backgrounds, which can make a huge difference to their individual approach. Many have been editors, some move over from selling rights in publishing houses to agenting and others have come from the sales and book-buying side of publishing. Each set of skills and experience has its own strengths.

My background is in sales and marketing. As a result, I approach things from a very commercial angle and spend almost as much time scouting for new opportunities as I do creating them. When I advise my clients, we talk about long-term objectives and career progression. The individual books are important, but I am always keen to find out what else an author can do and where they want to be.

An agent with an editorial background, however, may focus more on the individual manuscript. For some authors this is essential and they need this support, but others may already have confidence and feel secure in their writing, but they may need help to understand the market and publishing process and to pitch their story to the right audience and gatekeepers (i.e. publishers).

Part of this writer-development process, fostering authors of tomorrow, comes from the other professional hats I wear. Media training for authors, Events of Wonder and the festival I have run has given me a real insight into the life of a successful author today. Gone are the days of being able to write, send your script to an agent, sell your book and then start writing again. An author needs to promote and reach their audience. The first book you sell to a publisher will be the last before you add the role of juggler to your CV, as you tackle the balancing act of writing *and* promoting!

A larger agency will often have staff who specialise in rights, contract, legal, accounts and admin support. A smaller agency is more likely to have only a couple of these specialists, and sometimes they will have none; the agent may coordinate all aspects of the process. Which you prefer and works best for you is completely personal. Do you want to work with one person who answers everything, or do you wish to work with a team? Larger agencies may also be able to offer you other focused advice. For example, if you wish to write for adults, write plays or film scripts, they may have people on hand to advise or represent you beyond, for example, your initial work in young adult fiction. Smaller agencies can sometimes do this too, but tend to be more specialised.

Ideally, you should meet agents from both large and smaller agencies – that's if you are lucky enough to be offered representation by more than one agency. This will help you make an informed decision. It is in no one's interest for you to be with the wrong agent. Choosing the right agent is a balance of gut instinct and information; do your research before you contact them with your initial submission, and then again when they have shown interest in representing you.

One thing that everyone needs is an agent who is nice to work with, but also one who is an effective and strong dealmaker. When selecting your agent, there are some **key things to consider:**

1. How many clients do they have and who are they? If you feel that you will need and want a lot of hands-on support with your writing, a large agency may not be for you. If you are a confident writer and want someone who has big agency presence, then maybe the children's agent in a bigger agency would suit you.

2. Do they have clients that write in the same genre as you? This is a great indicator that they have strong contacts with the right commissioning editors and can sell this genre. But if they have lots of authors in this field, will you be competing with other clients within their agency? The balance needs to be right. So do look at their client list.

3. Where are they based? These days this seems to matter less and less but, if they are not near you, how often could you and they travel to a mutually sensible location (e.g. London)?

4. What sort of agent are they? Do you want an editor or commercial management? Do you have one book that you need an agent to sell, or do you have multiple ideas that you want someone to help you develop?

5. Can you relax and feel comfortable with them? You need to be able to communicate well with your agent. Is this someone you can work with? The relationship will become really important as you set off on the rollercoaster ride of getting published; you need to be yourself and have complete trust in your agent.

Always trust your gut instinct. If this is the agency and person you can imagine working with, then take the next step and sign up. Getting published is a long process, success doesn't come overnight, so who you share your journey with is important. Big agency or small agency, it's all about best fit and only you can decide which is right for you.

**Gill McLay** runs the Bath Literary Agency (www.bathliteraryagency.com) which specialises in children's books. She is co-founder of the annual Bath Festival of Children's Literature. She runs Events of Wonder (www.eventsofwonder.com) with her husband John McLay.

# Finding an agent for your picture book

Jodie Hodges explains the opportunities and options for aspiring picture book authors and illustrators, sharing her experience and essential advice on how to find representation and build a successful career in this creative sector.

I've been a literary agent for nearly 15 years; apart from a post-university six months as a bookseller, it is the only adult job I've ever known. Every day I count myself lucky that I was second choice for a position as assistant to Rosemary Canter at Peters, Fraser & Dunlop, one of the only children's literary agents at the time, and that her first choice turned down the job! Working with Rosemary, the agent of children's book luminaries like Giles Andreae, William Nicholson and Benjamin Zephaniah, was a privilege that gave me an incomparable grounding in the job of literary representation. We moved to United Agents in 2007 and, when Rosemary died in 2011, I inherited her list, combining it with my own fledging group of authors and illustrators of children's books. Working equally with new and established talent affords me a perspective on building careers – allowing me to see how things have changed and what remains the same, and I'm lucky enough to represent a fantastically varied list of creators across all age groups in children's publishing.

I love working with picture book creators; I enjoy the variety, the creativity, the collaboration. Picture book authors and illustrators in the children's market are in a particularly fortunate position, having the opportunity to publish multiple books (strategically managed by a good agent, of course!) and therefore to give themselves several chances of having a hit. I choose to represent both authors and illustrators of picture books, which gives me a full picture of this area of the market and the chance to work on lots and lots of different books (... I so enjoy doing this job, so why wouldn't I want to work on as many books as I can?).

## So what is a picture book?

When I say 'picture books', I'm mainly talking about colour illustrated books of around 12 double-page spreads with a text of about 500 words, aimed at a shared reading experience for adult and child under seven. Traditionally these would be fictional stories but, increasingly, narrative non-fiction is also published in this format. There are longer picture books, of course, and baby books, but the vast majority of picture books fall within that definition.

Picture books can be created by one person, an author-illustrator, such as Rob Biddulph. They can also be collaborations between an author and an illustrator, such as *The Littlest Yak* (Simon & Schuster Children's UK 2020) written by Lu Fraser and illustrated by Kate Hindley. When a picture book is a collaboration, it's usually the case that the publisher has acquired the text first and then searches for a suitable illustrator, commissioning them to bring the text to life visually. More rarely, a book might start from an illustrator's image or character which a publisher then commissions a writer to create a text for – as with *Dogs in Disguise* (HarperCollins Children's 2021) written by Peter Bently and illustrated by John Bond. Each collaborator is contracted separately – for most deals this will be an advance and royalty – and the royalty rate is usually split 50/50 between author and illustrator, although their advances are likely to vary as the illustrator has months of artwork to produce. The story may have started with the text, but it becomes a book when the illustrator comes on board – a true collaboration.

## An illustrator's essentials

If you want to get started as an illustrator of picture books, it's vital to have a really strong, targeted, market-specific portfolio, even if you only intend to illustrate your own stories. What sort of things come up in picture books? Animals, toddlers, dragons, friendship ... a varied mix. To give you some ideas for images, try going into a bookshop to take a look at the tables of new picture books, and making a list of their subjects, themes and settings.

Equally important is to find a stylistic voice of your own that also marries commercially with the market. Here again, research and inspiration are key. I think around 20 pages of work is about right for your portfolio, with a mixture of vignettes and spreads that allow you to show characterisation and how you would put a scene together. When your portfolio is ready, you can use this *Yearbook* to look up suitable agents to send it to (see the listings starting on page 218). There are literary agents and also illustration agents; it's wise to think about which of those might be right for you. As a literary agent, I represent my illustrators for their book work only, whereas an illustration agent might cover many other areas. Make a list of agents and then look them up on their websites, social media and trade press – who do they represent? Are they doing plenty of deals? Do you like the cut of their jib? Follow each agent's submission guidelines and hopefully someone will connect with your work and want to progress a conversation. If things go well, this might lead to representation.

## Advice for the picture book author

For authors of picture book texts, my first piece of advice is to embrace prolificacy. Write, write and write some more. Have lots of texts and lots of ideas. This is important for several reasons. Firstly, I assume you'd like to earn some money from your writing; advances for picture book texts are at the lower end of the scale, so selling and publishing multiple books each year is a way to increase your income.

Secondly, the picture book market moves quickly and is extremely focused on the new. You might have a text about a fussy-eating unicorn, but if your agent sends it to a publisher who has just bought a text about a fussy-eating dinosaur, or a unicorn with bad manners, then they're unlikely to have room for yours. It's not the fault of the text, but simply timing and elements that are out of your agent's control and yours. So, what do you do? Move on. Hopefully you've already got some other texts ready, and you try those.

The third reason to be prolific – which is also relevant to illustrators working on collaborative books – is that every new book, every new combination of text and illustration, is a new opportunity for a bestseller or an international success. The publishers use their market expertise to give the books the best possible chance, but sometimes it's simply alchemy. For example, the magical combination of Rachel Bright's words with my client Jim Field's illustrations in their bestselling series of books beginning with *The Lion Inside* (Orchard Books 2015) has meant both UK commercial success and many international partner publishers. We might have hoped for that – but it's never a given.

I would always advise an aspiring picture book author looking for an agent to use the same strategy they will need when they're published: if you submit some stories to agents and they're not picked up – press on and write some more. Use feedback, read, research, and go again. The next one might be the one. And then you'll need another one.

If an agent connects with your work, be it texts or illustrations, it's vital you feel able to have an honest, open, productive relationship with them. Meet them, ask all the questions you have in mind; if you're offered representation, take some time to mull over your meeting before making your decision. We all hope an agent-client relationship is going to be long-term, so don't rush into it.

## Dos and don'ts for authors and illustrators:

• If you're a picture book author, you **don't** need to find an illustrator yourself to be able to approach an agent. Have plenty of stories, make sure you're sending to agents representing picture book authors, and follow their guidelines – that's it.

• If you're an illustrator, you **don't** need to write a story. If you want to, and you've created a package that you feel could be a commercial picture book, that's great – but it's possible to have a very successful career as an illustrator who doesn't write.

• **Do** try to write your text with the book format in mind. It's good practice to write it out labelling the spreads 1–12. That way you can pace your story correctly and work with the page-turns to add jeopardy or humour.

• **Don't** provide extensive illustrative notes on your texts. If there's a visual joke that isn't spelt out in the text itself then, of course, mention it, but the reason a picture book royalty is split 50/50 is that the illustrator is equally as important as the author. I've seen projects completely transform when the illustrator takes the story to a different setting or casts it in a way the author just wouldn't have thought of. There will always be consultation; no one wants the author to be part of a book they don't recognise as their story any longer. More often than not, though, it's an extremely positive process.

• **Do** think about working outside the field of picture books. The skills used in writing and illustrating picture books can very often be transferred into other types of children's books – young fiction, chapter books, illustrated middle grade and young adult, non-fiction. It's thrilling to see creators branch out, with books like Rob Biddulph's *Peanut Jones* series (Macmillan Children's), or Jenny Løvlie illustrating both *The Boys* picture book (Caterpillar Books 2021) and the *Kitty* young fiction series (OUP 2019–). Once you've found an agent, you can talk about diversifying your writing or illustrating, or perhaps if you're struggling to find an agent with your picture book work, think about creating submissions for a different area of the market.

• **Don't** get carried away imagining the animated series and theme park of your picture book – even if you're lucky enough to have it published. It's natural, and desirable, to have ambitions, but expectation management is an undervalued and essential part of the publishing process and the life of an author and illustrator.

## Submission rules

I want to assure you the 'slush' pile is a friend of the aspiring picture book creator. An agent can read the texts, or look through portfolio work, much more quickly than they can read a novel. So use that to your advantage by making your submission as easy to navigate as possible. For me this means a clear, short covering email, and separate attachments for each text or a single pdf portfolio I can scroll through. Submitting in the good old-fashioned way is your best chance of finding an agent – I've taken on countless clients this way. So don't imagine there's a shortcut. No good agent is ignoring their submissions – we want to find gold in there. I hope I might see some of your work in my own inbox soon.

**Jodie Hodges** is an agent with United Agents, representing children's illustrators and authors of picture books, middle grade, teenage and young adult, including Rob Biddulph, Jim Field, Smriti Halls, Sophie McKenzie, Jamie Smart and Harriet Muncaster. She began working with Rosemary Canter at Peters, Fraser & Dunlop in 2006, becoming an agent in 2010. For more information see www.unitedagents.co.uk/jhodgesunitedagentscouk. Follow her on Twitter @jodiehodges31.

## See also...
- *Being an illustrator* and *a writer,* page 247
- *Choosing the right agent,* page 198

# Submitting your sci-fi/fantasy novel to an agent

Agent Molly Jamieson describes the magic of discovering well-written fantasy and science fiction for children, with absorbing narrative and world-building, and has advice for writers on the essential elements and qualities she looks for in a standout submission.

I didn't always know that I wanted to be an agent, but I started in publishing at Curtis Brown for an internship and then moved to United Agents as part of a maternity cover ... and I've been here ever since. I have worked for six years across both adult and children's lists, working on titles from board books right up to crime fiction, and I'm now building my own list with a particular focus on science fiction and fantasy titles for all ages.

Although I still work closely with Jodie Hodges, here at United Agents, on her list of children's authors and illustrators and review submissions for both of us, SFF (Science Fiction and Fantasy) is where my heart really lies. It is what I read in my spare time, what I gravitate towards naturally, and what I crave when I'm looking for comfort reading: something to really get lost in. When I was a kid, I went to see *The Lord of the Rings* in the cinema and I never looked back.

I love big stories with high stakes, both globally and personally, as well as quieter stories that focus on characters and the complexities of everyday relationships above all else. I like traditional stories of good trumping evil, but I'm also drawn to stories with shades of grey, that subvert expectations. I'm always on the lookout for new talent in this space, both in writing for adults and children, so I'm delighted to have the opportunity to help you get your submission to the best possible place. So, let's start with the basics ...

## Your submission package

For the most part, in a submission I look for the same things everyone else does. I hope that you'll get my name right (though it's not a deal breaker – I'd just prefer no 'Dear Sir's, if you can possibly help it) and I ask to see the synopsis and first three chapters.

While I know that agents' submission guidelines can feel restrictive, tricky, and often very tedious, we're not trying to trip you up with these; the traditional submission package is designed this way to make it as simple and straightforward as possible for us to review your work in its best light. You've got the opportunity to pitch it in the short form in your *cover letter*, to describe every major event in your *synopsis*, and to show me your most polished writing in the *first chapters* of your book – to draw me in. There are endless resources online, both free and paid for, to help you hone your pitch. Believe me, we know pitching isn't easy (if anyone understands that, it's us!), but it's a skill that is worth investing your time in, even at this early stage. It will serve you well for the rest of your career.

• **The synopsis**: ideally this would be about one A4 page but, if that means cramming it onto the single side of A4 with the narrowest margins and the tiniest font, I'd rather it just eked out onto a second page. Aim for 350-500 words and I'll be happy. If you're struggling with your synopsis, I always recommend having a trusted reader go through your manuscript and then describe, from memory, the major events of the story. As a writer, it can become so easy to get too close to your book – so much so that you can't necessarily see which information is vital for the synopsis. So fresh eyes are always a good idea.

• **First three chapters**: if your first three chapters are very short or your book isn't split into chapters, then feel free to send me the first 10,000 words. What I want to see is a good chunk of text that invites me into your story from the get-go. For me, it always comes down to the writing. A pitch might hook me, a synopsis might intrigue me, but when it comes to a final decision about taking a submission further, it's all about whether or not I love the writing. That is always going to be the deciding factor. So do make sure your draft is in the best shape possible. As with the synopsis, a fresh perspective on your manuscript is invaluable when you're struggling with edits or final touches so, ideally, I shouldn't be the first person to read it.

• **Cover letter**: there are common threads that run through my wish list for both the adult and children's SFF markets, and I don't necessarily look for the same thing in both places. In your cover letter for children's SFF, perhaps even more than in adult SFF, I want to see that you've got a good sense of the market as it is now. The easiest way to do this is to give me *comparison titles* for your book, which I know is not always the most straightforward process. I don't expect you to have read every book in your category, but I do think you should have a more contemporary comparison point for your book than *The Chronicles of Narnia* or *Harry Potter and the Philosopher's Stone* – there are so many great stories out there! Comparison titles are also useful, of course, because they help me to understand where you see your book on the shelf, and thus which publishers might be especially keen to see it.

## Fantasy and fun

For the younger end of science fiction and fantasy, the scope of possible things to write about is huge – but my particular favourite space is probably fantasy middle grade. I really love middle-grade fiction that leans into whimsy in a big way, with soaring and surreal imaginative scenes that take the protagonist(s) on a wondrous journey; you can see this in the market with the success of series like Jessica Townsend's *Nevermoor* (Orion Children's 2018–), A.F. Steadman's *Skandar and the Unicorn Thief* (Simon & Schuster 2022–) and Rob Biddulph's *Peanut Jones* (Pan Macmillan 2021–). A strong narrative voice plays a big part in this, as well as a sense of humour throughout. You can definitely be serious in this space, too, but balance is very important and, if you're going to err on one side, let that be on the side of funny.

## World-building that works

One thing I do look for in both adult and children's SFF is thorough world-building, and magic systems that have consistent rules. That's not to say I want to be overloaded with information about these things – far from it – but I want to feel that you, the author, have a really grounded understanding of the world or 'magics' you have created. Essentially, as a reader, I want to feel safe in your hands. The best way to show me how your world works is to let me watch a character live in it, let me walk its streets and interact with its society. This can be a character who has lived in this world all their life, or a fish out of water emerging into a new world for the first time, but the thing that matters most is that I get to experience the world alongside that character. I won't remember lists of names, or extensive histories, but I'll remember the particular scents of a bustling market or an old, dusty library. I may not remember every new magical term or name that you tell me, but I'll have a better chance of understanding it if I see how it is used by your protagonist (or against them).

When it comes to magic systems in books for children, you can arguably get away with a little more whimsy and looseness than in adult books. But any inconsistencies or breaks with the rules of magic should not just be incidental; they need to be used for maximum impact. Again, as a reader, I must believe that *you* know how it works – I don't need to understand how all of the cogs fit together, as long as I *feel* sure that they do. Similarly, with sci-fi (a famously impenetrable genre for the uninitiated) I'm always keen on seeing authors find ways to make it feel more approachable, especially for younger readers. You can do this by keeping technical jargon to a minimum and establishing clear stakes for the characters, key pieces of tech, and some strong grounding principles to help ease the reader into the unknown.

## Audience is key

Finally, it's important to remember, with any writing for children, that you need to bear in mind the age of your intended audience and know the limitations of formats for each age group. Anything for readers under the age of 13 is likely to be illustrated, so bear that in mind when considering your word count. Middle-grade fantasy is an overcrowded area of the market, and yet is still a genre which editors are actively acquiring and perhaps always will be. All areas of publishing run in cycles; a few years ago it seemed that YA was on the way out, but now it is having another resurgence, with a focus on that transitional 'New Adult/crossover' space. But there is also still an appetite for contemporary stories for teen readers. The main thing is to keep your audience in mind, always, and write what feels good rather than towards a particular trend.

There is so much fun to be had in writing science fiction and fantasy for children, and a delight in uncovering new stories in the genre. I can't wait to see what you write, and I wish you the best of luck with your journey to publication.

**Molly Jamieson** joined United Agents in 2017 as an assistant and is now an Associate Agent. She continues to work closely with Jodie Hodges and Emily Talbot on their lists of children's authors and illustrators as well as building her own list. For more information see www.unitedagents.co.uk/mjamiesonunitedagentscouk. Follow her on Twitter @MollyJamieson.

## See also...
- *Plotting and pace in your middle-grade adventure*, page 145
- *World-building in your fantasy fiction*, page 158
- *Writing magic into fiction*, page 136

# Why teachers make great children's writers

Kate Scarborough shares her thoughts on how a teacher's experience and skills can empower and benefit them as a children's writer, as well as the essential advice, tools and tips she can offer new writers since setting up her own agency.

If you are thumbing through this book wondering whether your dreams of becoming a published writer can become a reality, my story and practical advice might be useful. By giving you a little background into how and why I set up my literary agency – Tyild's Agency – in 2021, I hope to help you on that journey. (In the best teacherly tradition, I'll mark up in bold type the bits that are particularly pertinent to you, the aspiring writer).

Writers often talk about suffering from 'Imposter Syndrome' and, in this new post-pandemic publishing life I have created for myself, it's a condition I understand. As I dive deeper into the publishing world, I see fledgling writers revealing their unease through nervous tweets, published authors writing articles on how they can't believe they have been published, agents trying to find the next big thing, and publishers never being sure that a book they adore is going to fly on the open market. But amid all that self-doubt, I take comfort from accepting that **none of us really know for sure what makes a successful book and that the route to success is laced with huge amounts of luck.**

That said, it is easy to forget that **experience, planning, perseverance, persistence and craft account for a great deal.** I was an editor, writer and publisher in children's publishing for the first 14 years of my working life. I had a fabulous time, being creative, coming up with ideas, pitching them, putting them together and selling them, and ultimately being responsible for a team of people doing the same. Following a different dream, I then moved to teaching. Ironically – because I was always a bit of a rebel as a pupil, and *not* the teacher's favourite – I adored going back to the classroom, and loved planning ways to enthuse children about learning and especially about reading. The chance to use books in the classroom, find out what children particularly enjoy, and study how those books are written, was invaluable.

But upheavals, such as the pandemic, can have a dramatic effect on personal priorities. Like many, I found myself asking: What do I really want to do? What do I love doing? How do I make the most of my experience? I have always loved books and the creative process, and I know how to put them together. I love teaching and inspiring readers of all kinds. My wonderful colleague and friend for many years, Frances McKay (a successful illustrator's agent), gave me a nudge. Why not use these experiences to become an agent? There are many experienced, dynamic agents out there who have been digging out and nurturing writers for years. What could I bring to this market that would make my experience count? It had always struck me that **so many of our top children's authors previously worked in the classroom.** An agency that championed all those aspiring teacher writers might be exactly what I should do. And so Tyild's Agency was born.

**Starting from scratch is daunting.** I had to publicise my credentials and persuade authors to join the agency before I could begin to approach publishers with news that the agency was live. It is not easy to promote yourself – I had to work hard to remember that I was, in fact, qualified to do this job. However, this self-promotion is really important, and it is equally so for you, as authors. **In your covering letters to agents and publishers**, make sure you **mention all your training and your writing successes so far**. I had to spend a lot of time making connections through Twitter, LinkedIn, Facebook and Instagram. I could not have found my authors and developed the business without these tools. Teachers are one of the most communicative and vibrant communities online; they support and encourage one another across all these platforms and welcome newcomers with enthusiasm. And teacher writers are the best of these. I found that word spread quickly and, in no time, I had an inbox bulging with hopes and dreams.

Choosing authors to represent is extremely difficult, as there are so many talented writers out there. I have been fairly ambitious in my scope, in that I represent authors of picture books, chapter books and middle-grade titles. Most of the authors I have taken on, however, are keen to work across the age ranges, which is something I do look out for. Versatility and imagination are key, but it all starts with the initial email. And – forgive me – but if the email from a potential author is not addressed to me but has clearly been lumped in with a mailshot to lots of other agents, I tend not to prioritise it. **An agent will work very closely with an author and striking a good relationship right at the start is vital**. I check to see if an email shows that the sender has done their research and that they have followed my guidelines. The tone and style of the email also helps me to judge whether or not I should spend time reading the submission. When I started the agency, I had such high hopes of reading every word of each submission and of being able to give thoughtful feedback. I now know that this is absolutely impossible, given everything I need to do. And the same applies for all agents and publishers – so give yourself a head start, **do your research, follow the guidelines**, and **make it personal**.

Being a start-up, I am very conscious that the writers who have signed up with me are taking a gamble, and I speak to every potential writer to make sure that they understand this. It is a risk that is not for everyone and I understand that. The agency is in its infancy and each milestone – taking on new authors, meeting publishers, getting those first contracts signed – is fantastic, but (with a small child and a dog to support) I still have to earn in order to follow this dream. So, I am **not giving up the day job** ... yet. I tutor children in English, which I love because it ties in so well with the agency work. It means I am reading, studying and critiquing books with the target market, which provides the perfect insight.

But why do I feel so strongly that teachers can be great writers for children? And what can we learn from their experience to help our own writing? Some of the biggest names in children's publishing started in teaching – J.R. Tolkien, C.S. Lewis, Philip Pullman, Eva Ibbotson, David Almond, Michael Morpurgo – even J.K. Rowling and Julia Donaldson dabbled. On a Twitter exchange, **Philip Pullman** explained his journey by revealing that in class '... I told stories (not my own – myths, folk tales) because I thought it was a good thing to do. **I learned to tell [stories] by doing it**'. And **David Almond**, who said that teaching is central to his life as a writer, explained that in his lessons, he '... **wrote stories with the children**, inspired their own stories, dramatised stories with them. [This] helped me explore the varieties of form, and a connection to voice/movement'.

When writing for children, you need to **know your audience** in so many ways, from the practical (**what are they** *able* **to read**) to the inspirational (**what do they** *want* **to read**). A teacher works with children in the classroom, helping them to become readers. They can witness first-hand the impact stories have on young readers. The teacher will see which stories open eyes, widen horizons, encourage questions, unlock imagination and switch on light bulbs in their heads! Teachers also come to **know the book market** pretty well, especially those who take a professional interest in it. Most teacher writers will try out their own fledgling books on their class – who are always a willing audience. This can have a very direct effect, in that the teacher writer is able to edit on the fly and they quickly, even sometimes painfully (George, don't do that ...), **learn how to hold a reader's attention, how to build suspense, how to move them and how to make them laugh**.

It can seem that, as adults, we forget what it is like to be a child, but the teacher hopefully never forgets. Teachers are part of children's daily lives, and are there to share their joys, successes, struggles, battles and humour. This awareness of their audience that results from working with children means that teachers **never underestimate their reader**. Teaching children to write also lays bare the creative process for teachers. Every teacher writer that I work with writes with their pupils, and there is nothing more powerful than modelling writing for children, sharing what is good and exploring the difficulties. If children can see you struggle, change your mind, make mistakes and self-edit, then it is fine for them to do it. This **constant practice in editing helps hone a writer's craft**.

I spend a huge amount of my teaching time **exploring inference and empathy**. These are the skills you need to be a good reader (indeed, person), and which frankly give the child reader such a fantastic head start in life. As a writer, you need to know how to encourage inference and empathy in your reader, but you also must understand when your carefully crafted inference will go sailing right over the top of your reader's head. **Pitching it right for your reader** with enough to stretch children, and enough to help them begin to see it, is a delicate skill and the teacher writer has a distinct advantage with their insider knowledge. Good teachers **never stop learning**. There is so much help and support out there for writers, both of the teacher variety and others. My authors have writing groups, critical partners, go on courses for writing, attend conferences about the industry, join communities (see *Children's writing courses and conferences*, page 392 and *Societies, associations and organisations*, page 315). Using this book will help you to find those communities, as will the *Writers' & Artists'* website (www.writersandartists.co.uk; see *More than a book*, page ix).

Once your book is published you will need to do **school visits, festivals and presentations to children in order to market your work**. These are uplifting experiences, but can be extremely nerve-racking. Although – dare I say it – not to a teacher. Most teachers are more than happy to show off in front of children (any excuse) and know exactly how to manage that crowd so they don't lose them in the excitement. Not all great writers are teachers and not all teachers are great writers – but, if you talk to any writer who *has* taught, they will tell you the experience was invaluable. So, try to **get into a classroom and meet teachers**; they will be your strongest allies.

My own journey has really only just begun, and I hope the agency, which has been warmly welcomed by the publishing community, will flourish. I am and will go through the same highs and lows that everyone has in this industry. **It is not easy, but it is worth it**.

It is worth it for so many different reasons: you get to meet wonderful people; you share your creative vision; and ultimately, if all goes well, you get to inspire the next generation. You will feel what all teachers feel – that sense of vocation.

[With thanks to these teacher writers who shared their thoughts on Twitter: Gaynor Andrews, Barbara Henderson, Mark Smith, Catherine Bruton, Lindsay Galvin, David Almond and Philip Pullman.]

**Kate Scarborough** is the founder of Tyild's Agency, a literary agency particularly for teachers who write for children. She has, over the last 30 years, been an editor, writer, publisher and teacher and now combines all this experience and enthusiasm into promoting teacher–writers whose talent crosses over from the classroom to the page. For more information see www.tyildsagency.co.uk and follow on Twitter @TyildS.

Literary agents

# A message for under-represented writers: We Want You

Davinia Andrew-Lynch knows that, as well as a good story, agents and editors are also on the lookout for talented writers from groups and communities currently under-represented in the world of children's publishing. She has advice for marginalised writers on how to find the representation, confidence and support they need.

Despite the increasing number of children's books published each year, many budding authors find the world of publishing daunting. And, for those of you from under-represented groups (including, but not limited to, minority ethnic/religious, LGBTQ+ and working-class communities), this London-centric industry can seem wholly unwelcoming.

Things are changing, however. The vital importance of youngsters seeing themselves reflected in the books they read has become an issue more frequently recognised by 'gatekeepers' across the industry. The inclusion of these different narratives is not only good for society; it is also good for the health of our business. So, let's get practical. Whilst this book contains a plethora of information to get you on your way, the advice offered highlights how you, as an under-represented writer, can kick-start your career and get noticed.

When submitting to agents, always *do your research*. Does the agent you're looking at represent picture books, middle grade, young adult or all of these? What genres do they favour? Are they newer agents actively on the hunt for talent? Studying an agent's existing list will answer many of your questions, but Twitter can also provide you with extra up-to-date information. You never know, an agent's simple #MSWL (Manuscript Wish List) alert may just equate to the very book you've written. And check out #DVPit (strapline 'A Twitter Pitching Event for Marginalized Voices'); it's a great *free* opportunity.

At the same time, do not be deterred from approaching an agent whose list *doesn't* seem obviously inclusive. Time and time again I have met authors who have not submitted work to an agency because they didn't feel that they were reflected by an agent's existing clientele. And, do you know what? Often agents will say that they're just not hearing from marginalised writers, and that they don't understand *why*. Clearly there's a bit of a catch-22 situation going on here, because I for one know that you exist. Remember that agents are essentially looking for a good story and, granted, it is their job to look for talent in (and from) all forms and places; by not submitting your work, you are limiting your chance of discovery. If your story has the elements of a potential success, then the right agent will give you that chance of representation. So, if you like the look of an agent and think your work may appeal, type that email and hit Send!

If you are not yet ready to submit your manuscript, an extensive satellite industry of advice and support has developed to provide authors with the tools to navigate the world of publishing. And, now more than ever, many of these programmes are actively looking to reach out to those who may not have previously believed or found publishing to be a welcoming space. Often you will find events giving you access to many of the individuals on the 'inside', and these insiders (including agents and editors) want to hear from *you*. Understand, these gatekeepers are not wanting to pay lip service to a fad; they are driven by the satisfaction of finding and supporting genuine talent.

Writers' conferences and festivals can often be a good place to start. Yes, they can be an expense, but they can also be a worthwhile investment. Not only are they a vast source of information but, by giving you a couple of days to immerse yourself in a space which celebrates and encourages your writing, they can be the perfect boost for your confidence. You will have the opportunity to attend specific workshops, panel events, hear keynote speeches and often you can book a one-to-one appointment with an agent or editor. For many authors, these one-to-ones can be particularly valuable, and in fact I met one of my current clients at the Winchester Writers' Festival in this way. One of the most prominent such events, focusing on children's content, is hosted by SCBWI, a worldwide members network (see page 305). Their conference offers all of the above, but it also gives you access to a community of like-minded authors, and this can be a particular draw and comfort.

Do check the conference listings in this *Yearbook* (which start on page 392). As you will see, there are a number of them taking place around the country, at different times of the year and sometimes focusing on a specific area of publishing. But do understand, it is not about attending as many as possible. Assess your situation; consider what it is that you want to know about the industry and then do your research. If you are making the choice to spend your money in this way, then you should ensure that it is cash well spent – you want to leave that conference feeling better equipped to deal with what will, hopefully, be a future career. If the idea of a conference feels too much, then consider the many evening salons, day workshops and afternoon panel sessions offering more tailored advice. There really are events aplenty, and sometimes these are more affordable financially and timewise.

How do you find out about these events? Check out your local regional literary organisations, for instance, New Writing North/South, Writing West/East Midlands and Spread the Word (London) are a few of the most prominent (see *Societies, associations and organisations* section, starting on page 315). Each of these bodies work tirelessly to support new writers – and particularly those who may have to overcome varying barriers due to a, frankly, institutional bias (however unintentional). Not only do these organisations host their own events but they will often highlight and promote worthwhile external opportunities. A good example of this is the Free Reads Scheme organised by The Literary Consultancy (one of the largest editorial services companies in the country). In conjunction with the Arts Council, the scheme works with local literary organisations to find authors who may require and appreciate a subsidised manuscript assessment service. It is a brilliant opportunity which acknowledges that the choice to write is not necessarily an affordable one – a fact which in itself makes publishing seem as though it should only be for the privileged few. And, on the issue of expense, you may find that some of these services will offer bursaries for specific groups of people. They are there to help, not isolate. Do not hesitate to get in touch with those who are organising such events and ask whether there is anything you can apply for.

Do also keep an eye out for upcoming competitions; industry magazine the *Bookseller* often announces the most notable of these. While many are open to all writers, it is also worth investigating the increasing number which specifically target under-represented groups. These competitions may not land you with the hallowed publishing deal or representation but, depending on the scheme, they may offer the opportunity for you to get a foot in the door. For instance (and please excuse the personal plug here, ahem ahem ...): the FAB Prize (see page 336) was set up by Faber and my previous agency, ANDLYN,

Literary agents

looking specifically for un-agented and un-published BAME writing/illustrating talent. The individual category winners are awarded with mentoring, and an anthology of their work and the work of the runners-up is circulated around children's literary agents. Since the Prize's inception, a number of entrants have gone on to gain representation and get published. The prize was a *platform*, but these writers reached their goal off the back of their own merit. Be sure to use these opportunities – that is what they are there for.

I would be remiss not to mention the Arts Council (see page 315) in this context. Easily forgotten, but open to all, it has a number of grant schemes which provide writers with the time and space to focus on their writing. It has to be said that, particularly within children's publishing, the body is incredibly keen to help address the imbalance of marginalised voices. As mentioned, the financial implications of wanting to be a writer stretch far and wide; if this applies to you, see whether there is a grant for which you may qualify.

Having dealt with the practical side of pursuing your writing career, here's my take on how our identities can enrich the stories we tell. Children's publishing has always been synonymous with the idea that its stories and literature can teach children about the society in which they live. Yet statistics (most recently those led by BookTrust and CLPE – the Centre for Literacy in Primary Education – on multicultural diversity) show that there is a serious dearth of stories featuring characters from under-represented backgrounds. In my conversations with authors, the word 'diversity' seems to have inadvertently given way to the suggestion and/or impression that diverse stories should be 'issue'-led, that they should highlight the barriers or difficulties of 'other' lives. And, because there are so few novels in the market featuring minority groups and/or marginalised characters within a British context, it has become all too easy to associate particular kinds of stories with the different under-represented groups.

This means that, to some extent, an element of stereotyping has come in to play. But why? We can learn about each other within the framework of a simply entertaining and *mainstream* story. Your idea, *not* your identity, should be your USP. Remember you want (and deserve) to be measured on the same scale as any other author and, with that, there should be a freedom to write any kind of story. If you want to create an epic 'through the wardrobe'-style adventure, a young adult rom-com, or a rather left-of-centre comedy, then you must. Saying that, if you want to write a gritty issue-led tale, feel free to do that too! For those working within the industry, your ability to produce an excellent narrative is the attraction, but when your stories reflect you, your community, your *rarely seen world* – that is refreshing, and frankly a bonus.

There are many individuals within children's publishing who actively want to change the landscape so that its output is more inclusive. It cannot be denied, however, that our intentions are often left rattling around an echo chamber and that this message of inclusivity isn't necessarily being received on the 'outside'. So I am saying this very clearly now: as an industry we need your stories but, more importantly, we want you … *all of you, not just your demographic.* We look forward to hearing from you soon!

**Davinia Andrew-Lynch** is an agent at Curtis Brown and she specialises in children's and young adult fiction and content. She previously ran her own agency ANDLYN, worked as an associate agent at the Dench Arnold Agency, a film/TV agency, and as a freelance children's fiction editor and reader. Follow Davinia on Twitter @nocturnalreader.

## See also...
• *Opportunities for under-represented writers*, page 345

# The life and works of a literary scout

Sophie Clarke explains just what a literary scout's role and life entails, with its varied and challenging workload and often all-consuming pace, the buzz of staying well-informed and well-connected, and the satisfaction that comes from matching the right book to the right client.

Entitling this article 'the life and works of a literary scout' seems unusually apt because, as with many jobs in publishing, trying to separate the personal from the professional in the career of a literary scout is nigh on impossible. It is a job that relies on forming, maintaining and nurturing connections, assessing the industry with a finely-honed eye to see which way the winds are blowing, and on reading accurately and critically at speed. Your role is to deliver professional judgement with a personal touch to your clients, who need guidance or advice to help them find the books which will work best for them. You are, in effect, a literary matchmaker. The clients of a literary scout are foreign publishers seeking to buy titles originally published in one language in order to translate them into their own, for publication and sale in their territory or market. Scouts can work across a range of languages, for example all literature from the Scandinavian countries, or in one language, such as just the UK or USA.

## The information game

Literary scouts, unlike agents and editors, do not work directly with authors. They trade in information, gossip, industry buzz and foreign-market knowledge. A good scout has their finger on the pulse of the market they are scouting. They know which books are out on submission from agents to editors and, of those, which are making noise and going up for auction or being pre-empted. They are aware of which editors are moving between publishing houses, going on parental leave or sabbatical, or looking to acquire specific types of titles. They stay up-to-date on which new authors an agent might be representing; announcements on Twitter are particularly helpful for this. Before titles go on submission (the process where agents send manuscripts to editors for them to sign-up or 'buy' for publication), scouts actively check in with agents about any titles which sound particularly interesting, or any which might be particularly suited to specific clients of theirs.

In order to gather this information, at least half of the scout's role is to talk – and to as many people as possible. Scouts are in contact day-to-day with primary agents (representing authors), rights agents (selling titles internationally) and publishing editors (acquiring titles and working with authors) via email and WhatsApp, as well as via video, phone and in-person meetings. These conversations allow scouts to build up a picture of what is currently going on in UK publishing. The wider and warmer a scout's network of contacts, the better the overall picture they can provide, and the better informed their clients will be – ideally ahead of competitors – and thus able to make decisions faster. A scout's network is more than a directory of contacts. Most become friends or – at the very least – valued acquaintances. It's almost impossible not to build up a close relationship; a scout may talk to a client once a day in peak season to check in on a title that's moving quickly and being acquired widely. Over the course of many meetings and emails, both parties get to know each other well. But of course, the core aspect of the relationship requires that, however kindly one might think of a contact personally, each has professional duties to the other.

## Reading ... with a difference

The other half of a scout's role is to read, and to read quickly, professionally and widely in the area they scout in. Some scouts cover all genres; some specialise, for example in children's and young adult, like me. Reading and reporting on titles – providing a brief summary of the plot, information on the author and any notable facts or sales for the title – must be prioritised. Often, it must be done at speed. When titles are submitted for acquisition and begin to gather buzz domestically and/or internationally, translation sales begin to fall like dominoes in the right territories. A scout's reading does not always take place in the office or within office hours; with their clients in a variety of different time zones and territories, scouts must always be prepared to support and respond at any time of the day or night. As titles begin to move, auctions (multiple publishing houses bidding and offering on a title) and pre-empts (making an offer so convincing that the title is bought quickly and exclusively without the hassle of an auction) can happen overnight or even within a matter of hours from submission. This means that speed of reading, responding and reporting to clients is of the essence. You may be reading several manuscripts at one time, especially if you cover a broad range of titles. It's not uncommon for an individual scout to read between seven and ten titles a week – sometimes even more, around the busy book-fair seasons. You read with several different hats on, as there are many considerations: Will this title work in the UK market? Will it work in any of my client markets? Will any of the client's editors like it, even if it might not seem to be something for their market? Is it, objectively, any good? Do you, personally, like it – and would you be willing to recommend it, based on your own tastes, despite any other minor flaws to it? Addressing such questions, while reading to tight deadlines before reporting back to clients on a title, turns a seemingly simple task into one filled with nuance that requires a scout's expertise and professional knowledge.

## Networking nous

Networking, as with the reading, isn't entirely limited within office hours either. Scouts are a regular fixture at parties, book launches and other publishing industry events – in fact anywhere where it's possible to hobnob and mix with the widest possible number of people and have the most wide-ranging conversations, gleaning titbits of gossip and information. Breakfasts, lunches, coffees, dinners and drinks meetings all feature regularly in scout life as well – meaning that we're extremely well-fed, as well as well-informed! As a scout, you quickly become very comfortable with walking into events where you might only know a few people, and leaving having befriended at least a few more. This skill comes in particularly useful at the international trade book fairs. These happen throughout the year, but the main ones are in Frankfurt in the autumn, London and Bologna in the spring. Bologna is specifically focused on children's and young adult titles. Editors, agents and rights agents from a multitude of countries gather to buy, sell and discuss titles. Scouts are at the heart of it – talking to their clients, meeting with editors and rights agents from outside their home territory and attending as many events as possible to meet the maximum number of people. Rights fairs are key for rights sales and for getting material, authors and passion in front of editors' noses. A scout's enthusiasm for a particular title, and their awareness of information ahead of it being public knowledge, can create excitement and help their publisher clients strike deals.

## Author's friend

Indirectly, a scout is helping an author, even though they'll probably never meet and an author may be unaware of a scout's role across the publishing process. Across the course of many weeks, months or years, a scout may constantly re-flag an author's work or a specific title to their clients, demonstrating the momentum that a book or author is gathering both in their home territory and across other territories too. Sometimes, a book moves very quickly and there are swift acquisitions in the UK, the USA and a host of international territories – that's the dream scenario. But often books and authors take time to garner success and recognition and, as each building block of that process is achieved (e.g. sales figures, prize-shortlisting or -winning, accrued rights sales), a scout can be instrumental in reminding their clients of a title, seeing whose publishing list or taste might have changed enough to acquire it now, even if they passed over it previously.

To be a successful scout involves a high level of networking and reading, but of course there is far more to it than that. It also involves a huge volume of email traffic, lots of administration to stay on top of contacts – their changing roles and keeping up-to-date on correct territory contacts at each publisher and agency, organising meeting schedules for the book fairs, and reporting regularly to clients. All of this builds up to an ever-changing and shifting role – which is precisely what makes it one of the most exciting jobs in publishing. Scouts come from a variety of different backgrounds: some have started as interns at scouting agencies and worked their way up; others have previously worked at a publisher in rights or in editorial; others have come from a literary agency and are able to employ their already keen understanding of the industry. Most have some knowledge of a foreign language and culture, although almost all communication between scout and client is in English, and all reading is done in English too. Regardless of how they entered the industry, the key element a scout must have is a passion for, and deep knowledge of, the area of literature they are working in – no matter how broad or narrow that patch. Also helpful are the enthusiasm and energy to work more than occasional long hours, a curiosity about foreign markets, a desire to be well-informed about as much as possible, and the ability to read and network and manage emails beyond the office. And you need to be prepared – at peak book-fair season, when the pace becomes frenetic and the pressure to remain ahead of competitors becomes high – to be almost consumed by the job!

Reading back through this, I'm afraid I may have made scouting sound far too serious, when actually it's the most fun job I've ever had. There's a lot of stress, to be sure, but there also is a lot of laughter and camaraderie in the team as everyone works so closely together to deliver a great service to their clients. It's nigh on impossible to complain (and I certainly wouldn't now, amidst the pandemic) about drinks events and book launches and parties and trips to the book fairs, even if they are outside office hours. You read books months and even years before the general public sees them. It's fair to say that scouting, in both little and big ways, shapes your life because it dictates the structure of your social and professional weeks, months and seasons; but it also shapes the lives of authors. For a scout, when a client acquires a title that you loved – one that has the potential to be successful for them and you also know the deal will be wonderful for the author – it really is the best feeling. Literary match ... made.

**Sophie Clarke** is senior scout for children's and young adult books, Sci-fi and Fantasy, and romance across the UK and US at Daniela Schlingmann Literary Scouting (https://schlingmann.co.uk). She has previously worked at the publisher Penguin Random House Children's and at the literary agencies Curtis Brown and Bell Lomax Moreton.

# Children's literary agents UK and Ireland

The *Children's Writers' & Artists' Yearbook*, along with the Association of Authors' Agents and the Society of Authors, takes a dim view of any literary agent who asks potential clients for a fee prior to a manuscript being placed with a publisher. We advise you to treat any such request with caution and to let us know if that agent appears in the listings below. Agents may charge additional costs later in the process but these should only arise once a book has been accepted by a publisher and the author is earning an income. Authors should also check agents' websites before making an enquiry and should familiarise themselves with submission guidelines, agent preferences and manuscript formatting.

*Member of the Association of Authors' Agents
sae = self-addressed envelope

## The Agency (London) Ltd*
24 Pottery Lane, London W11 4LZ
*tel* 020-7727 1346
*email* childrensbooksubmissions@theagency.co.uk
*website* https://theagency.co.uk/childrens-books/childrens-home
*Twitter* @TheAgencyBooks
*Instagram* @theagencybooks
*Children's Book Agent* Jessica Hare, *Consultant* Hilary Delamere

Works in conjunction with overseas agents. The Agency also represents screenwriters, directors, playwrights and composers. Represents picture books, including novelty books, fiction for all ages including teenage fiction and series fiction. *Commission* Home 15%, overseas 20%. Submission guidelines on website. *Founded* 1995.

## Aitken Alexander Associates Ltd*
291 Gray's Inn Road, London WC1X 8QJ
*tel* 020-7373 8672
*email* reception@aitkenalexander.co.uk
*website* www.aitkenalexander.co.uk
*Twitter* @AitkenAlexander
*Instagram* @AitkenAlexander
*Agent* Amy St Johnston

Children's and YA fiction. Handles fiction for 9+ to young adults. *Commission* Home 15%, overseas 20%. Email submissions@aitkenalexander.co.uk with preliminary letter that includes a half-page synopsis and first 30 pages. No picture books. *Founded* 1977.

## Darley Anderson Children's Book Agency Ltd*
Unit 19, Matrix Studios, 91 Peterborough Road, London SW6 3BU
*tel* 020-7385 6652
*email* childrens@darleyanderson.com
*website* www.darleyandersonchildrens.com
*Twitter* @DA_Childrens
*Instagram* @da_childrens
*Managing Director* Darley Anderson, *Directors* Camilla Bolton, Clare Wallace, *Agents* Lydia Silver, Becca Langton, *Junior Agent* Chloe Davis, *Head of Rights* Kristina Egan, *TV and Film Rights* Sheila David

Children's fiction and non-fiction (for all ages from picture book to middle grade through to YA and crossover). For illustrators, please refer to the Darley Anderson Illustration Agency (see page 256). *Commission* Home 15%, USA/translation 20%, film/TV/radio 20%. Send covering letter, short synopsis and first three chapters by email. No scripts or screenplays.
  *Clients* include Mara Bergman, Mark Bradley, Gina Blaxill, Cathy Cassidy, John Connolly, Kate Foster, Lindsay Galvin, Ryan Hammond, A.M. Howell, Polly Ho-Yen, Rachel Morrisroe, Beth Reekles, Rashmi Sirdeshpande, Deirdre Sullivan, Efua Traoré. *Founded* 1988.

## ASH Literary*
*email* info@ashliterary.com
*website* www.ashliterary.com
*Twitter* @ashliterary
*Instagram* @ashliterary
*Agents* Alice Sutherland-Hawes, Saffron Dodd

Children's and YA focused agency representing authors and illustrators covering picture books to YA titles, including graphic novels. All genres represented. *Commission* Home 15%, translation/dramatisation 20%. Send first three chapters and synopsis through QueryManager. Does not handle adult fiction or non-fiction.
  *Clients* include Kereen Getten, Alex Falase-Koya, Radiya Hafiza, Jess McGeachin, Poonam Mistry, Úna Woods. *Founded* 2020.

## Bath Literary Agency*

5 Gloucester Road, Bath BA1 7BH
*email* submissions@bathliteraryagency.com
*website* www.bathliteraryagency.com
*Twitter* @BathLitAgency
*Instagram* @bathlitagency
*Contact* Gill McLay

Specialist in fiction for children and young adults. Also accepts submissions in picture books, non-fiction and author-illustrators. *Commission* UK 15%, overseas 20%, film/TV 20%. For full submission details, refer to the website.

*Clients* include Fox Benwell, Jake Biggin, Conor Busuttil, Philippa Forrester, Dr Jess French, Joe Haddow, Demelsa Haughton, Harry Heape, Laura James, Pippa Pixley, Dr Shini Somara, Tessa Strickland, Anna Terreros Martin, Tweedy, Chris Wakling. *Founded* 2011.

## The Bell Lomax Moreton Agency*

Suite C, Victory House, 131 Queensway, Petts Wood, Kent BR5 1DG
*tel* 020-7930 4447
*email* agency@bell-lomax.co.uk
*website* www.belllomaxmoreton.co.uk
*Twitter* @BLM_Agency
*Executives* Paul Moreton, Lauren Gardner, Jo Bell, Katie Fulford, Justine Smith, John Baker, Lorna Hemingway, Julie Gourinchas, Rory Jeffers, Sarah McDonnell

Will consider most fiction, non-fiction and children's (including picture books, middle grade and YA) book proposals. Submission guidelines on website. Physical submissions should be accompanied by sae for return and an email address for correspondence. Does not represent poetry, short stories or novellas, education textbooks, film scripts or stage plays. *Founded* 2000.

## The Bent Agency*

17 Kelsall Mews, Richmond TW9 4BP
*email* info@thebentagency.com
*website* www.thebentagency.com
*Agents* Nicola Barr, Jenny Bent, Victoria Cappello, Gemma Cooper, Claire Draper, Louise Fury, Molly Ker Hawn, James Mustelier, Zöe Plant, John Silbersack, Desiree Wilson

Full-service literary agency with offices in the UK and USA. Represents a diverse range of genres including history, humour, lifestyle, inspiration, memoir, literary fiction, children's and commercial fiction. Only accepts email queries. See website for detailed query and submission guidelines.

*Clients* include Faridah Abike-Iyimide, Sophie Anderson, Dhonielle Clayton, Stephanie Garber, Alwyn Hamilton, Hilary McKay, Mo O'Hara, Sibeal Pounder, Jo Spain, Robin Stevens, Angie Thomas, Jessica Townsend. *Founded* 2009.

## The BIA

*website* www.the-bia.com
*Twitter* @blindingbks
*Agents* Ben Illis, Rachel Hamilton

Children's and YA fiction specialist literary agency, with several notable prize-winning writers on the books. No picture books, fiction for under 7s or educational books. Currently closed to unsolicited submissions. Electronic submission only via website; send the first 50 pages and a synopsis for fiction or a detailed proposal for non-fiction. *Founded* 2012.

## The Blair Partnership*

PO Box 7828, London W1A 4GE
*tel* 020-7504 2520
*email* info@theblairpartnership.com
*website* www.theblairpartnership.com
*Twitter* @TBP_agency
*Instagram* @theblairpartnership_agency
*Founding Partner & Agent* Neil Blair, *Managing Director, Client Management* Rory Scarfe, *Lead Children's Agent* Rachel Petty, *Agents* Jordan Lees, Bea Fitzgerald

Represents a range of writers internationally from debut to established, with a strong focus on TV/film alongside literary publication. Considers fiction and non-fiction across YA and middle grade, graphic novels, and picture books. Will consider unsolicited MSS. Fiction: email the specific agent with a covering letter, one-page synopsis and first three chapters. Non-fiction: email a proposal document and writing sample. Picture books: email your query and full project. Not currently accepting screenplays, short stories or poetry.

*Clients* include Bana Alabed, JJ Arcanjo, Dawn Coulter-Cruttenden, Helena Duggan, Emma Farrarons, Sir Chris Hoy, Ramsey Hassan, Hazel Gardner, Frank Lampard, Kieran Larwood, Rose Lihou, J.K. Rowling, Nicki Thornton, Emanuel Wallace. *Founded* 2011.

## The Bright Agency*

103–105 St John's Hill, London SW11 1SY
*tel* 020-7326 9140
50 West Street, C12, New York, NY 10006
*tel* +1 646-578-6542
*website* https://thebrightagency.com/uk
*Founder* Vicki Willden-Lebrecht, *Director* Arabella Stein

Children's fiction and non-fiction, adult fiction and non-fiction, graphic novels and children's illustration. Other areas of representation include greeting and gift (cards, social stationery, giftwrap), design and advertising (editorial, branding, adult publishing, packaging, web and digital, typography), animation, and licensing (toys and games, digital gaming, fabric and apparel, and homewares). See website for illustration, writing and animation submissions guidelines. No submissions by post.

Literary agents

*Clients* include Benji Davies, David Litchfield, Yasmeen Ismail, Chris Chatterton, Diane Ewen, Laura Hughes, Galia Bernstein, Mechal Roe, Aura Lewis, Karl James Mountford, Jane Newland, Brenna Nation, Hannah Peck. *Founded* 2002.

## Jenny Brown Associates*
31 Marchmont Road, Edinburgh EH9 1HU
*email* childrens@jennybrownassociates.com
*website* www.jennybrownassociates.com
*Contact* Lucy Juckes

Writing and illustration for children, fiction and non-fiction. Has a preference for working with writers or illustrators based in Scotland. *Commission* Home 12.5%, overseas/translation 20%. A small agency which only reads submissions at certain points in the year; always check website before sending work.

*Clients* include Christopher Edge, Keith Gray, Helen Kellock, Emily MacKenzie, Jonathan Meres, Alison Murray. *Founded* 2002.

## Felicity Bryan Associates*
2A North Parade, Banbury Road, Oxford OX2 6LX
*tel* (01865) 513816
*email* agency@felicitybryan.com
*website* www.felicitybryan.com

Translation rights handled by Andrew Nurnberg Associates; works in conjunction with US agents. Fiction for children aged 8–14 and YA, and adult fiction and general non-fiction. *Commission* Home 15%, overseas 20%. All submissions and queries through website. No sci-fi and fantasy, horror, romance, graphic novels, scripts or poetry.

*Children's authors* include David Almond, Katya Balen, Matt Burton, Jenny Downham, Sally Gardner, Natasha Farrant, Clare Furniss, Liz Kessler, Annabel Pitcher, Meg Rosoff, Alom Shaha, Lauren St John, Chris Vick, Lisa Williamson, Lucy Worsley. *Founded* 1988.

## C&W Agency*
(previously Conville & Walsh)
Cunard House, 15 Regent Street, London SW1Y 4LR
*tel* 020-7393 4200
*website* www.cwagency.co.uk
*Twitter* @CWAgencyUK
*Instagram* @CWAgencyUK

A boutique and very select list of fiction for 5–8 and 9–12 years, teenage fiction, series fiction and film/TV tie-ins. Also handles adult literary and commercial fiction and non-fiction. *Commission* Home 15%, overseas 20%. Submissions welcome: first three chapters, cover letter and synopsis by email to the agent you would like to consider your work. Part of the Curtis Brown Group of Companies; simultaneous submission accepted. Not taking on picture books.

*Children's authors* include Katie Davies, Matt Haig, P.J. Lynch, Joshua Mowll, Paula Rawsthorne, Nicky Singer, Piers Torday, Steve Voake, the estate of John Burningham. *Founded* 2000.

## Georgina Capel Associates Ltd*
29 Wardour Street, London W1D 6PS
*tel* 020-7734 2414
*email* [firstname]@georginacapel.com
*website* www.georginacapel.com
*Agents* Georgina Capel, Rachel Conway, Simon Shaps, Irene Baldoni, Philippa Brewster

Children's and YA; literary and commercial fiction, history, biography; film and TV. *Commission* Home/overseas 15%. Postal submissions preferred, but does accept email. Include a covering letter, synopsis and first three chapters. *Founded* 1999.

## The Catchpole Agency
53 Cranham Street, Oxford OX2 6DD
*tel* 07789 588070
*email* james@thecatchpoleagency.co.uk
*website* www.thecatchpoleagency.co.uk
*Instagram* @thecatchpoles
*Proprietor* James Catchpole

Agents for authors and illustrators of children's books from picture books through to YA novels, with a specialism in editorial work. Email submissions@thecatchpoleagency.co.uk with a covering letter which includes a one- or two-sentence elevator pitch, the intended readership and a writing sample pasted directly into the body of the email. See additional submissions details on the website.

*Authors* include Polly Dunbar, S.F. Said, Michelle Robinson, Emer Stamp, Sean Taylor. *Founded* 1996.

## Anne Clark Literary Agency*
*email* submissions@anneclarkliteraryagency.co.uk
*website* www.anneclarkliteraryagency.co.uk
*Facebook* www.facebook.com/anneclarkliterary
*Twitter* @AnneClarkLit
*Contact* Anne Clark

Specialist in fiction, non-fiction and picture books for children and young adults. *Commission* Home 15%, overseas 20%. Submissions by email only. See website for details.

*Clients* include Mike Barfield, Anne Booth, Moira Butterfield, Lou Carter, Emily-Jane Clark, Pippa Goodhart, Cath Howe, Penny Joelson, Ruth Lauren, Leah Mohammed, Rebecca Patterson, Jason Rohan, Lucy Rowland. *Founded* 2012.

## Colwill & Peddle*
*email* submissions@colwillandpeddle.com
*website* www.colwillandpeddle.com
*Twitter* @colwillpeddle
*Instagram* @colwillandpeddle
*Agents* Charlotte Colwill, Kay Peddle

Focused on finding new voices and untold stories. Works with a number of foreign, film and TV co-agents to sell the rights to our clients' work internationally, in all formats and mediums. Charlotte is looking for adult fiction, children's fiction and non-fiction, and children's author-illustrators. Kay is looking for non-fiction: history, politics, essays, popular science, biography, memoir, travel, cookery and current affairs. *Commission* Home 15%, USA/foreign 20%. See website for detailed submission guidelines. Does not represent screenwriters or poets.

*Authors* include Kimberly McIntosh, Helen Graves, Joe Mulhall, It's a Continent, Kerri Andrews, Richard Smyth, Jess Morgan, Gianni Washington, Mark Illis, Kasia Delgado, Rupal Patel, Cecily Blench, Jemima Foxtrot, Samuel Blanchett. *Founded* 2022.

## Creative Authors Ltd

11A Woodlawn Street, Whitstable, Kent CT5 1HQ
*email* write@creativeauthors.co.uk
*website* www.creativeauthors.co.uk
*Twitter* @creativeauthors
*Instagram* @creativeauthors
*Director* Isabel Atherton

Children's fiction, picture books, YA, graphic novels and illustrators. Also fiction and non-fiction for adults. *Commission* Home 15%, overseas 20%. Only accepts email submissions.

*Authors and illustrators* include Guojing, Ged Adamson, Coll Muir, Colleen Kosinski. *Founded* 2008.

## Rupert Crew Ltd*

Southgate, 7 Linden Avenue, Dorchester DT1 1EJ
*tel* (01305) 260335
*email* info@rupertcrew.co.uk
*website* www.rupertcrew.co.uk
*Managing Director* Caroline Montgomery

International representation, handling accessible literary and commercial fiction and non-fiction for adult and children's (8+) markets. *Commission* Home 15%, overseas 20%, film/TV/radio 20%. No unsolicited MSS: see website for current submission guidelines. No picture books, plays, screenplays, poetry, journalism, sci-fi and fantasy or short stories. *Founded* 1927.

## Curtis Brown*

Cunard House, 15 Regent Street, London SW1Y 4LR
*tel* 020-7393 4400
*email* cb@curtisbrown.co.uk
*website* www.curtisbrown.co.uk, www.curtisbrowncreative.co.uk
*Twitter* @CBGBooks, @cbcreative
*Children's Agents* Isobel Gahan, Roxanne Edouard, Enrichetta Frizzato

Children's fiction ranges from picture books to YA novels across all genres. Represents prominent writers, from debut authors to established prize winners and bestsellers. Actively seeking talented new writers, particularly for books aimed at 8–12 years, adventure, fantasy, gothic stories and humour. Manages the international careers of authors with strong relationships in translation and US markets.

See website and individual agent webpages. Simultaneous submissions with C&W. *Founded* 1899.

## Dark House Literary & Screen Agency Ltd

19 Tottenhall Road, London N13 6HY
*tel* 07812 004546
*email* submission@darkhouse.uk
*website* www.darkhouse.uk
*Twitter* @DarkHouseAgency
*Managing Director* Andreas Charalambous

Represents the works of authors and creatives working within the horror and dark fantasy genres, including adult fiction, non-fiction, graphic novels, children's (with subtle horror themes) and YA. Also interested in screenplays for film and TV. Email submissions only. Fiction: attach a Word document that includes a brief synopsis and the first three chapters of the MS. Non-fiction: include a proposal, short synopsis and up-to-date CV. Does not represent works of poetry, picture books, theatrical scripts and any other genres bar horror and dark fantasy. *Founded* 2023.

## DHH Literary Agency*

23–27 Cecil Court, London WC2N 4EZ
*tel* 020-7836 7376
*email* enquiries@dhhliteraryagency.com
*website* www.dhhliteraryagency.com
*Facebook* www.facebook.com/dhhliteraryagency
*Twitter* @dhhlitagency
*Agents* David H. Headley, Broo Doherty, Harry Illingworth, Emily Glenister, Tom Drake-Lee

Children's fiction and YA fiction. Also adult fiction, women's commercial fiction, crime, literary fiction, sci-fi and fantasy; and non-fiction including history, cookery and humour. *Commission* UK 15%, overseas 15% (where a sub-agent is used 20%). Send informative preliminary email with first three chapters and synopsis. Consult website for correct email addresses for each agent. New authors welcome. No picture books, plays or scripts, poetry or short stories.

*Authors* include Matthew Crow, Phyllida Shrimpton, James Goodhand, Abi Elphinstone, Keris Stainton, Gabrielle Kent, Kate Mallinder, Amy Beashel, Morgan Owen. *Founded* 2008.

## Diamond Kahn & Woods Literary Agency*

Top Floor, 66 Onslow Gardens, London N10 3JX
*tel* 020-3514 6544
*email* info@dkwlitagency.co.uk
*email* submissions.ella@dkwlitagency.co.uk
*email* submissions.bryony@dkwlitagency.co.uk
*website* www.dkwlitagency.co.uk
*Twitter* @DKWLitAgency
*Agents* Ella Diamond Kahn, Bryony Woods

Children's, YA and crossover fiction; literary and commercial fiction (including all major genres) and non-fiction. Interested in new writers. *Commission* Home 15%, USA/translation 20%. Email submissions only. Send three chapters and synopsis to one agent.

*Clients* include Virginia Macgregor, Nicole Burstein, David Owen, Sharon Gosling, Sylvia Bishop, Sarah Baker, Katherine Orton, Dan Smith, Jamie Russell, Tom Huddleston, Caroline O'Donoghue, Daisy May Johnson. *Founded* 2012.

## Eddison Pearson Ltd*

West Hill House, 6 Swains Lane, London N6 6QS
*tel* 020-7700 7763
*email* enquiries@eddisonpearson.com
*website* www.eddisonpearson.com
*Contact* Clare Pearson

Small, personally run agency. Children's and YA books, fiction and non-fiction, poetry. *Commission* Home 10–15%, overseas 15–20%. Enquiries and submissions by email only; email for up-to-date submission guidelines. May suggest revision.

*Authors* include Valerie Bloom, Sue Heap, Caroline Lawrence, Robert Muchamore, Mary Murphy, Megan Rix. *Founded* 1997.

## Fraser Ross Associates

Larchwood, 42 Hadfast Road, Cousland, Midlothian EH22 2NZ
*email* agentlmfraser@gmail.com
*email* kjross@tiscali.co.uk
*website* www.fraserross.co.uk
*Facebook* www.facebook.com/fraserrossassociates
*Twitter* @FraserRossLA
*Instagram* @fraserrossassociates
*Partners* Lindsey Fraser, Kathryn Ross

Represents writers and illustrators. See website for submission guidelines. *Founded* 2002.

## The Good Literary Agency*

*email* info@thegoodliteraryagency.org
*website* www.thegoodliteraryagency.org
*Twitter* @thegoodagencyuk
*Instagram* @thegoodagencyuk

Represents authors from backgrounds under-represented in UK publishing including writers of colour, working class writers, disabled writers, LGBTQ+ writers and anyone who feels that they, or their stories, are under-represented. Children's and YA (all genres in fiction and non-fiction for readers 8+). Also adult fiction and non-fiction. For detailed submission guidelines, visit the website.

*Authors* include Patrick Gallagher, Nicola Garrard, Judy Hepburn, Lizzie Huxley-Jones, Ebinehita Iyere, Sharada Keats, Raj Kaur Khaira, Thomas Leeds, Jade Mutyora, Musa Okwonga, Kai Spellmeier, Clare Weze, Kimberly Whittam. *Founded* 2018.

## Annette Green Authors' Agency

5 Henwoods Mount, Pembury,
Tunbridge Wells TN2 4BH

*tel* (01892) 263252
*email* annette@annettegreenagency.co.uk
*website* www.annettegreenagency.co.uk
*Partners* Annette Green, David Smith

Fiction: literary, general, women's, historical, romance and fiction for older children. Non-fiction: popular culture, history and science. *Commission* Home 15%, overseas 20–25%. Preliminary email or letter, synopsis, sample chapter and sae essential. No picture books, dramatic scripts, poetry, sci-fi or fantasy. *Founded* 1998.

## The Greenhouse Literary Agency

*email* info@greenhouseliterary.com
*website* www.greenhouseliterary.com
*Director* Chelsea Eberly, *Agent* Kristin Ostby

Children's fiction and non-fiction: illustrators who write picture books, middle-grade through to teen/YA novels, and graphic novels. Some women's fiction. Submissions via QueryManager only; see website for submission guidelines. No poetry, short stories or film scripts.

*Authors* include Gavin Aung Than, Sarwat Chadda, Winifred Conkling, Andrea Contos, Alexandra Diaz, Bill Doyle, Theanne Griffith, Michelle Lam, Rebecca Mock, Kelis Rowe, Ali Standish, Emily Thiede, Ngozi Ukazu. *Founded* 2008.

## Greyhound Literary Agents*

49 Greek Street, London W1D 4EG
*email* info@greyhoundliterary.co.uk
*website* www.greyhoundliterary.co.uk
*Twitter* @GreyhoundLitAg
*Directors* Charlie Campbell, Sam Edenborough, *Agents* Charlotte Atyeo, Maria Brannan, Natalie Galustian, Philip Gwyn Jones, Dotti Irving, Julia Silk

Fiction and non-fiction for adults and children. Represent YA and some picture books for authors whose work is represented in other areas. *Commission* Home 15%, USA/film/TV 20%, translation 20%. Submissions via website. No plays, poetry or scripts.

*Clients* include Jennifer Lucy Allan, Beach, Victoria Belim, SJ Bennett, Edward Brooke-Hitching, Jen Campbell, Rebecca Front, Julian Gough, Ed Hawkins, Maisie Hill, Will Hill, Michael Holding, Anthony McGowan, Clare Seal, the estate of Alan Rickman. *Founded* 2022.

## Marianne Gunn O'Connor Literary, Film/TV Agency

Morrison Chambers, 32 Nassau Street, Dublin 2, D02 YE06, Republic of Ireland
*tel* +353 (0)16 669100
*email* submissions@mariannegunnoconnor.com
*website* www.mariannegunnoconnor.com
*Contact* Marianne Gunn O'Connor

Represents children's books, middle grade, YA, New Adult and crossover fiction, as well as literary fiction, upmarket fiction and non-fiction for adults. No screenplays. *Founded* 1996.

## Antony Harwood Ltd

103 Walton Street, Oxford OX2 6EB
*tel* (01865) 559615
*email* mail@antonyharwood.com
*website* www.antonyharwood.com
*Contacts* Antony Harwood, James Macdonald, Jo Williamson

General and genre fiction; general non-fiction. *Commission* Home 15%, overseas 20%. Will suggest revision.

*Children's authors* include Tamsyn Murray, Jennifer Gray, Peter Bunzl. *Founded* 2000.

## A.M. Heath & Co. Ltd*

6 Warwick Court, London WC1R 5DJ
*tel* 020-7242 2811
*email* enquiries@amheath.com
*website* www.amheath.com
*Twitter* @amheathltd
*Contact* Julia Churchill

Children's fiction and non-fiction from picture books to YA. Also handles adult literary and commercial fiction and non-fiction. *Commission* Home 15%, USA/translation 20%, film/TV 15–20% (by agreement). Digital submission via website. No screenplays, poetry or short stories except for collections.

*Authors* include Nicholas Allan, Sam Copeland, Sarah Crossan, Conn Iggulden, Pip Jones, Michelle Harrison, Az Dassu, Jenny McLachlan, Joanna Nadin, Amy Sparkes, Patricia Toht, Holly Webb and the estates of Noel Streatfeild, Joan Aiken, Christianna Brand. *Founded* 1919.

## Sophie Hicks Agency*

60 Gray's Inn Road, London WC1X 8LU
*email* info@sophiehicksagency.com
*website* www.sophiehicksagency.com
*Twitter* @SophieHicksAg
*Agents* Sophie Hicks, Sarah Williams

Fiction for 9+. Also handles adult fiction and non-fiction. *Commission* Home/USA 15%, translation 20%. Email submissions only, see website for guidelines. No poetry, scripts or illustrated books.

*Authors* include Herbie Brennan, Anne Cassidy, Lucy Coats, Eoin Colfer, Andrew Donkin, Kathryn Evans, Emerald Fennell, Rohan Gavin, Padraig Kenny, Sarah Mussi, Siobhan Parkinson, Kate Thompson, Shamim Sarif, Sif Sigmarsdóttir, Kiah Thomas. *Founded* 2014.

## David Higham Associates Ltd*

6th Floor, Waverley House, 7–12 Noel Street, London W1F 8GQ
*tel* 020-7434 5900
*email* dha@davidhigham.co.uk
*website* www.davidhigham.co.uk

*Managing Director* Lizzy Kremer, *Books* Veronique Baxter, Anthony Goff, Caroline Walsh, Christabel McKinley, *Children's Rights* Allison Cole, Olivia Hickman, *Film/TV/Theatre* Nicky Lund, Clare Israel, Georgie Smith

Children's fiction and non-fiction. 35% of the agency's list is for the children's market. Represented in all foreign markets. Also represents illustrators for children's book publishing. Handles novelty books, picture books, fiction for 5–8 and 9–12 years, teen and YA fiction, series fiction, poetry, plays, film/TV tie-ins, non-fiction and audio. Also handles adult fiction, general non-fiction, plays, film and TV scripts. *Commission* Home 15%, USA/translation 20%, scripts 10%. See website for submissions policy.

*Clients* include Emma Chichester Clark, Cressida Cowell, Nicola Davies, Anna Kemp, Geraldine McCaughrean, Tom McLaughlin, Michael Morpurgo, Kate O'Hearn, Catherine Rayner, Nick Sharratt, Jonathan Stroud, Jenny Valentine, Jacqueline Wilson and the estate of Roald Dahl. *Founded* 1935.

## Holroyde Cartey Ltd*

*email* claire@holroydecartey.com
*email* penny@holroydecartey.com
*website* www.holroydecartey.com
*Contacts* Claire Cartey, Penny Holroyde

A literary and artistic agency representing a list of award-winning and bestselling authors and illustrators. Welcomes submissions from debut and established authors. *Commission* Headline 15%. See website for submission guidelines. *Founded* 2015.

## Kate Hordern Literary Agency Ltd*

18 Mortimer Road, Clifton, Bristol BS8 4EY
*tel* (01179) 239368
*email* kate@khla.co.uk
*email* anne@khla.co.uk
*website* https://khla.co.uk
*Agents* Kate Hordern, Anne Williams

A small agency with an international reach representing a wide range of fiction, some non-fiction and some children's. See website for further details of what the agency is looking for and for submission guidelines. *Founded* 1999.

## Janklow & Nesbit (UK) Ltd*

66–67 Newman Street, Fitzrovia W1T 3EQ
*tel* 020-7243 2975
*email* submissions@janklow.co.uk
*website* www.janklowandnesbit.co.uk
*Twitter* @JanklowUK
*Instagram* @janklownesbituk
*Agents* Will Francis, Claire Paterson Conrad, Julia Eagleton, Emma Leong, *Foreign Rights* Mairi Friesen-Escandell, Nathaniel Alcaraz-Stapleton, Ellis Hazelgrove, Maimy Suleiman

Represents a bestselling, global and award-winning range of commercial and literary fiction and non-fiction, children's and YA. Handles translation rights directly or through sub-agents in all territories. US rights handled by Janklow & Nesbit Associates in New York. Send informative covering letter with full outline (non-fiction), synopsis and first three sample chapters (fiction) by email only. Include your name, the title of your work and the name of the agent you are submitting to in the email subject line. No plays or film/TV scripts.

*Clients* include Dr Rangan Chatterjee, Ed Yong, Rowan Coleman, Adam Rutherford, Mya-Rose Craig, Hannah Fry, Oliver Burkeman, Michel Faber, Sunjeev Sahota, Kiran Millwood Hargrave, M.J. Arlidge, Lucy Cooke, Sharna Jackson, Tsedal Neeley, Chukwuebuka Ibeh. *Founded* 2000.

## Johnson & Alcock Ltd*

West Wing, Somerset House, Strand, London WC2R 1LA
*tel* 020-7251 0125
*website* www.johnsonandalcock.co.uk
*Contact* Anna Power, Ed Wilson

All types of YA and teen fiction, particularly graphic novels. *Commission* Home 15%, USA/translation/film 20%. Send first three chapters (or 50 pages), full synopsis and brief covering letter with details of writing experience. For submission guidelines see website. Return postage essential. No short stories, poetry or board/picture books. *Founded* 1956.

## JQ Literary Agency

17 Carlton House Terrace, St James's, London SW1Y 5AH
*tel* 07396 344505
*email* joey@jq-agency.co.uk
*website* www.jq-agency.co.uk
*Instagram* @jq_literaryagency
*Director* Joey Quince

Actively looking for debut children's middle-grade fiction brimming with magic, fantasy, adventure and heart. Represents children's middle-grade, YA and fantasy fiction. Email in first instance with a summary of the book and an author biography. *Founded* 2019.

## Kane Literary Agency*

2 Dukes Avenue, London N10 2PT
*tel* 020-8351 9680
*website* www.kaneliteraryagency.com
*Director* Yasmin Kane

Interested in discovering new writers and launching the careers of first-time writers. Children's fiction: middle grade to YA. Also handles literary and commercial fiction for adults. *Commission* Home 15%, overseas 20%. Send submissions by email only; no submissions by post. For fiction, send a covering letter with the first three chapters and a synopsis; for non-fiction, send a covering letter and full book proposal plus two sample chapters. See website for further information. No picture books.

*Authors* include Christopher Moore, Richard Butchins, Colleen MacMahon, Sarah Harris, Ruchita Misra, Min Day. *Founded* 2004.

## LBA Books*

91 Great Russell Street, London WC1B 3PS
*tel* 020-7637 1234
*email* info@lbabooks.com
*website* www.lbabooks.com
*Twitter* @LBA_Agency
*Agents* Luigi Bonomi, Amanda Preston, Louise Lamont, Hannah Schofield

Fiction and non-fiction. Keen to find new authors and help them develop their careers. Works with foreign agencies and has links with film and TV production companies. YA and children's fiction, as well as adult fiction and non-fiction. *Commission* Home 15%, overseas 20%. Send preliminary letter, synopsis and first three chapters. No postal submissions. No poetry, short stories or screenplays.

*Authors* include Virginia Bergin, Anna Carey, Rebecca Cobb, Bea Fitzgerald, Julia Gray, Helen Hancocks, Anne Miller, Ben Miller, Nazneen Ahmed Pathak, S.A. Patrick, Lucy Strange, Tamsin Winter, Laura Wood, Katherine Woodfine, Emma Yarlett. *Founded* 2005.

## Lindsay Literary Agency*

East Worldham House, Alton, Hants GU34 3AT
*tel* (01420) 831430
*email* info@lindsayliteraryagency.co.uk
*website* www.lindsayliteraryagency.co.uk
*Twitter* @LindsayLit
*Founder* Becky Bagnell

Specialists in children's fiction and non-fiction, teen/YA, middle grade and picture books. *Commission* Home 15%, translation 20%. Send first three chapters, synopsis and covering letter by email. No submissions by post. Will suggest revision.

*Authors* include Pamela Butchart, Christina Collins, Donna David, Sam Gayton, Sital Gorasia Chapman, Ruth Hatfield, Larry Hayes, J.M. Joseph, Giles Paley-Phillips, Josh Silver, Daniel Tawse, Sharon Tregenza, Rachel Valentine, Sue Wallman, Joe Wilson. *Founded* 2008.

## The Literary Office

71–75 Shelton Street, London WC2H 9JQ
*tel* 07910 267336
*email* jenny.todd@theliteraryoffice.com
*website* www.theliteraryoffice.com
*Founder* Jenny Todd

Represents quality literary and commercial fiction, non-fiction, YA, film and TV. Drawn to works of originality by inventive, relevant and multi-faceted writers and artists, and committed to developing long-term strategies for their careers. *Commission* Home 15%, overseas 20%. Submissions via website. Send covering letter, synopsis and three sample chapters. *Founded* 2021.

## The Liverpool Literary Agency*

*tel* 07742 603459 , 07917 788964
*email* submissions@liverpool-literary.agency
*website* www.liverpool-literary.agency
*Twitter* @LiverpoolLit
*Agents* Clare Coombes, Matthew McKeown, Laura Bennett

Looking for adult fiction (all genres) and children's fiction, specifically chapter book (ages 5–7 and 7–9) and middle-grade fiction (ages 8–12). Only accepting submissions from writers born or currently living in the North of England. Submissions should include a synopsis and the first three chapters by email, with an author bio included in the covering email. See website for further submission guidelines. Does not accept children's picture books, scripts, non-fiction, poetry, short stories or YA.

*Authors* include David Beckler, Jack Byrne, Rachel Bowdler, Caron McKinlay, Ashleigh Nugent, Danielle Owen-Jones, Helen Parusel, Michael Sellars, Stephanie Sowden. *Founded* 2020.

## Luithlen Agency

88 Holmfield Road, Leicester LE2 1SB
*tel* 0116 273 8863
*email* penny@luithlenagency.com
*website* www.luithlenagency.com
*Agents* Jennifer Luithlen, Penny Luithlen

Children's fiction, all ages up to YA. *Commission* Home 15%, overseas 20%, performance rights 15%. See website for submission information. *Founded* 1986.

## Eunice McMullen Ltd

Low Ibbotsholme Cottage, Off Bridge Lane, Troutbeck Bridge, Windermere, Cumbria LA23 1HU
*tel* (01539) 448551
*email* eunice@eunicemcmullen.co.uk
*website* www.eunicemcmullen.co.uk
*Director* Eunice McMullen

Specialises exclusively in children's books, especially picture books and older fiction. Handles novelty books, picture books, fiction for all ages including teenage, series fiction and audio. *Commission* Home 15%, overseas 15%. No unsolicited scripts. Telephone or email enquiries only.

*Authors* include Alison Friend, Charles Fuge, Cally Johnson Isaacs, James Mayhew, Momoko Abe, Mark McKinley. *Founded* 1992.

## Marjacq Scripts Ltd*

The Space, 235 High Holborn, London WC1V 7DN
*tel* 020-7935 9499
*website* www.marjacq.com
*Twitter* @MarjacqScripts
*Contact* Catherine Pellegrino (children's and YA), Sandra Sawicka (YA only)

Handles all rights. In-house legal, foreign rights and book-to-film support. All genres represented.

*Commission* Home 15%, overseas 20%, film 20%. See website for submission guidelines.

*Clients* include James Campbell, Rose Edwards, Roopa Farooki, Steve Feasey, Gemma Fowler, Nick Garlick, Finbar Hawkins, T.C. Shelley, Claire Waller, Harriet Whitehorn. *Founded* 1973.

## MBA Literary and Script Agents Ltd*

62 Grafton Way, London W1T 5DW
*tel* 020-7387 2076
*website* www.mbalit.co.uk
*Twitter* @mbaagents
*Children's Book Agent* Sophie Gorell Barnes, *Film & TV Agent* Diana Tyler

Fiction, non-fiction, children's books. Foreign rights handled by Louisa Pritchard Associates. *Commission* Home 15%, overseas 20%, TV/theatre/radio 10%, film 15%. See website for submission guidelines.

*Clients* include Sufiya Ahmed, Sita Brahmachari, Christopher William Hill, Mark Wheeller. *Founded* 1971.

## Madeleine Milburn Literary, TV & Film Agency*

The Factory, 1 Park Hill, Clapham, London SW4 9NS
*tel* 020-7499 7550
*email* childrens@madeleinemilburn.com
*website* www.madeleinemilburn.co.uk
*Facebook* www.facebook.com/MadeleineMilburnLiteraryAgency
*Twitter* @MMLitAgency
*Instagram* @madeleinemilburn

Special interest in launching the careers of debut authors and illustrators. Represents a dynamic and prize-winning range of children's and YA fiction and non-fiction. Also award-winning and popular fiction including fantasy, real life/contemporary, YA thrillers, mystery, action, historical, sci-fi, romance, coming of age and film/TV tie-ins.

Represents British, American, Canadian and international authors. Handles all rights in the UK, US and foreign markets including film/TV/theatre/radio (for clients with book deal in place only) and digital. Areas include 6–8 years, 9–12 years, 12+, teen, YA, New Adult and books appealing to both children and adults. *Commission* Home 15%, USA/Canada/translation 20%, film/TV 20%. No submissions by post. See submission guidelines and agency news on website. Works editorially with all clients.

*Authors* include Holly Bourne, Anna Fargher, Kathryn Foxfield, Kate Weston, Ben Oliver, Danielle Jawando, Benjamin Dean, Lex Croucher, Katie Kirby, Jen Carney, Helen Rutter, Maisie Chan, Natasha Hastings, Jordan Lees, Laura Steven. *Founded* 2012.

## Miles Stott Children's Literary Agency Ltd*

East Hook Farm, Lower Quay Road, Hook, Haverfordwest, Pembrokeshire SA62 4LR

*tel* 07855 252043
*email* [firstname]@milesstottagency.co.uk
*website* www.milesstottagency.co.uk
*Twitter* @milesstott
*Instagram* @milesstott
*Director* Nancy Miles, *Associate Agents* Victoria
Birkett, Mandy Suhr

Specialist in children's novelty books, picture books,
fiction for 6–9 and 10–12 years, YA series fiction and
non-fiction. *Commission* Home 15%, overseas 20%,
film/TV 20%. Fiction submissions by email only to
fictionsubs@milesstottagency.co.uk including
covering letter, brief synopsis and first three chapters.
Picture book submissions by email only to
picturebooksubs@milesstottagency.co.uk including
covering letter, complete text and/or pdfs of sample
artwork.
  *Authors* include Kirsty Applebaum, Atinuke, Rachel
Bright, Stacy Gregg, Frances Hardinge, Caryl Hart,
Gill Lewis, Tom Percival, Tom Pollock, Mark
Sperring. *Founded* 2003.

## MMB Creative*

(Mulcahy Sweeney Associates Ltd)
The Old Truman Brewery, 91 Brick Lane,
London E1 6QL
*tel* 020-3582 9379
*email* mulcahyadmin@mmbcreative.com
*website* https://mmbcreative.com/books
*Twitter* @MulcahyLitAgent
*Contacts* Ivan Mulcahy, Sallyanne Sweeney, Edwina
de Charnace

Fiction and non-fiction. Biography, crime, finance,
historical, lifestyle, sport, thrillers, women's interests,
adult, children's, youth, commercial, literary. Send
query with synopsis, author bio and sample writing
via website only. See website for full guidelines.
  *Clients* include Ha-Joon Chang, Juno Dawson,
Felicity Everett, Ian Kelly, Steven Lenton, Lisa
McInerney, Alan McMonagle, Roisin Meaney, David
Mitchell, Simon Philip, E.M. Reapy, Robert Webb,
Dapo Adeola, Nathan Bryon, Brian Cox.
*Founded* 2016.

## Morgan Green Creatives Ltd

157 Ribblesdale Road, London SW16 6SP
*email* kirsty@morgangreencreatives.com
*website* www.morgangreencreatives.com
*Founder* Kirsty McLachlan

Actively looking for fresh talent and to be challenged
with new ideas, inspired and moved by great writing,
and to find unique and distinct voices with
compelling stories to tell. Represents fiction, non-
fiction and children's book writers. Submission by
email which includes a covering letter within the
body of the email, plus 30 pages of your work
attached. *Founded* 2020.

## Andrew Nurnberg Associates Ltd*

3–11 Eyre Street Hill, London EC1R 5ET
*tel* 020-3327 0400

*email* info@nurnberg.co.uk
*website* www.andrewnurnberg.com
*Twitter* @nurnberg_agency
*Managing Directors* Jenny Savill (ANA), Doug
Wallace (ANAI)

Represents adult and children's authors, agent and
publisher clients in the fields of literary and
commercial fiction and general non-fiction for the
sale of rights throughout the world via offices in the
UK and overseas. *Founded* 1977.

## Originate Literary Agency

71–75 Shelton Street, Covent Garden,
London WC2H 9JQ
*email* nataliejerome@originateliterary.co.uk
*Twitter* @OriginateLit
*Instagram* @originateliterary
*Founder & literary agent* Natalie Jerome

Actively looking to platform new voices who push
boundaries and want to create change on a global
stage. Represents a broad range of genres including
YA, commercial fiction and non-fiction. *Commission*
Home 15%, overseas 20%. Send a covering note
including a brief biography and the first three
chapters of your book (for illustrated titles send
sample spreads with your proposal) by email to
originatesubmissions@originateliterary.co.uk. Does
not represent academic and educational texts.
  *Clients* include Sir Lenny Henry (children's
publishing), David Harewood, Amir Khan, Eric
Collins. *Founded* 2023.

## Paper Lion Ltd

13 Grayham Road, New Malden, Surrey KT3 5HR
*tel* 07748 786199, (01276) 61322
*email* katyloffman@paperlionltd.com
*email* lesleypollinger@paperlionltd.com
*website* www.paperlionltd.com
*Agents* Katy Loffman, Lesley Pollinger

A cross-media literary agency. The client list includes
award-winning authors, literary estates and
publishers. Has a strong focus on the exploration of
digital opportunities and expertise in solving complex
copyright, dramatic rights and literary issues from the
present and past.
  *Clients* include Max Allen, Vince Cross, Catherine
Fisher, Dave Gatward, Saviour Pirottam, the estates
of authors including Gene Kemp, Bruce Hobson,
Cordelia Feldman and Gwynedd Rae. *Founded* 2017.

## Peters Fraser & Dunlop Ltd*

55 New Oxford Street, London WC1A 1BS
*tel* 020-7344 1000
*email* info@pfd.co.uk
*website* https://petersfraserdunlop.com
*Facebook* www.facebook.com/pfdagents
*Twitter* @PFDAgents
*Head of Children's Books* Silvia Molteni, *Agent* Lucy
Irvine

Represents authors of fiction and non-fiction, presenters and public speakers throughout the world. PFD runs its own digital publishing imprint called Agora Books Ltd (www.agorabooks.co). Email submissions addressed to individual agents. Include covering letter, synopsis or outline and first three chapters as well as author biographies. See website for submission guidelines. Does not represent scriptwriters.

*Authors* include Jeanette Winterson, Simon Schama, Edna O'Brien, Bear Grylls, Michael Caine, Onjali Q. Rauf, Lisa Thompson, Jamie Bartlett, Lesley Pearce, Chi-chi Nwanoku, Rose Tremain, Niall Williams, Jamie Susskind, Kenya Hunt, Ruby Wax. *Founded* 1924.

## Redhammer Management Ltd

*website* https://redhammer.info
*Vice President* Peter Cox

A boutique literary agency providing in-depth management for a restricted number of clients. Specialises in works with international book, film and TV potential. Participates in Pop-Up Submissions every Sunday; submit a title, brief description and first 700 words of the work. No radio or theatre scripts.

## Rogers, Coleridge & White Ltd*

20 Powis Mews, London W11 1JN
*tel* 020-7221 3717
*email* info@rcwlitagency.com
*website* www.rcwlitagency.com
*Twitter* @RCWLitAgency
*Instagram* @rcwliteraryagency
*Managing Director* Peter Straus, *Deputy Managing Director* Georgia Garrett, *Directors* Nelka Bell, Sam Copeland, Stephen Edwards, Natasha Fairweather, Laurence Laluyaux, Zoë Waldie, Claire Wilson, Jon Wood, *Agents* Cara Jones, Matthew Turner

International representation for all genres of fiction, non-fiction, children's and YA. *Commission* Home 15%, USA 20%, translation 20%. See website for submissions information.

*Clients* include David Baddiel, Frank Cottrell Boyce, Catherine Doyle, Lissa Evans, Hannah Gold, Anna James, Femi Fadugba, Tamzin Merchant, Alice Oseman, Katherine Rundell, A.F. Steadman, Holly Jackson, Katie and Kevin Tsang. *Founded* 1967 as Deborah Rogers Ltd, 1989 as Rogers, Coleridge & White Ltd.

## Sheil Land Associates Ltd

LABS House, Rm 9–25, 15–19 Bloomsbury Way, London WC1A 2TH
*tel* 020-7405 9351
*email* info@sheilland.co.uk
*website* www.sheilland.co.uk
*Twitter* @sheilland
*Agents UK & USA* Sonia Land, Gaia Banks, Piers Blofeld, Ian Drury, Natalie Barracliffe, *Film/Theatre/*

*TV* Lucy Fawcett, Rebecca Lyon, *Foreign Rights* Alba Arnau, Lauren Coleman

Represents book club, commercial and literary fiction: thrillers, crime, romance, drama, sci-fi and fantasy and YA; and non-fiction: biography, politics, history, military history, gardening, travel, cookery, humour. *Commission* Home 15%, USA/translation 20%. Welcomes approaches from new clients to start or to develop their careers. Send cover letter, synopsis and first three chapters. Please send submissions to submissions@sheilland.co.uk.

## Caroline Sheldon Literary Agency Ltd*

71 Hillgate Place, London W8 7SS
*tel* 020-7727 9102
*email* info@carolinesheldon.co.uk
*website* www.carolinesheldon.co.uk
*Twitter* @CarolineAgent
*Contacts* Caroline Sheldon, Millie Van Grutten

Represents in all areas of children's fiction, whether picture book, middle grade or YA. Looks for strong concepts, wonderful characterisation and excellent story-telling and compelling non-fiction. Also represents leading illustrators of children's books. Works closely with a media agent on film, TV and other opportunities. All genres of children's writing including fantasy, humour, contemporary life, thriller, stories set in schools and non-fiction. *Commission* Home 15%, USA/translation 20%, film/TV 20%. To submit work send an introductory email addressed to either Caroline Sheldon or Millie Van Grutten: in the subject line write 'Proposal and [title of the work]'; at the head of the email include a three-line synopsis; give further full information in the email about the work and yourself. Authors: send the first three chapters or equivalent length. Illustrators: attach work or include a link to your portfolio. *Founded* 1985.

## Hannah Sheppard Literary Agency

*email* enquiries@hs-la.com
*website* www.hs-la.com
*Twitter* @HS_LA_News
*Instagram* @HS_LA_News
*Founder & Literary agent* Hannah Sheppard

Actively seeking new authors, particularly from under-represented groups. Current wish lists can be found on the website. Represents children's fiction (primarily across middle grade, teen and YA), commercial adult fiction (with a focus on crime/thriller and women's fiction) and a very small amount of non-fiction. *Commission* Home 15%, overseas 20%, film/TV 20%. Submission via form on website. No poetry or screenplays.

*Clients* include Dee Benson, Jim Beckett, Sarah Bonner, Abi Elphinstone, Gabrielle Kent, Olivia Lara, Jon Lander, Chris McGeorge, Kate Mallinder, Morgan Owen, Keris Stainton. *Founded* 2023.

Literary agents

## Dorie Simmonds Agency Ltd*

*email* info@doriesimmonds.com
*website* https://doriesimmonds.com
*Twitter* @Dorie_Simmonds
*Contact* Dorie Simmonds

Children's fiction, general non-fiction and
commercial fiction. *Commission* Home 15%, USA
15%, translation 20%. Email the first three chapters
of your MS, with a query letter including your
background and relevant writing experience. Does
not represent poetry or screenplays. *Founded* 1997.

## Skylark Literary Ltd*

19 Parkway, Weybridge, Surrey KT13 9HD
*tel* 020-8144 7440
*email* info@skylark-literary.com
*email* submissions@skylark-literary.com
*website* www.skylark-literary.com
*Facebook* www.facebook.com/SkylarkLiteraryLtd
*Twitter* @skylarklit
*Directors* Joanna Moult, Amber Caraveo

Specialists in children's and YA fiction. Keen to
support new and established authors. Agents have
editorial backgrounds and will work closely with
clients on their manuscripts to increase chances of
publication. All genres considered. *Commission*
Home 15%, overseas 20%. Will consider unsolicited
submissions by email only. Will suggest revision
where appropriate. No adult fiction/non-fiction.
  *Clients* include Amy Wilson, Simon James Green,
Alyssa Hollingsworth, Rachel Burge, Nizrana Farook,
Lesley Parr, Em Lynas, Lily Dyu, Sarah Todd Taylor,
Naomi Gibson, Lucy Hope, Lee Newbery, Aislinn
O'Louglin, Clare Harlow, Eilish Fisher.
*Founded* 2014.

## The Soho Agency Ltd*

(previously LAW/Lucas Alexander Whitley Ltd)
16–17 Wardour Mews, 2nd Floor, London W1F 8AT
*tel* 020-7471 7900
*website* www.thesohoagency.co.uk
*Twitter* @TheSohoAgencyUK
*Managing Director* Rowan Lawton, *Agent* Philippa
Milnes-Smith

Novelty books, picture books, fiction for 5–8 and
9–12 years including series, YA, film/TV and non-
fiction. Special interests: projects with cross-media
potential, diverse voices, visual storytelling and
innovative non-fiction. *Commission* Home 15%,
overseas 20%. Representation in all markets.
Unsolicited and debut work considered. See website
for further information about the clients and genres
represented, plus essential information on
submissions. No postal submissions.
  *Clients* include Lauren Child, Steve Cole, Linda
Chapman, Gillian Cross, Emily Gravett, Chris Judge,
Sophie Kinsella, Philip Reeve, Chris Riddell, Niamh
Sharkey, Sarah Webb. *Founded* 1996.

## SP Literary Agency

*email* info@sp-agency.co.uk
*website* http://sp-agency.co.uk
*Facebook* www.facebook.com/sp.literary.agency
*Agents* Philippa Perry, Abigail Sparrow

Represents authors and illustrators across children's,
YA and adult fiction and non-fiction. Email
submissions preferred; attach a synopsis and the first
three chapters to a covering email. Children's or YA
submissions should be clearly marked in the subject
line.

## Abner Stein*

China House, Suite 137, 100 Black Prince Road,
London SE1 7SJ
*tel* 020-7373 0456
*email* info@abnerstein.co.uk
*website* www.abnerstein.co.uk
*Contacts* Caspian Dennis, Sandy Violette

Fiction, general non-fiction and children's.
*Commission* Home 15%, overseas 20%. Not taking on
any new clients at present.

## Rochelle Stevens & Co

2 Terretts Place, Upper Street, London N1 1QZ
*tel* 020-7359 3900
*email* info@rochellestevens.com
*website* www.rochellestevens.com
*Twitter* @TerrettsPlace
*Directors* Rochelle Stevens, Frances Arnold

Scripts for TV, theatre and radio. *Commission* Home
10%. Recommendation from industry professional
required. Email to introduce yourself and include the
recommendation. Will request a writing sample if
interested. Does not accept book submissions.
*Founded* 1984.

## Sarah Such Literary Agency

38 Church Road, Barnes, London SW13 9HN
*tel* 020-8741 2107
*email* info@sarah-such.com
*website* https://sarahsuchliteraryagency.tumblr.com
*Twitter* @sarahsuch
*Instagram* @sarahsuch1
*Director* Sarah Such

High-quality literary and commercial non-fiction and
fiction for adults and children. Always looking for
original children's and YA writers and projects.
Translation representation by The Buckman Agency.
Film/TV representation by Lesley Thorne, Aitken
Alexander Associates Ltd. Particular focus on debut
YA novels, topical middle-grade non-fiction,
children's fiction series, picture books and graphic
novels. *Commission* Home 15%, overseas 20%, film/
TV 20%. Will suggest revision. Submit synopsis and
three sample chapters (as a Word attachment by
email) and an author biography. No postal
submissions unless requested. No unsolicited MSS or
telephone enquiries. Film/TV scripts for established

clients only. No radio or theatre scripts, poetry, fantasy, self-help or short stories (unless full collections).

*Authors* include Matthew De Abaitua, Jeffrey Boakye, Kit Caless, Maxim Jakubowski, Antony Johnston, Amy Lankester-Owen, Louisa Leaman, Vesna Maric, Heather Martin, Sabrina Pace-Humphreys, Rachel Pashley, John Rowley, Caroline Sanderson, Nikhil Singh, Sara Starbuck. *Founded* 2007.

## Nick Turner Management Ltd

*tel* 020-3723 8833
*email* nick@nickturnermanagement.com
*website* https://nickturnermanagement.com
*Twitter* @nickturnermgmt
*Agents* Nick Turner, Phil Adie

Represents writers and directors for film, TV and radio worldwide. Specialises in TV drama, comedy, continuing drama and children's. *Commission* Home 10%, overseas 15–20%. *Founded* 2016.

## Two Piers Literary Agency

*email* hello@twopiersagency.com
*website* https://twopiersagency.com
*Facebook* www.facebook.com/TwoPiersAgency
*Twitter* @TwoPiersAgency
*Instagram* @twopiersagency
*Agent* Rufus Purdy

Represents fiction and non-fiction, including children's (from 7+) and memoir. Submissions through form on website. For fiction, submit the first three chapters and a one-page synopsis; for non-fiction, send three chapters and proposal. Submissions must include a covering letter. *Founded* 2021.

## Tyild's Agency

*email* submissionstotyildsagency@gmail.com
*website* www.tyildsagency.co.uk
*Twitter* @tyilds
*Agents* Kate Scarborough, Frances McKay

Set up particularly for teachers who write for children. Represents authors of picture books, young readers and middle-grade fiction, as well as non-fiction. Actively looking for new voices – wonderful storytellers with an innate understanding of children. *Commission* Home 15%, overseas 20%. See website for more details on how to send in submissions. *Founded* 2020.

## United Agents Ltd*

12–26 Lexington Street, London W1F 0LE
*tel* 020-3214 0800
*email* info@unitedagents.co.uk
*website* www.unitedagents.co.uk
*Agents* Jodie Hodges, Emily Talbot, Molly Jamieson

Fiction and non-fiction. *Commission* Home 15%, USA/translation 20%. See website for submission details. *Founded* 2008.

## Jo Unwin Literary Agency*

West Wing, Somerset House, London WC2R 1LA
*email* info@jounwin.co.uk
*website* www.jounwin.co.uk
*Twitter* @jounwin, @rachelphilippa
*Agents* Jo Unwin, Rachel Mann

Represents authors of literary fiction, commercial women's fiction, non-fiction, cookery, YA fiction and fiction for children aged 5+ (picture books only accepted if written by established clients). Email submissions only addressing a specific agent to submissions@jounwin.co.uk. Fiction: a covering letter, one- to two-page synopsis and first three chapters of your MS. Non-fiction: a proposal with a brief description of your work, an author bio, one or two sample chapters and a chapter outline.

*Authors* include Wibke Brueggemann, Janelle McCurdy, Jack Meggitt-Phillips, Sarah Moore Fitzgerald, Hayley Scott, Nadia Shireen, Emma-Jane Smith-Barton, Angharad Walker. *Founded* 2016.

## Watson, Little Ltd*

Suite 315, ScreenWorks, 22 Highbury Grove, London N5 2ER
*tel* 020-7388 7529
*email* office@watsonlittle.com
*website* www.watsonlittle.com
*Twitter* @watsonlittle
*Managing Director* James Wills, *Agents* Laetitia Rutherford, Megan Carroll, *Rights Director* Rachel Richardson

Offers a full service to its clients across all aspects of media. Handles a wide range of fiction and non-fiction for adults and children and works in conjunction with US agents and selected film and TV associates. YA and middle-grade fiction, picture books and children's non-fiction in all genres. *Commission* Home 15%, USA/translation 20%. Email submissions@watsonlittle.com with an informative preliminary letter, synopsis and sample chapters. No poetry, TV, play or film scripts.

*Authors* include Adam B, Tom Clempson, Rebecca Elliott, Tim Hall, Hayley Hoskins, Richard Joyce, Hiba Noor Khan, Lynne Reid Banks, Margaret Mahy. *Founded* 1970.

## Whispering Buffalo Literary Agency Ltd

97 Chesson Road, London W14 9QS
*tel* 020-7385 465 5
*email* info@whisperingbuffalo.com
*website* www.whisperingbuffalo.com
*Director* Mariam Keen

Commercial and literary fiction, non-fiction, children's and YA fiction. Special interest in book-to-screen adaptations; TV and film rights in novels and non-fiction handled in-house. *Commission* Home 15%, overseas 20%. Only accepts submissions by email. Will suggest revision. *Founded* 2008.

## Eve White Literary Agency Ltd*

15 Alderney Street, London SW1V 4ES
*tel* 020-7630 1155
*email* [firstname]@evewhite.co.uk
*website* www.evewhite.co.uk
*Twitter* @EveWhiteAgency
*Contacts* Eve White, Ludo Cinelli

Boutique agency representing young, middle grade, teenage and YA fiction, picture books and film/TV tie-ins. Also handles adult commercial and literary fiction and non-fiction; 35% of the list is for the children's market. *Commission* Home 15%, overseas 20%. Will suggest revision where appropriate. See website for up-to-date submission requirements. No submissions by post.
   *Clients* include Andy Stanton, Rae Earl, Tracey Corderoy, Elli Woollard, Sarah Naughton, Iona Rangeley, Simon Fox, Tia Fisher, James Bishop, Sarah Coyle, Ivan Brett. *Founded* 2003.

## Alice Williams Literary*

*tel* 020-7385 2118
*email* submissions@alicewilliamsliterary.co.uk
*website* www.alicewilliamsliterary.co.uk
*Twitter* @alicelovesbooks
*Contact* Alice Williams

Specialist literary agency representing writers and illustrators of picture books, children's fiction, teen/YA fiction and children's non-fiction. *Commission* Home 15%, USA/translation 20%, film/TV 20%. By email only; attach full typescript and synopsis, two or three picture book texts or illustration portfolio. See website for further guidelines.
   *Clients* include Fiona Barker, Lauren Beard, Jo Clarke, Ruby Clyde, Rachael Davis, Rachel Delahaye, Meg McLaren, Natelle Quek, Matt Ralphs, Rose Robbins, Fabi Santiago, Suzy Senior, Ciara Smyth, Clare Helen Welsh, Pete Williamson. *Founded* 2018.

## WME*

(William Morris Endeavour, UK)
100 New Oxford Street, London WC1A 1HB
*tel* 020-7534 6800
*email* ldnsubmissions@wmeagency.com
*website* www.wmeagency.com
*Books* Matilda Forbes Watson, Fiona Baird, Suzannah Ball, *Foreign Rights* James Munro, Florence Dodd, *TV* Antonia Melville, Tom Micelli

Worldwide talent and literary agency with offices in London, New York, Beverly Hills, Nashville and Sydney. Literary and commercial fiction, crime, thrillers, YA fiction, middle-grade fiction, memoir, self-help, lifestyle, sci-fi, fantasy, women's fiction, serious non-fiction and popular culture. *Commission* UK 15%, USA/translation 20%, film/TV 10%. Please submit via email to the address above with the first three chapters, a synopsis and a covering email.
   *Clients* include Mohsin Hamid, Alice Munro, Kiley Reid, Akala, Amor Towles, Greer Hendricks, Sarah

Pekkanen, Lori Gottlieb, Jhumpa Lahiri, Glennon Doyle, Soma Sara, Laura Dave, Dave Grohl, Ellie Goulding, Brené Brown. *Founded* 1898.

## Susan Yearwood Agency*

2 Knebworth House, Londesborough Road, London N16 8RL
*tel* 020-7503 0954
*email* submissions@susanyearwoodagency.com
*website* https://susanyearwoodagency.com
*Twitter* @sya_susan
*Contact* Susan Yearwood

Children's fiction 9+ and YA. *Commission* Home 15%, overseas 20%. Send submission with covering letter and brief synopsis via email. Submissions not accepted by hand or post. Tends not to read sci-fi and fantasy in adult fiction, short stories or poetry.
   *Authors* include Suzanne Snow, Fil Reid, Sarupa Shah. *Founded* 2007.

## YMU Books*

180 Great Portland Street, London W1W 5QZ
*tel* 020-8742 4950
*email* YMUBooksSubmissions@ymugroup.com
*website* www.ymugroup.com
*Twitter* @YMULiterary
*Instagram* @YMULiterary
*Managing Director* Amanda Harris

A bespoke literary division within talent management agency YMU Group. Represents authors who are elite in their field across fiction, non-fiction and children's. *Commission* Home 15%, USA 20%.
   *Clients* include Ant & Dec, Francis Bourgeois, Fearne Cotton, Tom Daley, Jane Dunn, Paloma Faith, Noel Fitzpatrick, Jake Humphrey, Matt Lucas, Ant Middleton, Stacey Solomon. *Founded* 2021.

## Zeno Agency Ltd*

Primrose Hill Business Centre,
110 Gloucester Avenue, London NW1 8HX
*tel* 020-7096 0927
*email* info@zenoagency.com
*website* www.zenoagency.com
*Twitter* @zenoagency
*Director* John Berlyne, *Agent* Stevie Finegan

Most adult fiction genres represented (commercial, crime/thriller, romance etc.) with a specialism in sci-fi, fantasy and horror. Children's fiction from picture books through YA. Non-fiction from specialists in their fields and authors with strong personal stories to tell (narrative, memoir, biography etc). Some illustrated non-fiction considered. *Commission* Home 15%, overseas 15% (via sub-agents 20%). Does not consider poetry, plays or film scripts.
   *Authors* include Ben Aaronovitch, Aliette De Bodard, Travis Baldree, Jonathan Carroll, Charlaine Harris, Grady Hendrix, William Gibson, Brandon Sanderson, Lavie Tidhar, the estate of Roger Zelazny. *Founded* 2008.

# Children's literary agents overseas

This list includes only a selection of agents across the English-speaking world. Before submitting material, writers are advised to visit agents' websites for detailed submission guidelines and to ascertain terms.

## AUSTRALIA AND NEW ZEALAND

### Alex Adsett Literary
PO Box 694, Tugun, QLD 4224
*email* agent@alexadsett.com.au
*website* https://alexadsett.com.au
*Literary agents* Alex Adsett, Rochelle Fernandez

Full service literary agency, representing quality works of fiction and non-fiction for children, teens and adults. Fiction: literary and commercial fiction, crime, mystery, romance, sci-fi and fantasy. Children's: chapter book, middle-grade and YA fiction (chapter or genre). Non-fiction: narrative non-fiction with a hook. Submission by invitation only; no unsolicited submissions. *Founded* 2008.

### ALM: Australian Literary Management
Suite 1, 2A Booth Street, Balmain, NSW 2041
*tel* +61 (0)2 9818 8557
*email* alphaalm8@gmail.com
*website* http://austlit.com
*Proprietor* Lyn Tranter

For full details of genres represented, see website. Unsolicited submissions welcome. Submissions should include a one- to two-page synopsis and covering letter. Writing sample on request. Does not consider TV or film scripts of any kind, poetry, self-help, sci-fi and fantasy or books for children by unpublished authors. Does not accept self-published work or previously published works, including ebooks, or writing by non-Australian authors. *Founded* 1980.

### Annabel Barker Agency
*email* hello@annabelbarker.com
*website* https://annabelbarker.com
*Instagram* @annabelbarkeragency
*Contact* Annabel Barker

Specialises in books for children and young adults. The agency has a focus on international rights and looks for work that showcases the depth of the Australian experience by writers and illustrators. Submissions are open in December only. Outside this period, submission is by invitation or referral only. *Founded* 2020.

### Curtis Brown (Australia) Pty Ltd
*email* submission@curtisbrown.com.au
*website* www.curtisbrown.com.au
*Twitter* @curtisbrownaus

Australia's oldest and largest literary agency representing a diverse range of Australian and New Zealander authors. Submissions open periodically throughout the year; check the website for current details and upcoming submission periods. Send cover email, synopsis and first three chapters. *Founded* 1967.

### Delaney Worner International
*email* info@delaneyworner.com
*website* www.delaneyworner.com
*Contacts* Joseph Delaney, Linda Worner, Joanne Delaney

Specialises in children's, teen and YA books but will consider all types of fiction. While the agency does not seek non-fiction or poetry submissions, it welcomes picture books which use rhyme as the text narrative. Submit the first three chapters and a synopsis by email. *Founded* 2016.

### Drummond Agency
PO Box 572, Woodend, VIC 3442
*tel* +61 (0)3 5427 3644
*email* info@drummondagency.com.au
*website* www.drummondagency.com.au/index.htm

Considers both fiction and non-fiction for adults and YA fiction, but no fantasy or sci-fi. Query by telephone, email or letter. Do not send attachments unless requested. Represents Australian and New Zealand citizens based in Australia. Does not represent educational materials, poetry, plays, film scripts or children's picture books.
 *Authors* include Randa Abdel-Fattah, Vikki Wakefield, Claire Zorn, Deborah Burrows, Margareta Osborn, Yvette Walker. *Founded* 1997.

### Sarah McKenzie Literary Management
*tel* +61 (0)4 1603 5061
*email* submissions@smlm.com.au
*website* www.smlm.com.au
*Contact* Sarah McKenzie

Provides advice, advocacy and representation for Australian and New Zealander authors, helping them to shape and polish their writing projects. Actively seeks established and emerging authors of commercial and literary fiction, non-fiction and children's fiction (including picture books, middle grade, YA and graphic novels). Submissions via email only. For fiction and memoir, include a covering letter, one- to two-page synopsis and 20 consecutive pages of the MS. For non-fiction, include a covering letter, one-page summary, author bio, one or two sample chapters and a table of contents. Does not represent works that have been previously self-published in any form, speculative fiction, novellas or poetry collections.

## CANADA

### CookeMcDermid

320 Front Street W #1105, Toronto, ON M5V 3B6
*tel* +1 647-788-4010
*email* admin@cookemcdermid.com
*website* https://cookemcdermid.com
*Agents* Dean Cooke, Martha Webb, Suzanne Brandreth, Ron Eckel, Rachel Letofsky, Paige Sisley, Cody Caetano, Hana El Niwairi, Sally Harding

Represents authors of literary, commercial, sci-fi and fantasy fiction; a broad range of narrative non-fiction; health and wellness resources; and middle-grade and YA books. Sells Canadian and American rights directly. The in-house rights team sells UK and translation rights, in conjunction with a network of co-agents around the world. CMD also sells film and TV rights directly, in addition to working with associates in New York and LA. Submission via online form.

*Clients* include John Irving, Geddy Lee, Cherie Dimaline, Omar el Akkad, Maye Musk, Jody Wilson-Raybould, Billy-Ray Belcourt, Michael Crummey, Claudia Dey, Elamin Abdelmahmoud, Robyn Doolittle, Scaachi Koul, Jen Agg, Robert Munsch, Ivan Coyote. *Founded* 2017.

### P.S. Literary Agency

2nd Floor, 2010 Winston Park Drive, Oakville, ON L6H 5R7
*email* info@psliterary.com
*website* www.psliterary.com
*Twitter* @PSLiterary
*President & Principal Agent* Curtis Russell, *Senior Literary Agents* Carly Watters (Senior Advisor), Maria Vicente (Advisor), Adria Goetz, *Literary Agents* Eric Smith, Claire Harris, *Associate Agents* Stephanie Winter, Cecilia Lyra

Represents both fiction and non-fiction works to publishers in North America, Europe and throughout the world. Categories include commercial, upmarket, literary, women's fiction, mystery, thriller, romance, sci-fi, fantasy, historical, LGBTQI+, YA, middle grade, picture books, graphic novels, memoir, history, politics, current affairs, business, wellness, cookery books, sports, humour, popular science, popular psychology, popular culture, design and lifestyle. Send queries to query@psliterary.com. Do not send email attachments unless specifically requested. Does not accept submissions via mail or telephone. *Founded* 2005.

### Transatlantic Agency

2 Bloor Street East, Suite 3500, Toronto, ON M4W 1A8
*tel* +1 416-488-9214
*website* www.transatlanticagency.com
*Facebook* www.facebook.com/TransLitAgency
*Twitter* @TransLitAgency

Represents more than 700 American, Canadian and internationally bestselling and award-winning clients, with a team of 20 experienced agents based in cities across North America. Offers a full spectrum of career representation to authors (adult, children's and YA, and illustrators) and storytellers (speakers, industry leaders and influencers) across all genres and formats for book, content development, speaking and TV & film. *Founded* 1993.

### Westwood Creative Artists

386 Huron Street, Toronto, ON M5S 2G6
*email* wca_office@wcaltd.com
*website* https://wcaltd.com
*Twitter* @WCA_LitAgency
*Instagram* @westwoodcreativeartists
*President* Jackie Kaiser, *Agents* Chris Casuccio, Emmy Nordstrom Higdon, Sara Harowitz, John Pearce, Meg Wheeler

Represents Canadian authors. Interested in high-quality writing and illustration for children, literary and commercial YA fiction and select graphic novels and illustrated works for all age catergories. Email submissions to submissions@wcaltd.com. Send a covering letter and 10–20 pages of MS in body of email. See website for full submission guidelines. Does not represent screenwriters, playwrights or poets.

## USA

*Member of the Association of American Literary Agents*

### Adams Literary*

7845 Colony Road, C4 Suite 215, Charlotte, NC 28226
*tel* +1 704-542-1440
*email* info@adamsliterary.com
*website* www.adamsliterary.com
*Twitter* @adamsliterary
*Instagram* @adamsliterary
*Agents* Tracey Adams, Josh Adams

Selectively children's from picture books to YA novels. Submissions currently closed; check website for updates.

*Authors* include John David Anderson, Anne Blankman, Margery Cuyler, Hafsah Faizal, Margaret Peterson Haddix, Amie Kaufman, Jay Kristoff, Cynthia Lord, Vaunda Micheaux Nelson, C.S. Pacat, Wendy Shang, Tom Taylor. *Founded* 2004.

## David Black Agency*

335 Adams Street, Suite 2707, Brooklyn, NY 11201
*tel* +1 718-852-5500
*email* dblack@dblackagency.com
*website* www.davidblackagency.com
*Facebook* www.facebook.com/davidblackagency
*Twitter* @dblackagency
*Contacts* David Black, Rica Allannic, Jennifer Herrera, Gary Morris, Susan Raihofer, Sarah Smith, Joy Tutela, Anna Zinchuk, Ellen Scott

Represents an extensive list of both prescriptive and narrative non-fiction including business, memoir, history, politics, fitness and sport. Also represents both commercial and literary fiction, middle grade and YA. Queries to be addressed to specific agent and by email, unless otherwise specified. For most up-to-date submission guidelines and agent preferences see website.
 *Clients* include Mitch Albom, Chris Kimball, Billie Jean King, Dann McDorman, Robert Simonson, Jonathan Eig, Julia Cameron, Ian O'Connor, Deborah Lipstadt, Danny Seo, Emily Timberlake, Lindy West, Rodney Scott, Jessie Damuck, Devon Price. *Founded* 1989.

## The Booker Albert Literary Agency

PO Box 20931, York, PA 17402
*email* bookeralbertinfo@gmail.com
*website* www.thebookeralbertagency.com
*Twitter* @BookerAlbertLit
*Agents* Brittany Carter, Jordy Albert, *Junior agents* Abigail Varnado, Helen Lane

Full service agency representing adult, YA and middle-grade fiction. Submission via QueryManager only. See agents' individual profiles on website for specific guidelines and areas of interest. No picture books, non-fiction or screenplays at this time.

## Bradford Literary Agency*

5694 Mission Center Road, Suite 347, San Diego, CA 92108
*email* queries@bradfordlit.com
*website* www.bradfordlit.com

Currently looking for picture books, chapter books, middle grade and YA in both fiction and non-fiction categories. Queries accepted only via QueryManager. See website for detailed submission guidelines and for links to each agent's QueryManager form. Not currently looking for poetry, screenplays, short stories, Westerns, inspirational/spiritual, horror, New Age, religion, crafts or gift books.

## Andrea Brown Literary Agency*

*website* www.andreabrownlit.com
*Facebook* www.facebook.com/AndreaBrownAgency
*Twitter* @andreabrownlit
*President* Andrea Brown, *Agents* Laura Rennert, Caryn Wiseman, Jennifer Laughran, Jennifer Rofé, Kelly Sonnack, Jamie Weiss Chilton, Jennifer

Mattson, Kathleen Rushall, Lara Perkins, Saritza Hernádez, Jennifer March Soloway, Jemiscoe Chambers-Black, Paige Terlip

Exclusively all kinds of children's books. Represents both authors and illustrators. Email and form submissions only. See website for guidelines. *Founded* 1981.

## Maria Carvainis Agency Inc.*

Rockefeller Center, 1270 Avenue of the Americas, Suite 2915, New York, NY 10020
*tel* +1 212-245-6365
*email* mca@mariacarvainisagency.com
*website* www.mariacarvainisagency.com
*President & Literary Agent* Maria Carvainis

YA fiction. Also handles adult fiction and non-fiction. *Commission* Home 15%, overseas 20%. Email and postal submissions are accepted. Send a query letter, a synopsis of the work, first 5–10 pages and a note of any writing credentials. See website for full submission guidelines. Does not represent screenplays, children's picture books, sci-fi, or poetry. *Founded* 1977.

## The Chudney Agency

72 North State Road, Suite 501, Briarcliff Manor, NY 10510
*tel* +1 201-758-8739
*email* steven@thechudneyagency.com
*website* https://thechudneyagency.com
*Contact* Steven Chudney

Represents authors of children's books and adult fiction. Submissions via email. Does not accept sci-fi, non-fiction, plays, screenplays or film scripts. *Founded* 2002.

## Corvisiero Literary Agency

1180 Avenue of the Americas, 8th Floor, New York, NY 10036
*email* info@corvisieroagency.com
*website* www.corvisieroagency.com
*Twitter* @CorvisieroLit
*Instagram* @corvisierolit
*Contacts* Marisa A. Corvisiero, Tessa Shaffer, Maggie Sadler, Kendyll Drilling

Offers international literary representation, management, and coaching services to fiction and non-fiction for all ages, in a wide spectrum of genres including screenplays. Only submit to one agent at a time via QueryManager. For fiction, send a query letter, one- to two-page synopsis and first five pages. For non-fiction, include a full proposal and sample chapter. For screenplays, include your logline, genre, and upload the first 20 pages of your script. Not currently representing collections of short stories, novellas, essays, or poetry. *Founded* 2012.

## Curtis Brown, Ltd*

228 East 45th Street, Suite 310, New York, NY 10017
*tel* +1 212-473-5400

**Literary agents**

*email* info@cbltd.com
*website* www.curtisbrown.com
*Twitter* @CurtisBrownLtd
*Instagram* @curtisbrown.ltd
*Ceo* Timothy Knowlton, *President* Peter Ginsberg, *Vice President* Elizabeth Harding, *Executive Vice President* Ginger Knowlton, *Contacts* Kerry D'Agostino, Jonathan Lyons, Jazmia Young, *Film & TV Rights* Holly Frederick, *Film & TV Rights Associate* Alexandra Franklin, *Translation Rights* Sarah Perillo

Fiction and non-fiction, juvenile, film and TV rights. No unsolicited MSS. See individual agents' entries on the Agents page of the website for specific query and submission information. *Founded* 1914.

## Liza Dawson Associates*
121 West 27th Street, Suite 1201, New York, NY 10001
*email* lwu@lizadawson.com
*website* www.lizadawsonassociates.com
*Twitter* @LizaDawsonAssoc
*Ceo* Liza Dawson

A full-service agency which draws on expertise as former publishers. YA and middle grade: thrillers, mysteries, romance, historical fiction, sci-fi and fantasy, contemporary. See website for full details of genres represented by individual agents, submission guidelines and email contacts.
   *Clients* include Annie Barrows, Bob Brier, Pierce Brown, Zen Cho, Britt Frank, Ross Gay, R.F. Kuang, Victoria Law, Julia Lee, Victoria Christopher Murray, David Santos Donaldson, Charles Stross and the estate of Eleanor Roosevelt. *Founded* 1996.

## Sandra Dijkstra & Associates*
PMB 515, 1155 Camino Del Mar, Del Mar, CA 92014
*tel* +1 858-755-3115
*website* www.dijkstraagency.com
*Contacts* Sandra Dijkstra, Elise Capron, Jill Marr, Thao Le, Andrea Cavallaro, Jessica Watterson, Jennifer Kim, Ariel Renner

YA sci-fi, fantasy and contemporary; middle-grade fiction and non-fiction; picture books by author/illustrators only. *Commission* Home 15%, overseas 20%. Works in conjunction with foreign and film agents. Email submissions only. Please see website for the most up-to-date guidelines.
   *Clients* include Amy Tan, Maxine Hong Kingston, Lisa See, Chitra Divakaruni, Jasmin Darznik, Eric Foner, Ian Morris, Walter Johnson, Erika Lee, Mae Ngai, Lillian Faderman, Roshani Chokshi, Elena Armas, Jessie Sima, Ali Hazelwood. *Founded* 1981.

## Dunham Literary Inc.*
*email* query@dunhamlit.com
*website* www.dunhamlit.com
*Contact* Jennie Dunham, Anjanette Barr

Children's books: handles picture books, fiction for 5–8 and 9–12 years and teenage fiction. Also handles adult literary fiction and non-fiction; 50% of list is for the children's market. *Commission* Home 15%, overseas 20%. Send query by email including a synopsis and first five pages in the body of the email. *Founded* 2000.

## Dystel, Goderich & Bourret LLC*
1 Union Square West, New York, NY 10003
*tel* +1 212-627-9100
*website* www.dystel.com
*Facebook* www.facebook.com/DGandB
*Twitter* @DGandBTweets
*Contacts* Michael Bourret, Jim McCarthy, Stacey Glick, John Rudolph, Lauren Abramo, Michaela Whatnall

Children's fiction: handles picture books, fiction for 5–8 and 9–12 years, teenage fiction and series fiction. Looking for quality YA fiction. Also handles adult fiction and non-fiction. *Commission* Home 15%, overseas 19%, film/TV/radio 15%. See website for submission guidelines. *Founded* 1994.

## The Ethan Ellenberg Literary Agency*
155 Suffolk Street, Suite 2R, New York, NY 10002
*tel* +1 212-431-4554
*email* agent@ethanellenberg.com
*website* www.ethanellenberg.com
*President & Agent* Ethan Ellenberg, *Senior Agent* Evan Gregory, *Agent* Bibi Lewis

Interested in all types of children's fiction: New Adult, YA, middle grade, chapter books and picture books. Will consider all genres: literary, mystery, romance, fantasy and sci-fi, humorous. Will consider other illustrated works. *Commission* Home 15%, overseas 20%. Accepts unsolicited MSS by email and seriously considers all submissions, including first-time writers. For fiction, submit synopsis and first three chapters. For shorter children's works, send complete MS. Illustrators should send four to five sample illustrations. Unable to return any material from overseas. No scholarly works, poetry, short stories or screenplays. *Founded* 1984.

## Fairbank Literary Representation*
21 Lyman Street, Waltham, MA 02452
*tel* +1 617-576-0030
*email* queries@fairbankliterary.com
*website* http://fairbankliterary.com
*Twitter* @FairbankLit
*Contacts* Sorche Elizabeth Fairbank

Represents more literary fiction than commercial. Seeking children's works (picture books and middle grade) by illustrator authors, as well as diverse illustrators of any type. Query by email preferred but accepted by mail as well. For full submission guidelines see website. *Founded* 2002.

## Flannery Literary
*email* jennifer@flanneryliterary.com
*website* https://flanneryliterary.com
*Contact* Jennifer Flannery

Specialises in children's and YA, juvenile fiction and non-fiction. *Commission* Home 15%, overseas 20%. Email submission only. Include 5–10 pages of MS in the body of the email. *Founded* 1992.

## Folio Literary Management*

The Film Center Building, 630 9th Avenue, Suite 1101, New York, NY 10036
*tel* +1 212-400-1494
*website* www.foliolit.com
*Twitter* @FolioLiterary
*Instagram* @folioliterary

Represents both first-time and established authors. Seeks upmarket adult fiction, literary fiction, commercial fiction that features fresh voices and/or memorable characters, and narrative non-fiction. Folio Jr is devoted exclusively to representing children's book authors and artists. Consult agents' submission guidelines on the website before making contact.

## Barry Goldblatt Literary LLC*

594 Dean Street, Brooklyn, NY 11238
*tel* +1 718-832-8787
*website* http://bgliterary.com
*Contact* Barry Goldblatt

Represents YA and middle-grade fiction, as well as adult sci-fi and fantasy. Has a preference for quirky, offbeat work. Submission via QueryManager only. No non-fiction. *Founded* 2000.

## Irene Goodman Literary Agency*

27 West 24th Street, Suite 804, New York, NY 10010
*email* agentfirstname.queries@irenegoodman.com
*website* www.irenegoodman.com
*Facebook* www.facebook.com/IreneGoodmanAgency
*Twitter* @IGLAbooks
*Instagram* @iglabooks
*Agents* Irene Goodman, Miriam Kriss, Barbara Poelle, Kim Perel, Victoria Marini, Whitney Ross, Pam Gruber, Natalie Lakosil, Lee O'Brien, Margaret Danko

Represents middle-grade and YA books, including fantasy. Also represents commercial fiction with an emphasis on women's voices, romantic novels, historical fiction, mystery, crime and suspense novels. Non-fiction areas of interest include narrative non-fiction of cultural, social or historical relevance, popular culture, biography, memoir, science and psychology. Works in collaboration with the foreign rights agency Baror International who deal with foreign publishers directly. Query by email and addressed to one agent only; send query letter and first ten pages of a manuscript for fiction, and a query letter for non-fiction. Does not represent picture poetry or screenplays. *Founded* 1989.

## The Greenhouse Literary Agency*

*website* www.greenhouseliterary.com
*Director* Chelsea Eberly, *Agent* Kristin Ostby

Children's fiction from picture book authors/ illustrators through to teen/YA. Occasional non-fiction projects and women's fiction will also be considered. Submissions via QueryManager only; see website for submission guidelines. No poetry, short stories or film scripts.

*Authors* include Gavin Aung Than, Sarwat Chadda, Winifred Conkling, Andrea Contos, Alexandra Diaz, Bill Doyle, Gabriela Epstein, Theanne Griffith, Michelle Lam, Rebecca Mock, Kelis Rowe, Ali Standish, Emily Thiede, Ngozi Ukazu. *Founded* 2008.

## The Joy Harris Literary Agency Inc.*

1501 Broadway, Suite 2605, New York, NY 10036
*tel* +1 212-924-6269
*email* contact@joyharrisliterary.com
*website* www.joyharrisliterary.com
*Twitter* @JoyHarrisAgency
*Instagram* @joyharrisliterary
*Agents* Joy Harris, Adam Reed, Alice Fugate

Represents adult and children's literary fiction and non-fiction. Submissions should be emailed, comprising a query letter and an outline or sample letter. See website for detailed submission guidelines. No unsolicited manuscripts. Does not currently accept poetry, screenplays, genre fiction or self-help submissions. *Founded* 1990.

## John Hawkins & Associates Inc.*

80 Maiden Lane, Suite 1503, New York, NY 10038
*tel* +1 212-807-7040
*email* jha@jhalit.com
*website* www.jhalit.com
*President* Moses Cardona, *Agents* Warren Frazier, Anne Hawkins

Fiction and non-fiction; YA. *Founded* 1893.

## HG Literary*

6 West 18th Street, Suite 7R, New York NY 10011
*email* [firstname]@hgliterary.com
*website* www.hgliterary.com
*Twitter* @HGLiterary
*Instagram* @hgliterary
*Contacts* Carrie Hannigan, Josh Getzler, Soumeya Bendimerad Roberts, Victoria Wells Arms, Julia Kardon, Rhea Lyons, Brianne Johnson, Jon Cobb, Ellen Goff, Hannah Popal.

Represents children's picture books, middle-grade and YA fiction. Represents a variety of both commercial and literary fiction, including women's literature, crime and mystery novels, historical fiction and thrillers. Non-fiction areas of interest include memoir and narrative non-fiction relating to business, current affairs, popular psychology, science, food and select works of photography. Query by email and addressed to one agent only. For full submission guidelines and agent preferences see website. *Founded* 2011.

## Janklow & Nesbit Associates

285 Madison, 21st Floor, New York, NY 10017
*tel* +1 212-421-1700
*email* info@janklow.com
*email* submissions@janklow.com
*website* www.janklowandnesbit.com
*Twitter* @JanklowNesbit
*President* Luke Nesbit

Commercial and literary fiction and non-fiction. Works in conjunction with Janklow & Nesbit (UK) Ltd. Submissions: send an informative cover letter, synopsis/outline and the first ten pages. For picture book submissions, include a dummy and at least one full-colour sample. For graphic novels, send ten illustrated pages with text and a synopsis. Address submissions to an individual agent, including your email address or a return envelope with sufficient postage for material to be returned. *Founded* 1989.

## kt literary*

9249 S. Broadway 200–543, Highlands Ranch, CO 80129
*tel* +1 720-344-4728
*email* queries@ktliterary.com
*website* https://ktliterary.com
*Twitter* @ktliterary
*Instagram* @ktliterary
*Agents* Kate Testerman, Sara Megibow, Renee Nyen, Hilary Harwell, Kelly Van Sant, Jas Perry, Kari Sutherland, Savannah Brooks, Tara Gilbert, Laurel Symonds, *Associate agent* Chelsea Hensley

Primarily middle-grade and YA fiction and graphic novels. Some picture books and select narrative non-fiction for children. Queries are accepted via QueryManager. No postal submissions.

*Clients* include Maureen Johnson, Stephanie Perkins, Matthew Cody, Ellen Booraem, Trish Doller, Amy Spalding, Jaleigh Johnson, Casey McQuiston, Rebecca Roanhorse, Stefan Bachmann. *Founded* 2008.

## Levine Greenberg Rostan Literary Agency*

307 Seventh Avenue, Suite 2407, New York, NY 10001
*tel* +1 212-337-0934
*email* submit@lgrliterary.com
*website* www.lgrliterary.com
*Twitter* @LGRLiterary
*Instagram* @lgrlit
*Principals* Jim Levine, Daniel Greenberg, Stephanie Rostan, *Agents* Sarah Bedingfield, Lindsay Edgecombe, Victoria Skurnick, Kerry Sparks, Danielle Svetcov, Monika Verma, Tim Wojcik, Courtney Paganelli

Represents literary and commercial fiction, non-fiction and books for young readers across a diverse range of genres. Submissions via online form.

## Gina Maccoby Literary Agency*

PO Box 60, Chappaqua, NY 10514
*tel* +1 914-238-5630
*email* query@maccobylit.com
*website* www.publishersmarketplace.com/members/GinaMaccoby/
*Contact* Gina Maccoby

Looking for high-quality upmarket fiction and non-fiction for adults and children. An engaging narrative voice and strong premise are most important; across all forms the agency is looking for compelling stories and fresh perspectives. Children's: YA and middle grade. Picture books of writer/illustrators only. Non-fiction areas of interest include history, biography, popular science, and narrative journalism. No unsolicited submissions. Query first via email. Due to the volume of submissions received, will only reply if interested. *Founded* 1986.

## McIntosh & Otis Inc.*

207 East 37th Street, Suite BG, New York, NY 10016
*tel* +1 212-687-7400
*email* info@mcintoshandotis.com
*website* https://mcintoshandotis.com
*Twitter* @McIntoshAndOtis
*Head of Children's Department* Christa Heschke

Board books, picture books (fiction and non-fiction), fiction for 5–8 and 9–12 years, teenage fiction, series fiction, poetry and non-fiction for children. For children and YA submissions, query letter, synopsis, and the first three chapters and any relevant illustrations. Does not represent poetry, screenplays, and original theatrical or dramatic works of any kind. *Founded 1928.*

## Erin Murphy Literary Agency

824 Roosevelt Trail, Suite #290, Windham, ME 04062
*website* https://emliterary.com
*President* Erin Murphy, *Senior Agents* Ammi-Joan Paquette, Tricia Lawrence, *Agents* Tara Gonzalez, Kevin Lewis, Miranda Paul

Children's books: fiction, non-fiction, picture books, middle grade and YA. *Commission* Home 15%, overseas 20–30%. No unsolicited queries or submissions; considers material only by referral or through personal contact such as at conferences or online pitch event requests. Some agents have submissions forms on QueryTracker. *Founded* 1999.

## Jean V. Naggar Literary Agency Inc.*

216 East 75th Street, Suite 1E, New York, NY 10021
*tel* +1 212-794-1082
*email* jvnla@jvnla.com
*website* www.jvnla.com
*Twitter* @JVNLA
*Instagram* @jvnlainc
*President & Agent* Jennifer Weltz, *Agents* Alice Tasman, Ariana Philips, Alicia Brooks

Mainstream commercial and literary fiction, non-fiction (narrative, memoir, journalism, psychology, history, pop culture, humour and cookery books), young readers (picture, middle grade, YA). Works in conjunction with foreign agents. Submit queries via form on website. *Founded* 1978.

## Olswanger Literary LLC*

*email* anna@olswangerliterary.com
*website* www.olswanger.com
*Contact* Anna Olswanger

Specialises in representing author-illustrators of picture books and graphic novels. Clients have won the Newbery Medal, Asian/Pacific American Award for Literature, Flora Stieglitz Strauss Award for Non-fiction, Orbis Pictus Award, PEN/Steven Kroll Award for Picture Book Writing, Parents' Choice Gold Award, Bank Street College of Education Best Children's Books, Sibert Award, Ezra Jack Keats Award, Sydney Taylor Award silver medal, Boston Globe-Horn Book Nonfiction Honor, International BolognaRagazzi Non-fiction Award, CCBC Choices and have been Junior Library Guild Selections and on the *New York Times* Bestseller list.

## Alison Picard, Literary Agent

PO Box 2000, Cotuit, MA 02635
*tel* +1 508-477-7192
*email* ajpicard@aol.com

Adult fiction and non-fiction, children's and YA. *Commission* Home 15%. Please send query via email (no attachments). No short stories, poetry, plays, screenplays or sci-fi and fantasy.
  *Clients* include David Housewright, Caryl Rivers, Jessica Fisher, David Alan Johnson, Susan Froetschel. *Founded* 1985.

## Pippin Properties Inc.

110 West 40th Street, Suite 1704, New York, NY 10018
*tel* +1 212-338-9310
*email* info@pippinproperties.com
*website* www.pippinproperties.com
*Facebook* www.facebook.com/pippinproperties
*Twitter* @LovethePippins
*Instagram* @pippinproperties
*Contacts* Holly McGhee, Elena Giovinazzo, Sara Crowe

Focuses on children's book authors and artists, including picture books, middle grade, graphic novels and YA novels, and adult trade books on occasion. *Commission* Home 15%, overseas 25%. Query specific agent by email. For authors, include the first chapter and short synopsis, or entire picture book. For illustrators, send a query letter detailing your background in illustration and links to website with a dummy or other examples of your work. *Founded* 1998.

## Rees Literary Agency*

One Westinghouse Plaza, Suite A203, Boston, MA 02136-2075
*tel* +1 617-227-9014
*email* [firstname]@reesagency.com
*website* www.reesagency.com
*Agents* Ann Collette, Lorin Rees, Rebecca Podos, Kelly Peterson, Taj McCoy

Represents literary and commercial fiction, memoirs, history, biography, business, YA and middle grade, self-help, psychology and science. *Commission* Home 15%. See the website for individual agents' submission guidelines. *Founded* 1983.

## Rodeen Literary Management

*email* submissions@rodeenliterary.com
*website* www.rodeenliterary.com
*Facebook* www.facebook.com/RodeenLiterary
*Twitter* @RodeenLiterary
*Instagram* @rodeenliterary
*Contact* Paul Rodeen

Open to submissions from writers and illustrators of all genres of children's literature including picture books, early readers, middle-grade fiction and non-fiction, graphic novels, YA fiction and non-fiction. Submit the first 50 pages of a novel (authors), a portfolio (illustrators) or a picture book dummy via email. *Founded* 2008.

## Susan Schulman Literary Agency LLC*

454 West 44th Street, New York, NY 10036
*tel* +1 212-713-1633
*email* susan@schulmanagency.com
*Twitter* @SSchulman

Agents for negotiation in all markets (with co-agents) of fiction and general non-fiction; for picture books, middle-grade and YA markets; and associated subsidiary rights including plays, TV adaptation and film. *Commission* Home 15%, UK 7.5%, overseas 20%. Return postage required. Email enquiries to queries@schulmanagency.com.

## Scovil Galen Ghosh Literary Agency, Inc.*

276 Fifth Avenue, Suite 708, New York, NY 10001
*tel* +1 212-679-8686
*email* info@sgglit.com
*website* www.sgglit.com
*Contacts* Russell Galen, Jack Scovil, Anna Ghosh, Ann Behar

Represents a wide range of commercial and literary fiction, with an emphasis on novels with strong characters and distinct, new voices. Non-fiction tastes generally lean towards the literary scale and favour works that have something new to teach their reader. Areas of interest include biography and memoir, business and politics, contemporary culture, journalism, nature, history, science and sport. Picture books, children's, middle-grade and YA fiction also of interest. Foreign rights handled by co-agency Baror International, Inc. Query by post or email to one agent. *Founded* 1992.

## Stimola Literary Studio, Inc.*

*tel* +1 508-696-9353
*website* www.stimolaliterarystudio.com
*President & Founder* Rosemary B. Stimola, *Vice President* Peter K Ryan, *Senior Agent* Erica Rand Silverman, *Agents* Adriana Stimola, Allison Hellegers, Allison Remcheck

Children's fiction and non-fiction, from preschool to YA; adult fiction, non-fiction, cookery books and lifestyle. *Commission* Home 15%, overseas 20%. Most clients come via referral. *Founded* 1997.

## 3 Seas Literary Agency*

PO Box 444, Sun Prairie, WI 53590
*tel* +1 608-332-3430
*website* www.threeseasagency.com
*Twitter* @threeseaslit
*Agents* Michelle Grajkowski, Cori Deyoe, Stacey Graham, Stephanie Stevens, Kara Grajkowski

A full-service literary agency representing authors who write romance, women's fiction, sci-fi and fantasy, thrillers, YA and middle-grade fiction, as well as select non-fiction titles and picture books. Accepts submissions through QueryManager only. Genre-specific submission guidelines can be found on the website. Will only reply if interested in your work. *Founded* 2000.

## Trident Media Group

355 Lexington Avenue, Floor 12, New York, NY 10017
*tel* +1 212-333-1511
*email* info@tridentmediagroup.com
*website* www.tridentmediagroup.com
*Facebook* www.facebook.com/TridentMediaGroup
*Twitter* @Trident_Media
*Instagram* @trident_media

Adult and children's fiction and non-fiction across a variety of genres. *Commission* Home 15%, overseas 20%, in conjunction with co-agents/theatre/films/TV 15%. Will suggest revision. Query one agent via online form. Writing sample on request. *Founded* 2000.

## WME

11 Madison Avenue, 18th Floor, New York, NY 10010
*tel* +1 212-586-5100
*website* www.wmeentertainment.com

Worldwide talent and literary agency with offices in New York, Beverly Hills, Nashville, Sydney and London. Represents bestselling authors, critically acclaimed literary writers, award-winning thought leaders and up-and-coming talent. *Founded* 1898.

## Writers House LLC*

120 Broadway, 22nd floor, New York, NY 10271
*tel* +1 212-685-2400
*website* www.writershouse.com

Fiction and non-fiction for adults and children, including film and TV rights. Represents literary and commercial fiction, women's fiction, sci-fi and fantasy, narrative non-fiction, history, memoirs, biographies, psychology, science, parenting, cookbooks, how-to, self-help, business, finance, YA and juvenile fiction/non-fiction and picture books. Send a query letter and a synopsis of your work addressed to one agent; email preferred. Does not represent screenplays. *Founded* 1973.

# Illustration
## Notes from a successful children's author and illustrator

Lauren Child describes how *Clarice Bean, That's Me* came to be published and shares her experiences of taking advice from publishers and editors.

My first attempt at writing a children's book was when I was 18 – my friend Bridget and I had an idea. Everything seemed simple – we were going to write a book, get it published and get on with something else. Almost immediately, and by sheer fluke, we had an interested publisher. We were invited along for a 'working lunch' to discuss the story development. The editor made some suggestions for improvement which we were quite happy about – we really had no objection to rewriting; we were happier still with the business lunch and were fuelled by the confidence of youth that life would always be this easy. We did nothing, of course, and the whole thing fell through which, with hindsight, was a relief – I think we would both be squirming now. It was a number of years later before I even thought to write anything else.

### Please yourself

The next time I learnt the hard way, by trekking around uninterested publishers with my portfolio – something it would be almost impossible to do now, as no one wants to see unsolicited work. I used any contacts I had, however distant. I forced myself to phone complete strangers in order to get appointments and advice, which I hated doing. When I met with publishers they seemed to have very set views on what a children's book should be. I listened to their advice and always tried to write the book they wanted me to write. But, whenever I went back to them with my work, there was always something missing – I could never write the book they had in mind.

So, unable to interest publishers, no matter how hard I tried to give them what they said they wanted, I forgot about the whole project and got on with other things. One day, having reached a rather low point in my life, and having looked at every possible career path, a friend suggested that I leave my portfolio of designs, drawings and ideas with her so she could show it to her business manager who had created and managed various successful companies. When I met with this woman, I mentioned I had an interest in film and animation and also designing products for children. Although I had no relevant training, she suggested that I try to write a children's book because, hopefully, it would prove I could create characters and invent a world for them. I think that I was just at a point where I was ready to listen – perhaps because she was very successful, perhaps because it made sense, perhaps because she was a complete stranger.

I started to write the odd sentence, then draw a character, then write a bit more … there was no order to it, no plot structure. I wasn't even sure what I was writing, all I knew was that I was interested when I hadn't been before. I think it helped enormously that I wasn't fixated on creating the perfect children's book – it was merely a means to an end, a way to get into something else. I stopped being self-conscious about what I was doing and stopped trying to please everyone else. When I took this book – *Clarice Bean, That's Me* – to publishers, the difference was very obvious – they were all interested! However, no one was willing to take it on – they all thought it was unpublishable and told me so. But I had written something that had at least got their attention.

## Listening to publishers

Nearly every publisher made suggestions of what I should change in order for this book to be published, some of them quite fundamental. I was told to drop the illustrations and simplify the text. I was told that varying fonts and integrating text and pictures was too complicated, that it would confuse young readers. I listened to them all; I considered what they had to say, but I knew they were all wrong – I knew they were wrong because I knew I wouldn't be happy with the end result. Because I had written something which felt right to me, it seemed better not to be published at all than to publish a book that wasn't really mine. After four or so long years, I eventually found a publisher who was willing to take the book on pretty much as it was.

And I think this is one of the most important things to know – how far will you go, how far *should* you go to be published? When it comes to this you have to follow your gut instinct. Despite my experience, I do think it is important to listen to what publishers have to say – it is always wise to listen, but it is not always right to take it on board. In the end, they can give you the benefit of their experience, but they cannot write the book for you, and you cannot write the book for them. As the writer, the book has to come from you. Of course, if more than one or two people pick up on the same thing then it may be worth following that advice, but for me it is never worth making a change when, after much consideration, it still feels wrong.

## Know who you are writing for

When it comes to the question of writing for the 6–9 year-old market, I would say there is no formula. I don't write for 6–9 year-olds, I write for myself. My books are for anyone who wants to read them. For me, writing young fiction is less about writing for a particular audience or age group and more about telling a story that interests me. I have never thought 'Is this a book for 6–9 year-olds?' or 'Is this a book for 8–12 year-olds?'. I feel the same when writing picture books; they are there to be enjoyed by both adults *and* children because while the child looks at the pictures, it is the adult who usually reads the story.

How does a writer come up with the interesting ideas in the first place? As an adult writing a children's book, is it helpful – even necessary – to have children of your own? My own view is that it is simply irrelevant. First, we have all been children and anyone who wants to write for children must have strong feelings from his or her own childhood to draw upon. But more importantly, good fiction writing is not about imitation – it is about imagination. Just as having children does not mean you have anything to say to them in book form, so not having children is no bar to writing in a manner to which they will respond. Writing for anyone is about having something to say – a point of view. Writing for children is no different. When it comes to writing fiction, I think that any good writer will see children as people first, and as children second. Of course the context of childhood experiences is different from those of adults, but there is no emotion experienced as a child which is not felt equally in adult life.

At the more practical level, I do not believe that there are any fixed rules. I know that many writers plot a book out before they start, and I had always been told that I needed to plot my books and understand where they were going if I was to write successfully. But I never begin writing a book knowing how it is going to end. I never normally know how it is going to start either. I generally just begin with a sentence taken at random. For me, it is all about an idea taking hold, and the writing tends to be more about a feeling than anything. *Clarice Bean, Don't Look Now* began as a book about love and ended up being a book more about loss than anything else. I wrote a few sentences about Clarice's inability to sleep and from that the whole mood of the book was determined. I started to write about insomnia and then wondered why Clarice might experience this, which led to thinking about her worries, which in turn led to the idea that she might be feeling very insecure and start questioning things around her. So, in a way, a few sentences shaped the whole plot because they reflected something that I felt personally at the time. I didn't try to force a story that I wasn't interested in writing; instead it became a book about Clarice's anxieties, her inability to explain the world to herself and some recognition on her part that not only is life something which cannot be controlled, but it's also something which can only be imperfectly understood.

I write a lot of material and read it over and over, until I see what themes are emerging and then I look for a way to hang it all together. Once it has a solid plot, I start to cut. Writing picture books is a very good discipline for writing novels because with just 800 or so words to play with, you have to decide what is important and what isn't: what exactly is this book *about*? Writing picture books makes you much less frightened of editing out the bits that you love. You really can't be indulgent, and have to pare your writing down to the essence of what that story is about. Although, of course, a novel gives you much more freedom – *Don't Look Now* was 42,000 words – I still consciously try to make sure that every chapter is pushing the story forward and has something to say.

## A good editor

That brings me on to another important part – your editor. I really have to trust who I am working with. I rely so much on my editor because of the patchwork way I work. A good editor will let you debate back and forth until you've finally reached a point where you know that you can't make something any better. You do have to trust them because it is so easy to lose your perspective about your own work. You may think it's great and not listen to criticism, but more often than not you will get doubtful and think it's all rubbish, and that's where an editor can keep you believing in your work.

If there's a single piece of advice I could offer for writing fiction, it would be to write from the heart. When I wrote *Clarice Bean, That's Me*, I became passionate about what I was writing and found it exciting. If you're bored when you're writing, you will write a boring book. And no matter how hard you find the early stages, keep going. You just need to write and write until you've written the imitation stuff out of you. It is hard but it is very rewarding too. Writing is one of the best things in the world – a licence to discuss ideas – even if it's just with yourself.

**Lauren Child's** picture books have won many awards, including the Kate Greenaway Medal in 2000 for *I Will Not Ever Never Eat a Tomato* (Orchard Books 2000); the Smarties Gold Award in 2002 for *That Pesky Rat* (Orchard Books 2002); and the Smarties Bronze Award for *Clarice Bean, That's Me* (Orchard Books 1999); *Beware of the Storybook Wolves* (Hodder Children's Books 2000); and *What Planet Are You From, Clarice Bean?*

Illustration

(Orchard Books 2001). In 2002 she published *Utterly Me, Clarice Bean* (Orchard Books), the first of three Clarice Bean novels. Three animated TV series of *Charlie & Lola* have been shown on CBBC and on channels around the world, and the series has won four BAFTAs. From 2011–16 she wrote the *Ruby Redfort* novels (HarperCollin's Children's Books), a six book adventure series for young teens and illustrated new editions of Astrid Lindgren's *Pippi Longstocking* series as well as P.L. Travis' *Mary Poppins* (HarperCollin's Children's Books). Her latest books are *Clarice Bean Scram* (2022) and *Clarice Bean Smile* (2024), both published by HarperCollins. Lauren has written and/or illustrated over 50 books. She was Children's Laureate 2017–19 and a Trustee for the Quentin Blake Centre for Illustration 2012–22. She is a Fellow of the Foundling Museum and Patron of Hastings Book Festival. Her websites are www.milkmonitor.me and www.staringintospace.me.

# The craft of the illustrator

Salvatore Rubbino describes how he finds inspiration by looking at the world around him with curiosity and wonder, and explains the exciting creative and collaborative process by which sketches and ideas are woven together into finished picture books.

## Looking is a wonderful thing

As a picture book illustrator, I spend my day drawing and thinking about stories. I love words – the music they make and the taste they leave behind in my mouth – but above all I think in pictures. My task is to shape a tangible graphic world where story events and characters can thrive, a world that the reader can believe in. Pictures are a perfect story-telling tool and stories help to give a context to experience and our lives. We simply can't live without them!

Looking at the world around me is where my ideas come from. Drawing roots me to the spot and turns an initial glance into a long hard stare. It connects me to my surroundings and reminds me how interesting and varied life can be. Looking and drawing is a process of discovery; it helps me to notice the 'overlooked' and feeds my imagination.

We live a good deal of our lives in the humdrum (punctuated every now and then, perhaps, with something extraordinary) but I find the 'everyday' and the tiniest events inspiring and full of poetry. I carry a notebook with me wherever I go, ready to capture those special moments; I have little books for drawing on crowded trains should I see a compelling face, and larger paper that I might lay out on the pavement for more sustained work. I like to collect characters – we are all interesting and everyone comes with a story, and I have certain themes that I often return to. Musicians give the city a rhythm; they perform to be noticed and I have pages full of expressive players, particularly accordionists, so I hope one day to weave my musical drawings into a tale.

I've overheard some astonishing phone conversations whilst out walking – albeit only one half of the exchange (if you're an illustrator you're allowed to be nosey!). We continue to be expressive, pulling faces and gesturing vigorously, even when we can't see the other person on the line, and this gives me the chance to record some wonderfully animated behaviour. I can never pass a group of gossiping ladies without straining to hear what they're talking about and capture them in a picture. To be an illustrator, it's also necessary to cultivate a sense of wonder. This starts with a willingness to look with curiosity and to train the eye to find meaning in everything around you. I'm still learning.

## From observation to imagination

City life has always inspired me – almost any street corner will do, although the busier the better, a spot where I can watch little everyday dramas unfold. My first picture book was set in New York (*A Walk in New York*; Candlewick Press 2009) and describes a walk over the course of a day. It follows a real route that a family might attempt (importantly no more than 3km), with stops for lunch and cheesecake – and no doubt the loo, too. It was quite a rigorous process to join up landmarks and beautiful views to form a satisfying sequence. When I was thinking about the characters, I asked myself, 'Well, who do you know?'. In the end I decided to have a dad based on me (more dapper and taller, why not? – after all, anything is possible in a story) and the boy who was a version of my son. At the time my son was only six months old, but I imagined him as a boy aged about seven, in a striped T-shirt and occasionally dragging his tired feet, even though in real life he had not yet learned to walk. I showed both of us craning our necks to look up at the skyscrapers, just as I did on my visit to the Big Apple when collecting ingredients for the book.

As a Londoner, I was excited when asked to make my next walk and subsequent book, *A Walk in London* (Candlewick Press 2011), about 'my' city. When you've lived somewhere all your life it's easy to feel you know it, the challenge was to see the city with fresh eyes. So, I bought a very large sketchbook and set out to audition locations and landmarks for a role in the book. One of my favourite places is Trafalgar Square. There's something quite joyful about a spurting fountain, especially on a hot day when you can put your hand in the water to cool down. I can't think of many national landmarks that you're allowed to climb, but, as long as you're careful, no one actually tells you off if you decide to sit on one of the lions guarding Nelson's column at the heart of the Square.

I am a little embarrassed to admit that I had never seen the Changing of the Guard ceremony in front of Buckingham Palace until I chose to include it in my story. It's a spectacle of synchronised walking accompanied by an orchestra and a cheerful tune. It begins with military precision at 11:27am, and I made sure I had a place in front of the palace in good time, as I knew it would get crowded. And then it happened – an elegant lady wearing a wide-brimmed hat walked out of a side door, accompanied by her entourage; she got into her car and drove away – it was, of course, the Queen! I was astonished, but the encounter triggered an idea. I introduced a 'spot the royals' game, with the royal car weaving its way through the book; it's not mentioned explicitly, but the characters (a girl and her mother this time) receive a royal wave on the last page. I doubt if I would have thought of the idea without this experience of 'meeting the Queen'.

My early visual thinking for all pages in the London book was a flat plan. It records a conversation I had with my publisher when we made decisions about what to include, what to say about London and how to organize everything into a coherent whole. There are crossing outs and several blank pages, so it is still a work in progress. Your publisher or editor may have different opinions, and – whilst it's important to have an honest discussion – it's worth remembering that they want to find the best treatment for the story too. Trust your creative instinct, but also be prepared to listen.

## Marshalling your creativity

The text for a story arrives, via the publisher rather than directly from an author, in a compact form – usually a couple of sides of A4, accompanied by a few notes from the publisher ending with 'Please let me know if you're interested' (I'm always very interested!). By the time it reaches me the text has already undergone a rigorous process of rewriting, and has a well-crafted plot and clear point of view. Being invited to illustrate someone else's words is like collaborating with someone else's imagination – it's extremely exciting. I may sometimes meet the author and discuss the project, but our paths don't cross very often. Our relationship is via the publisher, who realises that I need to respond to the text in my own way.

I tend to start with a slow read-through of the story and then I reread it whilst busily scribbling first impressions all over the manuscript. These notes might be about mood, a sense of place, character or anything that's particularly vivid. I don't start work straight away. Instead I let the story sink in over the next few days. I will try to visit places or find aspects of the story that I can see and draw. I don't want to illustrate the text word for word (like a list) but instead I slide up to the story … sideways. I'm trying to find a way into the heart of the story. I'm looking for interesting things to describe, dramatic moments full of visual friction with the potential for mark-making or moments that might allow me to draw the things that I like and a chance to celebrate beauty.

My first drawing attempts for a book are usually quite unrefined. There is no process or formula an illustrator has to follow, or indeed that I follow, for each new project. In every case, I'm meeting the book's characters for the first time, getting to know them and the world they inhabit. I might simply respond to one line or phrase to begin with, until eventually I feel confident enough to start mapping a composition on the page. A book takes time.

I tend to approach a new book rather like a method actor learning a role. *A Book of Feelings* (Walker Books 2015) allowed me to be expressive and play with character in a way I had not tried before. I purchased a mirror so that I could practice a grimace or gesture, in order to draw myself and understand the way in which the child characters in the story might feel and behave and look – even doing a range of voices to help inhabit each emotional state I was depicting. The face has over 40 muscles, which makes it a fantastically elastic communication tool. I try to think about situations in my own life that relate to those described in a story, to provide me with creative inspiration.

## What else can illustrators do?

If you are a commissioning editor reading this, I'd like to remind you that illustrators are resourceful people and good problem-solvers. Support them and help to celebrate images together. If you're an author, it's worth adding that illustrators make keen collaborators and will relish the chance to draw your story. And if you're an illustrator, why not consider sharing your appetite for creating pictures? Illustration can be a solitary business, but talking about pictures, running workshops or teaching can be very rewarding, as well as another way to support yourself financially. I'm often invited to take part in festivals and events and I like to cultivate this (time permitting). I also teach, as a visiting tutor, and regularly deliver activities at schools and museums.

I always find watching other people draw or demonstrate a technique quite magical. From humble beginnings something takes shape until it becomes more substantial, to form a face, an animal or a landscape full of life. We all seek to express ourselves, and drawing and creating is a perfect vehicle. People are keen to know 'how it's done' and as an illustrator you can take them on a behind-the-scenes tour.

The picture books I make often have a family at the heart of the story, doing things together; there's friction sometimes, but a good deal of understanding too. Running family activities allows me to observe how children and adults collaborate and eventually find a solution by working together, feeling proud of their achievements by the end of the task. One child might be busy cutting whilst their dad holds the card; another sibling is gluing, untroubled about sticky fingers, and at the same time mum or a grandparent may be helping to colour in. Explaining to others what I do, and thinking about pictures with others, makes me deeply aware of my own creative practice; at the same time it exposes me to lots of refreshingly different points of view – and so, whilst sharing, you never stop learning.

**Salvatore Rubbino** graduated from the Royal College of Art in 2005. His first picture book, *A Walk in New York,* was published in 2009 by Candlewick Press, followed by *A Walk in London* in 2011. His other books, all published by Walker Books, include *Just Ducks!* (2012) written by Nicola Davies, *A Walk in Paris* (2014), *A Book of Feelings* (2015), *Our Very Own Dog* (2016) written by Amanda McCardie, *Harry Miller's Run* (2015) by David Almond and *Ride the Wind* written by Nicola Davies (Walker Books 2020). His latest book is *Grandma's Story* (2022) written by Moira Butterfield. He received a BookTrust Best New Illustrators Award in 2011.

## See also...

- *Finding your voice and point of view,* page 85
- *How to write a picture book,* page 128

# Being an illustrator *and* a writer

Writer and illustrator of children's books, Liz Pichon, tells how persistence and hard work – and following the urge to create the kind of books *you* would have enjoyed as a child – can bring successful and very enjoyable results.

I always loved drawing and writing stories, but it wasn't something I ever thought I could do for a living. I was a bit hopeless at spelling (and still am). My route to becoming an author came through being asked to work on other people's stories as an illustrator. I found it too stressful sitting around waiting for someone else to give me a job, so I had a go at writing my own picture book ideas to illustrate as well. I already had an agent for my illustration work in books (Caroline Walsh at David Higham Associates), who was very encouraging (and has stuck by me for over 16 years).

My first picture book, *Square Eyed Pat*, was published in 2004. This was followed by *My Big Brother, Boris*, which won the Smarties Book Prize Silver Award (0–5 Years) and gave me more confidence to keep writing and drawing.

This year is the 10th anniversary of my *Tom Gates* series and I have just published the 18th book. The series started life as a picture book idea. Publishers said they liked the format but didn't think there was sufficient story. So eventually, after rewriting it in different formats, I sat down and wrote afresh the first pages in a school exercise book. I imagined Tom writing about a rotten camping holiday he'd had with his family which included his teacher's comments as well as lots of drawings and doodles.

This was about the third (or fourth) go I'd had at it. But when Caroline sent out this version we got seven offers from seven different publishers within two weeks – which of course had NEVER happened to me before.

Here's my advice to anyone who wants to write or illustrate children's books:
• Be persistent. I know lots of people who have had their first efforts turned down or ideas rejected. But if the comments from publishers are positive, keep going and don't give up. Take feedback on board, especially if you're being told the same thing from different publishers. (However, some of my best ideas have lingered around for a while.)
• Think about what kind of books YOU really enjoyed reading when you were a child. I was crazy about a series about a bear called Mary Plain. Looking at them now, I realise that the main stories didn't really engage me, but Mary used to write letters with lots of drawings and doodles as part of them. I loved these bits so much that I would skip through the whole book to devour her letters. This is exactly why the *Tom Gates* books have so many doodles and drawings in them: I wanted to write a book that I would have enjoyed as a child.

The *Children's Writers' & Artists' Yearbook* is a fantastic source of information, STUFFED full of useful FACTS to help you get writing (and drawing). So be sure to make good use of it. And if you're lucky enough to get a book published – ENJOY it! Put together an event and do anything you can to help it along the way. I love going to schools and doing events now, although I found it tricky at first. It's really fantastic to be invited to talk about your books and meet the children and other people who are reading them. I often get ideas from going out and about.

As I look back on ten years of *Tom Gates* and am working on the next book in the series, I can honestly say I've never worked so hard on anything or enjoyed myself so much. So keep going and don't give up!

Here's my feet                                        not touching the ground

– because that's what has happened to me since *The Brilliant World of Tom Gates* was published in April 2011.

**Liz Pichon** is a writer and illustrator of children's books, including *A Tale of Two Kitties* (Scholastic 2006), *Bored Bill* (Little Tiger Press 2008), *My Big Brother, Boris* (winner of the Smarties Book Prize Silver Award in 2004; Scholastic 2004), *The Very Ugly Bug* (Little Tiger Press 2004), *Spinderella* (Egmont 2002), *Square Eyed Pat* (Puffin 2003), *Penguins* (Gullane Children's Books 2008), *My Little Sister, Doris* (Scholastic 2008) and *The Three Horrid Pigs and the Big Friendly Wolf* (Little Tiger Press 2009). Her first standalone middle-grade title is *Shoe Wars* (Scholastic 2020). 2021 was the 10th anniversary of the *Tom Gates* series; it has sold over 16 million copies, has been a multiple No. 1 children's bestseller and has been translated into 46 languages. The latest title in the series is *Tom Gates: Happy to Help (eventually)* (Scholastic 2022). *The Brilliant World of Tom Gates* won the 2011 Roald Dahl Funny Prize (7–14 Years), the 2012 Red House Children's Book Award (Younger Readers) and the 2012 Waterstones Children's Book Prize (Best Fiction for 5–12s); *Tom Gates – Genius Ideas (Mostly)* won the 2013 Blue Peter Book Award for Best Story; and *Tom Gates – Epic Adventures* won the 2018 LOLLIES Laugh Out Loud Book Award. Liz co-wrote the script for *Tom Gates Live*, which toured around the UK and Ireland in 2019, and co-writes the scripts and songs and presents the DRAW IT section of the Sky Kids TV animated/magazine-style adaptation of *The Brilliant World of Tom Gates*. The first series won a Scottish BAFTA for Best Entertainment in 2021. Liz designed the official BBC Children in Need T-shirt. Find out more on her website http://lizpichon.com/ and follow her on Twitter @LizPichon.

## See also...
- *Notes from a successful children's author and illustrator*, page 239

# *Do* judge a book by its cover

Thomas Taylor explains how a good cover can tell you, at a glance, just how it feels to read the book, and he describes the key, defining, attention-grabbing elements that, thanks to the skills of designer, publisher and marketing team, combine to sell your book to the reader.

Not its contents, of course – I would never suggest that the quality of someone's writing or their ability to tell a story can be fairly assessed by how the book appears; but do judge the book as an object – by how it looks on the shelf or feels in your hand – because a lot of effort went into making it that way.

When my middle-grade novel *Malamander* (Walker Books 2019) was being prepared for publication, I was eager to do the cover art myself. I am, after all, an illustrator, and my first published piece of illustration – straight out of art school – was the cover art for *Harry Potter and the Philosopher's Stone* (Bloomsbury 1997) by J.K. Rowling. Editor Barry Cunningham contacted me, after seeing some sample drawings I left at the offices of Bloomsbury, and invited me to make a painting for the cover of a debut book by an unknown author. The brief was simple: paint Harry beside the Hogwarts Express, on Platform Nine and Three Quarters, and then paint a wizard ('any wizard will do') for the back cover. After some to-ing and fro-ing with rough sketches, I produced the paintings, which were then whisked into book cover shape by a designer. At the time I had little inkling what this 'whisking' entailed.

Given this experience – and the years of working on picture books that followed – it seemed only natural that I would do the cover art for my own middle-grade novel too, and not just the incidental interior drawings and the map. Indeed, I'd doodled and sketched right through the process of writing *Malamander*, so I was ready to go. But that's not what happened.

One of the questions I get asked most by up-and-coming writers looking to break into traditional publishing and asking for guidance is: 'Do I need to find an illustrator before I submit to publishers?'. This comes up especially frequently with picture book writers, who correctly sense the importance images will have as a vehicle for their storytelling, but don't always know how to handle it if they're not doing the art themselves. Well, there's some good news. The answer to this is: you *never* need to find an illustrator. Not if you are following the traditional publishing route.

Selecting the right visual match for your writing and storytelling is a complex business, and one the publishers will definitely want to be in control of. Art directors bring enormous expertise to this process, as well as the contact details of some of the best cover artists and designers in the industry. Actually, be *glad* that they'll handle all this for you; querying an agent or prospective publisher as a double act will make you much harder to deal with anyway, and will throw up unnecessary complications that no editor wants to deal with.

When you have a publishing contract, you may get some say in the look of the book – probably further down the line, once the work has essentially been done. But this is likely to be a polite request for comment, rather than an invitation to send the designers back to the storyboard. Well-established writers may be able to exert more influence on the process, perhaps thanks to a clause they (or more likely their agent) were able to insert into the contract. Whether they *should* or not is a point for debate, though; an author may have strong feelings about how the book should look, but their preferences may not marry up with current trends or other marketing factors that could be crucial to a book's success in a highly competitive market.

Sometimes it can be hard when an author sees their cover for the first time and it is nothing like they imagined it would or should be. The publishing process can often appear mysterious and veiled, especially for new writers, who may feel that they are on the receiving end of arcane decisions made in secret conclave. But it's important to trust that the publishers know the market and how to position your book successfully in it, and to remember that they are on your side and have every interest in seeing your book succeed. This isn't to say you shouldn't use your chance to comment on the cover design, or that you should be shy of sharing your ideas. Just be aware that your voice is only one of many.

The first thing I noticed when the cover art for *Malamander* was being discussed was just how many people had input or a say in the process – from publishing and sales directors, through marketing and PR reps, to representatives of export sales, special sales, book club sales, etc. Oh, and designers of course. And that's before factoring in key account (bookshop chains, for example) managers and buyers who will have to actually sell the book, and who may well have strong views on what does or doesn't work on the shop floor. And yes, these views are sometimes strong enough to get a book cover design changed, in order to secure a substantial order.

This process has become more intense since my own experience of producing the cover art for *Harry Potter* back in 1996, due not only to ever-increasing competition in children's fiction but also to the rise of digital platforms. For example, the question of how a cover will display as a thumbnail is more important than ever, because that tiny postage-stamp-sized image that scrolls down an iPhone screen in a second may be the book's only chance to connect with potential readers. If the actual physical book benefits from a foil finish, or sprayed edges or embossed lettering, it still has to look good at just 107 pixels wide by 160 high (standard thumbnail dimensions), where all these flourishes will be invisible. Delicate typography might vanish altogether at that resolution, and subtle artwork become little more than a blob.

For similar reasons, the spine of a book – so often overlooked – might be the only side of your work a browsing reader sees as they scan the shelves. But a good designer can tell them the author's name, the title, the publisher and something of the flavour of the story – all in the narrow strip of paper that holds the book together. And in a way that catches the eye too.

Series recognition and author branding often rests entirely on how that author's books appear. Get this right from the beginning and you can create a graphic language that tells us, at a glance, that the new book by X is out. Often this is achieved simply by choosing (and sticking with) a distinctive font for the author's name and making this the dominating graphic element of the cover. Think Rankin, Ellroy and Le Carré, and now you know where the term 'Big Name author' comes from.

They say a good cover tells you how it will *feel* to read the book. So alongside the practical considerations of text hierarchy – the relative graphic importance of the title, author's name, and straplines and quotes – there are other, less literal design components at play. Photography, painted or decorative elements that conjure a sense of the story for the reader and entice them in, are complex considerations and easy to overdo. Clever font choice can straddle both of these fields, clearly communicating key information, whilst also hinting at the regional or temporal flavour of the story or summing up that elusive 'feel'.

There's only so much 'room' on a book cover. Doing a lot with font, for example, means you can't also add complex imagery without potentially overloading the design and creating a mess that the eye struggles to read at a glance. And when it comes to selling books by cover alone, a glance might be all you get.

What is or is not a good design is not entirely subjective. There are certain key elements that are usually combined to create a harmonious whole: what the book is called and who wrote it; how reading the story will make you feel; how the book can grab attention on displays; how the book cover fares when miniaturised to a thumbnail or glimpsed from across the street in a bookshop window. I now have a far greater appreciation for what designers do than I did when I painted those *Harry Potter* cover pictures way back at the start of my career.

I had my own lesson in the importance of the content of book cover art too, when the wizard I painted for the back cover of *Harry Potter* (the 'any wizard will do' wizard I mentioned at the start) became the subject of much fan speculation, and even consternation. With the rise of Pottermania, the identity of the wizard I originally painted there became the subject of debate – even some conspiracy theories. I was accused by some of having secret advance information about the then unwritten books, and of deliberately leaving clues and toying with readers. Nobody wanted to hear that the character I painted was just a generic wizard based on my own dad! Bloomsbury asked me, some years later, to paint a replacement picture – the image of Albus Dumbledore that most fans seemed to expect – and my father's brief career as an infamous magician came to an end.

In the ever-narrowing bricks-and-mortar retail space, and across the expanding and fiercely visual digital landscape, the appearance of your book has probably never been more important. So while it's still true that a good cover should tell you how it feels to read the book, these days it can't hurt if it also looks stunning on a coffee table, turns heads from across the street or launches a viral 'This was totally a cover buy, but …' Instagram wave.

I didn't do the cover art for *Malamander* in the end. I quickly became overwhelmed by how complex the process was, and how much editing and writing time it would take away. It was genuinely a relief to pass the task over to George Ermos, whose gorgeous art adorns the cover now – subtly suggesting the tone of the story within and how it will feel to read it, whilst also making a splash in a bookshop window. And yes, thanks to George, it also looks fabulous in an Instagram post.

**Thomas Taylor** is an author and illustrator. He has illustrated and contributed to dozens of books, and has also written and illustrated four of his own picture books, including *The Loudest Roar* (2003) and *The Biggest Splash* (2005), both published by OUP. His most recent books, in the *Legends of Eerie-on-Sea* series published by Walker Books for middle-grade readers, are *Malamander* (2019), *Gargantis* (2020), *Shadowghast* (2021) and *Festergrimm* (2022). For more information see www.thomastaylor-author.com; follow him on Twitter @ThomasHTaylor.

## See also…
● *Being an illustrator* and *a writer*, page 247

# How to create a graphic novel

Isabel Greenberg has valuable advice for the would-be graphic novelist, provides tried-and-tested practical rules and tips for visual storytellers, and shares her knowledge of this creative and engaging medium.

Contrary to how they are often presented, graphic novels (or comics) are not a genre – like science fiction or fantasy or crime or historical fiction, but a medium – like film, poetry, interpretative dance or prose novels. They are a way of telling stories. I can introduce you to some of the conventions or 'un-conventional' aspects of this medium and talk you through my own process, but to instruct you in how to create a graphic novel in one short article is as impossible a task as instructing someone on how to write a novel or make a film. That said, what I can do is tell you how I make *my* graphic novels. I'll present you with some tips, pointers and thoughts that I think might be useful for anyone embarking on this creative route … for it is a mammoth undertaking.

## Definitions

Whether you choose to call it a graphic novel or a comic book, or just a story told in pictures, is entirely up to you. For me, if it's the length of a novel, I call it a graphic novel. This doesn't mean its content is necessarily more 'highbrow' than your average comic; for me it simply denotes the length of the book. A short episodic periodical or a zine, regardless of its content, I would refer to as a comic. But hot debate surrounds this issue, with many comic fans feeling that the term 'graphic novel' has been used to make the medium more palatable to audiences who might balk at reading 'comic books'. I tend to feel that whether this is true or not doesn't matter, so long as it means more readers are willing to access this wonderful medium.

## Where to start?

With your story of course – and how you begin to find this is up to you. For some writers, a character might be their catalyst; for others it's a plot or premise. This is a visual medium, however, so that is something worth thinking about. Much as a film-maker might struggle to make an arresting film that takes place entirely in a pitch-black room, so you, as a visual storyteller, might also (that being said, you may be up for a challenge!).

As with standard novels, graphic novels encompass a vast array of genres. You can read a graphic novel adventure, a thriller, horror, biography or history. And yes, there are graphic novels that feature superheroes! Autobiography is extremely popular too; the most well-known examples of the medium are *Persepolis* by Marjane Satrapi (Jonathan Cape 2003) and *Maus* by Art Speigelman (Pantheon Books 1991), to name two of the most seminal.

Many graphic novelists write and draw their own books. I am one of these. But if you are an aspiring writer who would like to team up with an artist, that is also possible. Some publishers may be willing to help facilitate this but, with such a visual medium, it is hard to pitch the project on words alone, and you might want to consider approaching an artist to work on the pitch with you. A note here: do not ask an artist to illustrate your graphic novel pitch free of charge, unless you are equally invested artistic partners in the project.

If you need someone to facilitate your vision, you must pay for this service. Illustrating a graphic novel is an extremely complex and time-consuming task.

For me, everything starts with the story. I would not even begin to sketch or imagine characters or setting until I had the bare bones of a premise to work upon. Even my first book, which was set in an imaginary world called Early Earth, started with a creation story, rather than the building of the world itself. Many people like to start by building the world, but this aspect can be addictive, and your world can swiftly become too huge to handle. Remember that you are sculpting a narrative; the richer your world, the better. Of course, you can and should know all the back stories and places that go on off the page – but keep your focus on the story you want to tell in your book.

My most recent graphic novel, *Glass House* (Jonathan Cape 2020), began with research, as it is part biography, part fantastical interpretation of the Bronte siblings' childhood world-building. Many graphic novelists write their words like a film script. I do this to some extent, but I often play with writing as prose, and I'll frequently break off from the script to draw little moments or scenes so I can see how they might play out.

## Rules to break or keep

I won't tell you how many panels should be on a page, or how many words should be in a speech bubble. Some of my favourite graphic novels are totally silent, such as *The Arrival* by Shaun Tan (Hachette Children's 2007) and *Bad Island* by Stanley Donwood (Hamish Hamilton 2020), and some have so many words it's almost a challenge to separate them from the images, so of course these rules and conventions are there to be broken. But there are a few important maxims I do try to stick to:

### • One action per panel

You cannot direct a character to cross a room and open a window in a single panel (writers who have written for film are often the worst culprits in this area). You are working with still images. A character may be pictured mid-stride, crossing a room in the first panel, and opening a window in the next.

### • Communication is paramount

Test your story out on a reader at every point. If they do not understand what is happening, if your images are too oblique or you have too much going on, then you will need to adapt. I particularly like to test my work out on readers who are not familiar with, or do not read a lot of, this medium. If a reader does not understand what you want them to, then you need to rethink how you are telling the story. Writers who work with artists can sometimes assume that the images can clear up confusing motives or explain things they do not want to say in words. Sometimes this is the case, but remember that – unlike with film – you cannot control how long your reader lingers on a moment or panel, or puzzles over the expression and emotion of a character. If there is something important you want them to know, you must endeavour to communicate it. Above all, remember that if your reader doesn't understand something, this is not their fault; the responsibility is on you, as the creator, to convey your own message adequately.

### • If a moment is important, make them stay

I just said above that you cannot control how long a reader lingers on a panel. This is quite true, but you can certainly try. If a moment is important, emotionally or as a crux to your story, let your reader know this. You could signify it with a full bleed spread for example (this is a single image that runs the entire width and height of your double page). It can create impact if not used too frequently in your story. This might be a point of emotional significance, or perhaps a scene-setting moment – to introduce a character's arrival in a certain setting, or to show a moment of excitement or action.

### • The page-turn is powerful

Don't show a big reveal as the last panel on a spread or page. Your reader will first see the page as one image before their eye adjusts and they read it as panels. This means you cannot stop spoilers if you show them on the same page. If you have a surprise, let the reader discover it as they turn the page.

### • If your picture is saying something, your words don't need to

If your images are showing or saying something, then there is no need for you to say it in words too. If your image shows a character looking into a beautiful sunrise, you do not need to say '[XX] looked at the beautiful sunrise'. But you might use your words to say something your image cannot convey, or to add another layer to the narrative: '[XX] had not seen a sunrise for nearly a year'. Or you may choose to let the image breathe, and speak for itself, letting your reader decide what your character is feeling at this moment of sunrise contemplation.

I tend to use narration in my work, rather than leaving the story to be told purely through dialogue and action. But this is a stylistic choice, and many writers and artists will try to avoid narration; it can seem like unnecessary, or obvious, exposition. I do use such exposition to capitalise on the humour of having an omniscient narrative voice.

### • Consider keeping your text on a separate layer

Whether you are hand lettering or using a font, this is worth considering. In all likelihood, your editor may come back to you with tweaks or spelling and grammatical corrections. I found early on that if I kept my text on a separate layer to my artwork, this made shuffling and changing much easier. Furthermore, it meant that when the works went into foreign translation, I was able to easily provide my font (which I made from my own handwriting) when appropriate, and when it needed to be re-lettered (for different alphabets) my text was easy to remove.

### Pitching

Most publishers will require a full synopsis and plot breakdown, as well as at least six to ten example spreads, showing your words and artwork together. Some will require even more of a completed script. When choosing your example spreads, pick a variety that can show your range. Perhaps you want some quiet, some dialogue-heavy spreads, and some action or full-page images, if your story will call for these, so that they can see the full visual scope of the story.

You may choose to approach an agent to represent you before approaching a publisher. Choose who you approach prudently. Not all publishers or agents will be right for your work. Pick a selection of graphic novels by writers or artists whose work you feel has a parallel with your own stylistically, and see who publishes or represents them. Remember you have to appeal to a publisher both visually and in terms of your story; one is no good without the other. Consider both of these things when deciding who to approach. Look through a publishers' back catalogue and see if they have a house 'style'. Don't attempt to change your work to fit that style, but do bear it in mind if you get a rejection – they just may not be the right place for you. An agent can advise you on this, and will guide you through the process of pitching, should you choose to get one.

## Making graphic novels your profession

Be aware that even the most generous advance from a publisher is unlikely to be enough for you to live on entirely whilst you make your book. The market is neither as large, nor as lucrative, as regular fiction, and the advances publishers offer will sadly reflect this. Most graphic novelists and comic artists will have several strings to their bow. Some may also do children's books, freelance writing, commercial illustration, hire themselves out to be the artist on another writers' work or have another day job completely.

## And finally ...

Good luck! Graphic novels are a mammoth undertaking. But they are also a unique medium in that you have the power to do absolutely everything: you are in charge of set design, lighting, script, costume and location. You are the director of your own world, and it can be created without having to source a million-dollar budget and deal with a staff of hundreds. This is a wonderful thing, so enjoy it.

Illustrator and writer **Isabel Greenberg** studied Illustration at the University of Brighton and completed an MA at the Royal College of Art in experimental animation. Her bestselling graphic novels, all published by Jonathan Cape in the UK, are *The Encyclopaedia of Early Earth* (2013), winner of the Best Book category at the British Comic Awards, *The One Hundred Nights of Hero* (2016), a *New York Times* Graphic Books Bestseller and *Glass Town* (2020). Her work also includes comics and illustration, animation and children's books. See www.isabelgreenberg.co.uk for more information, and follow her on Twitter @isabelgreenberg and @isabel_greenberg on instagram.

# Illustration agents

Before submitting work, artists are advised to make preliminary enquiries and to ascertain terms of work. Commission varies but averages 25–30%. The Association of Illustrators (see page 317) provides a valuable service for illustrators, agents and clients.

*Member of the Society of Artists Agents
†Member of the Association of Illustrators
sae = self-addressed envelope

## Advocate Art Ltd

Suite 7, The Sanctuary, 23 Oakhill Grove, Surbiton, Surrey KT6 6DU
*tel* 020-8390 6293
*email* mail@advocate-art.com
*website* www.advocate-art.com
*Facebook* www.facebook.com/advocateart
*Twitter* @advocateart01
*Directors* Edward Burns, Caroline Burns

Has 12 agents representing over 300 artists and illustrators. Bespoke illustration for children's books, greetings cards and fine art publishers, gift and ceramic manufacturers. For illustrators' submission guidelines see website. Animation, design and original content represented through LaB – Writers and Artists ColLaBorate. Also original art gallery, stock library and website in German, Spanish and French. Founded 1996.

## Allied Artists/Artistic License

*tel* 07971 111256
*email* info@allied-artists.net
*website* www.alliedartists-illustration.co.uk
*Contact* Gary Mills

Represents over 90 illustrators ranging in styles from realistic through stylised to cute, for all types of publishing but particularly children's illustration. Commission: 35%. Founded 1983.

## Darley Anderson Illustration Agency

Unit 19, Matrix Studios, 91 Peterborough Road, London SW6 3BU
*tel* 020-7385 6652
*website* www.darleyandersonillustration.com
*Instagram* @darleyanderson_illustration
*Managing Director & Agent* Clare Wallace, *Directors* Darley Anderson, Rosanna Bellingham, *Agents* Lydia Silver, Becca Langton (US), Chloe Davis

Represents bestselling and award-winning illustrators. Works across all areas of publishing, from picture books to gift titles to graphic novels, across fiction and non-fiction, collaborating with both adult and children's publishers worldwide. Actively looking for new talent, especially illustrators from under-represented backgrounds. Commission: 20%.

Submission guidelines: send an email with portfolio attached as a pdf or in the body of the email, along with information about yourself and links to social media channels used to display your work. Author-illustrators should send texts as pdf or Word attachments, along with a brief synopsis and illustration samples. Submissions should be made directly to the agent of choice. Founded 1988.

## Arena Illustration Ltd*†

31 Eleanor Road, London E15 4AB
*tel* 020-8555 9827
*website* www.arenaillustration.com
*Contact* Tamlyn Francis

Represents 29 artists. Average commission: 25%. Founded 1970.

## The Art Agency

21 Morris Street, Sheringham, Norfolk NR26 8JY
*tel* (01263) 823424
*email* artagency@me.com
*website* www.the-art-agency.co.uk
*Facebook* www.facebook.com/illustrationagency
*Director* Beryl Leitch

Provides non-fiction, reference and children's book illustration. Specialises in non-fiction illustrations across a wide variety of subjects and age groups. Submit up to six samples by email along with a link to your website. Founded 1990.

## The Artworks*

64 Cranbourne Avenue, London E11 2BQ
*email* submissions@theartworksinc.com
*website* www.theartworksinc.com
*Contacts* Stephanie Alexander-Jinks, Alex Hadlow, Lucy Scherer

Represents 35 illustrators for design and advertising work as well as for non-fiction children's books, book jackets, illustrated gift books and children's picture books. Commission: 30% design and advertising, 25% publishing advances, 15% royalties, 25% book jackets. Founded 1983.

## Astound US Inc

Suite 143, 61 Victoria Road, Surbiton KT6 4JX
*tel* 07465 772271

*email* contact@astound.us
*website* https://astound.us/publishing
*Director* Vince Verma

A new kind of artist representation business based in New York City and London. Offers contemporary children's book illustration, and both licensing and commercial art from around the world.

## Beehive Illustration

42A Cricklade Street, Cirencester, Glos. GL7 1JH
*tel* (01285) 644001
*email* enquiries@beehiveillustration.co.uk
*website* www.beehiveillustration.co.uk
*Contact* Paul Beebee

Represents 200 artists specialising in ELT, education and general children's publishing illustration. Commission: 25%. Founded 1989.

## The Big Red Illustration Agency

*tel* 0808 120 0996
*email* enquiries@bigredillustrationagency.com
*website* www.bigredillustrationagency.com
*Facebook* www.facebook.com/thebigredillustrationagency
*Twitter* @big_red_author
*Director* Adam Rushton

Represents a number of professional illustrators. Over the years has developed strong relationships with a wide range of clients including children's book publishers, design agencies, greetings card companies and toy manufacturers. Founded 2012.

## The Bright Agency*

103–105 St John's Hill, London SW11 1SY
*tel* 020-7326 9140
*US Office* 50 West Street, C12, New York, NY 10006
*tel* +1 646-604-0992
*email* mail@thebrightagency.com
*website* www.thebrightagency.com
*Ceo* Vicki Willden-Lebrecht, *Director* Arabella Stein

Areas of representation include: children's illustration, greeting and gift (cards, social stationery, giftwrap), design and advertising (editorial, branding, adult publishing, packaging, web and digital, typography), animation, literary (children's fiction and non-fiction, adult fiction and non-fiction, graphic novels) and licensing (toys and games, digital gaming, fabric and apparel, and homewares). For illustration, writing and animation submissions guidelines see website. No submissions by post. Clients include: Benji Davies, David Litchfield, Yasmeen Ismail, Chris Chatterton, Diane Ewen, Laura Hughes, Galia Bernstein, Mechal Roe, Aura Lewis, Karl James Mountford, Jane Newland, Brenna Nation and Hannah Peck. Founded 2002.

## Jenny Brown Associates – see page 220

## The Catchpole Agency

53 Cranham Street, Oxford OX2 6DD
*tel* 07789 588070
*email* james@thecatchpoleagency.co.uk
*email* celia@thecatchpoleagency.co.uk
*website* www.thecatchpoleagency.co.uk
*Proprietors* James Catchpole, Celia Catchpole

Agents for authors and illustrators of children's books from picture books through to YA novels, with a specialism in editorial work. See website for contact and submissions details. See also page 220. Founded 1996.

## The Copyrights Group Ltd

3 Pancras Square, London N1C 4AG
*tel* 020-3880 0134
*email* info@copyrightsgroup.com
*website* www.copyrightsgroup.com
*SVP UK Licensing & Retail* Rachel Clarke, *SVP Brand & International Licensing* Polly Emery, *VP Creative Services* Demi Patel

Full-service international brand licensing company offering strategic worldwide brand development, licensing and retail expertise. Focuses on the long-term development of IP and quality merchandise programmes. Properties include *Paddington Bear, Mush-Mush and the Mushables, Father Christmas, Fungus the Bogeyman*. Founded 1984.

## Good Illustration Ltd

118 Dumbreck Road, London SE9 1XD
*tel* 020-8123 0243 (UK) / +1 347-627-0243 (US)
*email* draw@goodillustration.com
*website* www.goodillustration.com
*Directors* Doreen Thorogood, Kate Webber, Tom Thorogood

Represents 50+ artists for advertising, design, publishing and animation. Send sae and samples. Commission: 25% publishing, 30% advertising. Founded 1977.

## Graham-Cameron Illustration

59 Hertford Road, Brighton BN1 7GG
*tel* (01273) 385890
*email* enquiry@gciforillustration.com
*Alternative address* The Art House, Uplands Park, Sheringham, Norfolk NR26 8NE
*tel* (01263) 821333
*website* www.gciforillustration.com
*Partners* Helen Graham-Cameron, Duncan Graham-Cameron

Represents 37+ artists and undertakes illustration for publishing and communications. Specialises in educational, children's and information books. Phone before sending A4 samples with sae or email samples or link to a website. No MSS. Founded 1985.

## David Higham Associates Ltd – see page 223

## IllustrationX*†

4th Floor, Silverstream House, 45 Fitzroy Street,
London W1T 6EB
*tel* 020-7720 5202
*email* hello@illustrationx.com
*website* www.illustrationx.com/uk
*Facebook* www.facebook.com/weareillustrationx
*Twitter* @illustrationx

Welcomes submissions from illustrators and
animators whose work is distinctive and innovative.
Only accepts applications from artists through
submissions page: www.illustrationx.com/
applications. Founded 1929.

## Inky Illustration

483 Green Lanes, London N13 4BS
*tel* 0121 330 1312
*email* info@inkyillustration.com
*website* https://inkyillustration.com/
*Facebook* www.facebook.com/inkyillustration
*Twitter* @inkyillo

The range of illustrators have experience working
with clients on international advertising campaigns,
publications and editorials, as well as commissions
for smaller companies. Always happy to receive new
work. New artists should fill out the application form
on the website or email to:
submissions@inkyillustration.com. Hard copies of
work are accepted with an sae if the work is to be
returned. Founded 2009.

## B.L. Kearley Art & Antiques

Glebe House, Bakers Wood, Denham,
Bucks. UB9 4LG
*tel* (01895) 832145
*email* christine.kearley@kearley.co.uk
*website* www.kearley.co.uk
*Agent* C.R. Kearley

Represents 30+ artists. Mainly specialises in children's
book and educational illustration for the domestic
market and overseas. Known for realistic figurative
work. Specialises in the sale of original book
illustration artwork. Commission: 25%.
Founded 1948.

## Kids Corner

1 Mailing Street, West Street, Lewes BN7 2NZ
*tel* 020-7593 0506
*email* claire@meiklejohn.co.uk
*website* www.kidscornerillustration.co.uk
*Managing Director* Claire Meiklejohn

Represents illustrators, from award-winning to
emerging artists for children's publishing. Styles
include fun, cute, stylised, picture book, young
fiction, reference, graphic, traditional, painterly and
digital. Founded 2015.

## Lemonade Illustration Agency

167–169 Great Portland Street, 5th Floor,
London W1W 5PF

*tel* 07891 390750
*email* gary@lemonadeillustration.com
*US office* 347 Fifth Ave, Suite 1402, New York, NY
10016
*website* www.lemonadeillustration.com

Represents 180+ international illustrators and
character development artists working in all media
from advertising brands to children's picture books.
The team work with many leading children's book,
children's literature, e-learning and educational
publishers across the world. Any submissions from
illustrators by email must contain a website link (no
attachments), or hard copies of samples can be sent
by post with an sae to the London office. Sadly
cannot reply to all submissions received due to the
volume received. Also has offices in Wakefield,
Sydney and Dubai. Founded 2001.

## David Lewis Illustration Agency

3 Somali Road, London NW2 3RN
*tel* 020-7435 7762 / 07931 824674
*email* info@davidlewisillustration.com
*Director* David Lewis, *Associate* Lisa Britton

Representing approx. 25 illustrators creating different
styles in varying mediums, mostly for all areas of
children's publishing, including educational,
merchandising and toys. Also considers complete
picture books with text. Send A4 colour or b&w
copies of samples with sae. Commission: 30%.
Founded 1974.

## Frances McKay Illustration

17 Church Road, West Mersea, Essex CO5 8QH
*tel* 07703 344334
*email* frances@francesmckay.com
*website* www.francesmckay.com
*Proprietor* Frances McKay

Represents 15–20 artists for illustration mainly for
children's books. For information on submissions
please look at website. Submit email with low-res
scans or colour copies of recent work; sae essential for
return of all unsolicited samples sent by post.
Commission: 25%. Founded 1999.

## The Monkey Feet Illustration Directory

*email* enquiries@monkeyfeetillustration.com
*website* www.monkeyfeetillustration.com

Presents portfolios for artists creating work for
children's book publishers, design agencies, greeting
cards and toy companies. Founded 2012.

## NB Illustration*

Home Farm, East Horrington, Somerset BA5 3EA
*tel* 07720 827328
*email* info@nbillustration.co.uk
*website* www.nbillustration.co.uk
*Directors* Joe Najman, Charlotte Dowson

Represents 50+ artists, 40% of whom produce
children's material for picture books and educational

publishing. For submission details see website. Commission: 30%. Founded 2000.

## The Plum Agency

Chapel House, St. Lawrences Way, Reigate, Surrey RH2 7AF
*tel* (01737) 244095
*email* letterbox@theplumagency.com
*website* https://theplumagency.com/
*Directors* Mark Mills, Hannah Whitt

Represents 200+ artists and authors, producing texts and illustrations for children's publishing, advertising, editorial, greeting cards and packaging. See website for submission procedure. Commission: 30%. Founded 2006.

## Sylvie Poggio Artists Agency

62 Ainsdale Road, London W5 1JX
*tel* 07775 894870
*email* sylvie-p@sylviepoggio.com
*website* www.sylviepoggio.com
*Facebook* www.facebook.com/Sylvie-Poggio-Artists-agency-700285410097943
*Twitter* @sylviepoggioart
*Directors* Sylvie Poggio, Bruno Caurat

Represents 40 artists producing illustrations for publishing and advertising. Founded 1996.

## Caroline Sheldon Literary Agency Ltd

71 Hillgate Place, London W8 7SS
*tel* 020-7727 9102
*email* info@carolinesheldon.co.uk
*website* www.carolinesheldon.co.uk
*Twitter* @CarolineAgent
*Contacts* Caroline Sheldon, Millie Van Grutten

Represents leading illustrators working in a broad range of styles, selling their work throughout the world and in all media. All genres of illustration. Commission: UK 15%, USA/translation 20%, film/TV 20%. Send an introductory email addressed to either Caroline Sheldon or Millie Van Grutten with work attached or a link to your work. In the subject line write 'Proposal from Illustrator', and include information about yourself and your work in the email. Clients: represents prominent, award-winning and bestselling clients in all fields including books, illustration, audio, digital and theatre. Works closely with a media agent on film, TV and other opportunities. See also page 227. Founded 1985.

## The Soho Agency Ltd

16–17 Wardour Mews, 2nd Floor, London W1F 8AT
*tel* 020-7471 7900
*website* www.thesohoagency.co.uk
*Contacts* Philippa Milnes-Smith

Illustrators for children's publishing for children 0–16 years. See website for submission requirements. Special interests: authors/artists creating their own projects, projects with cross-media potential, illustrators from diverse backgrounds, original talent. Commission: UK 15%, US 20%. Clients include Lauren Child, Emily Gravett, Chris Judge, Steve McCarthy, Jane Porter, Chris Riddell and Niamh Sharkey. See also page 228. Founded 1996.

## Tallbean

*tel* (01728) 454921
*email* heather@tallbean.co.uk
*website* www.tallbean.co.uk
*Founder* Heather Richards

Provides specialist illustrators offering a range of styles. The team of well-established and creative illustrators is kept relatively small to ensure a close working relationship. Founded 1996.

## Vicki Thomas Associates

195 Tollgate Road, London E6 5JY
*tel* 020-7511 5767
*email* vickithomasassociates@yahoo.co.uk
*website* www.vickithomasassociates.com
*Twitter* @VickiThomasA
*Instagram* @VickiThomasA
*Consultant* Vicki Thomas

Represents approx. 30 artists, 75% of whom produce children's material for all ages. Specialises in gift products and considers images for publishing, toys, stationery, clothing, decorative accessories. Email sample images, covering letter and CV. Commission: 30%. Founded 1985.

## United Agents LLP

12–26 Lexington Street, London W1F 0LE
*tel* 020-3214 0800
*email* info@unitedagents.co.uk
*website* www.unitedagents.co.uk
*Agents* Jodie Hodges, Emily Talbot

Illustrators of children's books for all ages. Commission: home 15%, USA/translation 20%. See website for submission details. Founded 2008.

# Magazines and newspapers
## Writing for teens

Chloe Rhodes describes the possibilities, challenges and rewards of writing for today's teenage magazine market, explains what writers need to bear in mind to find that crucial, supportive connection with young readers and provides essential tips on how to pitch your own ideas for features.

In a market that's often overly focused on looks, fashion and lifestyle, our magazine, *Teen Breathe*, gives attention to the fabric of readers' inner lives. It exists to provide a safe, reassuring and uplifting space at a time when many young adults are facing a crisis of confidence and experiencing worries that affect their physical and mental wellbeing. Published every seven weeks in print along with a digital edition, it's aimed at 11–14 year-olds (though some readers are as young as eight); its message is that *all* feelings and ways of being are valid, all questions readers might be asking themselves are normal, and that there are all kinds of ways to slow the pace and make meaningful connections in the world. Based on the experience I've had connecting with our readers (all 30,000 of them) at *Teen Breathe*, here is my advice on how to write for this demanding but rewarding market.

### Pick 'n' mix

*Teen Breathe* tries, in myriad ways, to suggest that thinking about who you are, why you feel as you do and how you experience the world can be enriching, especially during the formative teen years. That's not to say, however, that every feature has to offer profound insight or a therapeutic message. Creativity, humour and lightness are crucial ingredients too. Although they fall into the catch-all category of 'teens', our readers are as individual and unique as the rest of the population. Their family circumstances, cultural backgrounds, maturity levels, hobbies and interests vary wildly. As a result, we have no set list of subjects to constrain new contributors – just let the imagination flow! What the most powerful features we publish have in common are a) a curious approach, b) thorough, fact-backed research and c) the sense that there might be something interesting for readers to glean … something that sheds light on themselves or the world they're beginning to explore.

For would-be contributors, choosing a subject can be liberating and fun. The young reader's thirst for knowledge means that things adults might take for granted, like potted plants, book groups or their sense of smell, can be approached with fresh wonder. In every issue we aim for a mixture of topics, so pieces might range from bullying to baking, grief to gardening, perhaps alongside a recipe for boba pearl ice lollies and a DIY guide to building a wormery. But some areas are given a wide berth, including celebrity, romantic relationships and losing or gaining weight (anything to do with how to sculpt the so-called 'perfect body' is *not* for us). We also avoid using the term 'teenagers' (readers know that's what they are) and usually sidestep anything that's self-consciously cool or edgy. On the whole, we also try to steer clear of using online trends as a starting point for features. While it's important, of course, to acknowledge the role social media plays in readers' lives, its impact on young minds is complex. We're careful to present a balanced and nuanced picture.

## Tips on tone

While gentle guidance and suggestion is great, most readers, whatever their age, will baulk slightly if they feel they're being lectured – so we try hard to ensure content doesn't sound formal, condescending or overtly educational. Instead, we try to channel the voice of a supportive older sibling – chatty, warm, conversational – giving comfort and empathy while acknowledging that we're in it together in not having all the answers. The aim is to convey a positive message that no one needs to be perfect and that most people sometimes experience uncertainty as well as happiness, self-doubt as well as confidence, loneliness as well as friendship. We remind them there's support available to help with sad or challenging issues, ways to learn from mistakes and manageable methods which help bring balance and contentment.

## Wise words

From a practical perspective, language is important. Pieces need to be accessible to 12-year-olds, so it's best not to use overly complex vocabulary – but it's fine to include two or three tricky words per piece if they flow in the text and are explained by the surrounding sentences. Examples, quotes and points of reference also need to be suitable for this age group. Paragraphs are generally kept short (35–40 words) and features run to approximately 850 words.

## Pitch perfect

Every magazine will have its own submissions guidelines. At *Teen Breathe* we have a dedicated form for writers to use to send in a pitch (see www.teenbreathe.co.uk/contact-us). We welcome new voices and fresh perspectives, so please do get in touch if you'd like to collaborate with us on a feature. Follow these tips to give your idea the best chance of success:

1. Have at least one clear, age-appropriate idea for a feature you'd like to write. We receive a lot of enquiries from would-be writers who tell us how much they'd like to contribute to the magazine but forget to include a specific piece they have in mind. Links to websites or articles published elsewhere are useful background reading if your idea sounds promising, but you need to outline a clear, **concise and concrete proposal** that we can consider.
2. Give a **clear summary** of the piece. Ideally think of a title and write a sentence or two that could be used as a 'standfirst' – a compelling subheading that fills the reader in on what they can expect.
3. Do some **research**. We wouldn't expect you to have read every back issue, but being able to refer to a past article that you've enjoyed, or one that includes thematic parallels to your proposal, is helpful in two ways. Firstly, it tells us you know what kind of features work for a teen readership. Secondly, it allows us to imagine your piece alongside others we've commissioned.
4. If your subject matter would benefit from the inclusion of expert insight, make suggestions for **who you might interview**. Just a couple of pithy quotes from a professional in the relevant field can be invaluable and ensure the magazine is offering the right kind of help.
5. Provide suggestions for **how the piece might be presented**. We try to break up blocky text with subheadings, bullet points and panels, so include ideas for these, alongside exercises, writing prompts or activities that might complement the main article.

**6.** Include a brief outline of **your writing background** (with one or two links to previously published work, if appropriate) and any other relevant experience or subject-related qualifications. We'd like to know why you're the best person to write the piece.

## Handle with care

One of the joys of writing for teens is they're often open-minded, curious and compassionate. This makes exploring subjects like neurodiversity, self-acceptance or care for the natural world all the more rewarding. The feedback we receive from young adults, plus their guardians and teachers – via email and through social media – is that there's a willingness to see things from different perspectives and an interest in the experiences of others that is refreshing and inspiring.

The other side of this coin, though, is the challenge presented by writing for such an open-hearted audience; the sensitivities of some readers might not at first occur to older writers. This means thinking carefully about word choice, subtext and potential triggers. Some of the messages we receive from readers reveal the struggles and vulnerabilities they're facing and the important role the magazine plays in dealing delicately with raw emotions. It's important to consider every possible interpretation of what you're saying so that no one feels judged or hurt and to avoid making assumptions of any kind.

## Write for everyone

*Teen Breathe* has subscribers of all genders from all over the world, from the USA and Australia to Sweden and South Korea, so any activities suggested should be accessible and varied. It's impossible to cover every base, of course, but international examples should be in the mix. For example, local-interest stories or features based on a project targeted only at girls in one part of the UK, could leave readers who don't fit into those categories feeling as though they're on the outside of things. It's important, too, that all our readers feel valued – which means seeing themselves on the page. We encourage all our writers to cast their net wide when sourcing case studies and professionals, and try to include as diverse, representative and authentic a set of voices as possible.

## Consult your inner teen

There's one final point worth mentioning: writers sometimes think they need to have teenage children to write for the teen market. My own view is that – while that experience might equip you well to write parenting articles – the best preparation for writing for teens is simply to remember what it was like to *be* one. There's a gradual and natural loosening of the connection between the present version of yourself and the 'you' of your youth. But … if it's possible to re-inhabit that mindset for a little while, and even to let that teenage part of you pipe up with their ideas before you begin to write, you'll be better placed to get on readers' wavelength and connect with them more directly.

**Chloe Rhodes** is a commissioning editor at *Teen Breathe* (www.teenbreathe.co.uk). She is a former *Daily Telegraph* features commissioning editor and is also the author of several books on language and folklore published by Michael O'Mara and a series of reading books for children published by Oxford University Press. Her freelance work has been published in the *Guardian*, *The Sunday Times* and the *Independent*.

# Magazines and newspapers for children

Listings of magazines about children's literature and education start on page 268.

## Anorak

3rd Floor, 86–90 Paul Street, London EC2A 4NE
*email* anorakmagazine@gmail.com
*website* www.anorakmagazine.com
*Twitter* @AnorakMagazine
*Editor* Cathy Olmedillas
4 p.a. £8

Aimed at children aged 6+, and designed to encourage creativity. Founded 2006.

## Aquila

Studio 2, 67A Willowfield Road, Eastbourne, East Sussex BN22 8AP
*tel* (01323) 431313
*email* submissions@aquila.co.uk
*email* illustrators@aquila.co.uk
*website* www.aquila.co.uk
*Facebook* www.facebook.com/AquilaChildrensMagazine
*Twitter* @AquilaMag
*Instagram* @aquila.magazine
*Editorial Director* Freya Hardy
Monthly £60 p.a.

Dedicated to encouraging children aged 8–13 to reason and create, and to develop a caring nature. Short stories and serials of up to three parts. Occasional features commissioned from writers with specialist knowledge. Approach in writing with ideas and sample of writing style, along with sae or via e-mail (fiction and non-fiction pitches should be sent to the first email address above). Length: 700–800 words (features), 1,000–1,100 words (stories or per episode of a serial). Payment: by arrangement. Founded 1993.

## BBC Doctor Who Magazine

Panini UK, Brockbourne House, 77 Mount Ephraim, Tunbridge Wells TN4 8AR
*tel* (01892) 500100
*email* dwa@panini.co.uk
*website* https://doctorwhomagazine.com/
*Twitter* @DWMtweets
*Editor* Marcus Hearn
Monthly £6.99

Magazine for 6–12 year-old fans of *Doctor Who*. Readers are immersed into the world of the Doctor, taking them on an adventure into time and space, with monsters and creatures, excitement, action, adventure and humour. Founded 2006.

## Beano

D.C. Thomson & Co. Ltd, 2 Albert Square, Dundee DD1 1DD
*email* contactus@beano.com
*website* www.beano.com
*Facebook* www.facebook.com/BeanoOfficial
*Twitter* @BeanoOfficial
*Editor* John Anderson
50 p.a. £2.99

Comic strips for children aged 6–12. Series, 8–20 pictures. Artwork and scripts. Payment: on acceptance.

## Cocoa Boy

Studio 210, 134–146 Curtain Road, London EC2A 3AR
*email* admin@thecocoadream.com
*website* https://cocoaboy.com
*Instagram* @cocoaboymag
*Publisher and Creative Director* Serlina Boyd
4 p.a. £40 for two-year subscription

The first UK magazine aimed specifically at young Black boys. Includes empowering content aimed at teaching children about Black culture and celebrating role models. Actively encourages submissions from children aged 7–11 via the email address above. Founded 2020.

## Cocoa Girl

Studio 210, 134–146 Curtain Road, London EC2A 3AR
*email* admin@thecocoadream.com
*website* www.cocoagirl.com/submissions
*Instagram* @cocoagirlmag
*Publisher* Serlina Boyd, *Editor* Faith Boyd
4 p.a. £40 for two-year subscription

The first UK magazine aimed specifically at young Black girls. Includes empowering content aimed at teaching children about Black culture and celebrating role models. Actively encourages submissions from children aged 7–11 via the email address above. Winner of Launch of the Year at the British Society of Magazine Editors' 2020 Awards. Founded 2020.

## Commando

DC Thomson & Co Ltd., 2 Albert Square, Dundee, DD1 1DD
*email* generalenquiries@commandomag.com
*website* www.commandocomics.com/submissions
*Facebook* www.facebook.com/C0mmandoComics

*Twitter* @CommandoComic
*Instagram* @commandocomics
8 per month (four new, four reprints) £2.50

Fictional stories set in time of war told in pictures. Scripts: about 135 pictures. Synopsis required as an opener. See website (address above) for submissions information. Payment: on acceptance. Founded 1961.

## DOT

3rd Floor, 86–90 Paul Street, London EC2A 4NE
*email* anorakmagazine@gmail.com
*website* www.anorakmagazine.com/dot
*Editor* Cathy Olmedillas
4 p.a. £6.50

Ad-free magazine aimed at encouraging creativity and learning in the under-5s.

## Eco Kids Planet

Eco Kids Planet, 41 Claremont Road,
Barnet EN4 0HR
*tel* 0800 639 1365
*email* hello@ecokidsplanet.co.uk
*website* www.ecokidsplanet.co.uk
*Facebook* www.facebook.com/ecokidsplanet
*Instagram* @ecokidsplanetmag
*Editor* Anya Dimelow
11 p.a. £4.90

Aimed at 7–11 year-old children. Each issue is dedicated to a different ecosystem and contains facts, photographs, puzzles and projects. The magazine uses fun, fictional characters in a story format to convey facts about nature and the environment. It also provides children with real-world examples of how they can make a difference on the planet. Length: 500–1,200 words (themed articles). Requirements: well-researched, up-to-date, informative articles, creative approach and interesting language. Specially commissions most material. Payment: by arrangement. Founded 2014.

## FirstNews

7 Playhouse Court, 62 Southwark Bridge Road,
London SE1 0AT
*tel* 020-3195 2000
*email* info@firstnews.co.uk
*website* www.firstnews.co.uk
*Twitter* @First_News
*Editor-in-Chief* Nicky Cox
Weekly Fri £2.85

Covers news and events in the UK and internationally for children aged 8–14. Founded 2006.

## Girl Talk

Immediate Media Co. Ltd, Vineyard House,
44 Brook Green, London W6 7BT
*tel* 020-7150 5000
*email* hello@girltalkmagazine.com
*Instagram* @girltalkmag

*Editor* Clare Norman
Fortnightly £6.99

Magazine for children aged 7–12. Contains pop, TV and film celebrity features, personality features, quizzes, fashion, competitions and stories. Length: 500 words (fiction). Payment: by arrangement. All material is specially commissioned. Founded 1997.

## Headliners

200A Pentonville Road, London N1 9JP
*email* enquiries@headliners.org
*website* www.headliners.org
*Twitter* @HeadlinersUK
*Chief Executive* James Hunt

Award-winning journalism and multi-media charity, offering young people aged 8–18 the opportunity to write on issues of importance to them, for newspapers, radio and TV. Founded 1995.

## KiCK!

Kennedy Publishing, Greenway Farm, Bath Road,
Wick, Bristol BS30 5RL
*tel* 0117 937 3003
*email* info@kennedypublishing.co.uk
*Twitter* @KiCKmagazine
*Editor* Ash Rose
13 p.a. £5.99

Football magazine for readers aged 7–14. Reports on leading players and teams from a variety of divisions, including the Premier League; also includes puzzles, competitions and interviews.

## Kids Alive! (The Young Soldier)

The Salvation Army, 101 Newington Causeway,
London SE1 6BN
*tel* 020-7367 4911
*email* kidsalive@salvationarmy.org.uk
*website* www.salvationarmy.org.uk/kidsalive
*Editor* Justin Reeves, *Deputy Editor* Cara Mott
Weekly £52 p.a.

Children's magazine: scripts and artwork for cartoon strips, puzzles, etc; Christian-based articles with emphasis on education and lifestyle issues. Illustrations: half-tone, line and four-colour line, cartoons. Payment: by arrangement. Founded 1881.

## Marvel Legends

Panini UK, Brockbourne House, 77 Mount Ephraim,
Tunbridge Wells TN4 8AR
*tel* (01892) 500100
*email* astonspid@panini.co.uk
*website* www.panini.co.uk/shp_gbr_en/magazines-comics-books/marvel.html
Every 4 weeks £4.50

52pp of comic strips, including both contemporary and classic stories.

## Match!

Kelsey Media, The Granary, Downs Court,
Yalding Hill, Yalding, Kent ME18 6AL
*email* match.magazine@kelsey.co.uk
*website* www.matchfootball.co.uk
*Twitter* @matchmagazine
*Group Editor* Stephen Fishlock
Fortnightly £3.99

Aimed at teenage football fans. News, statistics and
information on leading Premier League, Football
League and Scottish Premier League teams.

## Match of the Day

Immediate Media Co. Ltd, Vineyard House,
44 Brook Green, London W6 7BT
*tel* 020-7150 5111
*email* shout@motdmag.com
*website* www.motdmag.com
Weekly £3.99

Aims to bring football-crazy youngsters closer to their
sporting heroes with interviews, facts and stats, the
latest transfer gossip and results, posters and quizzes,
as well as comic strips and funnies.

## National Geographic Kids

Unit 10, Tomas Seth Business Park, Argent Road,
Queenborough, Kent ME11 5TS
*email* kids@ngkids.co.uk
*website* www.natgeokids.co.uk
*Facebook* www.facebook.com/natgeokids
*Twitter* @natgeokidsuk
*Instagram* @natgeokidsuk
*Editor* Tim Herbert
Monthly From £39 p.a.

Fun facts, photos and features about animals, science,
geography, history, the environment and popular
culture, aimed at children aged 6–12.

## Okido

1–5 Vyner Street, London E2 9DG
*email* info@okido.com
*website* www.okido.com
*Facebook* www.facebook.com/OKIDO.OFFICIAL
*Twitter* @okido.official
Monthly £5

Award-winning, eco-friendly illustrated science and
arts magazine for children aged 3–7. Created by
scientists and educators to promote fun, immersive
STEAM learning, with a new topic to explore every
month. Each edition includes science experiments,
activities, recipes, doodles and games. Founded 2007.

## The Phoenix

29 Beaumont Street, Oxford OX1 2NP
*email* theeditor@thephoenixcomic.co.uk
*website* www.thephoenixcomic.co.uk
*Facebook* www.facebook.com/phoenixcomic
*Twitter* @phoenixcomicuk
*Instagram* @phoenixcomicuk

*Editor* Tom Fickling
Weekly £3.25

32pp weekly anthology comic for boys and girls aged
7–14. Features serialised stories and one-off stories as
well as non-fiction. Encourages reading for pleasure
and children's critical thinking, creative writing and
drawing skills. Contributors include Jamie Smart and
Neill Cameron. Founded 2011.

## PONY Magazine

DJ Murphy Publishers Ltd, Olive Studio,
The Timber Yard, Grange Road, Tilford, Farnham,
Surrey GU10 2DQ
*tel* (01428) 601020
*email* pony@djmurphy.co.uk
*website* www.ponymag.com
*Twitter* @PONY_mag
*Editor-in-Chief* Louise Kittle
13 p.a. from £3.99

Lively articles and short stories with a horsey theme
aimed at readers aged 8–16. Technical accuracy and
young, fresh writing essential. Length: up to 800
words. Payment: by arrangement. Illustrations:
drawings (commissioned), photos, cartoons.
Founded 1949.

## Storytime

61 Bridge Street, Kington HR5 3DJ
*email* hello@storytimemagazine.com
*website* www.storytimemagazine.com
*website* www.storytimeforschools.com
*Facebook* www.facebook.com/StorytimeMag
*Twitter* @StorytimeMag
Monthly From £38.99 p.a.

Illustrated bedtime story magazine for children aged
3–8. Accepting submissions from illustrators: see
website for full submission guidelines. Calls for
submissions from short-story writers also occur
periodically; check online for details of forthcoming
opportunities.

## Teen Breathe

GMC Publications, 86 High Street, Lewes BN7 1XN
*tel* (01273) 477374
*email* hello@breathemagazine.com
*website* www.teenbreathe.co.uk/submissions
*Publisher* Jonathan Grogan
Bi-monthly £4.99

Tips, exercises and ideas on how to make
mindfulness part of teenagers' lives so that they can
stay positive and improve their wellbeing.
Submissions welcomed from experienced or new
writers, and from illustrators; see website for specific
requirements for each type of potential contributor.

## 2000 AD

Rebellion Publishing, Riverside House, Osney Mead,
Oxford OX2 0ES
*website* www.2000adonline.com

*Twitter* @2000AD
*Instagram* @2000adcomic
Weekly £3.50

Cult science fiction and fantasy comic. Submissions accepted by post only. Founded 1977.

## The Week Junior

Future Publishing Limited, Quay House,
The Ambury, Bath BA1 1UA

*email* hello@theweekjunior.co.uk
*website* https://theweekjunior.co.uk
*Twitter* @theweekjunior
*Instagram* @theweekjunior
*Editorial Director* Anna Bassi
Weekly £3.50

Covers news and events in the UK and internationally for children aged 8–14. Companion publication focusing on science and nature also available.

# Magazines about children's literature and education

Listings of magazines and newspapers for children start on page 264.

## Armadillo

32 Cannon Court Road, Maidenhead SL6 7QN
*email* armadilloeditor@gmail.com
*website* www.armadillomagazine.co.uk
*Facebook* www.facebook.com/Armadillomag
*Twitter* @Armadillomag
*Instagram* @ArmadilloMagazine
*Editor* Louise Ellis-Barrett
4 p.a. Free

Online children's book review magazine including reviews, interviews, features, competitions, profiles and downloadable activities. Free weekly newsletter for subscribers. Weekly blog; daily social media posts; issues posted February, April, June, August, October, December. New reviewers and writers always welcome. Founded 1999.

## Books for Keeps

30 Winton Avenue, London N11 2AT
*tel* 020-8889 1292
*email* andrea@booksforkeeps.co.uk
*website* www.booksforkeeps.co.uk
*Twitter* @BooksforKeeps
*Editor* Andrea Reece
Bi-monthly Free

Children's book review journal including features, reviews and news on the genre. Readership is both professionals and parents. Founded 1980.

## The Bookseller

The Stage Media Company Ltd,
47 Bermondsey Street, London SE1 3XT
*tel* 020-3403 1818
*email* tom.tivnan@thebookseller.com
*website* www.thebookseller.com
*Twitter* @thebookseller
*Editor* Philip Jones, *Deputy Editor* Benedicte Page,
*Managing Editor* Tom Tivnan
Weekly £5.95

Journal of the UK publishing and bookselling trades. The *Children's Bookseller* supplement is published regularly and there is news on the children's book business in the main magazine. Produces the *Children's Buyer's Guide*, which previews children's books to be published in the following six months. The website features news on children's books, comment on the children's sector, author interviews and children's bestseller charts. Founded 1858.

## Children's Bookshelf

Publishers Weekly, 49 West 23 Street, Ninth Floor, New York, NY 10010, USA
*tel* +1 212-377-5500
*email* childrensbooks@publishersweekly.com
*website* www.publishersweekly.com
*Facebook* www.facebook.com/pubweekly
*Twitter* @PWKidsBookshelf
*Children's Books Editor* Diane Roback
Semi-weekly Free

E-newsletter about children's and young adult books. Published under the auspices of *Publishers Weekly*, which was founded in 1872. Children's book news, feature story ideas, new trends and pitches for author or illustrator interviews should be sent to the Editor. Visit website for PW's submission guidelines.

## Educate

National Education Union, Hamilton House, Mabledon Place, London WC1H 9BD
*tel* 020-7380 4708
*email* educate@neu.org.uk
*website* https://neu.org.uk/educate
*Editor* Max Watson
6 p.a. Free to NEU members

Articles, features and news of interest to all those involved in the education sector. Email outline in the first instance. Length: 500 words (single page), 1,000 (double page). Payment: NUJ rates to NUJ members.

## *Inis* – The Children's Books Ireland Magazine

Children's Books Ireland,
17 North Great George Street, Dublin D01 R2F1, Republic of Ireland
*tel* +353 (0)1 8727475
*email* jenny@childrensbooksireland.ie
*website* www.childrensbooksireland.ie
*Editor and Deputy CEO* Jenny Murray
3 p.a. €5

Solely devoted to children's books and the wider world of literature for young people. The three annual print issues each feature forty-four reviews of current or upcoming titles; the features section includes five-six articles, ranging from artist interviews, project overviews or a broader focus on a topic or theme. Each issue is printed in Ireland, distributed to Children's Books Ireland members and is available for individual purchase. Back issues become available online one year after print publication. The archive of back issues is available from childrensbooksireland.ie/our-recommendations. Founded 1989.

## Literacy

UK Literacy Association, Room 9 c/o VAL, 9 Newarke Street, Leicester LE1 5SN
*tel* 0116 254 4116
*website* https://onlinelibrary.wiley.com/journal/17414369
*Editors* Karen Daniels, Sam Duncan, Sinead Harmey, Rachael Levy and Lucy Taylor
3 p.a. Free to UKLA members or £98 p.a.

Official journal of the United Kingdom Literacy Association (see page 331), aimed at those interested in the study and development of literacy. Readership comprises practitioners, teachers, educators, researchers, undergraduate and graduate students. It offers educators a forum for debate through scrutinising research evidence, reflecting on analysed accounts of innovative practice and examining recent policy developments. Length: 2,000–6,000 words (articles). Illustrations: by arrangement. Formerly known as *Reading – Literacy and Language*. Founded 1966.

## Nursery World

MA Education, St Jude's Church, Dulwich Road, London SE24 0PB
*tel* 020-8501 6693
*email* karen.faux@markallengroup.com
*website* www.nurseryworld.co.uk
*Editor* Karen Faux
Fortnightly From £11 per month

For all grades of primary school, nursery and childcare staff, nannies, foster parents and all those concerned with the care of expectant mothers, babies and young children. Authoritative and informative articles, 800 or 1,300 words, and photos on all aspects of child welfare and early education, from 0–8 years, in the UK. Practical ideas, policy news and career advice. No short stories. Illustrations: by arrangement. Payment: by arrangement.

## Publishers Weekly

49 West 23 Street, Ninth Floor, New York, NY 10010, USA
*tel* +1 212-377-5500
*email* childrensbooks@publishersweekly.com
*website* www.publishersweekly.com
*Facebook* www.facebook.com/pubweekly
*Twitter* @PWKidsBookshelf
*Children's Books Editor* Diane Roback

International news magazine for the book industry. Covers all segments involved in the creation, production, marketing and sale of the written word in book, audio, video and electronic formats. In addition to reaching publishers worldwide, it influences all media dealing with the acquisition, sale, distribution and rights of intellectual and cultural properties.

Children's books for review published in the US market, from preschool to young adult, should be sent to Children's Books Reviews; note that all reviews are pre-publication. Also send story suggestions on children's publishing, new trends, author or illustrator interviews, etc for the semi-weekly *Children's Bookshelf* e-newsletter. Founded 1872.

## The School Librarian

School Library Association, 1 Pine Court, Kembrey Park, Swindon SN2 8AD
*tel* (01793) 401154
*email* tsl@sla.org.uk
*website* www.sla.org.uk
Quarterly Free to SLA members, £125 p.a. to others

Official journal of the School Library Association. Articles on news, best practice, education developments, school library management, literacy, publishing, developing reading, research skills and information literacy. Reviews of books, websites and other library resources from preschool to adult. Length: 1,200–1,800 words (articles). Payment: by arrangement. Founded 1937.

## Tes (The Times Educational Supplement)

70 Gray's Inn Road, London WC1X 8NH
*tel* 020-3194 3000
*email* newsdesk@tes.com
*email* features@tes.com
*website* www.tes.com
*Twitter* @tes
*Editor* Jon Severs
Daily £15 per quarter

Education magazine publishing daily online. The latest news, analysis and teaching and learning research for those who work in schools. Specialist knowledge required and ideas should be emailed to the relevant sector editor. Payment: by arrangement. Founded 1910.

## Tess (The Times Educational Supplement Scotland)

70 Gray's Inn Road, London WC1X 8NH
*email* henry.hepburn@tes.com
*website* www.tes.com/magazine/hub/scotland
*Twitter* @TesScotland
*Scotland Editor* Henry Hepburn
Updated daily; see website for subscription options

Online education magazine. Articles on education, preferably 500–600 words, written with special knowledge or experience. News items about Scottish educational affairs, especially those affecting schools. Payment: by arrangement. Founded 1965.

# Stage, screen and audio
## Adapting children's books for stage and screen

Emma Reeves offers her experience of the challenges and rewards of adapting other people's literary creations for the television or stage, with practical advice on securing rights and successfully reimagining and reshaping a story you love in a way that works for the new medium.

If you are a working writer for stage, screen or radio, whether you're writing for children, adults or both, it's highly likely that adaptations will form a regular part of your work – and income. Audio drama, film, TV and theatre have a voracious appetite for valuable IP (intellectual property) and the rights to successful books are fought over ruthlessly. TV companies working in children's television are constantly reading and keeping up with the latest events in children's publishing.

CBBC's two biggest home-grown brands are probably *Horrible Histories* (based on the books by Terry Deary) and *The Dumping Ground*, evolved from *Tracy Beaker Returns* (created by Elly Brewer and Ben Ward), an original TV series which continued the story of Jacqueline Wilson's popular protagonist, Tracy Beaker, and introduced a whole new set of characters and problems. Tracy and her world have now been a vital part of the CBBC landscape for nearly 20 years – yet the CBBC development exec who initially championed Tracy's cause admits that it was an uphill struggle to get the powers that be to buy into the realistic story of a brutally neglected child who experiences bed-wetting, meltdowns, rages and attachment issues as an all-too-plausible result of a heartbreaking upbringing. In the end, Tracy's inimitable spirit – and 20 years of fierce audience loyalty – won the day; but it's worth keeping in mind that, when it comes to commissioning, nothing is ever really a 'no-brainer' – and if you truly believe in an idea, it's probably worth fighting for.

Book adaptations have a strong appeal for TV and theatre producers, who like to have a tangible idea of what they're getting before commissioning a new series or play. This can be frustrating for new writers who are desperate to get their own big new idea out there. It does mean, though, that producers are often looking for the 'right' writer to match with a project, which can be a shortcut to a paid commission. And artistically, it can give you the chance to experience the joy, fear and pain of taking control of a group of beloved characters in a rich, well-realised world.

## Riding the highs and lows

The highs and lows of adaptation are dizzying. It's certainly not easier than original work. If you do happen to find it easier, I will sincerely try to be happy for you, but I enviously suspect that you're doing it wrong. In my personal experience, it doesn't hurt any less to fail as an adapter than as an originator – in fact, it's worse. You haven't just let yourself down, you've betrayed your original author, your guide, your travelling companion, maybe even your hero.

Of course, when things *do* work and people profess to love the resulting show, the Bad Voices in every writer's head lose no time in pointing out that *everything good is because of the original author ... everything bad is* your *fault.* And if those voices should ever abandon you (unlikely), there's always the internet ...

Which brings me to Rule One of adapting – no, Rule One of everything, ever: Never, *ever* search the internet. Just don't do it.

Rule Two: when you inevitably ignore my advice and search the internet – remember, they're just people, like you; maybe too much like you. As a child, I was an obsessive reader, and I still suffer from very strong 'fannish' tendencies. I know very well that there are certain books and authors of which no adaptation will ever satisfy me. The people who are hardest to please are the most devoted. If someone comes down hard on your adaptation, console yourself by imagining the review you'd give to any adaptation of *your* favourite book of all time.

The real high of adaptation is that you get to play inside someone else's incredible creation. And what could be better than that? As a stage adapter, I've been privileged to reimagine childhood favourites – *Little Women, Carrie's War, Anne of Green Gables, Sherlock Holmes, Cool Hand Luke, Doctor Jekyll and Mr Hyde* – and also to discover the work of a new generation of children's writers. I've written for *The Story of Tracy Beaker, Tracy Beaker Returns* and *The Dumping Ground* – all based on Jacqueline Wilson's work – and also worked on both the stage and TV versions of her *Hetty Feather*.

Every experience is different and brings its own challenges. Even within the same medium, there are different types of show. On TV, for example, at one end of the scale is the straight, closed-ended adaptation, where you are expected to more or less follow the story of the book. At the other end of the spectrum is the open-ended drama which may take nothing more from its source material than a few names and a situation, relying on the ingenuity of the script writers to come up with episodic plots. Most TV shows are somewhere in between – perhaps a novel may provide the protagonist's journey for series one, but then it's up to the writers to come up with new material.

## Check out the rights

A lot of my adaptation work has come about through people approaching me. But what if you've fallen in love with an original work and you just have to adapt it or write a sequel? What should you do? Before you type your first words, make sure the rights are available and that you've got a realistic chance of getting them. The only exception is for out-of-copyright material (where the author has been dead for 70 years or more). Otherwise, anything you write without the blessing of the author or their estate is basically fan fiction; you may enjoy it, your friends may enjoy it, but you can never reach a mass audience, and certainly never make any money, unless you want a lawsuit on your hands. So, if you're serious about sharing your vision with the world, check out the rights before doing anything else.

If you have an agent, or an interested production company, they will be able to help you approach the rights-holders. If not, you can search online for the writer's agent or go through the publisher. Bear in mind that the latest hot properties and surprise hits will almost always be optioned already – but options lapse, so it's worth enquiring about the length of the option and trying again at the appropriate time. Read more obscure work in the hope of finding an un-optioned gem.

Despite all this, securing book rights is comparatively easy compared to getting the rights to adapt film or TV shows. This is particularly tricky for lone writers, as TV and film properties tend to have multiple owners and sorting out the various claims requires an army of showbiz lawyers. As a general rule, it's only worth pursuing if you have a major producing force on your side (both to give you credibility and to pay those lawyers' fees!), but there are always exceptions. If you're really passionate about a project and you think you can persuade the rights-holders, go for it. Our business is built on stories of those few lucky people whose tenacity and love for their project enabled them to break all the rules and succeed.

## Reimagining the story

What happens next? A producer friend regularly chides me that he doesn't know why my scripts take so long, when all I have to do is copy down the book and cross out the description. Although I generally laugh bitterly at such comments, adaptation is a broad church and there are some gigs which are perhaps better described as abridging – such as when I worked out a three-hander version of *King Lear* and a four-hander version of *The Importance of Being Earnest* for a small touring company. Although you have to be a bit creative in situations like that, you're working within the intended medium and almost exclusively using the author's original text. At the other end of the scale of fidelity to the original work, I once worked on a children's TV show for two years before anyone informed me that it was actually based on a novel!

These two extremes aside, the job of the adapter is usually to reimagine the story in a way which works for the medium. For example, when I worked on the stage version of *Hetty Feather*, we started with Jacqueline's book and created the show in the rehearsal room with six actors. Using the wealth of material in the book, and even more which was generated by the actors, my job was to steer the story into a coherent structure which would fit into two hours' stage time, streamlining plot moments and making some tough calls about which brilliant bits to jettison. When I wrote episodes of the TV show, I had to come up with self-contained plots lasting half an hour. In the first case I had an overabundance of other people's material to deal with; in the second, it was up to me to tell new stories. People asked if I found it confusing but, to me, the worlds of *Hetty* the book, *Hetty* the stage show and *Hetty* the TV show were so different that I never struggled in that way. In some respects, the medium informs the writing experience possibly more than the original material does.

When you start to adapt a book, you are entering somebody else's world, and meeting their characters. In order to feel comfortable in that world, I always try to read as much of the writer's other work as I can. This may seem like obvious advice, but the benefits are so great that it's worth emphasising. If the author writes a lot about a specific time and place, that's useful for research and background colour. If they are preoccupied with certain ideas or social issues, you can get a greater understanding of where they were coming from when they wrote the book. I have actually transposed scenes from (out-of-copyright!) lesser-known works of authors, in order to illuminate important moments which I felt were glossed over somewhat in the work I was adapting. Cheeky perhaps, but it worked for me.

## Creating the shape

So, you've got a handle on the world and the characters. Everything may be clearly set out for you, or you may need to fill the gaps – or change certain elements. You may discover what you need to change as you go along. At this stage, you take a step back from the source material (and its potentially seductive prose) and ask the normal questions of dramatic writing: Whose story is it? What do they want? Who is trying to stop them getting it?

A specific problem I have encountered is that many beloved books are episodic in nature: this happens, then that happens, then this happens … In drama, stories tend to need ongoing hooks: this happens, SO that happens, SO that happens … I find I need to work hard to create a sense of building drama and inevitability. Also, coincidence feels much harder to mask in drama than in novels. I find myself investigating plot conveniences – are they really just happenstance? Or did someone plan it? If you can decide that the events are the result of someone's plan, it immediately feels easier to dramatise plausibly.

You have to keep your characters active and keep your hooks dangling. Keep your protagonist pushing through to the end. When you're watching previews, or in the edit, try to resist the temptation to keep a 'good bit' in if your gut is screaming at you that it's slowing down the story and risks letting the audience's interest drop. Sometimes that comedy interlude just sits too awkwardly at a moment when the hero has to make a life-or-death choice and risk everything. Sometimes it's time to stop piling torture, misery and despair on a character and let the audience know that they're ready to fight back. As an adapter, you need to take responsibility for the work as a whole – the shape is now up to you. And you may have to keep a mediocre bit at the expense of a good bit if, after a lot of consideration (and discussion with the director, editor or whoever), you realise that that's what the shape of the story needs.

Interestingly, not a word of the paragraph above couldn't also be usefully applied to original drama scripts.

So in summary: enjoy the highs, the fun and the privilege; appreciate the work that other people have done so you don't have to; but if something's not working, don't shrug it off as the original author's problem – look at it from all angles until you find a way to make it work for you. It's the very least that the author deserves. After all, it's probably their name that got you the gig.

**Emma Reeves** is a three times BAFTA-nominated writer. Her credits include adapting numerous Jacqueline Wilson titles, including *My Mum Tracy Beaker*, *The Beaker Girls*, *The Dumping Ground* and *Hetty Feather* (all for the BBC). Other TV credits include *Young Dracula* and a co-created original science fiction show, *Eve*, for CBBC. West End stage adaptations include *The Worst Witch*, *Carrie's War*, *Little Women*, *Hetty Feather* and *Cool Hand Luke*. *The Worst Witch* won the Olivier Award for Best Family Show, while *Hetty Feather* (the stage show) was nominated for an Olivier Award and won the first ever CAMEO award for best page-to-stage adaptation. She is currently Deputy Chair of the Writers' Guild of Great Britain. Follow her on Twitter @emmajanereeves.

# Children's literature on radio, podcast and audio

The technologies for transmitting the spoken word to children are developing rapidly. Neville Teller describes the fast-changing world of radio, podcasting and audio, and explores what a writer for the microphone needs to know to break into this market.

'Read me a story' – one of childhood's perennial cries. Until radio arrived, parents found little relief from it (palming it off on grandma or uncle was perhaps the best bet). But from its very beginning, radio included in its schedules stories read aloud for children. So, for part of the time at least, the loudspeaker was able to provide a fair substitute for mummy or daddy by providing literature, specially prepared for performance at the microphone, read by professional actors.

Very early on, actors learned that performing at the microphone was a new skill – the techniques were specialised and quite different from those required on the stage. Writers, too, had to acquire a whole range of new skills in preparing material for radio. Two things quickly became apparent. First, the time taken to read a complete book on the air would be far too long to be acceptable, and in consequence most books would need to be abridged. Second, literature simply read aloud from the printed page often failed to 'come across' to a listening audience, because material produced to be scanned by the eye is often basically unsuited to the requirements of the microphone.

Today there are two main outlets in this country for aspiring writers for children in the radio/podcasting sphere: online radio/audio/podcasts and audiobook publishers. How has this market reached its present position?

## Radio/podcast

Children's radio in the UK came into existence in December 1922, just a few weeks after the BBC itself was born, and for some 40 years the daily *Children's Hour* became an established and much-cherished feature of life.

However, in the 1960s the imminent death of radio was a generally accepted prognostication. Starting in 1961, in the belief that television was their preferred medium, children's radio was slowly but surely strangled.

The demise of children's radio naturally evoked a massive groundswell of protest. In response the BBC of the day did grant some sort of reprieve. *Story Time* – a programme of abridged radio readings – started life in the old *Children's Hour* slot with a strong bias towards children's literature. It was not long, however, before more general literature began to be selected, and finally, in 1982, that programme too was dropped. For the next 20 years the only regular children's programme left on BBC radio was *Listen with Mother*, the 15-minute slot for the under-fives.

Early in the new millennium, the BBC – moved, doubtless, by mounting evidence of the undiminished popularity of radio – decided to reintroduce a regular programme for children. All they could offer at the time was a 30-minute programme each Sunday evening on Radio 4 called *Go4It*, a magazine-type show which included a ten-minute reading, and I found myself abridging books for it like *The Lion, the Witch and the Wardrobe* by

C.S. Lewis and *The Wolves of Willoughby Chase* by Joan Aiken. Unfortunately, this renaissance was typically short-lived. *Go4It* was axed on 24 May 2009.

But the door had been pushed ajar, and in the autumn of 2002, when the BBC launched its new digital radio channel, BBC7, its schedules included, as a basic ingredient, daily programmes for children incorporating readings from children's literature, both current and classic. I prepared a considerable number of books for these programmes, including not only classical children's literature like *Robinson Crusoe* and *The Prince and the Pauper*, but also more general classics like *20,000 Leagues Under the Sea* and *Oliver Twist*. The programme for older children also featured up-to-the-moment favourites such as Anthony Horowitz's series about his boy secret agent, Alex Rider, the *Artemis Fowl* novels by Eoin Colfer, Terry Pratchett's *A Hat Full of Sky* and *The Amazing Maurice* and Jackie French's *Callisto* series. For younger listeners, I abridged books like the *Whizziwig* series by Malorie Blackman, the *Lily Quench* books by Natalie Jane Prior and Kaye Umansky's *The Silver Spoon of Solomon Snow*.

All seemed set fair, but towards the end of 2006 came news of major changes. The programme for younger listeners was converted into a radio extension of CBeebies, the BBC's digital television channel for the youngest children, while the BBC7 schedule included readings drawn from the programme's extensive archive, including my own abridgements of, among many others, *Bootleg* by Alex Shearer, *Stop the Train* by Geraldine McCaughrean, *Huckleberry Finn* by Mark Twain, *Slaves of the Mastery* and *Firesong* by William Nicholson, *Stig of the Dump* by Clive King, *The BFG* by Roald Dahl, *The Little House on the Prairie* by Laura Ingalls Wilder, *Dream Master* by Theresa Breslin and *Point Blanc* by Anthony Horowitz.

Nothing lasts for ever, and 2011 saw BBC7 transformed into BBC Radio 4 Extra. With the transformation came a new shape to children's radio – almost a return to the *Children's Hour* concept of yesteryear, *The Four O'Clock Show* always including abridged readings of children's literature. Among the specially commissioned readings I abridged *Chitty Chitty Bang Bang Flies Again* by Frank Cottrell Boyce, *Wonder* by R.J. Palacio and *Maggot Moon* by Sally Gardner.

Sadly, *The Four O'Clock Show* too succumbed to the rapidly changing technological needs of its audience. 30 April 2015 saw its final transmission. The axing of this hour of dedicated children's radio meant that there is no longer any children's programming on Radio 4 Extra, and its service licence has been amended to remove its commitment to the content.

However, the BBC is providing three online streams of children's programmes. CBeebies Radio is a daily web-based radio show for preschool children. They can either listen online on BBC Sounds through the CBeebies Radio Player or download and keep the podcast, choosing when and where is best for them to listen.

Meanwhile BBC Sounds has built up an impressive selection of radio programmes under its genre category 'Children's', including readings and drama. Audio productions provided online to be downloaded and retained are now generally known as podcasts. Find BBC Sounds podcasts for children at www.bbc.co.uk/sounds/category/childrens. In addition, the BBC provides CBeebies Radio, a web-based radio programme for children, and also a dedicated online service for 3–5 year-olds via its School Radio programme. The range of podcasts available for download can be found at https://www.bbc.co.uk/programmes/p007g5y4.

In addition to the BBC, there is a national digital radio station dedicated entirely to children aged 6–12. Fun Kids is a nationwide 18-station digital multiplex whose content is also available via its website (www.funkidslive.com). Its podcasts and videos include stories, drama and educational material. Storyline Online (https://storylineonline.net) provides readings from a wide range of children's books.

All these outlets require dedicated writers for children, prepared to adapt existing, or provide new, material in audio format specifically for young listeners.

## Audiobooks

Audiobooks are literary works of all types, read by actors and available as CDs or as downloads from the internet. For some years, audiobooks had been the fastest growing area of consumer publishing in the UK. Nielsen's most recent survey predicted audiobook sales totalling nearly 27 million units in 2022, valued at around £182m. This is compared to 26 million units in 2021, 23 million in 2020 and 18 million in 2019. A survey of the American audiobook market found 61% of parents saying their children listen to audiobooks, up from 35% in 2020.

Audible dominates the audiobook market and its sales are booming, but it faces growing competition from newcomers such as audiobooks.com, Kobo and BookBeat, as well as Google and Apple. Current estimates put the children's share of the market at 40% of the total.

The BBC's audio output, including the large and flourishing children's backlist, is now marketed through outlets such as Audible and Random House.

Nowadays, it is common for major publishers to launch a fair number of their new books, including books for older children, in printed and audiobook form simultaneously. Publishers of books for younger children often adopt the 'twin pack' concept – packaging book and audiobook together – so that children can read and listen at the same time. Such products are zero-rated for VAT. However VAT at 20% is still being charged on audiobooks; the UK book industry has mounted a campaign to have it removed.

## How children listen

The ways in which children listen to the readings intended especially for them are multiplying at what seems an ever-increasing rate. In addition to online radio heard via digital radio sets, computers, smartphones, tablets and smart speakers like Alexa, primary school teachers download BBC School podcasts and play them back in class.

Downloads are a growing method for children to access audiobooks especially for them. There are a range of online outlets, including Audible and Apple iTunes through its audiobooks ttore. Taken together, these DTO (download to own) providers have available an enormous and expanding list of children's books, and stories are proving a popular second-best to music for many children. Subscribers pay either a monthly fee for the right to download a specific number of titles or pay for downloads book by book. However, these days a surprising number of websites are offering free downloads of children's stories. One US website lists no less than 62 online sites from which children can download stories at no cost. The UK also has a fair number of such sites, including those run by the *Independent*, Storynory, Mashable, Oxford University Press and OpenCulture.

Amazon has some 30,000 children's audiobooks available to be purchased and downloaded. Users can start listening within seconds, transfer the audiobook to a Kindle, computer, tablet, iPod or other device, or burn it to a CD. Other specialist providers of audiobooks for children include Children's Storybooks Online (www.magickeys.com/books) and the Story Home (www.thestoryhome.com). All commission new stories for children.

Young people are increasingly accessing not only their social networks via their smartphones, but also audiobooks. Google, Amazon and Audible are providing access to audiobooks via the mobile phone, and other providers are crowding into the marketplace.

Amazon's ebook readers, the Kindle and Kindle Fire (which offers a colour touchscreen), have been runaway successes. The Kindle can download a book in about 30 seconds, either to be read on its 6-inch wide screen or to be read aloud to you (albeit in a somewhat robot-like voice). However audiobooks can also be downloaded, though the process is easier on the later versions of Kindle.

Kindle's biggest rivals as a non-print reading device are Kobo and Nook, and its growing number of tablet competitors, all of which can download audiobooks speedily, and have loudspeaker and headphone facilities.

In-car MP3 playback, via the car radio, now widely available, is becoming increasingly popular as a means of keeping children happy on long journeys. Children's audiobooks are also now part of in-flight entertainment on long-haul flights.

A recent phenomenon is 'podiobooks', or podcast audiobook novels, released on the internet in instalments and for free. They are commonly offered together with a range of stickers, ringtones and wallpapers – all designed to appeal to the younger market. The pioneer is Scott Sigler, whose website (https://scottsigler.com) offers free audio fiction, together with videos, ebooks and blog posts via social media. The whole concept is aimed particularly at teenagers and young people.

The message of all this for writers is that the radio/audio/podcast market is mushrooming, and that burgeoning technological developments and innovations seem designed to appeal particularly to the internet-savvy younger generations. If you are keen to break into the rapidly changing world of children's literature on radio and audio, this seems as favourable and opportune a time to succeed as ever. For contact details for children's radio, see *Children's television and radio* (page 284) or search online for children's audiobook publishers, and offer your services. Do not be discouraged by initial rejection – that is often a writer's early experience. Persevere. As in all professional fields, the tyro is faced with the classic catch-22 situation: radio producers and audio publishers are reluctant to offer commissions to people without a track record, while it is of course impossible to gain a track record without having won a commission or two. The only advice is to keep plugging away, hoping for that elusive lucky break – and the only consolation on offer is that even the most experienced of today's professionals was once a complete novice.

## Writing for the microphone

What of the techniques that need to be applied in converting material produced for the printed page into a script that can be performed by an actor with ease at the microphone, and bring real listening pleasure to the child at the other end?

Getting to grips with abridging books for the microphone requires, in the first instance, the application of some simple arithmetic. Take a book of around 70,000 words. CDs can accommodate some 70 minutes of airtime, which translates to about 10,500 words. So a 140-minute abridgement presented in the form of two CDs will allow the abridger about

21,000 words. Where the writer is called on to abridge specifically for download, the audiobook publishers will specify the length either in terms of time or wordage. Remember, an actor can normally get through about 2,200 words in 15 minutes.

What makes a good abridgement? To reproduce the sense of an original in fewer words while, in addition and quite as important, to retain the character of the original writing. That demands the capacity to respond sympathetically to the feel of an author's style and to be able to preserve it, even when large chunks of the original are being cut away.

How much liberty is the abridger allowed in translating the printed to the spoken word, while reducing the wordage? Some audiobook producers ask for the minimum of interference with the published text; some radio producers are content for the abridger to adapt the original freely, so as to enhance the actor's performance at the microphone. The different approaches reflect the fact that, in acquiring radio reading rights, the BBC retains editorial independence over the final product, while the granting of abridged audio rights is often conditional on the original writer's approval of the abridged text. So audio producers, reluctant to run the risk of rejection, sometimes allow the abridger very little freedom.

Nevertheless it is an undoubted fact that the requirements of eye and of ear do not always coincide, and that a message easily absorbed from the printed page can become surprisingly garbled if transmitted unamended at the microphone.

In crafting a radio/audio script, the needs of the listener must be one of the prime considerations. The needs of the actor who will read it at the microphone are another. The writer must keep in the forefront of their mind the fact that the script has to be performed. The words must, as Hamlet says, 'flow trippingly on the tongue'. With audio the listener is in control, and can switch on or off whenever convenient.

It is essential that the abridger of children's books reproduces, as far as possible, the plot, atmosphere and character of the original. The aim must be to leave the listener with as complete a feeling of the original book as possible, given the technical limitations of time and wordage. It is, in short, an essential aspect of the radio/audio writer's craft to keep faith with the author.

**Neville Teller** MBE has been contributing to BBC radio for over 50 years. He is credited with over 250 abridgements for radio readings, 50 radio dramatisations and 300 audiobook abridgements. His publications include *5-Minute Bedtime Stories*, based on classic children's tales he wrote for BBC radio. His radio dramatisation of *Ozma of Oz* by Frank Baum, broadcast across the USA, was included in his book *Audio Drama: 10 Plays for Radio and Podcast*. Included in his second book of radio plays, *Audio Drama 2*, is his dramatisation of the Zane Gray classic *Riders of the Purple Range*, also broadcast in the USA and Canada. Recent projects include his abridgement of *Bulldog Drummond* by Sapper, and *The First Men in the Moon* by H.G. Wells, both broadcast on BBC Radio 4 Extra. His own radio play *Little Boy Lost* was broadcast in 2022. He is a past chairman of the Society of Authors' Broadcasting Committee and of the Audiobook Publishing Association's Contributors' Committee. He was made an MBE in 2006 for 'services to broadcasting and to drama'.

## See also...
- *Children's audio publishers*, page 67
- *Children's television and radio*, page 284

Stage, screen and audio

# Writing for visual broadcast media

Jayne Kirkham shares her experience of writing for the ever-changing world of children's broadcast media, confident that the writer's role remains essentially unchanged: the writer needs to tell a story with characters and concepts that their audience will remember and love all their lives.

'Writing for kids' telly? Easy! I mean ... how hard can it be?'

So says someone who doesn't write for children. For a start, are kids actually watching a telly? If you watch much children's content (and, if you're interested in writing for children, you should) you'll know they are more likely to be watching YouTube on a phone. Depending on what it is, you may be even more inclined to think, 'No, seriously, how hard can it be?'. But what looks so simple has been put through a furnace of development: even a two-minute TikTok, if money is involved somehow, will have been shaped, moulded, reshaped, possibly with a good deal of firing, before it is finally hammered into something that perfectly suits a broadcaster's or platform's particular audience. And that audience is very particular; children have all the myriad tastes and genre preferences of adults but with the different stages of a child's personal, social and physical development thrown in. Furthermore, the content has to be fun or, as kids in a 2019 report put it, 'amazing/cool/excellent' (*Social Media, Television and Children Report 2019* by University of Sheffield, BBC Children's and Dubit). Even the serious stuff must engage or children simply won't watch.

When I started writing for children's TV, it was a hugely competitive but fairly straightforward world to navigate, with only a handful of broadcasters and producers that commissioned shows. If you went to the Children's Media Conference (CMC; or Showcomotion, as it was called then), you could fit everyone you needed to meet into one room. Nowadays, if you go to the Children's Media Conference (and if you're interested in writing for children, you should), everyone you need to meet will still be there – but that 'everyone' covers not just TV but online, games, books, apps and toys! Changes in children's media policy, and advances in technology, mean that children and young people have never known anything but access to content (what used to be called 'programmes') whenever and wherever they like, and in all sorts of formats. They might watch something on TV while accessing extra information about it on their tablet and simultaneously playing along on their phone; what's more, they are making and broadcasting their own content.

To write professionally, this looks like a much harder, more bewildering world to get into. But actually, whatever innovations arise and throw the industry into flux, for a writer the basics remain the same: know your audience and know how to tell a story, with characters and concepts that kids will remember and love all their lives. If you know your audience, you will know what they are watching and where. You will understand that they prefer to watch their content on YouTube rather than CBBC, and you will be aware of the growth of Sky Kids, TikTok, smart speakers and whatever new players are on the scene by the time you read this.

For a writer, things haven't changed as much as everyone would have us believe; children still enjoy drama, comedy, animation, game shows, documentaries and news made by professional media companies. Those companies need writers like you and me, but getting in touch with them can take a bit of detective work – and a decent pause button, so that you can read a programme's credits properly. Another source of information is the programme's entry on www.imdb.com (International Movie Database). Once you know the name of the production company, you can do an online search for their website where you can generally find contact details for particular producers and/or development departments. Before you contact anyone about writing for them, however, find out as much as you can about the producers, production companies and their intellectual properties (IP). What have they made in the past? What are they developing now? What do they want to develop? Remember, the show that you have just watched and enjoyed will probably have been written two years before; what are they doing now?

The children's channels or platforms also have websites you can explore. By 'platforms', I'm referring to online providers such as Disney+, Netflix, Amazon, Apple TV, Azoomee and Hopster, as well as the public service broadcasters (BBC, ITV, Channel 4 and Five) and the commercial digital channels (Nickelodeon, Pop, Cartoon Network, Disney, etc). To get beyond the shiny, public pages of games and fan chat, enter words like 'producer guidelines' or 'commissioning' into your search engine; you need to find the broadcasters' business pages which show what they are looking for. Remember, each channel/platform has its own brand identity, catering for a specific audience. Make sure you know the difference between a Nickelodeon and a Netflix show.

An easy way to compare and contrast the different platforms is to attend a trade event, such as the Children's Media Conference held in Sheffield every July (www.thechildrensmediaconference.com). There are other conferences and festivals, but the CMC is the best for UK children's media professionals; all the significant platforms and broadcasters attend and hold commissioning sessions where they explain what they want to produce in the next few years. It's also a great opportunity to meet producers and other professionals you may want to collaborate with or work for, with lots of time in the conference schedule for networking. While attending in person is best, it is possible to attend online if money and time are limited.

Having enjoyed a few years' respite from underfunding and lack of political support (thanks to the campaigning of organisations such as the Children's Media Foundation, and the WGGB (Writers' Guild of Great Britain; see page 300)), children's media is once more facing difficult times; government funds have been cut, advertising restrictions and other threats to the public service broadcasters (BBC, ITV, C4 and C5) are making it increasingly difficult to finance content. If you've been watching the credits carefully (and if you're interested in writing for children, you should), you will have noticed that very few shows are the product of one producer and one broadcaster. With the multinational streamers and international co-production as the norm, this means the writing has to appeal to an international audience. It can also mean that you are competing not just with British writers but writers from overseas. Rather than despair, let this open your eyes to other markets and territories. Countries like China, Brazil, India and many others have looked to the UK for writing talent in recent years. Annual international conferences, such as the Children's Media Conference here in the UK mentioned above, MIPJUNIOR in Cannes (www.mipjunior.com) and Kidscreen in Miami (http://kidscreen.com), are great places to meet international companies face to face. Attending these can be costly and time-consuming – it's easier and cheaper to subscribe to their regular newsletters for excellent insider information that you can follow up.

Stage, screen and audio

Working for an overseas company is one of the few reasons why a screenwriter might need an agent. I know a good number of non-agented writers working in the UK on existing shows; the contracts are generally straightforward and many follow WGGB guidelines. But when I have had overseas commissions, I've been grateful to have an agent used to dealing with other territories – not least getting the exchange rate and tax implications right.

It surely must be the dream of every screenwriter to get their own show produced. When the traditional broadcasters were the only players in town, new shows were generally commissioned from writers who had already proven themselves on other series. To get their ideas on screen, writers were dependent on the broadcaster's own producers or independent production companies and they often lost much creative control. The internet has created many more routes by which entrepreneurial writers can now reach their intended audience; for example, *Night Zookeeper* – now available on Sky Kids – started as a web-based teaching aid to encourage children to start writing their own stories.

However, no matter how you intend to get your idea in front of your audience, it needs to go through the same rigorous development process: interrogating the concept and the characters to make sure that it is age-appropriate and will engage the audience utterly, not just in its main format but also in different 'transmedia' guises (as an app, books, in social media, videogames). And don't forget to consider toys and other merchandising, as appropriate. Different genres will, of course, have different opportunities and limitations. A drama like *The Beaker Girls* is unlikely to sell as many lunchboxes as, say, preschool animation *Paw Patrol*, but that doesn't mean it shouldn't get made. Just remember to allow the potential revenue returns to determine the budget. Rather confusingly, industry people tend to bandy the term 'genre' in their own special way, using it to describe animation, drama, preschool or comedy. If you watch enough kids' content, you will know that nearly all dramas have a lot of comedy, that animation covers everything from wacky shorts to sitcoms to intense re-enactments for documentaries, and that preschool covers everything but in a way that's appropriate for the under-sixes. As I've mentioned, the specific requirements for each broadcaster/platform brand should be available on their websites.

Once you have sufficiently developed your idea – and in that development I would include writing some sample scripts to fully prove whether your idea works or not – and have researched the market, it is time to get it out there. Does your intended recipient give guidelines on submitting your IP? They may ask you to use an online submission portal. If there are no guidelines, write a brief email introducing yourself and your project as succinctly as possible. Can you pitch it in one sentence? Can you explain the series on a single sheet of A4 paper? Do you have a decent sample script to show off your writing talents? Some producers are wary of unsolicited attachments, so you may want to start with just the email and then follow up when they have responded. Again, be led by their specific guidelines.

If you have the opportunity to pitch in person, practise! These are very busy people, so clarity and passion are essential for you and your idea to stand out. Show that you know your audience and any business or creative constraints: how easy would it be to animate your idea? Would young actors be able to deliver your stunts? The first time I pitched in person, I was a quivering jelly and just about as coherent. But – you know what? – I wasn't eaten, and the world didn't end. It sounds silly, but producers and commissioners are people and, in this industry, they're usually lovely people at that.

Being realistic, it is unlikely that your first project will get picked up. The thing to remember is that this is a business and your IP is a commodity and your skills are a service for hire so don't take rejection personally. There is a lot to learn, so learn it; take feedback when it is offered and get better. It can feel galling to take what feels like a barrage of criticism from a '12-year-old' executive, but that '12 year-old' will know better than you do what works on their platform. And they may well be in a position to offer you work on another show. It happens. There can be many reasons why an executive doesn't like your project, but that doesn't mean they don't like you or your style of writing. They may not get back to you. But then again, I was once called out of the blue by a producer who had rejected an idea of mine several years before; I ended up writing an animation series and a feature film (and, while the feature is in interminable 'pre-production', I still enjoy the residual fees from the international sales of the TV series).

The best advice I was ever given as a new writer was that you only fail when you give up. So keep on writing; keep on submitting; keep on keeping on.

**Jayne Kirkham** is a screenwriter and a script and development consultant. With over 30 years' experience working with and writing for children and young people, she has worked on a wide range of theatre, film, TV, radio and online scripts, ranging in size from small conservation films in Africa to international feature films. She taught at the Northern Film School for 14 years, and is a member of the board of directors of the Children's Media Foundation. See her website https://jaynekirkham.com for more information.

# Children's television and radio

The information in this section has been compiled as a general guide for writers, artists, agents and publishers to the major companies and key contacts operating within the children's broadcasting industry. As personnel, corporate structures and commissioning guidelines can change frequently, please check the relevant websites for the most up-to-date information.

## REGULATION

### Advertising Standards Authority

Castle House, 37–45 Paul Street, London EC2A 4LS
*tel* 020-7492 2222
*website* www.asa.org.uk
*Facebook* www.facebook.com/adauthority
*Twitter* @ASA_UK
*Chief Executive* Guy Parker

The UK's independent regulator of advertising across all media. Its work includes acting on complaints and taking action against misleading, harmful or offensive advertisements.

### Ofcom

Riverside House, 2A Southwark Bridge Road, London SE1 9HA
*tel* 020-7981 3000, 0300 123 3000
*website* www.ofcom.org.uk
*Facebook* www.facebook.com/ofcom
*Twitter* @Ofcom
*Chief Executive* Melanie Dawes

Accountable to parliament and exists to further the interests of consumers by balancing choice and competition with the duty to encourage plurality, protect viewers and listeners, promote diversity in the media and ensure full and fair competition between communications providers.

## TELEVISION

### BabyTV

Baby Network Ltd, 3 Queen Caroline Street, Hammersmith, London W6 9PE
*email* info@babytvchannel.com
*website* www.babytv.com
*Facebook* www.facebook.com/BabyTVChannel
*Twitter* @BabyTVChannel

The world's leading baby and toddler network, for children under five and their parents, airing 24 hours a day and completely ad-free. BabyTV features top-quality shows created by child development experts, designed for child and parent to enjoy together.

### The BBC

BBC Broadcasting House, Portland Place, London W1A 1AA
*website* www.bbc.co.uk
*Director, Children's & Education* Patricia Hidalgo

Reina, *Head of Children's Content & Programming Strategy* Anna Taganov

The world's largest broadcasting organisation, with a remit to provide programmes that inform, educate and entertain. Established by Royal Charter, the BBC is a public service broadcaster funded by a licence fee. The Children's Director is responsible for the overall direction and management of all of the BBC's services for children, including CBeebies and CBBC channels and their websites.

### Commissioning

CBeebies and CBBC are self-commissioning and self-scheduling, and proposals may be submitted at any time throughout the year. All submissions for TV and online should be made via Pitch. For further details and commissioning guidelines visit:
    www.bbc.co.uk/commissioning/childrens
    www.bbc.co.uk/commissioning/childrens/0-6
    www.bbc.co.uk/commissioning/childrens/7-12
    www.bbc.co.uk/commissioning/pitch
    https://pitch.bbc.co.uk
  **BBC Cymru Wales** *Director* Rhuanedd Richards, *Head of Commissioning* Nick Andrews, *Commissioners* Christina Macaulay, Sian Harris, Paul Forde, Sorelle Neil
  **BBC Scotland** *Director* Stephen Carson, *Head of Multiplatform Commissioning* Louise Thornton, *Commissioners* Gareth Hydes, David Harron, Tony Nellany, Gavin Smith, Steve Allen, Gaynor Holmes, Muslim Alim, Ishbel Maclennan (Gaelic programming)
  **BBC Northern Ireland** *Senior Head of Content Comissioning* Eddie Doyle, *Comissioning executives* Fiona Keane (Ulster-Scots), Justin Binding, Karen Kirby (Irish Language)

### CBeebies

*website* www.bbc.co.uk/cbeebies

*Twitter* @CBeebiesHQ

*Head of Commissioning & Acquisitions (0–6)* Kate Morton, *Commissioning Editors (0–6)* Beth Gardiner, Julia Bond, *Commissioning Executives (0–6)* Joel Wilenius, Nick Hall, Dan Flint

CBeebies offers mixed genre output for TV, online and radio and is specifically produced for a young audience using a variety of formats including live action and animation. Content covers drama, comedy, entertainment and factual, and the target audience is children aged 0–6 years. CBeebies is on air daily from 6am–7pm.

## CBBC

*website* www.bbc.co.uk/cbbc

*Twitter* @cbbc

*Head of Commissioning & Acquisitions (7–12)* Sarah Mueller, *Senior Commissioning Editor (7–12)* Melissa Hardinge, *Commissioning Editors (7–12)* Kez Margrie, Amy Buscombe, *Commissioning Executives* Aubrey Clarke, Jo Allen

Online only from 2023, content covers drama, factual, comedy, entertainment, animation and news. The target audience is children aged 6–12 years.

## BBC Writersroom

*email* writersroom@bbc.co.uk

*website* www.bbc.co.uk/writersroom

*Facebook* www.facebook.com/BBCWriters

*Twitter* @bbcwritersroom

BBC Writersroom is a cross-genre department for scripted content, working with drama, comedy, CBeebies, CBBC, radio, online and others. It is the first port of call at the BBC for unsolicited scripts and new writers. Visit the website to discover:

• new opportunities for writers;
• writing tips and success stories;
• interviews and top tips from writers;
• competitions and events.
  The BBC Writersroom blog provides a wealth of behind-the-scenes commentary from writers and producers who have worked on BBC TV and radio programmes: www.bbc.co.uk/blogs/writersroom.

## Channel 4

124–126 Horseferry Road, London SW1P 2TX
*tel* 0345 076 0191
*website* www.channel4.com
*Facebook* www.facebook.com/Channel4
*Twitter* @Channel4
*Chief Executive* Alex Mahon
*Chief Content Officer* Ian Katz

A publicly owned television network that is freely available to all in the UK. Its commercially-funded, publicly owned structure enables all profit generated to be directly reinvested back into its public service remit. As a publisher-broadcaster, Channel 4 commissions UK content from the independent production sector and currently works with over 300 creative companies across the UK every year. It provides a digital streaming service, All 4, and a network of 12 television channels, aiming to create change by representing unheard voices and reinventing entertainment.
  Channel 4 is required to broadcast 330 hours of schools programmes every year. It focuses on content which tackles isuues and builds life skills relevant to those aged 10–19 years.

4Skills supports people to build their careers in the media industry across a range of disciplines. Visit https://careers.channel4.com/4skills.

## Commissioning

Information about commissioning and related processes and guidelines can be found at www.channel4.com/info/commissioning. Email addresses for most individuals named below can be found on the relevant parts of the website under 4Producers.

**Factual Entertainment**

*Head of Factual Entertainment* Alf Lawrie, *Commissioning Editors* Ian Dunkley, Lee McMurray, Daniel Fromm, Tim Hancock, Vivienne Molokwu, Luke Mcfarlane, Cal Turner

## Channel 5

17–29 Hawley Crescent, Camden Town, London NW1 8TT
*tel* 020-3580 3600
*website* www.channel5.com
*Facebook* www.facebook.com/channel5uk
*Twitter* @channel5_tv
*Director of Programming* Ben Frow

Channel 5 brands include Channel 5, 5Star, 5USA and 5Select, and an on-demand service, My5. Channel 5 broadcasts over 24 hours of children's programmes every week under the Milkshake! brand, which is aimed at children aged 2–5 years and airs daily from 6–9.15am (10am at weekends). Channel 5 commissions, co-produces and acquires preschool programming through a wide range of deals and arrangements.

## Commissioning

**Children's Programming: Milkshake!**

*General Manager Kids & Family* Louise Bucknole

## CITV

2 Waterhouse Square, 138–142 Holborn, London EC1N 2AE
*website* www.itv.com/watch/categories/children
*Facebook* www.facebook.com/childrensitv
*Chief Executive* Carolyn McCall

ITV is the UK's largest commercial TV network. The ITV network is responsible for the commissioning, scheduling and marketing of network programmes on ITV1 and its digital channel portfolio including ITV2, ITV3, ITV4, ITVBe and CITV. CITV is online only from Autumn 2023. Commissions and acquires a variety of programmes, including live action and animation, aimed at children up to age 12 years.

## Commissioning

*website* www.itv.com/commissioning/articles/citv-nbdhkx05-ckc52cce

See website for information about commissioning and how to submit an idea.

## Disney Channel UK

*website* www.disneyplus.com/en-gb/
*Facebook* www.facebook.com/DisneyPlusUK
*Twitter* @DisneyPlusUK
*President* Alisa Bowen

Channels run by the Walt Disney Company specialising in programming for children from preschoolers to teens. There are three channels: Disney Channel (9–17 years), Disney Junior (1–8 years) and Disney XD (6–11 years). They are available through the Disney+ subscription streaming service.

## Nickelodeon UK

17–29 Hawley Crescent, London NW1 8TT
*email* letterbox@nick.co.uk
*website* www.nick.co.uk
*Facebook* www.facebook.com/NickelodeonUK
*Twitter* @NickelodeonUK

Nickelodeon UK comprises of three channels with a target audience spanning children aged approximately 2–12 years: Nickelodeon aimed at children aged 2–12 years, NickToons (www.nicktoons.co.uk) aimed at children aged 7–11 years and NickJr (www.nickjr.co.uk) aimed at children aged 2–5 years.

## POP

Narrative Entertainment UK, 35 Inverness Street, London NW1 7HB
*email* info@popfun.co.uk
*website* www.popfun.co.uk

A free-to-air children's channel that broadcasts cartoons and live-action series for children aged 6–10 years. Has two sister channels.

## Tiny Pop

*email* info@tinypop.co.uk

*website* www.tinypop.com

*Twitter* @TinyPopTV

Cartoons and live action series for children aged 3–7 years.

## Pop Max

*website* www.popfun.co.uk/pop-max

Cartoons, sci-fi, action and anime for children aged 7–15 years.

## RTÉ

Donnybrook, Dublin 4, Republic of Ireland
*tel* +353 (0)20 83434
*email* info@rte.ie
*website* www.rte.ie
*Facebook* www.facebook.com/RTEjr
*Twitter* @RTEjr

RTÉ offers a comprehensive range of programmes for children and young people. RTÉjr broadcasts original and acquired live-action and animated content for children aged 2–7 years, airing each day from 7am–9pm. Additional content is made available on demand and online, as well as through RTÉjr radio. TRTÉ is aimed at children aged 7–15 and airs on RTÉ2.

## Commissioning

*Director of Content* Jim Jenning

*Deputy Director of Content* Niamh O'Connor

*Group Head of Arts & Culture* Ann-Marie Power

*Group Head of Cláracha Gaeilge (Irish Programs)* Niamh Ní Churnáin

*Acting Head of Drama* David Crean

*Group Head of Entertainment & Music* Alan Tyler

*Group Head of Factual* Sean MacGiollaPhadraig

*Group Head of Sport* Declan McBennett

*Head of Children's & Young People's Content* Suzanne Kelley

*Executive Producer* Eimear O'Mahony

*website* https://about.rte.ie/commissioning/commissioning-briefs/rte-young-peoples

See website for information about commissioning and submitting proposals for children and young people.

## S4C

Canolfan S4C Yr Egin, Carmarthen SA31 3EQ
*tel* 0370 600 4141
*website* www.s4c.cymru/en
*Facebook* www.facebook.com/S4C
*Twitter* @S4C

S4C is the world's only Welsh language TV channel, broadcasting programmes on sport, drama, music, factual, entertainment and culture. Cyw, a programming block for children aged 3–6 years, broadcasts every weekday from 6am–12pm. Stwnsh, a programming block for children aged 7–13 years, broadcasts every weekday from 4–6pm and on Saturdays from 9–11am.

# ORGANISATIONS CONNECTED TO TELEVISION BROADCASTING

## BARB

20 Orange Street, London WC2H 7EF
*email* enquiries@barb.co.uk
*website* www.barb.co.uk
*Twitter* @BARBtelevision
*Chief Executive* Justin Sampson

The Broadcasters Audience Research Board is the official source of viewing figures in the UK.

## Ipsos MORI

3 Thomas More Square, London E1W 1YW
*tel* 020-3059 5000

*website* www.ipsos.com/en-uk
*Twitter* @IpsosUK
*Ceo* Ben Page

One of the UK's leading research companies: conducts surveys for a wide range of major organisations (such as BARB and RAJAR), as well as for other market research agencies.

## Public Media Alliance

Room 02.101, Lawrence Stenhouse Building, University of East Anglia, Norwich NR4 7TJ
*tel* (01603) 592335
*email* info@publicmediaalliance.org
*website* www.publicmediaalliance.org
*Twitter* @PublicMediaPMA
*Ceo* Kristian Porter

World's largest association of public broadcasters. Provides advocacy, support, knowledge exchange, research and training opportunities for public media worldwide.

## Royal Television Society

3 Dorset Rise, London EC4Y 8EN
*tel* 020-7822 2810
*email* info@rts.org.uk
*website* www.rts.org.uk
*Facebook* www.facebook.com/RoyalTelevisionSociety
*Twitter* @RTS_media
*Ceo* Theresa Wise

An educational charity promoting the art and science of television and the leading forum for discussion and debate on all aspects of the TV community.

## RADIO

## BBC School Radio

*website* www.bbc.co.uk/schoolradio

BBC School Radio provides audio resources for primary schools including podcasts, downloads, audio and video clips, learning resources and teachers' notes that are curriculum-linked to Key Stages 1, 2, 3 and 4. Some Early Years Foundation Stage (EYFS) resources are also available.

## CBeebies Radio

*website* www.bbc.co.uk/cbeebies/radio

CBeebies Radio is aimed at encouraging preschool children to develop their listening skills. In addition to radio output, the website contains games, songs, make & colour and story-time activities.

## Fun Kids

*website* www.funkidslive.com

A British children's digital radio station (not national) providing programming to entertain children aged 7–12 years with a mixture of songs, stories, competitions and news. Fun Kids Jnr provides content for children under 7. Available to listen via the website or on DAB Digital Radio across London and south east England.

## ORGANISATIONS CONNECTED TO RADIO BROADCASTING

## Media.info

*email* info@media.info
*website* https://media.info/uk

This website provides detailed listings of UK radio stations alongside information about TV, newspapers, magazines and media ownership in the UK.

## The Radio Academy

Suite 303, Pill Box Studios, 115 Coventry Road, London E2 6GH
*tel* 0800 044 3811
*email* info@radioacademy.org
*website* www.radioacademy.org
*Facebook* www.facebook.com/radioacademy
*Twitter* @radioacademy
*Chair* Helen Thomas

The Radio Academy is a registered charity with branches across the UK dedicated to the promotion of excellence in radio broadcasting and production. For over 30 years the Radio Academy has run the annual Audio and Radio Industry Awards (ARIAS), which celebrate content and creativity in the industry.

## Radiocentre

15 Alfred Place, London WC1E 7EB
*tel* 020-7010 0600
*website* www.radiocentre.org
*Twitter* @Radiocentre
*Chief Executive* Matt Payton

Radiocentre is the voice of UK commercial radio. Works with government, policy makers and regulators, and provides a forum for industry-wide debate and discussion.

## RAJAR

15 Alfred Place, London WC1E 7EB
*tel* 020-7395 0630
*website* www.rajar.co.uk
*Twitter* @RAJARLtd
*Chief Executive* Jerry Hill

RAJAR – Radio Joint Audience Research – is the official body in charge of measuring radio audiences in the UK. It is jointly owned by the BBC and the RadioCentre on behalf of the commercial sector.

# Theatre for children

London and regional theatres are listed below; listings of touring companies start on page 292.

## LONDON

### Chickenshed Theatre

Chase Side, Southgate, London N14 4PE
*tel* 020-8292 9222
*email* info@chickenshed.org.uk
*website* www.chickenshed.org.uk
*Twitter* @CHICKENSHED_UK
*Managing Director* Louise Perry

Produces theatre for all ages as well as running successful education courses, outreach projects and membership programmes.

### Colour House Theatre

Merton Abbey Mills, Watermill Way,
London SW19 2RD
*tel* 020-8542 5511
*email* info@colourhousetheatre.co.uk
*website* www.colourhousetheatre.co.uk
*Facebook* www.facebook.com/The
ColourHouseTheatre
*Twitter* @ColourHouseThtr
*Founder and Chief Executive* Peter Wallder, *Resident Artistic Director* Charlie Shakespeare

Grade II-listed building in the riverside setting of Merton Abbey Millls, seating 50–70 people. The resident children's theatre has staged over 100 original musical adaptations of famous fairy tales during the past 25 years and achieved charitable status in 2008. The one-hour shows run at the weekends and school holidays (except July and August). The Theatre also hosts evening shows, music and comedy nights and is available to hire for events and private parties.

### Polka Theatre

240 The Broadway, London SW19 1SB
*tel* 020-8543 4888
*email* helenM@polkatheatre.com
*website* www.polkatheatre.com
*Twitter* @polkatheatre
*Artistic Director* Helen Matravers

Theatre of new work for children up to the age of 12, with targeted commissions. Founded 1967.

### The Questors Theatre

12 Mattock Lane, London W5 5BQ
*email* enquiries@questors.org.uk
*website* www.questors.org.uk
*Facebook* www.facebook.com/questorstheatre/
*Twitter* @questorstheatre

*Executive Director* Doug King

Largest independent community theatre in Europe. Produces 15–20 shows a year, specialising in modern and classical world drama. Visiting productions hosted too. No unsolicited scripts. Also runs a youth theatre for young people aged between 6–18, as well as summer workshops.

### Theatre-Rites

Unit 3, Energy Centre, Bowling Green Walk,
London N1 6AL
*tel* 020-7164 6196
*email* info@theatre-rites.co.uk
*website* www.theatre-rites.co.uk
*Facebook* www.facebook.com/TheatreRites
*Twitter* @TheatreRites
*Artistic Director* Sue Buckmaster, *Executive Producer* Claire Templeton

Creates devised theatre for family audiences and young people using a mix of performance, installation, puppetry, dance and sound. Working within the UK and internationally, the company creates site-specific and touring productions. Founded 1995.

### Unicorn Theatre

147 Tooley Street, London SE1 2HZ
*tel* 020-7645 0560
*email* hello@unicorntheatre.com
*website* www.unicorntheatre.com
*Facebook* www.facebook.com/unicorntheatre
*Twitter* @unicorn_theatre
*Artistic Director* Justin Audibert, *Co-Executive Director*s Bailey Lock, Helen Tovey

Produces a year-round programme of theatre for children and young people under 21. In-house productions of full-length plays with professional casts are staged across two auditoria, alongside visiting companies and education work. Rarely commissions plays from writers who are new to it, but it is keen to hear from writers who are interested in working with the theatre in the future.

Do not send unsolicited MSS, but rather a short statement describing why you would like to write for Unicorn along with a CV or a summary of your relevant experience.

### A Younger Theatre

*website* www.ayoungertheatre.com
*Facebook* www.facebook.com/AYoungerTheatre
*Twitter* @ayoungertheatre
*Instagram* @ayoungertheatre_

*Managing Director* Samuel Sims

Online theatre publication reviewing theatre both in London and across the UK, with features on high-profile industry names and discussions on issues facing young and marginalised people. Writers do so for free in return for seeing a show or in order to build a portfolio of work or promote their own performance work. Content is generally aimed at those aged 35 and under.

## REGIONAL

## Yvonne Arnaud Theatre Management Ltd

Millbrook, Guildford, Surrey GU1 3UX
*tel* (01483) 440077
*email* yat@yvonne-arnaud.co.uk
*website* www.yvonne-arnaud.co.uk
*Twitter* @YvonneArnaud
*Director and Chief Executive* Joanna Read

Producing theatre which also receives productions. Runs activities for education providers throughout the year.

## Bristol Old Vic Young Company

King Street, Bristol BS1 4ED
*tel* 0117 949 3993
*email* getinvolved@bristololdvic.org.uk
*website* https://bristololdvic.org.uk/interact/young-company
*Facebook* www.facebook.com/bristololdvic
*Director and Theatre Maker* Julia Head, *Writer*, *Director and Dramaturg* Krista Matthews

Large regional youth theatre hosting workshops, weekly sessions, masterclasses, community projects and performances for young people. Financial assistance is available for participants.

## Chichester Festival Theatre

Oaklands Park, Chichester, West Sussex PO19 6AP
*tel* (01243) 784437
*email* literary@cft.org.uk
*website* www.cft.org.uk
*Twitter* @chichesterFT
*Executive Director* Kate Bourne

Stages annual Summer Festival Season April–October in the Festival and Minerva Theatres together with a year-round education programme, winter touring programme and youth theatre Christmas show. Does not accept unsolicited scripts. The Learning, Education and Participation (LEAP) department runs a programme of events for all ages, including workshops, performances, talks and tours.

## Contact Theatre Company

Oxford Road, Manchester M15 6JA
*tel* 0161 274 0600
*website* https://contactmcr.com/
*Twitter* @ContactMcr

*Artistic Director and Chief Executive* Keisha Thompson, *Head of Creative Development* Laura Whitehurst

Multidisciplinary arts organisation focused on working with and for young people aged 13 and above. Offers a range of free projects, from writing to music and drama, including the Contact Young Company ensemble.

## Creation Theatre Company

*tel* (01865) 766266
*email* boxoffice@creationtheatre.co.uk
*website* www.creationtheatre.co.uk
*Facebook* https://en-gb.facebook.com/CreationTheatre
*Twitter* @creationtheatre
*Instagram* @creationtheatre
*Chief Executive and Creative Producer* Lucy Askew

Award-winning producing theatre company, specialising in digital and site-specific inventive theatre in extraordinary locations. Creators of Creation Home Delivery, live & interactive online drama classes for ages 5–16, designed to inspire a life-long love of stories and storytelling. Also delivers theatre and creativity classes for children during both term time and the school holidays. Does not accept unsolicited manuscripts.

## Derby Theatre

15 Theatre Walk, St Peter's Quarter, Derby DE1 2NF
*email* creatives@derbyplayhouse.co.uk
*website* www.derbytheatre.co.uk/about-us/in-good-company
*Facebook* www.facebook.com/DerbyTheatre
*Twitter* @DerbyTheatre
*Artistic Director and Chief Executive* Sarah Brigham,
*Creative Learning Director* Caroline Barth

Regional producing and receiving theatre. The In Good Company programme offers opportunities for theatre-makers and companies in the region.

## The Dukes

Moor Lane, Lancaster LA1 1QE
*tel* (01524) 598500
*email* ask@dukes-lancaster.org
*website* https://dukes-lancaster.org
*Twitter* @TheDukesTheatre
*Chief Executive* Karen O'Neill

Producing theatre and cultural centre. Its Young Writers scheme was launched in January 2017. See website for up-to-date information about the theatre's productions and programming approach.

## The Edge Theatre and Arts Centre

Manchester Road, Chorlton, Manchester M21 9JG
*tel* 0161 282 9776
*email* info@edgetheatre.co.uk
*website* www.edgetheatre.co.uk
*Twitter* @TheEdgeMcr

*Artistic Director and Chief Executive* Janine Waters, *Musical Director* Simon Waters

Produces and presents theatre for all ages, including families and children. Musical and children's theatre specialities. 70-seat flexible theatre space and studio spaces. Also runs classes, courses and workshops in theatre, dance, music, writing and other creative genres, including: Theatre Club for ages 6–8; Edge Youth Theatre for ages 9–12; Aspire for young people with learning challenges between 13–17; and the Young Actors' Company for ages 13–16. Founded 2011.

## The Egg

Sawclose, Bath BA1 1ET
*tel* (01225) 823409 (reception and administration)
*email* egg.reception@theatreroyal.org.uk
*website* www.theatreroyal.org.uk/the-egg
*Twitter* @theeggbath

Part of the Theatre Royal Bath. Purpose-built theatre for young people and their families. Hosts and produces shows for children and young people alongside a year-round participation and outreach programme for people aged 0–21. Opened 2005.

## Everyman Theatre Cheltenham

7 Regent Street, Cheltenham, Glos. GL50 1HQ
*tel* (01242) 512515
*email* admin@everymantheatre.org.uk
*website* www.everymantheatre.org.uk
*Twitter* @Everymanchelt
*Creative Director* Paul Milton

Regional presenting and producing theatre promoting a wide range of plays. Small-scale experimental, youth and educational work encouraged in The Studio Theatre. Contact the Creative Director before submitting material.

## Leeds Children's Theatre

c/o The Carriageworks Theatre, The Electric Press, 3 Millennium Square, Leeds LS2 3AD
*email* enquiry@leeds-childrens-theatre.co.uk
*website* www.leeds-childrens-theatre.co.uk
*Twitter* @LeedsCT

Oldest established Children's Theatre society in the UK. Its members (both adults and children) bring live theatre to young people, often for the very first time. Many of the plays produced are based on well-known children's literature. Stages two productions each year at the purpose-built Carriageworks Theatre, typically in spring (March/April) and late autumn (November). Welcomes school groups as well as families and friends. Founded 1935.

## Leeds Playhouse

Playhouse Square, Quarry Hill, Leeds LS2 7UP
*tel* 0113 213 7700
*website* https://leedsplayhouse.org.uk
*Twitter* @LeedsPlayhouse

*Artistic Director and Ceo* James Brining

Seeks out the best companies and artists to create theatre in the heart of Yorkshire. Its artistic development programme, Furnace, discovers and supports new voices, while developing work with established practitioners. It provides a creative space for writers, directors, companies and individual theatre-makers to refine their practice at all stages of their career. The Creative Engagement team works with more than 12,000 people every year reaching out to refugee communities, young people, students, older people and people with learning challenges.

## Live Theatre

Broad Chare, Quayside,
Newcastle upon Tyne NE1 3DQ
*tel* 0191 232 1232
*email* info@live.org.uk
*website* www.live.org.uk
*website* https://www.live.org.uk/children-young-people/schools-teachers
*Twitter* @LiveTheatre
*Executive Director & Joint Ceo* Jacqui Kell, *Artistic Director & Joint Ceo* Jack McNamara

New writing theatre company and venue. Stages 3–6 productions per year of new writing, plus touring plays from other new writing companies. The Live Youth Theatre programme is free and open to young people between the ages of 10 and 25. CPD and INSET support for teachers is also available.

## Norwich Puppet Theatre

St James, Whitefriars, Norwich NR3 1TN
*tel* (01603) 629921 (box office), (01603) 615564 (admin.)
*email* info@puppettheatre.co.uk
*website* www.puppettheatre.co.uk
*Facebook* www.facebook.com/NorwichPuppetTheatre
*Twitter* @norwich_puppet
*Instagram* @norwichpuppettheatre

Home to a professional theatre company which creates family puppet shows. The company tours to schools and venues around the country and occasionally internationally. As a venue, the Theatre also presents a programme of puppetry performances and workshops for family and adult audiences. Norwich Puppet Theatre is also a charity and a creative engagement organisation with an extensive outreach programme.

## Nottingham Playhouse

Nottingham Playhouse Trust Ltd, Wellington Circus, Nottingham NG1 5AF
*tel* 0115 941 9419
*website* https://nottinghamplayhouse.co.uk/get-involved/young-people/
*Twitter* @NottmPlayhouse
*Artistic Director* Adam Penford, *Chief Executive* Stephanie Sirr

Seeks to nurture new writers from the East Midlands primarily through its Artist Development programme, Amplify. Also offers a range of groups and youth theatres for young people aged 2 and above; see website above for full details.

## Pegasus
Magdalen Road, Oxford OX4 1RE
*tel* (01865) 812150
*email* info@pegasustheatre.org.uk
*website* https://pegasustheatre.org.uk/spark-artists/
*Twitter* @Pegatweet
*Instagram* @pegasusoxford
*Executive Director* Polly Cole

Theatre, dance and comedy for young people. Runs the two-year SPARK programme, which offers a range of support to artists, including development sessions, marketing and fundraising support, and rehearsal spaces. See website for details on future application windows.

## Queen's Theatre, Hornchurch
Billet Lane, Hornchurch, Essex RM11 1QT
*tel* (01708) 443333
*email* info@queens-theatre.co.uk
*website* www.queens-theatre.co.uk
*website* www.queens-theatre.co.uk/get-involved/youth-theatre
*Twitter* @QueensTheatreH
*Executive Director* Mathew Russell

Regional theatre working in outer East London, Essex and beyond. Each annual programme includes home-grown theatre, visiting live entertainment and learning and participation projects.

The Queen's Youth Theatre Programme (QYouth) provides the opportunity for young people aged 6–18 to develop creativity, confidence and teamwork, as well as offering valuable opportunities to perform on the Queen's Theatre stage and elsewhere. Younger members begin with the QSteps Programme before moving on to the Young Company Programme, which offers performance, technical and dance opportunities for those who wish to develop further a range of theatre skills. Founded 1953.

## Royal Shakespeare Company
The Royal Shakespeare Theatre, Waterside, Stratford-upon-Avon, Warks. CV37 6BB
*tel* (01789) 296655
*email* newwork@rsc.org.uk
*website* www.rsc.org.uk
*website* https://37plays.co.uk
*Facebook* www.facebook.com/thersc
*Twitter* @TheRSC
*Co-artistic Directors* Daniel Evans, Tamara Harvey, *Head of New Work* Pippa Hill

Produces Shakespeare's plays alongside new work by contemporary writers and the work of Shakespeare's contemporaries on its two main stages, the Royal Shakespeare Theatre and the Swan Theatre. In addition, its studio theatre, The Other Place, produces cutting-edge new work. For all its stages, the Company commissions new plays, new translations and new adaptations that illuminate the themes and concerns of Shakespeare and his contemporaries for a modern audience. The Literary department does not accept unsolicited work but rather seeks out writers it wishes to work with or commission, and monitors the work of writers in production in the UK and internationally. Writers are welcome to invite the Literary department to readings, showcases or productions by emailing the address above.

## Sherman Theatre
Senghennydd Road, Cardiff CF24 4YE
*tel* 029-2064 6900
*website* www.shermantheatre.co.uk/theatre-makers
*Twitter* @shermantheatre
*Chief Executive* Julia Barry, *Artistic Director* Joe Murphy

Produces two Christmas productions (for ages 3–6 in English and Welsh and an actor/musician-led production for ages 7+) and actively seeks high-quality work for children and young people as part of its programming. Participatory work with youth theatres. Founded 2007.

## Taking Flight Theatre Company
Chapter Arts Centre, Market Road, Cardiff CF5 1QE
*tel* 029-2023 0020
*email* louise@takingflighttheatre.co.uk
*website* www.takingflighttheatre.org.uk
*Facebook* www.facebook.com/Takingflightco
*Twitter* @takingflightco
*Instagram* @takingflighttheatre
*Artistic Director and Ceo* Elise Davison, *Executive Director* Louise Ralph

Boundary-pushing productions featuring Deaf, disabled and non-disabled performers.

## Theatr Clwyd
Mold, Flintshire CH7 1YA
*tel* (01352) 344101
*email* writers@theatrclwyd.com
*website* www.theatrclwyd.com
*Twitter* @ClwydTweets

Largest producing theatre in Wales, creating up to 14 productions each year in English, Welsh and bilingually. Productions are a mix of classic plays, contemporary revivals, musicals and new writing. Will consider plays by writers, particularly Welsh, Wales-based or with Welsh themes, and usually offers 6 writing residencies each year. No literary department, so authors should expect to wait for a response to unsolicited scripts.

## Visible Fictions

Suite 325/327, 4th Floor, 11 Bothwell Street,
Glasgow G2 6LY
*email* laura@visiblefictions.co.uk
*website* https://visiblefictions.co.uk
*Twitter* @visiblefictions
*Artistic Director* Dougie Irvine, *Producer* Laura Penny

Specialises in professional productions for young
audiences and their families across a range of
artforms, from theatre to film, puppetry to immersive
experiences. Also works in creative learning settings –
community, educational, institutional, and
professional – to make bespoke projects to
accompany and enhance artistic experiences of young
audiences.

# TOURING COMPANIES

## Arad Goch

Stryd y Baddon, Aberystwyth, Ceredigion SY23 2NN
*tel* (01970) 617998
*email* post@aradgoch.org
*website* www.aradgoch.cymru
*Twitter* @AradGoch
*Artistic Director* Jeremy Turner

Performs in Welsh and English and tours nationally
throughout Wales, and occasionally abroad. The
company is particularly interested in enabling
children and young people to recognise and
appreciate their own unique cultural identity through
theatre. Some of the company's work is based on
traditional material and children's literature, but it
also commissions new work from experienced
dramatists and new writers. Arad Goch performs in
theatres and other locations, including schools, and
also offers seminars/workshops for students and
teachers. The company has its own production house
in Aberystwyth which is used by other arts and
community organisations and where it programmes a
variety of participatory activities for young people. It
organises the biennial 'Agor Drysau–Opening Doors'
Wales International Festival of Performing Arts for
Young Audiences (www.agordrysau.cymru).
Founded 1989.

## Booster Cushion Theatre

75 How Wood, Park Street, St Albans,
Herts. AL2 2RW
*tel* (01727) 873874
*email* admin@booster-cushion.co.uk
*website* www.booster-cushion.co.uk
*Facebook* www.facebook.com/boostercushiontheatre
*Twitter* @BoosterCushion
*Director* Philip Sherman

Comic theatre company formed especially to re-tell
traditional tales to primary-school pupils and their
families using surprising Big Books. BCT has
performed to over 500,000 people in schools,
libraries, museums and theatres across the UK using
pop-up books up to 3m tall and concertina books
over 5m wide.

All productions are solo performing shows using
mime, voice and some sign language. They involve a
high level of audience participation. Each show is
completely portable and can be performed inside or
outside; technical requirements are minimal.
Founded 1989.

## Boundless Theatre

Big Local Works, 4 Market Place,
South Bermondsey, London SE16 3UQ
*tel* 020-7072 0140
*email* hello@boundlesstheatre.org.uk
*website* www.boundlesstheatre.org.uk
*website* https://boundlesstheatre.org.uk/projects/
accelerator
*Instagram* @boundlessabound
*Artistic Director and Ceo* Rob Drummer

Creates new plays with and for audiences aged 15–25.
Tours the UK and internationally. Its Accelerator
programme helps new voices develop their work;
there is a cash bursary of £2,500, alongside other
sources of support. Founded 2001 (as Company of
Angels).

## Cahoots NI

Cahoots NI, Cityside Retail Park,
100–150 York Street, Belfast BT15 1WA
*tel* 07434 661671
*email* info@cahootsni.com
*website* www.cahootsni.com
*Facebook* www.facebook.com/Cahoots NI
*Twitter* @CahootsNI
*Artistic Director* Paul Bosco McEneaney, *Creative
Engagement Manager* Emma Wilson

Professional children's touring company which
concentrates on the visual potential of theatre and
capitalises upon the age-old popularity of magic and
illusion as an essential ingredient in the art of
entertaining. The company tours in Ireland, the UK,
the US and Asia in theatres, schools and healthcare
settings. Founded 2001.

## Catherine Wheels Theatre Company

Brunton Theatre, Ladywell Way,
Musselburgh EH21 6AF
*tel* 0131 653 5255
*email* admin@catherinewheels.co.uk
*website* www.catherinewheels.co.uk
*Facebook* www.facebook.com/
CatherineWheelsCompany
*Twitter* @cwheelstheatre
*Artistic Director* Gill Robertson

Producing company that tours the UK and
internationally, performing for children and young
people. One of the founders of the Theatre in Schools
Scotland initiative.

## Fevered Sleep

15A Old Ford Road, London E2 9PJ
*tel* 020-3815 6430
*email* info@feveredsleep.co.uk
*website* www.feveredsleep.co.uk
*Facebook* www.facebook.com/feveredsleeponline/
*Twitter* @feveredsleep
*Instagram* @feveredsleep
*Co-Artistic Directors* Sam Butler, David Harradine

Creates performances, installations and digital art for children and adults that the company describes as 'collaborative, participatory, research-led art'. Founded 1996.

## Half Moon Theatre

43 White Horse Road, London E1 0ND
*tel* 020-7709 8900
*email* admin@halfmoon.org.uk
*website* www.halfmoon.org.uk
*Facebook* www.facebook.com/halfmoontheatre
*Twitter* @HalfMoonTheatre
*Instagram* @halfmoon_theatre
*Director and Ceo* Chris Elwell

Stages professional plays for young people and family audiences; also tours work around the UK. Youth theatre groups offer opportunities for participants aged 5–18.

## Hobgoblin Theatre Company

9 St George's Yard, Farnham, Surrey GU9 7LW
*tel* 0800 530 0384
*email* info@hobgoblintheatrecompany.co.uk
*website* www.hobgoblintheatrecompany.co.uk
*Facebook* www.facebook.com/hobgoblintheatrecompany
*Contacts* James Anthony, Daniel Foley, Hannah Foley

Live and online theatre productions for EYFS, Key Stage 1 and Key Stage 2 pupils, as well as Play in a Day workshops. More than 20 shows available, as well as yearly Christmas productions. Founded 2007.

## Hopscotch Theatre Company

Second Floor, 7 Water Row, Govan G51 3UW
*tel* 0141 440 2025
*email* info@hopscotchtheatre.com
*website* https://hopscotchtheatre.com
*Facebook* www.facebook.com/hopscotchtheatre
*Twitter* @HopscotchTC
*Instagram* @hopscotch_theatre
*Producer and General Manager* Thomas McCulloch, *Creative Learning Producer and General Manager* Stephanie Black-Daniels

Producer of touring theatre for young people aged 4–12 and families, including an annual pantomime tour. An artist-support programme for new writers and theatre-makers enables artists to make accessible work for young audiences. Founded 1988.

## Kazzum Arts

Oxford House, Derbyshire Street, London E2 6HG
*tel* 020-7749 1123
*email* hello@kazzum.org
*website* www.kazzum.org
*Facebook* www.facebook.com/Kazzum/
*Twitter* @KazzumArts
*Instagram* @kazzumarts
*Artistic Director* Alex Evans, *Executive Director* Lauren Irving

Facilitates innovative, playful and multi-disciplinary projects which encourage social and reflective skills, enabling young people to foster positive relationships and experience an increased sense of wellbeing. Founded 1989.

## Konflux Theatre in Education

4100 Park Approach, Thorpe Park, Leeds LS15 8GB
*tel* (01937) 832740
*email* info@konfluxtheatre.com
*website* www.konfluxtheatre.com
*Facebook* www.facebook.com/KonfluxTheatre/
*Twitter* @KonfluxTheatre
*Artistic Director* Anthony Koncsol

Theatre in Education company and Arts Award Supporter. Works with approx. 700 schools each year, building close working relationships with teachers and other education professionals and ensuring its programmes and their delivery are tailored to the needs of each organisation. Konflux offers over 70 curriculum-based Play in a Day workshops designed to build confidence and promote team work. They give pupils the opportunity to learn through drama, increase their acting skills and present a performance back to peers and parents. Founded 1998.

## Little Angel Theatre

14 Dagmar Passage, London N1 2DN
*tel* 020-7226 1787
*email* info@littleangeltheatre.com
*website* www.littleangeltheatre.com
*Twitter* @LittleATheatre
*Artistic Director* Samantha Lane, *Executive Director* Peta Swindell

Committed to working with children and families through schools, the local community and the wider community through its extensive touring programme. Little Angel Theatre develops innovative projects, implements improved access to their creative work, increases opportunities for participation and provides stimulating learning and creativity for all using puppetry. Productions last approx. one hour. Termly activities are run for children, families and schools, including INSET training for teachers. Regular introductory and professional development courses are held throughout the year for teenagers and adults.

**Stage, screen and audio**

## The London Bubble

(Bubble Theatre Company)
5 Elephant Lane, London SE16 4JD
*tel* 020-7237 4434
*email* admin@londonbubble.org.uk
*website* www.londonbubble.org.uk
*Twitter* @LBubble
*Instagram* @bubbletheatre
*Co-Ceos* Lucy Bradshaw, Marie Vickers

Aims to provide the artistic direction, skills,
environment and resources to create inspirational,
inclusive and involving theatre for the local
community and beyond. Also runs a number of
groups for children and young people as well as an
adult drama group.

## M6 Theatre Company

Studio Theatre, Hamer C.P. School,
Albert Royds Street, Rochdale, Lancs. OL16 2SU
*tel* (01706) 355898
*email* admin@m6theatre.co.uk
*website* https://m6theatre.co.uk
*Facebook* https://en-gb.facebook.com/M6Theatre
*Twitter* @M6Theatre
*Artistic Director* Gilly Baskeyfield

Touring theatre company specialising in creating and
delivering innovative theatre for young audiences.

## Oily Cart

Smallwood School Annexe, Smallwood Road,
London SW17 0TW
*tel* 020-8672 6329
*email* oilies@oilycart.org.uk
*website* www.oilycart.org.uk
*Twitter* @oilycart
*Artistic Director* Ellie Griffiths, *Executive Director* Zoë
Lally

Touring company staging interactive, sensory shows
across the UK and internationally. Reimagines theatre
for young audiences to make it more inclusive, and
all productions are created for and with children and
young people, regardless of age or perceived ability.
Considers scripts from new writers, but at present all
work is generated from within the company.
Founded 1981.

## The Pied Piper Theatre Company

1 Lilian Place, Coxcombe Lane, Chiddingfold,
Surrey GU8 4QA
*tel* (01428) 684022
*email* info@piedpipertheatre.co.uk
*website* www.piedpipertheatre.co.uk
*Twitter* @PiedPiperLive
*Artistic Director* Tina Williams

Specialises in bringing new writing for children to the
stage. Typically tours one show a year in the UK,
sometimes two, and occasionally tours in Europe and
Asia. Founded 1984.

## Prime Theatre

(formerly Sixth Sense Theatre for Young People)
c/o The Wyvern Theatre, Theatre Square,
Swindon SN1 1QN
*tel* (01793) 614864
*email* info@primetheatre.co.uk
*website* www.primetheatre.co.uk
*Twitter* @PrimeTheatreUK
*Artistic Director* Mark Powell

Professional theatre company prioritising work with
young people. Prime Theatre produces both issue-
based and creative theatre productions and performs
in schools, theatres and arts centres in the South-
West region and beyond. These productions are
supported by additional young people-led work,
workshops, training sessions and other projects.

## Proteus Theatre Company

Proteus Creation Space, Council Road, Basingstoke,
Hants RG21 3DH
*tel* (01256) 354541
*email* info@proteustheatre.com
*website* www.proteustheatre.com
*Twitter* @proteustheatre
*Artistic Director and Chief Executive* Mary Swan

Small-scale touring company particularly committed
to new writing and new work, education and
community collaborations. Produces up to 3 touring
shows per year plus community projects.
Founded 1981.

## Red Earth Theatre

122 Chapel Street, Belper DE56 0NT
*tel* 07584 046184
*email* admin@redearththeatre.com
*website* https://redearththeatre.com
*Facebook* www.facebook.com/redearththeatre
*Twitter* @redearththeatre
*Co-Artistic Directors* Wendy Rouse, Amanda Wilde

Sign-integrated theatre performances for children
and young people. Tours virtually and in person.
Founded 1999.

## Replay Theatre Company

East Belfast Network Centre,
55 Templemore Avenue, Belfast BT5 4FP
*tel* 028-9045 4562
*email* info@replaytheatre.co.uk
*website* www.replaytheatre.co.uk
*Twitter* @ReplayTheatreCo
*Chief Executive Officer* Brian Mullen, *Artistic Director*
Janice Kernoghan-Reid, *Finance and Operations
Manager* Hayley McBride, *Lead Artist Inclusion*
Andrew Stanford, *Research and Evaluation Officer*
Cristal Palacios

Innovative, high-quality work for audiences under
the age of 19, including school groups, children and
young people with disabilities, and families. Each
show is shaped through creative consultation with its

intended audience, and those who live and work with them. Tours locally, nationally and internationally. Founded 1988.

## Rhubarb Theatre

7 Queensway, Leadenham, Lincoln LN5 0PF
*tel* (01400) 275133
*email* info@rhubarbtheatre.co.uk
*website* www.rhubarbtheatre.co.uk
*Artistic Directors* Kirsty Mead, Philip Mead

Professional indoor theatre and street theatre predominantly aimed at family audiences (age 5+). Productions are newly created stories that include original music and lots of theatrical devices, i.e. masks, puppetry, dance, song, movement and mime. Most of Rhubarb's street shows are wordless and suitable for booking overseas. Tours nationally and performs in a host of different small- to middle-scale venues, including theatres, arts centres, village halls, rural touring schemes and schools, undertaking approx. 200 performances a year. Other activities include walkabout, interactive storytelling, workshops and teaching. Founded 2004.

## Spectacle Theatre Ltd

c/o The Factory, Jenkin Street, Porth CF39 9PP
*tel* 07900 493691
*email* steve.davis@spectacletheatre.co.uk
*website* www.spectacletheatre.co.uk
*Facebook* www.facebook.com/Theatr-Spectacle-Theatre
*Twitter* @SpectacleTheat1
*Manager/Creative Director* Steve Davis

Community theatre company. Bilingual performance, health and wellbeing workshops, training and volunteering opportunities.

## Tell Tale Hearts

c/o 4 Oxspring Road, Penistone, Sheffield S36 8AB
*email* info@telltalehearts.co.uk
*website* www.telltalehearts.co.uk
*Facebook* www.facebook.com/
TellTaleHeartsTheatreCo
*Twitter* @TellTaleHeart
*Artistic Director* Natasha Holmes

Produces participatory theatre for primary-school pupils and younger years in a range of settings, from theatres to schools and community venues. Also runs workshops, INSET training and offers other consultancy services. Rarely produces theatre from written work but actively seeks out collaborations with contributing artists. Occasionally works with a writer as part of its collaborative team, but this is to produce new work. Contact the Artistic Director before sending any work in order to gauge interest. Founded 2003.

## Theatr Iolo

Chapter, Market Road, Canton, Cardiff CF14 3HS
*tel* 029-2061 3782
*email* hello@theatriolo.com
*website* www.theatriolo.com
*Twitter* @theatriolo
*Artistic Director* Lee Lyford

Producing children's theatre company. Creates live theatre, workshops and activities in both English and Welsh. Its work for babies, children and teenagers is toured across Wales, the UK and internationally.

## Theatre Centre

The Albany, Douglas Way, Deptford,
London SE8 4AG
*tel* 020-7729 3066
*email* admin@theatre-centre.co.uk
*website* www.theatre-centre.co.uk
*Facebook* www.facebook.com/TheatreCentreUK
*Twitter* @TClive
*Artistic Director* Rob Watt, *Executive Director and Ceo* Emma Rees

Young people's theatre company producing plays and workshops which tour nationally across the UK. Productions are staged in primary and secondary schools, arts centres and other venues. Keen to nurture new and established talent, encouraging all writers to consider writing for young audiences. Also runs creative projects and manages writing awards: see website for details. Founded 1953.

## Theatre Hullabaloo

The Hullabaloo, Borough Road, Darlington DL1 1SG
*tel* (01325) 405681
*email* info@theatrehullabaloo.org.uk
*website* www.theatrehullabaloo.org.uk
*Twitter* @hullabalootweet
*Artistic Producer* Miranda Thain

Specialist theatre company that creates, promotes and tours work for young audiences, with a particular emphasis on early years. Encourages greater awareness of the value of theatre to children and young people by working with academic researchers, teachers and others through courses, events and publications. Tours professional theatre productions to schools and venues across the North East and nationally. Dedicated children's theatre and family venue, The Hullabaloo, offers theatre for children, creative play installations and more.

## Travelling Light Theatre Company

Barton Hill Settlement, 43 Ducie Road,
Lawrence Hill, Bristol BS5 0AX
*tel* 07305 085081
*email* info@travellinglighttheatre.org.uk
*website* www.travellinglighttheatre.org.uk
*Facebook* www.facebook.com/travellinglighttheatre
*Twitter* @tl_theatre
*Instagram* @tl_theatre
*Executive Director* Dienka Hines

Professional theatre company producing work for young audiences. Collaborates with many different arts organisations to create original, cross-artform productions that inspire and engage young people. Tours to theatres and festivals throughout the UK and abroad as well as to local schools. Also runs an extensive participation programme engaging with 0–25 year-olds through youth theatre groups, holiday and school projects, work experience, placements and mentoring. Founded 1984.

## Tutti Frutti Productions

Shine, Harehills Road, Harehills, Leeds LS8 5DR
*tel* 0113 388 0027
*email* emma@tutti-frutti.org.uk
*website* www.tutti-frutti.org.uk
*Twitter* @tuttifruttiprod

*Artistic Director* Wendy Harris, *Executive Director* Emma Killick

Professional theatre for family audiences (age 3+ and families/carers). Productions are adaptations of well-known stories or specially commissioned new shows with a focus on diversity, and have a very physical movement-based style with original music. Tours nationally and internationally and performs in a host of different small- and middle-scale venues in isolated or deprived areas, including theatres, arts centres, village halls, rural touring schemes and schools, undertaking approx. 250 performances a year. Also creates local arts engagement projects for children. Founded 1991.

# Societies, prizes and festivals

## Society of Authors

The Society of Authors (SoA) is the UK trade union for all types of writers, illustrators and literary translators at every stage of their careers.

Founded in 1884, the Society of Authors now has over 10,000 members. Members receive unlimited free advice on all aspects of the profession, including confidential clause-by-clause contract vetting, access to professional and geographic author communities and a wide range of exclusive offers. It campaigns and lobbies on the issues that affect authors and holds hundreds of events online and across the UK each year, offering opportunities for authors to network and learn from each other. It manages more than 58 literary estates, the income from which helps to fund the organisation's work.

### Members

SoA members include household names, such as Malorie Blackman, Neil Gaiman, Lemn Sissay and Joanne Harris, but they also include authors right at the start of their careers. Amongst the SoA membership are academic writers, biographers, broadcasters, children's writers, crime writers, dramatists, educational writers, ELT writers, health writers, ghostwriters, graphic novelists, historians, illustrators, journalists, medical writers, non-fiction writers, novelists, poets, playwrights, radio writers, scriptwriters, short story writers, translators, spoken word artists, YA writers and more.

The benefits available to all SoA members include the following:

• assistance with contracts, from negotiation and assessment of terms to clause-by-clause, confidential vetting;

## Membership

**The Society of Authors**
24 Bedford Row, London WC1R 4EH
*tel* 020-3880 2230
*email* info@societyofauthors.org
*website* www2.societyofauthors.org
*Chief Executive* Nicola Solomon

There are two membership bands: Full and Associate membership.

*Full membership* is available to professional writers, poets, translators and illustrators working in any genre or medium. This includes those who have had a full-length work traditionally published, broadcast or performed commercially; self-published or been published on a print-on-demand or ebook-only basis and who meet sales criteria; published or had broadcast or performed an equivalent body of professional work; or administrators of a deceased author's estate.

Authors at the start of their careers are invited to join as Associates.

*Associate membership* is available to anyone actively working to launch a career as an author. This includes authors who are starting out in self-publishing but who are not yet making a profit; authors who have been offered a contract for publication or agent representation but who are not yet published; students engaged on a course of at least one academic year's duration that will help them develop a career as an author, as well as other activities that mark the early stages of an author's career. Associate members enjoy all the same services and benefits as Full members.

Membership is subject to election and payment of subscription fees.

The subscription fee (tax deductible) starts at £29.25 per quarter, or £20.50 for those aged 35 or under. A concessionary rate for over 65s is available on request. Joint membership also available.

• unlimited advice on queries, covering any aspect of the business of authorship;
• taking up complaints on behalf of members on any issue concerned with the business of authorship;
• pursuing legal actions for breach of contract, copyright infringement and the non-payment of royalties and fees, when the risk and cost preclude individual action by a member and issues of general concern to the profession are at stake;
• conferences, seminars, meetings and other opportunities to network and learn from other authors;
• regular communications and a comprehensive range of publications, including the SoA's quarterly journal, *The Author*;
• discounts on books, exclusive rates on specialist insurance, special offers on products and services and free membership of the Authors' Licensing and Collecting Society (ALCS; see page 407);

• Authors with Disabilities and Chronic Illnesses – a peer support network for authors living and working with health challenges;
• Comics Creators Network – a professional support network for all types of comics creators;
• Children's Writers and Illustrators Group – a professional community of writers and illustrators who create content for the children's publishing market;
• Educational Writers Group – protecting the interests of educational authors in professional matters, especially contracts, rates of pay, digitalisation and copyright;
• Poetry and Spoken Word Group – a new, increasingly active group to which all new member poets are subscribed on joining SoA;
• Scriptwriters Group – representing members working in radio, TV, film and games development;
• Society of Authors in Scotland – organises a varied and busy calendar of activities in Scotland through a committee of volunteers;
• Translators Association – a source of expert advice for individual literary translators and a collective voice representing the profession;
• Carers Network – a new group designed to help keep writers writing when they take on caring responsibilities for someone with an illness or disability.

The SoA also coordinates a growing network of over 37 local author communities across the UK.

> 'It does no harm to repeat, as often as you can, "Without me the literary industry would not exist: the publishers, the agents, the sub-agents, the accountants, the libel lawyers, the departments of literature, the professors, the theses, the books of criticism, the reviewers, the book pages – all this vast and proliferating edifice is because of this small, patronised, put-down and underpaid person."' – *Doris Lessing*

## Campaigning and lobbying

The SoA is a voice for authors and works at a national and international level to improve terms and treatment of authors, negotiating with all parties including publishers, broadcasters, agents and governments. Current areas of campaigning include contract terms, copyright, freedom of expression, tax and benefits arrangements and Public Lending Right (PLR; see page 369) – which the SoA played a key role in establishing. With the ongoing impacts of the Covid-19 pandemic and Brexit, the SoA continues to lobby for better terms, benefits and rights for authors and other creative professionals.

In the UK the SoA lobbies parliament, ministers and departments and makes submissions on relevant issues, working closely with the Department for Culture, Media and Sport and the All Party Parliamentary Writers Group. The SoA is a member of the British Copyright Council and was instrumental in setting up ALCS. They chair the Creators for Rights Alliance (CRA), a partnership of unions and member organisations from across the creative industries, working together on common interests such as copyright, payment and credit, and in 2022 launched the cross-industry 'Pay the Creator' campaign. It is recognised by the BBC in the negotiation of rates for authors' contributions to radio drama, as well as for the broadcasting of published material.

The SoA is a member of the European Writers' Council and applies pressure globally, working with sister organisations as part of the international Authors' Foundation.

The SoA also works closely with other professional bodies, including the Association of Authors' Agents, the Booksellers Association, the Publishers Association, the Independent Publishers Guild, the British Council, the National Union of Journalists and the Writers' Guild of Great Britain.

## Awards and grants

The SoA supports authors through a wide range of awards and grants. Over £120,000 is given in prizes each year and more than £250,000 is distributed in grants.

The SoA administers the following awards:

- the annual SoA Awards – ten prizes for poetry, fiction and non-fiction, and illustration, awarding authors at the beginning of their careers as well as those well established;
- two audio drama prizes: the Imison Award for a writer new to radio drama and the Tinniswood Award;
- awards for translations from Arabic, Dutch/Flemish, French, German, Greek, Italian, Spanish and Swedish into English;
- the Authors' Foundation and K Blundell Trust, which give grants to assist authors working on their next book;
- the Francis Head Bequest and the Authors' Contingency Fund, which assist authors who, through physical mishap, are temporarily unable to maintain themselves or their families;
- the *Sunday Times* Charlotte Aitken Young Writer of the Year Award;
- the ALCS Educational Writers' Awards.

# WGGB (Writers' Guild of Great Britain)

The WGGB is the TUC-affiliated trade union for writers.

WGGB represents writers working in film, television, radio, theatre, books, poetry, animation, comedy and videogames. Formed in 1959 as the Screenwriters' Guild, the union gradually extended into all areas of freelance writing activity and copyright protection. It comprises professional writers in all media, united in common concern for one another and regulating the conditions under which they work.

Apart from necessary dealings with government and policies on legislative matters affecting writers, the WGGB is, by constitution, non-political, has no involvement with any political party and members pay no political levy.

WGGB employs a permanent general secretary and other permanent staff and is administered by an Executive Council of around 20 members.

## WGGB agreements

WGGB's core function is to negotiate minimum terms in those areas in which its members work. Those agreements form the basis of the individual contracts signed by members. It also gives individual advice to its members on contracts and other matters and maintains a welfare fund to help writers in financial trouble.

## Membership

**Writers' Guild of Great Britain**
First Floor, 134 Tooley Street, London SE1 2TU
*tel* 020-7833 0777
*email* admin@writersguild.org.uk
*website* www.writersguild.org.uk
*Facebook* www.facebook.com/thewritersguild
*Twitter* @The WritersGuild
*General Secretary* Ellie Peers

*Full membership*: Members pay approximately 1.2% of earnings from professional writing using a banding system (min. £198, max. £2,000 p.a.).

*Candidate membership*: £108 p.a. restricted to writers who have not had work published or produced at WGGB-approved rates.

*Student membership*: £30 p.a. for student writers aged 18 or over, studying at BA level or below.

*Affiliate membership*: £300 p.a. for people who work professionally with writers, e.g. agents, technical advisers.

Members receive a weekly email newsletter. The WGGB website contains full details of collective agreements and WGGB activities, plus a 'Find a Writer' service and a dedicated members' area; information is also made available on Twitter, Facebook and other social media channels. Other benefits include legal advice and contract vetting; free training; member events, discounts and special offers (subject to membership tier).

## Television

WGGB negotiates minimum terms agreements with the BBC, ITV, Pact (Producers' Alliance for Cinema and Television) and TAC (representing Welsh-language television producers).

WGGB TV agreements regulate minimum fees, residuals and royalties, copyright, credits and general conditions for television plays, series and serials, dramatisations and adaptations, soaps, sitcoms and sketch shows. One of the WGGB's most important achievements has been the establishment of pension rights for members. The BBC, ITV and independent producers pay a pension contribution on top of the standard writer's fee on the understanding that the WGGB member also pays a contribution.

The switch to digital television, video-on-demand and download-to-own services, mobile phone technology and the expansion of the BBC's commercial arm have seen WGGB in constant negotiation over the past decade. WGGB now has agreements for all of the BBC's digital channels and for its joint venture channels. In May 2012 it signed new agreements with the BBC extending minimum terms over online services such as iPlayer. From April 2015 the first payments under the Writers Digital Payments scheme (a not-for-profit company) were paid out to writers whose work had been broadcast on BBC iPlayer and ITV Player. In 2016 WGGB negotiated a 75% fee increase for writers working under its 2003 Pact agreement, and also started work on rewriting the agreement. In 2017 it negotiated a new script agreement for television and online with the BBC.

## Film

In 1985 an agreement was signed with two producer organisations: the British Film and Television Producers' Association and the Independent Programme Producers' Association (now known as Pact). Since then there has been an industrial agreement covering UK film productions and pension fund contributions have been negotiated for WGGB members. The agreement was renegotiated in February 1992 and consultations on an updated arrangement are in progress.

## Radio

WGGB has a standard agreement for Radio Drama with the BBC, establishing a fee structure that is reviewed annually. It was comprehensively renegotiated in 2005 resulting in an agreement covering digital radio. In 1985 the BBC agreed to extend the pension scheme already established for television writers to include radio writers. WGGB has special agreements for Radio 4's *The Archers* and for BBC iPlayer. A separate agreement covers the reuse of old comedy and drama material on digital BBC Radio 4 Extra. It has also negotiated rates for podcasts.

## Books

WGGB fought for the loans-based Public Lending Right (PLR, see page 369) to reimburse authors for books lent in libraries. The scheme is now administered by the British Library; WGGB is represented on its advisory committee. WGGB has a Books Committee, which works on behalf of book writers and poets. Issues affecting members include authors' earnings, self-publishing, print-on-demand services and ebooks, and in 2022 the union launched the 'Is It A Steal?' joint campaign with the Society of Authors to tackle bad practice in the hybrid/paid-for publishing sector.

## Theatre

In 1979 WGGB, together with the Theatre Writers' Union, negotiated the first industrial agreement for theatre writers. The Theatres National Committee Agreement (TNC) covers the Royal Shakespeare Company, the Royal National Theatre Company and the English Stage Company at the Royal Court. When their agreement was renegotiated in 2007, WGGB achieved a long-standing ambition of a minimum fee of £10,000 for a new play; this has since risen to £13,257.

In June 1986, a new agreement was signed with the Theatrical Management Association (now UK Theatre), which covers 95 provincial theatres. In 1993, this agreement was comprehensively revised and included a provision for a year-on-year increase in fees in line with the Retail Price Index. The agreement was renegotiated in 2015.

After many years of negotiation, an agreement was concluded in 1991 between WGGB and the Independent Theatre Council (ITC), which represents 200 of the smaller and fringe theatres as well as educational and touring companies. This agreement was revised in 2002 and the minimum fees are reviewed annually. WGGB is currently talking to the ITC about updating the agreement. The WGGB Theatre Committee holds an annual forum for Literary Managers and runs the Olwen Wymark Theatre Encouragement Award scheme. In 2022 the union launched a landmark New Play Commission Scheme to address the severe impact Covid-19 had on playwrights and new writing in the theatre sector, resulting in commissions for 18 new plays.

## Videogames

WGGB counts games writers amongst its members and holds regular networking events for them, as well as celebrating their achievements at the annual Writers' Guild Awards. The union publishes guidelines for games writers and those who work with them, outlining best practice in this growing area.

## Other activities

WGGB is in touch with government and national institutions wherever and whenever the interests of writers are in question or are being discussed, for example submitting evidence to a Parliamentary inquiry on the lack of working-class writers. It holds cross-party Parliamentary lobbies with Equity and the Musicians' Union to ensure that the various artforms they represent are properly cared for and writers' voices are heard during, for example, the Brexit transition and the Covid-19 pandemic. Working with the Federation of Entertainment Unions, WGGB makes its views known to bodies, such as Arts Council England and Ofcom on a broader basis.

WGGB is an active affiliate of the British Copyright Council, Creators' Rights Alliance and other organisations whose activities are relevant to professional writers.

Internationally, WGGB plays a leading role in the International Affiliation of Writers Guilds, which includes the American Guilds East and West, the Canadian Guilds (French and English) and the Irish, Mexican, French, Israeli, South African and New Zealand Guilds. When it is possible to make common cause, the guilds act accordingly. WGGB takes a leading role in the Fédération des Scénaristes d'Europe.

On a day-to-day basis, WGGB gives advice on contracts and takes up issues that affect the lives of its members as professional writers. Other benefits include access to free and discounted training, exclusive events and discounts and a dedicated online members' area. Full members are entitled to submit a profile for inclusion in the WGGB online *Find A Writer* directory; pay no joining fee for membership to Writers Guild of America East or West; and are eligible for Cannes accreditation. Regular committee meetings are held by specialist WGGB Craft Committees, and its active branches across the UK organise panel discussions, talks and social events. WGGB also has an Equality & Diversity Committee where activists have been involved in many initiatives, including an access rider to reduce access barriers for freelance writers.

Recent campaigns include Equality Writes, following an independent report commissioned by WGGB which revealed the shocking lack of gender equality in the UK screen industries. The union has also campaigned against the privatisation of Channel 4, and to tackle bullying and harassment in the creative industries. In 2019 it declared a 'climate emergency' and pledged to put the climate crisis at the heart of everything it does. It has also taken a stand against proposed government anti-strike legislation.

Each year WGGB presents the Writers' Guild Awards, covering all the areas in which its members work. These are the only cross-media awards in which writers are honoured by their peers.

# Alliance of Independent Authors

ALLi is the professional association for self-publishing writers and advisors.

The Alliance of Independent Authors (ALLi) is a global organisation with a mission of fostering ethics and excellence in self-publishing and advocating for author-publishers.

Founded in 2012 at the London Book Fair by author, poet and creative mentor, Orna Ross, ALLi is headquartered in London but with members all over the world. In addition to its member services, the organisation offers outreach education to the self-publishing community through its popular online Self-Publishing Advice Center, which features a blog, podcast, bi-annual online conference and series of guidebooks, and supports Ross's annual Self-Publishing Advice Conference.

ALLi has an Advisory Board of author-publishers, educators and service providers, and an active Watchdog desk which rates self-publishing services and provides community alerts. It also publishes a directory of vetted services, ranging from large global players like Amazon KDP and Ingram Spark to local freelancers. Many of these services offer discounted services to ALLi authors.

ALLi advocates for the interests of independent authors within and outside the literary, publishing and bookselling sectors and works with ambassadors, other authors associations and grassroots organisations to promote diversity and accessibility, through a 'Self-Publishing for All' campaign.

Other campaigns include 'Open Up To Indie Authors', which urges the inclusion of author–publishers in literary programmes and events; 'AskALLi', which pledges to answer any self-publishing question anyone might have; and 'Self-Publishing 3.0', a campaign to raise the average income for authors and poets through use of technology and creative business practice.

## Membership

**The Alliance of Independent Authors**
7 Bell Yard, City of Westminster, London WC2A 2JR
*email* info@allianceindependentauthors.org
*website* www.allianceindependentauthors.org, https://selfpublishingadvice.org
*Twitter* @IndieAuthorALLi

ALLi offers three grades of membership for authors:

*Associate membership* (£69 p.a.) is open to writing/publishing students with an interest in self-publishing and non-published writers (or translators) preparing a book for self-publication.

*Author membership* (£89 p.a.) is open to writers or translators of books for adults who have self-published a full-length title (55,000+ words) or series of shorter books; writers of children's/young adult books who have self-published one or more titles.

*Authorpreneur membership* (£119 p.a.) is open to full-time self-publishing authors who earn their living from their author business and can show evidence of 50,000 book sales in the last two years; applications are assessed.

Benefits include self-publishing advice, guidance and community; vetted services, service ratings and watchdog desk; legal and contract appraisal; discounts and deals; professional and business development; campaigns and advocacy.

ALLi also has two partner memberships: for self-publishing services; and for other authors' organizations that align with ALLi's ethos.

# Society of Children's Book Writers & Illustrators

The Society of Children's Book Writers & Illustrators (SCBWI) is the only international professional organisation for authors and illustrators of books for children and young adults. It is a global community of writers, illustrators, translators, publishers, librarians, advocates, and other industry professionals working to establish a more imaginative and inclusive world through the power of children's literature.

**Society of Children's Book Writers and Illustrators**

SCBWI's mission is to support the creation of an abundance of quality children's books, so that young people everywhere have the books they need and deserve. They state that 'We believe there can never be too many good children's books, and this simple belief guides everything we do. We are committed to breaking down barriers and opening doors for everyone with a story to tell. By harnessing the collective power of this vibrant global community, we make the children's publishing industry more inclusive and elevate the art of children's literature.'

Whether you are a professional children's writer or illustrator, or a newcomer to the field, SCBWI has plenty to offer, from local to national to international events, from advice on getting your first deal to help in navigating your career. Established in 1971, SCBWI now has over 26,000 members in 70 regional chapters worldwide; SCBWI serves as a consolidated voice for members within the publishing industry. Membership benefits include professional development and networking opportunities, marketing information, events, publications, online profiles, grants and awards. Through awards, events and publications SCBWI provides established writers, illustrators and translators tools and resources to manage and develop their careers, as well as educate those just starting out.

## What does SCBWI British Isles do?

SCBWI British Isles is a dynamic and friendly chapter of over 1,000 members, which aims to support aspiring and published writers and illustrators and provide opportunities for them to network, market their work, hone their craft, make industry connections and develop their careers. Events include an annual two-day conference, a fiction and picture book retreat, an annual Agents' Party, the Industry Insiders series (six talks a year in London aimed at professional development on a variety of topics), the illustrators' masterclasses (Saturday workshops with a hands-on craft element), sketch and scrawl crawls, author masterclasses, webinars, PULSE events (SCBWI PULSE provides professional development opportunities for published members) and an author and illustrator

**Further information**

**Society of Children's Book Writers & Illustrators**
*website* www.scbwi.org,
https://britishisles.scbwi.org
*Co-Regional Advisors (Co-chairs)* Natascha Biebow and Alison Gardiner
*email* ra@britishscbwi.org
*Membership Coordinator* Anita Loughrey
*email* membership@britishscbwi.org
*Membership* £95 p.a.; £65 p.a. for students

showcase. A network of regional organisers run local critique groups, workshops and social events across the British Isles. SCBWI British Isles is committed to offering free and subsidised places to attend and participate in all of its events and initiatives (see below for details).

## What SCBWI does for its members

• SCBWI is a professional guild. It speaks as a consolidated global voice for professional children's writers and illustrators. In recent years, SCBWI has successfully lobbied for such issues as new copyright legislation, equitable treatment of authors and artists, and fair contract terms.

• It offers a showcase of authors' and illustrators' work through the Find a Speaker Directory, Featured Illustrator Showcase and Member Awards, Celebrations & Achievements Showcase (www.scbwishowcase.org).

• It keeps members up to date with industry developments through the SCBWI PULSE series of events, with opportunities to learn more about the 'business' of writing and illustrating, including marketing and publicity, school and festival visits, and exclusive networking events with librarians and booksellers.

• It offers members invaluable exposure to editors, art directors and agents through one-to-one manuscript or portfolio reviews at the annual conference and retreats, the members-only Agents' Party, the Slush Pile Challenge and biennial SCBWI Undiscovered Voices (www.undiscoveredvoices.com) competitions.

• It supports professional development for members to hone their craft through the Masterclass series, conference workshops and highly successful critique groups.

• It gives members increased visibility online with a free profile on its website, which is a port of call for agents, art directors and editors.

• It provides support and a network of like-minded people, helping to answer members' queries through a variety of online resources including a popular social networking site.

• It facilitates networking opportunities with professionals worldwide.

• Publications include the *Bulletin*, the SCBWI international magazine; *Insight* and *PRO-Insider* e-newsletters; weekly *Words & Pictures* newsletter blog with weekly content (www.wordsandpics.org) and resources including annual publications, market guides and *The Book: The Essential Guide to Children's Publishing*.

• Website resources include book launch parties, members' bookshop, discussion boards, illustrator gallery, Find a Speaker Directory, webinars and podcasts.

## Awards and grants

The SCBWI administers a number of awards and grants.

## British Isles Regional Grants

• There are six Conference Scholarships to attend the annual SCBWI-BI conference.

• A number of scholarship places are awarded at all British Isles region events for underrepresented groups in children's publishing, including SCBWI British Isles members who have financial need; SCBWI British Isles members and non-members who identify as BAME, LGBTQIA+, disabled or working class.

• SCBWI British Isles also offers scholarship memberships to the All Stories Mentorship programme and Undiscovered Voices competition for participants who have been traditionally underrepresented in children's publishing.

## For SCBWI Members

• Several Work-in-Progress Grants are available each year to assist children's book writers. illustrators and translators in the completion of a specific project currently not under contract, in the categories of Picture Book Text, Chapter Books/Early Readers, Middle Grade, Young Adult Fiction, Non-fiction, and Multicultural Fiction or Non-Fiction.

• The Stephen Fraser Encouragement Fund offers three no-strings attached yearly grants of $2,000 each to three children's book authors, artists or translators who have traditionally published at least one book.

## For Writers

• A. Orr Fantasy Grant: For young adult and middle-grade writers working in the fantasy or science fiction genre.

• Ann Whitford Paul – Writer's Digest Manuscript Award: For the Most Promising Picture Book manuscript.

• BIPOC Scholarship: For an all-expense paid trip to the Winter or Summer Conference for a writer who identifies as Black, Indigenous, or a Person of colour.

• The Emerging Voices Award: For fostering the emergence of diverse voices in children's books.

• Karen Cushman Late Bloomer Award: For a work-in-progress from an unpublished author over age 50.

• Out from the Margins Award: For early career under-represented creators of children's literature.

• Volemos – The Meg Medina Grant: For authors of Hispanic/Latinx/Ibero-American heritage who are in the early stages of their career (between 1 and 3 traditionally published books) or not yet traditionally published.

• The Russell Freedman Award for Non-Fiction for a Better World (currently closed): For a work of non-fiction that contributes to our understanding of how to make our world and society better.

## For Illustrators

• Bologna Illustrators Scholarship: For two illustrators to receive a ticket to the Bologna Book Fair, travel fare, and a stipend for accommodations.

• Don Freeman Work-in-Progress Grant: For assisting illustrators in the completion of a book dummy or portfolio.

• Ezra Jack Keats Showcase Prize: For a promising BIPOC illustrator.

• Narrative Art Award: For an illustrator of promise based on a given prompt.

• Out from the Margins Award: For early career under-represented creators of children's literature.

• The Tomie dePaola Professional Development Award (currently closed): For grants of $3,500 and $1,500 to two early-career illustrators in need of professional development funding.

• The Portfolio Award: For the best art portfolio on view at the Juried Portfolio Display at the Summer or Winter Conference.

• Student Illustrator Scholarships: For Summer or Winter Conference tuition for full-time university students studying illustration.

## For PAL Published Members

• The Book Launch Award: Provides authors or illustrators with $2,000 in funds to help the promotion of their newly published work and taking the marketing strategy into their own creative hands.

• The Golden and Crystal Kite Awards: For the most outstanding books published by SCBWI members each year, voted for by SCBWI peers.

## For Independently Published Members

• Independently Published Pre-publication Grant provides $2,500 to help offset the price of self-publishing.

• The annual Spark Award recognises excellence in a children's book published through a non-traditional publishing route.

## Community Grants

• Amber Brown Grant commemorates author and beloved school speaker Paula Danziger. One school is awarded each year with an author or illustrator visit and new books to continue Paula's love of connecting children with creative influences.

• The SCBWI Disability Fund gives grants to disabled members for anything that would help them create children's literature. For non-members with disabilities, the funds may support memberships and/or registration to events.

• The SCBWI Emergency Fund gives a grant of up to $1,500 to a member for anything that would help them create children's literature. For non-members with disabilities, the funds may support memberships and/or registration to events.

## See also...

• *Seven Stories – The National Centre for Children's Books*, page 309
• *Federation of Children's Book Groups*, page 311
• *Opportunities for under-represented writers*, page 345

# Seven Stories – The National Centre for Children's Books

At Seven Stories the rich heritage of British children's books is collected, explored and celebrated.

**seven stories**
National Centre for Children's Books

Once upon a time an idea was born on the banks of the Tyne to create a national home for children's literature – a place where the original work of authors and illustrators could be collected, treasured and celebrated. After ten years of pioneering work by founding directors Elizabeth Hammill and Mary Briggs, that dream became a reality. In August 2005 Seven Stories, the Centre for Children's Books, opened in an award-winning converted seven storey Victorian granary in the Ouseburn Valley, a stone's throw from Newcastle's vibrant quayside. Seven Stories is now officially known as The National Centre for Children's Books, following approval by Arts Council England in 2012. It is the only accredited museum in the UK that specialises in children's books.

## The collection

At the heart of Seven Stories is a unique and growing collection of manuscripts, artwork and other pre-publication materials. These treasures record the creative process involved in making a children's book and provide illuminating insights into the working lives of modern authors and illustrators. The collection focuses on work created in modern Britain. It already contains thousands of items by authors such as Judith Kerr, Peter Dickinson, Michael Morpurgo, Enid Blyton, Berlie Doherty, Jan Mark, Philip Pullman, Michael Rosen, Robert Westall and Ursula Moray Williams; illustrators like Edward Ardizzone, Faith Jaques, Harold Jones, Anthony Maitland, Pat Hutchins, Helen Cooper, Jan Ormerod and Jane Ray; and editors and other practitioners such as Kaye Webb. Many more bodies of work are pledged. A catalogue of the collection is available via the Seven Stories website. In 2022, Seven Stories launched an new platform designed to attract and encourage new audiences to explore its collections and widen access to a digitised archive of children's literature through https://sevenstories.online.

## Exhibitions

A celebration of creativity underpins the Seven Stories project: its collection documents the creative act, and its exhibitions and programmes interpret this original material in unconventional but meaningful ways. The aim is to cultivate an appreciation of books and their making, and inspire creativity in its audience.

Seven Stories has been mounting exhibitions since 1998 – first in borrowed venues and now in its own home. Here it provides the only exhibition space in the UK wholly dedicated to showcasing the incomparable legacy of British writing and illustrating for children. With exhibitions changing every year, Seven Stories have profiled the work of children's authors such as Judith Kerr, Michael Morpurgo and David McKee, as well as working alongside communities to showcase their collection in ways that reflect a modern and ever-changing landscape.

Throughout its seven storeys – from the galleries, Story Station to the independent bookshop and coffee shop to the Attic – visitors of all ages are invited to engage in a unique, interactive exploration of creativity, literature and art. In this ever-changing literary playground and landscape for the imagination, they can become writers, artists, explorers, designers, storytellers, readers or collectors, in the company of storytellers, authors, illustrators and Seven Stories' own facilitators and learning team.

Seven Stories aims to place children, young people and their books at the heart of the UK's national literary culture. An independent educational charity, it is committed to access for all and has initiated several innovative participation projects working with its regional universities to develop their collection while utilising the archive of over one million items from the making of children's literature to broaden access and improve inclusivity.

Seven Stories is dedicated to the celebration of children's literature. It is supported by Arts Council England and Community Foundation Newcastle Culture Investment Fund.

## Further information

**Seven Stories – The National Centre for Children's Books**

30 Lime Street, Ouseburn Valley, Newcastle upon Tyne NE1 2PQ

*tel* 0300 330 1095

*email* info@sevenstories.org.uk

*website* www.sevenstories.org.uk

*Twitter* @7stories

*Public opening hours* Thurs–Tues, 10am–5pm. Open daily during school holidays.

*Admission charges* General admission free. Events, story time, and workshops tickets start at £2.

Please check the website for the most up-to-date opening and booking information.

## See also...

- *Society of Children's Book Writers & Illustrators*, page 305
- *Federation of Children's Book Groups*, page 311

# Federation of Children's Book Groups

'The Federation of Children's Book Groups, has, in its own quiet, single-minded way, done more for reading than almost anyone else' – *Anthony Horowitz*

The achievements of the Federation of Children's Book Groups were publicly recognised in 2011 when it was nominated for and subsequently won the Eleanor Farjeon Award. Its aim is simple: to bring children and books together, promote children's books and inspire a love of reading through its national and local events. If you are a parent, carer, author, illustrator or professional with a passion for encouraging children to read, the Federation will be of interest to you.

## Federation history

The Federation of Children's Book Groups was formed in 1968 by Anne Wood to co-ordinate the work of the many different children's book groups already in existence across the country, and in 2018 it celebrated 50 years of bringing children and books together.

Celebrating its 40th anniversary in 2020, the Children's Book Award is the only national award voted for entirely by children. Throughout the year Federation Testing Groups read and vote on new fiction supplied by publishers. Each year 100,000 votes are cast involving nearly 250 schools and families across the UK. A shortlist (Top Ten) is drawn up with four picture books in the Younger Children category, three shorter novels for Younger Readers and three novels for Older Readers, with children from all over the UK voting in their groups or online. You do not have to be a member to vote in the Top Ten. The Award has a track record of identifying future bestsellers: the first Overall Winner was *Mr Magnolia* by Quentin Blake; other winners include *The Hunger Games*, and the *Harry Potter* and *Percy Jackson* books. For over ten years the Award was supported by Red House, with award ceremonies held at a number of prestigious venues, including the Queen Elizabeth Hall, in London as part of the Imagine: Writers and Writing for Children (see page 352).

In 1976 National Tell-A-Story-Week was established and it has now grown into National Share-A-Story-Month (NSSM), which takes place each May. It enables groups to focus on the power of story and to hold events which celebrate all forms of storytelling. The theme in 2023 is 'Sail Away in a Story'. The website hosts the NSSM pack, full of ideas and activities, which is sent to each book group and can also be downloaded by non-members.

In 1977, the first Federation anthology was published, and since then they have compiled booklists covering the whole age range from picture books to the latest teen and young adult novels; these are available on request free of charge via the website as downloads.

In 2010 the Federation created National Non-Fiction Day to celebrate the quality and variety of information books available for children; this takes place on the first Thursday of each November, with a host of events focused on non-fiction. It has expanded to be

National Non-Fiction November; further details can be found on the website. The theme for 2022 was 'Communication', and there are always resources to download for free.

Each year the Federation holds a conference: three days of author and illustrator events, panel discussions and seminars enable group and individual members, publishers, authors, illustrators, teachers, librarians and booksellers to meet and exchange ideas. Delegates are inspired by meeting others who share their passion. The 2023 Conference was held in April at Rugby School, entitled 'Portable Magic: How to Catch a Reader'. See http://fcbg.org.uk/conference for more details about future events.

## The Children's Book Groups

Federation Book Groups exist throughout the UK: from Plymouth to Dundee, from Ipswich to St David's and from Harrogate to Lewes. Their activities are as varied and diverse as the groups themselves, serving their own community's needs, including author and illustrator visits, bonfire parties, museum and library events, book swaps and parties. But, above all, FCBG are passionate about children's books, bringing together ordinary book-loving families, empowering parents, grandparents, carers and children to become enthusiastic and excited about all kinds of good books. Some book groups are based around schools run by enthusiastic librarians and teachers. You can still be a member of the Federation if there is no book group near you. Individual and professional membership enables everyone to participate in sharing their passion for children's books.

> ### Further information
>
> **Federation of Children's Book Groups**
> Wakananai Firs Road, Mardy, Abergavenny,
> Wales NP7 6NA
> *tel* 07591 380434
> *email* info@fcbg.org.uk
> *website* http://fcbg.org.uk

### See also...
- *Society of Children's Book Writers & Illustrators*, page 305
- *Seven Stories – The National Centre for Children's Books*, page 309

# National Literacy Trust

Authors and artists can spark a lifelong love of reading – it just takes one book. Jonathan Douglas explains how the National Literacy Trust is raising literacy levels across the UK.

Writers and artists are essential to the National Literacy Trust's mission to raise literacy levels in the UK. We work to improve reading, writing, speaking and listening abilities in the most disadvantaged communities. Creators are not just our natural allies, they are key partners in our campaign to make a difference. It goes without saying that a literacy charity cannot exist without books.

**Further information**

**National Literacy Trust**
68 South Lambeth Road, London SW8 1RL
*tel* 020-7587 1842
*email* contact@literacytrust.org.uk
*website* https://literacytrust.org.uk
*Facebook* www.facebook.com/nationalliteracytrust
*Twitter* @Literacy_Trust

The literacy challenge in the UK is significant: in 2022, over a quarter of children left primary school unable to read and write at the expected level, with children from disadvantaged backgrounds falling even further behind. With 4.3 million children already living in poverty and the cost-of-living crisis set to grow this at a faster rate than any time in the last century, the literacy levels of the most vulnerable children are at risk.

Authors have the power to transform the way a child engages with books and in doing so unlock a lifetime of benefits. Our research shows that visits from authors to schools have a tangible impact on literacy skills: twice as many children and young people who had a writer visit to their school read above the expected level for their age compared with their peers who didn't have such a visit. What's more, children who have had an author visit to their school also have higher levels of confidence in their reading and enjoy reading and writing more. We are grateful when writers ask how they can collaborate with us, and are always looking for support with our campaigning. As a charitable organisation, we are thankful to the people who help us spread the word about our initiatives. Every new like, comment or share is vitally important in helping us reach the people who need our assistance.

One of the National Literacy Trust's priorities is increasing access to books by transforming and equipping primary school libraries. 1 in 7 state primary schools does not have a designated library space and over three-quarters of a million children (that's nearly 1 in 10 children from disadvantaged backgrounds) in the UK do not own, or have access to, books at home. To combat this, the Primary School Library Alliance was founded in November 2021 by the National Literacy Trust and Penguin Random House UK. The Alliance works with its flagship partners to address the chronic lack of investment in primary school libraries and brings together relevant parties to help solve this urgent issue. The aim is to transform 1,000 primary school libraries by 2025. In its first twelve months, the Alliance involved 334 schools in its programmes to transform school reading spaces in underserved communities in the UK, including donating 165,840 books. We believe that bringing together expertise and resources from partners across a number of sectors can more effectively support children's educational outcomes and ensure the wider emotional and economic benefits of reading for pleasure can be felt by all children.

The unequal impact of school closures during the recent pandemic, coupled with the pressures of the cost-of-living crisis, highlights the urgent need for our work helping children, young people, families, teachers and communities. Our Arts Council England-funded project 'Connecting Stories' is in its second year and is an excellent example of our work to make deep connections with communities where engagement with reading for pleasure is traditionally low. Publishers large and small are donating books and writers' time to encourage children in 14 areas with low literacy levels to read for pleasure, enjoy their local libraries, and boost their wellbeing. Since its launch, Connecting Stories has reached more than 200,000 individuals. It has been supported by 43 publishers and 95 authors and creatives, including celebrated children's writers Cressida Cowell, Matt Haig and Waterstones Children's Laureate Joseph Coelho (see Joseph's *Foreword* on page xv).

We are working hard to make sure more children will have greater access to books and their brilliant benefits. We will continue our work developing programmes, resources, activities and materials to give children across the country the best chance to develop literacy skills that will benefit them throughout their lives.

**Jonathan Douglas** CBE is the Chief Executive of the National Literacy Trust.

## See also...
• *Opportunities for under-represented writers*, page 345

# Societies, associations and organisations

The societies and associations listed here include appreciation societies devoted to specific authors, professional bodies and national institutions. Some also offer prizes and awards (see page 333).

## AccessArt

6 West Street, Comberton, Cambridge CB23 7DS
*tel* (01223) 262134
*website* www.accessart.org.uk

Inspires and enables high-quality visual arts teaching, learning and practice. The website features over 1,200 unique resources to inspire practice.

## Action for Children's Arts

c/o Mousetrap Theatre Projects,
33 Shaftesbury Avenue, London W1D 7EH
*website* www.childrensarts.org.uk
*Facebook* www.facebook.com/ActionChildrensArts
*Twitter* @childrensarts
*Membership* £18 student and school; £30 p.a. individual; from £50 p.a. organisation

A membership charity organisation that values children, childhood and the arts. It embraces the UN Convention on the Rights of the Child by campaigning for the right of all children in the UK to experience high-quality arts as an integral part of their childhood; by connecting people within and across the cultural and education sectors, across art forms and across the regions and nations of the UK; and by celebrating achievement, dedication and best practice in artistic activity for and with children.

## Louisa May Alcott's Orchard House

Orchard House, 399 Lexington Road, Concord, MA 01742, USA
*email* admin@louisamayalcott.org
*website* www.louisamayalcott.org
*Facebook* www.facebook.com/
louisamayalcottsorchardhouse
*Twitter* @LouisaMayAlcott

A not-for-profit historic site dedicated to public education and historic preservation, providing guided tours, educational programmes and special events that honour and interpret the legacy of the Alcotts, a unique 19th-century family who contributed to the fields of literature, education, philosophy, art and social justice. Founded 1911.

## Alliance of Independent Authors – see page 304

## American Booksellers Association

333 Westchester Avenue, Suite S202, White Plains, NY 10604, USA
*tel* +1 800-637-0037
*email* info@bookweb.org
*website* www.bookweb.org

A national non-profit trade organisation that works with booksellers and industry partners to ensure the success and profitability of independently owned book retailers and to assist in expanding the book community. Provides education and information dissemination, offers business products and services, creates relevant awareness programmes and engages in public policy. Founded 1900.

## American Society of Composers, Authors and Publishers

250 West 57th Street, New York, NY 10107, USA
*tel* 020-7439 0909
*website* www.ascap.com
*Facebook* www.facebook.com/ascap
*Twitter* @ascap
*Instagram* @ascap

An organisation founded and governed by its members, it is the leading performance rights organisation representing more than 850,000 songwriters, composers and music publishers.

## Arts Council/An Chomhairle Ealaíon

70 Merrion Square, Dublin D02 NY52,
Republic of Ireland
*tel* +353 (0)1 618 0200
*website* www.artscouncil.ie/home
*Facebook* www.facebook.com/artscouncilireland
*Twitter* @artscouncil_ie
*Instagram* @artscouncilireland

The national development agency for the arts in Ireland. Promotes the arts through funding, research, information sharing, setting standards and encouraging appreciation. Founded 1951.

## Arts Council England

*tel* 0161 934 4317
*website* www.artscouncil.org.uk
*Facebook* www.facebook.com/artscouncilofengland
*Twitter* @ace_national
*Instagram* @aceagrams

The national development agency for arts and culture in England, distributing public money from the government and the National Lottery. Organisations, artists, events and initiatives can receive funding to help achieve the Council's mission of providing art and culture for everyone. There are nine regional offices: Newcastle, Leeds, Manchester, Nottingham, Birmingham, Cambridge, Brighton, Bristol and London. Visit the website for information on funding support and advice, an online funding finder and funding FAQs. Founded 1946.

## Arts Council of Northern Ireland

Linen Hill House, 23 Linenhall Street,
Lisburn BT28 1FJ
*tel* 028-9262 3555
*email* info@artscouncil-ni.org
*website* www.artscouncil-ni.org
*Chief Executive* Roisín McDonough

Promotes and encourages the arts throughout Northern Ireland. Artists in drama, dance, music and jazz, literature, the visual arts, traditional arts and community arts can apply for support for specific schemes and projects. The value of the grant will be set according to the aims of the programme. Artists of all disciplines and in all types of working practice, who have made a contribution to artistic activities in Northern Ireland for a minimum period of one year within the last five years, are eligible.

## Arts Council of Wales

Bute Place, Cardiff CF10 5AL
*tel* 0330 124 2733
*website* https://arts.wales
*Twitter* @Arts_Wales_

The official body that funds and develops the arts in Wales. The funding it distributes comes from both the Welsh government and the National Lottery; most funding goes to artists and arts organisations carrying out programmes of work across Wales. Founded 1994.

### North Wales Regional Office

Princes Park II, Princes Drive, Colwyn Bay LL29 8PL

### Mid and West Wales Regional Office

The Mount, 18 Queen Street, Carmarthen SA31 1JT

## Association for Library Service to Children

American Library Association, 225 N Michigan Ave, Suite 1300 Chicago, IL 60601, USA
*tel* +1 800-545-2433
*email* alsc@ala.org
*website* www.ala.org/alsc
*Facebook* www.facebook.com/
Associationforlibraryservicetochildren
*Twitter* @wearealsc

Develops and supports the profession of children's librarianship by enabling and encouraging its practitioners to provide the best library service to US children.

## Association for Scottish Literature

c/o Dept of Scottish Literature,
University of Glasgow, 7 University Gardens,
Glasgow G12 8QH
*tel* 0141 330 5309
*email* office@asls.org.uk
*website* www.asls.org.uk
*President* David Goldie, *Secretary* Moira Hansen,
*Director* Duncan Jones
*Membership* £65 p.a. individuals; £18 p.a. UK students; £100 p.a. corporate

Promotes the study, teaching and writing of Scottish literature and furthers the study of the languages of Scotland. Publishes annually *New Writing Scotland*, an anthology of new Scottish writing; an edited text of Scottish literature; a series of academic journals; and the eZine *The Bottle Imp*. Also publishes *Scotnotes* (comprehensive study guides for major Scottish writers), literary texts and commentaries designed to assist the classroom teacher, and a series of occasional papers. Organises two conferences a year. Founded 1970.

## Association of American Literary Agents

302A West 12th Street, Suite 122, New York,
NY 10014, USA
*email* assistant@aalitagents.org
*website* https://aalitagents.org

A professional organisation of over 415 agents who work with authors and illustrators. Founded 1991.

## Association of American Publishers

455 Massachusetts Avenue, NW Suite 700,
Washington, DC 20001, USA
*tel* +1 202-347-3375
*email* info@publishers.org
*website* https://publishers.org
*Twitter* @AmericanPublish

AAP is the largest trade association for US books, journals and education publishers, providing advocacy and communications on behalf of the industry and its priorities nationally and worldwide. Founded 1970.

## The Association of Authors' Agents

c/o The Society of Authors, 24 Bedford Row,
London WC1R 4EH
*tel* 020-3880 2230
*website* www.agentsassoc.co.uk
*President* Catherine Clarke, *Secretary* Camille Burns

The AAA exists to provide a forum which allows member agencies to discuss issues arising in the profession; a collective voice for UK literary agencies in public affairs and the media; and a code of conduct to which all members commit themselves. Please note that the AAA is not able to offer advice on finding representation by an agent or getting published. Founded 1974.

## Association of Canadian Publishers

401 Richmond Street W, Studio 257A, Toronto,
ON M5V 3A8, Canada
*tel* +1 416-487-6116
*email* admin@canbook.org
*website* https://publishers.ca
*Executive Director* Kate Edwards

Represents approximately 115 Canadian-owned and
controlled book publishers from across the country.
Activities include government and public relations,
marketing initiatives, research and communications,
and professional development. Founded 1976.

## Association of Freelance Editors, Proofreaders and Indexers of Ireland

*email* info@afepi-ireland.com
*website* www.afepi-ireland.com
*Facebook* www.facebook.com/AFEPI.Ireland
*Twitter* @AFEPI_Ireland

AFEPI Ireland is a professional organisation for
publishing and editorial freelancers in Ireland. It
fosters high standards in editing, proofreading and
indexing; protects the interests of its members; and
helps to match authors, indie writers, publishers,
businesses, public bodies and charitable organisations
with suitable editorial freelancers. Membership is
available to experienced professional editors,
proofreaders and indexers. For services for publishers
and authors, see the online directory of freelance
professional editors, proofreaders and indexers based
in Ireland and Northern Ireland. Founded 1985.

## The Association of Illustrators

Somerset House, Strand, London WC2R 1LA
*tel* 020-7759 1010
*email* info@theaoi.com
*website* www.theaoi.com
*Facebook* www.facebook.com/theaoi
*Twitter* @theaoi

Trade association which supports illustrators with
licensing and contract advice, promotes illustration
and encourages professional standards in the
industry. Presents an annual programme of events
and holds an annual competition, the World
Illustration Awards, in partnership with the *Directory
of Illustration.* Founded 1973.

## Australia Council

PO Box 576, Pyrmont, NSW 2009, Australia
*tel* +61 (0)2 9215 9000
*website* www.australiacouncil.gov.au
*Ceo* Adrian Collette

Provides a broad range of support for the arts in
Australia, embracing music, theatre, literature, visual
arts and crafts, dance, First Nations arts, community
and experimental arts.

## Australian Copyright Council

PO Box 1986, Strawberry Hills, NSW 2012, Australia
*tel* +61 (0)2 9101 2377

*email* info@copyright.org.au
*website* www.copyright.org.au
*Facebook* www.facebook.com/AusCopyrightCouncil
*Twitter* @AusCopyright
*Instagram* @AusCopyrightCouncil
*Chief Executive Officer* Eileen Camilleri

Provides easily accessible and affordable practical
information, legal advice, education and forums on
Australian copyright law for content creators and
consumers. It represents the peak bodies for
professional artists and content creators working in
Australia's creative industries and Australia's major
copyright collecting societies, including the Australian
Society of Authors, the Australian Writers' Guild and
the Australian Publishers Association.

The Council advocates for the contribution of
creators to Australia's culture and economy and the
importance of copyright for the common good. It
works to promote understanding of copyright law
and its application, advocate for appropriate law
reform and foster collaboration between content
creators and consumers. Founded 1968.

## Australian Publishers Association

60/89 Jones Street, Ultimo, NSW 2007, Australia
*tel* +61 (0)2 9281 9788
*website* www.publishers.asn.au
*Twitter* @AusPublish

The APA is the industry body for Australian book,
journal and electronic publishers. Founded 1948.

## Australian Writers' Guild

Level 4, 70 Pitt Street, Sydney, NSW 2000, Australia
*tel* +61 (0)2 9319 0339
*email* admin@awg.com.au
*website* www.awg.com.au

The professional association representing writers for
stage, screen, radio and online. Has protected and
promoted their creative and professional interests for
60 years. Founded 1962.

## Authors Aloud UK

72 Castle Road, St Albans, Herts. AL1 5DG
*tel* (01727) 893992
*email* info@authorsalouduk.co.uk
*website* www.authorsalouduk.co.uk
*Facebook* www.facebook.com/Authors-Aloud-UK-
497942623573822
*Twitter* @AuthorsAloudUK
*Instagram* @AuthorsAloudUK
*Directors* Naomi Cooper, Annie Everall

An author booking agency which brings together
authors, illustrators, poets, storytellers and trainers
with schools, libraries and festivals, in the UK and
internationally, to promote enthusiasm for reading,
both for enjoyment and information. Works with
children's authors who wish to visit schools and
libraries, in person and virtually, and who are
published by mainstream children's publishers.

Also arranges author tours and book-related events for publishers and other organisations.

## Authors' Licensing and Collecting Society – see page 407

## Quentin Blake Centre for Illustration

Rear of 28 Amwell Street, London EC1R 1XU
*email* info@qbcentre.org.uk
*website* https://qbcentre.org.uk
*Twitter* @qbcentre
*Instagram* @qbcentre

Will open the UK's permanent national Centre for Illustration in London in 2024. The Centre will have exhibition galleries, an education studio, community gardens and a permanent gallery for the archive of the organisation's founder, Quentin Blake. Until it reopens, the centre's work continues, with online talks and workshops and a UK-wide programme of touring exhibitions.

## Enid Blyton Society

*email* tony@enidblytonsociety.co.uk
*website* www.enidblytonsociety.co.uk

Provides a focal point for collectors and enthusiasts of Enid Blyton through its magazine *The Enid Blyton Society Journal* (three each year) and website. Founded 1995.

## Book Marketing Society

*email* admin@bookmarketingsociety.co.uk
*website* www.bookmarketingsociety.co.uk
*Twitter* @BMSoc

Launched with the objective of becoming the representative body of marketing within the book industry. It provides a forum for sharing best practice, inspiration and creativity across the sector through regular awards and a lively programme of member meetings, development workshops, masterclasses and social events. Anyone who works for a book publisher, book retailer or book wholesaler is eligible for membership, including those working in associated areas of the publishing and book retailing industry.

## Books Council of Wales/Cyngor Llyfrau Cymru

Castell Brychan, Aberystwyth, Ceredigion SY23 2JB
*tel* (01970) 624151
*email* castellbrychan@books.wales
*website* https://llyfrau.cymru/en
*website* www.gwales.com
*Ceo* Helgard Krause

A national charity which supports and develops the publishing industry in Wales. It promotes literacy and reading for pleasure through a range of public campaigns, activities and events across Wales, often working in partnership with schools, libraries and other literary organisations. The Council works with publishers to nurture new talent and content in Welsh and English as well as offering specialist editing, design, marketing and distribution services. It administers grants to publishers and independent booksellers. Partly funded by the Welsh government through Creative Wales and from the commercial operations of its wholesale book distribution centre. Founded 1961.

## The Booksellers Association

6 Bell Yard, London WC2A 2JR
*tel* 020-7421 4640
*email* mail@booksellers.org.uk
*website* www.booksellers.org.uk
*Twitter* @BAbooksellers
*President* Hazel Broadfoot

A membership organisation for all booksellers in the UK and Ireland, representing over 95% of bookshops. Key services include National Book Tokens, Batch Payment Services and BatchLine. Founded 1895.

## BookTrust

G8 Battersea Studios, 80 Silverthorne Road, London SW8 3HE
*tel* 020-7801 8800
*email* query@booktrust.org.uk
*website* www.booktrust.org.uk
*Twitter* @Booktrust
*Ceo* Diana Gerald, *Chair of Trustees* John Coughlan

The UK's largest children's reading charity, dedicated to getting children reading because children who read are happier, healthier, more empathetic and more creative; they also do better at school. BookTrust gets children reading in lots of different ways, but its priority is to get children excited about books and stories.

Reviews at least one children's book each day and runs the Waterstones Children's Laureate, BookTrust Storytime Prize and BookTrust Lifetime Achievement Award.

## BookTrust Represents

G8 Battersea Studios, 80 Silverthorne Road, London SW8 3HE
*tel* 020-7801 8826
*email* booktrust.represents@booktrust.org.uk
*website* www.booktrust.org.uk/booktrustrepresents
*Twitter* @Booktrust

A project to support and promote authors and illustrators of colour and to reach more readers through school visits, special events and festivals. The project also supports aspiring and new authors and illustrators of colour with training, mentoring, events and an online community. Find out more about the project and the associated research into the ethnicity of authors and illustrators in the UK on the website. Founded 2019.

## The British Council

Bridgewater House, 58 Whitworth Street,
Manchester M1 6BB
*tel* 0161 957 7755
*website* www.britishcouncil.org
*Facebook* www.facebook.com/britishcouncil
*Twitter* @BritishCouncil
*Chief Executive* Scott McDonald, *Director of Cultural Engagement* Mark Stephens

The UK's international organisation for cultural relations and educational opportunities. Builds connections, understanding and trust between people in the UK and other countries through arts and culture, education and the English language. Working in close collaboration with book trade associations, the Literature team participates in major international book fairs.

Collaborates with offices overseas to broker relationships and create activities which link artists and cultural institutions around the world. Works with writers, publishers, producers, translators and other sector professionals across literature, publishing and education. The Visual Arts team shares UK visual arts around the world, connecting professionals internationally through collaborative exhibition programmes, digital networking, training and development and delegations. Manages and develops the British Council Collection and the British Pavilion at the Venice Biennale.

## Canadian Authors Association

19 Machell Avenue, Aurora, ON L4G 2R6, Canada
*tel* +1 877-905-1921 ext. 800
*email* office@canadianauthors.org
*website* www.canadianauthors.org
*Facebook* www.facebook.com/
canadianauthorsassociation
*Twitter* @canauthors
*Administrative Director* Brandi Tanner

A membership-based organisation for writers in all areas of the profession. Has branches across Canada that provide writers with a wide variety of programmes, services and resources to help them develop their skills in the craft and business of writing. Founded 1921.

## The Canadian Children's Book Centre

5th Floor, 30 Wellington Street West,
Toronto ON M5L 1E2, Canada
*tel* +1 416-975-0010
*email* info@bookcentre.ca
*website* https://bookcentre.ca
*Facebook* www.facebook.com/kidsbookcentre
*Twitter* @kidsbookcentre
*Instagram* @kidsbookcentre

CBBC is a national, not-for-profit organisation that is dedicated to encouraging, promoting and supporting the reading, writing, illustrating and publishing of Canadian books for young readers. Programmes, publications and resources help teachers, librarians, booksellers and parents select the very best for young readers. Founded 1976.

## Canadian Publishers' Council

Suite 6060, 3080 Yonge Street, Toronto,
ON M4N 3N1
*tel* +1 647-255-8880
*email* dswail@pubcouncil.ca
*website* https://pubcouncil.ca
*Twitter* @pubcouncil_ca
*President* David Swail

Represents the interests of Canadian publishing companies that publish books and other media for schools, colleges and universities, professional and reference markets, the retail and library sectors. Founded 1910.

## Canadian Society of Children's Authors, Illustrators & Performers

720 Bathurst Street, Suite 412, Toronto,
ON M5S 2R4, Canada
*tel* +1 416-515-1559
*email* office@canscaip.org
*website* www.canscaip.org
*Twitter* @CANSCAIP
*Administrative Director* Helena Aalto
*Membership* $85 p.a. member; $45 p.a. friend

CANSCAIP is a membership-based non-profit organisation that supports the professional development of Canada's community of authors, illustrators and performers for children and teens. Founded 1977.

## The Lewis Carroll Society

*email* secretary@lewiscarrollsociety.org.uk
*email* membership@lewiscarrollsociety.org.uk
*website* https://lewiscarrollsociety.org.uk
*Facebook* www.facebook.com/groups/68678994062
*Twitter* @LewisCarrollSoc
*Membership* £25 p.a. UK; £30 p.a. Europe; £35 p.a. elsewhere; special rates for students and institutions

Promotes interest in the life and works of Lewis Carroll (Revd Charles Lutwidge Dodgson, 1832–98) and encourages research. Activities include regular meetings, exhibitions and a publishing programme that includes the first annotated, unexpurgated edition of his diaries in nine volumes, the society's journal *The Carrollian*, a newsletter, *Bandersnatch*, and the *Lewis Carroll Review*. An archive hosting 50 years of scholarly journals is available to members through an online portal. Founded 1969.

## Lewis Carroll Society of North America

*email* president@lewiscarroll.org
*website* www.lewiscarroll.org
*Facebook* www.facebook.com/LCSNA
*Twitter* @AliceAmerica
*President* Arnold Hirshon
*Membership* $42 p.a.

An organisation of Carroll admirers, of all ages and interests, dedicated to furthering Carroll studies, increasing accessibility of research material, and maintaining public awareness of Carroll's contributions to society. Has a worldwide membership and meets twice a year. Maintains an active publication programme and members receive copies of the society's magazine *Knight Letter*. An interest in Lewis Carroll or a simple love for Alice (or the Snark for that matter) qualifies for membership. Founded 1974.

## The Center for Children's Books

School of Information Sciences,
501 East Daniel Street, Champaign, IL 61820, USA
*tel* +1 217-244-9331
*email* ccb-asst@illinois.edu
*website* https://ccb.ischool.illinois.edu
*Twitter* @iSchoolCCB

CCB houses a non-circulating collection of recent and historically significant trade books for children, plus review copies of nearly all trade books published in the USA in the current year.

There are professional and reference books on the history and criticism of literature for youth, literature-based library and classroom programming, and storytelling. The collection is available for examination by scholars, teachers, librarians, students and other educators.

## Centre for Literacy in Primary Education

Webber Street, London SE1 8QW
*tel* 020-7401 3382/3
*email* info@clpe.org.uk
*website* https://clpe.org.uk
*Facebook* www.facebook.com/
CentreforLiteracyinPrimaryEducation
*Twitter* @clpe1

The CLPE is a small independent charity working with all those involved in teaching literacy in primary schools. Raises the achievement of children by helping schools to teach literacy more effectively and by showing teachers how quality children's literature can be placed at the heart of all learning.

## The Children's Book Council and Every Child A Reader

54 West 39th Street, 14th Floor, New York, NY 10018, USA
*email* cbc.info@cbcbooks.org
*website* www.cbcbooks.org
*website* www.everychildareader.net

The CBC is the non-profit trade association of North American publishers and packagers of trade books and related materials for children and young adults. Runs Every Child a Reader, its charitable component that sponsors Children's Book Week; the Kids' Book Choice Awards; Get Caught Reading; and the National Ambassador of Young People's Literature, in conjunction with the Library of Congress.

Offers children's publishers the opportunity to work together on educational programming, diversity advocacy, and national literacy and public awareness campaigns. The CBC connects member publishers to librarians, teachers, booksellers and caregivers across the country, providing reading lists, student resources and community outreach in coordination with prominent national organisations.

## The Children's Book Council of Australia

Level 2 State Library of Queensland, Stanley Place, South Brisbane, QLD 4101, Australia
*email* admin@cbca.org.au
*website* www.cbca.org.au
*Facebook* www.facebook.com/theCBCA
*Twitter* @theCBCA

Fosters children's enjoyment of books through managing the Children's Book of the Year Awards; providing information on and encouragement to authors and illustrators; organising exhibitions and activities during Children's Book Week; supporting children's library services; and promoting high standards in book reviewing, along with promoting greater equity of access to reading through community projects.

## The Children's Book Guild of Washington DC

*email* membership.cbg@gmail.com
*website* www.childrensbookguild.org
*Facebook* www.facebook.com/bookguilddc
*Twitter* @BOOKGUILDDC
*Instagram* @bookguilddc

A regional association of writers, artists, librarians and other specialists dedicated to the field of children's literature. Its aims are to uphold and stimulate high standards of writing and illustrating for children; to increase knowledge and use of better books for children in the community; and to cooperate with other groups having similar purposes. Founded 1945.

## Children's Book North

*email* childrensbooknorth@gmail.com
*website* https://childrensbooknorth.blogspot.com
*Twitter* @books_north
*Instagram* @childrens_books_north
*Co-founders* Emma Layfield, Tilda Johnson, Liz Scott

A voluntary network group which connects published children's authors, illustrators and publishing professionals living in the North West, North East, Yorkshire and Scotland. The network seeks to promote their members' work, new books and events, and highlights the importance of regional diversity in children's books and the publishing industry.

## Children's Books Ireland
17 North Great George's Street, Dublin D01 R2F1, Republic of Ireland
*tel* +353 (0)1 872 7475
*email* info@childrensbooksireland.com
*website* www.childrensbooksireland.ie
*Ceo* Elaina Ryan, *Deputy Ceo* Jenny Murray, *Programme & Events Manager* Aoife Murray

Champions every child's right to develop a love of reading. They aim to engage young people in reading, foster a greater understanding of books for young people and act as a core resource for those with an interest in books for children in Ireland. Celebrates the importance of authors and illustrators and work in partnership with the people and organisations who enhance children's lives through books. Core projects include: the Children's Books Ireland International Annual Conference; the KPMG Children's Books Ireland Awards and its Junior Juries' programme for school groups and book clubs; the annual Children's Books Ireland Reading Guide; nationwide Book Clinics; various book gifting initiatives including the Every Child A Reader Reading Communities and Bookseed; and *Inis* magazine in print and online – a forum for discussion, debate and critique of Irish and international books. Also administers the Laureate na nÓg project on behalf of the Arts Council and runs live literature events throughout the year. Founded 1996.

## Children's Literature Association
ChLA, 140B Purcellville Gateway Drive, Suite 120, Purcellville, VA 20132, USA
*tel* +1 630-571-4520
*email* info@childlitassn.org
*website* https://chla.memberclicks.net
*Facebook* www.facebook.com/ChildLitAssn
*Twitter* @chlatweets
*Membership* From $40 p.a. (dependent on income)

An organisation encouraging high standards of criticism, scholarship, research and teaching in children's literature.

## CIEP (Chartered Institute of Editing and Proofreading)
8 Devonshire Square, London EC2M 4YJ
*tel* 020-8785 6155
*email* office@ciep.uk
*website* www.ciep.uk
*Facebook* www.facebook.com/EditProof
*Twitter* @The_CIEP

A membership organisation promoting excellence in English language editing, and setting and demonstrating editorial standards. It is a community, training hub and support network for editorial professionals – the people who work to make text accurate, clear and fit for purpose. The CIEP runs online courses and workshops in copy-editing, proofreading and related skills, for people starting an editorial career and those wishing to broaden their competence. Its also maintains an online directory of experienced editorial professionals. In addition to providing professional training, publishes factsheets and guides on various aspects of editing and business skills for the self-employed. Was known as the Society for Editors and Proofreaders before being awarded its Royal Charter in 2019.

## Contact An Author
2 Burns Close, Carshalton SM5 4PY
*tel* 020-8642 0884
*email* info@contactanauthor.com
*website* https://contactanauthor.co.uk
*Facebook* www.facebook.com/contactanauthor
*Twitter* @contactanauthor
*Instagram* @contactanauthor

An author-booking agency that connects children with compassionate and creative people to enhance education. Helps schools, libraries, festivals and organisations all over the world to book authors for their events. Its mission is to celebrate books and help to arrange as many author visits as possible. Always happy for authors to join. Founded 2006.

## Coram Beanstalk
Coram Campus, 41 Brunswick Square, London WC1N 1AZ
*tel* 020-7729 4087
*email* admin@corambeanstalk.org.uk
*website* www.beanstalkcharity.org.uk
*Facebook* www.facebook.com/Beanstalkreads
*Twitter* @beanstalkreads
*Instagram* @beanstalkreads

Recruits, trains and supports volunteers to provide consistent, one-to-one reading support to children aged 3–13 who need help. Reading helpers give them the support they need to improve their reading skills, reading ability and confidence. Also provides training to people within the school community who want to help children learn to read for pleasure whilst improving their reading skills.

## Creative Scotland
Waverley Gate, 2–4 Waterloo Gate, Edinburgh EH1 3EG
*email* enquiries@creativescotland.com
*website* www.creativescotland.com
*Twitter* @CreativeScots

The public body that supports the arts, screen and creative industries across all parts of Scotland on behalf of everyone who lives, works or visits there. Through distributing funding from the Scottish government and the National Lottery, Creative Scotland enables people and organisations to work in and experience the arts, screen and creative industries in Scotland by helping others to develop great ideas and bring them to life. Creative Scotland supports writers and publishers based in Scotland through a range of funds and initiatives.

## Creative UK

Tomorrow Building, 130 Broadway, 2nd Floor, Suite 7, MediaCityUK, Salford M50 2UW
*tel* 0333 023 5240
*email* info@wearecreative.uk
*website* www.wearecreative.uk
*Facebook* www.facebook.com/WeAreCreativeUK
*Twitter* @WeAreCreativeUK
*Instagram* @wearecreativeuk

The national network for the creative industries. Champions the social and economic value of the creative industries by connecting and supporting talent, businesses and organisations, providing development opportunities at a local and national level through their network of partners, offering tailor-made resources and financial expertise.

## The Roald Dahl Museum and Story Centre

81–83 High Street, Great Missenden,
Bucks HP16 0AL
*tel* (01494) 892192
*email* hello@roalddahlmuseum.org
*website* www.roalddahl.com/museum
*Facebook* www.facebook.com/roalddahlmuseum
*Twitter* @roalddahlmuseum

Houses Roald Dahl's unique archive and is situated in the Buckinghamshire village where Roald Dahl lived and worked for 36 years. The museum features interactive galleries and the Story Centre provides activities and events to inspire young writers. Hosts school visits and creative workshops for young people year round.

## Discover Children's Story Centre

383–387 High Street, Stratford, London E15 4QZ
*tel* 020-8536 5555
*email* bookings@discover.org.uk
*website* https://discover.org.uk
*Facebook* www.facebook.com/
DiscoverChildrensStoryCentre
*Twitter* @Discover_Story
*Instagram* @Discover_Story

The UK's first hands-on creative literacy centre for children aged 0–11 years and their families, carers and teachers. Discover's mission is to spark children's and adults' imagination, curiosity and creativity in a magical and stimulating environment through creative play. It offers a variety of programmes including creative family events led by children's writers and illustrators, community and education projects, school workshops and artist residencies. Support is given to new and upcoming artists

working with children and families. Artists are also commissioned to create multisensory installations, exhibitions and sets for performative storytelling.

## Editors' and Proofreaders' Alliance of Northern Ireland

*email* info@epani.org.uk
*website* www.epani.org.uk
*Twitter* @epa_ni
*Coordinator* Averill Buchanan

Establishes and maintains high professional standards in editorial skills in Northern Ireland. For services for authors, see the directory of freelance professional editors, proofreaders and indexers.

## Empathy Lab

*email* info@empathylab.uk
*website* https://www.empathylab.uk
*Facebook* www.facebook.com/EmpathyLabUK
*Twitter* @EmpathyLabUK

A non-profit with a mission to raise an empathy-educated generation. EmpathyLab builds children's empathy, literacy and social activism through high-quality literature. Their strategy is built on scientific evidence showing that empathy is learnable and that reading is a crucial tool to build this skill. EmapathyLab provides training, free resources, an in-depth schools programme and an annual Read for Empathy Book Collection. Empathy Day, a festival led by children's authors and illustrators, takes place each June and is streamed for free online. Empathy Action Month takes place in November. Founded 2014.

## English Association

University Road, Leicester LE1 7RH
*email* hello@englishassociation.ac.uk
*website* www.englishassociation.ac.uk
*President* Rob Penman

Both a membership association and a learned society for people passionate about English language, literature and creative writing. Brings together individuals and organisations with a wealth of expertise from all sectors of education and all areas of English studies, and has a long history of engagement with national and international bodies. The elective Fellowship recognises outstanding achievement in English studies, and Officers and Committee members are leaders in their field. Through a large portfolio of publications, an events programme, networking and campaigning, the association has shaped the discipline and continues to connect English teachers in schools, colleges and universities. Founded 1906.

## Federation of Children's Book Groups – see page 311

## Federation of European Publishers

Chaussee d'Ixelles, 29/35 Box 4, 1050 Brussels,
Belgium
*tel* +32 2770 1110
*email* info@fep-fee.eu
*website* www.fep-fee.eu
*Twitter* @FEP_EU

Represents the interests of European publishers on
EU affairs and informs members on the development
of EU policies which could affect the publishing
industry. Founded 1967.

## Forward Arts Foundation

*tel* 020-8187 9861
*email* info@forwardartsfoundation.org
*website* www.forwardartsfoundation.org

Promotes appreciation and engagement with poetry
through programmes and initiatives that run
throughout the year. As well as advocating for the
positive social impact of poetry and growing poetry
audiences, the foundation supports and celebrates
poets, works closely with schools and libraries,
organises National Poetry Day each year and runs the
Forward Prizes for Poetry.

## The Gaelic Books Council/Comhairle nan Leabhraichean

32 Mansfield Street, Glasgow G11 5QP
*tel* 0141 337 6211
*email* alison@gaelicbooks.org
*website* www.gaelicbooks.org
*Director* Alison Lang

Stimulates Scottish Gaelic publishing by awarding
publication grants for new books, commissioning
new works from established and emerging authors
and providing editorial advice and guidance to Gaelic
writers and publishers. Has a bookshop in Glasgow
that stocks all Gaelic and Gaelic-related books in
print. All stock is listed on the website.
Founded 1968.

## Greeting Card Association

PO Box, Teddington TW11 1EL
*tel* 020-7619 9266
*email* hello@gca.cards
*website* www.gca.cards
*Facebook* www.facebook.com/
GreetingCardAssociation
*Twitter* @GCAUK
*Instagram* @GCA_UK
*Chief Executive* Amanda Fergusson

## Guernsey Arts Commission

Candie Museum, Candie Road, St Peter Port,
Guernsey GY1 2UG
*tel* (01481) 220711
*email* info@arts.gg

Helps promote, develop and support the arts in
Guernsey through exhibitions, a community arts
programme and public events.

## IBBY

Nonnenweg 12, CH–4055, Switzerland
*tel* +41 61-272 2917
*email* ibby@ibby.org
*website* www.ibby.org
*Facebook* www.facebook.com/ibby.international
*Twitter* @IBBYINT
*Instagram* @ibby.international

IBBY (the International Board on Books for Young
People) is a non-profit organisation which represents
an international network of people from all over the
world who are committed to bringing books and
children together. Its aims are to promote
international understanding through children's
books; to give children everywhere the opportunity to
have access to books with high literary and artistic
standards; to encourage the publication and
distribution of quality children's books, especially in
developing countries; to provide support and training
for those involved with children and children's
literature; and to stimulate research and scholarly
works in the field of children's literature.

IBBY is composed of National Sections all over the
world and represents countries with well-developed
book publishing and literacy programmes, and other
countries with only a few dedicated professionals who
are doing pioneer work in children's book publishing
and promotion. Founded 1953.

## IBBY UK

71 Addiscombe Court Road, Croydon CR0 6TT
*website* www.ibby.org.uk
*Facebook* www.facebook.com/IBBYUK
*Twitter* @IBBYUK

IBBY (the International Board on Books for Young
People) is a unique international alliance of everyone
interested in children's literature including
academics, librarians, publishers, booksellers, writers,
illustrators, teachers, literacy workers, parents and
others.

## Imaginate

30B Grindlay Street, Edinburgh EH3 9AX
*tel* 0131 225 8050
*email* info@imaginate.org.uk
*website* www.imaginate.org.uk
*Chief Executive* Belinda McElhinney, *Festival Director*
Noel Jordan

The national organisation in Scotland which
promotes, develops and advocates for theatre and
dance for children and young people. Works to
enable more children in Scotland to experience work
that is deeply engaging, innovative and inspiring, and
believes that all children deserve the opportunity to
develop their creativity, emotional intelligence and
reach their true potential. Runs the Edinburgh

International Children's Festival, delivers a year-round programme for schools, and provides a year-round Creative Development Programme for artists who make theatre and dance for children, including projects to develop artistic practice and support productions, networking events, mentoring and a Go and See Fund.

## Imaginative Book Illustration Society

*email* ibissec@martinsteenson.co.uk
*website* www.bookillustration.org
*Membership enquiries* Martin Steenson

IBIS was established to encourage research into, and to facilitate, the exchange of information on book and periodical illustrations, the artists and their publishers. The society has a worldwide membership including artists, collectors, bibliographers, writers and general enthusiasts. Whilst IBIS embraces all aspects of illustrative art, the main emphasis is on the illustration of texts in English since the 1830s. Founded 1995.

## Independent Publishers Guild

PO Box 12, Llain, Login SA34 0WU
*tel* (01437) 563335
*email* info@independentpublishersguild.com
*website* www.independentpublishersguild.com
*Chief Executive* Bridget Shine
*Membership* Open to new and established publishers from all sectors and of all sizes, plus suppliers and service providers.

The IPG is the UK's largest network of publishers and has served, supported and represented independents for over 60 years. It delivers two popular annual conferences featuring speakers from across publishing and beyond, a range of other events and numerous resources to help members do better business. Coordinates the Independent Publishing Awards, a mentoring programme, collective stands at book fairs and training via the IPG Skills Hub; and provides members with weekly ebulletins and special deals on publishing products and services. Founded 1962.

## Independent Theatre Council

The Albany, Douglas Way, London SE8 4AG
*tel* 020-7403 1727
*email* admin@itc-arts.org
*website* www.itc-arts.org
*Facebook* www.facebook.com/
independenttheatrecouncil
*Twitter* @itc_arts
*Membership* £190 p.a.

Enables the creation of high-quality professional performing arts by supporting, representing and developing the people who manage and produce it. It has over 450 members from a wide range of companies, venues and individuals in the fields of drama, dance, opera, musical theatre, puppetry, mixed media, mime, physical theatre and circus. Founded 1974.

## International Authors Forum

6th Floor, International House,
1 St Katherine's Way, London E1W 1UN
*tel* 020-7264 5707
*email* luke.alcott@internationalauthors.org
*website* www.internationalauthors.org
*Twitter* @IntAuthors
*Executive Administrator* Luke Alcott

Represents authors around the world and has a membership made up of authors' organisations from every continent. Campaigns for authors' rights at the UN and national levels. Organises events, publications and opportunities for knowledge sharing to promote the importance of creative work financially, socially and culturally. Keeps members up to date with international developments in copyright law.

## International Publishers Association

23 Avenue de France, 1202 Geneva, Switzerland
*tel* +41 22-704 1820
*email* info@internationalpublishers.org
*website* www.internationalpublishers.org
*Facebook* www.facebook.com/
InternationalPublishersAssociation
*Twitter* @IntPublishers
*President* Karine Pansa, *Secretary-General* José Borghino

The IPA is a federation of national, regional and international publishers' associations. It promotes and protects publishing worldwide, with a focus on copyright and freedom to publish. Its membership comprises 92 organisations from 76 countries worldwide. Founded 1896.

## Irish Writers Centre

19 Parnell Square, Dublin D01 E102,
Republic of Ireland
*tel* +353 (0)1 872 1302
*email* info@writerscentre.ie
*website* https://irishwriterscentre.ie
*Facebook* www.facebook.com/irishwritersctr
*Twitter* @IrishWritersCtr
*Director* Valerie Bistany

National support and development centre and membership organisation for Irish writers, carrying out its work online and in-person. The IWC works with writers of all types and talents, and actively encourages writers from all communities to engage in creative writing. Provides opportunities for skill development, gaining industry knowledge and networking with other writers. Founded 1991.

## The Kipling Society

Bay Tree House, Doomsday Garden, Horsham,
West Sussex RH13 6LB
*email* michaelrkipling@gmail.com
*website* www.kiplingsociety.co.uk
*Chairman* Dr Alex Bubb

*Membership* £29 p.a. UK; £31 p.a. Europe; £35 p.a. rest of world; £10 p.a. student

Encourages discussion and study of the work and life of Rudyard Kipling (1865–1936) by assisting in the study of his writings, holding discussion meetings, publishing a quarterly journal and website (with a readers' guide to Kipling's work), maintaining a Kipling Library at Haileybury School in Hertfordshire and running an annual writing competition.

## The C.S. Lewis Society (New York)

84–23 77th Avenue, Glendale, NY 11385–7706, USA
*email* subscribe@nycslsociety.com
*email* csarrocco@aol.com
*website* www.nycslsociety.com
*Secretary* Clare Sarrocco

The oldest society for the appreciation and discussion of C.S. Lewis (1898–1963). Founded 1969.

## Literature Wales

Glyn Jones Centre, Wales Millennium Centre, Bute Place, Cardiff CF10 5AL
*tel* 029-2047 2266
*email* post@literaturewales.org
*website* www.literaturewales.org
*Facebook* www.facebook.com/LlenCymruLitWales
*Twitter* @LitWales
*Instagram* @llencymru_litwales

The national company for the development of literature in Wales. Works to inspire communities, develop writers and celebrate Wales' literary culture. Activities include the Wales Book of the Year Award; the Children's Laureate Wales and Bardd Plant Cymru schemes; creative writing courses at Tŷ Newydd Writing Centre; the professional development scheme Representing Wales; writer's bursaries and mentoring; the National Poet of Wales initiative and more. The organisation is a member of the Arts Council of Wales' Arts Portfolio Wales.

## Little Theatre Guild of Great Britain

*tel* 07971 474721
*email* secretary@littletheatreguild.org
*website* www.littletheatreguild.org
*Secretary* Anne Gilmour

Promotes closer cooperation amongst the little theatres constituting its membership, acts as a coordinating and representative body on behalf of the little theatres, maintains and advances the highest standards in the art of theatre, and assists in encouraging the establishment of other little theatres.

## LoveReading4Kids

157 Shooters Hill, London SE18 3HP
*tel* 020-3004 7204
*website* www.lovereading4kids.co.uk
*Facebook* www.facebook.com/lovereading4kids
*Twitter* @lovereadingkids

A book recommendation site for children's books ranging from toddlers to teens. Ensures that whatever their age or interest, there is a steady stream of book recommendations available. Offers a variety of free services for parents and anyone who is interested in buying the best books for children. Supports parents, teachers and school librarians in helping engender a lifelong love of reading in children. The website features Kids' Zone, an area designed specifically for children, with competitions, quizzes and book-related material.

## The Mythopoeic Society

*website* www.mythsoc.org
*Twitter* @mythsoc

A non-profit international literary and educational organisation for the study, discussion and enjoyment of fantastic and mythic literature, especially the works of Tolkien, C.S. Lewis and Charles Williams. 'Mythopoeic' (myth-oh-PAY-ik or myth-oh-PEE-ik) means 'mythmaking' or 'productive of myth' and aptly describes much of the fictional work of the three authors who were also prominent members of an informal Oxford literary circle (1930s–50s) known as the Inklings. Membership is open to all scholars, writers and readers of these literatures. The society sponsors three periodicals: *Mythprint* (a bulletin of book reviews, articles and events), *Mythlore* (scholarly articles on mythic and fantastic literature), and *Mythic Circle* (a literary annual of original poetry and short stories). Each summer the society holds an annual conference, Mythcon. Founded 1967.

## National Association for the Teaching of English

Marshall House, 2 Park Avenue, Sale, Manchester M33 6HE
*tel* 0161 929 7302
*email* membership@nate.org.uk
*website* www.nate.org.uk
*Twitter* @Natefeed

NATE is a professional association for English teachers that works regionally, nationally and internationally at all key stages. Works to promote standards of excellence in the teaching of English from early years to university; research curriculum design and assessment; promote innovative and original ideas that have practical classroom outcomes; support teachers' professional development through access to current research, publications and national and regional conferences; provide an informed national voice on matters concerning the teaching of English and its related subjects; and encourage sharing and collaboration between teachers and learners of English and its related subjects. Founded 1963.

## National Association of Writers and Groups

Old Vicarage, Scammonden, Huddersfield HD3 3FT
*email* info@nawg.co.uk
*website* www.nawg.co.uk
*Facebook* www.facebook.com/NAWGNews

*Twitter* @NAWGnews
*Secretary* Chris Huck
*Membership* £50 p.a. per group; £25 p.a. individuals

Advances the education of the general public throughout the UK, including the Channel Islands, by promoting the study and art of writing in all its aspects. Publishes *LINK*, a bi-monthly magazine, and a bi-monthly newsletter; holds the Festival of Writing annually in August/September; runs competitions with cash prizes (open to all and some free for members); and facilitates online workshops and writing weekends. New members always welcome. Founded 1995.

## National Association of Writers in Education

Tower House, Mill Lane, off Askham Fields Lane, Askham Bryan, York YO23 3FS
*email* admin@nawe.co.uk
*website* www.nawe.co.uk
*Twitter* @NaweWriters
*Membership* £75 p.a. professional; £37.50 professional graduate; £30 p.a. student/associate/overseas

National membership organisation which furthers knowledge, understanding and enjoyment of creative writing and supports good practice in its teaching and learning at all levels. NAWE promotes creative writing as both a distinct discipline and an essential element in education generally. Its membership includes those working in higher education, the many freelance writers working in schools and community contexts, and the teachers and other professionals who work with them. It runs a national database of writers, produces a weekly opportunities bulletin, publishes a journal, *Writing in Education*, and holds a national conference. Professional Membership includes public liability insurance cover.

## National Centre for Writing

Dragon Hall, 115–123 King Street, Norwich NR1 1QE
*email* info@nationalcentreforwriting.org.uk
*website* https://nationalcentreforwriting.org.uk
*Facebook* www.facebook.com/NationalCentreforWriting
*Twitter* @WritersCentre
*Instagram* @writerscentre

Celebrates and explores the artistic and social power of creative writing and literary translation. An ongoing programme of innovative collaborations engages writers, literary translators and readers in projects that support new voices and new stories and respond to the rapidly changing world of writing. Based at the historic Dragon Hall in Norwich, where workshops and mentoring are regularly available for writers at all levels, both face-to-face and online. Projects range from the Desmond Elliott Prize to vibrant festivals such as the City of Literature strand of Norfolk & Norwich Festival. Founded 2018.

## National Literacy Trust – see page 313

## National Society for Education in Art and Design

3 Masons Wharf, Potley Lane, Corsham, Wilts. SN13 9FY
*tel* (01225) 810134
*email* info@nsead.org
*website* www.nsead.org
*Twitter* @NSEAD1
*General Secretary* Michele Gregson

The leading national authority concerned with art, craft and design across all phases of education in the UK. Offers the benefits of membership of a professional association, a learned society and a trade union. Has representatives on national and regional committees concerned with art and design education. Publishes *International Journal of Art and Design Education* online (four each year; Wiley Blackwell) and *AD* magazine for teachers. Founded 1888.

## The Edith Nesbit Society

21 Churchfields, West Malling, Kent ME19 6RJ
*email* edithnesbit@gmail.com
*website* www.edithnesbit.co.uk
*Membership* £10 p.a. individual; £12 p.a. joint; £15 p.a. organisations

Promotes an interest in the life and works of Edith Nesbit (1858–1924) by means of talks, a regular newsletter and other publications, and visits to places associated with her. Founded 1996.

## New Writing North

Northumbria University, Newcastle upon Tyne NE1 8ST
*email* office@newwritingnorth.com
*website* https://newwritingnorth.com
*Facebook* www.facebook.com/newwritingnorth
*Twitter* @NewWritingNorth

Supports writing and reading in the North of England. Commissions new work, creates development opportunities and nurtures talent. Founded 1996.

## Newcastle University Library

Philip Robinson Library, Jesmond Road West, Newcastle upon Tyne NE2 4HQ
*tel* 0191 208 7662
*email* libraryhelp@ncl.ac.uk
*website* www.ncl.ac.uk/library
*Facebook* www.facebook.com/NULibraries
*Twitter* @libraryncl, @nclibspeccoll

A modern academic library with multi-disciplinary collections, including historical children's books. The Library's Special Collections hold many unique archives and rare books. These materials provide great scope for original research for many subject areas and the potential to complement teaching and learning at the university. There are a number of collections and archives dedicated to children's literature. See website for details.

## The Office for Standards in Education, Children's Services and Skills

Piccadilly Gate, Store Street, Manchester M1 2WD
*tel* 0300 123 1231
*email* enquiries@ofsted.gov.uk
*website* www.gov.uk/ofsted

Ofsted is a non-ministerial government department. It regulates and inspects to achieve excellence in the care of children and young people, and in education and skills for learners of all ages. It regulates and inspects childcare and children's social care, and inspects the Children and Family Court Advisory and Support Service (Cafcass), schools, colleges, initial teacher training, further education and skills, adult and community learning, and education and training in prisons and other secure establishments. It assesses council children's services, and inspects services for looked after children, safeguarding and child protection.

## Pen to Print

*tel* 020-8227 2267
*email* pentoprint@lbbd.gov.uk
*website* https://pentoprint.org
*Facebook* www.facebook.com/OfficialPentoPrint
*Twitter* @Pen_to_Print
*Instagram* @officialpentoprint

A free writer development programme based in libraries. As an Arts Council–funded library, it provides a safe, collaborative environment to develop writers' authentic voices. Aspiring writers, especially those from backgrounds that are under-represented in publishing, are encouraged to reach communities with their stories and inspire potential in others. Free activities include writing classes and workshops; competitions including The Book Challenge; author talks; ReadFest literary festival; *Write On!* magazine (print); *Write On! Extra* magazine (online); and *Write On! Audio* podcast.

## PICSEL (Picture Industry Collecting Society for Effective Licensing)

112 Western Road, Brighton, East Sussex BN1 2AB
*tel* 07377 535095
*email* info@picsel.org.uk
*website* www.picsel.org.uk

A not-for-profit collecting society that ensures that all visual artists, creators and representative rights holders of images receive fair payment for various secondary uses of their works following the initial publication, such as copying pages from books and magazines for use in schools and universities. It works to ensure that all licence fees collected are distributed equitably, efficiently and in a transparent manner. Founded 2016.

## The Poetry Book Society – see page 184

## The Poetry Society – see page 184

## Poetry Society Education – see page 188

## Pop Up Projects: Transforming Lives Through Literature

5 Paper Mill Buildings, City Garden Row, London N1 8DW
*email* info@pop-up.org.uk
*website* www.pop-up.org.uk
*Facebook* www.facebook.com/popupfestival
*Twitter* @PopUpProjectsUK
*Instagram* @popupprojectsuk

A national literature and publishing organisation which believes that all children should find themselves, and discover others, through the stories they read. Their work includes creating courses and training for aspiring children's book illustrators and writers from under-represented backgrounds, publishing books for children and young people that celebrate difference, and providing author-led programmes in special educational needs schools. Founded 2011.

## The Beatrix Potter Society

*email* info@beatrixpottersociety.org.uk
*website* www.beatrixpottersociety.org.uk
*Facebook* https://en-gb.facebook.com/beatrixpottersociety
*Twitter* @BeatrixPotterSo
*Instagram* @beatrixpottersociety

Promotes the study and appreciation of the life and works of Beatrix Potter (1866–1943) as author, artist, diarist, farmer and conservationist. Regular lectures, meetings, conferences and events in the UK and USA. Distributes a journal and newsletter three times a year. Small publishing programme. Founded 1980.

## Publishers Association

First Floor, 50 Southwark Street, London SE1 1UN
*email* mail@publishers.org.uk
*website* www.publishers.org.uk
*Twitter* @PublishersAssoc
*President* Antonia Seymour, *Ceo* Dan Conway

A member organisation for UK publishing, representing companies of all sizes and specialisms – including children's books. Their members produce digital and print books, research journals and educational resources across genres and subjects. The Publishers Association exists to champion publishing to the wider world and to provide their members with everything they need to thrive. They have helped change laws, improved business conditions and inspired people to become publishers. Founded 1896.

## Publishers Association of New Zealand

Level 6, 19 Como Street, Takapuna, Auckland 0622, New Zealand

tel +64 (0)9 280 3213
email admin@publishers.org.nz
website www.publishers.org.nz
Twitter @Publishers_NZ

PANZ represents book, educational and digital publishers in New Zealand. Members include both the largest international publishers and companies in the independent publishing community.

## Publishing Ireland/Foilsiú Éireann

63 Patrick Street, Dun Laoghaire, Dublin A96 WF25, Republic of Ireland
website www.publishingireland.com
Facebook www.facebook.com/PublishingIreland
Twitter @PublishingIRL
General Manager Orla McLoughlin

Enables publishers to share expertise and resources in order to benefit from opportunities and solve problems that are of common concern to all. It comprises most of the major publishing houses in Ireland with a mixture of trade, general and academic publishers as members. Founded 1970.

## Publishing Scotland

Scott House, 10 South St Andrew Street, Edinburgh EH2 2AZ
tel 0131 228 6866
email enquiries@publishingscotland.org
website www.publishingscotland.org
Chief Executive Marion Sinclair

A network for trade, training and development in the Scottish publishing industry. Runs events throughout the year, including workshops and courses, spotlights opportunities and supports the Scottish publishing industry and those who work within it. Founded 1973.

## The Arthur Ransome Society Ltd

Abbot Hall Museum, Kendal, Cumbria LA9 5AL
email tarsinfo@arthur-ransome.org
website www.arthur-ransome.org

Exists to celebrate the life, promote the works and diffuse the ideas of Arthur Ransome (1884–1967), author of the world-famous *Swallows and Amazons* series of books for children. The society seeks in particular to encourage children and others to engage, with due regard to safety, in adventurous pursuits; educate the public generally about Ransome and his work; sponsor research in relevant areas; and be a communications link for those interested in any aspect of Arthur Ransome's life and works. Founded 1990.

## Read for Good

26 Nailsworth Mills, Avening Road, Nailsworth, Glos. GL6 0BS
tel (01453) 839005
email reading@readforgood.org
website www.readforgood.org
Facebook www.facebook.com/readforgood

Twitter @ReadforGoodUK
Instagram @readforgood

The charity wants all children and young people in the UK to be able to develop a life-long love of reading, positively shaping their futures and creating a more equal society. The charity runs Readathon and Track My Read programmes in thousands of schools, motivating children to read for pleasure. The Read for Good in Hospitals programme provides a regular supply of books and storyteller visits to children in the UK's major children's hospitals.

## The Reading Agency

24 Bedford Row, London WC1R 4EH
tel 07933 181889
email info@readingagency.org.uk
website www.readingagency.org.uk
Facebook www.facebook.com/readingagency
Twitter @readingagency
Instagram @readingagency

A charity whose mission is to tackle life's big challenges through the proven power of reading. Works closely with public libraries, publishers, health partners and volunteers to bring reading programmes to children across the UK. Funded by Arts Council England, The Reading Agency supports a wide range of reading initiatives for children including the Summer Reading Challenge, run in partnership with libraries, which helps get around three-quarters of a million children into libraries each year; and Chatterbooks reading clubs, which help children build a lifelong reading habit.

## RNIB Reading Services

RNIB, Northminster House, Northminster, Peterborough PE1 1YN
tel 0303 123 9999
website www.rniblibrary.com
website https://readingservices.rnib.org.uk
website www.rnibbookshare.org

The largest specialist library for readers with sight loss in the UK. It offers a comprehensive range of books and accessible information for children and adults in braille and Talking Books. Books are also available for download in audio and braille. RNIB Bookshare opens up the world of reading in education for learners with a print-disability, including those with dyslexia or who are blind or partially sighted.

## The Malcolm Saville Society

27 Whitehills Way, Kingsthorpe, Northampton, Northamptonshire NN2 8EW
email mystery@witchend.com
website www.witchend.com
Membership £15 p.a. UK; £17.50 p.a. Europe; £21 p.a. elsewhere

Promotes interest in the work of children's author Malcolm Saville (1901–82). Regular social activities, library, book and merchandise sales and a magazine (up to four each year). Founded 1994.

## Scattered Authors' Society

*email* scatteredauthorssociety@gmail.com
*website* www.scatteredauthors.org

Provides a forum for informal discussion, contact and support for professional writers in children's fiction. Founded 1998.

## School Library Association

1 Pine Court, Kembrey Park, Swindon SN2 8AD
*tel* (01793) 530166
*email* info@sla.org.uk
*website* www.sla.org.uk
*Facebook* www.facebook.com/schoollibraryassociation
*Twitter* @uksla

The SLA is a UK-focused charity which supports everyone involved in school libraries. It believes that every pupil is entitled to effective school library provision and the educational, emotional and developmental benefits that come with it. Provides training, networking and an information service, publishes guidelines for school library and resource centres, book lists and a quarterly journal which includes current book and digital resources for all school-age children.

## Scottish Book Trust

Sandeman House, Trunk's Close, 55 High Street, Edinburgh EH1 1SR
*tel* 0131 524 0160
*email* info@scottishbooktrust.com
*website* www.scottishbooktrust.com
*Facebook* www.facebook.com/scottishbktrust
*Twitter* @ScottishBkTrust

Scotland's national agency for the promotion of reading, writing and literature. Programmes include: Bookbug, a free universal book-gifting programme which encourages families to read with their children from birth; an ambitious schools programme including national tours; the virtual events programme Authors Live; the Live Literature funding programme, a national initiative enabling Scottish citizens to engage with authors, playwrights, poets, storytellers and illustrators; a writer development programme, offering mentoring and professional development for emerging and established writers; and a readership development programme featuring a national writing campaign, as well as Book Week Scotland, during the last week in November. Founded 1998.

## Scottish Storytelling Forum

Scottish Storytelling Centre, 43–45 High Street, Edinburgh EH1 1SR
*tel* 0131 652 3273
*email* storytelling@tracscotland.org
*website* www.scottishstorytellingcentre.com
*website* www.storytellingforum.co.uk
*Facebook* www.facebook.com/ScotStoryForum
*Twitter* @ScotStoryCentre, @scotstoryforum

Scotland's national charity for oral storytelling, established to encourage and support the telling and sharing of stories across all ages and sectors of society, in particular those who, for reasons of poverty or disability, are sometimes excluded from artistic experiences. The Scottish Storytelling Centre is the Forum's resource and training centre which presents a year-round programme of storytelling and traditional arts events, workshops and the Scottish International Storytelling Festival in the autumn. The Storytelling Network has over 150 professional storytellers across Scotland. Founded 1992.

## Seven Stories – The National Centre for Children's Books – see page 309

## Society for Storytelling

Lytchett House, 13 Freeland Park, Wareham Road, Poole BH16 6FA
*tel* 07942 344259
*email* membership@sfs.org.uk
*website* www.sfs.org.uk
*Facebook* www.facebook.com/societyforstorytelling
*Twitter* @sfs_uk
*Instagram* @sfsintheuk

SfS is a registered charity and community organisation for both professional and non-professional oral storytellers. It provides information on oral storytelling, events, storytellers and traditional stories. Its volunteers have specialist knowledge of storytelling in education, health, therapy and business settings. To increase public awareness of the art of storytelling it promotes National Storytelling Week. The SfS provides a network for anyone interested in the art of oral storytelling whether they are full-time storytellers, use storytelling in their work, tell stories for the love of it or just want to listen. Founded 1993.

## Society of Artists Agents

*website* https://saahub.com
*Twitter* @SaaAgents

Formed to promote professionalism in the illustration industry and to forge closer links between clients and artists through proper terms and conditions that protect the interests of both. Actively campaigns to protect copyright and intellectual property. Founded 1992.

## Society of Authors
– see page 297

## SCBWI (Society of Children's Book Writers and Illustrators) – see page 305

## Society of Editors

Stationers Hall, Ave Maria Lane, London EC4M 7DD
*tel* 07599 954636
*email* office@societyofeditors.org
*website* www.societyofeditors.org
*President* Kamal Ahmed

Formed from the merger of the Guild of Editors and the Association of British Editors, it has members in national, regional and local newspapers, magazines, broadcasting and digital media, journalism, education and media law. It campaigns for media freedom, self regulation, the public's right to know and the maintenance of standards in journalism.

## Society of Young Publishers

c/o The Publishers Association, First Floor,
50 Southwark Street, London SE1 1UN
*email* sypchair@thesyp.org.uk
*website* www.thesyp.org.uk
*Twitter* @SYP_UK, @SYPIreland, @SYP_LDN,
@SYPNorth, @SYP_Oxford, @SYPScotland,
@SYP_SouthWest
*Instagram* @syp_uk, @syp_london, @syp.north,
@oxford_syp, @sypscotland, @syp_southwest
*Membership* £30 p.a. employed standard; £24 p.a.
student/unemployed; £18 p.a. digital membership

The SYP supports those of any age looking to get into publishing, or those within the first ten years of their career who are looking to get ahead. It is made up of six regional committees (Ireland, London, North, Oxford, Scotland and South West), and a UK team responsible for the organisation's oversight. These committees organise mentorship schemes for current and aspiring publishers based in the UK and Ireland. Two annual conferences are held, as well as numerous in-person and digital events each month – including socials, career panels and more. Founded 1949.

## Speaking of Books

*tel* 07931 929325
*email* elle@speakingofbooks.co.uk
*website* www.speakingofbooks.co.uk
*Twitter* @speakingofbks

Arranges school visits from writers, illustrators, poets and storytellers, plus other high-quality speakers and workshop facilitators. Also provides speakers for festivals and events relating to literacy and the arts.

## Spread the Word

The Albany, Douglas Way, London SE8 4AG
*email* hello@spreadtheword.org.uk
*website* www.spreadtheword.org.uk
*Facebook* www.facebook.com/spreadthewordwriters
*Twitter* @STWevents
*Instagram* @spreadthewordwriters

London's literature development agency, a charity and a National Portfolio client of Arts Council England. Develops the careers and creative talents of London's under-represented writers. Initiates change-making research and developmental programmes that prioritise equity and access. Partners with people and organisations to diversify storytelling and enrich the UK's literature ecology. Founded by Bernardine Evaristo and Ruth Borthwick.

## The Robert Louis Stevenson Club

*website* https://robert-louis-stevenson.org/rls-club

Fosters interest in Robert Louis Stevenson's life (1850–94) and writings through various events and a quarterly newsletter. Founded 1920.

## The Story Museum

42 Pembroke Street, Oxford OX1 1BP
*tel* (01865) 790050
*email* hello@storymuseum.org.uk
*website* www.storymuseum.org.uk
*Facebook* www.facebook.com/TheStoryMuseum
*Twitter* @TheStoryMuseum
*Instagram* @thestorymusuem

Celebrates story in all forms and ensures that everyone has the opportunity to engage with stories. Includes a library, activity spaces, a 100-seat theatre and temporary exhibition spaces. As well as inviting public visitors and school groups, it delivers a programme of funded community and school participation projects with targeted groups, and an extensive public programme which includes skills courses, workshops, drop-in activities and access visits.

## Story Therapy

1 Sugworth Lane, Radley, Abingdon-on-Thames, Oxon OX14 2HZ
*email* admin@storytherapyresources.co.uk
*website* www.storytherapyresources.co.uk
*Facebook* www.facebook.com/storytherapy
*Twitter* @StoryTherapy
*Contact* Hilary Hawkes

A non-profit social enterprise creating stories and resources, especially story-themed resources, that support children's emotional health and mental wellbeing. Founded 2016.

## The Swedish Institute for Children's Books

*email* info@barnboksinstitutet.se
*website* www.barnboksinstitutet.se

Svenska barnboksinstitutet is a research and information centre for children's and YA literature with a special library open to the public. Founded 1965.

## The Tolkien Society

*website* www.tolkiensociety.org
*Facebook* www.facebook.com/TolkienSociety
*Twitter* @TolkienSociety
*Instagram* @tolksoc
*Membership* Postal: £35 p.a. UK; £40 p.a. EU; £50 p.a. rest of world; add £15 p.a. for family membership; Online: £30 p.a.; £10 p.a. students

An educational charity and literary society devoted to the study and promotion of the life and works of J.R.R. Tolkien.

## United Kingdom Literacy Association

Room 9 c/o VAL, 9 Newarke Street,
Leicester LE1 5SN
*tel* 0116 254 4116
*website* www.ukla.org
*Twitter* @The_UKLA
*Membership* £65 p.a. individuals; £30 p.a.
concessionary

UKLA is a registered charity, which has as its sole
object the advancement of literacy in education. It
conducts research into literacy education and
encourages teachers and librarians to take an active
role in finding and sharing a wider range of books
that children will love. Members receive access to a
community focused on improving literacy, resources
and guides, literacy journals, *English 4-11* magazine
and conference discounts. Founded 1963.

## Voice of the Listener & Viewer

The Old Rectory Business Centre, Springhead Road,
Northfleet DA11 8HN
*tel* (01474) 338716
*email* info@vlv.org.uk
*website* www.vlv.org.uk
*Facebook* www.facebook.com/VLVUK
*Twitter* @vlvuk
*Administrator* Lucy Regan
*Membership* From £30 p.a.; academic, corporate and
student rates available

VLV's mission is to campaign for accountability,
diversity and excellence in UK broadcasting, seeking
to sustain and strengthen public service broadcasting
to the benefit of civil society and democracy in the
UK. It holds regular conferences and seminars and
publishes a bulletin and an e-newsletter.
Founded 1983.

## Writers Advice Centre for Children's Books

Riverbank House, 1 Putney Bridge Approach,
London SW6 3JD
*tel* 020-7801 6300
*email* info@writersadvice.co.uk
*website* www.writersadvice.co.uk
*Facebook* www.facebook.com/writersadvice
*Twitter* @writersadvice
*Managing Editor* Louise Jordan

Dedicated to helping new and published children's
writers by offering both editorial advice and tips on
how to get published. The Centre also runs
workshops, an online children's writing
correspondence course and publishes a small list of
its own under the name of Wacky Bee Books.
Founded 1994.

## WGGB (Writers' Guild of Great Britain) – see page 300

## Writing East Midlands

The Garage Studios, Unit 4, 41-43 St Mary's Gate,
Notts. NG1 1PU
*tel* (01157) 934110
*email* info@writingeastmidlands.co.uk
*website* https://writingeastmidlands.co.uk
*Facebook* www.facebook.com/WritingEM
*Twitter* @WritingEM
*Instagram* @writingeastmidlands

Removes barriers and encourages equal access to
writing and publishing by supporting writers
throughout their careers. Services include workshops
and writing courses, mentorships and career
development, MS appraisals, organising festivals,
conferences and events, and facilitating residencies
for writers in schools, libraries and museums. Also
works with specific groups of under-represented
people such as refugees, migrants, domestic abuse
survivors, offenders and the elderly.

## Young at Art

Cotton Court, 30–42 Waring Street, Belfast BT1 2ED
*tel* 028-9023 0660
*website* www.youngatart.co.uk
*Twitter* @Young_at_Art

Coordinates the annual Belfast Children's Festival as
well as a wide variety of projects that encourage
children and young people to enjoy the arts, develop
awareness of its impact on their lives, and have a say
in what their arts provision should be. These include
engagement programmes, workshop programmes,
commissions, seminars, training, research and online
resources. Founded 2000.

## Young V&A

Cambridge Heath Road, Bethnal Green,
London E2 9PA
*tel* 020-7942 2000
*website* www.vam.ac.uk/info/young
*Facebook* www.facebook.com/youngvam
*Twitter* @young_vam

A world-leading museum of design and creativity for
children and young people, which reopened in 2023
after extensive redevelopment.
 Inspires young people to be active citizens and
creative change-makers in their communities;
empowers educators to drive forward creative
education in art, design and performance from early
years to secondary school; connects young people
with the creative ingenuity of designers,
entrepreneurs, innovators, inventors and each other;
and influences the sector through child-centred
museum practice.

## Youth Libraries Group

CILIP, 7 Ridgmount Street, London WC1E 7AE
*email* secretary.YLG@cilip.org.uk
*website* www.cilip.org.uk/ylg

*Twitter* @youthlibraries
*Secretary* Alison Cassels

YLG is open to all members of the Chartered Institute for Library and Information Professionals (CILIP) who are interested in children's work. At a national level its aims are to influence the provision of library services for children and the provision of quality literature; to inspire and support all librarians working with children and young people; to liaise with other national professional organisations in pursuit of such aims.

At a local level, the YLG organises regular training courses, supports professional development and provides opportunities to meet colleagues. It holds an annual conference and judges the Yoto Carnegie and Kate Greenaway Awards (see page 342).

# Children's book and illustration prizes and awards

This list provides details of prizes, competitions and awards relevant to children's writers and artists. Check individual websites for entry guidelines and deadlines.

## Academy of British Cover Design: Annual Cover Design Competition

Underbelly, 11 Hoxton Square, London N1 6NU
*website* https://abcoverd.co.uk
*Twitter* @ABCoverD

Awards covers produced for any book published between 1 January and 31 December each year, by any designer in the UK, for a UK or overseas publisher. Designers may enter their own work or the work of other designers. There are three children's categories: Children's (0–5) and (6–12), and Young Adult. Entry is free. Voting opens to the public for two hours before the award ceremony.

## The Adrien Prize

*Twitter* @AdrienPrize

Created by author Elle McNicoll and named after a neurodivergent character in her second novel, *Show Us Who You Are*. The award recognises middle-grade and YA fiction that includes a positive portrayal of a protagonist with a disability. The novel must be longer than 20,000 words, must show a nuanced portrayal of disability and the main character with the disability must not die. A group of young readers are asked to read the shortlist and their reviews help the judge to pick the final winner. The winner receives a trophy. Founded 2023.

## ALCS Educational Writers' Award

The Society of Authors, 24 Bedford Row, London WC1R 4EH
*tel* 020-3880 2230
*email* prizes@societyofauthors.org
*website* www.societyofauthors.org/ALCS-award

Alternates each year between books in the 5–11 and 11–18 age groups. It is given to an outstanding example of traditionally published non-fiction (with or without illustrations) that stimulates and enhances learning. The work must have been first published in the UK, in the English language, within the previous two calendar years. The total value of the prizes is £2,000.

## The Alligator's Mouth Award for Illustrated Early Fiction

2A Church Court, Richmond, Surrey TW9 1JL
*tel* 020-8948 6775
*email* award@thealligatorsmouth.co.uk
*website* www.thealligatorsmouth.co.uk/award

Celebrates highly illustrated early fiction. The children's book prize, launched by The Alligator's Mouth and the Bright Agency in 2018, celebrates the best books for 6–8-year-olds and champions authors and illustrators. The official partner is the book wholesaler Gardners. The award is open to books first published in the UK in English from the last year which have illustrations on the majority of the internal spreads. Entry form, submissions criteria and entry rules can be downloaded from the website. Longlist announced in March. The winner of the prize receives a trophy. 2022 winner: Pippa Curnick for *Indigo Wilde and the Creatures at Jellybean Crescent* (Hodder Children's Books).

## The Hans Christian Andersen Awards

International Board on Books for Young People, Nonnenweg 12, CH–4055, Basel, Switzerland
*tel* +41 61-272 2917
*email* ibby@ibby.org
*website* www.ibby.org
*Facebook* www.facebook.com/ibby.international
*Twitter* @IBBYINT
*Instagram* @ibby.international

Given every other year by IBBY, they recognise lifelong achievement and are presented to an author and an illustrator whose complete works have made an important, lasting contribution to children's literature. The selection criteria include the aesthetic and literary qualities of writing and illustrating, as well as the ability to see things from the child's point of view and the ability to stretch the child's curiosity and imagination. The complete works of the author and of the illustrator are taken into consideration. The Author's Award has been given since 1956 and the Illustrator's Award since 1966.

## Association for Library Service to Children Awards

American Library Association, 225 N Michigan Ave, Suite 1300, Chicago, IL 60601, USA
*tel* +1 800-545-2433
*email* alsc@ala.org
*website* www.ala.org/alsc/awardsgrants/bookmedia
*Facebook* www.facebook.com/Associationforlibraryservicetochildren
*Twitter* @wearealsc

The following awards are administered by ALSC:

The Caldecott Medal (named in honour of the 19th-century English illustrator Randolph Caldecott) awarded annually to the artist of the most distinguished US picture book for children;

The Newbery Medal (named after the 18th-century British bookseller John Newbery) awarded annually to the author of the most distinguished contribution to US literature for children;

The Geisel Medal (named after the world-renowned children's author a.k.a. Dr Seuss) given annually to the author(s) and illustrator(s) of the most distinguished contribution to the body of children's literature known as beginning reader books published in the USA during the preceding year;

The Robert F. Sibert Informational Book Medal given annually to the author of the most distinguished informational book published in English during the preceding year;

The Children's Literature Legacy Award honouring authors and illustrators published in the US whose books have made a substantial and lasting contribution to literature for children;

The Excellence in Early Learning Digital Media Award given to a digital media producer that has created distinguished digital media for an early learning audience;

The Batchelder Award awarded annually to an outstanding children's book translated from a language other than English and originally published in a country other than the United States;

The Belpré Awards presented annually to a Latino/Latina writer and illustrator whose work best portrays, affirms and celebrates the Latino cultural experience;

The Odyssey Award given for the best audio book produced for children and/or young adults. Co-administered with YALSA and Booklist.

## Bardd Plant Cymru (Welsh-Language Children's Poet Laureate)

Books Council of Wales, Castell Brychan, Aberystwyth, Ceredigion SY23 2JB
*tel* (01970) 624151
*email* castellbrychan@books.wales
*website* https://llyfrau.cymru/en

Raises the profile of poetry amongst children and to encourage them to compose and enjoy poetry. During their term of office the bard will visit schools as well as help children to create poetry through electronic workshops. The scheme's partner organisations are: S4C, the Welsh Government, the Books Council of Wales, Urdd Gobaith Cymru and Literature Wales.

## J.M. Barrie Outstanding Achievement Award

c/o Mousetrap Theatre Projects,
33 Shaftesbury Avenue, London W1D 7EH

*email* admin@childrensarts.org.uk
*website* www.childrensarts.org.uk/celebrate
*Facebook* www.facebook.com/ActionChildrensArts
*Twitter* @childrensarts

Administered by Action for Children's Arts annually to a children's arts practitioner or organisation for a lifetime's achievement in delighting children whose work, in the view of the trustees, will stand the test of time. Also delivers a Lifetime Achievement Award.

## The Bath Children's Novel Award

PO Box 5223, Bath BA1 0UR
*email* info@bathnovelaward.co.uk
*website* www.bathnovelaward.co.uk
*Twitter* @bathnovelaward

This annual international prize is for unpublished or independently published writers of novels for children or young adults. Submissions: first 5,000 words plus one-page synopsis. Entries open June until November. Entry fee: £29 per novel with sponsored places available for low-income writers. Children and teenagers vote for the shortlist, with the winner chosen by a literary agent. Prize: £3,000.

## International Award for Illustration Bologna Children's Book Fair – Fundación SM

*email* illustratori@bolognafiere.it
*website* www.bolognachildrensbookfair.com

Supports the illustration work of young artists, the special quality of whose work has yet to be acknowledged. This annual award is granted to one of the young illustrators selected each year from the Bologna Children's Book Fair Illustrators Exhibition. Founded 2009.

## BolognaRagazzi Award

Piazza Costituzione 6, 40128 Bologna, Italy
*tel* +39 051-282111
*email* bolognaragazziaward@bolognafiere.it
*website* www.bolognachildrensbookfair.com/premi/bolognaragazzi-award/8382.html
*Facebook* www.facebook.com/BolognaChildrensBookFair
*Twitter* @BoChildrensBook

One of the world's most highly regarded international prizes in the sector of children's publishing, it celebrates the finest illustrated children's books and honours the best productions in terms of their graphic and editorial qualities, providing an international launch pad for authors and illustrators thanks to the high profile recognition that the winners receive during the fair. There are four main award categories: Fiction, Non-fiction, Opera Prima (for unpublished authors and illustrators) and Comics. Special categories are introduced each year (Photography for 2023). A special New Horizons award is made to a particularly innovative book. Founded 1966.

## Books Are My Bag Readers Awards

*website* www.nationalbooktokens.com/vote

Curated by bookshops and chosen by readers, categories include: Fiction, Non-Fiction, Poetry, Young Adult Fiction, Children's Fiction, Breakthrough Author, and Readers' Choice, which is nominated exclusively by readers.

## BookTrust Storytime Prize

BookTrust, G8 Battersea Studios, 80 Silverthorne Road, London SW8 3HE
*tel* 020-7801 8826
*email* StoryTimePrize@booktrust.org.uk
*website* www.booktrust.org.uk/what-we-do/awards-and-prizes

Celebrates the best books for sharing with young children aged 0–5 with a particular focus on books that have a wide appeal to parents and carers across our diverse nation, and for stories which can be read and enjoyed over and over again. The prize is run in collaboration with public libraries and librarians and the shortlisted titles are shared with families. Publishers are invited to enter up to five books per imprint.

## The Branford Boase Award

30 Winton Avenue, London N11 2AT
*tel* 023-8899 3369
*email* anne.marley@tiscali.co.uk
*website* www.branfordboaseaward.org.uk
*Facebook* www.facebook.com/branfordboaseaward
*Twitter* @BranfordBoase

An annual award of £1,000 is made to a first-time writer of a full-length children's novel (age 7+) published in the preceding year; the editor is also recognised. Encourages new writers for children and recognises the role of perceptive editors in developing new talent. The award was set up in memory of the outstanding children's writer Henrietta Branford and the gifted editor and publisher Wendy Boase who both died in 1999. Closing date for nominations: end of December. Founded 2000.

## Caledonia Novel Award

*email* caledoniaaward@gmail.com
*website* https://thecaledonianovelaward.com

Award for unpublished and self-published novelists. Novels can be of any genre for adults or young adults. The award is open to writers of any nationality who are over 18. Entries cost £25, with the winner receiving £1,500, and the writer of the best novel from the UK and Ireland winning a free place on a writing course at Moniack Mhor Creative Writing Centre. The award provides a number of sponsored places to low-income writers who are unable to afford the fee. For more information, see the competition rules on the website.

## Carnegie Medal – see The Yoto Carnegies

## The Caterpillar Poetry Prize

Ardan Grange, Milltown, Belturbet, Co. Cavan H14 K768, Republic of Ireland
*tel* + 353 (0)87 265 7251
*email* enquiries@thecaterpillarmagazine.com
*website* www.thecaterpillarmagazine.com

For a single unpublished poem written by an adult for children. The winners are chose by a different judge each year; previous judges have included Michael Morpurgo and Michael Rosen. 1st prize: €1,000 and a week at Circle of Misse in France; 2nd prize: €500; 3rd prize: €250. Winning poems appear in the *Irish Times* online. The prize is open to anyone over the age of 16. The entry fee is €15 and writers can submit as many poems as they like. Closing date 31 March. For full entry details and guidelines, see the website.

## Cheltenham Illustration Awards

*email* pittvillepress@gmail.com
*website* www.cheltenham-illustration-awards.com

The awards are divided into two sections: Student (aged 18 and over), and Emerging and Established Illustrators. Entries must relate to that year's theme. The selected work will be showcased in an exhibition and published in the *Cheltenham Illustration Awards Annual*, which will be distributed to education institutions and publishers.

## The Cheshire Novel Prize

*website* https://cheshirenovelprize.com
*Facebook* www.facebook.com/cheshirenovelprize
*Twitter* @prize_novel
*Instagram* @cheshirenovelprize

Only accepts entries from unagented writers; self-published writers may apply. Every unsuccessful entrant will receive at least one paragraph of feedback explaining why they were not longlisted. Submit a one-page synopsis and the first 5,000 words of a novel for adults or young adults (not children). Entry fee £25; sponsored entries are available for writers who are under-represented in publishing. 1st prize: £1,500; 2nd prize: £500.

## The Children's Book Award

*email* childrensbookaward@fcbg.org.uk
*website* https://fcbg.org.uk/childrens-book-award-2023
*Twitter* @FCBGNews

Awarded annually to authors and illustrators of children's fiction published in the UK. Children participate in the judging of the award and their votes are the deciding factor. Awards are made in the following categories: Books for Younger Children, Books for Younger Readers, and Books for Older Readers. Founded 1980.

## The KPMG Children's Books Ireland Awards

Children's Books Ireland, 17 North Great George's Street, Dublin 1 D01 R2F1, Republic of Ireland

*tel* +353 (0)1 872 7475
*email* info@childrensbooksireland.ie
*website* www.childrensbooksireland.ie

Leading annual children's book awards in Ireland. The awards are: Book of the Year, Eilís Dillon Award (for a first children's book), Honour Award for Fiction, Honour Award for Illustration, Judges' Special Award and Junior Juries Award. Schools and reading groups nationwide take part in the Junior Juries programme: participating groups make their own selection of suitable titles from the books shortlisted for the awards in March, using a specially devised activity pack to guide them in their reading; each group then votes for their favourite book. Closing date: November for work published between 1 January and 31 December of an awards year. Shortlist announced in February; winners announced in May. Founded 1990.

## The Children's Laureate

BookTrust, Studio G8, Battersea Studios, 80 Silverthorne Road, London SW8 3HE
*tel* 020-7801 8800
*email* childrenslaureate@booktrust.org.uk
*website* www.childrenslaureate.org.uk
*Twitter* @UKLaureate

The idea for the Children's Laureate originated from a conversation between (the then) Poet Laureate Ted Hughes and children's writer Michael Morpurgo. The post was established to celebrate exceptional children's authors and illustrators and to acknowledge their importance in creating the readers of tomorrow. Current Children's Laureate is Joseph Coelho (2022–24). Founded 1999.

## CLiPPA (Centre for Literacy in Primary Poetry Award)

CLPE, Webber Street, London SE1 8QW
*tel* 020-7401 3382/3
*email* info@clpe.org.uk
*website* https://clpe.org.uk/poetry/CLiPPA
*Facebook* www.facebook.com/CentreforLiteracyinPrimaryEducation
*Twitter* @clpe1
*Instagram* @clpe.org.uk

Honours excellence in children's poetry. Organised by the Centre for Literacy in Primary Education (CLPE), it is presented annually for a book of poetry published in the preceding year. The book can be a single-poet collection or an anthology. Submissions deadline: end of January/early February. Founded 2003.

## English Association English 4–11 Children's Picture Book Awards

The English Association, Leicester LE1 7RH
*email* awards@englishassociation.ac.uk
*website* https://englishassociation.ac.uk/english-4-11-picture-book-awards

Presented by the English Association to the best children's picture books of the year, both fiction and non-fiction, in the age ranges 4–7 years and 7–11 years. The winning books are chosen by the editorial board of *English 4-11*, the journal for primary teachers published by the English Association, from a shortlist selected by a panel of teachers and primary specialists. Each year, one of the books submitted is selected as the recipient of the Margaret Mallett Prize for Children's Non-Fiction. Founded 1995.

## Etisalat Award for Arabic Children's Literature

*email* info@uaebby.org.ae
*website* www.etisalataward.org.ae
*Facebook* www.facebook.com/EtisalatAward
*Twitter* @EtisalatAward

The prize of 1.2 million UAE dirhams is open only to children's literature written in the Arabic language; translated content is not eligible. Has widened its scope since its inception, adding new categories in order to highlight the individual achievements of writers, illustrators and publishers. The value of the award is distributed between four fixed categories and a fifth which changes every two years. Also runs the Warsha-Etisalat Workshops for Children's Books, an initiative aimed at nurturing a new generation of Arab authors, illustrators and publishers of Arabic children's books.

## FAB Prize for Undiscovered Talent

*email* prize@fabfaber.co.uk
*website* www.fabprize.org
*Twitter* @FaberChildrens

Set up by Faber Children's and Andlyn Literary Agency, this is an annual competition for unagented and unpublished writers and illustrators from Black, Asian and/or non-white minority ethnic backgrounds. Now with the additional backing of BookTrust and the Association of Illustrators, the competition winners and runners up are offered mentoring and exposure to literary agents and editors alongside access to training and shadowing schemes. The prize provides a unique opportunity to kick-start a writing or illustrating career and get a foot in the door. Entries must be text or artwork for children aged 1–18 years. 1st prize: £1,500 each for text and illustration plus a bundle of support; 2nd prize: £500 each; one commended writer: a place on a five-part programme, Insights into the Publishing Process. Founded 2017.

## FeedARead.com Book Awards

*tel* 07948 392634
*email* edward@youwriteon.com
*website* www.youwriteon.com

Arts Council–funded publishing site which facilitates awards for new fiction and non-fiction writers. Random House and Orion provide free professional critiques for the highest rated new writers' opening chapters and short stories on FeedaRead.com each month. The three adult fiction or non-fiction books judged to be the best books each year are published by FeedaRead.com as Award Winner Editions. The publishing awards are worth £1,000, including publishing, advertising and online sales. Writers can enter at any time throughout the year: closing date is 31 December each year. Founded 2010.

## The Klaus Flugge Prize

*email* klausfluggeprize@gmail.com
*website* www.klausfluggeprize.co.uk
*Twitter* @KlausFluggePr
*Instagram* @klausfluggeprize

Awarded to the most promising and exciting newcomer to children's picture book illustration. It honours the work of publisher Klaus Flugge in the field of illustration and children's picture books. The winning debut illustrator receives £5,000.

## Foyle Young Poets of the Year Award – see page 188

## Indie Book Awards

6 Bell Yard, London WC2A 2JR
*tel* 020-7421 4656
*email* emma.bradshaw@booksellers.org.uk
*website* www.booksaremybag.com/IndieBookAwards/About
*Facebook* www.facebook.com/booksaremybag
*Twitter* @booksaremybag
*Instagram* @booksaremybag

The only awards given to an author or illustrator on behalf of independent bookshops. The awards showcase the best paperback reads for the summer. Awards are given in four categories: Fiction, Non-Fiction, Children's Fiction, and Picture Book. For entry guidelines and shortlist details see the website.

## Jhalak Children's & YA Prize

*email* info@jhalakprize.com
*website* www.jhalakprize.com/childrens-ya
*Twitter* @jhalakprize
*Instagram* @jhalakprize

Seeks out the best books by British or British resident BAME writers and awards one winner £1,000, along with a unique work of art created by artists of colour for the annual Jhalak Art Residency. All shortlisted authors receive one year of complementary membership of The London Library; the winner receives two years. Entries can be for fiction, non-fiction, short stories, graphic novels, poetry, picture books and all other genres intended for children and young adult readers. The prize exists to celebrate the achievements of writers of colour. For submission guidelines and details of key dates see the website. Founded 2020.

## The Kelpies Prizes for Writing and Illustration

Floris Books, Canal Court, 40 Craiglockhart Avenue, Edinburgh EH14 1LT
*email* kelpiesprize@florisbooks.co.uk
*website* https://discoverkelpies.co.uk/kelpies-prizes

Annual awards for emerging writers and illustrators who are committed to developing their skills and creating quality books for children. The Kelpies Prizes are open to anyone who lives or works in Scotland. The winners will receive £500 cash, nine months of mentoring with an experienced editorial or design team, and consideration for a publishing contract with Floris Books. Submit writing or illustration samples and entry form online; see website for full details. Closing date: end February.

## Kindle Storyteller Award

*website* www.amazon.co.uk/b?ie=UTF8&node=12061299031

Open to submissions of new English-language books in any genre. Titles must be previously unpublished and be available as an ebook and in print via Kindle Direct Publishing. The award shortlist is decided by reader feedback and a panel of industry judges. The winning author will receive £20,000. Competition entry period runs from 1 May to 31 August.

## Lancashire Book of the Year Award

*tel* 0300 123 6703
*website* www.lancashire.gov.uk/libraries-and-archives/libraries/lancashires-book-of-the-year

Awarded to the best work of fiction for children in the 12–14 year group, published in the UK. It is the longest-running regional book award in the country and the award is voted for by Year 9 students in high schools around the county of Lancashire. Winner announced in July.

## Laureate na nÓg/Ireland's Children's Laureate

Children's Books Ireland, 17 North Great George's Street, Dublin 1 D01 R2F1, Republic of Ireland
*tel* +353 (0)18 727475
*email* info@childrenslaureate.ie
*website* www.childrenslaureate.ie
*Project Manager* Ruth Ní Eidhin

Recognises the role and importance of literature for children in Ireland. Established to engage young people with high-quality literature and to underline the importance of children's literature in Ireland's cultural and imaginative life. It was awarded for the first time in 2010. The Laureate participates in selected events and activities around Ireland and internationally during their three-year term.

The Laureate is chosen in recognition of their widely recognised high-quality children's writing or illustration and the positive impact they have had on readers as well as other writers and illustrators. The current Laureate is Áine Ní Ghlinn (2020–23).

## The Astrid Lindgren Memorial Award

Borgvagen 1–5, Stockholm, Sweden
*tel* +46 8-51926400
*email* literatureaward@alma.se
*website* https://alma.se/en

Honours the memory of Astrid Lindgren, Sweden's favourite author, and promotes children's and youth literature around the world. The award is five million Swedish kronas, the world's largest for children's and youth literature, and the second-largest literature prize in the world. It is awarded annually to one or more recipients, regardless of language or nationality.

Authors, illustrators, storytellers and promoters of reading are eligible. The award is for life-long work or artistry rather than for individual pieces. The prize can only be awarded to living people. The winner is selected by a jury based on nominations for outstanding achievement from selected nominating bodies around the world. Administered by the Swedish Arts Council. Founded 2002.

## Little Rebels Children's Book Award

*email* info@letterboxlibrary.com
*website* https://littlerebels.org
*Twitter* @littlerebsprize

Recognises children's fiction for readers aged 0–12 years which promotes social justice or social equality, challenges stereotypes or is informed by anti-discriminatory concerns. The award is given by the Alliance of Radical Booksellers. Winning prize: £2,000. See website for submission guidelines. Founded 2010.

## The Macmillan Prize for Illustration

Macmillan Children's Books, 6 Briset Street, London EC1M 5NR
*email* macmillanprize@macmillan.co.uk
*website* www.panmacmillan.com/mac-prize-entry-page

Three prizes are awarded annually for unpublished children's book illustrations by art students in higher education institutions in the UK. The books should be between 24–32 pages, the text can be fiction or non-fiction and the artwork must meet the specifications given on the website. 1st prize: £1,000; 2nd prize: £500; 3rd prize: £250. Founded 1985.

## The Mythopoeic Fantasy Award for Children's Literature

*email* awards@mythsoc.org
*website* www.mythsoc.org

Honours books for younger readers (from YA novels to picture books for beginning readers) in the tradition of *The Hobbit* or *The Chronicles of Narnia*. The Mythopoeic Awards are chosen from books nominated by individual members of the Mythopoeic Society and selected by a committee of society members. Authors, publishers and their representatives may not nominate their own books for any of the awards, nor are books published by the Mythopoeic Press eligible for the awards. The Mythopoeic Society does not accept or review unsolicited manuscripts.

## Nero Book Awards

9–15 Neal Street, Covent Garden, London WC2H 9PW
*email* info@nerobookawards.com
*website* https://nerobookawards.com
*Facebook* www.facebook.com/NeroBookAwards
*Twitter* @nerobookawards
*Instagram* @nerobookawards

Administered by the Booksellers Association and in partnership with Brunel University London and Right to Dream. Recognises books which are popular with readers across four categories: Fiction, Debut Fiction, Non-Fiction and Children's Books. Judging panel includes publishing professionals, authors, booksellers and influencers. Shortlist announced in November, category winners in January and overall winner in February. 1st prize: £5,000 in each category; one overall winner receives the Nero Gold Prize and £30,000. Submissions accepted from publishers only. Founded 2023.

## New Anglia Manuscript Prize

*email* newangliaprize@laxfieldliterary.com
*website* https://laxfieldliterary.com/new-anglia-manuscript-prize

Sponsored by the National Centre for Writing in Norwich, it is open to unpublished writers from Suffolk and Norfolk. Applicants must submit a completed manuscript of at least 30,000 words. Winning entries are awarded £500 and receive representation from Laxfield Literary Associates. There is no fee to enter. Founded 2020.

## New Zealand Book Awards for Children and Young Adults

c/o NZ Book Awards Trust,
72 Te Wharepōuri Street, Wellington 6023, New Zealand
*tel* +64 (0)27 773 9855
*email* childrensawards@nzbookawards.org.nz
*website* www.nzbookawards.nz/new-zealand-book-awards-for-children-and-young-adults

Celebrates excellence in, and provides recognition for, the best children's books published in New Zealand. Awards are presented in six categories: Picture Book, Junior Fiction (the Wright Family Foundation Esther Glen Award), Young Adult Fiction, Non-Fiction (the Elsie Locke Award), Illustration (the Russell Clark Award) and te reo Māori (the Wright Family Foundation Te Kura

Pounamu Award). Each of these awards carries prize money of $7,500. The overall prize, the Margaret Mahy Book of the Year award, carries a further prize of $7,500. A $2,500 prize (The NZSA Best First Book Award) is also awarded to a previously unpublished author or illustrator. Eligible books must have been published in New Zealand between April and March in the period preceding the awards' August ceremony date.

## North East Book Award

Cramlington Learning Village, Cramlington, Northumberland NE23 6BN
*tel* (01670) 712311
*email* earmstrong@cramlingtonlv.co.uk
*website* www.nebookawards.org.uk
*Contact* Eileen Armstrong

Awarded to a book written by a UK/Ireland resident author and first published in paperback the previous year. The shortlist is selected by school librarians, teachers and the previous year's student judges. The final winner is decided entirely by the student judges (Year 7/8) and is announced in June. The 2022 winner was *When the Sky Falls* by Phil Earle (Andersen Press).

## North East Teen Book Award

Cramlington Learning Village, Cramlington, Northumberland NE23 6BN
*tel* (01670) 712311
*email* earmstrong@cramlingtonlv.co.uk
*website* https://www.nebookawards.org.uk
*Contact* Eileen Armstrong

Awarded to a book written by a UK/Ireland resident author and first published in paperback during the previous year. The shortlist is selected by school librarians, teachers and the previous year's student judges. The final winner is decided entirely by the student judges (Year 9+) and is announced in June.

## Nottingham Children's Book Awards

Nottingham Library Service, Culture and Libraries, Aspley Library, Nottingham NG8 5DD
*email* charlotte.blount@nottinghamcity.gov.uk
*website* www.nottinghamcity.gov.uk/ncba
*Facebook* www.facebook.com/NottmLibraries
*Twitter* @readingnottm
*Contact* Charlotte Blount

Nottingham children aged 2–4 years choose their favourite picture books from books published the previous year. The shortlist of titles is drawn up by the end of July with the help of local schools and nurseries. In the autumn, library staff visit settings to read the three books to preschool children, asking them to vote for their favourite. Families can also vote in libraries and via the website. The winner is announced at the beginning of December. Founded 1999.

## Oscar's Book Prize

*email* info@oscarsbookprize.co.uk
*website* www.oscarsbookprize.co.uk
*Facebook* www.facebook.com/oscarsbookprize
*Twitter* @oscarsbookprize
*Instagram* @oscarsbookprize

This £10,000 prize, supported by Amazon and in partnership with the *Evening Standard*, CLPE and Read for Good, is awarded to the preschool book published in the UK in the previous year that the judges consider to be the best. Publishers may enter up to five books per imprint. Collections and anthologies are not eligible. Previously published, self-published books and ebooks are not eligible. Founded 2013.

## The People's Book Prize

*website* www.peoplesbookprize.com
*Facebook* www.facebook.com/pages/The-Peoples-Book-Prize/200637717319384
*Twitter* @PeoplesBkPrize
*Founder & Prize Administrator* Tatiana Wilson, *Patron Emeritus* Frederick Forsyth, *Founding Patron* Dame Beryl Bainbridge

Awards are given in three categories: Fiction, Non-Fiction, and Children's. Titles must be submitted by publishers, with a limit of three titles per category.

## Phoenix Award

140B Purcellville Gateway Drive, Suite 120, Purcellville, VA 20132, USA
*tel* +1 630-571-4520
*email* info@childlitassn.org
*website* www.childlitassn.org

Presented by the Children's Literature Association (ChLA) for the most outstanding book for children originally published in the English language 20 years earlier which did not receive a major award at the time of publication. It is intended to recognise books of high literary merit. Founded 1985.

## The Queen's Knickers Award

The Society of Authors, 24 Bedford Row, London WC1R 4EH
*tel* 020-3880 2230
*email* prizes@societyofauthors.org
*website* www.societyofauthors.org/Prizes/Society-of-Authors-Awards/The-Queens-Knickers-Award
*Twitter* @Soc_of_Authors

An annual prize, generously funded by the author of *The Queen's Knickers*, Nicholas Allan, for outstanding children's illustrated books for ages 0–7. The prize recognises books that strike a quirky, new note, in any combination of words and/or pictures and in any physical format including pop-ups, flap books and board books. Submissions must be made by the print publisher. The winner receives £5,000 as well as a golden Queen's Knickers badge, and the runner-up receives £1,000 and a silver badge. The prize will be shared between the author and illustrator if applicable.

## The Royal Society Young People's Book Prize

The Royal Society, 6–9 Carlton House Terrace, London SW1Y 5AG
*tel* 020-7451 2500
*email* education@royalsociety.org
*website* https://royalsociety.org/grants-schemes-awards/book-prizes/young-peoples-book-prize
*Facebook* www.facebook.com/theroyalsociety
*Twitter* @royalsociety

Open to books for under-14s that have science as a substantial part of their content, narrative or theme. An expert adult panel chooses the shortlist, but the winner is chosen by groups of young people in judging panels across the UK. The winning entry receives £10,000 and shortlisted entries receive £2,500. Entries open in December each year. Pure reference works including encyclopedias, educational textbooks and descriptive books are not eligible. The Prize is offered thanks to the generosity of an anonymous donor. Founded 1988.

## Rubery Book Award

PO Box 15821, Birmingham B31 9EA
*email* enquiries@ruberybookaward.com
*website* www.ruberybookaward.com

An annual award for published books on any subject, including children's books, with prizes totalling £2,800 (Book of the Year receives £2,000 and category winners £200 each). Books published by independent presses and self-published books are eligible.

## SCBWI Awards and Grants – see Society of Children's Book Writers & Illustrators

## Scholastic Laugh Out Loud Book Awards

*email* laughoutloud@scholastic.co.uk
*website* https://shop.scholastic.co.uk/lollies
*Twitter* @lolbookawards

Known as The Lollies, they are awarded to books in seven categories: Illustrator of the Year, Best Picture Book, 6–8-year-olds, 9–12-year-olds, Teens, Non-Fiction and Poetry. A judging panel selects four books to make up a shortlist for each category, but winners are decided entirely by children's votes, with voting taking place via the website and promoted through Scholastic Book Clubs and Book Fairs. See website for full entry and submission guidelines.

## Searchlight Writing for Children Awards

*email* hello@searchlightawards.co.uk
*website* www.searchlightawards.co.uk
*Facebook* www.facebook.com/WritingAwards

*Twitter* @WritingAwards
*Instagram* @searchlight_awards

An international competition for aspiring authors writing for children or young adults. There are two competition categories: Best Children's Picture Book (text only) and Best Novel Opening for Children or Young Adults. Entries open 1st May 2023 until 31st August 2023. Entry fee: £9 – picture book; £14 – novel opening. Winners are chosen by high-profile industry judges. 1st prize: £500 – picture book; £1000 – novel opening. The top ten stories in both categories will feature in an agent/publisher pitch book. See website for further details and submission guidelines. Founded 2021.

## Sheffield Children's Book Award

Schools Library Service, Stadia Technology Park, 60 Shirland Lane, Sheffield S9 3SP
*tel* 0114 250 6840
*email* sheffieldchildrensbookaward@sheffield.gov.uk
*website* www.sheffield.gov.uk/home/libraries-archives/book-awards

Presented annually in November to the book chosen as the most enjoyable by the children of Sheffield. Categories include: Baby Books, Toddler Books, Picture Books, Emerging Reads, Shorter Novel, Longer Novel and Young Adult.

## Wilbur Smith Adventure Writing Prize

The Wilbur & Niso Smith Foundation, Unit 9, 5–7 Wells Terrace, London N4 3JU
*email* submissions@wilbur-niso-smithfoundation.org
*website* www.wilbur-niso-smithfoundation.org/awards/intro
*Facebook* www.facebook.com/WNSmithFoundation
*Twitter* @Wilbur_Niso_Fdn

Supports and celebrates today's best adventure writing. Open to writers of any nationality, writing in English. Awards are presented for fiction in three categories. The Best Published Novel (prize: £10,000) and New Voices Award (prize: one year of editorial support and one-to-one mentoring) are for full-length novels for adults or young adults. The Author of Tomorrow award (prizes: £150–£1,000 depending on age category, plus book tokens and digital publication) seeks to find the adventure writers of the future and is open to young people across the world (in age categories 16–21 years, 12–15 years and age 11 and under) who have completed a short piece of adventure writing in English. Submission guidelines, eligibility criteria, entry fees, shortlist dates and details of the previous winners for each category can be found on the website.

## The Stephen Spender Prize

41 Wellington Square, Oxford OX4 2JF
*email* prize@stephen-spender.org
*website* www.stephen-spender.org/stephen-spender-prize

Celebrates poetry in translation, with categories for adults and young people, as well as an annually rotating spotlight highlighting a language spoken widely in the UK and a prize for schools. Entrants should translate into English any poem from any language. Overall winner will receive a £1,000 cash prize. Open to adults from all over the world; youth entrants must be UK or Irish citizens or residents, or pupils at a British school overseas. Founded 2004.

## The Edward Stanford Travel Writing Awards

Stanfords, 7 Mercer Walk, Covent Garden, London WC2H 9FA
*tel* 020-7836 1321
*website* https://www.stanfords.co.uk/edward-stanford-travel-writing-awards

Administered by Stanfords, a specialist retailer of maps, travel books and other travel accessories, they recognise exceptional travel writing published in the previous year. The categories include: Travel Book of the Year, Children's Travel Book of the Year, New Travel Writer of the Year, and Outstanding Contribution to Travel Writing. The winner in each category receives a personalised handmade globe trophy.

## The Week Junior Book Awards

*website* www.theweekjuniorbookawards.co.uk
*Facebook* www.facebook.com/Theweekjunior
*Twitter* @theweekjunior
*Instagram* @theweekjunior

Celebrates authors, illustrators and publishers who inspire children to read for pleasure and recognise original ideas, captivating illustration and intelligent storytelling. Books can be nominated by fellow authors, illustrators and publishers across nine categories: Fiction (Younger and Older), Non-Fiction (Younger and Older), STEM Book, Illustrated Book, Audiobook, Cover and New Author. Winners receive coverage in *The Week Junior* and *The Bookseller* and are part of the marketing campaign which supports the awards.

## TikTok Book Awards

6th Floor, One London Wall, London EC2Y 5EB
*website* www.tiktok.com
*Facebook* www.facebook.com/tiktok
*Twitter* @tiktok_uk
*Instagram* @tiktok_uk

Celebrates the best books and authors discussed on TikTok and the most popular creators who post videos about them. Awarded across nine categories including Best BookTok Revival and Best Book I Wish I Could Read Again For The First Time. Judged by a panel of authors and publishing professionals, TikTok users vote on a shortlist in July and winners are announced in August. Founded 2023.

## The Times/Chicken House Children's Fiction Competition

Chicken House, 2 Palmer Street, Frome, Somerset BA11 1DS
*tel* (01373) 454488
*email* competitions@chickenhousebooks.com
*website* www.chickenhousebooks.com
*Twitter* @chickenhsebooks
*Contact* Jazz Bartlett Love

Open to unpublished writers of a full-length children's novel (age 7–18). Entrants must be over 18 and novels must not exceed 80,000 words in length. There are two winners, both of whom are announced in *The Times* and receive a worldwide publishing contract with Chicken House with a royalty advance of £10,000 and £7,500 respectively. The winner is selected by a panel of judges which includes children's authors, journalists, publishers, librarians and other key figures from the world of children's literature. For competition opening and closing dates, consult the Chicken House website.

## Tir na n-Og Awards

Books Council of Wales, Castell Brychan, Aberystwyth, Ceredigion SY23 2JB
*tel* (01970) 624151
*email* wbc.children@books.wales
*website* https://llyfrau.cymru/en/gwobrau/tir-na-nog
*Facebook* www.facebook.com/LlyfrDaFabBooks
*Twitter* @LlyfrDaFabBooks

Established to promote and raise the standard of children's and young people's books in Wales. Three awards (prize: £1,000 each) are presented annually by the Welsh Books Council and are sponsored by the Chartered Institute of Library and Information Professionals Cymru/Wales: The best English-language book of the year with an authentic Welsh background: fiction and factual books originally in English are eligible, translations from Welsh or any other language are not eligible; the best original Welsh-language book aimed at the primary school sector; the best original Welsh-language book aimed at the secondary school sector. Founded 1976.

## Christopher Tower Poetry Competition – see page 189

## UKLA Book Awards

*tel* 07933 724030
*website* www.ukla.org/awards/ukla-book-award

The only UK children's book awards voted for by teachers. Encourage teachers and school librarians to increase their knowledge of recently published children's books and to share them with their students. The selection committee is looking for books that can be read aloud, studied, discussed and inspire creative classroom activities. Teachers are looking for books which evocatively express ideas and offer layered meanings through the use of language, imaginative expression and rich illustration/graphics.

## The V&A Illustration Awards

Victoria & Albert Museum, London SW7 2RL
*email* villa@vam.ac.uk
*website* www.vam.ac.uk/info/va-illustration-awards

Biennial awards open to illustrators living or publishing in the UK and students who have attended a course in the UK over the last two years. Previous awards included the following categories: Book Illustration, Book Cover Design, and Illustrated Journalism; the categories are currently being reviewed for the next awards. Winners each receive £3,000, with the overall winner receiving £8,000. Founded 1972.

## The Warwick Prize for Women in Translation

*email* womenintranslation@warwick.ac.uk
*website* https://warwick.ac.uk/fac/cross_fac/womenintranslation
*Coordinator* Holly Langstaff

Addresses the gender imbalance in translated literature and increases the number of international women's voices accessible to a British and Irish readership. Awarded annually to the best eligible work of fiction, poetry, literary non-fiction, work of fiction for children or young adults, graphic novel or play text, written by a woman, translated into English by a translator (or translators) of any gender, and published by a UK or Irish publisher. The £1,000 prize is divided between writer and translator. Founded 2017.

## Waterstones Children's Book Prize

Waterstones, 203–206 Piccadilly, London W1J 9HD
*email* childrensbookprize@waterstones.com
*website* www.waterstones.com

Rewards and champions new and emerging children's writers, voted for by booksellers. There are three categories: Illustrated Books, Books for Younger Readers and Books for Older Readers. Submission criteria:

*Illustrated Books.* Illustrated books authored and illustrated by the same person: the author/illustrator may not have previously published more than two titles of any fiction genre worldwide (educational titles are exempt). Author/illustrator partnerships: neither the author nor illustrator may have previously solely published more than two titles of any fiction genre (which includes picture books) worldwide (educational titles are exempt). The partnership may not have previously published more than two titles together.

*Books for Younger Readers* and *Books for Older Readers*. No more than one previously published title of any fiction genre worldwide (educational titles are exempt). The title must make sense as a standalone novel. If the title is illustrated, and the illustrator matches submission criteria for Illustrated Books, then the illustrator will be considered eligible for this category. Narrative non-fiction is also eligible for submission.

There will be an overall winner from the category winners.

## Wildlife Photographer of the Year

The Natural History Museum, Cromwell Road, London SW7 5BD
*website* www.nhm.ac.uk/visit/wpy/competition.html

Open to photographers of all experience levels, aged 18 and over. There are 16 categories, ranging from Animal Portraits to Photojournalism and Urban Wildlife to Underwater Photography. The Grand Title award is given to the photographer whose individual image is judged to be the most striking and memorable. Prizes range in value depending on the category. The Young Wildlife Photographer of the Year recognises photographers aged 17 and under.

## World Illustration Awards

Association of Illustrators, Somerset House, Strand, London WC2R 1LA
*tel* 020-7759 1010
*email* awards@theaoi.com
*website* www.theaoi.com/world-illustration-awards
*Facebook* www.facebook.com/theaoi
*Twitter* @theaoi
*Instagram* @WorldIllustrationAwards

Presented in partnership with the *Directory of Illustration*, the awards programme celebrates contemporary illustration across the globe. A panel of international judges create a 500–strong longlist and shortlists 200 projects, which are celebrated in an online showcase, a catalogue and with an online industry events programme. For submission guidelines, categories and prizes, see the website.

## YA Book Prize

*email* caroline.carpenter@thebookseller.com
*website* www.yabookprize.com
*Facebook* www.facebook.com/YABookPrize
*Twitter* @yabookprize

First prize to specifically focus on fiction for young adults. Organised by *The Bookseller*, in partnership with the Edinburgh International Book Festival. Open for titles published between 1st January and 31st December of the previous year. Author must be living in the UK or Ireland at publication. Publishers must submit on behalf of an author. Winner receives £2,000. Founded 2014.

## The Yoto Carnegies

Room 150 British Library, 96 Euston Road, London NW1 2DB
*email* carnegies@cilip.org.uk
*website* www.yotocarnegies.org.uk

Nominations for the following two awards are invited from members of CILIP (the library and information association), who are asked to submit one title per Medal, accompanied by an explanation of how the book they have selected meets the medal criteria. The awards are selected by librarian judges from the Youth Libraries Group of CILIP. One title from each shortlist will receive a prize awarded by children vote for their favourites as part of the awards' shadowing scheme.

### Yoto Carnegie Medal for Writing

Awarded annually for an outstanding book for children (fiction or non-fiction) written in English and first published in the UK during the preceding year or co-published elsewhere within a three-month time lapse. The Yoto Carnegie Medal for Writing winner is awarded £5,000 prize money from the Colin Mears Award annually.

### Yoto Carnegie Medal for Illustration

Awarded annually for an outstanding illustrated book for children first published in the UK during the preceding year or co-published elsewhere within a three-month time lapse. Books intended for older as well as younger children are included, and reproduction will be taken into account. The Yoto Carnegie Medal for Illustration winner is awarded £5,000 from the Colin Mears Award fund each year.

# Prize winners

This is a selection of high-profile literary prize winners from the last year presented chronologically. See individual awards websites for details. Entries for many of these prizes are included in the *Yearbook*, starting on page 333.

## February 2022

**Scholastic Laugh Out Loud Book Awards**
*101 Bums* by Sam Harper, illustrated by Chris Jevons (Picture book); *Cats React to Science Facts* by Izzi Howell (Book for 6–8 year-olds); *The Super Miraculous Journey of Freddie Yates* by Jenny Pearson, illustrated by Rob Biddulph (Book for 9–13 year-olds)

## May

**KPMG Book of the Year Award**
*Gut Feelings* by C.G. Moore

**Tir na n-Og Awards**
*Gwag y Nos* by Sioned Wyn Roberts (Primary); *Y Pump* edited by Elgan Rhys (Secondary)

**Scottish Teenage Book Prize (Scottish Book Trust)**
*Fin & Rye & Fireflies* by Harry Cook

**Jhalak Children's & YA Prize**
*Danny Chung Does Not Do Maths* by Maisie Chan, illustrated by Anh Cao

**YA Book Prize**
*Hani and Ishu's Guide to Fake Dating* by Adiba Jaigirdar

## June

**The Macmillan Prize for Children's Picture Book Illustration**
*The Queue* by Heike Scharrer

**The Yoto Carnegie Medal**
*October, October* by Katya Balen

**The Yoto Kate Greenaway Medal**
*Long Way Down* by Jason Reynolds, illustrated by Danica Novgorodoff

## July

**Lancashire Book of the Year Award**
*Last One To Die* by Cynthia Murphy

**UKLA Book Awards**
*Barbara Throws a Wobbler* by Nadia Shireen and *The Invisible* by Tom Percival (3–6+ years); *October, October* by Katya Balen (7–10+ years); *Punching the Air* by Ibi Zoboi and Yusef Salaam (11–14+ years)

**CLiPPA (Centre for Literacy in Primary Poetry Award)**
*Stars with Flaming Tails* by Valerie Bloom, illustrated by Ken Wilson-Max

**Branford Boase Award**
*Danny Chung Does Not Do Maths* by Maisie Chan (and her editor Georgia Murray)

## October

**Mythopoeic Fantasy Award for Children's Literature (USA)**
*Pahua and the Soul Stealer* by Lori M. Lee and *Root Magic* by Eden Royce

## January 2023

**BookBug Picture Book Prize (Scottish Book Trust)**
*My First Book of Sea Creatures* by Zoe Ingram

## March

**BolognaRagazzi Award**
*Everything That Happened Before You Arrived* by Yael Frankel (Fiction); *Art of Protest* by De Nichols, illustrated by Diana Dagadita, Saddo, Olivia Twist, Molly Mendoza and Diego Bacas (Non-fiction); *The Purse* by Maria José Ferrada, illustrated by Ana Palmero Cáceres (New Horizons); *Mariedl. A Gigantic Story* by Laura Simonati (Opera Prima)

# Opportunities for under-represented writers

There has been an acknowledgement across the publishing industry that many voices have not found it easy to be heard and promoted amongst the many hundreds and thousands of books published every year. Publishers, agents, authors and prize-awarding organisations have collectively started to actively encourage and nurture a more diverse range of writers who have new stories to tell. There has been an increase in open submissions, prizes, bursaries and other schemes aimed at previously less represented groups. Some of the awards have full entries in other sections of this *Yearbook* (as indicated below) and some are listed in full here.

## PRIZE AND AWARDS

### The Diverse Book Awards

*email* hello@thediversebookawards.co.uk
*website* www.thediversebookawards.co.uk

Administered by author Abiola Bello and publicist Helen Lewis to celebrate diversity in book publishing in the UK and Ireland. There are four fiction award categories: Adult, YA, Children's and, new from 2023, Picture Books. Entries can be traditionally or self-published but must have been published in the preceding year. The winner in each category receives a trophy as well as access to a range of opportunities including marketing workshops, inclusion in *Pen&inc* magazine, panel spots and more. 2022 winners: Kia Abdullah, *Next of Kin* (Adult); Natasha Bowen, *Skin of the Sea* (YA); Benjamin Dean, *Me, My Dad and the End of the Rainbow* (Children's). Founded 2020.

### Golden Egg Award – see page 392

### Jhalak Children's & YA Prize – see page 337

### The London Writers' Awards

The Albany Centre, Douglas Way, London SE8 4AG
*email* bobby@spreadtheword.org.uk
*website* www.spreadtheword.org.uk/projects/london-writers-awards

Set up by Spread the Word for London-based prose writers who identify as being from a background currently under-represented in publishing: disabled, LGBTQIA+, working class or writers of colour. The awards are given across four genres: literary fiction (including short stories), commercial fiction, narrative non-fiction, and children's (including middle-grade and YA fiction, excluding picture books). Founded 2018.

### SCBWI Diversity Awards and Grants – see page 305

### The Times/Chicken House, Children's Fiction Competition – see page 241

## EVENTS, BURSARIES AND OTHER SCHEMES

### All Stories

*email* info@allstories.org.uk
*website* www.allstories.org.uk
*Facebook* www.facebook.com/AllStoriesWrite
*Twitter* @AllStoriesWrite
*Instagram* @allstorieswrite

An initiative offering free opportunities for children's book writers from under-represented groups to develop their work, supported by the ALCS, Arts Council England and SCBWI. Under-represented is used broadly and includes writers who are people of colour, disabled, neurodiverse, LGBTQIA+, working class or socio-economically marginalised; the programme is also intended for those who would not otherwise be able to pay for writing support. Opportunities available include mentorships with experienced editors, writing workshops from award-winning authors and book career guidance for students.

### The Malorie Blackman Scholarships for Unheard Voices

*website* www.citylit.ac.uk/malorie-blackman-scholarships

Three annual awards worth up to £1,000 each, to fund one year's study within the Creative Writing department at City Lit. Writers are welcome from under-represented groups, including (but not exclusive to) people with disabilities, who are members of the LGBTQIA+ community, who are from lower socioeconomic backgrounds or who are from BAME backgrounds. Founded 2020.

## Book Edit Writers' Prize

*email* writersprize@thebookedit.co.uk
*website* www.thebookedit.co.uk/writers-prize

Supports unpublished novelists who are from backgrounds and communities under-represented in publishing. Eight winners will be selected to read their work at an Agent Showcase in front of industry professionals, including literary agents. The selected writers will receive training and an opportunity to practise reading their work aloud, and an anthology of the readings will be published online. All entrants receive advice on mentoring, courses and editing. Entrants should submit the first 1,000 words of a novel, a synopsis of the novel and details of their writing experience to date. Founded 2021.

## BookTrust Represents – see page 318

## Breakthrough x Black Ballad Mentoring Programme

*email* help@curtisbrowncreative.co.uk
*website* www.curtisbrowncreative.co.uk/course/
breakthrough-black-ballad-mentoring-programme-
0523

A mentoring programme for Black women writers, run in collaboration between Curtis Brown Creative and Black Ballad. Four writers will receive guidance from a published mentor over nine months and a tutorial with a literary agent. Entrants can apply with a writing project at any stage, from just starting to redrafting, in one of the following categories: Children's or YA Novel, Adult Novel, Short Stories, Memoir, or Narrative Non-Fiction. Applicants should submit 3,000 words of their project, a one-page synopsis and a completed entry form. Three of the mentorships are reserved for Black Ballad members (including new members) and one place is available for a low-income writer who cannot afford membership. Founded 2023.

## Creative Access

c/o ITV, Westworks, 195 Wood Lane,
London W12 7FQ
*email* info@creativeaccess.org.uk
*website* www.creativeaccess.org.uk
*Facebook* www.facebook.com/CreativeAccessUK
*Twitter* @_CreativeAccess
*Instagram* @_CreativeAccess

One of the UK's leading diversity, equity and inclusion organisations which provides career support and fosters development for those from under-represented communities. Working with leading creative organisations across the UK, Creative Access provides a range of services to help support employer partners create inclusive workplaces, including recruitment programmes, research-driven consultancy and training. Founded 2012.

## Curtis Brown Creative – see page 392

## Design. Publishing. Inclusivity.

*email* contact@dpi.org.uk
*website* www.dpi.org.uk
*Twitter* @dpi_org
*Instagram* @dpi_org

The mentorship scheme runs twice a year and offers ten applicants an opportunity to develop skills to pursue a career in book design. No prior education or experience is required, but existing designers are eligible to apply. Each successful applicant is matched with a mentor for six months. Applicants must be from an under-represented background, including Black, Asian and minority ethnicity, disabled, neurodivergent, LGBTQIA+ or working class. Founded 2022.

## Emerging Writers Programme

*tel* 020-7766 4765
*email* emergingwriters@londonlibrary.co.uk
*website* www.londonlibrary.co.uk/about-us/ll-
emerging-writers

Open to all writers above the age of 16, the programme offers writers, in all genres, one year's free membership to The London Library, writing development masterclasses and literary networking opportunities. The Virago Participation Bursary (funded by Virago Books) is awarded to Black women and Black nonbinary writers to assist with any financial issues that might prevent them from accessing the full programme. Founded 2019.

## Hachette Children's Group Picture Book Open Day

*email* picturebookopenday@hachettechildrens.co.uk

A virtual open day to find new picture book writers and illustrators from the North of England, Scotland and Ireland. Participants get the chance to engage with the publishing team at Hachette Children's Group and receive feedback on a work-in-progress. There are 30 places available. Applicants must not have previously been published or self-published, or have a contract to have their work published in the future. Writers should submit a complete picture book in rhyme or prose (not exceeding 700 words); illustrators should submit three coloured pieces from their portfolio; writer-illustrators should submit both. The submitted work should be aimed at children aged 3–5, include a memorable character and a strong hook or theme. For more information see: www.hachette.co.uk/wp-content/uploads/2022/12/HCG-NORTH-OPEN-DAY-2023-FINAL.pdf.

## HarperCollins Author and Design Academy

Westerhill Road, Bishopsbriggs, Glasgow G64 2QT
*email* enquiries@harpercollins.co.uk
*website* www.harpercollinsacademy.co.uk

*Facebook* www.facebook.com/
HarperCollinsPublishersUK
*Twitter* @harpercollinsuk
*Instagram* @harpercollinsuk

A training programme for writers from BAME
backgrounds who are under-represented in
publishing. Courses run twice a year for six weeks
and are available in three genres: fiction, non-fiction
and writing for children. A design course runs once a
year. All successful applicants also receive publishing
masterclasses and support from a mentor. Applicants
must not be represented by a literary agent and
should apply online to one of the three courses.
Founded 2021.

## Inscribe
*email* contact@peepaltreepress.com
*website* www.peepaltreepress.com/inscribe
*Twitter* @INSCRIBEwriters

Supports writers of colour in England to
professionally advance their creative work and their
careers through coaching, mentoring, workshops,
residentials, training, newsletters, publications and
general advice. Founded 2009.

## Megaphone Writer Development Scheme
*email* megaphone.write@gmail.com
*website* https://megaphonewrite.com
*Twitter* @MegaphoneWrite

An Arts Council England–funded project which
offers a year of one-to-one mentoring and
masterclasses for writers of colour based in England
who are writing a novel for children or teenagers.
Bursaries are available for writers who cannot afford
the fees.

## The Octopus Scheme
*email* hello@thenovelry.com
*website* www.thenovelry.com/scholarships

Established by The Novelry to offer fully funded
scholarships for places on their Ninety Day Novel
course for under-represented writers. Applicants can
include writers from a low-income background,
primary carers, ex-offenders, writers with a disability,
writers of colour and writers from the LGBTQIA+
community. Successful applicants will also receive
one-to-one coaching. Applicants should follow the
instructions on the website to apply. Scholarships are
sponsored by authors including Sophie Kinsella,
Rachel Joyce and Ajay Chowdhury. Founded 2022.

## Pathways Into Children's Publishing
Pop Up Projects, 5 City Garden Row,
London N1 8DW
*email* pathways@pop-up.org.uk
*website* https://pop-up.org.uk/courses/pathways-into-
childrens-publishing
*Facebook* www.facebook.com/PathwaysINTO

*Twitter* @PathwaysINTO
*Instagram* @PathwaysInto

Two-year illustration programme for talented artists
from under-represented backgrounds who want to
become the next generation of children's illustrators.
The programme is designed and organised by Pop
Up Projects, with support from over 20 publishers
and leading universities.
Pathways also runs a series of masterclasses and
short courses for all aspiring illustrators looking to
improve their practice and learn about creating
successful children's books. The courses are run by
award-winning illustrators and highly-experienced
publishers and provide practical, creative advice as
well as a real insight into children's publishing.

## Storymix — see page 69

## TLC/Arts Council England Free Reads Scheme
East Side, Platform 1, Kings Cross Station,
London N1C 4AX
*tel* 020-3751 0757 ext. 800
*email* info@literaryconsultancy.co.uk
*website* www.literaryconsultancy.co.uk/editorial/ace-
free-reads-scheme
*Director* Aki Schilz

In 2001, TLC received funding from Arts Council
England to enable the provision of bursaried
manuscript assessments for writers from low-income
households. The scheme is known as the Free Reads
Scheme and offers access to TLC's core services to
writers who might not be able to afford them. Free
Reads are selected by a range of literature
development bodies from across the UK, and there
are currently 17 organisations benefitting from the
scheme. For detailed submission guidelines and
eligibility information, see the website.
Founded 2001.

## WriteNow Programme
WriteNow - The Penguin Random House Group,
20 Vauxhall Bridge Road, London SW1V 2SA
*email* writenow@penguinrandomhouse.co.uk
*website* www.penguin.co.uk/company/creative-
responsibility/writenow/whats-on-offer.html
*Twitter* @PenguinUKBooks

A programme by PRH which nurtures and publishes
new, unpublished writers from under-represeneted
communities. All applicants attend workshops that
provide the aspiring writer with tools, contacts,
information and access to the publishing and TV
industries. Shortlisted applicants receive feedback
from an editor and their submission is shared with
BBC Studios for consideration. Successful applicants
receive one year of mentoring with a Penguin editor
to develop their writing and career and a £1,000

writing grant. All applicants should submit 1,000 words from a book they are working on and shortlisted writers will be required to submit a further 5,000 words.

## Writers & Artists

Bloomsbury Publishing plc, 50 Bedford Square, London WC1B 3DP
*tel* 020-7631 5985

*email* AccessWA@bloomsbury.com
*website* www.writersandartists.co.uk/accessible-to-all
*website* www.writersandartists.co.uk/bursary-opportunities

Financial assistance to a combined value of £4,000 has been made available to help ensure that everything W&A offers – events, writing courses and editing services – is accessible to all. See the website for more details and eligibility.

# Children's literature festivals and trade fairs

Some of the literature festivals in this section are specifically related to children's books and others are general arts festivals which include literature events for children.

## Aspects Irish Literature Festival

Town Hall, The Castle, Bangor BT20 4BT
*website* www.aspectsfestival.com
*Twitter* @aspectsfestival
*Takes place* September–October

An annual celebration of contemporary Irish writing, based in Bangor, with novelists, poets and playwrights. Includes readings, children's events and exhibitions.

## Aye Write! Glasgow's Book Festival

Glasgow Life, Commonwealth House,
38 Albion Street, Glasgow G1 1LH
*tel* 0141 287 4350
*email* ayewrite@glasgowlife.org.uk
*Facebook* www.facebook.com/AyeWrite
*Twitter* @AyeWrite
*Takes place* May

Brings together the best undiscovered local talent with a wealth of established writers from the city and nationwide. A free children's festival, Wee Write, runs in tandem with the main festival. Creative writing workshops and masterclasses are on offer. Founded 2005.

## Barnes Children's Literature Festival

*website* www.barneskidslitfest.org
*Facebook* www.facebook.com/BarnesKidsLitFest
*Twitter* @kidslitfest
*Takes place* June

Dedicated children's literature festival with more than 100 family friendly events, performances and workshops. Barnes is also the home of the largest free literature festival for primary school programmes in England, available to every state-maintained school in London.

## Bath Children's Literature Festival

*tel* (01225) 463362
*email* info@bathfestivals.org.uk
*website* https://bathfestivals.org.uk/childrens-literature
*Twitter* @bathkidslitfest
*Takes place* 29 September–8 October

Annual dedicated children's literature festival with events for families featuring writers and illustrators.

## Beyond the Border: Wales' International Storytelling Festival

*tel* 029-2166 0501
*email* info@beyondtheborder.com
*website* www.beyondtheborder.com

An international festival celebrating oral tradition and bringing together storytellers, poets and musicians from around the world. This is the largest event of its type in the UK and features storytelling, poetry, music, singing, theatre, circus and film.

## Black British Book Festival

Izabella House, 24–26 Regents Place,
Jewellery Quarter, Birmingham B1 3NJ
*email* selina@blackbritishbookfestival.com
*website* https://blackbritishbookfestival.com
*Twitter* @BBBookFestival
*Instagram* @bbbookfestival
*Takes place* October

Europe's largest festival dedicated to celebrating Black writers across all genres and at all stages of their career. Supports Black writers and increases accessibility by demystifying the publishing process and providing opportunities. Also promotes literacy and a love of reading in both children and adults. Founded 2021.

## Bologna Children's Book Fair

Piazza Costituzione 6, 40128 Bologna, Italy
*tel* +39 051-282111
*email* bookfair@bolognafiere.it
*website* www.bolognachildrensbookfair.com
*Facebook* www.facebook.com/BolognaChildrensBookFair
*Twitter* @BoChildrensBook
*Takes place* Spring

The leading children's publishing event. Publishers, authors and illustrators, literary agents, app developers, e-publishing professionals, licensors and licensees and many other members of the children's content community meet in Bologna. Attendees buy and sell copyrights, establish new contacts and strengthen their professional relationships, discover new illustrators, develop new business opportunities, learn about the latest trends and developments and explore children's educational materials, including new media products. Entry is restricted to professionals in children's content.

## Baillie Gifford Borders Book Festival

Harmony House, St Mary's Road, Melrose TD6 9LJ
*email* info@bordersbookfestival.org
*website* www.bordersbookfestival.org
*Facebook* www.facebook.com/bordersbookfestival
*Twitter* @BordersBookFest
*Instagram* @bordersbookfest
*Takes place* June

An annual festival with a programme of events featuring high-profile and bestselling writers, including a Family Festival programme. Winner of the Walter Scott Prize for Historical Fiction is announced during the festival. Founded 2004.

## Boswell Book Festival

*website* www.boswellbookfestival.co.uk
*Facebook* www.facebook.com/boswellbookfestival
*Twitter* @bozzyfest
*Instagram* @boswellbookfest

The world's only festival of biography and memoir, named after Ayrshire biographer James Boswell. The festival is programmed around stories taken from the inspirational lives of people past and present, shared through writing, drama, art and music. A children's festival runs alongside the main festival, featuring popular children's authors, illustrators and performers, and a school's programme encourages primary and secondary students to engage in storytelling.

## Bradford Literature Festival

Horton Building, University of Bradford, Richmond Road, Bradford BD7 1DP
*tel* (01274) 044140
*email* info@bradfordlitfest.co.uk
*website* www.bradfordlitfest.co.uk
*Facebook* www.facebook.com/bradfordlitfest
*Twitter* @BradfordLitFest
*Founder & Director* Syima Aslam
*Takes place* June–July

An annual arts event and year-round cultural outreach programme that hosts a diverse range of authors, poets, speakers, musicians and artists from Bradford, the UK and around the world. Taking place over ten days, the programme includes over 400 events with a mix of topic-led events, author talks, poetry line-ups, live music, film, theatre and more. Operates an extensive ethical ticketing policy, offering free or discounted tickets to those who might otherwise be unable to attend the festival. Founded 2014.

## Budleigh Salterton Literary Festival

10 Fairfield Close, Exmouth EX8 2BN
*tel* (01395) 262635
*email* festival@budlitfest.org.uk
*website* https://budlitfest.org.uk
*Facebook* www.facebook.com/
BudleighSaltertonLiteraryFestival
*Twitter* @BudleighLitFest
*Director* Annie Ashworth, *Chair* Sue Briggs
*Takes place* 20–24 September 2023

Held beside the sea on the Jurassic Coast, the festival features leading writers and celebrities, events for families and workshops for writers. Includes an outreach programme in schools and is one of the biggest literary festivals in the South West. Founded 2009.

## Cambridge Literary Festival

*tel* (01223) 515335
*email* hello@cambridgeliteraryfestival.com
*website* https://cambridgeliteraryfestival.com
*Facebook* www.facebook.com/CamLitFest
*Twitter* @camlitfest
*Takes place* April and November

Brings together an eclectic mix of writers, thinkers and speakers, covering poetry, politics, fiction, finance, history, hip-hop, comedy and current affairs. Founded 2003.

## Cardiff Children's Lit Fest

County Hall, Atlantic Wharf, Cardiff CF10 4UW
*email* events@cardiff.gov.uk
*website* www.cardiffkidslitfest.com
*Facebook* www.facebook.com/CDFKidsLitFest
*Twitter* @CDFKidsLitFest
*Takes place* April

Aimed at young people who appreciate the magic of books and grown-ups who want to write them. The festival includes events with local and national authors and comprises a number of educational sessions for schools.

## The Times and Sunday Times Cheltenham Literature Festival

Hub8, The Brewery Quarter, Cheltenham GL50 3FF
*tel* (01242) 850270
*email* boxoffice@cheltenhamfestivals.com
*website* www.cheltenhamfestivals.com/literature
*Facebook* www.facebook.com/cheltenhamfestivals
*Twitter* @cheltlitfest
*Takes place* 6–15 October 2023

This annual festival is one of the oldest literary events in the world. Features adult, family and schools programmes, with around 500 events over ten days. Events for families and schools include presentations from the very best children's authors and illustrators alongside workshops, shows, storytellers, story trails, discussions and free drop-in craft activities. Founded 1949.

## Chiswick Book Festival

St Michael & All Angels Parish Hall, Priory Avenue, Chiswick, London W4 1TX
*email* admin@chiswickbookfestival.net
*website* www.chiswickbookfestival.net
*Facebook* www.facebook.com/chiswickbookfestival

*Twitter* @W4BookFest
*Instagram* @chiswickbookfest
*Takes place* 6–13 September 2023

Brings writers and readers together to support reading-related charities. Since its inception it has raised over £120,000. Hosts a range of literary events, covering history, poetry, biography, fiction, thrillers, gardens, food, wine, politics, creative writing and self-help. Children's book events are also central to the festival, encouraging a love of both reading and writing. Founded 2009.

## Creative Folkestone Book Festival

Quarterhouse, Mill Bay, Folkestone, Kent CT20 1BN
*tel* (01303) 760740
*email* info@creativefolkestone.org.uk
*website* www.creativefolkestone.org.uk/folkestone-book-festival
*Facebook* www.facebook.com/FolkestoneBookFestival
*Twitter* @CreativeFstone
*Instagram* @creativefstone

An opportunity to gather, tell stories, exchange ideas and encourage debate on a wide range of topics. Founded 2002.

## Cuckfield Book Festival

*email* info@cuckfieldbookfest.co.uk
*website* https://cuckfieldbookfest.co.uk
*Facebook* www.facebook.com/cuckfieldbookfest
*Twitter* @CuckfieldBF
*Instagram* @cuckfieldbookfest
*Takes place* 5–8 October 2023

Includes talks and workshops featuring authors from a wide range of genres across fiction, non-fiction and poetry. Also a programme of events for young people. Founded 2016.

## Deptford Literature Festival

*email* festival@spreadtheword.org.uk
*website* http://deptfordlitfest.com
*Takes place* March

Celebrates the diversity and creativity of Deptford and Lewisham through words, stories and performance. Run by Spread the Word, each year the festival is curated around a different theme. The festival features writers, artists and arts organisations based in the area, and hosts creative writing workshops and a programme of events for children and families.

## Derby Book Festival

13 Lavender Row, Darley Abbey, Derby DE22 1DF
*email* hello@derbybookfestival.co.uk
*website* www.derbybookfestival.co.uk
*Facebook* www.facebook.com/DerbyBookFestival
*Twitter* @DerbyBookFest
*Instagram* @derby_book_festival
*Takes place* Spring and Autumn

Celebrates the joy of books and reading for all ages

and interests, with a programme featuring great writers, poets, historians, politicians, illustrators, storytellers and musicians. Each year the festival welcomes internationally celebrated bestselling authors as well as a broad range of local writing talent. In addition to its core programme of events, the organisers operate community-focused projects across Derby and in schools. Founded 2015.

## Edinburgh Comic Art Fair

*Facebook* www.facebook.com/comicartfestival
*Twitter* @edinburghcomic
*Takes place* November

ECAF is a gathering of artists, comic authors, fans and readers that expands the reach and creativity of the genre and offers unique events, from writing poetry graphic novels to illustrating folk tales. Comic creators take part in panels, talks, workshops and portfolio reviews.

## Edinburgh International Book Festival

Edinburgh College of Arts, 74 Lauriston Place, Edinburgh EH3 9DF
*tel* 0131 718 5666
*email* admin@edbookfest.co.uk
*website* www.edbookfest.co.uk
*Twitter* @edbookfest
*Takes place* 12–28 August 2023

A key event in Edinburgh's annual August festival season and one of the largest public celebrations of words and ideas in the world. Around 600 UK and international writers appear in over 500 events for adults, children and schools. Programme details available in June. Founded 1983.

## Edinburgh International Children's Festival

30B Grindlay Street, Edinburgh EH3 9AX
*tel* 0131 225 8050
*email* info@imaginate.org.uk
*website* www.imaginate.org.uk
*Takes place* May/June

Presents theatre and dance for young audiences aged 0–15, with performances that are deeply engaging, innovative and inspiring. With an emphasis on striking visual productions, the international programme goes beyond expectations of children's and young people's work. The shows include a mix of theatre and dance and attract an audience of over 17,000 children, families and schools every year. The festival regularly attracts over 300 industry delegates from around the world.

## Hay Festival

The Drill Hall, 25 Lion Street, Hay-on-Wye HR3 5AD
*tel* (01497) 822620
*email* submissions@hayfestival.org
*website* www.hayfestival.com
*Facebook* www.facebook.com/hayfestival

*Twitter* @hayfestival
*Instagram* @hayfestival
*Takes place* May; Hay Festival Winter Weekend takes place 23–26 November

Brings together writers, musicians, filmmakers, historians, politicians, environmentalists and scientists from around the world to communicate challenging ideas. The 2023 festival featured Margaret Atwood, Caleb Azumah Nelson, Alexander McCall Smith and Marina Hyde. Hundreds of events over ten days. Within the annual festival is a festival for families and children, HAYDAYS, which introduces children, from toddlers to teenagers, to their favourite authors and holds workshops. Programme published April. Founded 1987.

## I Am Writing Festival

*email* iamwriting@iaminprint.co.uk
*website* https://iaminprint.co.uk
*Twitter* @iaminprint
*Instagram* @iaminprint
*Directors* Sarah Post, Elane Retford
*Takes place* May

A festival for writers who are based in Bristol and working towards publication; all abilities are welcome, from beginners to those ready to approach agents and publishers. The festival hosts a variety of workshops, talks and panels featuring debut and bestselling authors, agents and publishers across all book genres. Includes creative writing classes, competition announcements and the opportunity for manuscript feedback. A pitch party takes place on the Friday. Founded 2022.

## Ilkley Literature Festival

9 The Grove, Ilkley LS29 9LW
*tel* (01943) 601210
*email* info@ilkleylitfest.org.uk
*website* www.ilkleyliteraturefestival.org.uk
*Facebook* www.facebook.com/ilkleylitfest
*Twitter* @ilkleylitfest
*Director* Erica Morris, *Programme Manager* Becky Wholley
*Takes place* 7–23 October

One of the UK's longest-running and widest-ranging literature festivals with over 100 events, from author discussions to workshops, readings, literary walks, children's events and a festival fringe. Founded 1973.

## Imagine: Writers and Writing for Children

Southbank Centre, London SE1 8XX
*tel* 020-7960 4200
*website* www.southbankcentre.co.uk/whats-on/festivals-series/imagine-childrens-festival
*Twitter* @southbankcentre
*Takes place* February

Annual festival celebrating writing for children featuring a selection of poets, storytellers and illustrators.

## Independent Bookshop Week

*website* www.booksaremybag.com/IndependentBookshopWeek
*Facebook* www.facebook.com/booksaremybag
*Twitter* @booksaremybag
*Instagram* @booksaremybag
*Takes place* June

An annual celebration of independent bookshops, part of the Books Are My Bag campaign to promote high-street bookshops and shopping locally and sustainably. Founded 2006.

## Jewish Book Week

Raymond Burton House, 129–131 Albert Street, London NW1 7NB
*email* info@jewishbookweek.com
*website* https://jewishbookweek.com
*Twitter* @JewishBookWeek
*Festival Director* Claudia Rubenstein
*Takes place* February/March

A ten day festival of writing, arts and culture, with contributors from around the world and sessions in London and nationwide. Includes events for children and teenagers. Founded 1952.

## London Literature Festival

*email* literatureandspokenword@southbankcentre.co.uk
*website* www.southbankcentre.co.uk
*Facebook* www.facebook.com/southbankcentre
*Twitter* @southbankcentre
*Takes place* 19–29 October 2023

Combines the best of the year-round literature events with an engaging festival programme, encompassing free public programming, thematically focused talks and debates, newly commissioned performances and a family offer to coincide with the half-term school holiday. Founded 1967.

## Manchester Children's Book Festival

Manchester Metropolitan University, All Saints Building, Manchester M15 6BH
*email* mcbf@mmu.ac.uk
*website* www.mmu.ac.uk/mcbf
*Facebook* www.facebook.com/MCBFestival
*Twitter* @MCBFestival
*Instagram* @mcbfestival

Year-round activities celebrating the very best writing for children, inspiring young people to engage with literature and creativity across the curriculum and offering extended projects and training to ensure the events have an impact and legacy in classrooms. Founded 2009.

## Marlborough Literature Festival

*email* general@marlboroughlitfest.org
*website* www.marlboroughlitfest.org
*Facebook* www.facebook.com/MarlboroughLitFest
*Twitter* @MarlbLitFest
*Festival Patron* Sir Simon Russell Beale
*Takes place* 28 September–1 October 2023

An annual literary festival in the market town of Marlborough, celebrating the best in writing and reflecting the legacy of writers linked to the town such as Siegfried Sassoon, John Betjeman and William Golding. Champions new and upcoming writers as well as established names and offers a varied programme of events for all ages, including fiction, non-fiction, poetry, children's events and creative writing workshops in local venues in and around Marlborough. Has a strong outreach programme, delivering free author talks to local schools. Founded 2010.

## Monty Lit Fest

Montgomery Town Hall, Broad Street, Montgomery, Powys SY15 6PH
*email* enquiries@montylitfest.com
*website* https://montylitfest.com
*Facebook* www.facebook.com/montylitfest
*Twitter* @montylitfest
*Instagram* @montylitfest
*Takes place* June

A diverse programme of events brings together a wide range of audiences to celebrate writers who live in or write about Wales. Founded 2016.

## National Poetry Day

*email* info@forwardartsfoundation.org
*website* https://nationalpoetryday.co.uk
*Facebook* www.facebook.com/PoetryDayUK
*Twitter* @PoetryDayUK
*Instagram* @nationalpoetryday
*Takes place* 6 October 2023

Organised by the Forward Arts Foundation to encourage poetry reading and writing. Combines poetry recommendations and teaching resources with nationwide events to highlight the artistic and social value of poetry. Each year it takes place on the first Thursday in October and explores a different theme. Founded 1999.

## Off the Shelf Festival of Words Sheffield

Cathedral Court, 46 Church Street, Sheffield S1 2GN
*tel* 0114 222 3895
*email* offtheshelf@sheffield.ac.uk
*website* www.offtheshelf.org.uk
*Takes place* 13–29 October 2023

A diverse festival featuring children's authors and illustrators with activities and events for children, young people and families. Events in Sheffield and South Yorkshire.

## Oundle Festival of Literature

*email* kidlithillfield@live.com
*website* www.oundlelitfest.org.uk
*Facebook* www.facebook.com/OundleFestivalOfLiterature
*Twitter* @OundleLitEvents
*Festival Director* Helen Shair
*Takes place* Early March

Kid Lit Week includes a writing competition and events for infant and junior school children. Also runs a programme of year-round events aimed at exciting, informing, entertaining and educating a wide variety of people through talks, discussions and workshops by award-winning and local authors and poets. Held in a variety of venues in the market town of Oundle. Founded 2002.

## FT Weekend Oxford Literary Festival

c/o Critchleys, Beaver House,
23–28 Hythe Bridge Street, Oxford OX1 2EP
*email* info@oxfordliteraryfestival.org
*website* https://oxfordliteraryfestival.org
*Takes place* March/April

An annual festival for both adults and children held in venues across the city and university. Presents topical debates, fiction and non-fiction discussion panels, and adult and children's authors who have recently published books. Topics range from contemporary fiction to discussions on politics, history, science, gardening, food, poetry, philosophy, art and crime fiction. Founded 1998.

## Paisley Book Fest

*email* bookfest@renfrewshire.gov.uk
*website* https://paisleybookfest.com
*Facebook* www.facebook.com/BookPaisley
*Twitter* @bookpaisley
*Instagram* @paisleybookfest
*Takes place* February

Celebrates Scottish arts and culture. Events include author talks, writing workshops and publishing advice, covering a range of genres including poetry, flash fiction and memoir. Also runs a Writer in Residence scheme and a schools programme. Facilitates the Janet Coats Memorial Prize.

## Scottish International Storytelling Festival

43–45 High Street, Edinburgh EH1 1SR
*tel* 0131 556 9579
*email* reception@scottishstorytellingcentre.com
*website* www.scottishstorytellingcentre.co.uk
*Festival Director* Donald Smith
*Takes place* October

A celebration of Scottish storytelling set in its international context, complemented by music, ballad and song. Takes place at the Scottish Storytelling Centre and partner venues across Edinburgh and Scotland.

## The Self-Publishing Conference

*tel* 0116 279 2299
*email* books@troubador.co.uk
*website* www.selfpublishingconference.org.uk
*Twitter* @Selfpubconf

The UK's longest-established self-publishing conference. This annual event covers all aspects of self-publishing from production through to marketing and distribution. The conference offers plenty of networking opportunities and access to over 16 presentations. Founded 2013.

## China Shanghai Children's Book Fair

*email* ccbf@bfchina.net
*website* www.ccbookfair.com/en
*Facebook* www.facebook.com/ccbookfair
*Twitter* @ccbookfair
*Instagram* @ccbookfair
*Takes place* 17–19 November

The leading fair entirely dedicated to books and specific content for children aged 0–16 in Asia Pacific. Offers unique opportunities for face-to-face interaction with publishers, popular authors, translators and illustrators from the region. Located on the ground floor of the Shanghai World Expo Exhibition and Convention Centre. Founded 2013.

## StAnza: Scotland's International Poetry Festival

*tel* (01334) 475000 (box office)
*email* stanza@stanzapoetry.org
*website* www.stanzapoetry.org
*Facebook* www.facebook.com/stanzapoetry
*Twitter* @StAnzaPoetry
*Instagram* @stanzapoetry
*Operations Manger* Suzie Kirk Dumitru
*Takes place* March

Dedicated to programming a wide diversity of poetries and poets, alongside other art forms such as music and visual art. It is international in focus and has a hybrid format, including both live and digital events. Founded 1997.

## Stratford-upon-Avon Literary Festival

*email* info@stratfordliteraryfestival.co.uk
*website* www.stratlitfest.co.uk
*Facebook* www.facebook.com/stratfordlitfest
*Twitter* @StratLitFest
*Instagram* @stratfordlitfest
*Takes place* May with events in autumn

A feast of workshops, panel discussions, celebrity and author events. The festival also runs a programme of educational events and projects for families and regional schools aimed at entertaining and inspiring children and encouraging literacy, as well as events in the community and writing workshops in prisons. Founded 2008.

## The Summer Festival of Writing

4 Acer Walk, Oxford OX2 6EX
*tel* 0345 459 9560
*email* info@jerichowriters.com
*website* https://jerichowriters.com/events/summer-festival-of-writing
*Takes place* June–August

A three-month online festival for all writers to connect with others from across the world. Writers have the opportunity to hear from literary agents, publishers and professional authors. This includes pitching work to literary agents, receiving live feedback from industry professionals and entering writing competitions.

## Wigtown Book Festival

11 North Main Street, Wigtown, Dumfries and Galloway DG8 9HN
*email* mail@wigtownbookfestival.com
*website* https://wigtownbookfestival.com
*Facebook* www.facebook.com/WigtownBookFestival
*Twitter* @WigtwonBookFest
*Takes place* 22 September–1 October 2023

Ten-day annual festival in Scotland's National Book Town, bringing readers, aspiring writers and published authors together across 200 events. In addition to the festival, runs events throughout the year, facilitates a mentorship programme for writers and administers two prizes. Also runs Hooked Festival for Young Readers and Writers. Founded 1999.

## Wimbledon Book Fest

35 Wimbledon Hill Road, London SW19 7NB
*email* info@wimbledonbookfest.org
*website* www.wimbledonbookfest.org
*Twitter* @Wimbookfest
*Takes place* 12–22 October 2023

Fosters a space for art and culture within the community. Guest speakers include writers from all genres, with a focus on inspiring stories, diversity and inclusion. Runs educational workshops and projects for young people during the festival and throughout the year. Founded 2006.

## World Book Day

*email* wbd@education.co.uk
*website* www.worldbookday.com
*Facebook* www.facebook.com/worldbookdayuk
*Twitter* @WorldBookDayUK
*Ceo* Cassie Chadderton
*Takes place* First Thursday in March

Its mission is to promote reading for pleasure, offering every child and young person the opportunity to have a book of their own. Reading for pleasure is the single biggest indicator of a child's future success – more than their family circumstances, their parents' educational background or their income. Encourages more children, particularly those from disadvantaged backgrounds,

to form a life-long habit of reading for pleasure and the improved life chances this brings them.
Founded 1988.

## YALC (Young Adult Literature Convention)

*email* yalc@showmastersevents.com
*website* https://londoncomicconwinter.com/YALC

*Facebook* www.facebook.com/ukYALC
*Twitter* @yalc_uk

YALC is a celebration of the best YA books and authors. It is an interactive event where YA fiction fans can meet their favourite authors, listen to panel discussions and take part in workshops.
Founded 2014.

# Publishing advice and resources

## How to hire a freelance editor

Jenny Bowman has helpful advice for the self-publishing author on how to set about hiring the ideal editor. She clarifies what is involved in the editorial process, what to look for in an editor and why their role is essential in ensuring your book is perfectly polished and ready for publication.

Self-publishing has become a widely accepted avenue for publishing children's books, from picture books to young adult novels. In contrast to the traditional way of publishing a book, self-published authors can bypass the need for an agent, as well as maintain complete creative control of their manuscript from start to finish. Self-publishing can be particularly attractive to picture book authors who prefer to select and collaborate with their illustrators.

There are many reasons an author might decide to self-publish their book: maybe they have researched the traditional route and decided it's just not the path they want to take; they might be writing to fill a need for a specific audience; or they may plan to write just one book. Being clear on motivation for self-publishing is important and will guide you through every step of the process. Since self-published books forgo the rigorous editing performed when a book is acquired by a publisher, hiring a freelance editor is a must. It's important to understand the different types of editorial services available to authors, and the order in which they are typically employed.

## Types of editing

### 1. Developmental editing

Developmental editing is the first editing step; it is a comprehensive process that reviews the major backbone of a manuscript while also looking at the details, and then at how it all works together. Developmental editors will evaluate your manuscript as a whole and will offer relevant writing advice, constructive criticism and – if they're good – words of encouragement. Developmental editors typically evaluate:

• the book's core intentions and goals;
• the underlying premise and the story;
• character development and dialogue;
• narrative voice;
• the book's overall pacing, style and language;
• the age of the readership in relationship to themes and category.

Look for someone who is willing to offer a fluid working relationship and who will communicate openly on major changes. Out of all the editors you may hire, you will do the most rigorous revisions while working with your developmental editor.

### 2. Copy-editing

A copy-editor will check your manuscript making sure the syntax is smooth and the writing adheres to the conventions of grammar. They will spot minor inconsistencies in plot and story or character development, and comment on readability. They will bring your manuscript to a professional level before you format your book in preparation for a proof-read and print. Copy-editors typically evaluate:

- overall readability;
- grammatical conventions and punctuation;
- consistency in content layout, such as chapters or sections, and content delivery;
- syntax and sentence structure;
- overall style and tone of the manuscript.

## 3. Proofreading

A proofreader is the detail-oriented, 'fan-of-the-red-pen' person whose job it is to make sure your book is error-free. Both you and your editor will know your manuscript inside and out; this means that errors such as simple grammar, formatting and spelling mistakes might easily be overlooked. Hiring a proofreader is an absolute must for authors wishing to self-publish. Many self-published authors even hire two proofreaders before going to print. Proofreaders typically:

- evaluate and correct grammar, typos and punctuation;
- ensure the document is error-free and consistent in style;
- review formatting and ensure that the book is ready for print.

## Hiring an editor

There are hundreds of children's book editors available, and the range of editorial services is wide. With so many editors available, how do you know which one to choose? To start, select an editor who specialises in writing for children. You want someone who understands the complex category systems within the umbrella of children's books. This is especially important when you are at the developmental stage, or if you are unsure which category your children's book falls within. Are you writing a picture book, chapter book or easy reader? Is your book for middle-grade readers or young adults? How many words should your book have in order to be age-appropriate? What themes or topics are typically relevant? These are some of the more generalised questions your developmental editor can answer for you.

## Where to start

A Google search for a children's book editor is the best place to start. Look for an editor who is specialised, or who has edited books similar to your own. An easy way to do this is to open a few of your favourites in tabs and check out each editor's website and 'About me' section. Take a look at their testimonials; see if any stand out to you.

Another resource to check out are the acknowledgements in your favourite children's book. For example, if you're writing a middle-grade novel, hop to the back of your most recent read and see who the author thanked. Even traditionally published authors hire freelance editors, and they often return to these same editors time and again. This is a fantastic way to narrow your search down stylistically.

Check out the Editorial Freelancers Association (EFA) – a vetted, members-only organisation. The EFA website (www.the-efa.org) has a user-friendly search tool for narrowing down your selections, and provides information such as years worked in editing and editor bios, all in one place. The UK equivalent is the Chartered Institute of Editing and Proofreading (CIEP), which includes a directory of contacts, www.ciep.uk/directory (see page 321). Use the *Children's Writers' & Artists' Yearbook*, or *The Book* from the Society of

Children's Book Writers and Illustrators (SCBWI; see page 305). Both publications have listings for editorial services.

## What to look for in an editor

Once you have a list of prospective editors, study their websites to narrow down your choices. Some qualifications you might look for are:

- How long have they been editing?
- Have they edited books similar to your own?
- What do their testimonials say?
- What are their rates, if published online?
- Besides a list of services, does their website offer helpful resources for new and emerging authors?
- Is there helpful information about self-publishing children's books?

## When to contact an editor

Once you have narrowed down your options to a few editors, get in touch with them. If they have a contact form on their website, use it to submit the information they need to offer a quote on services, rates and timeline. If not, send your core questions via email. You might ask the following:

- What editing services will you provide?
- Do you have experience of editing books in my category and/or genre?
- What are your rates?
- What is your turnaround time and when are you available to start?
- Do you offer an opportunity for a follow-up call?

Communicating via email is often enough to get your questions answered. If not, find out if the editor is willing to talk with you about your project before being hired. Most editors will include the opportunity to chat at some point during the process. Be mindful of the time you are requesting; if you have a 500-word manuscript that needs a copy-edit, it's unrealistic to ask a freelance editor to attend an hour-long interview before getting hired.

## Key points to remember

### Budget

Be up-front about your budget. Most freelance editors publish their fees online, so you can get a sense of what you'll be spending. If you find that your dream editor, and their rates, are out of reach, think twice before asking for a discount, as this may come across as devaluing the freelancer's qualifications and expertise. Rather, be proactive. Ask if the editor will consider a payment plan, or look for another editor who fits your budget.

### Timing

Plan ahead. Many freelance editors are booked well in advance. If you have a tight deadline, or you have prearranged other services such as illustrations, or have a launch date goal in mind, be sure to get your editor booked. Expect to wait a month or more once you find your editor.

### About sample edits

The editor's web presence, testimonials and credentials should be enough to qualify them for hire. It's unrealistic to ask for a sample edit. Sample edits are not reflective of the multiple manuscript reviews, suggested rewrites, inline edits and comments that are part of a full edit. It's equally unrealistic to ask an editor to send a sample of something they've previously edited, since most editors work under an agreement of confidentiality with their authors.

## What to expect after hire

Typically, editors will outline the process – from hire to project completion – by email. After you initiate hire, you should receive a comprehensive contract that outlines the entire process. Most editors do line edits using 'track changes' in MS Word. Certainly with a developmental edit, and sometimes with a copy-edit and proofread, you will receive an editorial assessment of the document as well; this will review any problem areas, with steps to tackle revisions, and will also point out the areas that are really strong and working well. While editing your manuscript, editors will reach out if any pressing questions come up. When editing is complete, they will provide an in-depth review of their recommendations and answer any questions you may have.

## Special considerations for picture book writers

• Picture books take a surprising amount of work – every word matters. The overall structure of the book, as well as specific placement of each word or sentence, each refrain, really matters. You will want to hire an editor who has unique experience in editing picture books.

• Is your book in rhyme? If so, hire an editor who is an old hand with poetry. Your rhyme and metre will need to be deliberately crafted with purpose. Today's market is choosy when it comes to rhyming picture books; there is definitely an art to writing a successful one.

• Hire your editor *before* you commission illustrations. Quality illustrations are pricey. How heartbreaking it is when an author completes illustrations, only to realise during the editing process that major changes are needed to their book which make those illustrations obsolete. Hire your illustrator when all editing, apart from the final proofread, is complete. Finding an editor to collaborate with is an essential step in producing a polished and complete book for publication. It can also be a rewarding learning experience, especially at the developmental stage, when it comes to the craft of writing for kids. Self-publishing your children's book is an exciting path to follow, with one of the most satisfying endings – the joy of holding your first printed book, and then revisiting that feeling every time someone reads your story. Happy writing!

**Jenny Bowman** is a creative writer and children's book editor with experience editing books on the *New York Times* bestseller list, and books with international acclaim. Having edited over 100 books for children to young adults, Jenny is well-versed in all genres of children's literature. She is an active member of the EFA, the Society for Children's Books Writers and Illustrators, the Children's Literature Association, and participates annually in both the 12x12 Picture Book Challenge and Inked Voices. Her website is www.jennybowman.com.

# How BookTok can help you engage with your readers

Author Beth Reekles reveals the huge potential and reach of BookTok, a community within TikTok that is built on a 'shared joy over all things bookish', offering an almost limitless and varied audience for authors to tap into. She has advice on using BookTok to engage with and grow your readership in your own individual way, and describes its power to boost confidence and creativity, as well as sales.

We've all seen those articles doing the rounds on Twitter. You know the ones: someone gained a certain amount of viral fame and now they're signing an impressive book deal and living out their dreams – *your* dreams – of being a published author. There's a sensationalism about it that can go one of two ways. Either you want to burst with excitement (the book sounds great and, if it can happen to anybody, why not you?) or scream into a pillow and cry (because … why *wasn't* it you?).

I was one of those authors back in 2012. I'd written a YA romance (*The Kissing Booth*) that I shared on story-sharing platform Wattpad when I was 15 and then, after it gained over 19 million hits, I was offered a publishing deal at age 17. That was practically unheard of at the time – Twitter was still relatively new, and I was just getting my first iPhone. The press dubbed me simultaneously 'The Dickens of the iPad Generation' and 'Fifty Shades of Youth' (apparently, I had the range). Nowadays, of course, the real powerhouse you hear about is TikTok – or, more specifically, BookTok. You'll see plenty of articles about book deals signed after the author gained some kind of notoriety on the app, and probably you'll have seen the stands in WHSmith or stickers on book covers in The Works declaring: 'As seen on BookTok!', rather than simply trying to showcase them as 'new' or 'bestselling'.

For those who are unfamiliar with BookTok, let's break it down. Simply put, BookTok is the name given to the bookish side of TikTok, encompassing everything from reader reviews, pretty aesthetics of bookshelves or unboxings of a Waterstones haul, authors discussing their writing process or promoting new books, character cosplays, mood boards of fictional worlds, reactions to snippets of an audiobook… It's a niche, yes, but it is by no means small. At the time of writing, the hashtag #booktok has over 143 billion views, and that's not counting all the denominations like #romancetok, #fantasytok, #authorsoftiktok, #booktoker, etc. BookTok is often cosy, but it's also vibrant and friendly and excited. It's a place where people can connect with a community and feel at home in this shared joy over all things bookish. This sense of community is what drives sales in such huge numbers, carves out new genres, and helps to lift up new writers and allows them to secure book deals.

Bea Fitzgerald, known on TikTok as @chaosonolympus, may be best recognised for applying viral soundbites from pop culture to classic Greek myths, but she also posts videos sharing her publishing journey with her debut YA romance *Girl, Goddess, Queen* (Penguin 2023). The name Serena Terry might not ring a bell, but chances are you've laughed at her comedy skits of life as an Irish mum on her channel @mammybanter – and 22 million views later, she landed a book deal with Harper Collins. Her debut novel *The Secret Life of an Uncool Mum* was published in 2021, complete with a roundel on the cover declaring '*From the viral TikTok sensation*'.

One particularly notable novel that gained massive traction on BookTok is Travis Baldree's cosy fantasy *Legends & Lattes* (Tor 2022). I first heard about this book in videos that started, 'If you like playing Dungeons and Dragons, you'll like these novels …' but before long, I was seeing it everywhere. It featured in videos that racked up hundreds of thousands of views, gaining such massive reach from 'word of mouth' alone, to the point where 'cosy fantasy' has now become its own established subgenre – and a corner of BookTok with over 3.9 million views (although it's worth noting that the US spelling, #cozyfantasy, has over 25 million views). When a book finds its audience on TikTok, it well and truly finds its audience and, most importantly, often *continues* to gain traction after that initial wave of views and engagement.

The rise in BookTok also speaks to the shift in social media, both for readers and writers/publishers. There's often an expectation for authors and illustrators to leverage their social media presence to help sell their book (easier said than done), but these days that focus is less on Twitter and Facebook or even Instagram, and more about tapping into that massive reach that BookTok has. The *New York Times* reported last year that BookTok helped authors sell 20 million (printed) books in 2021. And while romance is consistently a high-selling but under-recognised genre in certain traditional print media, BookTokers are loud and proud about their love for it. Huge romance hits like Ali Hazelwood's *The Love Hypothesis* (Sphere 2021) or Elena Armas's *The Spanish Love Deception* (Simon & Schuster 2021) will be touted under headings like 'TikTok made me buy it', and this isn't down to things like in-app ads but word of mouth – people shouting about a book they loved, and sharing it with others.

Part of what allows BookTok to have such a chokehold on the market is the 'For You Page' (FYP), a key feature of TikTok that's been quickly adopted by other social media platforms in the last few years. The FYP is less concerned with showing you content from accounts you follow, but cares more about what you interact with (which videos you spend time watching, sharing, liking, commenting on) in order to show you more of that. Pushing content it thinks you want to see, rather than only videos from the people you've chosen to follow, makes it a great tool for offering readers new book recommendations. If you are sharing a lot of fanart videos of Sarah J. Maas's *A Court Of Thorns And Roses* (Bloomsbury 2020) with your friends, for instance, the app will realise you enjoy fantasy romance novels and start pushing BookTokers showcasing other fantasy romances you might like. Recommendations are usually driven by how a reader felt, what the vibes of the book were, rather than a critical deconstruction and analysis of the storytelling.

The FYP is obviously a fantastic tool if you're a reader (I know my TBR pile has grown exponentially since downloading TikTok) but it also works its magic for authors. Previously, you would have needed a large following on social media to get your content seen by as many eyes as possible – but that's not the case here. The majority of views on any given video will come from the FYP, not necessarily directly from existing followers, so the potential audience for anything you upload is practically limitless. The appeal of having social media profiles as an author is very simple and straightforward: it's a free way to promote your books, but also a chance to interact directly with readers. For a career that can be, in large part, sitting alone behind a computer screen indulging your imagination, being able to hear that someone is excited about your new book or loved your characters is a wonderful feeling.

It's not essential to have a big online following to sign an agent or get a publishing deal; there are obviously cases when it might help new writers prove that there is interest in their story, but that won't always be the case. And it's not essential to have any online presence in order to get published, but it can help – and it's never too early to start. Sure, you could be one of the lucky few who build such a dedicated audience that it ultimately lays the path to getting you that book deal. Or maybe you'll just share an idea you're working on and find that two or three comments saying 'I love this! I'd read that!' is all the encouragement you need to finish your manuscript and gather the courage to submit it to an agent. These are both equally valuable outcomes – don't lose sight of that. Writing can be a lonely profession, so it's important to find community where you can.

Utilising your social media presence to build your readership can be tricky and, for a lot of people, it's a daunting experience to put yourself out there as a 'brand' rather than simply sharing photos and memes with your close friends. Many people find just the thought of being on camera uncomfortable enough but, the good news is, there are ways around this. The beauty (ironically) of BookTok (and its Instagram equivalent, Bookstagram) is that you can show as much or as little of yourself as you want. Your content might feature you chatting directly to the camera, or maybe just filming your morning coffee-making routine and then showing off your desk set-up while you do a voiceover – or even just add some text and lo-fi music so that your video doesn't have either your face or voice in it. BookTok loves everything from quiet bookshelf videos to clever, choppy transitions between different paperbacks, to chatty reviews, to Pedro Pascal eating a sandwich next to some text summarising the plot of a book in one line. Its content is as varied as its audience, which is a further part of its appeal on both sides of the screen.

One struggle that creators face with TikTok is the complexity of its seemingly ineffable algorithm. Compared to the more straightforward algorithms of previous Twitter/Instagram/Facebook iterations which made for an easy rinse-repeat success model, TikTok's is both unnervingly specific and wildly inaccurate – all in the same five-minute scroll. This can be frustrating for creators, as you're never totally sure which of your videos will take off, even if you follow 'the formula' (for instance, by using a trending CapCut (www.capcut.com) template and sound, posting when most of your followers are active – usually around 8pm, using the appropriate keywords in both your caption and as a text overlay in the video, and avoiding pushing traffic to external websites/sources). For example, I recently posted a video with the 'Pedro Pascal eating a sandwich' meme promoting my new book, and it did ten times better than other recent videos. And yet it only did half as well as a random 15-second rant about dating which I filmed carelessly and uploaded within under a minute. Like I said, the algorithm can be unpredictable.

The complexity of the algorithm shouldn't be disheartening or intimidating, though. Let me put it this way: there's no telling exactly *which* of your videos will be the one to gain traction, and there's something very freeing about that. It allows you – encourages you – to try new things ... to be a bit silly, a bit serious, to have fun with it. To experiment with filters and filming techniques. One thing that's clear about TikTok is that it rewards people who engage and try new things. When you see someone else's video in your niche going viral, it's easy to wonder – why not yours? Just as when you see articles about someone else's book getting a publishing deal, that same jealousy can rear its head. But things like BookTok are a great reminder that – it *can* be yours. It can always be. If not this video, maybe the next. If not this exact moment or stage in your career, maybe the next. Any one of your videos could hit the algorithm at just the right time, finding just the right people, and take you from hundreds of views to hundreds of thousands. Even if your book only finds one or two new readers each time you post a video – well, those readers can add up pretty quickly.

BookTok is a behemoth. Its boundless potential in allowing you to access new readers directly means that it's worth a try, whether you're an established writer with published books under your belt or are only just beginning that journey.

**Beth Reekles** is the author of the bestselling young adult series *The Kissing Booth* (now a Netflix film trilogy) and several other rom-com novels. Aged 17 she was offered a three-book publishing deal with Penguin Random House before completing her degree in Physics at Exeter University. Beth's first book *The Kissing Booth* (Corgi Children's) was published in 2013; the series also includes *The Beach House* (2019), *Going the Distance* (2020) and *One Last Time* (2021). Her debut adult novel *Love, Locked Down* was published by Sphere in 2022, and her most recent books are *Faking It* (Sphere 2023) and *Sincerely Yours, Anna Sherwood* (Penguin 2023). Beth lives in South Wales. See www.authorbethreekles.com for more information. Follow her on Instagram @authorbethreekles and on TikTok @bethreekles

# ISBNs: what you need to know

The Nielsen BookData ISBN Agency for UK & Ireland receives a large number of enquiries about the ISBN system. The most frequently asked questions are answered here; for more information visit www.nielsenisbnstore.com.

## What is an ISBN?

An ISBN is an International Standard Book Number and is 13 digits long.

## What is the purpose of an ISBN?

An ISBN is a product number, used by publishers, booksellers and libraries for ordering, listing and stock control purposes. It enables them to identify a particular publisher and allows the publisher to identify a specific edition of a specific title in a specific format within their output.

### Contact details

**Nielsen BookData ISBN Agency for UK and Ireland**
3rd Floor, Midas House, 62 Goldsworth Road, Woking GU21 6LQ
*tel* (01483) 712215
*email* isbn.agency@nielseniq.com
*website* www.nielsenisbnstore.com

## Does an ISBN protect copyright?

A widely held belief is that an ISBN protects copyright. It doesn't, it is an identifier, a product code. The copyright belongs to the author. In general, publishers don't tend to buy copyrights for books. They license the copyrights, which the author retains.

## What is a publisher?

The publisher is generally the person or organisation taking the financial and other risks in making a product available. For example, if a product goes on sale and sells no copies at all, the publisher loses money. If you get paid anyway, you are likely to be a designer, printer, author or consultant of some kind.

## What is the format of an ISBN?

The ISBN is 13 digits long and is divided into five parts separated by spaces or hyphens.
• Prefix element: for the foreseeable future this will be 978 or 979
• Registration group element: identifies a geographic or national grouping. It shows where the publisher is based
• Registrant element: identifies a specific publisher or imprint
• Publication element: identifies a specific edition of a specific title in a specific format
• Check digit: the final digit which mathematically validates the rest of the number
The four parts following the prefix element can be of varying length.
Prior to 1 January 2007 ISBNs were ten digits long; any existing ten-digit ISBNs must be converted by prefixing them with '978' and the check digit must be recalculated using a Modulus 10 system with alternate weights of 1 and 3. The ISBN Agency can help you with this.

## Do I *have* to have an ISBN?

There is no legal requirement in the UK and Ireland for an ISBN and it conveys no form of legal or copyright protection. It is simply a product identification number.

## Why should I use an ISBN?

If you wish to sell your publication through major bookselling chains, independent bookshops or internet retailers, they will require you to have an ISBN to assist their internal processing and ordering systems.

The ISBN also provides access to bibliographic databases, such as the Nielsen BookData Database, which use ISBNs as references. These databases help booksellers and libraries to provide information for customers. Nielsen BookData has a range of bibliographic metadata and retail sales monitoring services which use ISBNs and are vital for the dissemination, trading and monitoring of books in the supply chain. The ISBN therefore provides access to additional marketing opportunities which could help sales of your product.

## Where can I get an ISBN?

ISBNs are assigned to publishers in the country where the publisher's main office is based. This is irrespective of the language of the publication or the intended market for the book.

The ISBN Agency is the national agency for the UK and Republic of Ireland and British Overseas Territories. A publisher based elsewhere will not be able to get numbers from the UK Agency (even if you are a British Citizen) but can contact the Nielsen BookData ISBN Agency for details of the relevant national Agency.

If you are based in the UK and Ireland you can purchase ISBNs online from the Nielsen BookData ISBN Store: www.nielsenisbnstore.com.

## How long does it take to get an ISBN?

If you purchase your ISBNs online from the Nielsen BookData ISBN Store you will receive your ISBN allocation within minutes. If you are purchasing ISBNs direct from the ISBN Agency via an off-line application, it can take up to five days. The processing period begins when a correctly completed application is received in the ISBN Agency and payment is received.

## How much does it cost to get an ISBN?

ISBNs can be bought individually or in blocks of ten or more; visit the ISBN Store to find out more. Refer to www.nielsenisbnstore.com or email the ISBN Agency: isbn.agency@nielseniq.com.

## Who is eligible for ISBNs?

Any individual or organisation who is publishing a qualifying product for general sale or distribution to the market. By publishing we mean making a work available to the public.

## Which products do NOT qualify for ISBNs?

Any publication that is without a defined end should not be assigned an ISBN. For example, publications that are regularly updated and intended to continue indefinitely are not eligible for an ISBN.

**Some examples of products that do not qualify for an ISBN are:**
• Journals, periodicals, serials, newspapers in their entirety (single issues or articles, where these are made available separately, may qualify for ISBN);
• Abstract entities such as textual works and other abstract creations of intellectual or artistic content;
• Ephemeral printed materials such as advertising matter and the like;

- Customised print-on-demand publications (Publications that are available only on a limited basis, such as customised print-on-demand publications with content specifically tailored to a user's request shall not be assigned an ISBN. If a customised publication is being made available for wider sale, e.g. as a college course pack available through a college book store, then an ISBN may be assigned);
- Printed music;
- Art prints and art folders without title page and text;
- Personal documents (such as a curriculum vitae or personal profile);
- Greetings cards;
- Music sound recordings;
- Software that is intended for any purpose other than educational or instructional;
- Electronic bulletin boards;
- Emails and other digital correspondence;
- Updating websites;
- Games.

Following a review of the UK market, it is now permissible for ISBNs to be assigned to calendars and diaries, provided that they are not intended for purely time-management purposes and that a substantial proportion of their content is textual or graphic.

### What is an ISSN?

An International Standard Serial Number. This is the numbering system for journals, magazines, periodicals, newspapers and newsletters. It is administered by the British Library, *tel* (01937) 546959; *email* issn-uk@bl.uk; *website* www.bl.uk/help/Get-an-ISBN-or-ISSN-for-your-publication#

### Where do I put the ISBN?

The ISBN should appear on the reverse of the title page, sometimes called the copyright page or the imprint page, and on the outside back cover of the book. If the book has a dust jacket, the ISBN should also appear on the back of this. If the publication is not a book, the ISBN should appear on the product, and on the packaging or inlay card. If the publication is a map, the ISBN should be visible when the map is folded and should also appear near the publisher statement if this is elsewhere.

### I am reprinting a book with no changes – do I need a new ISBN?

No.

### I am reprinting a book but adding a new chapter – do I need a new ISBN?

Yes. You are adding a significant amount of additional material, altering the content of the book.

### I am reprinting a book with a new cover design – should I change the ISBN?

No. A change of cover design with no changes to the content of the book should not have a new ISBN.

### I am changing the binding on the book to paperback rather than hardback. Do I need a new ISBN?

Yes. Changes in binding always require new ISBNs even if there are no changes to the content of the book.

## I am changing the price – do I need a new ISBN?

No. Price changes with no other changes do not require new ISBNs and in fact must not change the ISBN.

# Public Lending Right

Under the PLR system, payment is made from public funds to authors and other contributors (writers, illustrators/photographers, translators, adapters/retellers, ghostwriters, editors/compilers/abridgers/revisers, narrators and producers) whose books (print, audiobook and ebook) are lent from public libraries. Payment is annual; the amount authors receive is proportionate to the number of times that their books were borrowed during the previous year (July to June).

## How the system works

From the applications received, the PLR office compiles a database of authors and books (the PLR Register). A representative sample of book issues is recorded, consisting of all loans from selected public libraries. This is then multiplied in proportion to total library lending to produce, for each book, an estimate of its total annual loans throughout the country. The estimated loans are matched against the database of registered authors and titles to discover how many loans are credited to each registered book for the calculation of PLR payments, using the ISBN printed in the book (see below).

Parliament allocates a sum each year (£6.6 million for 2021/22) for PLR. This fund pays the administrative costs of PLR and reimburses local authorities for recording loans in the sample libraries (see below). The remaining money is divided by the total estimated national loan figure for all registered books in order to work out how much can be paid for each estimated loan of every registered ISBN.

### Further information

**Public Lending Right – British Library**
Boston Spa, Wetherby, West Yorkshire LS23 7BQ
*tel* (01937) 546030
*website* www.bl.uk/plr, www.plrinternational.com
*Contact* Head of PLR Operations

The UK PLR scheme is administered by the British Library from its offices in Boston Spa. The UK PLR office also provides registration for the Irish PLR scheme on behalf of the Irish Public Lending Remuneration office.

Application forms, information and publications are all obtainable from the PLR Office. See website for further information on eligibility for PLR, loans statistics and forthcoming developments.

**British Library Advisory Committee for Public Lending Right**

Advises the British Library Board, the PLR Head of Policy and Engagement and Head of PLR Operations on the operation and future development of the PLR scheme.

## Limits on payments

If all the registered interests in an author's books score so few loans that they would earn less than £1 in a year, no payment is due. However, if the books of one registered author score so high that the author's PLR earnings for the year would exceed £6,600, then only £6,600 is paid. (No author can earn more than £6,600 in PLR in any one year.) Money that is not paid out because of these limits belongs to the fund and increases the amounts paid that year to other authors.

## The sample

Because it would be expensive and impracticable to attempt to collect loans data from every library authority in the UK, a statistical sampling method is employed instead. The sample represents only public lending libraries – academic, school, private and commercial libraries are not included. Only books which are loaned from public libraries can earn PLR; consultations of books on library premises are excluded.

Publishing advice and resources

The sample consists of the entire loans records for a year from libraries in more than 41 public library authorities spread through England, Scotland and Wales, and whole data is collected from Northern Ireland. Sample loans represent around 20% of the national total. All the computerised sampling points in an authority contribute loans data ('multi-site' sampling). The aim is to increase the sample without any significant increase in costs. In order to ensure representative sampling, at least seven libraries are replaced every year and a library cannot stay in the sample for more than four years. Loans are totalled every 12 months for the period 1 July–30 June.

An author's entitlement to PLR depends on the loans accrued by his or her books in the sample. This figure is averaged up to produce first regional and then finally national estimated loans.

## ISBNs

The PLR system uses ISBNs (International Standard Book Numbers) to identify books lent and correlate loans with entries on the PLR Register so that payments can be made. ISBNs are required for all registrations. Different editions (e.g. 1st, 2nd, hardback, paperback, large print) of the same book have different ISBNs. See *ISBNs: what you need to know* on page 365.

## Authorship

In the PLR system the author of a printed book or ebook is any contributor such as the writer, illustrator, translator, compiler, editor or reviser. Authors must be named on the book's title page, or be able to prove authorship by some other means (e.g. receipt of royalties). The ownership of copyright has no bearing on PLR eligibility. Narrators, producers and abridgers are also eligible to apply for PLR shares in audiobooks and e-audiobooks.

**Co-authorship/illustrators.** In the PLR system the authors of a book are those writers, translators, editors, compilers and illustrators as defined above. Authors must apply for

---

### Summary of the 40th year's results

**Registration: authors.** When registration closed for the 40th year (30 June 2022) there were 60,104 authors and assignees.

**Eligible loans.** The loans from UK libraries credited to registered books – approximately 33% of all library borrowings – qualify for payment. The remaining loans relate to books that are ineligible for various reasons, to books written by dead or foreign authors, and to books that have simply not been applied for.

**Money and payments.** PLR's administrative costs are deducted from the fund allocated to the British Library Board annually by Parliament. Total government funding for 2021/22 was £6.6 million. The amount distributed to authors was just over £6 million. The Rate per Loan for 2021/22 was 30.53 pence.

The numbers of authors in various payment categories are as follows:

| | | |
|---|---|---|
| *303 | payments at | £5,000–6,600 |
| 372 | payments between | £2,500–4,999.99 |
| 828 | payments between | £1,000–2,499.99 |
| 898 | payments between | £500–999.99 |
| 3,034 | payments between | £100–499.99 |
| 15,592 | payments between | £1–99.99 |
| 21,034 | TOTAL | |

\* Includes 205 authors whose book loans reached the maximum threshold registration before their books can earn PLR and this can be done via the PLR website. There is no restriction on the number of authors who can register shares in any one book as long as they satisfy the eligibility criteria.

**Writers and/or illustrators**. At least one contributor must be eligible and they must jointly agree what share of PLR each will take based on contribution. This agreement is necessary even if one or two are ineligible or do not wish to register for PLR. The eligible authors will receive the share(s) specified in the application.

**Translators.** Translators may apply for a 30% fixed share (to be shared equally between joint translators).

**Editors and compilers.** An editor or compiler may apply to register a 20% share if they have written at least 10% of the book's content or more than ten pages of text in addition to normal editorial work and are named on the title page. Alternatively, editors may register 20% if they have a royalty agreement with the publisher. In the case of joint editors/compilers, the total editor's share should be divided equally.

**Audiobooks.** PLR shares in audiobooks are fixed by the UK scheme and may not be varied. *Writers* may register a fixed 60% share in an audiobook, providing that it has not been abridged or translated. In cases where the writer has made an additional contribution (e.g. as narrator), she/he may claim both shares. *Narrators* may register a fixed 20% PLR share in an audiobook. *Producers* may register a fixed 20% share in an audiobook. *Abridgers* (in cases where the writer's original text has been abridged prior to recording as an audiobook) qualify for 12% (20% of the writer's share). *Translators* (in cases where the writer's original text has been translated from another language) qualify for 18% (30% of the writer's share). If there is more than one writer, narrator, etc the appropriate shares should be divided equally.

**Dead or missing co-authors.** Where it is impossible to agree shares with a co-author because that person is dead or untraceable, then the surviving co-author or co-authors may submit an application to register a share which reflects their individual contribution to the book.

**Transferring PLR after death.** First applications may not be made by the estate of a deceased author. However, if an author registers during their lifetime the PLR in their books can be transferred to a new owner and continues for up to 70 years after the date of their death. The new owner can apply to register new titles if first published one year before, or up to ten years after, the date of the author's death. New editions of existing registered titles can also be registered posthumously.

**Residential qualifications.** To register for the UK PLR scheme, at the time of application authors must have their only home or principal home in the UK or in any of the other countries within the European Economic Area (i.e. EC member states plus Iceland, Norway and Liechtenstein).

## Eligible books

In the PLR system each edition of a book is registered and treated as a separate book. A book is eligible for PLR registration provided that:

- it has an eligible author (or co-author);
- it is printed and bound (paperbacks count as bound);
- it has already been published;
- copies of it have been put on sale, i.e. it is not a free handout;

• the authorship is personal, i.e. not a company or association, and the book is not crown copyright;
• it has an ISBN;
• it is not wholly or mainly a musical score;
• it is not a newspaper, magazine, journal or periodical.

**Audiobooks.** An audiobook is defined as an 'authored text' or 'a work recorded as a sound recording and consisting mainly of spoken words'. Applications can therefore only be accepted to register audiobooks which meet these requirements and are the equivalent of a printed book. Music, dramatisations and live recordings do not qualify for registration. To qualify for UK PLR in an audiobook contributors should be named on the case in which the audiobook is held; or be able to refer to a contract with the publisher; or be named within the audiobook recording.

**Ebooks.** Previously only ebooks downloaded to fixed terminals in library premises and then taken away on loan on portable devices to be read elsewhere qualified for PLR payment. Information provided by libraries suggested that the vast majority of ebook and digital audio lending was carried out 'remotely' to home PCs and mobile devices, which meant the loan did not qualify for PLR.

On 27 April 2017 the Digital Economy Bill, which included provision to extend the UK PLR legislation to include remote loans of ebooks from public libraries, received Royal Assent. The new arrangements took effect officially from 1 July 2018, and remote ebook loans data is now collected, and the first payments arising from the newly eligible loans were made in February 2020. The PLR website provides updated information on this legislation.

## Statements and payment

Authors with an online account may view their statement online. Only registered authors with an offline account and no registered email address receive a statement posted to their address if a payment is due.

### Most popular authors and titles for PLR year 2021/22

| Top 10 authors | Top 10 titles |
| --- | --- |
| 1 Julia Donaldson | 1 *The Thursday Murder Club* – Richard Osman |
| 2 James Patterson | 2 *The Man Who Died Twice* – Richard Osman |
| 3 Daisy Meadows | 3 *The Midnight Library* – Matt Haig |
| 4 David Walliams | 4 *The Sentinel* – Lee Child |
| 5 Lee Child | 5 *The Darkest Evening* – Ann Cleeves |
| 6 Jeff Kinney | 6 *The Long Call* – Ann Cleeves |
| 7 Ann Cleeves | 7 *Harry Potter and the Philosopher's Stone* – J.K. Rowling |
| 8 Roald Dahl | 8 *The Heron's Cry* – Ann Cleeves |
| 9 David Baldacci | 9 *Shuggie Bain* – Douglas Stuart |
| 10 Adam Blade | 10 *Trust Me* – T.M. Logan |

These two lists are based on loans data collected from a sample of UK public libraries between 1 July and 30 June each year. A grossing-up calculation is then applied at the end of the reporting year to provide a national estimate. They are based on PLR sample loans in the period July 2021–June 2022. They include all writers, both registered and unregistered, but not illustrators where the book has a separate writer. Writing names are used; pseudonyms have not been combined.

PLR's 'most borrowed' lists are based on loans data collected from a sample of UK public libraries between 1 July and 30 June each year. A grossing-up calculation is then applied at the end of the reporting year to provide a national estimate. See www.bl.uk/plr/popular-loans for more information.

## Sampling arrangements

To help minimise the unfairness that arises inevitably from a sampling system, the scheme specifies the eight regions within which authorities and sampling points have to be designated and includes libraries of varying size. Part of the sample drops out by rotation each year to allow fresh libraries to be included. The following library authorities were designated for the year 1 July 2022–30 June 2023 (all are multi-site authorities). This list is based on the nine government regions for England plus Northern Ireland, Scotland and Wales. The composition of the PLR library authority sample changes annually and not all regions have to be represented each year.

- East – Peterborough, Suffolk
- East Midlands – Leicester, Leicestershire, Nottinghamshire
- London – Bromley, Camden, Croydon, Harrow, The Royal Borough of Kensington and Chelsea (RBKC)
- North East – Newcastle, Northumberland, Stockton-on-Tees
- North West & Merseyside – Bury, St Helens, Wirral
- South East – Bracknell Forest, Medway, Oxfordshire, Southampton, West Sussex
- South West – Cornwall, Gloucestershire, Isle of Wight, Wiltshire
- West Midlands – Dudley, Shropshire, Wolverhampton
- Yorkshire & The Humber – Calderdale, Kingston Upon Hull, Leeds, North Lincolnshire
- Northern Ireland – The Northern Ireland Library Authority
- Scotland – Glasgow, Highland, Stirling
- Wales – Bridgend, Carmarthenshire, Newport, Pembrokeshire, Powys, Swansea.

Participating local authorities are reimbursed on an actual cost basis for additional expenditure incurred in providing loans data to the PLR Office. The extra PLR work mostly consists of modifications to computer programs to accumulate loans data in the local authority computer and to transmit the data to the PLR Office.

## Reciprocal arrangements

Reciprocal PLR arrangements now exist with the German, Dutch, Austrian and other European PLR schemes. Authors can apply for overseas PLR for most of these countries through the ALCS (Authors' Licensing and Collecting Society; see page 407). The exception to this rule is Ireland. Authors should now register for Irish PLR through the UK PLR Office. Further information on PLR schemes internationally and recent developments within the EC towards wider recognition of PLR is available from the PLR Office or on the international PLR website.

**Publishing advice and resources**

# Libraries

Libraries are not just repositories for books and a source of reference. They provide an increasing range of different services, using a multitude of media to reach more diverse audiences. Countless writers attest to the importance of libraries in shaping and helping develop their creative ambitions. Local libraries are a good source of information about the writing process and how to get published. They often hold author events, reading groups and creative writing classes.

## TYPES OF LIBRARIES

• **Public libraries** are accessible to the general population and are usually funded by a local or district council. They typically offer a mix of lending and reference facilities. Public libraries are distinct from research libraries, subscription libraries and other specialist libraries in terms of their funding and access, but may offer some of the same facilities to visitors. Public library services are facing financial challenges and cuts to funding, so many library authorities are looking for new approaches to working with communities in order to build sustainable library services for the future.
• A list of **community libraries** in the UK can be found at www.publiclibrariesnews.com.
• An **academic library** is usually affiliated to an educational institution and primarily serves the students and faculty of that institution. Many are accessible to the public.
• A **subscription library** is one that is funded via membership or endowments. Access is often restricted to members but membership is sometimes extended to groups who are non-members, such as students.
• Many libraries belong to the Association of Independent Libraries and a list of members can be found on the Association's website (see below).
• Consult this website to find your nearest and local UK public libraries: www.gov.uk/local-library-services.

## SOME OF THE BEST

Britain has such a wealth of comprehensive and historic libraries that a full list of them is not possible in this publication. Here is just a small selection of public libraries with outstanding collections in the UK.

### Barbican Library
Barbican Centre, Silk Street, London EC2Y 8DS
*tel* 020-7638 0569
*email* barbicanlib@cityoflondon.gov.uk
*website* www.barbican.org.uk/your-visit/during-your-visit/library
*Facebook* www.facebook.com/Barbicanlibrary
*Twitter* @barbicanlib

The largest of London's lending libraries with a strong arts and music section, a London collection, literature events programme and reading groups.

### Belfast Central Library
Royal Avenue, Belfast BT1 1EA
*tel* 028-9050 9150
*email* belfast.central@librariesni.org.uk
*website* www.librariesni.org.uk/libraries/greater-belfast/belfast-central-library
*Facebook* www.facebook.com/BelfastCentralLibrary
*Twitter* @BelfastCentLib

The library's reference library holds the greatest number of titles in Northern Ireland. The library houses a number of special collections including a digital film archive and the Northern Ireland Music Archive.

### Library of Birmingham
Centenary Square, Broad Street, Birmingham B1 2ND
*tel* 0121 242 4242
*email* enquiries@libraryofbirmingham.com
*website* www.birmingham.gov.uk/info/50132/visiting_the_library_of_birmingham
*Facebook* www.facebook.com/libraryofbirmingham
*Twitter* @LibraryofBham
*Instagram* @the_library_of_birmingham

The largest public library in the UK and the largest regional library in Europe. Houses locally relevant collections of archives, photography and rare books. Facilities include an art gallery space. It is also home to the BFI Mediatheque, providing free access to the National Film Archive.

### Bristol Central Library
Deanery Road, City Centre, Bristol BS1 5TL
*tel* 0117 903 7250
*email* bristol.library.service@bristol.gov.uk
*website* www.bristol.gov.uk/libraries-archives/central-library

Includes collections related to Bristol's slave trade, 19th-century travel and art. An appointment must be made by email or phone five working days in advance to view rare items.

### Canterbury Library
18 High Street, Canterbury, Kent CT1 2RA
*tel* 03000 413131

*email* canterburylibrary@kent.gov.uk
*website* www.kent.gov.uk/libs

The main library for the city of Canterbury. Canterbury Library was the first publicly funded library in Great Britain, through innovative interpretation of the Museums Act 1845 for provision of a museum of arts and science. It is now part of a large network of public libraries managed by Kent County Council. For services see website.

## Cardiff Central Library
The Hayes, Cardiff CF10 1FL
*tel* 029-2038 2166
*email* centrallibrary@cardiff.gov.uk
*website* https://cardiffhubs.co.uk/hub/central-library-hub/

The largest public library in Wales, opened in 2009, houses 90,000 books, 10,000 of which are in Welsh.

## Leeds Library
18 Commercial Street, Leeds LS1 6AL
*tel* 0113 245 3071
*email* enquiries@theleedslibrary.org.uk
*website* www.theleedslibrary.org.uk
*Facebook* www.facebook.com/leedslibrary
*Twitter* @theleedslibrary

Founded in 1768 as a proprietary subscription library, it is now the oldest surviving example of this sort of library in the UK. It includes specialist collections in travel, topography, biography, history and literature. There are long runs of periodicals, popular novels, children's books, and Civil War pamphlets and Reformation Tracts. About 1,500 new books and audio/visual items are added every year.

## Liverpool Central Library
William Brown Street, Liverpool L3 8EW
*tel* 0151 233 3069
*email* refbt.central.library@liverpool.gov.uk
*website* https://liverpool.gov.uk/libraries/find-a-library/central-library/

The collection includes 15,000 rare books, some of which date back to the 13th century.

## London Library
14 St James's Square, London SW1Y 4LG
*tel* 020-7766 4700
*email* reception@londonlibrary.co.uk
*website* www.londonlibrary.co.uk
*Facebook* www.facebook.com/thelondonlibrary
*Twitter* @thelondonlib

A subscription lending library containing more than one million books and periodicals in over 50 languages, the collection includes works from the 16th century to the latest publications in print and electronic form. Over 6,000 new books are added each year. Membership is open to all. The library's emerging writers' programme offers writers, in all genres, one year's free membership of The London

Library and includes writing development masterclasses, literary networking opportunities, peer support and guidance in use of the Library's resources. For details: www.londonlibrary.co.uk/about-us/ll-emerging-writers.

## Manchester Central Library
St Peter's Square, Manchester M2 5PD
*tel* 0161 234 1983
*email* libraries@manchester.gov.uk
*website* www.manchester.gov.uk/centrallibrary

Manchester's main library, the second biggest public lending library in the UK, houses a number of specialist collections such as Elizabeth Gaskell, Bellot Chinese and Thomas Penson De Quincey collections.

## Mitchell Library
North Street, Glasgow G3 7DN
*tel* 0141 287 2999
*email* libraries@glasgowlife.org.uk
*website* www.glasgowlife.org.uk/libraries/venues/the-mitchell-library
*Facebook* www.facebook.com/GlasgowLibraries
*Twitter* @GlasgowLib

One of the largest public reference library in Europe housing almost two million volumes. Holds an unrivalled collection of material relating to the city of Glasgow. The archives are open Tuesday, Wednesday and Thursday. To contact the special collections team, email specialcollections@glasgowlife.org.uk or phone 0141 287 2988.

## Newcastle City Library
Charles Avison Building, 33 Newbridge Street West, Newcastle upon Tyne NE1 8AX
*tel* 0191 277 4100
*email* information@newcastle.gov.uk
*website* www.newcastle.gov.uk/services/libraries-culture/your-libraries/city-library-community-hub
*Facebook* www.facebook.com/NewcastleLibraries
*Twitter* @ToonLibraries

Newcastle's main public library includes a café, exhibition spaces, a rare books and watercolours collection, a viewing deck and six floors of books.

## Westminster Reference Library
35 St Martin's Street, London WC2H 7HP
*tel* 020-7641 6200 (press 2)
*email* referencelibrarywc2@westminster.gov.uk
*website* www.westminster.gov.uk/westminster-reference-library
*Twitter* @WCClibraries

Specialist public reference library with collections in performing arts and art and design. Hosts regular and varied events, includes an exhibition space and a Business Information Point. Also has a range of business resources including market research, company and legal databases. Includes collection from Westminster Music Library.

## LIBRARIES OF LEGAL DEPOSIT IN THE UK AND IRELAND

A library of legal deposit is a library that has the power to request (at no charge) a copy of anything published in the UK. There are six legal deposit libraries in the UK and Ireland. To obtain a copy of a book, five out of the six legal deposit libraries must make a request in writing to a publisher within one year of publication of a book, newspaper or journal. Different rules apply to the British Library in that all UK libraries and Republic of Ireland publishers have a legal responsibility to send a copy of each of their publications to the library, without a written request being made. The British Library is the only legal deposit library with its own Legal Deposit Office. Since April 2013, legal deposit also covers material published digitally and online, so that the legal deposit libraries can provide a national archive of the UK's non-print published material, such as websites, blogs, e-journals and CDs.

### Agency for the Legal Deposit Libraries (ALDL)

Unit 21 Marnin Way, Edinburgh EH12 9GD
*tel* 0131 334 2833
*email* publisher.enquiries@legaldeposit.org.uk
*website* www.legaldeposit.org.uk

The ALDL requests and receives copies of publications for distribution to five major libraries (not the British Library). It is maintained by five legal deposit libraries and ensures that they receive legal deposit copies of British and Irish publications. The agency must request copies on behalf of the libraries within 12 months of the date of publication. On receiving such a request, a publisher must supply a copy for each of the requesting libraries under the terms of the Legal Deposit Libraries Act 2003 (UK) and the Copyright and Related Rights Act 2000 (Ireland).

### Bodleian Libraries of the University of Oxford

Broad Street, Oxford OX1 3BG
*tel* (01865) 277162
*email* reader.services@bodleian.ox.ac.uk
*website* www.bodleian.ox.ac.uk
*Facebook* www.facebook.com/bodleianlibraries
*Twitter* @bodleianlibs

With over 13 million items and including 80,000 e-journals and vast quantities of materials in many other formats, the Bodleian Libraries together form the second-largest library in the UK after the British Library, and is the main reference library of Oxford University. It is one of the oldest libraries in Europe. It holds special collections in classics and ancient history, English, history, history of science, local history, philosophy, reference, theology and patristics.

### The British Library

St Pancras Building, 96 Euston Road, London NW1 2DB
*tel* 0330 333 1144 (switchboard)
Legal Deposit Office: The British Library, Boston Spa, Wetherby, West Yorkshire LS23 7BQ
*tel* (01937) 546268
*email* legal-deposit-books@bl.uk
*website* www.bl.uk
*Facebook* www.facebook.com/britishlibrary
*Twitter* @britishlibrary

### Cambridge University Library

West Road, Cambridge CB3 9DR
*tel* (01223) 333000
*email* library@lib.cam.ac.uk
*website* www.lib.cam.ac.uk

Cambridge University Library houses its own collection and also comprises four other libraries within the university. The library dates back to the 15th century and now has a collection of over eight million books and other items. It is the only legal deposit library that keeps a large percentage of its books on open access. To visit the rare books collection email: rarebooks@lib.cam.ac.uk.

### National Library of Scotland

George IV Bridge, Edinburgh EH1 1EW
*tel* 0131 623 3700
*email* enquiries@nls.uk
*website* www.nls.uk
*Facebook* www.facebook.com/NationalLibraryOfScotland
*Twitter* @natlibscot

The National Library of Scotland holds over 24 million items. It is the world's central source for research relating to Scotland and the Scots. The library also holds a copy of the Gutenberg Bible, a First Folio of Shakespeare, and the last letter written by Mary Queen of Scots. It contains important items relating to Jane Austen, Lord Byron and Sir Arthur Conan Doyle.

### National Library of Wales

Aberystwyth, Ceredigion SY23 3BU
*tel* (01970) 632800
*email* gofyn@llgc.org.uk
*website* www.library.wales
*Facebook* www.facebook.com/llgcymranlwales
*Twitter* @nlwales

The National Library of Wales was established in 1907 and holds 6.5 million books and newspapers, including many important works such as the first book printed in Welsh and the first Welsh translation of the Bible.

### Trinity College Library Dublin

College Green, Dublin 2, Republic of Ireland
*tel* +353 (0)1 896 1127

*email* library@tcd.ie
*website* www.tcd.ie/library
*Facebook* www.facebook.com/tcdlibrary
*Twitter* @tcdlibrary

Trinity College Library is the largest library in Ireland and is home to the *Book of Kells* – two of the four volumes are on permanent public display. The library houses sound recordings, maps, databases, and a digital collection. Currently it has over seven million printed volumes with extensive collections of journals, manuscripts, maps and music reflecting over 400 years of academic development.

## DESIGNATED OUTSTANDING COLLECTIONS

The Designated Outstanding Collections scheme was established in 1997 by the Museums and Galleries Commission to identify collections of national and international importance in non-national museums and galleries. In 2005 the scheme was extended to include libraries and archives. The scheme is now administered by Arts Council England and there are currently 154 Designated Outstanding Collections in England. To find out if there is a Designated Outstanding Collection library near you, visit the Designation section of the Arts Council website (www.artscouncil.org.uk/designated-collections).

## SPECIALIST LIBRARIES IN THE UK

Writers often need access to specialised information sources in order to research their work. The following are a sample of specialist libraries in the UK. In addition to the libraries listed below, many university libraries hold special collections which are accessible to the public, usually by appointment. Check individual university library websites for details.

### BBC Written Archives Centre

Peppard Road, Caversham Park, Reading RG4 8TS
*tel* 020-8008 5661
*email* heritage@bbc.co.uk
*website* www.bbc.co.uk/archive/written-archives-centre-visiting-the-archive/zfqpwty

Home of the BBC's written records. Holds thousands of files, scripts and working papers, dating from the BBC's formation in 1922, together with information about past programmes and the history of broadcasting. Does not have recordings or information about current programmes. Accredited students or staff members at a higher education institution, writers commissioned for a publication or those working towards commercial projects can arrange a visit for research purposes. By appointment only, between 10am to 5.00pm, Wednesday to Friday.

### BFI National Archive and Reuben Library

Belvedere Road, South Bank, London SE1 8XT
*tel* 020-7255 1444
*email* library@bfi.org.uk
*website* www.bfi.org.uk/archive-collections
*Facebook* www.facebook.com/BritishFilmInstitute
*Twitter* @BFI

Established in 1933, the BFI National Archive is one of the largest film and television collections anywhere. Dating from the earliest days of film to the 21st century, it contains nearly a million titles. The archive holds over 800,000 items of film – including television programmes, documentaries, newsreels, as well as educational and training films – and is updated daily. The majority of the collection is British material but it also features internationally significant holdings. The Archive also collects films which feature key British actors and the work of British directors. Using the latest preservation methods, the BFI cares for a variety of often obsolete formats. The BFI Reuben Library at BFI Southbank is home to a huge collection of books, journals, documents and audio recordings about the world of film and television.

### British Library for Development Studies (BLDS)

Institute of Development Studies at the University of Sussex, Brighton BN1 9RE
*tel* (01273) 678163
*email* blds@ids.ac.uk
*website* https://guides.lib.sussex.ac.uk/

Europe's largest research collection on economic and social change in developing countries.

### British Newspaper Archive

*tel* (01382) 210100
*website* www.britishnewspaperarchive.co.uk
*Facebook* www.facebook.com/TheBritishNewspaperArchive
*Twitter* @BNArchive

The British Newspaper Archive gives access to over three million historical local, national and regional newspaper pages from across the UK and Ireland. The Archive is currently in partnership with the British Library and findmypast.co.uk to digitise up to nearly 63 million newspaper pages from the British Library's vast collection.

### Caird Library and Archive

Greenwich, London SE10 9NF
*tel* 020-8312 6516
*email* library@rmg.co.uk
*website* www.rmg.co.uk/collections/caird-library

Specialist maritime research library at the National Maritime Museum in Greenwich.

Publishing advice and resources

## Catholic National Library

Centre for Catholic Studies,
Department of Theology and Religion,
University of Durham, Abbey House, Palace Green,
Durham DH1 3RS
*tel* 0191 334 1656
*email* ccs.admin@durham.ac.uk
*website* www.dur.ac.uk/theology.religion/ccs

Holds over 70,000 books, pamphlets and periodicals
on theology, spirituality and related subjects,
biography and history.

## Chained Library

Hereford Cathedral Library and Archives,
Hereford Cathedral, 5 College Cloisters,
Cathedral Close, Hereford HR1 2NG
*tel* (01432) 374200
*email* library@herefordcathedral.org
*website* www.herefordcathedral.org/chained-library

Hereford Cathedral has housed a collection of books
accessible to the public from the 12th century. The
chaining of books was a widespread security system
in European libraries from the Middle Ages to the
18th century; this is the largest to survive with all its
chains, rods and locks intact. The library is open
Tuesday, Wednesday and Thursday 10am to 4pm
and the first Saturday in each month 10am until
1pm.

## Chawton House Library

Chawton, Alton, Hants. GU34 1SJ
*tel* (01420) 541010
*email* info@chawton.net
*website* https://chawtonhouse.org/the-library/using-
the-library/
*Facebook* www.facebook.com/ChawtonHouse
*Twitter* @ChawtonHouse

The collection focuses on women's writing in English
from 1600 to 1830 and includes some manuscripts.
The library also houses the Knight Collection, which
is the private library belonging to the Knight family,
the owners of Chawton House for over 400 years.

## Chetham's Library

Long Milgate, Manchester M3 1SB
*tel* 0161 834 7961
*email* fwilde@chethams.org.uk
*website* https://library.chethams.com
*Facebook* www.facebook.com/chethamslibrary
*Twitter* @chethamslibrary

Founded in 1653, this is the oldest public library in
the English-speaking world. In addition to a
collection of early printed books, it includes
manuscript diaries, letters and deeds, prints, paintings
and glass lantern slides. Use of the library is free, no
membership or reader's ticket is required.
Researchers need a prior appointment by phone or
email (above) at least one working day in advance to
consult library material.

## Commonwealth Library and Archives

Commonwealth Secretariat, Marlborough House,
Pall Mall, London SW1Y 5HX
*tel* 020-7747 6164 (librarian) / 020-7747 6167
(archivist)
*email* library@commonwealth.int
*website* https://thecommonwealth.org/library-and-
archives
*Facebook* www.facebook.com/commonwealthsec
*Twitter* @commonwealthsec

Collection covers politics and international relations,
economics, education, health, gender, environment
and management. Holds a comprehensive collection
of Commonwealth Secretariat publications and its
archives. Opening hours are Monday to Friday from
10am to 4.45pm.

## Crafts Council Research Library

Crafts Council, 44A Pentonville Road,
London N1 9BY
*tel* 020-7806 2500
*email* reception@craftscouncil.org.uk
*website* www.craftscouncil.org.uk
*Facebook* www.facebook.com/CraftsCouncilUK/
*Twitter* @CraftsCouncilUK

This is a reference library which normally opens to
the public two days a week by appointment. Houses a
large collection of contemporary craft books and
catalogues as well as journals. Covers ceramics,
textiles, jewellery, fashion accessories and paper.

## The Dana Research Centre and Library

165 Queens Gate, London SW7 5HD
*tel* 020-7942 4242
*email* smlinfo@sciencemuseum.ac.uk
*website* www.sciencemuseum.org.uk/researchers/
dana-research-centre-and-library
*Facebook* www.facebook.com/sciencemuseumlondon
*Twitter* @sciencemuseum

Allows access to around 500,000 items covering
museum studies, the history and biography of science
technology and medicine and the philosophical and
social aspects of these subjects. Open Thursdays and
Fridays 11am until 5pm.

## University of Exeter Library, Special Collections

Old Library, Prince of Wales Road, Exeter EX4 4SB
*tel* (01392) 263867
*email* libspc@exeter.ac.uk
*website* www.exeter.ac.uk/departments/library/
special-collections

Bill Douglas Cinema Museum is home to one of the
largest collections of material relating to the moving
image in Britain. It is both an accredited public
museum and an academic research facility and we
hold a collection of over 85,000 items. Special
collections include the Agatha Christie archive, which

houses correspondence between Agatha Christie and Edmund Cork, between Cork and American literary agent, Harold Ober, and other interested parties. There are between 5,000-6,000 letters in the collection.

## Feminist Library
The Sojourner Truth Community Centre,
161 Sumner Rd, Peckham, London SE15 6JL
*tel* 020-7261 0879
*email* admin@feministlibrary.co.uk
*website* www.feministlibrary.co.uk
*Facebook* www.facebook.co/feministlibrary
*Twitter* @feministlibrary

The Feminist Library holds a large archive collection of women's liberation movement literature, particularly second-wave materials dating from the late 1960s to the 1990s.

## Gladstone's Library
Church Lane, Hawarden, Flintshire CH5 3DF
*tel* (01244) 532350
*email* enquiries@gladlib.org
*website* www.gladstoneslibrary.org

Britain's first residential library, the building houses 20,000 of Gladstone's books. Since the library opened in 1902, it has continued to acquire books specialising in those subjects that were of most interest to Gladstone: theology, history, philosophy, classics, art and literature. Researchers seeking an extended period of quiet study can stay in one of 26 rooms in the Gothic stone building.

## Goethe-Institut London Library
50 Princes Gate, Exhibition Road, London SW7 2PH
*tel* 020-7596 4040
*email* library@london.goethe.org
*email* info-london@goethe.org
*website* https://www.goethe.de/ins/gb/en/sta/lon/bi2.html
*Facebook* www.facebook.com/goethe.institut.london
*Twitter* @GI_London1

Specialises in German literature, especially contemporary fiction and drama, film DVDs and books/audiovisual material on German culture and recent history. The e-library gives access to Goethe Institut libraries in the UK, Ireland and the Netherlands and allows electronic downloading of ebooks, e-audiobooks and electronic newspapers for a predetermined period of time.

## Guildhall Library
Aldermanbury, London EC2V 7HH
*tel* 020-7332 1868/1870
*email* guildhall.library@cityoflondon.gov.uk
*website* https://www.cityoflondon.gov.uk/things-to-do/history-and-heritage/guildhall-library
*Twitter* @GuildhallLib

Books collection comprises over 200,000 titles dating from the 15th century to the 21st century and includes books, pamphlets, periodicals, trade directories and poll books. Covers all aspects of life in London, past and present.

## Imperial War Museum Archive and Reading Room
IWM London, Lambeth Road, London SE1 6HZ
researchroom@iwm.org.uk
*website* www.iwm.org.uk/research/research-facilities
*Facebook* www.facebook.com/iwm.london
*Twitter* @I_W_M

Responsible for a unique national reference library with over 150,000 items on 20th- and 21st-century conflict involving British and Commonwealth countries. Along with material on military units and campaign histories, contains biographies, manuals, items relating to the economic, social and cultural aspects of war, journals, newspapers, ephemera, propaganda and digital resources. The Archive and Research Room is open three days a week (Wednesdays, Thursdays and Fridays 10am until 3pm) to nine researchers who can order up to ten items at a time per day.

## Lambeth Palace Library
15 Lambeth Palace Road, London SE1 7JT
*tel* 020-7898 1400
*email* archives@churchofengland.org
*website* www.lambethpalacelibrary.org
*Facebook* www.facebook.com/LambethPalaceLibrary
*Twitter* @lampallib

The historic library of the Archbishops of Canterbury and the principal library and record office for the Church of England. The library opens one Saturday every month, 10am to 5pm. Check website for details. To book a spot in the reading room please fill out the contact form on the website.

## The Library of the Society of Friends
Friends House, 173–177 Euston Road, London NW1 2BJ
*tel* 020-7663 1135
*email* library@quaker.org.uk
*website* www.quaker.org.uk/resources/library/visit-the-library

The library has over 80,000 books and pamphlets, including a unique collection of 17th-century Quaker and anti-Quaker material. Open to researchers Tuesdays, Wednesdays and Thursdays 10am to 5pm (with a lunchbreak 1pm to 2pm). To be able to use a desk space and work with collection material you need to register and book an appointment. Please email library@quaker.org.uk.

## Linen Hall Library
17 Donegall Square North, Belfast BT1 5GB
*tel* 028-9032 1707
*email* info@linenhall.com
*website* www.linenhall.com
*Facebook* www.facebook.com/LinenHallLibraryBelfast

*Twitter* @thelinenhall

Renowned for its Irish and Local Studies Collection, including early Belfast and Ulster printed books and 350,000 items in the Northern Ireland Political Collection (NIPC). Also large General Lending Collection. Open Monday to Friday, 9.30am to 5.30pm.

## National Art Library

Victoria & Albert Museum, Cromwell Road, London SW7 2RL
*tel* 020-7942 2000
*email* hello@vam.ac.uk
*website* www.vam.ac.uk/info/national-art-library
*Facebook* www.facebook.com/victoriaandalbertmuseum
*Twitter* @V_and_A

Houses around one million books but also holds prints, drawings, paintings, photographs, ceramics and glass, textiles and fashion, furniture, design, metalwork and sculpture. The collections range from medieval manuscripts to contemporary artists' books and armorial bindings to comics and graphic novels. Anyone can register to visit its collection, which focuses on the decorative arts in the museum's collection. Currently open Tuesdays, Wednesdays and Thursdays from 11am until 5pm.

## Natural History Museum Library and Information Services

Cromwell Road, London SW7 5BD
*tel* 020-7942 5000 (switchboard)/ 020-7942 5460 (archives/general library) / 020-7942 6156 (ornithology library, Tring)
*email* library@nhm.ac.uk
*website* www.nhm.ac.uk/research-curation/science-facilities/library
*Facebook* www.facebook.com/naturalhistorymuseum
*Twitter* @NHM_Library

Online catalogue contains all library material acquired since 1989 and about 80% of earlier items. The library collection contains more than one million items. For contact and opening times see website.

## RNIB National Library Service

PO Box 173, Peterborough PE2 6WS
*tel* 0303 123 9999 (library); 0300 303 8313 (bookshare)
*email* library@rnib.org.uk
*website* https://readingservices.rnib.org.uk; www.rnibbookshare.org/cms
*Facebook* www.facebook.com/rnibuk
*Twitter* @RNIB

The largest specialist library for readers with sight loss in the UK. It offers a comprehensive range of books and accessible information for children and adults in braille and Talking Books. Audio books are also available for download. RNIB Bookshare opens up the world of reading in education for learners with a print-disability, including those with dyslexia or who are blind or partially sighted.

## John Rylands Research Institute and Library

150 Deansgate, Manchester M3 3EH
*tel* 0161 306 0555
*email* uml.special-collections@manchester.ac.uk
*website* www.library.manchester.ac.uk/rylands/
*Facebook* www.facebook.com/JohnRylandsLibrary
*Twitter* @UoMLibrary

The library is part of the University of Manchester but is open to the public. Home to 1.4 million items, including books, manuscripts, maps, artworks and objects.

## Tate Library & Archive

Tate Britain, Millbank, London SW1P 4RG
*tel* 020-7887 8838
*email* reading.rooms@tate.org.uk
*website* www.tate.org.uk/visit/tate-britain/library-archive-reading-rooms/library

Located at Tate Britain, broadly covers those areas in which the Tate collects. The library include over 115,000 books and monographs, 175,000 recent and historic exhibition catalogues, over 10,000 artists' books, zines and serials, 3,000 print and e-journals, printed ephemera, audio and video recordings, as well as microfilm and microfiche collections and half a million press cuttings.

## Wellcome Library

Wellcome Collection, 183 Euston Road, London NW1 2BE
*tel* 020-7611 8722
*email* library@wellcome.ac.uk
*website* http://wellcomelibrary.org/
*Facebook* www.facebook.com/Wellcomelibrary/
*Twitter* @WellcomeLibrary

One of the world's major resources for the study of medical history. Also houses an expanding collection of material relating to contemporary medicine and biomedical science in society.

## Westminster Music Library and Archives

35 St Martin's Street, Westminster, London WC2H 7HP
*tel* 020-7641 6200
*email* musiclibrary@westminster.gov.uk
*website* www.westminster.gov.uk/leisure-libraries-and-community/library-opening-times-and-contact-details/westminster-music-library

Holds a wide range of scores, orchestral sets, books on music, music journals and a collection of Mozart sound recordings, formerly the GLASS collection.

## Women's Library @ LSE

Lionel Robbins Building,
The London School of Economics and Political

Science, 10 Portugal Street, Westminster,
London WC2A 2HD
*tel* 020-7955 7229
*email* library.enquiries@lse.ac.uk
*website* www.lse.ac.uk/library/collection-highlights/
the-womens-library
*Twitter* @LSELibrary

Houses the most extensive collection of women's
history in the UK. Part of the London School of
Economics. Open Monday to Friday, 10am to 4pm.

## Wordsworth Library

Dove Cottage, Grasmere, Cumbria LA22 9SH
*tel* (01539) 435544
*email* enquiries@wordsworth.org.uk
*website* https://wordsworth.org.uk/
*Facebook* www.facebook.com/WordsworthTrust/

William Wordsworth's home, Dove Cottage, houses a
small library which is situated in a two-storey
converted coach house adjacent to the cottage
museum. It contains treasures of all kinds related to
the Romantic movement, from books to paintings
and Wordsworth's manuscripts.

## Working Class Movement Library

Jubilee House, 51 The Crescent, Salford M5 4WX
*tel* 0161 736 3601
*email* enquiries@wcml.org.uk
*website* www.wcml.org.uk
*Facebook* www.facebook.com/wcmlibrary
*Twitter* @wcmlibrary

Records over 200 years of organising and
campaigning by ordinary men and women. The
collection provides an insight into working people's
daily lives. Collection contains: books, pamphlets,
archives, photographs, plays, poetry, songs, banners,
posters, badges, cartoons, journals, biographies,
reports.

## Wren Library

Trinity College Cambridge, Cambridge CB2 1TQ
*email* wren.library@trin.cam.ac.uk
*email* archives@trin.cam.ac.uk
*website* www.trin.cam.ac.uk/library/wren-library

This library houses the manuscript of Winnie-the-
Pooh and the papers of philosopher Ludwig
Wittgenstein. As an academic library it's only open to
the public for two hours each day during term time.
To view rare books and manuscripts use the first
email above. To view the college archive and modern
manuscripts use the second email above.

## Zoological Society of London Library

Outer Circle, Regent's Park, London NW1 4RY
*tel* 020-7449 6293
*email* library@zsl.org
*website* www.zsl.org/about-us/library
*Facebook* www.facebook.com/officialzsl
*Twitter* @officialzsl

Contains a unique collection of journals and books
on zoology and animal conservation.

## ORGANISATIONS THAT SUPPORT LIBRARIES

There are many organisations which are affiliated to,
and champion the use of libraries in the UK. These
include:

## APPG for Libraries Information & Knowledge in Parliament

*website* www.cilip.org.uk/page/APPGLInK

The goal of the APPG for Libraries Information &
Knowledge in Parliament is to provide information
and opportunities for debate about the important
role libraries play in society and their future; to
highlight the contribution that a wide variety of
library and information services make, including
those in public, school, government, health sector,
colleges, private companies and university libraries;
and to promote and discuss themes in the wider
information and knowledge sector including the
impact of technology, skills and training, professional
standards and broader issues.

## Arts Council England

*website* www.artscouncil.org.uk

Arts Council England is the developmental agency for
libraries in England and has responsibility for
supporting and developing libraries. See also
page 185.

## Association of Independent Libraries

Church Lane, Doncaster DN5 7AU
*email* emma.marigliano@gmail.com
*website* http://independentlibraries.co.uk

Developes the conservation, restoration and public
awareness of independent libraries in the UK.
Together, its members possess over two million
books and have many listed buildings in their care.
Founded 1989.

## Association of Senior and Children's Education Librarians (ASCEL)

*website* www.ascel.org.uk

A national membership network of Senior Children's
and Education Librarians. It aims to stimulate
innovation and share initiatives relating to children
and young people using public libraries and
educational services.

## BookTrust

*website* www.booktrust.org.uk

Aims to give everyone access to books and the chance
to benefit from reading. See also page 318.

## Chartered Institute of Library and Information Professionals (CILIP)

7 Ridgmount Street, London WC1E 7AE
*tel* 020-7255 0500
*email* info@cilip.org.uk
*website* www.cilip.org.uk

The leading professional body for librarians, information specialists and knowledge managers. Aims for a fair and economically prosperous society underpinned by literacy, access to information and the transfer of knowledge. A registered charity. Offices in London, Wales, Scotland and Northern Ireland.

## The Community Knowledge Hub for Libraries

*website* https://libraries.communityknowledgehub. org.uk/content/community-knowledge-hub

Unites expert guidance and resources with an interactive community of organisations and local authorities involved with community-managed and supported libraries.

## Friends of Libraries

Many libraries in the UK have Friends of Libraries organisations affiliated to them which support library use through charitable means. Sometimes Friends groups are set up to campaign against a potential council closures of libraries or reductions in budgets. They have been known to set up their own community libraries.

## Friends of National Libraries

*website* www.friendsofnationallibraries.org.uk

A registered charity. Founded in 1931. Helps libraries in the UK acquire books, manuscripts and archives, in particular those that might otherwise leave the UK.

## Internet Library for Librarians

*email* info@itcompany.com
*website* www.itcompany.com/inforetriever/index.htm

Internet Library for Librarians has been one of the most popular information resource sites for librarians since 1994. It is an information portal specifically designed for librarians to locate internet resources related to their profession.

## Libraries Connected

*email* info@librariesconnected.org.uk
*website* www.librariesconnected.org.uk

A charity, previously known as the Society of Chief Librarians (SCL). Partly funded by Arts Council England as the Sector Support Organisation for libraries. This funding provides increased capacity with a new team of staff and trustees to work alongside members. Remains a membership organisation, made up of every library service in England, Wales and Northern Ireland.

## Libraries Week

*website* www.librariesweek.org.uk

The first Libraries Day took place in February 2012 and is now a week-long annual event in the UK dedicated to the celebration of libraries and librarians. Author talks and competitions are arranged by local authorities, universities, library services and local community groups.

## The Library Campaign

*website* www.librarycampaign.com

Aims to advance the lifelong education of the public by the promotion, support, assistance and improvement of libraries through the activities of friends and user groups.

## Library Planet

*website* https://libraryplanet.net/

A crowdsourced travel guide for the libraries of the world. The intention is to inspire library travellers.

## National Literacy Trust

*website* www.literacytrust.org.uk

Aims to improve reading, writing, speaking and listening skills in disadvantaged communities, in part through access to libraries. See also page 313.

## Private Libraries Association

*email* info@plabooks.org
*website* www.plabooks.org

An international society of book collectors and lovers of books. Membership: £30 p.a. Publications include *The Private Library* (quarterly), annual *Private Press Books*, and other books on book collecting. Founded 1956.

## Public Library News

*website* www.publiclibrariesnews.com

Promotes knowledge about libraries in the UK.

## The Reading Agency

*website* https://readingagency.org.uk

Aims to give everyone an equal chance in life by helping people become confident and enthusiastic readers, and that includes supporting library use.

## School Library Association (SLA)

1 Pine Court, Kembrey Park, Swindon SN2 8AD
*tel* (01793) 530166
*email* info@sla.org.uk
*website* www.sla.org.uk

The main goal of the SLA is to support people involved with school libraries, promoting high-quality reading and learning opportunities for all. Founded 1937.

# Software for writers

This is a selection of software programmes and applications designed to enhance your writing experience and aid productivity. Each product has its own selection of features; we recommend you check the cost carefully, as many involve a fixed-term subscription or licence fee but do also offer free trials.

## WRITING SOFTWARE

### Aeon Timeline
*website* https://timeline.app
£47.99 one-off fee

Includes tools and features to help you understand characters, avoid plot holes and inconsistencies, and visualise your story in new ways.

### Atticus
*website* www.atticus.io
$147 one-off fee (exc. tax)

Allows authors to use the same platform for writing and formatting; writing can also be imported. A word counter and goal tracker allow you to monitor your progress.

### Bear
*website* https://bear.app
Free; pro $1.49 monthly; $14.99 p.a.

A note-taking tool that allows you to link notes to create an outline and apply hashtags to organise notes, and provides a focus feature to aid concentration.

### Bibisco
*website* https://bibisco.com
Community edition: free; supporters edition: pay what you want

Designed to allow a writer to focus on their characters and develop rounded and complex narratives, with particular emphasis on the manuscript's geographical, temporal and social context.

### Dabble
*website* www.dabblewriter.com
From $10 monthly; from $72 p.a.

Gives writers the freedom to plot, write and edit on a desktop, in a browser or offline, and automatically syncs all versions across your devices. Features include plot grids, progress tracking and goal setting.

### Evernote
*website* https://evernote.com
Free; tiered from £5.75 monthly

Note-taking tool which allows you to sync notes across devices, identify tasks and assign schedules, and mark-up webpages and add them to your notes along with documents, images, videos and audio files.

### FocusWriter
*website* https://gottcode.org/focuswriter
Free

Provides a simple and distraction-free writing environment with a hide-away interface, so you can focus solely on your writing.

### MasterWriter
*website* https://masterwriter.com
$9.95 monthly; $99.95 p.a.

An extensive catalogue of words and phrases that can help improve and enrich the vocabulary in your writing. The search function will return synonyms, words used in similar contexts, common phrases, rhymes and figures of speech.

### Novel Factory
*website* www.novel-software.com
From $75 p.a.

Plan your book with confidence by using the Roadmap feature which provides tools and structures to suit your needs. Includes detailed character overviews including biographies and images, as well as scene tabs and writing statistics about your work.

### Novel Suite
*website* www.novelsuite.com/novel-writing-software
$12 monthly; $99 p.a.

An all-in-one novel writing application that can be used across all devices. Manage multiple books using character profiles, scene outlines and writing template tools.

### Novelize
*website* www.getnovelize.com
$9 monthly; $65 p.a.

Developed for fiction writers, this web-based writing app means you can work on your book anywhere on any device. Keep your research in one place in the notebook displayed on the writing screen and track your progress.

### NovelPad
*website* https://novelpad.co
$15 monthly; $120 p.a.

A writing and editing application that provides plot boards, scene cards and a consistency checker which filters your writing for specific characters and plot lines.

## Obsidian

*website* https://obsidian.md
Free

A mapping structure which helps writers to make new connections and identify relationships between ideas and key terms in order to create a coherent narrative.

## Plottr

*website* https://plottr.com
$25 p.a.; $99 one-off fee

Created to aid book planning and story mapping. Tracks characters and plots for easy reference, provides templates for plot outlining and visualisation, and creates an automated outline of your writing.

## Scrivener

*website* www.literatureandlatte.com/scrivener/overview
From £42.49 one-off fee

Tailored for long writing projects with everything you need housed in one place; it is a typewriter, ring binder and scrapbook, allowing you to optimise your digital workspace.

## SmartEdit Writer

*website* www.smart-edit.com/Writer
Free

Organically build your book one scene or one chapter at a time, then drag and drop to arrange these on your document tree. Store your research images, URLs and notes alongside work for easy access, then export your manuscript into a single Word document when ready.

## Ulysses

*website* https://ulysses.app
$5.99 monthly; $39.99 p.a.

Document management for all writing projects, with flexible export options including pdf, Word, ebook and HTML which are appropriately formatted and styled.

## WriteItNow

*website* www.ravensheadservices.com
From $59.95 one-off fee

Includes sophisticated world-building features to create detailed and complex settings and characters. Recommends suitable names for your characters based on the historical period and geographical setting of your story.

# EDITING SOFTWARE

## After the Deadline

*website* www.afterthedeadline.com
Free

A context-driven grammar and spelling checker, it underlines potential issues and gives a suggestion with an explanation of how you can rectify the error.

## AutoCrit

*website* www.autocrit.com
Free; pro from $30 monthly

Analyses your entire manuscript and suggests insightful improvements in the form of an individual summary report, showing where your strengths and weaknesses lie.

## Ginger

*website* www.gingersoftware.com
$13.99 monthly; $84 p.a.

Combines a grammar checker with tools to improve your writing, including a synonym suggester and text rephrasing.

## Grammarly

*website* www.grammarly.com
Free; premium from £10 monthly

Provides accurate and context-specific suggestions when the application detects grammar, spelling, punctuation, word choice and style mistakes in your writing.

## Hemingway Editor

*website* https:/hemingwayapp.com
$19.99 one-off fee

Helps you write with clarity and confidence. This application is like a spellchecker but for style. It will highlight any areas that need tightening up by identifying adverbs, passive voice, and uninspiring or over-complicated words.

## iA Writer

*website* https://ia.net/writer
From $29.99 one-off fee

Provides tools to help you improve your writing: syntax colour-coding identifies repetitive and extraneous text, text blocking allowing moving whole sections of text, and a style checker highlights cliches and weak phrases.

## Linguix

*website* https://linguix.com
Free; pro $60 p.a.; $85 one-off fee

Combines a range of editing tools: checks your grammar, suggests ways to paraphrase your writing to make it more succinct and aids with style and flow for non-native English writers.

## PerfectIt

*website* https://intelligentediting.com
From £76 p.a.

Proofreading software which checks consistency, for example by applying style rules and highlighting undefined abbreviations.

## ProWritingAid

*website* https://prowritingaid.com
Free; pro from £30 monthly; £120 p.a.; £399 one-off fee

For use via the web, or as an add-on to word processing software, it analyses your work for a multitude of potential issues such as passive voice, clichés, missing dialogue tags and pace, and suggests how you can rectify any errors or make style improvements.

## SmartEdit

*website* www.smart-edit.com
$77 one-off fee; pro $139 one-off fee

Sits inside Microsoft Word and runs 25 individual checks whilst you work, flagging areas that need attention, including highlighting repeated words, listing adverbs and foreign phrases used and identifying possible misused words.

## Vellum

*website* https://vellum.pub
£169.99 (ebook only); £209.99 (ebook and print)

Print and ebook formatting package that provides templates for front and endmatter, styles pages and generates versions for different platforms. Allows the user to update ebooks after they have been published. Only available for Mac.

## WordRake

*website* www.wordrake.com
$17 monthly; $129 p.a.

When you click the 'rake' button in Microsoft Word, the text editor will read your document and suggest edits to tighten and add clarity to your work.

## Wordtune

*website* www.wordtune.com
Free; premium from $9.99 monthly

An extension which can be added to browsers, email providers, social media and Microsoft Word. Provides a rephrasing and rewriting tool and suggests ways to shorten sentences, expand your ideas and alter your tone.

Publishing advice and resources

# Glossary of publishing terms

## advance

Money paid by a publisher to an author before a book is published which will be covered by future royalties. A publishing contract often allows an author an advance payment against future royalties; the author will not receive any further royalties until the amount paid in advance has been earned by sales of the book.

## advance information (AI) sheet

A document that is put together by a publishing company to provide sales and marketing information about a book before publication and can be sent several months before publication to sales representatives. It can incorporate details of the format and contents of the book, key selling points and information about intended readership, as well as information about promotions and reviews.

## backlist

The range of books already published by a publisher that are still in print.

## blad (book layout and design)

A pre-publication sales and marketing tool. It is often a printed booklet that contains sample pages, images and front and back covers which acts as a preview for promotional use or for sales teams to show to potential retailers, customers or reviewers.

## blurb

A short piece of writing or a paragraph that praises and promotes a book, which usually appears on the back or inside cover of the book and may be used in sales and marketing material.

## book club edition

An edition of a book specially printed and bound for a book club for sale to its members.

## co-edition

The publication of a book by two publishing companies in different countries, where the first company has originated the work and then sells sheets to the second publisher (or licenses the second publisher to reprint the book locally).

## commissioning editor

A person who asks authors to write books for the part of the publisher's list for which he or she is responsible or who takes on an author who approaches them direct or via an agent with a proposal. Also called acquisitions editor or acquiring editor (more commonly in the USA). A person who signs-up writers (commissions them to write) an article for a magazine or newspaper.

## copy-editor

A person whose job is to check material ready for printing for accuracy, clarity of message and writing style and consistency of typeface, punctuation and layout. Sometimes called a desk editor.

## copyright

The legal right, which the creator of an original work has, to only allow copying of the work with permission and sometimes on payment of royalties or a copyright fee. An amendment to the Copyright, Designs and Patents Act (1988) states that in the UK most works are protected for 70 years from the creator's death. The 'copyright page' at the start of a book asserts copyright ownership and author identification.

## distributor

Acts as a link between the publisher and retailer. The distributor can receive orders from retailers, ship books, invoice, collect revenue and deal with returns. Distributors often handle books from several publishers. Digital distributors handle ebook distribution.

## double-page spread

Two facing pages of an illustrated book.

## editor

A person in charge of publishing a newspaper or magazine who makes the final decisions about the content and format. A person in book publishing who has responsibility for the content of a book and can be variously a senior person (editor-in-chief) or day-to-day contact for authors (copy-editor, development editor, commissioning editor, etc).

## endmatter

Material at the end of the main body of a book which may be useful to the reader, including references, appendices, indexes and bibliography. Also called back matter.

## extent

The number of pages in a book.

## folio

A large sheet of paper folded twice across the middle and trimmed to make four pages of a book. Also a page number.

## frontlist

New books just published (generally in their first year of publication) or about to be published by a publisher. Promotion of the frontlist is heavy, and the frontlist carries most of a publisher's investment. On the other hand, a backlist which continues to sell is usually the most profitable part of a publisher's list.

## imprint

The publisher's or printer's name which appears on the title page of a book or in the bibliographical details; a brand name under which a book is published within a larger publishing company, usually representing a specialised subject area.

## inspection copy

A copy of a publication sent or given with time allowed for a decision to purchase or return it. In academic publishing, lecturers can request inspection copies to decide whether to make a book/textbook recommended reading or adopt it as a core textbook for their course.

## ISBN

International Standard Book Number.

## ISSN

International Standard Serial Number. An international system used on periodicals, magazines, learned journals, etc. The ISSN is formed of eight digits, which refer to the country in which the magazine is published and the title of the publication.

## literary agent

Somebody whose job is to negotiate publishing contracts, involving royalties, advances and rights sales on behalf of an author and who earns commission on the proceeds of the sales they negotiate.

## moral right

The right of people such as editors, authors or illustrators to have some say in the publication of a work to which they have contributed, even if they do not own the copyright.

## out of print or o.p.

Relating to a book of which the publisher has no copies left and which is not going to be reprinted. Print on demand technology, however, means that a book can be kept 'in print' indefinitely.

## packager

A company that creates a finished book for a publisher.

## PDF/pdf

Portable Document Format. A data file generated from PostScript that is platform-independent, application-independent and font-independent. Acrobat is Adobe's suite of software used to generate, edit and view pdf files.

## picture researcher

A person who looks for pictures relevant to a particular topic, so that they can be used as illustrations in, for example, a book, newspaper or TV programme.

## prelims

The initial pages of a book, including the title page and table of contents, which precede the main text. Also called front matter.

## pre-press

Before a book goes to press.

## print on demand or POD

The facility to print and bind a small number of books at short notice, without the need for a large print run, using digital technology. When an order comes through, a digital file of the book can be printed individually and automatically.

## production controller

A person in the production department of a publishing company who deals with printers and other suppliers.

## proofreader

A person whose job is to proofread texts to check typeset page presentation and text for errors and to mark up corrections.

## publisher

A person or company that publishes books, magazines and/or newspapers.

## publisher's agreement

A contract between a publisher and the copyright holder, author, agent or another publisher, which lays down the terms under which the publisher will publish the book for the copyright holder.

## publishing contract

An agreement between a publisher and an author by which the author grants the publisher the right to publish the work against payment of a fee, usually in the form of a royalty.

## reading fee

Money paid to somebody for reading a manuscript and commenting on it.

## recto

Relating to the right-hand page of a book, usually given an odd number.

## reprint

Copies of a book made from the original, but with a note in the publication details of the date of reprinting and possibly a new title page and cover design.

## rights

The legal right to publish something such as a book, picture or extract from a text.

## rights manager

A person who negotiates and coordinates rights sales (e.g. for subsidiary, translation or foreign rights). Often travels to book fairs to negotiate rights sales.

## royalty

Money paid to a writer for the right to use his or her property, usually a percentage of sales or an agreed amount per sale.

## royalty split

The way in which a royalty is divided between several authors or between author and illustrator.

## royalty statement

A printed statement from a publisher showing how much royalty is due to an author.

## sans serif

A style of printing letters with all lines of equal thickness and no serifs. Sans faces are less easy to read than seriffed faces and they are rarely used for continuous text, although some magazines use them for text matter.

## sensitivity reader

Assesses a manuscript with a particular issue of representation in mind, usually one that they have personal experience of.

## serialisation

Publication of a book in parts in a magazine or newspaper.

## serif

A small decorative line added to letters in some fonts; a font that uses serifs, such as Times. The addition of serifs keeps the letters apart while at the same time making it possible to link one letter to the next, and makes the letters distinct, in particular the top parts which the reader recognises when reading.

## slush pile

Unsolicited manuscripts which are sent to publishers or agents, and which may never be read.

## style sheet

A guide listing all the rules of house style for a publishing company which has to be followed by authors and editors.

## sub-editor

A person who corrects and checks articles in a newspaper before they are printed.

## subsidiary rights

Rights other than the right to publish a book in its first form, e.g. paperback rights; rights to adapt the book; rights to serialise it in a magazine; film and TV rights; audio, ebook, foreign and translation rights.

## territory

Areas of the world where the publisher has the rights to publish or can make foreign rights deals.

## trade discount

A reduction in price given to a customer in the same trade, as by a publisher to another publisher or to a bookseller.

## trade paperback (B format)

A paperback edition of a book that is superior in production quality to a mass-market paperback edition and is similar to a hardback in size 198 x 129mm.

## trim size or trimmed size

The measurements of a page of a book after it has been cut, or of a sheet of paper after it has been cut to size.

## typesetter

A person or company that 'sets' text and prepares the final layout of the page for printing. It can also now involve XML tagging for ebook creation.

## typographic error or typo

A mistake made when keying text or typesetting.

## verso

The left-hand page of a book, usually given an even number.

## volume rights

The right to publish the work in hardback or paperback (this can now sometimes include ebook).

## XML tagging

Inserting tags into the text that can allow it to be converted for ebooks or for use in electronic formats.

# Publishing services for independent authors

This is a selection of the expanding list of companies that offer editorial, production, marketing and distribution support predominantly (but not exclusively) for authors who want to publish independently. As with all the organisations mentioned in the *Yearbook*, we recommend that you check carefully what companies offer and their fees; also be aware of any minimum commitment requirements. A longer list of companies and individuals who provide similar services is included in our subscription service: www.writersandartists.co.uk/shop/subscriptions.

POD = print on demand

## Amolibros

Loundshay Manor Cottage, Preston Bowyer, Milverton, Somerset TA4 1QF
*tel* (01823) 401527
*email* amolibros@aol.com
*website* www.amolibros.com
*Director* Jane Tatam

Services include print and ebook design, production, copy-editing and distribution through online retailers. Sales and marketing services include design and production of adverts, leaflets, author websites, distribution of press releases and direct mail campaigns.

## Blue Elephant Storyshaping

*email* hello@blueelephantstoryshaping.com
*website* www.blueelephantstoryshaping.com
*Director* Natascha Biebow MBE

Offers professional, bespoke editorial and project management services for picture book creators (authors and author/illustrator teams) who wish to self-publish. Includes storyshaping from idea to finished, print-ready PDF, including text shaping and editing, development of roughs to final artwork cover concept and copy, marketing pitch and final proofread. Authors can collaborate with an experienced picture book expert to create their envisaged book. See website for full details of services available.

## Blue Falcon Publishing

The Mill, Pury Hill Business Park, Alderton Road, Towcester, Northants NN12 7LS
*tel* 07955 002040
*email* books@bluefalconpublishing.co.uk
*website* www.bluefalconpublishing.co.uk
*Facebook* www.facebook.com/bluefalconpublishing
*Twitter* @bluefalconpub
*Instagram* @bluefalconpub

Small independent company publishing children's fiction books with a focus on high-quality, personal service. Services include: editing; typesetting; publishing and ebook production. See website for package and individual service prices.

## BookPrinting UK

Remus House, Coltsfoot Drive, Woodston, Peterborough PE2 9BF
*tel* (01733) 898102
*email* info@bookprintinguk.com
*website* www.bookprintinguk.com
*Twitter* @BookPrintingUK

Colour and b&w printing and POD books in a range of bindings. Can provide custom illustration and interior layout options, as well as typesetting. Supplies templates for formatting manuscript files before sending. Can also distribute print books direct to customers. Prints bookmarks, posters and flyers.

## eBook Versions

27 Old Gloucester Street, London WC1N 3AX
*website* www.ebookversions.com
*Proprietor* John Ransley

Offers ebook, paperback, hardback and audiobook self-publishing and distribution through Amazon Kindle Direct Publishing, Barnes & Noble, Google Play Book Store, IngramSpark, iTunes and Kobo Books. Fees begin at £95 for ebook conversion of a manuscript of up to 100,000 words. POD paperback and hardback pre-press production is available from £295, and audiobook production from £195. OCR scanning of hardbacks, paperbacks and typescripts is also offered

## Frank Fahy Publishing Services

5 Barna Village Centre, Barna, Co. Galway, H91 DF24, Republic of Ireland
*tel* +353 (0)86 2269330
*email* frank.fahy0@gmail.com
*website* https://frankfahypublishing.wordpress.com/

Specialises in preparing manuscripts for book production, either as printed books or digital ebooks. This can include, as required, copy-editing and/or proofreading, or preparing presentations for submission to publishers. Estimates are free of charge and authors' individual requirements discussed. Publishing projects of all kinds considered, from individuals, institutions or businesses. Founded 2007.

## Grosvenor House Publishing

Link House, 140 The Broadway, Tolworth, Surrey KT6 7HT
tel 020-8339 6060
website www.grosvenorhousepublishing.co.uk
Facebook www.facebook.com/
GrosvenorHousePublishing
Founder Kim Cross

Publishes across a range of genres including children's and non-fiction in colour, b&w, POD, paperback, hardback and ebook formats. Offers a £795 publishing package which includes typesetting and five free print copies as well as an ISBN, and print and ebook distribution via online retailers. Marketing services include producing posters and postcards, and website set-up from template with two years' hosting. Ebook publishing costs £195 if the print edition of the book has been produced by the company and £495 otherwise. Print costs and royalties depend on book specification. A proofreading service is offered at a rate of £5 per 1,000 words. See website for full list of costs.

## Jelly Bean Self-Publishing

Candy Jar Ltd, Mackintosh House, 136 Newport Road, Cardiff CF24 1DJ
tel 029-211 57202
email submissions@jellybeanselfpublishing.co.uk
website www.jellybeanselfpublishing.co.uk
Twitter @Jelly_BeanUK
Director Shaun Russell

Self-publishing imprint of Candy Jar Books. Services include editing, typesetting, illustration, cover design, website design, audiobook production and marketing support. Can accommodate authors of various genres, budgets and timetables. Welsh Self-Publisher of the Year 2020. Founded 2012.

## Kindle Direct Publishing

website https://kdp.amazon.com
Facebook www.facebook.com/KindleDirectPublishing
Twitter @AmazonKDP

Ebook self-publishing and distribution platform for Kindle and Kindle Apps. Its business model offers up to a 70% royalty (on certain retail prices between $2.99–$9.99) in many countries and availability in Amazon stores worldwide. POD options are also available. Note that KDP Select makes books exclusive to Amazon (which means they cannot be sold through an author's personal website, for example), but authors can share in the Global Fund amount every time the book is borrowed from the Kindle Owners' Lending Library.

## Kobo Writing Life

email writinglife@kobo.com
website www.kobo.com/p/writinglife
Facebook www.facebook.com/KoboWritingLife
Twitter @kobowritinglife
Instagram @kobo.writing.life

Ebook self-publishing platform where authors can upload manuscripts and cover images. These files are then converted into ebooks before being distributed through the Kobo Store. Authors are able to set pricing and DRM territories, as well as track sales. Royalty rates vary depending on price or territory; enquire directly. Free to join. Owned by Rakuten.

## Little Steps

Vicarage House, 58–60 Kensington Church Street, London W8 4DB
email info@littlestepspublishing.co.uk
website www.littlestepspublishing.co.uk
Facebook www.facebook.com/littlestepspublishinguk
Instagram @littlestepspublishinguk

Provides a complete service for the aspiring children's author, including printing, design, marketing, editing, proofreading, public relations, production and distribution. Authors invest financially in their own books, entitling them to receive majority royalties. Founded in the UK 2019; has been operating for over 10 years in Australia.

## Manuscripts & Mentoring

25 Corinne Road, London N19 5EZ
tel 07973 300276
email manuscriptmentoring@gmail.com
website www.genevievefox.com
Twitter @genevievefox21
Contact Genevieve Fox

Helps both fledgling and experienced writers of fiction, non-fiction, memoir and YA fiction get from first draft to finished manuscript. Primary services include editing, manuscript overviews as well as advice on structure, plot, themes and characterisation. One-to-one tutoring, mentoring and coaching, writing plans, ghostwriting; and creative writing courses also available. Genevieve Fox is a published author and holds a doctorate in Creative Writing.

## Matador

Troubador Publishing Ltd, Unit E2, Airfield Business Park, Harrison Road, Market Harborough, Leics. LE16 7UL
tel 0116 279 2299
email books@troubador.co.uk
website www.troubador.co.uk/matador
Facebook www.facebook.com/matadorbooks
Twitter @matadorbooks
Managing Director Jeremy Thompson, Operations Director Jane Rowland

Self-publishing imprint of Troubador Publishing. Offers POD, short-run digital- and litho-printed books as well as audiobooks and ebook production, with distribution through high-street bookshops and online retailers. Also worldwide ebook distribution. Author services include all book, ebook and audiobook production, trade and retail marketing, plus bookshop distribution and sales representation by Star Book Sales. Founded 1999.

## MJV Literary Author Services

71–75 Shelton Street, London WC2H 9JQ
*email* authors@mjvliterary.com
*website* www.mjvliterary.com
*Contact* Matt McAvoy

Offers professional proofreading, copy-editing and beta-reading services for self-published and traditionally published authors of all genres, including fiction, non-fiction and children's books, as well as a popular ebook and KDP-ready Kindle-book creation service, at $49. As part of the company's #ReturnToRealBooks campaign, KDP-formatted print-ready typesetting is offered free with all proofreading and copy-editing instructions. Other services include translation into English with full copy-editing, for non-English language authors. Editing services start from $6.95 per 1,000 words, and all instructions include two human editor passes and software checks as standard. Trees planted with every job.

## Peahen Publishing

*tel* 0117 427 0126
*email* info@peahenpublishing.com
*website* www.peahenpublishing.com
*Twitter* @peahenbooks
*Instagram* @peahenbooks
*Contact* Carly Corlett

Produces a range of titles for independent authors, from picture books to rhyming books, YA novels to short story collections. Authors are guided through the publishing process, from initial manuscript consultation to choosing an illustrator, from paper and font selection to delivering bookshelf-ready books. No minimum print run. Founded 2015.

## PublishNation

Suite 544, Kemp House, 152 City Road, London EC1V 2NX
*email* david@publishnation.co.uk
*website* www.publishnation.co.uk
*Publisher* David Morrison

Offers POD paperback and Kindle format ebooks, available through Amazon. Publication in both print and digital formats costs £325 or £175 for Kindle format. Images may be included from £3.95 each. A range of book sizes is available, as are free template book covers. Enhanced cover design costs £40. Marketing services include creation of a press release, social media accounts and author website. Standard proofreading is £8 per 1,000 words, while an 'express' option from £125 focuses on the beginning of the manuscript. Editorial critique reports range in price from £99 for manuscripts of up to 15,000 words to £219 for manuscripts of up to 120,000 words.

## The Joey Quince Editorial and Ghostwriting Agency

17 Carlton House Terrace, London SW1Y 5AH
*tel* 07396 344505
*email* joey@jq-agency.co.uk
*website* www.jq-agency.co.uk
*Editor* Joey Quince

Provides a range of services, taking authors from initial idea to final product across multiple genres including fiction, business and academic books, children's writing, memoir and sport. Founded 2019.

## SilverWood Books

14 Small Street, Bristol BS1 1DE
*tel* 0117 910 5829
*email* enquiries@silverwoodbooks.co.uk
*website* www.silverwoodbooks.co.uk
*Twitter* @SilverWoodBooks
*Publishing Director* Helen Hart

Complete self-publishing service for adult and children's books (including picture books), from manuscript feedback to editing and proofreading, professional cover and page design, typesetting, ebook hand-formatting and conversion, b&w and colour POD, short-run and lithographic printing, one-to-one support and coaching. Distributes to bookshops via wholesalers and to online retailers including Amazon. See website for price information.

## The Stardust Experience

*email* alex@thestardustexperience.com
*website* www.thestardustexperience.com
*Facebook* www.facebook.com/thestardustexperience
*Instagram* @the.stardust.experience
*Creative Director* Alex Peart-Johnson

Works with both traditionally published writers and independent authors around the world, providing a range of ghostwriting services for children's books, including idea creation, outlining, developmental editing, writing picture books and writing chapter books. Editorial support also available. Prices start from £195 for 250 words; see website for cost estimates depending on requirements.

## WRITERSWORLD

2 Bear Close Flats, Bear Close, Woodstock, Oxon OX20 1JX
*tel* 0800 121 4960
*email* enquiries@writersworld.co.uk
*website* www.writersworld.co.uk
*Founder & Owner* Graham Cook

Specialises in self-publishing, POD books and book reprints. Also issues ISBNs on behalf of authors, pays them 90% of the royalties and supplies them with copies of their books at print cost. Worldwide book distribution. Founded 2000.

# Children's writing courses and conferences

Contact your local library, college or university for further information about the courses that might be most suited to you and the stage you are at with your writing. While many courses are now going ahead in person once more, some may have an online component.

## Blue Elephant Storyshaping

*email* hello@blueelephantstoryshaping.com
*website* www.blueelephantstoryshaping.com
*Editor, Coach and Mentor* Natascha Biebow MBE

Offers one-to-one coaching, individual manuscript reviews and marketing advice to writers and author/illustrators of picture books up to middle grade fiction. The Cook Up a Picture Book online course offers coaching and mentoring, and is aimed at picture-book writers who wish to fine-tune their work, plus illustrators who would like to write and illustrate. The Small-Group Coaching Course is a six-week course featuring weekly, one-to-one detailed editorial feedback and top tips on key aspects of picture book craft and publishing. The aim is to create at least one marketable picture book. There is the opportunity to submit to an editor or agent at the end of this course. See website for full details of services available.

## Curtis Brown Creative

Cunard House, 15 Regent Street, London SW1Y 4LR
*tel* 020-7393 4201
*email* help@curtisbrowncreative.co.uk
*website* www.curtisbrowncreative.co.uk
*Facebook* www.facebook.com/CurtisBrownCreative
*Twitter* @cbcreative
*Instagram* @curtisbrowncreative

Creative writing school offering courses in London and online. Over 200 students to date have subsequently signed publishing deals; alumni include Bonnie Garmus, Kirsty Capes, Alex Hay and Julia Armfield. Subjects covered include fiction, memoirs, short stories, screenwriting and children's picture books. Curtis Brown Creative also runs the Breakthrough Writers' Programme, which offers free courses, mentoring and scholarships for under-represented writers.

## The Federation of Children's Book Groups Conference

*email* info@fcbg.org.uk
*website* www.fcbg.org.uk/conference
*Facebook* www.facebook.com/fcbgnews
*Twitter* @FCBGnews
*Takes place* April

Held annually, guest speakers include well-known children's authors as well as experts and publishers in the field of children's books. Publishers also exhibit their newest books and resources.

## The Golden Egg Academy

The Wool House, 6 Cork Street, Frome, Somerset BA11 1BL
*email* info@goldeneggacademy.co.uk
*website* www.goldeneggacademy.co.uk
*Twitter* @TheGEAcademy
*Founder and Managing Director* Imogen Cooper

Runs writing courses for authors who want to develop their writing to publication standard. All courses are run online and include: Write Your Successful Children's Novel; Writing for Children and Young Adults; Work on Your Novel; How to be a Picture Book Writer; and Writing Picture Books for Young Children. Selective courses comprise virtual workshops, one-to-one editorial surgeries and regular online group seminars.

Students also have the opportunity to meet industry professionals and benefit from presentations by some of the best writers in their field. Middle Grade and Young Adult fiction writers enjoy an exclusive non-binding 'First Look' deal with Chicken House; Lower Middle Grade with Scholastic/Chicken House and Young Series Fiction with Nosy Crow; picture book writers with Andersen Press. Also runs the Golden Egg Award for BAME, LGBTQ+, disabled and financially disadvantaged groups.

## IBBY Congress

Nonnenweg 12, CH-4055-Basel, Switzerland
*tel* +41 61-272 2917
*email* ibby@ibby.org
*website* www.ibbycongress2022.org
*Twitter* @IBBYINT

IBBY's biennial international congresses bring together IBBY (the International Board on Books for Young People) members and other people involved in children's books and reading development from all over the world. The congresses are excellent occasions to make contacts, exchange ideas and open horizons. Every two years a different National Section hosts the Congress. Several hundred people attend the lectures, panel discussions, seminar sessions and workshops on current congress themes. An IBBY International

Congress also serves as a framework not only for the General Assembly and other meetings, but also for the presentation of different exhibitions and celebrations such as the Hans Christian Andersen Awards and the IBBY Honour List.

## Jericho Writers

Box 321, 266 Banbury Road, Oxford OX2 7DL
tel 0345 459 9560 / +1 646-974-9060 (US)
email info@jerichowriters.com
website https://jerichowriters.com
Twitter @JerichoWriters
Instagram @JerichoWriters
Founder Harry Bingham

Inclusive online writing organisation offering editorial services and events for all genres, including writing for children, and tutored courses. Also available: guidance for self-publishers, masterclasses, AgentMatch (a database of over 1,000 literary agents), a free community for writers to connect, and expert guides to writing and publishing. See website for information on Festival of Writing.

## The London School of Journalism

tel 020-7432 8140
email admin@lsjournalism.com
website www.lsj.org/courses/distance-learning/writing-for-children

Part of the School's distance learning programme, the year-long Writing for Children course guides the writer as they work in their chosen genre, including picture books, story books, early readers, teenage fiction, activity books, non-fiction and books for the education market. Students will learn how to construct a story that children will enjoy reading, including how to create believable characters and realistic dialogue.

## Oxford University Short Courses

Oxford University Department of Continuing Education, Rewley House, 1 Wellington Square, Oxford OX1 2JA
tel (01865) 270360
email enquiries@conted.ox.ac.uk
website www.conted.ox.ac.uk
Contact Day School Administrator

Online and in-person creative writing courses including Writing for Young Adults and Writing for Children. Courses range from day schools to weekly learning programmes.

## SCBWI-BI Annual Conference and Masterclass Series

email scbwi@scbwi.org
website https://britishisles.scbwi.org/conference
website www.scbwi.org
Twitter @scbwi
Instagram @scbwi_british_isles
Contacts Natascha Biebow and Alison Gardiner

Annual series of author masterclasses, fiction and picture book retreats and conference, offering a mix of craft-based seminars, industry professional one-to-ones, inspiration and networking opportunities for writers and author/illustrators, both published and unpublished. Check website for information on future events.

## SCBWI-BI Writers' Events

email araevents@britishscbwi.org
website https://britishisles.scbwi.org/events
Twitter @scbwi
Instagram @scbwi_british_isles

Online listings of retreats and other writing and literary events across the UK organised by the Society of Children's Book Writers and Illustrators.

## Swanwick, The Writers' Summer School

Hayes Conference Centre, Swanwick, Derbyshire DE55 1AU
tel (01290) 552248
email secretary@swanwickwritersschool.org.uk
website www.swanwickwritersschool.org.uk
Facebook www.facebook.com/SwanwickWriters
Twitter @swanwickwriters

Extensive choice of courses, talks and workshops. Offers several highly subsidised places for writers aged between 18 and 30, and assistance for writers unable to afford the full course fee. Full details of the programme and information on how to apply for the TopWrite Programme and Assisted Places Scheme are available on the website.

## Tŷ Newydd Writing Centre

Tŷ Newydd, Llanystumdwy, Criccieth, Gwynedd LL52 0LW
tel (01766) 522811
email tynewydd@literaturewales.org
website www.tynewydd.wales
Twitter @ty_newydd

Residential creative writing courses for writers of all abilities over the age of 16. Courses cover everything from poetry and popular fiction to writing for the theatre and developing a novel for young adults. No qualifications are necessary; staff can advise on the suitability of courses. Also offers courses for schools, corporate courses and awaydays for companies. Tŷ Newydd is home to Nant, the writers' retreat cottage located on site. Run by Literature Wales, the national organisation for the development of literature in Wales.

## Writers & Artists

Bloomsbury Publishing plc, 50 Bedford Square, London WC1B 3DP
tel 020-7631 5985
email writersandartists@bloomsbury.com
website www.writersandartists.com
Facebook www.facebook.com/WritersArtistsYearbook

Publishing advice and resources

*Contacts* James Rennoldson, Clare Povey, Amelia Brown

Hosts online and offline masterclasses, conferences and writing courses throughout the year. Masterclasses and conferences are run independently or in collaboration with literary festivals, universities and charities such as Book Aid International, Literature Works and the Open University. A series of events dedicated to writing and illustrating books for children and young adults is held in March each year. Online writing courses – which cover a variety of genres – take place on weekday evenings.

Also offers a range of editing services, and works regularly with literary agents to provide guidance on the submission process. The W&A platform is free to join, contains hundreds of writing and publishing advice articles, and offers a lively community area and personalisation features.

## UNIVERSITY COURSES

### Bath Spa University
Newton Park, Newton St Loe, Bath BA2 9BN
*tel* (01225) 876180
*email* admissions@bathspa.ac.uk
*website* www.bathspa.ac.uk/courses/course-index-a-z/

Offers a variety of postgraduate courses on subjects including Creative Writing, Writing for Young People, Travel and Nature Writing, Scriptwriting, and Children's Publishing.

### University of Central Lancashire
School of Arts and Media,
University of Central Lancashire, Preston PR1 2HE
*tel* (01772) 893364
*email* mstuart1@uclan.ac.uk
*website* www.uclan.ac.uk

Offers MA Children's Book Illustration, a taught master's course which explores the practice of illustration for children's picture and story books, including graphic novels and other formats for children's publishing. The course is designed to encourage the pursuit of a unique and personal line of research into an artist's chosen area of children's book illustration. Many graduates have gone on to careers as published illustrators. The course runs both full and part time.

### University of Chichester
Bishop Otter Campus, College Lane, Chichester,
West Sussex PO19 6PE
*tel* (01243) 816000
*email* h.frey@chi.ac.uk
*email* h.dunkerley@chi.ac.uk
*website* www.chi.ac.uk
*Contacts* Professor Hugo Frey (Head of Department), Professor Hugh Dunkerley (MA Creative Writing Programme Coordinator)

Offers BA, MA and PhD Creative Writing. Students work with practising writers. Specialisms include: novels, short stories, creative non-fiction, writing for children, screenwriting and poetry. Hosts regular visits by high-profile writers, editors and agents. Visiting professors: Kate Mosse and Alison MacLeod. Many students go on to publish and win prizes.

### University of Cumbria
Fusehill Street, Carlisle CA1 2HH
*tel* 0808 291 6578
*email* enquirycentre@cumbria.ac.uk
*website* www.cumbria.ac.uk/study/courses/postgraduate/literature-romanticism-and-the-english-lake-district
*Facebook* www.facebook.com/universityofcumbria
*Twitter* @CumbriaUni

Courses offered include MA Literature, Romanticism and the English Lake District.

### University of London, Goldsmiths
Goldsmiths, University of London,
London SE14 6NW
*tel* 020-7919 7171
*website* www.gold.ac.uk
*Facebook* www.facebook.com/GoldsmithsUoL
*Twitter* @GoldsmithsUoL
*Instagram* @goldsmithsuol

Postgraduate courses include Artists' Film and Moving Image, Art Psychotherapy, Art and Ecology, Arts and Learning, Black British Literature, Children's Literature, Children's Book Illustration, Computational Arts, Computer Games Art and Design, Creative and Life Writing, Creative Writing and Education, Curating, Digital Media, Dramaturgy and Writing for Performance, Film and Screen Studies, Filmmaking, Fine Art, Journalism, Performance Making, Radio, Script Writing and Translation.

### The Manchester Writing School at Manchester Metropolitan University
Grosvenor East Building, Cavendish Street,
Manchester M15 6BG
*tel* 0161 247 2000
*email* writingschool@mmu.ac.uk
*website* www.mmu.ac.uk/english/mcr-writing-school
*Twitter* @McrWritingSchl
*Creative Director* Professor Carol Ann Duffy, *Contact (admission and general enquiries)* James Draper

Courses offered include Master of Fine Arts (MFA) and Master of Arts (MA) in Creative Writing with specialist routes in Novel, Poetry, Writing for Children & Young Adults, Scriptwriting and Creative Non-Fiction. Campus-based and international online distance learning, available to study full-time (MA: one year, MFA: two years) or part-time (MA: two years; MFA: three years). September and January enrolment. Scholarships available (including Joyce

Nield Fund for non-UK Commonwealth students). Evening taught, with strong industry links. MFA students complete a full-length book/script. MA in Publishing presented in collaboration with the iSchool at Manchester Met and industry partners. PhD in Creative Writing, including PhD by practice.

## Nottingham Trent University

School of Arts and Humanities, Clifton Lane, Nottingham NG11 8NS
*tel* 0115 848 4200
*email* rory.waterman@ntu.ac.uk
*email* hum.enquiries@ntu.ac.uk
*website* www.ntu.ac.uk/course/english-linguistics-creative-writing
*Twitter* @ntuhum
*Programme Leader* Dr Rory Waterman

Offers a long-established and practice-based MA Creative Writing. Close links to the writing industry, an annual anthology, a programme of guest talks and workshops and many successful graduate writers. Diverse module options include: Fiction, Poetry, Writing for Stage, Radio and Screen, and Children's and Young Adult Fiction.

## Plymouth Marjon University

Derriford Road, Plymouth, PL6 8BH
*tel* (01752) 636890
*email* admissions@marjon.ac.uk
*website* www.marjon.ac.uk/courses/ma-literature-for-children/
*Course Leader* Dr Leah Phillips

Offers MA Literature for Children and Young Adults, which includes creative writing modules.

## University of Roehampton

Grove House, Roehampton Lane, London SW15 5PJ
*tel* 020-8392 3000
*website* www.roehampton.ac.uk/postgraduate-courses/childrens-literature-distance-learning
*Facebook* www.facebook.com/roehamptonuni
*Twitter* @RoehamptonUni
*Instagram* @uni_roehampton

Postgraduate courses include Children's Literature.

## University of Southampton

Avenue Campus, Highfield Road, Southampton, Hampshire SO17 1BF
*tel* 023-8059 5000
*email* enquiries@southampton.ac.uk
*website* www.southampton.ac.uk/courses/creative-writing-masters-ma
*Course Leader* Carole Burns

Offers MA Creative Writing, and Publishing which includes modules on Writing for Children and Young People, Scriptwriting, Narrative Non-Fiction and Fiction Writing. Lecturers include writers Toby Litt, Philip Hoare, Rebecca Smith, Kevin Brazil, Devorah Baum and Carole Burns.

## University of Suffolk

Waterfront Building, 19 Neptune Quay, Ipswich IP4 1QJ
*tel* (01473) 338833
*email* Lindsey.Scott@uos.ac.uk
*website* www.uos.ac.uk/courses/pg/ma-creative-and-critical-writing
*Course Leader* Dr Lindsey Scott

The MA Creative and Critical Writing offers Children's Literature, a module focused on writing middle grade and young adult fiction. Other modules offered are Writing Historical Fiction, Adaptation, and Writers in Residence (residencies have included international art galleries, museums, and schools). A programme of events with industry professionals runs throughout the academic year, including the annual Children's Literature Festival.

**Publishing advice and resources**

# Copyright and contracts
## Copyright 101: top tips

Sarah Burton of the Society of Authors provides answers and advice for writers, illustrators and translators on copyright, with valuable tips on how to protect your work and avoid any pitfalls.

## 1. What is copyright, and what does 'in the public domain' mean?

Copyright is what allows you – whether you're an author, an illustrator or a translator – to control and make money from the exploitation of your work. A copyright owner has the exclusive right to copy the work, issue copies of the work to the public, rent or lend the work to the public, perform, show or play the work in public, communicate the work to the public, edit or adapt the work (including translation or dramatisation), sell or licence the copyright for use by others. Generally speaking, copyright in the UK lasts until 70 years after the end of the year of the creator's death. However, there are variations when it comes to unpublished or posthumously published works by older authors.

Copyright also gives you **moral rights**. You should check that your publishing contract upholds, rather than asks you to waive, your moral rights. These include:

• The right to be named as the author, translator or illustrator of your work. This right needs to be asserted in writing.

• The right to object to derogatory treatment, which means no one can distort or mutilate your work. In essence, significant changes cannot be made without your consent.

• The right of false attribution. This protects you from being named as the author of a work you did not create.

• There is also the moral right of privacy if someone is easily identifiable in a photograph or still from a film, taken for private purposes.

In the context of copyright, a work that is **in the public domain** is out of copyright and therefore can be freely used by anyone. Be careful when it comes to older works, though; for example, an old work that is out of copyright in the UK might still be protected in the USA.

## 2. Can I use quotations or images from other writers in my book?

You might wish to use a quotation as an epigram at the head of a chapter, for example, or include lyrics from a song, or lines from a poem, that a character recites. Be aware that you need to seek permission if you are using a 'substantial' amount of material from works that are in copyright. 'Substantial' is not defined in the Copyright Designs and Patents Act 1988 – but is a matter of fact and degree. It has often been said that the test is much more about quality than quantity. A short extract may be a vital part of a work. A few sentences taken from a long novel or biography are unlikely to constitute a 'substantial part', but a few lines of poetry may be. It can be helpful to imagine you are the rights holder – how would you feel about the proposed use?

There are some very specific circumstances, known as **copyright exceptions**, in which you can reproduce limited extracts from in-copyright works without consent, even if it's a substantial part.

You can quote without needing permission *if all of the following apply*:

• The use is 'fair dealing' (consider if the amount of the original being used is reasonable and appropriate, and whether you are affecting the market for the original work).

• The work you are quoting from has been previously published.

• You quote no more than is required by the specific purpose for which it is used.

• The use is genuinely for the purpose of quotation – for example in the context of criticism or review.

• You include proper acknowledgement (generally the title and author).

For a fuller explanation of fair dealing and copyright exceptions, the Society of Authors (SoA; see page 297) has a *Guide to Copyright Permissions* or you can find details on the Intellectual Property Office website (www.gov.uk/topic/intellectual-property/copyright).

If you are quoting from song lyrics or from films, some rights holders are notoriously rigorous about charging even for very short extracts, taking the view that any quotation, however short, is de facto 'substantial'. They often have deep pockets, can be litigious, and the fees they charge can be high. Even if they are overreaching, they are often large companies and you may wish to avoid a legal battle.

The use of an in-copyright work as an epigram is generally regarded as substantial because its use is decorative, rather than forming an integral part of the text, and it would not be considered fair dealing.

### 3. I'm a self-published author and want to use a famous painting on the cover for my book. Is that okay?

If you wish to reproduce an in-copyright painting on the cover of your book, you will need permission. If you find an image online of the painting you want to use, do not assume it's copyright-free. You should also be aware that if you find a photograph of a painting, that photograph will have its own separate copyright for which permission is required. Whether or not an image is still in copyright, its owner (be they an individual, museum, picture library) may deny access or charge a reproduction fee. Picture libraries sometimes also charge loan fees for temporary access to images under their control. Such fees are separate from and in addition to any consent needed from a copyright owner.

If you're considering using a photograph of an easily identifiable living individual, you should be aware that people have a legal right not to have their privacy unreasonably invaded and you won't be able to reproduce the photo without their consent. For more information on this subject, the SoA has a *Guide to Licensing Rights in Images*.

### 4. How do I protect my story from plagiarism? Can I trust an agent or publisher I submit to?

Your work is automatically protected by copyright as soon as it is written or recorded, but it makes sense to keep drafts and notes should you ever need to prove ownership. Standard advice used to be for authors to post a copy to themselves and keep it unopened; now that most authors will have date-stamped digital files, that is rarely necessary. However, if you're very uneasy, using the old-fashioned method will do no harm!

It's good practice always to mark your work with your name, the copyright symbol and the date when you submit. It's also sensible to make it clear you are submitting your work in strictest confidence. This means the recipient cannot share your work without your consent and gives you protection under the law of confidentiality. Remember: there is no copyright in an idea or facts per se, but only in the unique arrangement of words you use to express those ideas or facts. You should therefore be particularly mindful of confidentiality when submitting ideas that are not fully developed.

Do your homework on any agent or publisher you wish to submit work to, and be wary of any unsolicited approach. It can be difficult to distinguish between legitimate offers and scams. The SoA is always happy to advise authors on any offer they receive.

## 5. When do I need to clear permissions for quotations and images in my book? Who does this – the author or the publisher?

Many contracts make the author responsible both for clearing and paying for permissions, and whether that is fair and/or negotiable depends on the work in question. It may be possible to negotiate with a publisher for them to cover the cost, share the cost, or pay upfront and deduct a corresponding sum from your royalties. If it's your responsibility, allow as much time as possible, particularly as your contract may say you need to deliver clearances at the same time as your book. Some publishers' permissions departments operate on a 12-16 week turnaround.

## 6. What can I do if I have written to seek permission but there has been no response from the rights holder?

If you're seeking permission for use of published material, it is best to write first to the publisher of the original edition of the book. Most publishers' websites tell you how to contact the Permissions Department. If the original publisher does not control the rights, it should let you know who does. The website for Writers, Artists and Their Copyright Holders (https://norman.hrc.utexas.edu/watch) is a very helpful resource. And if you still cannot discover or get a response from the rights holder, see the Intellectual Property Office's online guidance on **diligent search** (www.gov.uk/government/publications/orphan-works-diligent-search-guidance-for-applicants).

## 7. How do I earn money from a translation of my book or if a TV programme is made based on my story?

Anyone wishing to translate and publish your book in another language, or to create a TV, film or stage adaptation of your work, will need an agreement with you to do so and we would expect the terms of that agreement to include payment.

If you have granted translation rights and dramatisation rights to your publisher, they will handle any such deal on your behalf and split the income with you in the proportions agreed in your publishing contract. If you have retained the rights, either you or your agent (if you have one) will negotiate the deal directly. Members are welcome to consult the SoA on any proposed agreement.

## 8. My stories for 8-10 year-olds are retellings of fairy stories – do I need permission from anywhere to 'use' these original tales?

Very old tales, such as those first collected and published by Charles Perrault in the 17th century and the Brothers Grimm in the 19th century, are now out of copyright. But, as the nature of a fairy tale is to evolve each time someone writes it down, be careful you are not relying on an in-copyright version. An individual author's unique expression of a fairy tale will be protected, and permission is needed if you wish to reproduce a substantial amount of the text. Be mindful, too, of translations – even if the original work is out of copyright, a translation holds its own separate copyright and may still be protected.

## 9. If I forget to get permission to use a picture or quotation in my novel, will I be prosecuted?

You could be sued by a third party if you use a substantial amount of their in-copyright work without consent and therefore infringe their copyright. However, before taking legal action, any claimant must first take steps to settle the matter out of court. Anyone making a claim against you is usually entitled to claim the damage they have suffered by the infringement. Damages can be difficult to calculate, but typically they amount to the licence fee the claimant would have charged for authorised use; they could also include other sums, such as compensation for the loss of another contract due to the unauthorised use, or damage arising from the possibility of loss of reputation through a failure to credit the author.

For further information on what is a complex area, the SoA has a *Guide to Copyright Infringements* or see the online guidance provided by the Intellectual Property Enterprise Court (www.gov.uk/courts-tribunals/intellectual-property-enterprise-court).

## 10. I'm a YouTuber and use BookTok to advocate for children's books and reading. Do I need permission to read a(nother) writer's work online?

Yes, the usual rules apply: if you are reading a substantial amount of another author's work, you will need their permission to do so (or their publisher's, depending on who holds the relevant rights) unless you are confident that a copyright exception applies (see question 2 above).

This article is inevitably a brief summary of a very complex topic. Authors should also be aware of other potential danger areas, notably privacy, libel, trademarks and 'passing off'. The SoA's advisory team is always pleased to offer members confidential guidance on all business aspects of the writing profession.

**Sarah Burton** is head of the Contracts Advisory Team and senior publishing contracts advisor at the Society of Authors (https://societyofauthors.org), where she also handles literary estates.

### See also...
- *Copyright Licensing Agency Ltd*, page 405
- *DACS (Design and Artists Copyright Society)*, page 409
- *Society of Authors*, page 297

# Author–Publisher contracts

Publishing contracts can be lengthy; it's helpful to know what types of clauses they are likely to include and why they are there.

If you have an agent, they will negotiate your publishing contract on your behalf. Organisations such as the of the Society of Authors (see page 297) and WGGB (see page 300) offer contract review services. A contract is a legal agreement between two parties and exists to protect both author and publisher. It includes clauses on rights and obligations to avoid ambiguity as to the responsibilities of both parties. The clauses in your publishing contract are likely to include those listed below.

**Definitions** used throughout the contract will often be included at the beginning or in an appendix, and might include terms such as 'Net Receipts', 'Hybrid Product', 'First Serial', 'Territory' and 'Electronic Book'.

**Legal operation and enforcement** of the contract is covered by a few standard clauses, such as those relating to 'Interpretation', 'Arbitration', 'Confidentiality', 'Notices' and 'Entire Agreement'.

## Free to publish

The author confirms that they are able to enter into the agreement and that the book they are writing is a unique, new property, their own work and will not contain any legally compromising material. Note that the first example below indicates the style of legalese in which your contract is likely to be couched:

**Exclusivity** 'The Author hereby grants to the Publishers during the legal term of copyright the sole and exclusive licence to publish the said work in volume form.'

**Warranty and indemnity** are confirmed, meaning the author states that they are freely able to enter into the agreement, is the sole author, owns the rights in the 'work' and that it is unique, i.e. has not been published elsewhere previously. It also confirms the work does not contain any libellous or defamatory material or content that isn't the author's to include, i.e. that is someone else's copyright and that the author has cleared permissions with the copyright holder for any part of somebody else's work being reproduced in the book. The author agrees to cover any legal costs, other fees or losses if they are in any way in breach of the warranty.

## Territory

This is the geographical areas where the book can be sold, for example UK and Europe, or North American, or World territories.

## Rights

**Legal Term** is the period that the contract covers, from date of signature of the contract by both parties or until rights are reverted to the author.

**Granting and Reversion** is when an author agrees that the publisher is allowed to publish their Work during the legal term. Rights might revert (back to the author) automatically when sales dip below a minimum annual level, of say, 50 copies. An author may negotiate to have rights in their book reverted and will be able to purchase any remaining stock. At that stage the contract is also formally terminated.

**Termination** might also occur if either party breaches any of the terms of the contract, for example if the author fails to deliver a manuscript of the quality expected on time and if it is found to be plagiarised. Late delivery alone would not usually be grounds for termination, but an author should always inform the agent or publisher if a contracted delivery date cannot be fulfilled.

**Copyright Notice and Infringement** This covers how the author's name will appear in the book, i.e. © [name of author], 202X. These clauses confirm that copyright in the Work is the property of the author. They will also make it clear that, if the publisher decides to protect the copyright of a book insofar as it threatens the value of the rights sold to a publisher, the author will assist the publisher (at the publisher's expense).

**Subsidiary rights** include:
• Anthology and quotation rights
• Broadcast reading and audiobook rights
• Digital and electronic rights
• Dramatisation, film, documentary, television sound broadcasting video or other mechanical reproduction rights
• English language rights (royalty exclusive)
• First serial rights (e.g. in a magazine where an extract from an original Work is serialised or published)
• Large print, educational, reprint or paperback rights licensed to a book club or to another publisher
• Micrography reprography, merchandising and manufacturing rights
• Second serial rights (rights sold subsequent to the first serial rights, see above)
• Single-extract or digest or book condensation rights
• Translation rights (royalty exclusive)
• US rights (royalty exclusive)

Each set of rights will be subject to a royalty percentage, payable to the author when these rights have been exercised. Some rights are held back or retained by an agent or author, so they might be exploited at another time and be subject to negotiation with a third party after publication. These tend to be the potentially more lucrative rights if exploited, such as dramatisation and film, translation or audio. Some 'hybrid' authors will license print rights to a publisher but retain digital book rights to allow them to self-publish in that format; a contract would make clear in which territories each edition might be sold.

## Practicalities

**Delivery** includes a realistic delivery date and the specifications as to what will be delivered in what format (e.g. complete digital manuscript), to what extent (70,000 words including any endmatter) and accompanied by any material (extracts, quotations) for which copyright might need to be cleared.

## Payments

**Advances** are an example of financial goodwill, a pact that author and editor have cemented through the contract to agree to work together and to make money from the activity. It is usually paid in two or three equal tranches, payable on signature of the contract, on delivery and approval of the final manuscript, and on first publication. The advance against royalties means a payment made before any actual revenue from sales of a book have been received.

**Royalties** are the fees paid to an author on the sale of copies of their book and are subject to sliding scales, so that as a book becomes more successful an author benefits more. As more and more copies are sold the investment the publisher made in producing the first print run will be recouped; subsequent runs might become very profitable for the publisher and rightly an agent will argue for an author to profit from this success too. Such rising royalty rates for a published price contract might look something like this:

• **on home sales**: 7.5% of the published price on the first ten thousand (10,000) copies sold; 10% of the published price up to twenty thousand (20,000) copies sold and 12.5% of the published price on all copies sold thereafter, such royalty not to be deemed a precedent between the publishers and author or agent;

• **on home sales where the discount is 52.5% or more**: four-fifths (4/5ths) of the prevailing royalty; on home sales where the discount is 60% or more: three-fifths (3/5ths) of the prevailing rate.

**Free and presentation** copies will be provided to the author (anywhere between six and 15 free copies) on publication and to potential reviewers as part of a promotional campaign; royalty payments are not made against these gratis copies. Authors may purchase copies of their own book at discount.

**Payment process**, accounting periods and other details about how and when the publisher will remunerate the author (or their agent on the author's behalf) will be included.

## Publishing process

**Author corrections** and their proofreading responsibilities might be clearly laid out, covering what checking tasks an author will be expected to undertake and when and which might be carried out and paid for by the publisher, such as having an index prepared or clearing permissions for images or quotations. It might also include a clause in which the publisher 'reserves the right to charge the Author' for the cost of author corrections to page proofs if these are over and above the usual level of alterations. Such costs might be debited against the author's royalty account.

**Promotion** clauses advise that a publisher shall advertise, promote and market the Work as they deem appropriate 'in their sole discretion'. If an author feels strongly that they wish to be consulted about any aspect of promotion or cover design they could ask for such clauses to be modified. The most an author is likely to get is an amendment that agrees they will be 'consulted' and asked to 'agree' to the publisher's plan and that their agreement 'will not be unreasonably withheld'.

**Publication date** might not be firmly set when the contract is signed but the publisher's commissioning editor should have a clear idea of what quarter they would like the book to appear in. An agreement would usually stipulate that the book should be published within twelve months of date of delivery and acceptance 'unless prevented by circumstances over which they have no control or unless mutually agreed'.

**New and updated editions** for non-fiction titles might be referred to, defining what would constitute a 'new' rather than a 'revised' edition and how much new content it might include, say at least 10% new material. The author would be offered first refusal on preparing a new edition, but the publisher would want to include a clause to allow them to ask another writer to complete such a project if they perceived there was a market for it, but the original author was unable or unwilling to take on the commission.

The contract should not daunt an author. It is supposed to be a joint declaration and not biased in favour of one party or the other.

By **Alysoun Owen**, Editor of the *Writers' & Artists' Yearbook* and author of the *Writers' & Artists' Guide to Getting Published* (Bloomsbury 2019).

# Copyright Licensing Agency

The Copyright Licensing Agency (CLA) is a non-profit body established to help organisations to legally copy and share extracts from published works.

The CLA is recognised by the government (www.gov.uk/copyright-licensing-agency-licence) as the collective licensing body for the reuse of text and images from books, journals and magazines. More information on collective licensing bodies can be found at: www.gov.uk/guidance/licensing-bodies-and-collective-management-organisations.

It licenses on behalf of its four members: ALCS (the Authors' Licensing and Collecting Society), PLS (Publishers' Licensing Services), DACS (The Design and Artists Copyright Society) and PICSEL (Picture Industry Collecting Society for Effective Licensing).

CLA's licences permit limited copying, including photocopying, scanning and emailing of articles and extracts from books, journals and magazines, as well as digital copying from electronic publications, online titles and websites. CLA issues its licences to schools, further and higher education, businesses and government bodies. The money collected is distributed to the copyright owners to ensure that they are fairly rewarded for the use of their intellectual property. It gives licensees protection against the risk of copyright infringement and includes an indemnity against legal action, offering a simple solution to copyright compliance.

## How CLA helps creators and users of copyright work

CLA provides content users with access to millions of titles worldwide. In return, CLA ensures that creators, artists, photographers and writers, along with publishers, are paid royalties for the copying, sharing and re-use of limited extracts of their published work.

> **Further information**
>
> **Copyright Licensing Agency**
> 1 St Katharine's Way, London E1W 1UN
> *tel* 020-7400 3100
> *email* cla@cla.co.uk
> *website* www.cla.co.uk

Through this collective licensing system CLA provides users with the simplest and most cost-effective means of obtaining authorisation for the use of their work.

CLA has licences which enable digitisation of existing print material, enabling users to scan and electronically send extracts from print copyright works as well as copy digital electronic and online publications, including websites.

## Who is licensed?

CLA offers licences to three principal sectors:
• education (schools, further and higher education);
• government (central departments, local authorities, public bodies); and
• business (businesses, industry and the professions).

The licences meet the specific needs of each sector and user groups within each sector. Depending upon the requirement, there are both blanket and transactional licences available. Every licence allows copying from most print and digital books, journals, magazines and periodicals published in the UK.

Copyright and contracts

## The international dimension

Many countries have established equivalents to CLA and the number of such agencies is set to grow. Nearly all these agencies, including CLA, are members of the International Federation of Reproduction Rights Organisations (IFRRO).

Through reciprocal arrangements covering 38 overseas territories, including the USA, Canada and most EU countries, CLA's licences allow copying from an expanding list of international publications. CLA receives monies from these territories for the copying of UK material abroad, passing it on to UK rights holders.

## Distribution of licence fees

The fees collected from licensees are forwarded to ALCS, PLS, DACS and PISCEL for distribution to publishers, writers and visual artists. The allocation of fees is based on subscriptions, library holdings and detailed surveys of copying activity (see www.cla.co.uk/who-we-represent and read the 'Distribution Model Report'). CLA has collected and distributed over £1.5 billion as royalties to over 200,000 authors, publishers, and visual artists since 1983.

## Copyright made simple

The CLA exists to simplify copyright for content users and copyright owners. They help their customers to legally access, copy and share published content while making sure copyright owners are paid royalties for the use of their work.

Their rights, licences and innovative digital services (including the Digital Content Store for Higher Education; and the Education Platform for UK schools (www.educationplatform.co.uk)) make it easy for content users to use and manage digitalised content and digital versions of books. By doing so they simplify access to the work of 117,000 authors, 25,000 visual artists and 3,500 publishers and play an important part in supporting the creative industries.

# Authors' Licensing and Collecting Society

ALCS is the rights management society for UK writers.

ALCS is the largest writers' organisation in the UK with a membership of over 117,000. Between September 2022 and March 2023, ALCS paid their eligible members over £39.8 million (net) in royalties. Once you've paid your £36 lifetime membership fee, whatever you've earned in secondary royalties is paid into your bank account during twice yearly distributions. You can be part of this organisation which is committed to ensuring that writers' intellectual and moral rights are fully respected and fairly rewarded. ALCS represents all types of writers and includes educational, research and academic authors drawn from the professions, scriptwriters, adapters, playwrights, poets, editors and freelance journalists, across the print and broadcast media.

## Membership

**Authors' Licensing and Collecting Society Ltd**
6th Floor, International House, 1 St Katharine's Way, London E1W 1UN
*tel* 020-7264 5700
*email* alcs@alcs.co.uk
*website* www.alcs.co.uk
*Twitter* @ALCS_UK
*Chief Executive* Barbara Hayes

Membership is open to all writers and successors to their estates at a one-off fee of £36. Members of the Society of Authors, the Writers' Guild of Great Britain, National Union of Journalists, Chartered Institute of Journalists and British Association of Journalists have free membership of ALCS. Operations are primarily funded through a commission levied on distributions and membership fees. The commission on funds generated for Ordinary members is currently 10%. Most writers will find that this, together with a number of other membership benefits, provides good value.

Established in 1977, ALCS (a non-profit company) was set up in the wake of the campaign to establish a Public Lending Right (see page 369) to help writers protect and exploit their collective rights. The organisation now represents the interests of all UK writers and aims to ensure that they are fairly compensated for any works that are copied, broadcast or recorded.

Internationally recognised as a leading authority on copyright matters and authors' interests, ALCS is committed to fostering an awareness of intellectual property issues among the writing community. It maintains a close watching brief on all matters affecting copyright, both in the UK and internationally, and makes regular representations to the UK government and the European Union.

ALCS collects fees that are difficult, time-consuming or legally impossible for writers and their representatives to claim on an individual basis, money that is nonetheless due to them. To date, it has distributed over £600 million in secondary royalties to writers. Over the years, ALCS has developed highly specialised knowledge and sophisticated systems that can track writers and their works against any secondary use for which they are due payment. A network of international contacts and reciprocal agreements with foreign collecting societies also ensures that UK writers are compensated for any similar use overseas.

Copyright and contracts

The primary sources of fees due to writers are secondary royalties from the following:

## Photocopying and scanning

The single largest source of income, this is administered by the Copyright Licensing Agency (CLA; see page 405). Created in 1982 by ALCS and the Publishers' Licensing Services (PLS), CLA grants licences to users for copying books and serials. This includes schools, colleges, universities, central and local government departments, as well as the British Library, businesses and other institutions. Licence fees are based on the number of people who benefit and the number of copies made. The revenue from this is then split between the rights holders: authors, publishers and artists. Money due to authors is transferred to ALCS for distribution. ALCS also receives photocopying payments from foreign sources.

## Foreign Public Lending Right

The Public Lending Right (PLR) system pays authors whose books are borrowed from public libraries. Through reciprocal agreements, ALCS members receive payment through a number of overseas Public Lending Right (PLR) schemes, currently from Germany, Belgium, the Netherlands, France, Austria, Estonia and Ireland. Please note that ALCS does not administer the UK Public Lending Right; this is managed directly by the UK PLR Office (see page 369).

## Simultaneous cable retransmission

This involves the simultaneous showing of one country's television signals in another country, via a cable network. Cable companies pay a central collecting organisation a percentage of their subscription fees, which must be collectively administered. This sum is then divided by the rights holders. ALCS receives the writers' share for British programmes containing literary and dramatic material and distributes it to them.

## Educational recording

ALCS, together with the main broadcasters and rights holders, set up the Educational Recording Agency (ERA) in 1989 to offer licences to educational establishments. ERA collects fees from the licensees and pays ALCS the amount due to writers for their literary works.

Other sources of income include a blank tape levy and small, miscellaneous literary rights.

## Tracing authors

ALCS is dedicated to protecting and promoting authors' rights and enabling writers to maximise their income. It is committed to ensuring that royalties due to writers are efficiently collected and speedily distributed to them. One of its greatest challenges is finding some of the writers for whom it holds funds and ensuring that they claim their money.

Any published author or broadcast writer could have some funds held by ALCS for them. It may be a nominal sum or it could run into several thousand pounds. Either call or visit the ALCS website – see **Membership** box for contact details.

# DACS (Design and Artists Copyright Society)

Established by artists for artists, DACS is the UK's leading visual artists' rights management organisation.

DACS is the flagship rights management organisation for visual artists in the UK. Passionate about transforming the financial landscape for visual artists, DACS acts as a trusted broker for 180,000 artists worldwide.

DACS is a leading voice in campaigning for artists' rights, championing their

**Contact details**

**DACS**
33 Old Bethnal Green Road, London E2 6AA
*tel* 020-7336 8811
*email* info@dacs.org.uk
*website* www.dacs.org.uk
*Membership* Free to join

sustained and vital contribution to the creative economy. Through its services, DACS collects and distributes royalties to visual artists and their estates through Payback, Artist's Resale Right, Copyright Licensing and Artimage.

## Payback

Every year, DACS pays artists for the use of artworks that are published in UK books, magazines and shown on TV. If their artwork has been published or broadcast on television, artists could be entitled to a share of millions in royalties. DACS' latest distribution saw the annual Payback scheme pay thousands of artists and their representatives a share of over £4.6 million.

## Artist's Resale Right

The Artist's Resale Right is a royalty that is due when a work is resold by an art market professional for over €1,000 or the equivalent in pound sterling. DACS collects resale royalties and provide a quick, efficient payment service trusted by thousands of UK artists and estates. Artists can sign up as a member and DACS will monitor sales of artwork by auction houses, galleries and dealers and collect royalties on their behalf.

## Copyright Licensing and Artimage

DACS has over 35 years of experience helping artists generate income through the licensed use of their work. Its dedicated team collaborate with artists and leading brands to facilitate partnerships that both parties can be proud of, while making sure artists' rights are always protected.

Artimage is DACS' curated image platform, which makes available over 30,000 hi-res, artist or estate-approved images to a wide range of clients. Through Artimage DACS offers a wraparound service: putting licences in place, collecting royalty fees, and releasing quality image files.

## Additional Benefits for Members

DACS' Artist's Resale Right, Copyright licensing and Artimage members can all access DACS' Copyright Advice Service free of charge. This service includes advice and guidance about copyright matters and reviews of relevant sections in agreements. DACS also have a copyright enforcement service for licensing members which aims to protect artists' rights and artistic integrity by pursuing action when work is misused.

# Money, tax and benefits
## Managing your finances: a guide for writers

Chartered accountants Jonathan and Louise Ford of Writers Tax Limited set out a clear view of the various financial issues that a writer needs to understand and consider at each stage of their writing career, with helpful links and valuable advice.

In some ways the financial issues of being a writer are no different to pursuing any other occupation. You earn money for your skill, you deduct the costs you have incurred earning your money, and you pay tax on what's left. However, there are several factors that, in combination, make the situation of a writer unique; many writers have income from multiple sources, as well as overseas tax issues and matters concerning copyright.

We'll look at the different stages of a writer's career and the financial aspects you may need to consider as your career develops: 1) getting started – unpaid writing done for love not money; 2) paid writing often running alongside traditional employed income; 3) paid writing as main source of income; and 4) lifelong considerations.

## Stage 1: getting started

When you're at an early stage of your writing career and not earning any money from it, there is little you need to do to stay compliant. However, there are still some important things you can consider.

## Setting up a dormant limited company

If you are planning to write a book and you would like the royalty income of that book to be held in a limited company, then consider setting up a company even before you start writing. This will allow you to write the book on behalf of your company. If you wait to set the company up until the book is complete, and publishers are interested, then you

### Do I need an accountant?

If your financial situation is straightforward, there may be no need for you to appoint an accountant. If you are employed, then PAYE usually does a reasonable job of collecting the right amount of tax. Your writing income may be quite modest so it should be straightforward to deal with and – if the numbers are not very big – it may not cause too many issues if you get things wrong. To help you as your career develops, a good accountant can do the following:

- Deal with HMRC on your behalf;
- Submit your tax returns on time, so you don't get penalties for being late;
- Make sure you are claiming for the things you can claim for (and not claiming for things you shouldn't);
- Advise you on ways of saving tax legitimately;
- Help you to keep your records accurately;
- Help you to avoid nasty surprises and unexpected tax bills;
- Be on hand for all your tax-related questions.

Anybody can call themselves an accountant, even if they have no qualifications or experience. Try to choose someone who is a member of a professional accountancy body, such as ICAEW, ICAS, AAT, ACCA or CIOT. It is also worth getting recommendations from other writers. Social media groups can be a useful source when looking for accountants who act for lots of writers and understand their needs.

would have to transfer the copyright of the book to the company at market value; this could cause issues in terms of valuing the copyright and can create a tax problem that could have been avoided. To decide whether this is right for you, you need to weigh up the cost and hassle of having a dormant limited company against the possible future advantages.

## Creative averaging

There are a number of conditions you need to satisfy to be eligible for creative averaging; more details are available on HMRC Helpsheet HS234. One such condition is that you cannot use your first year of trading as part of any creative averaging calculation. Using the example given in the box, Theo would need to be submitting information to HMRC about his writing business from the 2019/20 tax year to be able to claim Creative averaging in 2021/22.

## Loss relief against other income

It is possible for a sole trader to make a loss and to set that loss against other income. This can be beneficial for tax reasons. For example, if an author makes a loss of £5,000 and they also have *employed income* of £30,000, they could offset the £5,000 loss against their employed income so that they only have to pay tax on £25,000. To be able to offset losses against other income, you need to be able to show HMRC that the loss has been incurred on a commercial basis with a view to making a profit. A vague idea that one day you might write a book on Greece would not be sufficient evidence to get a tax deduction on the costs of your holiday.

> ### Creative averaging example
>
> Theo earns nothing in the tax year 2020/21 while he is writing his novel.
>
> In 2021/22 his book is published and he makes a profit of £30,000. Without creative averaging his tax bill in 2020/21 would be nothing, but in 2021/22 he would owe £3,486 income tax and £1,997.48 in National Insurance – a total of £5,483.48.
>
> If he elects to use creative averaging, his £30,000 profit would be split across both tax years, giving him a total tax bill of £1,153.60 in 2020/21 and of £1,133.48 in 2021/22. By choosing to use creative averaging, Theo would have saved £3,194.40 over the two tax years.

## Pre-trading expenses

If you haven't been reporting expenditure to HMRC as losses, then it is still possible to get tax relief for 'pre-trading expenditure'. The relief allows you to claim for expenditure incurred within seven years of starting to trade and, in effect, gives tax relief as if it was incurred on the first day of trading. The 'wholly and exclusive' rule will still apply, so it is important to be able to link the expenditure you are claiming to the income you are receiving. The stronger the link, the more likely HMRC are to accept it. In order to maximise any possible pre-trading expenditure claim, it is important to try and keep records and receipts *just in case* you might need them in the future.

## Stage 2: paid writing as additional income

Most writers at this stage will still be running their writing business as a sole trader (or freelancer – there is no difference in terms of tax). Legally you don't need to do anything to set up as a sole trader. As soon as you start writing with a view to making a profit, you've become a sole trader. The tax system is very flexible. You can have a part-time employed job, be a partner in a bookshop and be a published author, all at the same time. Important things to consider at this stage are:

## Registering with HMRC

If you earn more than £1,000 from self-employment you need to register as a sole trader with HMRC. You can do this at www.gov.uk/register-for-self-assessment/self-employed. You need to register by 5 October in your second tax year (tax years run from 6 April to 5 April).

For example, if you started on 20 November 2022 (tax year 2022/23) then you would need to register with HMRC by 5 October 2023 (tax year 2023/24). You would then get sent a tax return to complete by 31 January 2024 if filing online or 31 October 2023 if filing by paper.

Two or more writers working together may also need to consider if they are in partnership with each other. A partnership has to be registered in its own right with HMRC and submit a tax return each year.

## Submitting a tax return

The tax system is called Self Assessment and this means that it is necessary for you to assess what rules and regulations apply to your tax position. There are a range of penalties that HMRC levy and, although it is possible in certain circumstances to appeal the penalties, it is well worth doing all you can to avoid them in the first place.

## Keeping records

A self-employed person needs to keep records for at least 5 years from 31 January following the tax year they relate to. For example, if you have transactions in the tax year to 5 April 2023, you need to keep your records until 31 January 2029. You can keep records digitally or on paper. You should keep copies of bank statements, contracts, receipts for expenditure you are claiming for and any invoices you have raised. It is also worth keeping a note of any unusual non-business transactions. If you win £1,000 at the races or get a generous gift from Aunt Ethel, you want to be able to prove this wasn't undeclared income from writing.

It is usually a good idea to have a separate business bank account that you use just for your writing income. This will help to keep things organised and could give you a little more privacy, as your accountant – and possibly HMRC – don't have to look through all your private outgoings.

### HMRC Self Assessment penalties

#### Late filing

Up to 3 months late £100, plus

after 3 months £10 per day for 90 days, plus

after 3 months penalties accrue at regular intervals based on 5% of the tax due or £300 – whichever is the greater.

You can estimate your penalty at www.gov.uk/estimate-self-assessment-penalties.

#### Late payment of tax

5% of tax due if not paid within 30 days with further 5% penalties every 6 months.

Interest is also charged (currently 3%).

#### Incorrect returns

Penalties are charged for tax returns that HMRC consider to be incorrect. There is an appeals process. The penalties are all behaviour based and are as follows:

• Careless errors – 0% to 30% of the additional tax due.

• Deliberate errors – 20% to 70% of the additional tax due.

• Deliberate and concealed errors – 30% to 100% of the additional tax due.

## Claiming expenses

A writer pays tax on their profit. Profit is income less allowable costs, often referred to as 'expenses'. Sometimes people talk about things being 'tax deductible', which means they can be deducted from your profit before calculating the tax bill, rather than being deducted from your tax bill. For example, if a higher-rate tax payer spends £100 on stationery, this is tax deductible and so it will reduce her profits by £100 and save income tax at 40%, i.e. £40.

## Trading allowance

You can claim a £1,000 trading allowance against your self-employed income instead of claiming for expenses you have incurred. You cannot claim the trading allowance and expenses at the same time. Claiming the trading allowance would be suitable when the trading allowance is more than the expenses incurred. However, you can't use the trading allowance to turn your profit into a loss. There are also restrictions to prevent you from using the trading allowance if the income is received from a business controlled by you, or by someone connected to you.

## What can you claim for?

The rule is that an expense must be 'wholly and exclusively' for the purpose of your business. Typical costs are:

• Accountancy
• Advertising
• Agent commission
• Bank charges
• Computing and IT
• Printing, postage and stationery
• Professional subscriptions
• Internet and telephone
• Software subscriptions
• Research
• Travel

Some costs may have an element of private use. In this case, HMRC will allow the cost to be apportioned provided you can justify the calculation. For example:

• Motor expenses – may be apportioned according to business use.
• Home as office – apportioned according to rooms and time spent in use.

Alternatively, you may be able to use HMRC Simplified Expenses. You can find more details at www.gov.uk/simpler-income-tax-simplified-expenses.

---

### Cloud bookkeeping

Recent years have seen the development of relatively cheap, simple bookkeeping packages like Xero and Quickbooks. These allow you to link up your business bank account to your accounting records, so you can quickly and accurately keep track of your income and expenditure. They have the advantage of being regularly backed up, less prone to error, and easy to use. You can also store your receipts and paperwork digitally. As the UK moves towards a new system of reporting called Making Tax Digital from April 2026 (delayed from the original date of April 2023), it will become more important to be able to easily record and report your income.

## Prizes and bursaries

There are many prizes and awards open to authors and other creatives, and entering competitions or seeking awards is a normal part of these professions and a good way for them to obtain extra income from their work. Such prizes are usually taxable. However, there are exceptions. When a prize is unsolicited, and awarded as a mark of honour, distinction or public esteem in recognition of outstanding achievement in a particular field, it won't be taxable. For example, if your publisher or agent enters you for a competition without your knowledge or consent, any prize money received should not be taxable.

## Payments on account

For self-employed people the tax system can require payments on account of tax to be made every six months. Each payment on account is half of the previous year's tax bill.

For example: Jo's first year of trading is the tax year 2022/23; she owes tax of £4,000 for the 2022/23 tax year which is due for payment by 31 January 2024. Also, on 31 January 2024 she'll need to pay a payment on account of £2,000 towards her 2023/24 tax bill. She'll have to make a further payment of £2,000 in July 2024. Her actual tax bill for 2023/24 is £5,000. In January 2025 her payments will be:

|  | £ |
|---|---|
| Tax due for tax year 2023/24 | 5,000 |
| *Less:* |  |
| Payment on account - paid 31 January 2024 | 2,000 |
| Payment on account - paid 31 July 2024 | 2,000 |
| Balance for 2023/24 | 1,000 |
| *Add:* |  |
| Payment on account for 2024/25 (50% of £5,000) | 2,500 |
| Total due 31 January 2025 | 3,500 |

When income is rising, payments on account can catch out the unwary, as each January there is both a shortfall of tax and a new, higher payment on account to pay. A sensible approach is to save for your tax throughout the year and to complete your tax return early in the tax year, so you have plenty of notice if the bill is higher than expected.

When income is falling (or ceasing) then it is possible to make a claim to HMRC to reduce payments on account so that you don't pay tax in advance that is more than necessary. If the payments on account you make are more than your tax bill, these will be offset against your next payments on account or refunded to you.

## Setting up a limited company as a 'money box'

If you already have a paid job, then it's possible that your additional income from writing may take your total income into a higher tax band. If you don't need the money now, setting up a limited company could mean that the company pays corporation tax at a lower rate.

For example, Jamie earns £50,000 through his employment; he also receives £1,820 in Child Benefit in respect of his two children. He earns a further £10,000 in profit as a writer. He doesn't need to access the additional money now and is happy to leave it in his company.

His tax liability as a sole trader can be compared with that of the limited company as follows:

| Sole trader | £ |
|---|---|
| Income tax on £10,000 @ 40% | 4,000 |
| High Income Child Benefit Tax Charge | 1,820 |
| Total due | 5,820 |

| Limited company | £ |
|---|---|
| Corporation tax on £10,000 @ 19% | 1,900 |
| Total due | 1,900 |

Although this is an extreme example, it shows that through using a limited company Jamie has saved £3,920 of tax on £10,000 of income. Once Jamie wants to take the money out of the company, it will be taxable on him personally, but he can control the amount paid so that it is covered by his personal allowance entirely or subject to a lower rate of tax than he is paying now. If Jamie's plans are to build up a savings buffer, so that one day he can take the plunge and become a full-time writer, then this could be of real benefit.

From 1 April 2023 the rate of corporation tax has increased. The first £50,000 of profit will continue to be taxed at 19%. Profits between £50,000 and £250,000 are taxed at a marginal rate of 26.5% and profits over £250,000 at 25%. There are also special rules that reduce the tax bands where more than one company is controlled by the same people.

## Stage 3: writing as main source of income

Typically, a writer at this stage will either be self-employed or trade through a limited company. A limited company has to be 'incorporated' at Companies House and, once it is set up, it exists as a legal entity. It can enter into contracts, have a bank account, and exist without you. It is possible to trade both as a sole trader and through a limited company. It may even be the case that an author has some of their books taxed as a sole trader and other titles taxed within a limited company.

## Issues on incorporation

If you do trade through a limited company, it is important to ensure that the underlying paperwork is correct. Here are some issues to bear in mind:
• For a company to receive copyright income, it must be legally entitled to the income. This can be achieved by ensuring the company exists before the book has been written and a service contract is in place between the director (i.e. the author) and the company.

### IR35

IR35 was introduced in April 2000 to stop the practice of employees setting up a limited company (a 'personal service company') and invoicing their employer for their work rather than being paid as an employee. This practice led to a large tax saving for both the employer and the employee.

IR35 only applies to limited companies, so a writer who is trading as a sole trader can ignore it. From April 2021 both public entities and larger private companies will have to look at the status of people working through personal service companies and, if necessary, deduct tax and National Insurance.

For most writers operating through a personal service company, it will be clear that they are not working for anyone as disguised employment. For other writers the situation may be more uncertain. For example, a copywriter with their own company providing weekly content for a client who describes them as their 'Content Manager', pays them a regular salary, expects them to attend meetings on site and doesn't allow a substitute, may be caught by the IR35 rules.

The IR35 rules are complex and, if caught by the rules, your limited company has to pay out most of the money it receives as a salary to the employee – together with Employers National Insurance.

Specialist help should be sought if you think your company may be affected by IR35.

fp• It isn't sufficient to simply 'bank' any proceeds into your company. All contracts need to be properly drawn up in the company's name.

• If you simply give your copyright to your company, it can create a tax issue; HMRC will expect you to pay income tax on the market value of the gift and will also expect the company to pay tax on the income it receives. In effect, the same income could be taxed twice.

• It is possible to sell the copyright to the company. This results in a better tax position, as the company would be able to get some tax relief for the cost of the copyright, but it will require a valuation of the copyright which brings with it costs and some uncertainty.

• Once your company owns the copyright, royalty income is 'locked' into being paid to the company. If you wished to own the copyright personally, it would need to be transferred out of the company at a fair value. You may find you have a company for a much longer time than you first anticipate, because it may not be practical to close it down until the copyright has a negligible value.

## VAT

VAT (Value Added Tax) is a tax that businesses are required to charge their customers for goods or services. A writer is no different from any other business and therefore must charge VAT when supplying writing services. The standard UK rate of VAT is currently 20%. VAT is a complicated subject and much of it is beyond the scope of this book. However, there are some key things a writer should be aware of.

A VAT-registered business usually submits a quarterly VAT return within one month and seven days of the end of the VAT quarter. Any VAT due is then paid by the same deadline. Being VAT-registered is not entirely bad news; a VAT-registered business has to charge VAT on their relevant services, but they can also claim back VAT on things they buy for their business. For example, in the VAT quarter ending 31 December 2022 a writer gets a publishing deal for £10,000 plus £2,000 of VAT. Their agent charges them £1,500 plus £300 VAT, and they buy a computer for writing for £500 plus £100 VAT. They would submit a VAT return to HMRC by 7 February 2023 and pay over £1,600, as follows:

|  | £ |
| --- | --- |
| VAT charged | 2,000 |
| *Less:* | |
| VAT on agent's fees | 300 |
| VAT on computer | 100 |
| *Paid to HMRC* | 1,600 |

Although this may make you feel worse off, especially when you are paying £1,600 to HMRC, you are in fact better off by £400 – this being the difference between the VAT you have been paid and the VAT you have paid out.

## VAT registration threshold

A business needs to register for VAT when the level of sales exceeds the VAT threshold. The VAT threshold is currently £85,000 and it applies to the last 12 months. To know whether you need to register or not, you have to look back at your cumulative sales over the last 12 months and, if these exceed the VAT threshold, you must register. You are also required to register if you believe your sales in the next 30 days alone will be more than the VAT threshold – for example if you bag a big publishing deal.

**Money, tax and benefits**

## Sole trader or limited company – the key differences

| Sole trader | Limited company |
|---|---|
| *Starting up* | |
| Nothing legal required | Must be incorporated at Companies House |
| *Closing down* | |
| Nothing legal required | Must be formally struck off at Companies House |
| *Legal protection* | |
| None – you and the business are one and the same | Limited liability (but watch out for contracts that pass on liabilities to directors) |
| If you are sued, then all your assets are at stake | If the company is sued, then only the assets of the company are at stake |
| *Tax on profits* | |
| Income tax paid depending on total earnings from all sources in the year; rates may be 0%, 20%, 40% or 45% depending on income | Corporation tax paid; rates are between 19% and 26.5% |
| *Tax on profits extracted* | |
| Not applicable – you pay tax on profit whether extracted or not | Dividend tax due at rates of 0%, 8.75%, 33.75% or 39.35% depending on income |
| *National Insurance* | |
| Pay Class 2 National Insurance and Class 4 National Insurance earn over the limit | Only pay National Insurance on salaries paid to employees if they earn over the limit |
| *Reporting* | |
| Must complete an individual Self Assessment tax return each year | Must file accounts each year with Companies House |
| | Must submit a Confirmation Statement each year to Companies House |
| | Must file a corporation tax return each year with HMRC |
| | May have to run a payroll and report to HMRC |
| | Likely that director/shareholder will have to complete an individual Self Assessment tax return each year |
| *Separate business bank account* | |
| Advisable | Essential |
| *VAT* | |
| Can be VAT registered; it is a person that is VAT registered, not a business, which may have unintended consequences | Can be VAT registered |
| *Creative averaging* | |
| Can be used | Cannot be used |
| *Why choose this one?* | |
| Simple; cheap; you want to take all the money out of business when it's earned, not concerned about legal liability; provides legal liability protection | Possible to save tax if you don't require all the money or are able to take advantage of splitting income |

Some writers will make an early 'protective' VAT registration, so that they know they are registered and don't have to worry about tripping over the VAT threshold. It is important to remember that the turnover figure is not necessarily the amount you receive. For example, a writer gets an advance of £10,000; their agent deducts 15% plus their VAT and so the writer only receives £8,200. The figure that counts towards the VAT threshold is £10,000. You do not need to include employment income in your turnover calculation or non-UK income (such as royalties from Amazon).

Finally, you need to include services you buy that are subject to the 'reverse charge' rules in your turnover calculation. For example, a writer who uses Facebook and Amazon advertising and spends, on average, more than £7,083 per month on this type of service would be required to register for VAT even if they are not making any sales themselves that are subject to VAT.

## Voluntary registration

You can voluntarily register for VAT even if your sales are under the VAT registration threshold. The reason you may want to do this is to recover the VAT you are being charged – typically by your agent. For example, a writer gets a publishing deal for £25,000; their agent charges 15% commission plus VAT. If they are not VAT-registered, they'll lose the agent VAT of £750 but, if they are VAT-registered, they'd be able to recover this.

Being in the 'VAT club' will allow you to recover VAT on all your other business expenditure, such as computer costs and accountancy fees. Whether it is a good idea to register early depends on your circumstances. If you're not incurring much VAT, then it may not be worth the hassle.

## What to include in your sales for VAT

You need to include all your UK sales and any foreign sales collected by your UK publisher. You can exclude any direct foreign sales (such as Amazon self-publishing or sales you or your agent have agreed with a foreign publisher). If you're a sole trader, you can exclude any employed income. But, if you are self-employed as something else too (e.g. you're both a plumber and a writer), you need to aggregate both sets of income. The VAT registration belongs to the *person*, not the *business*.

## Claiming back VAT

When you first register for VAT, you can reclaim VAT on goods purchased up to four years prior to registration provided those goods are still held when registration takes place. VAT on services supplied in the six months prior to registration may also be reclaimed. To claim VAT you'll need a valid VAT receipt; a credit card receipt isn't enough, and a VAT inspector will disallow any expenditure that you can't produce a valid VAT receipt for – even if it's obvious that you would have paid VAT.

Not all expenditure has VAT charged on it:

| Usually has VAT | Usually has no VAT |
| --- | --- |
| Agent commission | Trains, planes and taxis |
| Accountancy fees | Software subscriptions from overseas |
| Stationery | Postage |
| Computers and UK software | Entertainment |
| Internet and mobile phone | Insurance |

## Withholding tax and double taxation relief

Writers will often receive some or, in the case of an author selling via Amazon Kindle Direct Publishing (KDP), most of their income from an overseas source. Many foreign countries will charge a 'withholding tax' on such royalty payments, for example 30% in the case of the USA. Once withholding tax is paid, it is often not cost effective to try to recover it from the country in question, as doing so may require local professional advice and tax returns to be submitted to the country in question.

It is often possible to avoid any withholding tax being deducted in the first instance by completing the information required by the overseas publisher, so they don't have to apply withholding tax. Amazon KDP has an online tax interview to make it as easy as possible for you to comply. Other publishers in other countries will have to follow their own rules and will often ask for a Certificate of Residence to prove you are a UK tax payer. There are more details on applying for a Certificate of Residence at www.gov.uk/guidance/get-a-certificate-of-residence.

If you do suffer withholding tax, then it may be possible to use the foreign tax you have paid to offset against your tax liability on the same income when you complete your tax return. A word of warning though: you may not get back the full amount of foreign tax paid and relief is restricted to the amount of UK tax you would have to pay on the same income or the amount of foreign tax you would have paid had you complied with the requirements to avoid withholding tax.

## Stage 4: Lifelong considerations

As a writer's career becomes more established, there are other financial considerations.

### Pensions
#### State Pension

To qualify for the new State Pension, you need a minimum of 10 qualifying years and at least 35 qualifying years to receive the maximum payments. You can check your pension entitlement online at www.gov.uk/check-state-pension. If you have gaps in your pension contribution history, then you can consider making voluntary contributions.

#### Writers' Guild Pension Fund

For their members writing for TV, radio and film, WGGB (Writers' Guild of Great Britain) have negotiated agreements with the BBC, ITV and PACT so that pension contributions are made to the Writers' Guild Pension Fund. In return for the writer making a contribution to the fund, the production company will also make a contribution, in addition to the writer's fee. More details are available from WGGB (see page 300 for contact details).

#### Private pensions

If you have been employed, you may have an occupational pension from your employment in place. Most writers who have been self-employed will depend upon their own pension arrangements using 'defined contribution' schemes. Contributions to a private pension by an individual are made net of basic rate income tax. This means that a contribution of £80 actually means the amount invested is £100, with £20 being claimed by the pension company from the government. A higher-rate tax payer would save another £20 in income tax, making the cost of putting £100 into a pension just £60. There are rules regarding how much you can invest each year and many people will need professional advice as to what scheme they invest in.

## Insurances

Being a self-employed writer does mean that you don't have the same safety net that many employees may have. It is sensible to think about how you and your family would manage if you died or, through injury or illness, were unable to continue to earn a living. There are insurance policies that are available to help.

- **Life insurance** can provide a lump sum or a monthly income for a period of time if you die.
- **Critical illness insurance** can provide a lump sum or a monthly income for a period of time if you are diagnosed with a critical illness.
- **Income protection insurance** can provide a monthly income if you are unable to work due to ill health.

## Wills

Making a will is important for a number of reasons. Amongst other things, you can specify who inherits your assets, make tax efficient choices and provide instructions as to who looks after your minor children. A writer also needs to consider what happens with any copyright they hold as part of their estate. Copyright can last up to 70 years after death, so it may represent a valuable asset. You may also have particular instructions as to what happens to your personal papers and unpublished works. It is also worth thinking about what happens with digital assets such as blogs, social media accounts, online videos, and access to cloud storage services like Dropbox. A bit of forward planning may save a lot of trouble for the people dealing with your estate.

### Further advice: useful websites

**HMRC**
www.gov.uk/government/organisations/hm-revenue-customs

**Institute of Chartered Accountants in England and Wales**
www.icaew.com

**Institute of Chartered Accountants of Scotland**
www.icas.com
*These author associations offer support and advice on financial matters to their members.*

**National Union of Journalists**
www.nuj.org.uk

**Society of Authors**
www2.societyofauthors.org (see page 297)

**WGGB (Writers' Guild of Great Britain)**
https://writersguild.org.uk (see page 300)
*Accountancy and business software tools include:*

**Sage**
www.sage.com/en-gb/cp/accounting

**Quickbooks**
https://quickbooks.intuit.com/uk

**Xero**
www.xero.com/uk

**Jonathan Ford** BSC FCA MSWW and **Louise Ford** BA FCA are the directors of Writers Tax Ltd, a firm of chartered accountants that specialises in helping authors, scriptwriters and other professional writers with their tax and accountancy needs, which they established in 2020. They both qualified as chartered accountants with Price Waterhouse in Liverpool. Jonathan worked at Grant Thornton and later as Financial Controller at Mersey TV before setting up his own company. See their website https://writers.tax for more information.

# National Insurance contributions

Sarah Bradford sets out the facts about National Insurance, explaining the contributory principle that underlies it, the various classes of contribution payable by workers (both employed and self-employed), the related benefit entitlements and information on current rates and earnings thresholds.

## Nature of National Insurance contributions

The payment of National Insurance contributions secures access to the state pension and to contributory benefits. This is the contributory principle of National Insurance. National Insurance contributions are payable by employed earners and their employers and also by self-employed earners. People who do not have any earnings or whose earnings are not sufficient to trigger a liability to pay National Insurance contributions can choose to pay National Insurance contributions voluntarily to maintain their contribution record.

If sufficient National Insurance contributions of the right type are paid or credited for a tax year, the year will be a qualifying year for National Insurance purposes. A person needs 35 qualifying years in order to receive the full state pension when they reach state pension age. Where a person has at least ten qualifying years, they will receive a reduced state pension.

## Classes of National Insurance

There are various different classes of National Insurance contribution. The class (or classes) that you pay will depend on whether you are an employed earner, a self-employed earner, an employer or a voluntary contributor. Contributions may be earnings-related, payable on profits or payable at a flat rate, depending on the class.

The different classes of contribution are shown in the box below. Class 1, 2 and 4 contributions are only payable once earnings exceed certain thresholds and limits. The rates and thresholds applying to 2023/24 are set out in the box on page 428.

### Classes of National Insurance

| Nature of contribution | Payable by |
|---|---|
| *Class 1* Earnings-related | Employed earners (primary Class 1 contributions) |
| | Employer (secondary Class 1 contributions) |
| *Class 1A* Earnings-related | Employer on taxable benefits in kind and taxable termination payments and sporting testimonials |
| *Class 1B* Earnings-related | Employer on items included within a PAYE Settlement Agreement and on the tax due under that agreement |
| *Class 2* Flat rate | Self-employed earners |
| *Class 3* Flat rate | Voluntary contributions |
| *Class 3A* Variable amount | Payable between 12 October 2015 and 5 April 2017 voluntarily by those who reached state pension age before 6 April 2016 to boost their state pension |
| *Class 4* Profits-related | Self-employed earners |

## Contributions payable by writers and artists

As for other earners, the class of National Insurance payable by writers and artists depends on whether they are a self-employed earner or an employed earner. This is not something that they can choose – it will depend on the facts of the engagement. It is important that the employment status of the writer or artist is categorised correctly as this will affect not only what class (and therefore how) they pay, but also what benefits they are entitled to.

## Categorisation – employed earner v self-employed earner

To ensure that writers and artists pay the correct class of National Insurance contributions, it is important they are correctly categorised. Employed earners will pay Class 1 National Insurance contributions, whereas self-employed earners will pay Class 2 and Class 4 contributions.

A worker's categorisation depends on the characteristics of the engagement. In many cases, it will be clear whether a worker is an employed earner or a self-employed earner. For example, a writer who is employed by a publishing firm and has a contract of employment will be an employed earner and will pay Class 1 National Insurance contributions on their earnings, whereas a freelance writer who undertakes commissions for a variety of people and is paid a fee for each commission will be a self-employed earner and will pay Class 2 and Class 4 contributions.

## Characteristics of employment

The following characteristics apply to an engagement where the worker is an employed earner:
• they are required to work regularly unless they are unwell or on leave;
• they are expected to work a minimum number of hours a week and expect to be paid for the time that they work;
• a manager or supervisor is responsible for their workload and will say when a job should be finished or how it should be done;
• they must do the work themselves – they can't send someone else to do it instead;
• the business deducts tax and National Insurance from their pay;
• they are entitled to paid holiday;
• they are entitled to statutory payments;
• they can join the business's pensions scheme;
• they are subject to grievance and disciplinary procedures;
• the contract sets out the procedure applying in the event of redundancy;
• they work at the business premises or at a location specified by the business;
• they work for only that business or, if they have another job, it is completely separate;
• the offer letter and contract refer to the 'employee' and the 'employer'.

For example, a staff writer who is paid a salary and contracted to work 35 hours a week would be an employed earner.

## Characteristics of self-employment

The following characteristics indicate that the writer or artist is a self-employed earner:
• they are in business for themselves and are responsible for the success or failure of the business and can make a profit or a loss;
• they decide what work they take on and where and how they do it;
• they can hire someone else to do the work;

• they are responsible for fixing unsatisfactory work in their own time;

• they agree a fixed price for a job – the fee is the same regardless of how long it takes them to do the work;

• they use their own money to buy any equipment needed and to cover the running costs of the business;

• they work for more than one client.

A writer who is commissioned to write specific articles for different publications and who works for a number of publishers, being paid a fee for each article, would be a self-employed earner.

## Marginal cases

It will not always be clear whether a writer or artist is an employed earner or a self-employed earner. In this situation, it is necessary to look at the overall picture and see whether, on balance, the writer or artist is employed or self-employed. It should be noted that there is not one single definitive test, rather a question of seeing what characteristics of employment and what characteristics of self-employment are present.

In reaching a decision, the following factors need to be considered:

• The nature of the contract and the written terms – a contract for *services* indicates employment and a contract of *service* indicates self-employment.

• The nature of the engager's business and the nature of the job.

• Right of substitution – a right to send a substitute indicates self-employment.

• Mutuality of obligation – for a contract for services there must be minimum mutual obligations; the employer is obliged to offer work and the employee is obliged to do that work.

• Right of control – a high degree of control (on the part of the employer) over how and where the worker performs the work suggests employment.

• Provision of equipment – the provision by the worker of their own equipment suggests self-employment.

• Financial risk – a person who is self-employed bears a higher degree of financial risk than an employee.

• Opportunity to profit – a person who is self-employed has the opportunity to profit if they do the job quicker or under-budget.

• Length of engagement – while this is not a decisive factor, an open-ended contract is more likely to indicate employment.

• Part and parcel of the organisation – a worker who is seen as 'part and parcel' of the organisation is likely to be an employee.

• Entitlement to benefits – a worker who is entitled to employee-type benefits, such as a pension, is more likely to be an employee.

• Personal factors – a highly skilled worker may not need supervising but may still be an employee.

• Intention – while intention alone cannot determine status, it can be useful in forming an opinion on whether the worker is employed or self-employed.

## Check Employment Status for Tax (CEST) tool

HMRC have produced a tool – the Check Employment Status for Tax (CEST) tool – which can be used to reach a decision on whether a writer or artist is employed or self-employed.

The tool asks a series of questions on the engagement, which must be answered honestly, in order to reach a decision. As long as the information provided is accurate and represents the reality of the engagement, HMRC will stand by the decision that is reached. The CEST tool is available on the government website at www.gov.uk/guidance/check-employment-status-for-tax.

## Workers providing their services through a personal service company

Anti-avoidance rules apply where services are provided through a personal limited company or another intermediary to an end client. There are two sets of rules to consider – the off-payroll working rules and the IR35 rules. The rules that apply depend on the nature of the end client.

### • Off-payroll working rules

The off-payroll working rules were introduced from 6 April 2017. They apply from the date when services were provided through an intermediary to a private sector body. The rules were extended from 6 April 2021, and from that date they also apply when the end client is a medium or large private sector organisation.

The end client must carry out a status determination to ascertain whether the worker would be an employee of the end client if they provided their services to them directly. Where this is the case, the end client must deduct tax and National Insurance from payments made to the worker's personal company (after adjusting the bill for VAT and the cost of any materials), and report this to HMRC. The worker receives credit for the tax and National Insurance on payment made to them by their personal limited company. They do not need to consider the IR35 rules because the off-payroll working rules apply instead.

### • IR35

From 6 April 2021 onwards, the IR35 rules only apply where a worker provides their services to a small private sector organisation through an intermediary, such as a personal service company. The worker's personal service company must determine whether the worker would be an employee of the small private sector organisation if they provided their services directly. If the answer is 'yes' the IR35 rules apply. The intermediary must calculate the deemed employment payment at the end of the tax year, and account for tax and National Insurance on that payment to HMRC.

## Employed earners – Class 1 National Insurance

Class 1 National Insurance is payable on the earnings of an employed earner. The employed earner pays primary contributions and the secondary contributor (which is generally the employer) pays secondary contributions. The payment of primary Class 1 National Insurance contributions by the employed earner is the mechanism by which the employed earner earns the right to the state pension and contributory benefits. Secondary Class 1 contributions, payable by the employer, do not earn benefit entitlement – they are akin to a tax on the employee's earnings.

Contributions are calculated by reference to earnings for the earnings period on a non-cumulative basis; no account is taken of earnings previously in the tax year, only those for the earnings period. The earnings period will normally correspond to the pay interval.

However, directors have an annual earnings period, regardless of their actual pay frequency. The employer must deduct primary contributions from the employee's pay and pay them over to HMRC together with tax deducted under PAYE and the employer's secondary contributions.

## • Primary Class 1 National Insurance

Primary Class 1 National Insurance contributions are payable by employees aged 16 and over until they reach state pension age (which depends on their date of birth). No contributions are payable until earnings reach the *lower earnings limit* (set at £123 per week, £533 per month, £6,396 per year for 2023/24). They are then payable at a notional zero rate until earnings reach the primary threshold. This is important as it secures the year as a qualifying year for National Insurance purposes (as long as earnings are paid above the lower earnings limit for each earnings period in the tax year). Where earnings are below the lower earnings limit, the year is not a qualifying year (although may become one if the worker receives National Insurance credits or pays voluntary contributions).

Contributions are payable on earnings above the *primary threshold* at the main primary rate of 12% until earnings reach the *upper earnings limit*. The primary threshold is set at £242 per week (£1,048 per month, £12,570 per year) for 2023/24 and is aligned with the personal allowance applying for tax purposes. The upper earnings limit is set at £967 per week, £4,189 per month and £50,270 per year for 2023/24. Contributions are payable at the additional primary rate of 2% on earnings above the upper earnings limit. For 2023/24 only, the main primary rate is set at 12% and the additional primary rate is set at 1%.

## • Secondary Class 1 contributions

Secondary contributions are payable by the secondary contributor, which in most cases is the employed earner's employer. They are payable on the earnings of an employee aged 16 and above; unlike primary contributions, the secondary liability does not stop when the employed earner reaches state pension age.

Contributions are payable at the secondary rate of 13.8% on earnings in excess of the *secondary threshold* (set at £175 per week, £758 per month, £9,100 per year for 2023/24).

A higher secondary threshold applies to the earnings of employees under the age of 21 (the upper secondary threshold for under 21s), to those of apprentices under the age of 25 (the apprentice upper secondary threshold) and to armed forces veterans in the first year of their first civilian employment since leaving the armed forces. Each of these thresholds are aligned with the upper earnings limit for primary Class 1 purposes (set at £967 per week, £4,189 per month and £50,270 per year for 2023/24). A separate secondary threshold applies to the earnings of a new Freeport employee in the first 36 months of their employment with an employer with physical premises in a Freeport tax zone. This threshold is set at £481 per week, £2,083 per month and £25,000 per year. These thresholds only apply for secondary Class 1 purposes; the employee or apprentice pays the usual primary contributions.

Eligible employers can claim the Employment Allowance which is offset against their secondary Class 1 National Insurance liability. To qualify, their secondary Class 1 National Insurance liability must be less than £100,000 for 2022/23. Companies where the sole employee is also a director do not qualify for the allowance. The Employment Allowance is set at £5,000 for 2023/24 (capped at the employer's secondary Class 1 liability where this is lower).

## • Earnings for Class 1 purposes

Class 1 contributions are calculated on the earnings for the earnings period. The definition of 'earnings' includes any remuneration or profits derived from the employment. This will include payments of wages and salary, but will also include other items such as statutory sick pay, statutory payments, and certain share-based remuneration. Comprehensive guidance on what to include in earnings for National Insurance purposes can be found in the HMRC guidance CWG2 *Employer further guide to PAYE and National Insurance contributions*. The 2023/24 edition is available on the government website at www.gov.uk/government/publications/cwg2-further-guide-to-paye-and-national-insurance-contributions.

## • Class 1A National Insurance contributions

Class 1A National Insurance contributions are employer-only contributions payable on taxable benefits in kind and also on taxable termination payments in excess of the £30,000 tax-free threshold and taxable sporting testimonials in excess of the £100,000 tax-free threshold. They are payable at the Class 1A rate, which for 2023/24 is set at 13.8%.

## • Class 1B National Insurance

Class 1B National Insurance contributions are employer-only contributions payable in place of the Class 1 or Class 1A liability that would otherwise arise on items included within a PAYE Settlement Agreement (PSA), and also on the tax due under the PSA. The Class 1B rate is aligned with the secondary Class 1 rate and is set at 13.8% for 2023/24.

## Self-employed earners – Class 2 and Class 4 National Insurance contributions

Where a writer or artist is a self-employed earner, if their profits are high enough, they will pay Class 2 contributions, and also Class 4 contributions on their profits. Class 2 and Class 4 National Insurance contributions are payable via the Self Assessment system and must be paid by 31 January after the end of the tax year to which they relate (i.e. by 31 January 2025 for 2023/24 contributions).

## • Class 2 National Insurance contributions

Self-employed earners are able to build up entitlement to the state pension and to certain contributory benefits through the payment of Class 2 National Insurance contributions. Contributions must be paid for the full year for the year to be a qualifying year.

Class 2 National Insurance contributions are flat-rate contributions payable by self-employed earners whose profits exceed the *lower profits threshold*, set at £12,570 for 2023/24. Class 2 National Insurance contributions are payable at the rate of £3.45 per week for 2023/24. Where a self-employed earner has profits between the small profits threshold (set at £6,725 for 2023/24) and the lower profits threshold, from 2022/23 onwards, they are treated as if they have paid Class 2 contributions at a zero rate. This provides them with a qualifying year for state pension purposes without actually having to pay Class 2 National Insurance contributions. A self-employed individual whose profits from self-employment are below the small profits threshold can pay Class 2 National Insurance contributions voluntarily. This is a cheap way to build up pension entitlement.

## • Class 4 National Insurance contributions

Class 4 National Insurance contributions are payable by self-employed earners on their profits. They do not provide any benefit entitlement, and in effect are a tax on profits.

## National Insurance rates and thresholds 2023/24

| National Insurance class | Rate or threshold |
| --- | --- |
| **Class 1** | |
| Lower earnings limit | £123 per week |
| | £533 per month |
| | £6,396 per year |
| Primary threshold | £242 per week |
| | £1,048 per week |
| | £12,570 per year |
| Secondary threshold | £175 per week |
| | £758 per month |
| | £9,100 per year |
| Upper earnings limit | £967 per week |
| | £4,189 per month |
| | £50,270 per year |
| Upper secondary threshold for under 21s | £967 per week |
| | £4,189 per month |
| | £50,270 per year |
| Apprentice upper secondary threshold | £967 per week |
| | £4,189 per month |
| | £50,270 per year |
| Veterans upper secondary threshold | £967 per week |
| | £4,189 per month |
| | £50,270 per year |
| Freeport upper secondary threshold | £481 per week |
| | £2,083 per month |
| | £25,000 per year |
| *Primary (employee) contributions* | |
| On earnings between the primary threshold and the upper earnings limit | 12% |
| On earnings above the upper earnings limit | 2% |
| *Secondary (employer) contributions* | |
| On earnings above the relevant secondary threshold | 13.8% |
| **Class 1A and Class 1B** | |
| Contribution rate (employer only) | 13.8% |
| **Class 2** | |
| Flat rate contribution | £3.45 per week |
| Small profits threshold | £6,725 a year |
| Lower profits threshold | £12,570 per year |
| **Class 3** | |
| Flat rate contribution | £17.45 per week |
| **Class 4** | |
| Lower profits limit | £12,570 a year |
| Upper profits limit | £50,270 a year |
| Main rate on earnings between the lower profits limit and the upper profits limit | 9% |
| Additional rate on profits in excess of the upper profits limit | 2% |

No contributions are payable on profits below the *lower profits threshold*, set at £12,570 for 2023/24. For 2023/24, Class 4 contributions are payable at the rate of 9% on profits between the lower profits limit and the *upper profits limit*, set at £50,270 for 2023/24, and on profits in excess of the upper profits limit, at the additional Class 4 rate of 2%.

## Voluntary contributions – Class 3

A person can pay voluntary Class 3 contributions to plug gaps in their contributions record. Class 3 contributions are payable at the rate of £17.45 per week. Where a person has profits from self-employment below the *small profits threshold* (set at £6,725 for 2023/24), they can instead pay Class 2 contributions voluntarily; at £3.45 per week for 2023/24 this is a much cheaper option.

## Maximum contributions

Where a person has more than one job, or is both employed and self-employed, there is a cap on the contributions that are payable for the year. The calculations are complex.

## National Insurance credits

National Insurance credits are available in certain circumstances where people are unable to work or because they are ill. There are two types of credit. Class 1 credits count towards state pension and contributory benefits, while Class 3 credits only count towards the state pension. Further detail on National Insurance credits can be found on the government website at www.gov.uk/national-insurance-credits.

## Benefit entitlement

The payment of National Insurance contributions (and the award of National Insurance credits) earns entitlement to the state pension and certain contributory benefits. Only the payment of primary Class 1, Class 2 and Class 3 contributions confer benefit entitlement. Benefit entitlement depends on the class of contribution paid.

| Benefit entitlement | |
| --- | --- |
| **Class of contributions** | **Benefit entitlement** |
| Primary Class 1 (employed earner) | State Pension, contribution-based Jobseeker's Allowance, contribution-based Employment and Support Allowance, Maternity Allowance and Bereavement Payment, Bereavement Allowance, Widowed Parent's Allowance, Bereavement Support Payment. |
| Class 2 (self-employed earners) | State Pension, contribution-based Employment and Support Allowance, Maternity Allowance and Bereavement Allowance. |
| Class 3 (voluntary contributions) | State Pension and Bereavement Payment, Bereavement Allowance, Widowed Parent's Allowance. |

**Sarah Bradford** BA (Hons), FCA CTA (Fellow) is the director of WriteTax Ltd and the author of *National Insurance Contributions 2022/23* (and earlier editions) published by Bloomsbury Professional. She writes widely on tax and National Insurance contributions.

# Index

# Writers & Artists

## W&A WRITING COURSES

- Expert guidance on the writing process

- Small workshop groups

- Recordings, takeaway exercises and manuscript critiques

- Genre-specific courses include: children's and YA, non-fiction, horror, crime

- Storytelling essentials: Writing Better Fiction; Find Your Voice

*"The weeks flew. I feel I've improved as a writer and also as a reader."*

For full course outlines and an up-to-date schedule of our one-off **masterclass evenings, full-day conferences** and events with **literary agents,** visit:

www.writersandartists.co.uk/events-and-courses